TAKING SIDES

Clashing Views on Controversial

Issues in 20th Century American History

Selected, Edited, and with Introductions by

Larry Madaras
Howard Community College

McGraw-Hill/Dushkin
A Division of The McGraw-Hill Companies

To Maggie

Photo Acknowledgment
Cover image: Corbis/Royalty Free

Cover Acknowledgment
Maggie Lytle

Manufactured in the United States of America

First Edition

123456789DOCDOC98765

0-07-311162-7
1554-3218

Printed on Recycled Paper

Preface

The success of the past eleven editions of *Taking Sides Clashing Views on Controversial Issues in American History,* Volumes One and Two, as well as the two editions of *Taking Sides American History Since 1945* has encouraged me to develop a *Taking Sides 20th Century American History.* Our aim has been to create an effective instrument to enhance classroom learning and to foster critical thinking. Historical facts present in a vacuum are of little value to the educational process. For students, whose search for historical truth often concentrates on *when* something happened rather than on *why,* and on specific events rather than on the *significance* of those events, *Taking Sides* offers an interesting and valuable departure. The understanding that the reader arrives at based on the evidence that emerges from the clash of views encourages the reader to view history as an *interpretive* discipline, not one of rote memorization.

The issues are arranged in chronological order and can be easily incorporated into any American history survey course. Each issue has an issue *introduction,* which sets the stage for the debate that follows in the pro and con selections and provides historical and methodological background to the problem that the issues examine. Each issue concludes with a *postscript* that ties the readings together, briefly mentions alternative interpretations, and supplies detailed *suggestions for further reading* for the student who wishes to pursue the topics raised in the issue. Also, Internet site addresses (URLs), which should prove useful as starting points for further research, have been provided on the *On the Internet* page that accompanies each part opener. At the back of the book is a listing of all the *contributors to this volume* with a brief biographical sketch of each of the prominent figures whose views are debated here.

A Word to the Instructor *An Instructor's Manual With Test Questions* (multiple-choice and essay) is available through the publisher for the instructor using *Taking Sides* in the classroom. A general guidebook, *Using Taking Sides in the Classroom,* which discusses methods and techniques for integrating the pro-con approach into any classroom setting, is also available. An online version of *Using Taking Sides in the Classroom* and a correspondence service for Taking Sides adopters can be found at `http://www.dushkin.com/usingts/`.

Taking Sides: Clashing Views on Controversial Issues in 20th Century American History is only one title in the Taking Sides series. If you are interested in seeing the table of contents for any other titles, please visit the Taking Sides Web site at `http://dushkin.com/takingsides/`.

Acknowledgments Many individuals have contributed to the successful completion of this edition. We appreciate the evaluations submitted to McGraw-Hill/Dushkin by those who have used Taking Sides in the classroom. Special thanks to those who responded with specific suggestions.

Gary Best
University of Hawaii–Hilo

James D. Bolton
Coastline Community College

Mary Borg
University of Northern Colorado

John Whitney Evans
College of St. Scholastica

Mary Hickerson
Chaffey College

Maryann Irwin
Diablo Valley College

Tim Koerner
Oakland Community College

Gordon Lam
Sierra College

Jon Nielson
Columbia College

Andrew O'Shaugnessy
University of Wisconsin–Oshkosh

Manian Padma
DeAnza College

Elliot Pasternack
Middlesex County College (N.J.)

Robert M. Paterson
Armstrong State College

Charles Piehl
Mankato State University

Ethan S. Rafuse
University of Missouri–Kansas City

John Reid
Ohio State University–Lima

Murray Rubinstein
CUNY Baruch College

Neil Sapper
Amarillo College

Preston She
Plymouth State College

Jack Traylor
William Jennings Bryan College

I am partially indebted to Maggie Cullen, Jim and Cindy SoRelle, the late Barry A. Crouch, Joseph and Helen Mitchell, Chris Higgins, Rob Bailey, Robert Levene, Fred Campbell, and Larry Fischer, who shared their ideas for changes, pointed me toward potentially useful historical works and provided significant editorial assistance. Susan E. Myers, Jean Soto, Elu Ciborowski, Sharon Frey, Sharen Gover, James Johnson, Chart Chalungsooth, Marie Kottis, and Lucy Gardner in the library at Howard Community College provided essential help in acquiring books, articles, videos, Internet sources and inter-library loan materials. I am grateful over the years for help and guidance from former Dushkin senior development editor David Brackley and former list managers David Dean and Ted Knight.

Finally two kudos are extended to typist Lynn Wilder who has been able to decipher my handwriting and spelling errors. Jill Peter, the current editor-in-charge of the *Taking Sides* series, has carefully guided, with great patience, this project from its origins to its conclusion.

Larry Madaras
Howard Community College

Contents In Brief

Contents

NO: Roger Biles, from *A New Deal for the American People* (Northern Illinois University Press, 1991) *134*

Professor of history Gary Dean Best argues that Roosevelt established an antibusiness environment with the creation of the New Deal regulatory programs, which retarded the nation's economic recovery from the Great Depression until World War II. Professor of history Roger Biles contends that, in spite of its minimal reforms and non-revolutionary programs, the New Deal created a limited welfare state that implemented economic stabilizers to avert another depression.

Issue 7. Did President Roosevelt Deliberately Withhold Information About the Attack on Pearl Harbor from the American Commanders? 143

YES: Robert A. Theobald, from *The Final Secret of Pearl Harbor: The Washington Contribution to the Japanese Attack* (Devin-Adair, 1954) *145*

NO: Roberta Wohlstetter, from *Pearl Harbor: Warning and Decision* (Stanford University Press, 1967) *155*

Retired Rear Admiral Robert A. Theobald argues that President Franklin D. Roosevelt deliberately withheld information from the commanders at Pearl Harbor in order to encourage the Japanese to make a surprise attack on the weak U.S. Pacific Fleet. Historian Roberta Wohlstetter contends that even though naval intelligence broke the Japanese code, conflicting signals and the lack of a central agency coordinating U.S. intelligence information made it impossible to predict the Pearl Harbor attack.

PART 3 AMERICAN HIGH, 1945–1963 169

Issue 8. Was the United States Responsible for the Cold War? 170

YES: Thomas G. Paterson, from *Meeting the Communist Threat: Truman to Reagan* (Oxford University Press, 1988) *172*

NO: John Lewis Gaddis, from *Russia, the Soviet Union, and the United States: An Interpretive History,* 2d ed. (McGraw-Hill, 1990) *180*

Professor of history Thomas G. Paterson argues that the Truman administration exaggerated the Soviet threat after World War II because the United States had expansionist political and economic global needs. Professor of history John Lewis Gaddis argues that the power vacuum that existed in Europe at the end of World War II exaggerated and made almost inevitable a clash between the democratic, capitalist United States and the totalitarian, communist USSR.

Issue 9. Did Communism Threaten America's Internal Security After World War II? 192

YES: John Earl Haynes and Harvey Klehr, from *Venona: Decoding Soviet Espionage in America* (Yale University Press, 1999) *194*

NO: Richard M. Fried, from *Nightmare in Red: The McCarthy Era in Perspective* (Oxford University Press, 1990) *205*

History professors John Earl Haynes and Harvey Klehr argue that army code-breakers during World War II's "Venona Project" uncovered a disturbing number of high-ranking U.S. government officials who seriously damaged American interests by passing sensitive information to the Soviet Union. Professor of history Richard M. Fried argues that the early 1950s were a "nightmare in red" during which American citizens had their First and Fifth Amendment rights suspended when a host of national and state investigating committees searched for Communists in government agencies, Hollywood, labor unions, foundations, universities, public schools, and even public libraries.

Issue 10. Did Lee Harvey Oswald Kill President Kennedy by Himself? 218

YES: President's Commission on the Assassination of President John F. Kennedy, from *The Warren Report: Report of the President's Commission on the Assassination of President John F. Kennedy* (September 24, 1964) *220*

NO: Michael L. Kurtz, from *Crime of the Century: The Kennedy Assassination From a Historian's Perspective,* 2d ed. (University of Tennessee Press, 1993) *227*

The President's Commission on the Assassination of President John F. Kennedy argues that Lee Harvey Oswald was the sole assassin of President Kennedy and that he was not part of any organized conspiracy, domestic or foreign. Professor of history Michael L. Kurtz argues that the Warren Commission ignored evidence of Oswald's connections with organized criminals and with pro-Castro and anti-Castro supporters, as well as forensic evidence that points to multiple assassins.

PART 4 FROM LIBERATION THROUGH WATERGATE, 1963–1974 247

Issue 11. Was Martin Luther King, Jr.'s Leadership Essential to the Success of the Civil Rights Revolution? 248

YES: Adam Fairclough, from "Martin Luther King, Jr. and the Quest for Nonviolent Social Change," *Phylon* (Spring 1986) *250*

NO: Clayborne Carson, from "Martin Luther King, Jr.: Charismatic Leadership in a Mass Struggle," *Journal of American History* (September 1987) *262*

Professor of history Adam Fairclough argues that Martin Luther King, Jr., was a pragmatic reformer who organized nonviolent direct-action protests in strategically targeted local communities, which provoked violence from his opponents, gaining publicity and sympathy for the civil rights movement. Professor of history Clayborne Carson concludes that the civil rights struggle would have followed a similar course of development even if King had never lived because its successes depended upon mass activism, not the actions of a single leader.

Issue 12. Was America's Escalation of the War in Vietnam Inevitable? 269

YES: Brian VanDeMark, from *Into the Quagmire: Lyndon Johnson and the Escalation of the Vietnam War* (Oxford University Press, 1991) *271*

NO: H. R. McMaster, from *Dereliction of Duty: Lyndon Johnson, Robert McNamara, the Joint Chiefs of Staff, and the Lies That Led to Vietnam* (HarperCollins, 1997) *280*

Professor of history Brian VanDeMark argues that President Lyndon Johnson failed to question the viability of increasing U.S. involvement in the Vietnam War because he was a prisoner of America's global containment policy and because he did not want his opponents to accuse him of being soft on communism or endanger support for his Great Society reforms. H. R. McMaster, an active-duty army tanker, maintains that the Vietnam disaster was not inevitable but a uniquely human failure whose responsibility was shared by President Johnson and his principal military and civilian advisers.

Issue 13. Has the Women's Liberation Movement Been Harmful to American Women? 291

YES: F. Carolyn Graglia, from *Domestic Tranquility: A Brief Against Feminism* (Spence, 1998) *293*

NO: Sara M. Evans, from "American Women in the Twentieth Century," in Harvard Sitkoff, ed., *Perspectives on Modern America: Making Sense of the Twentieth Century* (Oxford University Press, 2001) *302*

Writer and lecturer F. Carolyn Graglia argues that women should stay at home and practice the values of "true motherhood" because contemporary feminists have discredited marriage, devalued traditional homemaking, and encouraged sexual promiscuity. According to Professor Sara M. Evans, despite class, racial, religious, ethnic and regional differences, women in America experienced major transformations in their private and public lives in the twentieth century.

Issue 14. Was Richard Nixon America's Last Liberal President? 319

YES: Joan Hoff-Wilson, from "Richard M. Nixon: The Corporate Presidency," in Fred I. Greenstein, ed., *Leadership in the Modern Presidency* (Harvard University Press, 1988) *321*

NO: Bruce J. Schulman, from *The Seventies: The Great Shift in American Culture, Society, and Politics* (The Free Press/Simon & Schuster, 2001) *331*

According to professor of history Joan Hoff-Wilson, the Nixon presidency reorganized the executive branch and portions of the federal bureaucracy and implemented domestic reforms in civil rights, welfare, and economic planning, despite its limited foreign policy successes and the Watergate scandal. According to professor Bruce J. Schulman, Richard Nixon was the first conservative president of the post–World War II era who undermined the Great Society legislative program of President Lyndon Baines Johnson and built a new Republican majority coalition of white, northern, blue-collar workers, and southern and sunbelt conservatives.

PART 5 POSTINDUSTRIAL AMERICA AND THE END OF THE COLD WAR, 1974–2005 347

Issue 15. Did President Reagan Win the Cold War? 348

YES: John Lewis Gaddis, from *The United States and the End of the Cold War: Implications, Reconsiderations, Provocations* (Oxford University Press, 1992) *350*

NO: Daniel Deudney and G. John Ikenberry, from "Who Won the Cold War?" *Foreign Policy* (Summer 1992) *360*

Professor of history John Lewis Gaddis argues that President Reagan combined a policy of militancy and operational pragmatism to bring about the most significant improvement in Soviet-American relations since the end of World War II. Professors of political science Daniel Deudney and G. John Ikenberry contend that the cold war ended only when Soviet President Gorbachev accepted Western liberal values and the need for global cooperation.

Issue 16. Should America Remain a Nation of Immigrants? 372

YES: Tamar Jacoby, from "Too Many Immigrants?" *Commentary* (April 2002) *374*

NO: Patrick J. Buchanan, from *The Death of the West: How Dying Populations and Immigrant Invasions Imperil Our Country and Civilization* (Thomas Dunne Books, 2002) *385*

Social scientist Tamar Jacoby maintains that the newest immigrants keep America's economy strong because they work harder and take jobs that native-born Americans reject. Syndicated columnist Patrick J. Buchanan argues that America is no longer a nation because immigrants from Mexico and other Third World Latin American and Asian countries have turned America into a series of fragmented multicultural ethnic enclaves that lack a common culture.

Issue 17. Environmentalism: Is the Earth Out of Balance? 397

YES: Otis L. Graham, Jr., from "Epilogue: A Look Ahead," in Otis L. Graham, Jr., ed., *Environmental Politics and Policy, 1960s–1990s* (Pennsylvania State University Press, 2000) *399*

NO: Bjorn Lomborg, from "Yes, It Looks Bad, But . . . ," "Running on Empty," and "Why Kyoto Will Not Stop This," *The Guardian* (August 15, 16, & 17, 2001) *411*

Otis L. Graham, Jr., a professor emeritus of history, maintains that the status of the biophysical basis of our economies, such as "atmospheric pollution affecting global climate, habitat destruction, [and] species extinction," is negative and in some cases irreversible in the long run. Associate professor of statistics Bjorn Lomborg argues that the doomsday scenario for earth has been exaggerated and that, according to almost every measurable indicator, humankind's lot has improved.

Contributors 424
Index 430

Introduction

The Study of History

In a pluralistic society such as ours, the study of history is bound to be a complex process. How an event is interpreted depends not only on the existing evidence but also on the perspective of the interpreter. Consequently, understanding history presupposes the evaluation of information, a task that often leads to conflicting conclusions. An understanding of history, then, requires the acceptance of the idea of historical relativism. Relativism means the redefinition of our past is always possible and desirable. History shifts, changes, and grows with new and different evidence and interpretations. As is the case with the law and even with medicine, beliefs that were unquestioned 100 or 200 years ago have been discredited or discarded since.

Relativism, then, encourages revisionism. There is a maxim that says, "The past must remain useful to the present." Historian Carl Becker argues that every generation should examine history for itself, thus ensuring constant scrutiny of our collective experience through new perspectives. History, consequently, does not remain static, in part because historians cannot avoid being influenced by the times in which they live. Almost all historians commit themselves to revising the views of other historians, by either disagreeing with earlier interpretations or creating new frameworks that pose different questions.

Schools of Thought

Three predominant schools of thought have emerged in American history since the first graduate seminars in history were given at the Johns Hopkins University in Baltimore, Maryland, in the 1870s. The *progressive* school dominated the professional field in the first half of the twentieth century. Influenced by the reform currents of populism, progressivism, and the New Deal, these historians explored the social and economic forces that energized America. The progressive scholars tended to view the past in terms of conflicts between groups, and they sympathized with the underdog.

The post–World War II period witnessed the emergence of a new group of historians who viewed the conflict thesis as overly simplistic. Writing against the backdrop of the Cold War, these neo-conservative and consensus historians argued that Americans possess a shared set of values and that the areas of agreement within the nation's basic democratic and capitalistic framework are more important than the areas of disagreement.

In the 1960s, however, the civil rights movement, women's liberation, and the student rebellion (with its condemnation of the war in Vietnam) fragmented the consensus of values upon which historians of the 1950s centered their interpretations. This turmoil set the stage for the emergence of another group of scholars. *New Left* historians began to reinterpret the past once again. They emphasized the significance of conflict in American history, and they resurrected interest in those groups ignored by the consensus school. In addition, New Left historians critiqued the expansionist policies of the United States and emphasized the difficulties confronted by Native Americans, African Americans, women, and urban workers in gaining full citizenship status.

Progressive, consensus, and New Left history is still being written. The most recent generation of scholars, however, focuses upon social history. Their primary concern is to discover what the lives of "ordinary Americans" were really like. These new social historians employ previously overlooked court and church documents, house deeds and tax records, letters and diaries, photographs, and census data to reconstruct the everyday lives of average Americans. Some employ new methodologies, such as quantification (enhanced by advancing computer technology) and oral history, while others borrow from the disciplines of political science, economics, sociology, anthropology, and psychology for their historical investigations.

The proliferation of historical approaches, which are reflected in the issues debated in this book, has had mixed results. On the one hand, historians have become so specialized in their respective time periods and methodological styles that it is difficult to synthesize the recent scholarship into a comprehensive text for the general reader. On the other hand, historians now know more about new questions or ones that previously were considered to be germane only to scholars in other social sciences. Although there is little agreement about the answers to these questions, the methods employed and the issues explored make the "new history" a very exciting field to study.

The topics that follow represent a variety of perspectives and approaches. Each of these controversial issues can be studied for its individual importance to twentieth century American history. Taken as a group, they interact with one another to illustrate larger historical themes. When grouped thematically, the issues reveal continuing motifs in the development of American history.

Political Movements

Issue 1 explores the various progressive reform movements that ushered in the twentieth century. Professor Richard Abrams maintains that progressivism was a failure because it tried to impose a uniform set of values upon a culturally diverse people and never seriously confronted the inequalities that still exist in American society. Professors Arthur Link and Richard McCormick argue that the progressives were a diverse group of reformers who confronted and ameliorated the worst abuses that emerged in urban-industrial America during the early 1900s.

A second reform movement took place in the 1930s. The Great Depression of the 1930s remains one of the most traumatic events in U.S. history. The characteristics of that decade are deeply etched in American folk memory, but the remedies that were applied to these social and economic ills–known collectively as the New Deal—are not easy to evaluate. In Issue 6, Roger Biles contends that the economic stabilizers created by the New Deal programs prevented the recurrence of the Great Depression. Gary Dean Best, on the other hand, criticizes the New Deal from a 1990s conservative perspective. In his view, because New Deal agencies were antibusiness, they overregulated the economy and did not allow the free enterprise system to work out of the depression that FDR's programs prolonged.

The 1960s brought about a third era of domestic reforms. President Lyndon Johnson named through the early 1960s, the Great Society anti-poverty programs and civil rights laws. Did his successor Richard Nixon continue or attempt to kill the Great Society? In Issue 14, Professor Joan Hoff-Wilson believes the Nixon presidency reorganized the executive branch and portions of the federal bureaucracy and implemented domestic reforms in civil rights, welfare, and economic planning, despite its limited foreign policy successes and the Watergate scandal. But Professor Bruce Schulman argues Nixon was not the last liberal twentieth-century president, but America's first modern conservative executive. By 1971, Nixon had recognized the center of the American political spectrum had shifted rightward, and he shifted his policies accordingly in the areas of civil rights, environmentalism, and welfare reform.

The Outsiders: Blacks, Women, and Immigrants

In recent years, historians have shifted their focus toward social issues, and groups previously ignored have been given renewed attention. Issue 2 asks whether Booker T. Washington's philosophy and actions betrayed the interests of African Americans. The most famous black intellectual, W. E. B. Du Bois, a founding member of the National Organization for the Advancement of Colored People, argues that Booker T. Washington failed to articulate the legitimate demands of African Americans for full civil and political rights. Professor of history Louis R. Harlan portrays Washington as a political realist whose policies and actions were designed to benefit black society as a whole.

It was a long struggle from the Washington era of the early twentieth century to the civil rights revolution of the 1960s. Would the movement have occurred differently without the leadership of Martin Luther King, Jr.? In Issue 11, professor of history Adam Fairclough argues that Martin Luther King, Jr., was a pragmatic reformer who organized nonviolent direct-action protests in strategically targeted local communities, which provoked violence from his opponents, gaining publicly and sympathy for the civil rights movement. Professor of history Clayborne Carson concludes that the civil rights struggle would have followed a similar course of development even if King had never lived because its success depended upon mass activism, not the actions of a single leader.

A direct lineage of the civil rights revolution was the women's liberation movement of the 1970s. Did it help or harm women? In Issue 13, writer an lecturer F. Carolyn Graglia argues that women should stay at home and tice the values of "true motherhood" because contemporary femir discredited marriage, devalued traditional homemaking, and encouraged sexual promiscuity. But feminist and activist scholar Sara M. Evans takes a much more positive view of the women's movements for sufferage and liberation in the past 100 years. Despite their class, racial, religious, ethnic, and regional differences, Evans argues that women in America experienced major transformations in their private and public lives in the twentieth century.

Social Conflicts and Conspiracy Theories

Americans often resort to oversimplified conspiracy theories to explain why certain historical events have taken place. Issue 5 ponders why the Ku Klux Klan emerged in the 1920s. Was the KKK an extremist movement? Professor of history David H. Bennett argues that the Ku Klux Klan was supported mainly by fundamentalist Protestants who were opposed to the changing values associated with the Catholic and Jewish immigrants. Professor of history Stanley Coben believes that local Klansmen were solid middle-class citizens who were concerned about the decline in moral standards in their communities.

Issue 7 seems even more relevant today in light of the 9/11 terrorist attacks. Did President Franklin Roosevelt know in advance that the Japanese had planned to attack Pearl Harbor on December 7, 1941? Retired Rear Admiral Robert A. Theobald argues that FDR deliberately withheld information from the commanders at Pearl Harbor in order to encourage the Japanese to make a surprise attack on the weak U.S. Pacific Fleet. Historian Roberta Wohlstetter contends that even though naval intelligence broke the Japanese code, conflicting signals and the lack of a central agency coordinating U.S. intelligence information made it impossible to predict the Pearl Harbor attack.

America's victory in the Second World War over the fascist powers—Nazi German and imperial Japan—did not provide an extended period of world peace. If anything, America felt more insecure than ever, threatened by the spread of communism throughout the Soviet Union, eastern Europe, and China. Was communism a real threat to America's political and social institutions in the 1940s and 1950s? History professors John Earl Haynes and Harvey Klehr argue in Issue 9 that army code-breakers during World War II's "Venona Project" uncovered a disturbing number of high-ranking U.S. government officials who seriously damaged American interests by passing sensitive information to the Soviet Union. Professor of history Richard M. Fried argues that the early 1950s were a "nightmare in red" during which American citizens had their First and Fifth Amendment rights suspended when a host of national and state investigating committees searched for communists in government agencies, Hollywood, labor unions, foundations, universities, public schools, and even public libraries.

Everyone over age 50 can remember where they were on November 22, 1963 when President Kennedy was assassinated. Did Lee Harvey Oswald kill JFK by himself, or was the President a victim of a vast conspiracy? Thousands of books, articles, and films have dissected this event. In the first selection in Issue 10, the summary of the President's Commission on the Assassination of President John F. Kennedy, formed in 1964 by President Lyndon Johnson, argues that Lee Harvey Oswald was the sole assassin of President Kennedy and that he was not part of any organized conspiracy, domestic or foreign. Professor of history Michael L. Kurtz argues that the Warren Commission ignored evidence of Oswald's connections with organized criminals and with pro-Castro and anti-Castro supporters, as well as forensic evidence that points to multiple assassins.

The United States and the World

As the United States developed a preeminent position in world affairs, the nation's politicians were forced to consider the proper relationship between their country and the rest of the world. To what extent, many asked, should the United States seek to expand its political, economic, and moral influence around the world? This was a particularly intriguing question for early twentieth-century American Presidents Roosevelt, Taft, and Wilson, who actively intervened in the internal affairs in the Caribbean basin of Cuba, Haiti, and the Dominican Republic as well as in the Central American countries of Mexico, Nicaragua and Panama. Were these forays spurred by a need for security or by economic concerns? In Issue 3, the well-known diplomatic historian Walter LaFeber argues that the United States developed a foreign policy that deliberately made the Caribbean nations its economic dependents from the early nineteenth century on. Professor of history David Healy maintains that the two basic goals of American foreign policy in the Caribbean were to provide security against the German threat and to develop the economies of the Latin American nations, whose peoples were considered to be racially inferior.

Issue 4 explores the role of the controversial President Woodrow Wilson in world affairs. Did Wilson set the tone for a moralistic and naively idealistic streak that permeates much of America's twentieth-century foreign policy? Or was Wilson ahead of his time in his attempt to force the United States to abandon its traditional isolationist foreign policy by joining the League of Nations and working in concert with other nations to solve international problems? In the first reading, former national security adviser and political scholar Henry Kissinger characterizes President Woodrow Wilson as a high-minded idealist whose views have made it difficult for later presidents to develop a logical foreign policy based on national self-interest. But the late William G. Carleton, a popular professor of political science at the University of Florida, in his classic article on Woodrow Wilson, provides a spirited defense of Wilson and argues that Woodrow Wilson understood better than his nationalistic opponents the new international role that America would play in world affairs.

The atomic bomb ended the hot war, but friction within the grand alliance over the divisions of Europe and Asia led to a Cold War. Because the United States had become the world's major superpower—both economically as well as militarily—did it bear the primary responsibility for the Cold War? In Issue 8, professor of history Thomas G. Paterson argues that the Truman administration exaggerated the Soviet threat after World War II because the

United States had expansionist political and economic global needs. Professor of history John Lewis Gaddis argues that the power vacuum that existed in Europe at the end of World War II exaggerated and made almost inevitable a clash between the democratic, capitalist United States and the totalitarian, communist USSR.

No discussion of American foreign policy is complete without some consideration of the Vietnam War. Was America's escalation of the war inevitable in 1965? In Issue 12, Brian VanDeMark argues that President Lyndon Johnson was a prisoner of America's global "containment" policy and was afraid to pull out of Vietnam because he feared that his opponents would accuse him of being soft on communism and that they would also destroy his Great Society reforms. H.R. McMaster blames Johnson and his civilian and military advisers for failing to develop a coherent policy in Vietnam.

Now that the Cold War is over, historians must assess why it ended so suddenly and unexpectedly. Did President Ronald Reagan's military buildup in the 1980s force the Soviet Union into economic bankruptcy? In Issue 15, John Lewis Gaddis gives Reagan high marks for ending the cold war. By combining a policy of militancy and operational pragmatism, he argues, Reagan brought about the most significant improvement in Soviet-American relations since the end of World War II. According to Daniel Deudney and G. John Ikenberry, however, the cold war ended only when the Soviets saw the need for international cooperation to end the arms race, prevent a nuclear holocaust, and liberalize their economy. They contend that Western global ideas, not the hard-line containment policy of the early Reagan administration, caused Soviet president Mikhail Gorbachev to abandon Russian communism.

The final issue in this book, Issue 17, is of great concern to most Americans: Is the earth out of balance? In other words, is there really an environmental crisis? Otis L. Graham, Jr., concedes that severe increases in population and declines in forests and water and air quality did not occur as some futurists had projected. However, he holds that the status of the biophysical basis of our economies—"atmospheric pollution affecting global climate, habitat destruction, [and] species extinction"—is negative and, in some cases, irreversible in the long run. Bjorn Lomborg, in reply, argues that the doomsday scenario for earth has been exaggerated and that, by about every measurable indicator, humankind's lot has improved.

Conclusion

The process of historical study should rely more on thinking than on memorizing data. Once the basics of who, what, when, and where are determined, historical thinking shifts to a higher gear. Analysis, comparison and contrast, evaluation, and explanation take command. These skills not only increase our knowledge of the past, but they also provide general tools for the comprehension of all the topics about which human beings think.

The diversity of a pluralistic society, however, creates some obstacles to comprehending the past. The spectrum of differing opinions on any particular subject eliminates the possibility of quick and easy answers. In the final analysis, conclusions are often built through a synthesis of several different interpretations, but even then they may be partial and tentative.

The study of history in a pluralistic society allows each citizen the opportunity to reach independent conclusions about the past. Since most, if not all, historical issues affect the present and future, understanding the past becomes necessary if society is to progress. Many of today's problems have a direct connection with the past. Additionally, other contemporary issues may lack obvious direct antecedents, but historical investigation can provide illuminating analogies. At first, it may appear confusing to read and to think about opposing historical views, but the survival of our democratic society depends on such critical thinking by acute and discerning minds.

Larry Madaras

On the Internet . . .

Internet Web sites containing historical material relevant to the subjects discussed in Part 1 can be reached through the McGraw-Hill history site.

http://www.mhhe.com/socscience/history/usa/link/linktop.htm

Gilded Age and Progressive Era Resources

This page of the department of history at Tennessee Technological University offers over 100 links to sites on the Gilded Age and the Progressive Era. Links include general resources, political leaders, transformation of the West, the rise of big business and American workers, and literary and cultural resources.

http://www.tntech.edu/www/acad/hist/gilprog.html

PART 1

The Response to Industrialism and America's Emergency as a World Power, 1900–1919

The maturing of the industrial system, a major economic depression, agrarian unrest, and labor violence all came to a head in 1898 with the Spanish-American War. The victory gave overseas territorial possessions to the United States and served notice to the world that the United States was entering the twentieth century as a "great power."

The emergence of three strong presidents—Roosevelt, Taft, and Wilson—in the first two decades of the twentieth century brought about a proactive foreign policy and major domestic reforms. The Panama Canal was built in 1913, linking the two oceans through the Caribbean, and military force was used in the area under the pretext of the Monroe Doctrine to protect America's security and emerging business interests. America's role as a mediator and arbitrator of global conflicts was pushed to the limit when Wilson tried to get the United States to join the League of Nations at the end of World War I.

Reformers known as the Progressives attempted to ameliorate the worst abuses brought about in the factories and slums of America's cities. On the national level, all three presidents strengthened enforcement of the anti-trust laws and created regulatory agencies to curb the power that the giant corporations exerted over the economy.

It is argued, however, that the most serious problems of inequality were never addressed by the Progressives. At the end of the nineteenth century, the African American population began fighting for civil rights, political power, and integration into society. Spokespersons for blacks began to emerge, but their often unclear agenda frequently touched off controversy among both black and white people.

ISSUE 1

Did the Progressives Fail?

YES: Richard M. Abrams, from "The Failure of Progressivism," in Richard Abrams and Lawrence Levine, eds., *The Shaping of the Twentieth Century*, 2d ed. (Little, Brown, 1971)

NO: Arthur S. Link and Richard L. McCormick, from *Progressivism* (Harlan Davidson, 1983)

ISSUE SUMMARY

YES: Professor of history Richard M. Abrams maintains that progressivism was a failure because it tried to impose a uniform set of values upon a culturally diverse people and never seriously confronted the inequalities that still exist in American society.

NO: Professors of history Arthur S. Link and Richard L. McCormick argue that the Progressives were a diverse group of reformers who confronted and ameliorated the worst abuses that emerged in urban-industrial America during the early 1900s.

Progressivism is a word used by historians to define the reform currents in the years between the end of the Spanish-American War and America's entrance into the Great War in Europe in 1917. The so-called Progressive movement had been in operation for over a decade before the label was first used in the 1919 electoral campaigns. Former president Theodore Roosevelt ran as a third-party candidate in the 1912 election on the Progressive party ticket, but in truth the party had no real organization outside of the imposing figure of Theodore Roosevelt. Therefore, as a label, "progressivism" was rarely used as a term of self-identification for its supporters. Even after 1912, it was more frequently used by journalists and historians to distinguish the reformers of the period from socialists and old-fashioned conservatives.

The 1890s was a crucial decade for many Americans. From 1893 until almost the turn of the century, the nation went through a terrible economic depression. With the forces of industrialization, urbanization, and immigration wreaking havoc upon the traditional political, social, and economic structures of American life, changes were demanded. The reformers responded in a variety of ways. The proponents of good government believed that democracy was threatened because the cities were ruled by corrupt political machines while the state legislatures were dominated by corporate interests. The cure was to purify democracy and place government directly in the hands of the people through such devices as the initiative, referendum, recall, and the direct election of local school board officials, judges, and U.S. senators.

Social justice proponents saw the problem from a different perspective. Settlement workers moved into cities and tried to change the urban environment. They pushed for sanitation improvements, tenement house reforms, factory inspection laws, regulation of the hours and wages of women, and the abolition of child labor.

A third group of reformers considered the major problem to be the trusts. They argued for controls over the power of big business and for the preservation of the free enterprise system. Progressives disagreed on whether the issue was size or conduct and on whether the remedy was trust-busting or the regulation of big business. But none could deny the basic question: How was the relationship between big business and the U.S. government to be defined?

How successful was the Progressive movement? What triggered the reform impulse? Who were its leaders? How much support did it attract? More important, did the laws that resulted from the various movements fulfill the intentions of its leaders and supporters?

In the following selections, Richard M. Abrams distinguishes the Progressives from other reformers of the era, such as the Populists, the Socialists, the mainstream labor unions, and the corporate reorganization movement. He then argues that the Progressive movement failed because it tried to impose a uniform set of middle-class Protestant moral values upon a nation that was growing more culturally diverse, and because the reformers supported movements that brought about no actual changes or only superficial ones at best. The real inequalities in American society, says Abrams, were never addressed.

In contrast, Arthur S. Link and Richard L. McCormick view progressivism from the point of view of the reformers and rank it as a qualified success. They survey the criticisms of the movement made by historians since the 1950s and generally find them unconvincing. They maintain that the Progressives made the first real attempts to change the destructive direction in which modern urban-industrial society was moving.

Richard M. Abrams

YES

The Failure of Progressivism

Our first task is definitional, because clearly it would be possible to beg the whole question of "failure" by means of semantical niceties. I have no intention of being caught in that kind of critics' trap. I hope to establish that there was a distinctive major reform movement that took place during most of the first two decades of this century, that it had a mostly coherent set of characteristics and long-term objectives, and that, measured by its own criteria—not criteria I should wish, through hindsight and preference, to impose on it—it fell drastically short of its chief goals.

One can, of course, define a reform movement so broadly that merely to acknowledge that we are where we are and that we enjoy some advantages over where we were would be to prove the "success" of the movement. In many respects, Arthur Link does this sort of thing, both in his and William B. Catton's popular textbook, *American Epoch*, and in his article, "What Happened to the Progressive Movement in the 1920's?" In the latter, Link defines "progressivism" as a movement that "began convulsively in the 1890's and waxed and waned afterward to our own time, to insure the survival of democracy in the United States by the enlargement of governmental power to control and offset the power of private economic groups over the nation's institutions and life." Such a definition may be useful to classify data gathered to show the liberal sources of the enlargement of governmental power since the 1890's; but such data would not be finely classified enough to tell us much about the *non*-liberal sources of governmental power (which were numerous and important), about the distinctive styles of different generations of reformers concerned with a liberal society, or even about vital distinctions among divergent reform groups in the era that contemporaries and the conventional historical wisdom have designed as progressive. . . .

Now, without going any further into the problem of historians' definitions which are too broad or too narrow—there is no space here for such an effort—I shall attempt a definition of my own, beginning with the problem that contemporaries set themselves to solve and that gave the era its cognomen, "progressive." That problem was *progress*—or more specifically, how American society was to continue to enjoy the fruits of material progress without the accompanying assault upon human dignity and the erosion of the conventional values and moral assumptions on which the social order appeared to rest. . . .

To put it briefly and yet more specifically, a very large body of men and women entered into reform activities at the end of the nineteenth century to translate "the national credo" (as Henry May calls it) into a general program for social action. Their actions, according to Richard Hofstadter, were "founded upon the indigenous Yankee-Protestant political tradition [that] assumed and demanded the constant disinterested activity of the citizen in public affairs, argued that political life ought to be run, to a greater degree than it was, in accordance with general principles and abstract laws apart from and superior to personal needs, and expressed a common feeling that government should be in good part an effort to moralize the lives of individuals while economic life should be intimately related to the stimulation and development of individual character."

The most consistently important reform impulse, among *many* reform impulses, during the progressive era grew directly from these considerations. It is this reform thrust that we should properly call "the progressive movement." We should distinguish it carefully from reform movements in the era committed primarily to other considerations.

The progressive movement drew its strength from the old mugwump reform impulse, civil service reform, female emancipationists, prohibitionists, the social gospel, the settlement-house movement, some national expansionists, some world peace advocates, conservation advocates, technical efficiency experts, and a wide variety of intellectuals who helped cut through the stifling, obstructionist smokescreen of systematized ignorance. It gained powerful allies from many disadvantaged business interests that appealed to politics to redress unfavorable trade positions; from some ascendant business interests seeking institutional protection; from publishers who discovered the promotional value of exposes; and from politicians-on-the-make who sought issues with which to dislodge long-lived incumbents from their place. Objectively it focused on or expressed (1) a concern for responsive, honest, and efficient government, on the local and state levels especially; (2) recognition of the obligations of society—particularly of an affluent society—to its underprivileged; (3) a desire for more rational use of the nation's resources and economic energies; (4) a rejection, on at least intellectual grounds, of certain social principles that had long obstructed social remedies for what had traditionally been regarded as irremediable evils, such as poverty; and, above all, (5) a concern for the maintenance or restoration of a consensus on what conventionally had been regarded as *fixed moral* principles. "The first and central faith in the national credo," writes Professor May, "was, as it always had been, the reality, certainty, and eternity of moral values. . . . A few thought and said that ultimate values and goals were unnecessary, but in most cases this meant that they believed so deeply in a consensus on these matters that they could not imagine a serious challenge." Progressives shared this faith with most of the rest of the country, but they also conceived of themselves, with a grand sense of stewardship, as its heralds, and its agents.

The progressive movement was (and is) distinguishable from other Contemporary reform movements not only by its devotion to social conditions regarded, by those within it as well as by much of the generality, as *normative*, but also by its definition of what forces threatened that order. More specifically, progressivism directed its shafts at five principal enemies, each in its own way representing reform:

1. The *socialist reform movement*—because, despite socialism's usually praiseworthy concern for human dignity, it represented the subordination of the rights of private property and of individualistic options to objectives that often explicitly threatened common religious beliefs and conventional standards of justice and excellence.
2. The corporate reorganization of American business, which I should call *the corporate reform movement* (its consequence has, after all, been called "the corporate revolution")—because it challenged the traditional relationship of ownership and control of private property, because it represented a shift from production to profits in the entrepreneurial definition of efficiency, because it threatened the proprietary small-business character of the American social structure, because it had already demonstrated a capacity for highly concentrated and socially irresponsible power, and because it sanctioned practices that strained the limits of conventionality and even legality.
3. *The labor union movement*—because despite the virtues of unionized labor as a source of countervailing force against the corporations and as a basis for a more orderly labor force, unionism (like corporate capitalism and socialism) suggested a reduction of individualistic options (at least for wage-earners and especially for small employers), and a demand for a partnership with business management in the decision-making process by a class that convention excluded from such a role.
4. *Agrarian radicalism*, and populism in particular—because it, too, represented (at least in appearance) the insurgency of a class conventionally believed to be properly excluded from a policy-making role in the society, a class graphically represented by the "Pitchfork" Bens and "Sockless" Jerrys, the "Cyclone" Davises and "Alfalfa" Bills, the wool hat brigade and the rednecks.
5. *The ethnic movement*—the demand for specific political and social recognition of ethnic or ex-national affiliations—because accession to the demand meant acknowledgment of the fragmentation of American society as well as a retreat from official standards of integrity, honesty, and efficiency in government in favor of standards based on personal loyalty, partisanship, and sectarian provincialism.

Probably no two progressives opposed all of these forces with equal animus, and most had a noteworthy sympathy for one or more of them. . . .

So much for what progressivism was not. Let me sum it up by noting that what it rejected and sought to oppose necessarily says much about what it was—perhaps even more than can be ascertained by the more direct approach.

My thesis is that progressivism failed. It failed in what it—or what those who shaped it—conceived to be its principal objective. And that was, over and above everything else, to restore or maintain the conventional consensus on a particular view of the universe, a particular set of values, and a particular constellation of behavioral modes in the country's commerce, its industry, its social relations, and its politics. Such a view, such values, such modes were challenged by the influx of diverse religious and ethnic elements into the nation's social and intellectual stream, by the overwhelming economic success and power of the corporate form of business organization, by the subordination of the work-ethic bound up within the old proprietary and craft enterprise system, and by the increasing centrality of a growing proportion of low-income, unskilled, wage-earning classes in the nation's economy and social structure. Ironically, the *coup de grâce* would be struck by the emergence of a philosophical and scientific rationale for the existence of cultural diversity within a single social system, a rationale that largely grew out of the very intellectual ferment to which progressivism so substantially contributed.

Progressivism sought to save the old view, and the old values and modes, by educating the immigrants and the poor so as to facilitate their acceptance of and absorption into the Anglo-American mode of life, or by excluding the "unassimilable" altogether; by instituting antitrust legislation or, at the least, by imposing regulations upon corporate practices in order to preserve a minimal base for small proprietary business enterprise; by making legislative accommodations to the newly important wage-earning classes—accommodations that might provide some measure of wealth and income redistribution, on-the-job safety, occupational security, and the like—so as to forestall a forcible transfer of policy-making power away from the groups that had conventionally exercised that power; and by broadening the political selection process, through direct elections, direct nominations, and direct legislation, in order to reduce tensions caused unnecessarily by excessively narrow and provincial cliques of policymakers. When the economic and political reforms failed to restore the consensus by giving the previously unprivileged an ostensible stake in it, progressive energies turned increasingly toward using the force of the state to proscribe or restrict specifically opprobrious modes of social behavior, such as gaming habits, drinking habits, sexual habits, and Sabbatarian habits. In the ultimate resort, with the proliferation of sedition and criminal syndicalist laws, it sought to constrict political discourse itself. And (except perhaps for the disintegration of the socialist movement) *that* failed, too.

One measure of progressivism's failure lies in the xenophobic racism that reappeared on a large scale even by 1910. In many parts of the country, for example, in the far west and the south, racism and nativism had been fully blended with reform movements even at the height of progressive activities there. The alleged threats of "coolie labor" to American living standards, and of "venal" immigrant and Negro voting to republican institutions generally, underlay the alliance of racism and reform in this period. By and large, however, for the early progressive era the alliance was conspicuous only in the south and on the west coast. By 1910, signs of heightening ethnic animosities, most notably anti-Catholicism, began appearing in other areas of the country as well. As John Higham has written, "It is hard to explain the rebirth of anti-Catholic ferment [at this time] except as an outlet for expectations which progressivism raised and then failed to fulfill." The failure here was in part the inability of reform to deliver a meaningful share of the social surplus to the groups left out of the general national progress, and in part the inability of reform to achieve its objective of assimilation and consensus.

The growing ethnic animus, moreover, operated to compound the difficulty of achieving assimilation. By the second decade of the century, the objects of the antagonism were beginning to adopt a frankly assertive posture. The World War, and the ethnic cleavages it accentuated and aggravated, represented only the final blow to the assimilationist idea; "hyphenate" tendencies had already been growing during the years before 1914. It had only been in 1905 that the Louisvilleborn and secular-minded Louis Brandeis had branded as "disloyal" all who "keep alive" their differences of origin or religion. By 1912, by now a victim of anti-Semitism and aware of a rising hostility toward Jews in the country, Brandeis had become an active Zionist; before a Jewish audience in 1913, he remarked how "practical experience" had convinced him that "to be good Americans, we must be better Jews, and to be better Jews, we must become Zionists."

Similarly, American Negroes also began to adopt a more aggressive public stance after having been subdued for more than a decade by antiblack violence and the accommodationist tactics suggested in 1895 by Booker T. Washington. As early as 1905, many black leaders had broken with Washington in founding the Niagara Movement for a more vigorous assertion of Negro demands for equality. But most historians seem to agree that it was probably the Springfield race riot of 1908 that ended illusions that black people could gain an equitable share in the rewards of American culture by accommodationist or assimilationist methods. The organization of the NAACP in 1909 gave substantive force for the first time to the three-year-old Niagara Movement. The year 1915 symbolically concluded the demise of accommodationism. That year, the Negro-baiting movie, "The Birth of a Nation," played to massive, enthusiastic audiences that included notably the president of the United States and the chief justice of the Supreme Court; the KKK was revived; and Booker T. Washington died. The next year, black nationalist Marcus Garvey arrived in New York from Jamaica.

Meanwhile, scientific knowledge about race and culture was undergoing a crucial revision. At least in small part stimulated by a keen self-consciousness of his own "outsider" status in American culture, the German Jewish immigrant Franz Boas was pioneering in the new anthropological concept of "cultures," based on the idea that human behavioral traits are conditioned by historical traditions. The new view of culture was in time to undermine completely the prevailing evolutionary view that ethnic differences must mean racial inequality. The significance of Boas's work after 1910, and that of his students A. L. Kroeber and Clyde Kluckhohn in particular, rests on the fact that the racist thought of the progressive era had founded its intellectual rationale on the monistic, evolutionary view of culture; and indeed much of the progressives' anxiety over the threatened demise of "the American culture" had been founded on that view.

Other intellectual developments as well had for a long time been whittling-away at the notion that American society had to stand or fall on the unimpaired coherence of its cultural consensus. Yet the new work in anthropology, law, philosophy, physics, psychology, and literature only unwittingly undermined that assumption. Rather, it was only as the ethnic hostilities grew, and especially as the power of the state came increasingly to be invoked against dissenting groups whose ethnic "peculiarities" provided an excuse for repression, that the new intelligence came to be developed. "The world has thought that it must have its culture and its political unity coincide," wrote Randolph Bourne in 1916 while chauvinism, nativism, and antiradicalism were mounting; now it was seeing that cultural diversity might yet be the salvation of the liberal society—that it might even serve to provide the necessary countervailing force to the power of the state that private property had once served (in the schema of Locke, Harrington, and Smith) before the interests of private property became so highly concentrated and so well blended with the state itself.

The telltale sign of progressivism's failure was the violent crusade against dissent that took place in the closing years of the Wilson administration. It is too easy to ascribe the literal hysteria of the postwar years to the dislocations of the War alone. Incidents of violent repression of labor and radical activities had been growing remarkably, often in step with xenophobic outbreaks, for several years before America's intervention in the War. To quote Professor Higham once more. "The seemingly unpropitious circumstances under which antiradicalism and anti-Catholicism came to life [after 1910] make their renewal a subject of moment." It seems clear that they both arose out of the sources of the reform ferment itself. When reform failed to enlarge the consensus, or to make it more relevant to the needs of the still disadvantaged and disaffected, and when in fact reform seemed to be encouraging more radical challenges to the social order, the old anxieties of the 1890's returned.

The postwar hysteria represented a reaction to a confluence of anxiety-laden developments, including the high cost of living, the physical and social dislocations of war mobilization and the recruitment of women and Negroes into war production jobs in the big northern cities, the Bolshevik Revolution, a series of labor strikes, and a flood of radical literature that exaggerated the capabilities of radical action. "One Hundred Per Cent Americanism" seemed the only effective way of meeting all these challenges at once. As Stanley Coben has written, making use of recent psychological studies and anthropological work on cultural "revitalization movements"; "Citizens who joined the crusade for one hundred per cent Americanism sought, primarily, a unifying forte which would halt the apparent disintegration of their culture. . . . The slight evidence of danger from radical organizations aroused such wild fear only because Americans had already encountered other threats to cultural stability."

Now, certainly during the progressive era a lot of reform legislation was passed, much that contributed genuinely to a more liberal society, though more that contributed to the more absolutistic moral objectives of progressivism. Progressivism indeed had real, lasting effects for the blunting of the sharper edges of self-interest in American life, and for the reduction of the harsher cruelties suffered by the society's underprivileged. These achievements deserve emphasis, not least because they derived directly from the progressive habit of looking to standards of conventional morality and human decency for the solution of diverse social conflicts. But the deeper nature of the problem Confronting American society required more than the invocation of conventional standards; the conventions themselves were at stake, especially as they bore upon the allocation of privileges and rewards. Because most of the progressives never confronted that problem, in a way their efforts were doomed to failure.

In sum, the overall effect of the period's legislation is not so impressive. For example, all the popular government measures put together have not Conspicuously raised the quality of American political life. Direct nominations and elections have tended to make political campaigns so expensive as to reduce the number of eligible candidates for public office to (1) the independently wealthy; (2) the ideologues, especially on the right, who can raise the needed campaign money from independently wealthy ideologues like themselves, or from the organizations set up to promote a particular ideology; and (3) party hacks who payoff their debt to the party treasury by whistle-stopping and chicken dinner speeches. Direct legislation through the Initiative and Referendum device has made cities and states prey to the best-financed and -organized special-interest group pressures, as have so-called nonpartisan elections. Which is not to say that things are worse than before, but only that they are not conspicuously better. The popular government measures did have the effect of shaking up the established political organizations of the day, and that may well have been their only real purpose.

But as Arthur Link has said, in his text, *The American Epoch*, the popular government measures "were merely instruments to facilitate the capture of political machinery. . . . They must be judged for what they accomplished or failed to accomplish on the higher level of substantive reform." Without disparaging the long list of reform measures that passed during the progressive era, the question remains whether all the "substantive reforms" together accomplished what the progressives wanted them to accomplish.

Certain social and economic advantages were indeed shuffled about, but this must be regarded as a short-term achievement for special groups at best. Certain commercial interests, for example, achieved greater political leverage in railroad policy-making than they had had in 1900 through measures such as the Hepburn and Mann-Elkins Acts—though it was not until the 1940's that any real change occurred in the general rate structure, as some broad regional interests had been demanding at the beginning of the century. Warehouse, farm credits, and land-bank acts gave the diminishing numbers of farm owners enhanced opportunities to mortgage their property, and some business groups had persuaded the federal government to use national revenues to educate farmers on how to increase their productivity (Smith-Lever Act, 1914); but most farmers remained as dependent as ever upon forces beyond their control—the bankers, the middlemen, the international market. The FTC, and the Tariff Commission established in 1916, extended the principle of using government agencies to adjudicate intra-industrial conflicts ostensibly in the national interest, but these agencies would develop a lamentable tendency of deferring to and even confirming rather than moderating the power of each industry's dominant interests. The Federal Reserve Act made the currency more flexible, and that certainly made more sense than the old system, as even the bankers agreed. But depositers would be as prey to defaulting banks as they had been in the days of the Pharaoh—bank deposit insurance somehow was "socialism" to even the best of men in this generation. And despite Woodrow Wilson's brave promise to end the banker's stifling hold on innovative small business, one searches in vain for some provision in the FRA designed specifically to encourage small or new businesses. In fact, the only constraints on the bankers' power that emerged from the era came primarily from the ability of the larger corporations to finance their own expansion out of capital surpluses they had accumulated from extortionate profits during the War.

A major change almost occurred during the war years when organized labor and the principle of collective bargaining received official recognition and a handful of labor leaders was taken, temporarily, into policy-making councils (e.g., in the War Labor Board). But actually, as already indicated, such a development, if it had been made permanent, would have represented a defeat, not a triumph, for progressivism. The progressives may have fought for improved labor conditions, but they jealously fought against the enlargement of union power. It was no aberration that once the need for wartime productive efficiency evaporated, leading progressives such as A. Mitchell Palmer, Miles Poindexter, and Woodrow Wilson himself helped civic and employer organizations to bludgeon the labor movement into disunity and docility. (It is possible, I suppose, to argue that such progressives were simply inconsistent, but if we understand progressivism in the terms I have outlined above I think the consistency is more evident.) Nevertheless, a double irony is worth noting with respect to progressivism's objectives and the wartime labor developments. On the one hand, the progressives' hostility to labor unions defeated their own objectives of (1) counterbalancing the power of collectivized capital (i.e., corporations), and (2) enhancing workers' share of the nation's wealth. On the other hand, under wartime duress, the progressives did grant concessions to organized labor (e.g., the Adamson Eight-Hour Railway Labor Act, as well as the WLB) that would later serve as precedents for the very "collectivization" of the economic situation that they were dedicated to oppose.

Meanwhile, the distribution of advantages in the society did not change much at all. In some cases, from the progressive reformers' viewpoint at least, it may even have changed for the worse. According to the figures of the National Industrial Conference Board, even income was as badly distributed at the end of the era as before. In 1921, the highest 10 percent of income recipients received 38 percent of total personal income, and that figure was only 34 percent in 1910. (Since the share of the top S percent of income recipients probably declined in the 1910–20 period, the figures for the top 10 percent group suggest a certain improvement in income distribution at the top. But the fact that the share of the lowest 60 percent also declined in that period, from 35 percent to 30 percent, confirms the view that no meaningful improvement can be shown.) Maldistribution was to grow worse until after 1929.

American farmers on the whole and in particular seemed to suffer increasing disadvantages. Farm life was one of the institutional bulwarks of the mode of life the progressives ostensibly cherished. "The farmer who owns his land" averred Gifford Pinchot, "is still the backbone of the Nation; and one of the things we want most is more of him, . . . [for] he is the first of homemakers." If only in the sense that there were relatively fewer farmers in the total population at the end of the progressive era, one would have to say farm life in the United States had suffered. But, moreover, fewer owned their own farms. The number of farm tenants increased by 21 percent from 1900 to 1920; 38.1 percent of all farm operators in 1921 were tenants; and the figures look even worse when one notices that tenancy *declined* in the most *impoverished* areas during this period, suggesting that the family farm was surviving mostly in the more marginal agricultural areas. Finally, although agriculture had enjoyed some of its most prosperous years in history in the 1910–20 period, the 21 percent of the nation's gainfully employed who were in agriculture in 1919 (a peak year) earned only 16 percent of the national income.

While progressivism failed to restore vitality to American farming, it failed also to stop the vigorous ascendancy of corporate capitalism, the most conspicuous challenge to conventional values and modes that the society faced at the beginning of the era. The corporation had drastically undermined the very basis of the traditional rationale that had supported the nation's free-wheeling system of resource allocation and had underwritten the permissiveness of the laws governing economic activities in the nineteenth century. The new capitalism by-passed the privately-owned proprietary firm, it featured a separation of ownership and control, it subordinated the profit motive to varied and variable other objectives such as empire-building, and, in many of the techniques developed by financial brokers and investment bankers, it appeared to create a great gulf between the making of money and the producing of useful goods and services. Through a remarkable series of judicial sophistries, this nonconventional form of business enterprise had become, in law, a *person*, and had won privileges and liberties once entrusted only to men, who were presumed to be conditioned and restrained by the moral qualities that inhere in human nature. Although gaining legal dispensations from an obliging Supreme Court, the corporation could claim no theoretical legitimacy beyond the fact of its power and its apparent inextricable entanglement in the business order that had produced America's seemingly unbounded material success.

Although much has been written about the supposed continuing vitality of small proprietary business enterprise in the United States, there is no gainsaying the continued ascendancy of the big corporation nor the fact that it still lacks legitimation. The fact that in the last sixty years the number of small proprietary businesses has grown at a rate that slightly exceeds the rate of population growth says little about the character of small business enterprise today as compared with that of the era of the American industrial revolution; it does nothing to disparage the apprehensions expressed in the antitrust campaigns of the progressives. To focus on the vast numbers of automobile dealers and gasoline service station owners, for example, is to miss completely their truly humble dependence upon the very few giant automobile and oil companies, a foretold dependence that was the very point of progressives' anticorporation, antitrust sentiments. The progressive movement must indeed be credited with placing real restraints upon monopolistic tendencies in the United States, for most statistics indicate that at least until the 1950's business concentration showed no substantial increase from the turn of the century (though it may be pertinent to note that concentration ratios did increase significantly in the decade immediately following the progressive era). But the statistics of concentration remain impressive—just as they were when John Moody wrote *The Truth About the Trusts* in 1904 and Louis Brandeis followed it with *Other People's Money* in 1914. That two hundred corporations (many of them interrelated) held almost one-quarter of all business assets, and more than 40 percent of all corporate assets in the country in 1948; that the fifty largest manufacturing corporations held 35 percent of all industrial assets in 1948, and 38 percent by 1962; and that a mere twenty-eight corporations or one one-thousandth of a percentage of all nonfinancial firms in 1956 employed 10 percent of all those employed in the nonfinancial industries, should be sufficient statistical support for the apprehensions of the progressive era—*just as it is testimony to the failure of the progressive movement to achieve anything substantial to alter the situation.*

Perhaps the crowning failure of progressivism was the American role in World War I. It is true that many progressives opposed America's intervention, but it is also true that a great many more supported it. The failure in progressivism lies not in the decision to intervene but in the futility of intervention measured by progressive expectations.

Arthur S. Link and
Richard L. McCormick

NO

Progressivism in History

Convulsive reform movements swept across the American landscape from the 1890s to 1917. Angry farmers demanded better prices for their products, regulation of the railroads, and the destruction of what they thought was the evil power of bankers, middlemen, and corrupt politicians. Urban residents crusaded for better city services and more efficient municipal government. Members of various professions, such as social workers and doctors, tried to improve the dangerous and unhealthy conditions in which many people lived and worked. Businessmen, too, lobbied incessantly for goals which they defined as reform. Never before had the people of the United States engaged in so many diverse movements for the improvement of their political system, economy, were calling themselves progressives. Ever since, historians have used the term *progessivism* to describe the many reform movements of the early twentieth century.

Yet in the goals they sought and the remedies they tried, the reformers were a varied and contradictory lot. Some progressives wanted to increase the political influence and control of ordinary people, while other progressives wanted to concentrate authority in experts. Many reformers tried to curtail the growth of large corporations; others accepted bigness in industry on account of its supposed economic benefits. Some progressives were genuinely concerned about the welfare of the "new" immigrants from southern and eastern Europe; other progressives sought, sometimes frantically, to "Americanize" the newcomers or to keep them out altogether. In general, progressives sought to improve the conditions of life and labor and to create as much social stability as possible. But each group of progressives had its own definitions of improvement and stability. In the face of such diversity, one historian, Peter G. Filene, has even argued that what has been called the progressive movement never existed as a historical phenomenon ("An Obituary for 'The Progressive Movement,'" *American Quarterly*, 1970).

Certainly there was no *unified* movement, but, like most students of the period, we consider progessivism to have been a real, vital, and significant phenomenon, one which contemporaries recognized and talked and fought about. Properly conceptualized, progressivism provides a useful framework for the history of the United States in the late nineteenth and early twentieth centuries.

One source of confusion and controversy about progressives and progressivism is the words themselves. They are often used judgmentally to describe people and changes which historians have deemed to be "good," "enlightened," and "farsighted." The progressives themselves naturally intended the words to convey such positive qualities, but we should not accept their usage uncritically. It might be better to avoid the terms progressive and progressivism altogether, but they are too deeply embedded in the language of contemporaries and historians to be ignored. Besides, we think that the terms have real meaning. In this [selection] the words will be used neutrally, without any implicit judgment about the value of reform.

In the broadest sense, progressivism was the way in which a whole generation of Americans defined themselves politically and responded to the nation's problems at the turn of the century. The progressives made the first comprehensive efforts to grapple with the ills of a modern urban-industrial society. Hence the record of their achievements and failures has considerable relevance for our own time.

Who Were the Progressives?

Ever since the early twentieth century, people have argued about who the progressives were and what they stood for. This may seem to be a strange topic of debate, but it really is not. Progressivism engaged many different groups of Americans, and each group of progressives naturally considered themselves to be the key reformers and thought that their own programs were the most important ones. Not surprisingly, historians ever since have had trouble agreeing on who really shaped progressivism and its goals. Scholars who have written about the period have variously identified farmers, the old middle classes, professionals, businessmen, and urban immigrants and ethnic groups as the core group of progressives. But these historians have succeeded in identifying *their* reformers only by defining progressivism narrowly, by excluding other reformers and reforms when they do not fall within some specific definition, and by resorting to such vague, catch-all adjectives as "middle class." . . .

The advocates of the middle-class view might reply that they intended to study the leaders of reform, not its supporters, to identify and describe the men and women who imparted the dominant character to progressivism, not its mass base. The study of leadership is surely a valid subject in its own right and is particularly useful for an understanding of progressivism. But too much focus on leadership conceals more than it discloses about early twentieth-century reform. The dynamics of progressivism were crucially generated by ordinary people—by the sometimes frenzied mass supporters of progressive leaders, by rank-and-file voters willing to trust a reform candidate. The chronology of progressivism can be traced by events which aroused large numbers of people—a sensational muckraking article, an outrageous political scandal, an eye-opening legislative investigation, or a tragic social calamity. Events such as these gave reform its rhythm and its power.

Progressivism cannot be understood without seeing how the masses of Americans perceived and responded to such events. Widely circulated magazines gave people everywhere the sordid facts of corruption and carried the clamor for reform into every city, village, and county. State and national election campaigns enabled progressive candidates to trumpet their programs. Almost no literate person in the United States in, say, 1906 could have been unaware that ten-year-old children worked through the night in dangerous factories, or that many United States senators served big business. Progressivism was the only reform movement ever experienced by the whole American nation. Its national appeal and mass base vastly exceeded that of Jacksonian reform. And progressivism's dependence on the people for its objectives and timing has no comparison in the executive-dominated New Deal of Franklin D. Roosevelt or the Great Society of Lyndon B. Johnson. Wars and depressions had previously engaged the whole nation, but never reform. And so we are back to the problem of how to explain and define the outpouring of progressive reform which excited and involved so many different kinds of people.

A little more than a decade ago, Buenker and Thelen recognized the immense diversity of progressivism and suggested ways in which to reorient the study of early twentieth-century reform. Buenker observed that divergent groups often came together on one issue and then changed alliances on the next ("The Progressive Era: A Search for a Synthesis," *Mid-America,* 1969). Indeed, different reformers sometimes favored the same measure for distinctive, even opposite, reasons. Progressivism could be understood only in the light of these shifting coalitions. Thelen, in his study of Wisconsin's legislature, also emphasized the importance of cooperation between different reform groups. "The basic riddle in Progressivism," he concluded, "is not what drove groups apart but what made them seek common cause."

There is a great deal of wisdom in these articles, particularly in their recognition of the diversity of progressivism and in the concept of shifting coalitions of reformers. A two-pronged approach is necessary to carry forward this way of looking at early twentieth-century reform. First, we should study, not an imaginary unified progressive movement, but individual reforms and give particular attention to the goals of their diverse supporters, the public rationales given for them, and the results which they achieved. Second, we should try to identify the features which were more or less common to different progressive reforms.

The first task—distinguishing the goals of a reform from its rhetoric and its results—is more difficult than it might appear to be. Older interpretations of progressivism implicitly assumed that the rhetoric explained the goals and that, if a proposed reform became law, the results fulfilled the intentions behind it. Neither assumption is a sound one: purposes, rationale, and results are three different things. Samuel P. Hays' influential article, "The Politics of Reform in Municipal Government in the Progressive Era" (*Pacific Northwest Quarterly,* 1964), exposed the fallacy of automatically equating the democratic rhetoric of the reformers with their true purposes. The two may have coincided, but the historian has to demonstrate that fact, not take it for granted. The unexamined identification of either intentions or rhetoric with results is also invalid, although it is still a common feature of the scholarship on progressivism. Only within the last decade have historians begun to examine the actual achievements of the reformers. To carry out this first task, in the following . . . we will distinguish between the goals and rhetoric of individual reforms and will discuss the results of reform whenever the current literature permits. To do so is to observe the ironies, complexities, and disappointments of progressivism.

The second task—that of identifying the common characteristics of progressivism—is even more difficult than the first but is an essential base on which to build an understanding of progressivism. The rest of this [selection] focuses on identifying such characteristics. The place to begin that effort is the origins of progressivism. . . .

The Character and Spirit of Progressivism

Progressivism was characterized, in the first place, by a distinctive set of attitudes toward industrialism. By the turn of the century, the overwhelming majority of Americans had accepted the permanence of large-scale industrial, commercial, and financial enterprises and of the wage and factory systems. The progressives shared this attitude. Most were not socialists, and they undertook reform, not to dismantle modern economic institutions, but rather to ameliorate and improve the conditions of industrial life. Yet progressivism was infused with a deep outrage against the worst consequences of industrialism. Outpourings of anger at corporate wrongdoing and of hatred for industry's callous pursuit of profit frequently punctuated the course of reform in the early twentieth century. Indeed, antibusiness emotion was a prime mover of progressivism. That the acceptance of industrialism *and* the outrage against it were intrinsic to early twentieth-century reform does not mean that progressivism was mindless or that it has to be considered indefinable. But it does suggest that there was a powerful irony in progressivism: reforms which gained support from a people angry with the oppressive aspects of industrialism also assisted the same persons to accommodate to it, albeit to an industrialism which was to some degree socially responsible.

The progressives' ameliorative reforms also reflected their faith in progress—in mankind's ability, through purposeful action, to improve the environment and the conditions of life. The late nineteenth-century dissidents had not lacked this faith, but their espousal of panaceas bespoke a deep pessimism: "Unless this one great change is made, things will get worse." Progressive reforms were grounded on a broader assumption. In particular, reforms could protect the people hurt by industrialization, and make the environment more humane. For intellectuals of the era, the achievement of such goals meant that they had to meet Herbert Spencer head on and confute his absolute "truths." Progressive thinkers, led by Lester Frank Ward, Richard T. Ely, and, most important, John Dewey, demolished social Darwinism with what Goldman has called "reform Darwinism." They asserted that human adaptation to the environment did not interfere with the evolutionary process, but was, rather, part and parcel of the law of natural change. Progressive intellectuals and their popularizers produced a vast literature to condemn laissez faire and to promote the concept of the active state.

To improve the environment meant, above all, to intervene in economic and social affairs in order to control natural forces and impose a measure of order upon them. This belief in interventionism was a third component of progressivism. It was visible in almost every reform of the era, from the supervision of business to the prohibition of alcohol John W. Chambers II, *The Tyranny of Change: America in the Progressive Era, 1900–1917,* 1980). Interventionism could be both private and public. Given their choice, most progressives preferred to work noncoercively through voluntary organizations for economic and social changes. However, as time passed, it became evident that most progressive reforms could be achieved only by legislation and public control. Such an extension of public authority made many progressives uneasy, and few of them went so far as Herbert Croly in glorifying the state in his *The Promise of American Life* (1909) and *Progressive Democracy* (1914). Even so, the intervention necessary for their reforms inevitably propelled progressives toward an advocacy of the use of governmental power. A familiar scenario during the period was one in which progressives called upon public authorities to assume responsibility for interventions which voluntary organizations had begun.

The foregoing describes the basic characteristics of progressivism but says little about its ideals. Progressivism was inspired by two bodies of belief and knowledge—evangelical Protestantism and the natural and social sciences. These sources of reform may appear at first glance antagonistic to one another. Actually, they were complementary, and each imparted distinctive qualities to progressivism.

Ever since the religious revivals from about 1820 to 1840, evangelical Protestantism had spurred reform in the United States. Basic to the reform mentality was an all-consuming urge to purge the world of sin, such as the sins of slavery and intemperance, against which nineteenth-century reformers had crusaded. Now the progressives carried the struggle into the modern citadels of sin—the teeming cities of the nation. No one can read their writings and speeches without being struck by the fact that many of them believed that it was their Christian duty to right the wrongs created by the processes of industrialization. Such belief was the motive force behind the Social Gospel, a movement which swept through the Protestant churches in the 1890s and 1900s. Its goal was to align churches, frankly and aggressively, on the side of the downtrodden, the poor, and working people—in other words, to make Christianity relevant to this world, not the next. It is difficult to measure the influence of the Social Gospel, but it seared the consciences of millions of Americans, particularly in urban areas. And it triumphed in the organization in 1908 of the Federal Council of Churches of Christ in America, with its platform which condemned exploitative capitalism and proclaimed the right of workers to organize and to enjoy a decent standard of living. Observers at the Progressive party's national convention of 1912 should not have been surprised to hear the delegates sing, spontaneously and emotionally, the Christian call to arms, "Onward, Christian Solders!"

The faith which inspired the singing of "Onward, Christian Soldiers!" had significant implications for progressive reforms. Progressives used moralistic appeals to make people feel the awful weight of wrong in the world and to exhort them to accept personal responsibility for its eradication. The resultant reforms could be generous in spirit, but they could also seem intolerant to the people who were "reformed." Progressivism sometimes seemed to envision life in a small town Protestant community or an urban drawing room—a vision sharply different from that of Catholic or Jewish immigrants. Not every progressive shared the evangelical ethos, much less its intolerance, but few of the era's reforms were untouched by the spirit and techniques of Protestant revivalism.

Science also had a pervasive impact on the methods and objectives of progressivism. Many leading reformers were specialists in the new disciplines of statistics, economics, sociology, and psychology. These new social scientists set out to gather data on human behavior as it actually was and to discover the laws which governed it. Since social scientists accepted environmentalist and interventionist assumptions implicitly, they believed that knowledge of natural laws would make it possible to devise and apply solutions to improve the human condition. This faith underpinned the optimism of most progressives and predetermined the methods used by almost all reformers of the time: investigation of the facts and application of social-science knowledge to their analysis; entrusting trained experts to decide what should be done; and, finally, mandating government to execute reform.

These methods may have been rational, but they were also compatible with progressive moralism. In its formative period, American social science was heavily infused with ethical concerns. An essential purpose of statistics, economics, sociology, and psychology was to improve and uplift. Leading practitioners of these disciplines, for example, Richard T. Ely, an economist at the University of Wisconsin, were often in the vanguard of the Social Gospel. Progressives blended science and religion into a view of human behavior which was unique to their generation, which had grown up in an age of revivals and come to maturity at the birth of social science.

All of progressivism's distinctive features found expression in muckraking—the literary spearhead of early twentieth-century reform. Through the medium of such new ten-cent magazines as *McClure's, Everybody's* and *Cosmopolitan*, the muckrakers exposed every dark aspect and corner of American life. Nothing escaped the probe of writers such as Ida M. Tarbell, Lincoln Steffens, Ray Stannard Baker, and Burton J. Hendrick—not big business, politics, prostitution, race relations, or even the churches. Behind the exposes of the muckrakers lay the progressive attitude toward industrialism: it was here to stay, but many of its aspects seemed to be deplorable. These could be improved, however, if only people became aware of conditions and determined to ameliorate them. To bring about such awareness, the muckrakers appealed to their readers' consciences. Steffens' famous series, published in book form as *The Shame of the Cities* in 1904, was frankly intended to make people feel guilty for the corruption which riddled their cities. The muckrakers also used the social scientists' method of careful and painstaking gathering of data—and with devastating effects. The investigative function—which was later largely taken over by governmental agencies—proved absolutely vital to educating and arousing Americans.

All progressive crusades shared the spirit and used the techniques discussed here, but they did so to different degrees and in different ways. Some voiced a greater willingness to accept industrialism and even to extol its potential benefits; others expressed more strongly the outrage against its darker aspects. Some intervened through voluntary organizations; others relied on government to achieve changes. Each reform reflected a distinctive balance between the claims of Protestant moralism and of scientific rationalism. Progressives fought among themselves over these questions even while they set to the common task of applying their new methods and ideas to the problems of a modern society. . . .

In this analysis we have frequently pointed to the differences between the rhetoric, intentions, and results of progressive reform. The failure of reform always to fulfill the expectations of its advocates was not, of course, unique to the progressive era. Jacksonian reform, Reconstruction, and the New Deal all exhibited similar ironies and disappointments. In each case, the clash between reformers with divergent purposes, the inability to predict how given methods of reform would work in practice, and the ultimate waning of popular zeal for change all contributed to the disjuncture of rationale, purpose, and achievement. Yet the gap between these things seems more obvious in the progressive era because so many diverse movements for reform took place in a brief span of time and were accompanied by resounding rhetoric and by high expectations for the improvement of the American social and political environment. The effort to change so many things all at once, and the grandiose claims made for the moral and material betterment which would result, meant that disappointments were bound to occur.

Yet even the great number of reforms and the uncommonly high expectations for them cannot fully account for the consistent gaps which we have observed between the stated purposes, real intentions, and actual results of progressivism. Several additional factors, intrinsic to the nature of early twentieth-century reform, help to explain the ironies and contradictions.

One of these was the progressives' confident reliance on modern methods of reform. Heirs of recent advances in natural science and social science, they enthusiastically devised and applied new techniques to improve American government and society. Their methods often worked; on the other hand, progressive programs often simply did not prove capable of accomplishing what had been expected of them. This was not necessarily the reformers' fault. They hopefully used untried methods even while they lacked a science of society which was capable of solving all the great problems which they attacked. At the same time, the progressives' scientific methods made it possible to know just how far short of success their programs had sometimes fallen. The evidence of their failures thus was more visible than in any previous era of reform. To the progressives' credit, they usually published that evidence—for contemporaries and historians alike to see.

A second aspect of early twentieth-century reform which helps to account for the gaps between aims and achievements was the deep ambivalence of the progressives about industrialism and its consequences. Individual reformers were divided, and so was their movement as a whole. Compared to many Americans of the late 1800s, the progressives fundamentally accepted an industrial society and sought mainly to control and ameliorate it. Even reformers who were intellectually committed to socialist ideas often acted the part of reformers, not radicals.

Yet progressivism was infused and vitalized, as we have seen, by people truly angry with their industrial society. Few of them wanted to tear down the modern institutions of business and commerce, but their anger was real, their moralism was genuine, and their passions were essential to the reforms of their time.

The reform movement never resolved this ambivalence about industrialism. Much of its rhetoric and popular passion pointed in one direction—toward some form of social democracy—while its leaders and their programs went in another. Often the result was confusion and bitterness. Reforms frequently did not measure up to popular, antibusiness expectations, indeed, never were expected to do so by those who designed and implemented them. Even conservative, ameliorative reformers like Theodore Roosevelt often used radical rhetoric. In doing so, they misled their followers and contributed to the ironies of progressivism.

Perhaps most significant, progressives failed to achieve all their goals because, despite their efforts, they never fully came to terms with the divisions and conflicts in American society. Again and again, they acknowledged the existence of social disharmony more fully and frankly than had nineteenth-century Americans. Nearly every social and economic reform of the era was predicated on the progressive recognition that diverse cultural and occupational groups had conflicting interests, and that the responsibility for mitigating and adjusting those differences lay with the whole society, usually the government. Such recognition was one of the progressives' most significant achievements. Indeed, it stands among the most important accomplishments of liberal reform in all of American history. For, by frankly acknowledging the existence of social disharmony, the progressives committed the twentieth-century United States to recognizing—and to lessening—the inevitable conflicts of a heterogeneous industrial society.

Yet the significance of the progressives' recognition of diversity was compromised by the methods and institutions which they adopted to diminish or eliminate social and economic conflict. Expert administrative government turned out to be less neutral than the progressives believed that it would be. No scientific reform could be any more impartial than the experts who gathered the data or than the bureaucrats who implemented the programs. In practice, as we have seen, administrative government often succumbed to the domination of special interests.

It would be pointless to blame the progressives for the failure of their new methods and programs to eradicate all the conflicts of an industrial society, but it is perhaps fair to ask why the progressives adopted measures which tended to disguise and obscure economic and social conflict almost as soon as they had uncovered it. For one thing, they honestly believed in the almost unlimited potentialities of science and administration. Our late twentieth-century skepticism of these wonders should not blind us to the faith with which the progressives embraced them and imbued them with what now seem magical properties. For another, the progressives were reformers, not radicals. It was one thing to recognize the existence of economic and social conflict, but quite another thing to admit that it was permanent. By and large, these men and women were personally and ideologically inclined to believe that the American society was, in the final analysis, harmonious, and that such conflicts as did exist could be resolved. Finally, the class and cultural backgrounds of the leading progressives often made them insensitive to lower-class immigrant Americans and their cultures. Attempts to reduce divisions sometimes came down to imposing middle-class Protestant ways on the urban masses. In consequence, the progressives never fulfilled their hope of eliminating social conflict. Reformers of the early twentieth century saw the problem more fully than had their predecessors, but they nonetheless tended to consider conflicts resolved when, in fact, they only had been papered over. Later twentieth-century Americans have also frequently deceived themselves in this way.

Thus progressivism inevitably fell short of its rhetoric and intentions. Lest this seem an unfairly critical evaluation, it is important to recall how terribly ambitious were the stated aims and true goals of the reformers. They missed some of their marks because they sought to do so much. And, despite all their shortcomings, they accomplished an enormous part of what they set out to achieve.

Progressivism brought major innovations to almost every facet of public and private life in the United States. The political and governmental systems particularly felt the effects of reform. Indeed, the nature of political participation and the uses to which it was put went through transitions as momentous as those of any era in American history. These developments were complex, as we have seen, and it is no easy matter to sort out who was helped and who was hurt by each of them or by the entire body of reforms. At the very least, the political changes of the progressive era significantly accommodated American public life to an urban-industrial society. On balance, the polity probably emerged neither more nor less democratic than before, but it did become better suited to address, or at least recognize, the questions and problems which arose from the cities and factories of the nation. After the progressive era, just as before, wealthier elements in American society had a disproportionate share of political power, but we can hardly conclude that this was the fault of the progressives.

The personal and social life of the American people was also deeply affected by progressivism. Like the era's political changes, the economic and social reforms of the early twentieth century were enormously complicated and are difficult to summarize without doing violence to their diversity. In the broadest sense, the progressives sought to mitigate the injustice and the disorder of a society now dominated by its industries and cities. Usually, as we have observed, the quests for social justice and social control were extricably bound together in the reformers' programs, with each group of progressives having different interpretations of these dual ends. Justice sometimes took second place to control. However, before one judges the reformers too harshly for that, it is well to remember how bad urban social conditions were in the late nineteenth century and the odds against which the reformers fought. It is also well to remember that they often succeeded in mitigating the harshness of urban-industrial life.

The problems with which the progressives struggled have, by and large, continued to challenge Americans ever since. And, although the assumptions and techniques of progressivism no longer command the confidence which early twentieth-century Americans had in them, no equally comprehensive body of reforms has ever been adopted in their place. Throughout this study, we have criticized the progressives for having too much faith in their untried methods. Yet if this was a failing, it was also a source of strength, one now missing from reform in America. For the essence of progressivism lay in the hopefulness and optimism which the reformers brought to the tasks of applying science and administration to the high moral purposes in which they believed. The historical record of their aims and achievements leaves no doubt that there were many men and women in the United States in the early 1900s who were not afraid to confront the problems of a modern industrial society with vigor, imagination, and hope. They of course failed to solve all those problems, but no other generation of Americans has done conspicuously better in addressing the political, economic, and social conditions which it faced.

POSTSCRIPT

Did the Progressives Fail?

In spite of their differences, both Abrams's and Link and McCormick's interpretations make concessions to their respective critics. Link and McCormick, for example, admit that the intended reforms did not necessarily produce the desired results. Furthermore, the authors concede that many reformers were insensitive to the cultural values of the lower classes and attempted to impose middle-class Protestant ways on the urban masses. Nevertheless, Link and McCormick argue that in spite of the failure to curb the growth of big business, the progressive reforms did ameliorate the worst abuses of the new urban industrial society. Although the Progressives failed to solve all the major problems of their times, they did set the agenda that still challenges the reformers of today.

Abrams also makes a concession to his critics when he admits that "progressivism had real lasting effects for the blunting of the sharper edges of self-interest in American life, and for the reduction of the harsher cruelties suffered by the society's underprivileged." Yet the thrust of his argument is that the progressive reformers accomplished little of value. While Abrams probably agrees with Link and McCormick that the Progressives were the first group to confront the problems of modern America, he considers their intended reforms inadequate by their very nature. Because the reformers never really challenged the inequalities brought about by the rise of the industrial state, maintains Abrams, the same problems have persisted to the present day.

Historians have generally been sympathetic to the aims and achievements of the progressive historians. Many, like Charles Beard and Frederick Jackson Turner, came from the Midwest and lived in model progressive states like Wisconsin. Their view of history was based on a conflict between groups competing for power, so it was easy for them to portray progressivism as a struggle between the people and entrenched interests.

It was not until after World War II that a more complex view of progressivism emerged. Richard Hofstadter's *Age of Reform* (Alfred A. Knopf, 1955) was exceptionally critical of the reformist view of history as well as of the reformers in general. Born of Jewish immigrant parents and raised in cities in New York, the Columbia University professor argued that progressivism was a moral crusade undertaken by WASP families in an effort to restore older Protestant and individualistic values and to regain political power and status. Both Hofstadter's "status revolution" theory of progressivism and his profile of the typical Progressive have been heavily criticized by historians. Nevertheless, he changed the dimensions of the debate and made progressivism appear to be a much more complex issue than had previously been thought.

Most of the writing on progressivism for the past 20 years has centered around the "organizational" model. Writers of this school have stressed the role of the "expert" and the ideals of scientific management as basic to an understanding of the Progressive Era. This fascination with how the city manager plan worked in Dayton or railroad regulation in Wisconsin or the public schools laws in New York City makes sense to a generation surrounded by bureaucracies on all sides. Two books that deserve careful reading are Robert Wiebe's *The Search for Order, 1877–1920* (Hill & Wang, 1967) and the wonderful collection of essays by Samuel P. Hayes, *American Political History as Social Analysis* (Knoxville, 1980), which brings together two decades' worth of articles from diverse journals that were seminal in exploring ethnocultural approaches to politics within the organizational model.

In a highly influential article written for the *American Quarterly* in spring 1970, Professor Peter G. Filene proclaimed "An Obituary for the 'Progressive Movement.'" After an extensive review of the literature, Filene concluded that since historians cannot agree on its programs, values, geographical location, members, and supporters, there was no such thing as a Progressive movement. Few historians were bold enough to write progressivism out of the pantheon of American reform movements. But Filene put the proponents of the early-twentieth-century reform movement on the defensive. Students who want to see how professional historians directly confronted Filene in their refusal to attend the funeral of the Progressive movement should read the essays by John D. Buenker, John C. Burnham, and Robert M. Crunden in *Progressivism* (Schenkman, 1977).

Three works provide an indispensable review of the literature of progressivism in the 1980s. Link and McCormick's *Progressivism* (Harlan Davidson, 1983) deserves to be read in its entirety for its comprehensive yet concise coverage. More scholarly but still readable are the essays on the new political history in McCormick's *The Party Period and Public Policy: American Politics From the Age of Jackson to the Progressive Era* (Oxford University Press, 1986). The more advanced student should consult Daniel T. Rodgers, "In Search of Progressivism," *Reviews in American History* (December 1982). While admitting that Progressives shared no common creed or values, Rodgers nevertheless feels that they were able "to articulate their discontents and their social visions" around three distinct clusters of ideas: "The first was the rhetoric of antimonopolism, the second was an emphasis on social bonds and the social nature of human beings, and the third was the language of social efficiency."

ISSUE 2

Did Booker T. Washington's Philosophy and Actions Betray the Interests of African Americans?

YES: W. E. B. Du Bois, from *The Souls of Black Folk* (1903, Reprint, Fawcett Publications, 1961)

NO: Louis R. Harlan, from "Booker T. Washington and the Politics of Accommodation," in John Hope Franklin and August Meier, eds., *Black Leaders of the Twentieth Century* (University of Illinois Press, 1982)

ISSUE SUMMARY

YES: W. E. B. Du Bois, a founding member of the National Organization for the Advancement of Colored People, argues that Booker T. Washington failed to articulate the legitimate demands of African Americans for full civil and political rights.

NO: Professor of history Louis R. Harlan portrays Washington as a political realist whose policies and actions were designed to benefit black society as a whole.

In the late nineteenth and early twentieth centuries, most black Americans' lives were characterized by increased inequality and powerlessness. Although the Thirteenth Amendment had fueled a partial social revolution by emancipating approximately four million Southern slaves, the efforts of the Fourteenth and Fifteenth Amendments to provide all African Americans with the protections and privileges of full citizenship had been undermined by the United States Supreme Court.

By 1910, seventy-five percent of all African Americans resided in rural areas. Ninety percent lived in the South, where they suffered from abuses associated with the sharecropping and crop-lien systems, political disfranchisement, and antagonistic race relations, which often boiled over into acts of violence, including race riots and lynchings. Black Southerners who moved north in the decades preceding World War I to escape the ravages of racism instead discovered a society in which the color line was drawn more rigidly to limit black opportunities. Residential segregation led to the emergence of racial ghettos. Jim Crow also affected Northern education, and competition for jobs produced frequent clashes between black and white workers. By the early twentieth century, then, most African Americans endured a second-class citizenship reinforced by segregation laws (both customary and legal) in the "age of Jim Crow."

Prior to 1895, the foremost spokesman for the nation's African American population was former slave and abolitionist Frederick Douglass, whose crusade for blacks emphasized the importance of civil rights, political power, and immediate integration. August Meier has called Douglass "the greatest living symbol of the protest tradition during the 1880s and 1890s." At the time of Douglass's death in 1895, however, this tradition was largely replaced by the emergence of Booker T. Washington. Born into slavery in Virginia in 1856, Washington became the most prominent black spokesman in the United States as a result of a speech delivered at the Cotton States Exposition in Atlanta, Georgia. Known as the "Atlanta Compromise," this address, with its conciliatory tone, found favor among whites and gave Washington, who was president of Tuskegee Institute in Alabama, a reputation as a "responsible" spokesman for black America.

What did Booker T. Washington really want for African Americans? Did his programs realistically address the difficulties confronted by blacks in a society where the doctrine of white supremacy was prominent? Is it fair to describe Washington simply as a conservative whose accommodationist philosophy betrayed his own people? Did the "Sage of Tuskegee" consistently adhere to his publicly stated philosophy of patience, self-help, and economic advancement?

One of the earliest and most outspoken critics of Washington's program was his contemporary, W. E. B. Du Bois. In a famous essay in *The Souls of Black Folk*, Du Bois levels an assault upon Washington's narrow educational philosophy for blacks and his apparent acceptance of segregation. By submitting to disfranchisement and segregation, Du Bois charges, Washington had become an apologist for racial injustice in the United States. He also claims that Washington's national prominence was bought at the expense of black interests throughout the nation.

Louis R. Harlan's appraisal of Washington, while not totally uncritical, illuminates the complexity of Washington's personality and philosophy. Washington, according to Harlan, understood the reality of Southern race relations and knew what he was capable of accomplishing without endangering his leadership position, which was largely controlled by whites. He was, then, a consummate politician—master of the art of the possible in turn-of-the-century race relations.

W. E. B. Du Bois

YES

Of Mr. Booker T. Washington and Others

Easily the most striking thing in the history of the American Negro since 1876 is the ascendancy of Mr. Booker T. Washington. It began at the time when war memories and ideals were rapidly passing; a day of astonishing commercial development was dawning; a sense of doubt and hesitation overtook the freedmen's sons,—then it was that his leading began. Mr. Washington came, with a single definite programme, at the psychological moment when the nation was a little ashamed of having bestowed so much sentiment on Negroes, and was concentrating its energies on Dollars. His programme of industrial education, conciliation of the South, and submission and silence as to civil and political rights, was not wholly original; . . . But Mr. Washington first indisolubly linked these things; he put enthusiasm, unlimited energy, and perfect faith into this programme, and changed it from a by-path into a veritable Way of Life. And the tale of the methods by which he did this is a fascinating study of human life.

It startled the nation to hear a Negro advocating such a programme after many decades of bitter complaint; it startled and won the applause of the South, it interested and won the admiration of the North; and after a confused murmur of protest, it silenced if it did not convert the Negroes themselves.

To gain the sympathy and coöperation of the various elements comprising the white South was Mr. Washington's first task; and this, at the time Tuskegee was founded, seemed, for a black man, well-nigh impossible. And yet ten years later it was done in the word spoken at Atlanta: "In all things purely social we can be as separate as the five fingers, and yet one as the hand in all things essential to mutual progress." This "Atlanta Compromise" is by all odds the most notable thing in Mr. Washington's career. The South interpreted it in different ways: the radicals received it as a complete surrender of the demand for civil and political equality; the conservatives, as a generously conceived working basis for mutual understanding. So both approved it, and to-day its author is certainly the most distinguished Southerner since Jefferson Davis, and the one with the largest personal following.

Next to this achievement comes Mr. Washington's work in gaining place and consideration in the North. Others less shrewd and tactful had formerly essayed to sit on these two stools and had fallen between them; but as Mr. Washington knew the heart of the South from birth and training, so by singular insight he intuitively grasped the spirit of the age which was dominating the North. And so thoroughly did he learn the speech and thought of triumphant commercialism, and the ideals of material prosperity, that the picture of a lone black boy poring over a French grammar amid the weeds and dirt of a neglected home soon seemed to him the acme of absurdities. One wonders what Socrates and St. Francis of Assisi would say to this.

And yet this very singleness of vision and thorough oneness with his age is a mark of the successful man. It is as though Nature must needs make men narrow in order to give them force. So Mr. Washington's cult has gained unquestioning followers, his work has wonderfully prospered, his friends are legion, and his enemies are confounded. To-day he stands as the one recognized spokesman of his ten million fellows, and one of the most notable figures in a nation of seventy millions. One hesitates, therefore, to criticise a life which, beginning with so little, has done so much. And yet the time is come when one may speak in all sincerity and utter courtesy of the mistakes and shortcomings of Mr. Washington's career, as well as of his triumphs, without being thought captious or envious, and without forgetting that it is easier to do ill than well in the world.

The criticism that has hitherto met Mr. Washington has not always been of this broad character. In the South especially has he had to walk warily to avoid the harshest judgments,—and naturally so, for he is dealing with the one subject of deepest sensitiveness to that section. Twice—once when at the Chicago celebration of the Spanish-American War he alluded to the color-prejudice that is "eating away the vitals of the South," and once when he dined with President Roosevelt—has the resulting Southern criticism been violent enough to threaten seriously his popularity. In the North the feeling has several times forced itself into words, that Mr. Washington's counsels of submission overlooked certain elements of true manhood, and that his educational programme was unnecessarily narrow. Usually, however, such criticism has not found open expression, although, too, the spiritual sons of the Abolitionists have not been prepared to acknowledge that the schools founded before Tuskegee, by men of broad ideals and self-sacrificing spirit, were wholly failures or worthy of ridicule. While, then, criticism has not failed to follow Mr. Washington, yet the prevailing public opinion of the land has been but too willing to deliver the solution of a wearisome problem into his hands, and say, "If that is all you and your race ask, take it."

Among his own people, however, Mr. Washington has encountered the strongest and most lasting opposition, amounting at times to bitterness, and even to-day continuing strong and insistent even though largely silenced in outward expression by the public opinion of the nation. Some of this opposition is, of course, mere envy; the disappointment of displaced demagogues and the spite of narrow minds. But aside from this, there is among educated and thoughtful colored men in all parts of the land a feeling of deep regret, sorrow, and apprehension at the wide currency and ascendancy which some of Mr. Washington's theories have gained. These same men admire his sincerity of purpose, and are willing to forgive much to honest endeavor which is doing something worth the doing. They coöperate with Mr. Washington as far as they conscientiously can; and, indeed, it is no ordinary tribute to this man's tact and power that, steering as he must between so many diverse interests and opinions, he so largely retains the respect of all.

But the hushing of the criticism of honest opponents is a dangerous thing. It leads some of the best of the critics to unfortunate silence and paralysis of effort, and others to burst into speech so passionately and intemperately as to lose listeners. Honest and earnest criticism from those whose interests are most nearly touched,—criticism of writers by readers, of government by those governed, of leaders by those led,—this is the soul of democracy and the safeguard of modern society. If the best of the American Negroes receive by outer pressure a leader whom they had not recognized before, manifestly there is here a certain palpable gain. Yet there is also irreparable loss,—a loss of that peculiarly valuable education which a group receives when by search and criticism it finds and commissions its own leaders. The way in which this is done is at once the most elementary and the nicest problem of social growth. History is but the record of such group-leadership; and yet how infinitely changeful is its type and character! And of all types and kinds, what can be more instructive than the leadership of a group within a group?—that curious double movement where real progress may be negative and actual advance be relative retrogression. All this is the social student's inspiration and despair.

Now in the past the American Negro has had instructive experience in the choosing of group leaders, founding thus a peculiar dynasty which in the light of present conditions is worth while studying. When sticks and stones and beasts form the sole environment of a people, their attitude is largely one of determined opposition to and conquest of natural forces. But when to earth and brute is added an environment of men and ideas, then the attitude of the imprisoned group may take three main forms,—a feeling of revolt and revenge; an attempt to adjust all thought and action to the will of the greater group; or, finally, a determined effort at self-realization and self-development despite environing opinion. The influence of all of these attitudes at various times can be traced in the history of the American Negro, and in the evolution of his successive leaders. . . .

Booker T. Washington arose as essentially the leader not of one race but of two,—a compromiser between the South, the North, and the Negro. Naturally the Negroes resented, at first bitterly, signs of compromise which surrendered their civil and political rights, even though this was to be exchanged for larger chances of economic development. The rich and dominating North, however, was not only weary of the race problem, but was investing largely in Southern enterprises, and welcomed any method of peaceful coöperation. Thus, by national opinion, the Negroes began to recognize Mr. Washington's leadership; and the voice of criticism was hushed.

Mr. Washington represents in Negro thought the old attitude of adjustment and submission; but adjustment at such a peculiar time as to make his programme unique. This is an age of unusual economic development, and Mr. Washington's programme naturally takes an economic cast, becoming a gospel of Work and Money to such an extent as apparently almost completely to overshadow the higher aims of life. Moreover, this is an age when the more advanced races are coming in closer contact with the less developed races, and the race-feeling is therefore intensified; and Mr. Washington's programme practically accepts the alleged inferiority of the Negro races. Again, in our own land, the reaction from the sentiment of war time has given impetus to race-prejudice against Negroes, and Mr. Washington withdraws many of the high demands of Negroes as men and American citizens. In other periods of intensified prejudice all the Negro's tendency to self-assertion has been called forth; at this period a policy of submission is advocated. In the history of nearly all other races and peoples the doctrine preached at such crises has been that manly self-respect is worth more than lands and houses, and that a people who voluntarily surrender such respect, or cease striving for it, are not worth civilizing.

In answer to this, it has been claimed that the Negro can survive only through submission. Mr. Washington distinctly asks that black people give up, at least for the present three things,—

First, political power,

Second, insistence on civil rights,

Third, higher education of Negro youth,—

and concentrate all their energies on industrial education, the accumulation of wealth, and the conciliation of the South. This policy has been courageously and insistently advocated for over fifteen years, and has been triumphant for perhaps ten years. As a result of this tender of the palm-branch, what has been the return? In these years there have occurred:

1. The disfranchisement of the Negro.
2. The legal creation of a distinct status of civil inferiority for the Negro.
3. The steady withdrawal of aid from institutions for the higher training of the Negro.

These movements are not, to be sure, direct results of Mr. Washington's teachings; but his propaganda has, without a shadow of doubt, helped their speedier accomplishment. The question then comes: Is it possible, and probable, that nine millions of men can make effective progress in economic lines if they are deprived of political rights, made a servile caste, and allowed only the most meagre chance for developing their exceptional men? If history and reason give any distinct answer to these questions, it is an emphatic *No.* And Mr. Washington thus faces the triple paradox of his career:

1. He is striving nobly to make Negro artisans business men and property-owners; but it is utterly impossible, under modern competitive methods, for workingmen and property-owners to defend their rights and exist without the right of suffrage.
2. He insists on thrift and self-respect, but at the same time counsels a silent submission to civic inferiority such as is bound to sap the manhood of any race in the long run.
3. He advocates common-school and industrial training, and depreciates institutions of higher learning; but neither the Negro common-schools, nor Tuskegee itself, could remain open a day were it not for teachers trained in Negro colleges, or trained by their graduates.

This triple paradox in Mr. Washington's position is the object of criticism by two classes of colored Americans. One class is spiritually descended from Toussaint the Savior, through Gabriel, Vesey, and Turner, and they represent the attitude of revolt and revenge; they hate the white South blindly and distrust the white race generally, and so far as they agree on definite action, think that the Negro's only hope lies in emigration beyond the borders of the United States. And yet, by the irony of fate, nothing has more effectually made this programme seem hopeless than the recent course of the United States toward weaker and darker peoples in the West Indies, Hawaii, and the Philippines,—for where in the world may we go and be safe from lying and brute force?

The other class of Negroes who cannot agree with Mr. Washington has hitherto said little aloud. They deprecate the sight of scattered counsels, of internal disagreement; and especially they dislike making their just criticism of a useful and earnest man an excuse for a general discharge of venom from small-minded opponents. Nevertheless, the questions involved are so fundamental and serious that it is difficult to see how men like the Grimkes, Kelly Miller, J. W. E. Bowen, and other representatives of this group, can much longer be silent. Such men feel in conscience bound to ask of this nation three things:

1. The right to vote.
2. Civic equality.
3. The education of youth according to ability.

They acknowledge Mr. Washington's invaluable service in counselling patience an courtesy in such demands; they do not ask that ignorant black men vote when ignorant whites are debarred, or that any reasonable restrictions in the suffrage should not be applied; they know that the low social level of the mass of the race is responsible for much discrimination against it, but they also know, and the nation knows, that relentless color-prejudice is more often a cause than a result of the Negro's degradation; they seek the abatement of this relic of barbarism, and not its systematic encouragement and pampering by all agencies of social power from the Associated Press to the Church of Christ. They advocate, with Mr. Washington, a broad system of Negro common schools supplemented by thorough industrial training; but they are surprised that a man of Mr. Washington's insight cannot see that no such educational system ever has rested or can rest on any other basis than that of the well-equipped college and university, and they insist that there is a demand for a few such institutions throughout the South to train the best of the Negro youth as teachers, professional men, and leaders.

This group of men honor Mr. Washington for his attitude of conciliation toward the white South; they accept the "Atlanta Compromise" in its broadest interpretation; they recognize, with him, many signs of promise, many men of high purpose and fair judgment, in this section; they know that no easy task has been laid upon a region already tottering under heavy burdens. But, nevertheless, they insist that the way to truth and right lies in straightforward honesty, not in indiscriminate flattery; in praising those of the South who do well and criticising uncompromisingly those who do ill; in taking advantage of the opportunities at hand and urging their fellows to do the same, but at the same time remembering that only a firm adherence to their higher ideals and aspirations will ever keep those ideals within the realm of possibility. They do not expect that the free right vote, to enjoy civic rights, and to be educated, will come in a moment; they do not expect to see the bias and prejudices of years disappear at the blast of a trumpet; but they are absolutely certain that the way for a people to gain their reasonable rights is not by voluntarily throwing them away and insisting that they do not want them; that the way for a people to gain respect is not by continually belittling and ridiculing themselves; that, on the contrary, Negroes must insist continually, in season and out of season, that voting is necessary to modern manhood, that color discrimination is barbarism, and that black boys need education as well as white boys.

In failing thus to state plainly and unequivocally the legitimate demands of their people, even at the cost of opposing an honored leader, the thinking classes of American Negroes would shirk a heavy responsibility,—a responsibility to themselves, a responsibility to the struggling masses, a responsibility to the darker races of men whose future depends so largely on this American experiment, but especially a responsibility to this nation,—this common Fatherland. It is wrong to encourage a man or a people in evil-doing; it is wrong to aid and abet a national crime simply because it is unpopular not to do so. The growing spirit of kindliness and reconciliation between the North and South after the frightful difference of a generation ago ought to be a source of deep congratulation to all, and especially to those whose mistreatment caused the war; but if that reconciliation is to be marked by the industrial slavery and civic death of those same black men, with permanent legislation into a position of inferiority, then those black men, if they are really men, are called upon by every consideration of patriotism and loyalty to oppose such a course by all civilized methods, even though such opposition involves disagreement with Mr. Booker T. Washington. We have no right to sit silently by while the inevitable seeds are sown for a harvest of disaster to our children, black and white.

First, it is the duty of black men to judge the South discriminatingly. The present generation of Southerners are not responsible for the past, and they should not be blindly hated or blamed for it. Furthermore, to no class is the indiscriminate endorsement of the recent course of the South toward Negroes more nauseating than to the best thought of the South. The South is not "solid"; it is a land in the ferment of social change, wherein forces of all kinds are fighting for supremacy; and to praise the ill the South is to-day perpetrating is just as wrong as to condemn the good. Discriminating and broad-minded criticism is what the South needs,—needs it for the sake of her own white sons and daughters, and for the insurance of robust, healthy mental and moral development.

To-day even the attitude of the Southern whites toward the blacks is not, as so many assume, in all cases the same; the ignorant Southerner hates the Negro, the workingmen fear his competition, the money-makers wish to use him as a laborer, some of the educated see a menace in his upward development, while others—usually the sons of masters—wish to help him to rise. National opinion has enabled this last class to maintain the Negro common schools, and to protect the Negro partially in property, life, and limb. Through the pressure of the money-makers, the Negro is in danger of being reduced to semi-slavery, especially in the country districts; the workingmen, and those of the educated who fear the Negro, have united to disfranchise him, and some have urged his deportation; while the passions of the ignorant are easily aroused to lynch and abuse any black man. To praise this intricate whirl of thought and prejudice is nonsense; to inveigh indiscriminately against "the South" is unjust; but to use the same breath in praising Governor [Charles B.] Aycock, exposing Senator [John T.] Morgan, arguing with Mr. Thomas Nelson Page, and denouncing Senator Ben Tillman, is not only sane, but the imperative duty of thinking black men.

It would be unjust to Mr. Washington not to acknowledge that in several instances he has opposed movements in the South which were unjust to the Negro; he sent memorials to the Louisiana and Alabama constitutional conventions, he has spoken against lynching, and in other ways has openly or silently set his influence against sinister schemes and unfortunate happenings. Notwithstanding this, it is equally true to assert that on the whole the distinct impression left by Mr. Washington's propaganda is, first, that the South is justified in its present attitude toward the Negro because of the Negro's degradation; secondly, that the prime cause of the Negro's failure to rise more quickly is his wrong education in the past; and, thirdly, that his future rise depends primarily on his own efforts. Each of these propositions is a dangerous half-truth. The supplementary truths must never be lost sight of: first, slavery and race-prejudice are potent if not sufficient causes of the Negro's position; second, industrial and common-school training were necessarily slow in planting because they had to await the black teachers trained by higher institutions,—it being extremely doubtful if any essentially different development was possible, and certainly a Tuskegee was unthinkable before 1880; and, third, while it is a great truth to say that the Negro must strive and strive mightily to help himself, it is equally true that unless his striving be not simply seconded, but rather aroused and encouraged, by the initiative of the richer and wiser environing group, he cannot hope for great success.

In his failure to realize and impress this last point, Mr. Washington is especially to be criticised. His doctrine has tended to make the whites, North and South, shift the burden of the Negro problem to the Negro's shoulders and stand aside as critical and rather pessimistic spectators; when in fact the burden belongs to the nation, and the hands of none of us are clean if we bend not our energies to righting these great wrongs.

The South ought to be led, by candid and honest criticism, to assert her better self and do her full duty to the race she has cruelly wronged and is still wronging. The North—her co-partner in guilt—cannot salve her conscience by plastering it with gold. We cannot settle this problem by diplomacy and suaveness, by "policy" alone. If worse come to worst, can the moral fibre of this country survive the slow throttling and murder of nine millions of men?

The black men of America have a duty to perform, a duty stern and delicate,—a forward movement to oppose a part of the work of their greatest leader. So far as Mr. Washington preaches Thrift, Patience, and Industrial

Training for the masses, we must hold up his hands and strive with him, rejoicing in his honors and glorying in the strength of this Joshua called of God and of man to lead the headless host. But so far as Mr. Washington apologizes for injustice, North or South, does not rightly value the privilege and duty of voting, belittles the emasculating effects of caste distinctions, and opposes the higher training and ambition of our brighter minds,—so far as he, the South, or the Nation, does this,—we must unceasingly and firmly oppose them. By every civilized and peaceful method we must strive for the rights which the world accords to men, clinging unwaveringly to those great words which the sons of the Fathers would fain forget: "We hold these truths to be self-evident: That all men are created equal; that they are endowed by their Creator with certain unalienable rights; that among these are life, liberty, and the pursuit of happiness."

Louis R. Harlan

NO

Booker T. Washington and the Politics of Accommodation

It is ironic that Booker T. Washington, the most powerful black American of his time and perhaps of all time, should be the black leader whose claim to the litle is most often dismissed by the lay public. Blacks often question his legitimacy because of the role that favor by whites played in Washington's assumption of power, and whites often remember him only as an educator or, confusing him with George Washington Carver, as "that great Negro scientist." This irony is something that Washington will have to live with in history, for he himself deliberately created the ambiguity about his role and purposes that has haunted his image. And yet, Washington was a genuine black leader, with a substantial black following and with virtually the same long-range goals for Afro-Americans as his rivals. This presentation is concerned with Washington's social philosophy, such as it was, but it also addresses his methods of leadership, both his Delphic public utterances that meant one thing to whites and another to blacks and his adroit private movements through the brier patch of American race relations. It does not try to solve the ultimate riddle of his character.

Washington's own view of himself was that he was the Negro of the hour, whose career and racial program epitomized what blacks needed to maintain themselves against white encroachments and to make progress toward equality in America. The facts of his life certainly fitted his self-image. He was the last of the major black leaders to be born in slavery, on a small farm in western Virginia in 1856. Growing up during the Reconstruction era in West Virginia, he believed that one of the lessons he learned was that the Reconstruction experiment in racial democracy failed because it began at the wrong end, emphasizing political means and civil rights acts rather than economic means and self-determination. Washington learned this lesson not so much through experiences as a child worker in the salt works and coal mines as by what he was taught as a houseboy for the leading family of Malden, West Virginia, and later as a student at Hampton Institute in Virginia. Hampton applied the missionary method to black education and made its peace with the white South.

After teaching school in his home town, Washington briefly studied in a Baptist seminary and in a lawyer's office. But he soon abandoned these alternative careers, perhaps sensing that disfranchisement and the secularization of society would weaken these occupations as bases for racial leadership. He returned to Hampton Institute as a teacher for two years and then founded Tuskegee Normal and Industrial Institute in Alabama in 1881. Over the next quarter of a century, using Hampton's methods but with greater emphasis on the skilled trades, Washington built up Tuskegee Institute to be an equal of Hampton.

Washington's bid for leadership went beyond education and institution-building, however. Symbolic of his fresh approach to black-white relations was a speech he gave in 1895 before a commercial exposition, known as the Atlanta Compromise Address, and his autobiography, *Up from Slavery* (1901). As Washington saw it, blacks were toiling upward from slavery by their own efforts into the American middle class and needed chiefly social peace to continue in this steady social evolution. Thus, in the Atlanta Compromise he sought to disarm the white South by declaring agitation of the social equality question "the merest folly" and proclaiming that in "purely social" matters "we can be as separate as the fingers, yet one as the hand in all things essential to mutual progress." These concessions came to haunt Washington as southerners used segregation as a means of systematizing discrimination, and northerners followed suit. And they did not stop at the "purely social."

Washington's concessions to the white South, however, were only half of a bargain. In return for downgrading civil and political rights in the black list of priorities, Washington asked whites to place no barriers to black economic advancement and even to become partners of their black neighbors "in all things essential to mutual progress." Washington saw his own role as the axis between the races, the only leader who could negotiate and keep the peace by holding extremists on both sides in check. He was always conscious that his unique influence could be destroyed in an instant of self-indulgent flamboyance.

Washington sought to influence whites, but he never forgot that it was the blacks that he undertook to lead. He offered blacks not the empty promises of the demagogue but a solid program of economic and educational progress through struggle. It was less important "just now," he said, for a black person to seek admission to an opera house than to have the money for the ticket. Mediating diplomacy with whites was only half of Washington's strategy; the other half was black solidarity, mutual aid, and institution-building. He thought outspoken complaint against injustice was necessary but insufficient, and he thought factional dissent among black leaders was self-defeating and should be suppressed.

Washington brought to his role as a black leader the talents and outlook of a machine boss. He made Tuskegee Institute the largest and best-supported black educational institution of his day, and it spawned a large network of other industrial schools. Tuskegee's educational function is an important and debatable subject, of course, but the central concern here is Washington's use of the school as the base of operations of what came to be known as the Tuskegee Machine. It was an all-black school with an all-black faculty at a time when most black colleges were still run by white missionaries. Tuskegee taught self-determination. It also taught trades designed for economic independence in a region dominated by sharecrop agriculture. At the same time, by verbal juggling tricks, Washington convinced the southern whites that Tuskegee was not educating black youth away from the farms. Tuskegee also functioned as a model black community, not only by acquainting its students with a middle-class way of life, but by buying up the surrounding farmland and selling it at low rates of interest to create a community of small landowners and home-owners. The Institute became larger than the town.

Washington built a regional constituency of farmers, artisans, country teachers, and small businessmen; he expanded the Tuskegee Machine nation-wide after the Atlanta Compromise seemed acceptable to blacks all over the country, even by many who later denounced it. His first northern black ally was T. Thomas Fortune, editor of the militant and influential New York *Age* and founder of the Afro-American Council, the leading forum of black thought at the time. Washington was not a member, but he usually spoke at the annual meetings, and his lieutenants so tightly controlled the council that it never passed an action or resolution not in Washington's interest. Seeking more direct allies, Washington founded in 1900 the National Negro Business League, of which he was president for life. The league was important not so much for what it did for black business, which was little, but because the local branch of the league was a stronghold of Washington men in every substantial black population center.

Other classes of influential blacks did not agree with Washington's stated philosophy but were beholden to him for the favors he did them or offered to do for them. He was not called the Wizard for nothing. White philanthropists who approved of him for their own reasons gave him the money to help black colleges by providing for a Carnegie library here, a dormitory there. Through Washington Andrew Carnegie alone gave buildings to twenty-nine black schools. Not only college administrators owed him for favors, but so did church leaders, YMCA directors and many others. Though never much of a joiner, he became a power in the Baptist church, and he schemed through lieu-tenants to control the secret black fraternal orders and make his friends the high potentates of the Pythians, Odd Fellows, and so on. Like any boss, he turned every favor into a bond of obligation.

It was in politics, however, that Washington built the most elaborate ten-tacle of the octopus-like Tuskegee Machine. In politics as in everything else, Washington cultivated ambiguity. He downgraded politics as a solution of black problems, did not recommend politics to the ambitious young black man, and never held office. But when Theodore Roosevelt became president in 1901 and asked for Washington's advice on black and southern appointments, Washington consented with alacrity. He became the chief black advisor of both Presidents Roosevelt and William Howard Taft. He failed in his efforts to liber-alize Republican policy on voting rights, lynching, and racial discrimination, however, and relations between the Republican party and black voters reached a low ebb.

In patronage politics, however, Washington found his opportunity. For a man who minimized the importance of politics, Washington devoted an inor-dinate amount of his time and tremendous energy to securing federal jobs for his machine lieutenants. These men played a certain role in the politics of the period, but their first obligation was to the Tuskegean. Washington advised the presidents to replace the old venal officeholding class of blacks with men who had proven themselves in the independent world of business, but in practice it took only loyalty to Washington to cleanse miraculously an old-time political hack. . . .

Washington's outright critics and enemies were called "radicals" because they challenged Washington's conservatism and bossism, though their tactics of verbal protest would seem moderate indeed to a later generation of activists. They were the college-educated blacks, engaged in professional pursuits, and proud of their membership in an elite class—what one of them called the Talented Tenth. The strongholds of the radicals were the northern cities and southern black colleges. They stood for full political and civil rights, liberal education, free expression, and aspiration. They dreamed of a better world and believed Booker T. Washington was a menace to its achievement. . . .

Washington dismissed his black critics by questioning their motives, their claim to superior wisdom, and—the politician's ultimate argument—their numbers. Washington understood, if his critics did not, that his leadership of the black community largely depended on his recognition by whites as the black leader. If he did not meet some minimal standards of satisfactoriness to whites, another Washington would be created. He obviously could not lead the whites; he could not even divide the whites. He could only, in a limited way, exploit the class divisions that whites created among themselves. He could work in the cracks of their social structure, move like Brer Rabbit through the brier patch, and thus outwit the more numerous and powerful whites.

While Washington recognized the centrality of black-white relations in his efforts to lead blacks, he was severely restricted by the historical context of his leadership. It was an age of polarization of black and white. The overheated atmosphere of the South at the turn of the century resembled that of a crisis center on the eve of war. Lynching became a more than weekly occurrence; discrimination and humiliation of blacks were constant and pervasive and bred a whole literature and behavioral science of self-justification. Race riots terrorized blacks in many cities, and not only in the South. It would have required not courage but foolhardiness for Washington, standing with both feet in Alabama, to have challenged this raging white aggression openly and directly. Even unqualified verbal protest would have brought him little support from either southern blacks or white well-wishers. Du Bois took higher ground and perhaps a better vision of the future when he urged forthright protest against every white injustice, on the assumption that whites were rational beings and would respond dialectically to black protest. But few white racists of the early twentieth century cared anything for the facts. And when Du Bois in his Atlanta years undertook to implement his protest with action, he was driven to the negative means of refusing to pay his poll tax or refusing to ride segregated streetcars and elevators.

Instead of either confronting all of white America or admitting that his Faustian bargain for leadership had created a systemic weakness in his program, Washington simply met each day as it came, pragmatically, seeking what white allies he could against avowed white enemies. A serious fault of this policy was that Washington usually appealed for white support on a basis of a vaguely conceived mutual interest rather than on ideological agreement. For example, in both the South and the North Washington allied himself with the white upper class against the masses. In the South he joined with the planter class and when possible with the coal barons and railroad officials against the populists and other small white farmer groups who seemed to him to harbor the most virulent anti-black attitudes born of labor competition. Similarly, in the North, Washington admired and bargained with the big business class. The bigger the businessman, the more Washington admired him, as the avatar and arbiter of American society. At the pinnacle in his measure of men were the industrialists Carnegie, John D. Rockefeller, and Henry H. Rogers and the merchant princes Robert C. Ogden and Julius Rosenwald. To be fair to Washington, he appreciated their philanthropic generosity at least as much as he admired their worldly success, but his lips were sealed against criticism of even the more rapacious and ungenerous members of the business elite.

Washington made constructive use of his philanthropic allies to aid not only Tuskegee but black education and black society as a whole. He guided the generous impulse of a Quaker millionairess into the Anna T. Jeanes Foundation to improve the teaching in black public schools. He persuaded the Jewish philanthropist Julius Rosenwald to begin a program that lasted for decades for building more adequate black schoolhouses all over the South. Washington's influence on Carnegie, Rockefeller, Jacob Schiff, and other rich men also transcended immediate Tuskegee interests to endow other black institutions. In short, Washington did play a role in educational statesmanship. There were limits, however, to his power to advance black interests through philanthropy. When his northern benefactors became involved in the Southern Education Board to improve the southern public school systems, for example, he worked repeatedly but without success to get this board to redress the imbalance of public expenditures or even to halt the rapid increase of discrimination against black schools and black children. He had to shrug off his failure and get from these so-called philanthropists whatever they were willing to give.

Having committed himself to the business elite, Washington took a dim view of the leaders of the working class. Immigrants represented to him, as to many blacks, labor competitors; Jews were the exception here, as he held them up to ambitious blacks as models of the work-ethic and group solidarity. He claimed in his autobiography that his disillusionment with labor unions went back to his youthful membership in the Knights of Labor and stemmed from observation of their disruption of the natural laws of economics. In his heyday, however, which was also the age of Samuel Gompers, Washington's anti-union attitudes were explained by the widespread exclusion of blacks from membership in many unions and hence from employment in many trades. There is no evidence that Washington ever actively supported black strikebreaking, but his refusal to intervene in behalf of all-white unions is understandable. It was more often white employees rather than employers who excluded blacks, or so Washington believed. He worked hard to introduce black labor into the non-union, white-only cotton mills in the South, even to the extent of interesting northern capitalists in investing in black cotton mills and similar enterprises.

Washington was a conservative by just about any measure. Though he flourished in the Progressive era it was not he, but his opponents who were the men of good hope, full of reform proposals and faith in the common man. Washington's vision of the common man included the southern poor white full of rancor against blacks, the foreign-born anarchist ready to pull down the temple of American business, and the black sharecropper unqualified by education or economic freedom for the ballot. Though Washington opposed the grandfather clause and every other southern device to exclude the black man from voting solely on account of his color, Washington did not favor universal suffrage. He believed in literacy and property tests, fairly enforced. He was no democrat. And he did not believe in woman suffrage, either.

In his eagerness to establish common ground with whites, that is, with some whites, Washington overstepped his purpose in public speeches by telling chicken-thief, mule, and other dialect stories intended to appeal to white stereotypes of blacks, and he occasionally spoke of the Afro-American as "a child race." No doubt his intent was to disarm his listeners, and before mixed audiences he often alternately addressed the two groups, reassuring whites that blacks should cooperate with their white neighbors in all constructive efforts, but saying to blacks that in their cooperation there should be "no unmanly cowering or stooping." At the cost of some forcefulness of presentation, Washington did have a remarkable capacity to convince whites as well as blacks that he not only understood them but agreed with them. It is one of Washington's intangible qualities as a black leader that he could influence, if not lead, so many whites. The agreement that whites sensed in him was more in his manner than in his program or goals, which always included human rights as well as material advancement for blacks.

In his constant effort to influence public opinion, Washington relied on the uncertain instruments of the press and the public platform. A flood of books and articles appeared over his name, largely written by his private secretary and a stable of ghostwriters, because he was too busy to do much writing. His ghostwriters were able and faithful, but they could not put new words or new ideas out over his signature, so for the crucial twenty years after 1895, Washington's writings showed no fresh creativity or real response to events, only a steady flood of platitudes. Washington's speeches generally suffered from an opposite handicap, that he was the only one who could deliver them. But he was too busy making two or three speeches a day to write a new one for each occasion, so the audiences rather than the speeches changed. But everywhere he went, North, South, or West, he drew large crowds ready to hear or rehear his platitudes.

Washington did try to change his world by other means. Some forms of racial injustice, such as lynching, disfranchisement, and unequal facilities in education and transportation, Washington dealt with publicly and directly. Early in his career as a leader he tried to sidestep the lynching question by saying that, deplorable though it was, he was too busy working for the education of black youth to divide his energies by dealing with other public questions. Friends and critics alike sharply told him that if he proposed to be a leader of blacks, he was going to have to deal with this subject. So he began an annual letter on lynching that he sent to all the southern white dailies, and he made Tuskegee Institute the center of statistical and news information on lynching. He always took a moderate tone, deplored rape and crime by blacks, but always denied that the crime blacks committed was either the cause of or justification for the crime of lynching. He tried to make up for his moderation by persistence, factual accuracy, and persuasive logic. Disfranchisement of black voters swept through the South from Texas to Virginia during Washington's day. He publicly protested in letters to the constitutional conventions and legislatures in Alabama, Georgia, and Louisiana and aided similar efforts in several other states. He failed to stop lynching, to prevent the loss of voting rights, and to clean up the Jim Crow cars or bring about even minimal standards of fairness in the public schools. But he did try.

As for social segregation, Washington abided by southern customs while in the South but forthrightly declared it unreasonable for white southerners to dictate his behavior outside of the South. His celebrated dinner at the White House in 1901, therefore, though it caused consternation and protest among white southerners, was consistent with his lifetime practice. Tuskegee Institute underwent an elaborate ritual of segregation with every white visitor, but the man who came to dinner at the White House, had tea with the queen of England, and attended hundreds of banquets and private meals with whites outside the South certainly never internalized the attitudes of the segregators.

What Washington could not do publicly to achieve equal rights, he sought to accomplish secretly. He spent four years in cooperation with the Afro-American Council on a court case to test the constitutionality of the Louisiana grandfather clause, providing funds from his own pocket and from northern white liberal friends. In his own state of Alabama, Washington secretly directed the efforts of his personal lawyer to carry two grandfather-clause cases all the way to the U.S. Supreme Court, where they were lost on technicalities. He took the extra precaution of using code names in all the correspondence on the Atlabama cases. Through private pressure on railroad officials and congressmen, Washington tried to bring about improvement in the Jim Crow cars and railroad waiting rooms. He had more success in the Dan Rogers case, which overturned a criminal verdict against a black man because blacks were excluded from the jury. He also secretly collaborated with two southern white attorneys to defend Alonzo Bailey, a farm laborer held in peonage for debt; the outcome here was also successful, for the Alabama peonage law was declared unconstitutional. These and other secret actions were certainly not enough to tear down the legal structure of white supremacy, but they show that Washington's role in Afro-American history was not always that of the accommodationist "heavy." He was working, at several levels and in imaginative ways, and always with vigor, toward goals similar to those of his critics. If his methods did not work, the same could be said of theirs. And he did not take these civil rights actions as a means of answering criticism, because he kept his part in the court cases a secret except to a handful of confidants, a secret not revealed until his papers were opened to historians in recent decades.

There was another, uglier side of Washington's secret behavior, however—his ruthless spying and sabotage against his leading black critics. Washington never articulated a justification for these actions, perhaps because, being secret, they did not require defense. And yet Washington and Emmett Scott left the evidence of his secret machinations undestroyed in his papers, apparently in the faith that history would vindicate him when all the facts were known. Then, too, Washington was not given to explaining himself. . . .

The Booker T. Washington who emerges into the light of history from his private papers is a complex, Faustian character quite different from the paragon of self-uplift and Christian forbearance that Washington projected in his autobiography. On the other hand, there is little evidence for and much evidence against the charge of some of his contemporaries that he was simply an accommodationist who bargained away his race's birthright for a mess of pottage. Nor does he fit some historians' single-factor explanations of his career: that he offered "education for the new slavery," that he was a proto-black-nationalist, that he was or must have been psychologically crippled by the constraints and guilt feelings of his social role.

Washington's complexity should not be overstressed, however, for the more we know about anybody the more complex that person seems. And through the complexity of Washington's life, its busyness and its multiple levels, two main themes stand out, his true belief in his program for black progress and his great skill in and appetite for politics, broadly defined, serving both his goals and his personal power.

First, let us look closely at Washington's industrial education and small business program. It may have been anachronistic preparation for the age of mass production and corporate gigantism then coming into being, but it had considerable social realism for a black population which was, until long after Washington's death, predominantly rural and southern. Furthermore, it was well attuned to the growth and changing character of black business in his day. Increasingly, the nineteenth-century black businesses catering to white clients surrendered predominance to ghetto businesses such as banks, insurance companies, undertakers, and barbers catering to black customers. These new businessmen, with a vested interest in black solidarity, were the backbone of Washington's National Negro Business League. Washington clearly found congenial the prospect of an elite class of self-made businessmen as leaders and models for the struggling masses. There was also room for the Talented Tenth of professional men in the Tuskegee Machine, however. Washington welcomed every college-educated recruit he could secure. Directly or through agents, he was the largest employer in the country of black college graduates.

Second, let us consider Washington as a powerful politician. Though he warned young men away from politics as a dead-end career, what distinguished Washington's career was not his rather conventional goals, which in public or private he shared with almost every other black spokesman, but his consummate political skill, his wheeling and dealing. . . .

Washington's program was not consensus politics, for he always sought change, and there was always vocal opposition to him on both sides that he never tried to mollify. Denounced on the one hand by the Niagara Movement and the NAACP for not protesting enough, he was also distrusted and denounced by white supremacists for bringing the wooden horse within the walls of Troy. All of the racist demagogues of his time—Benjamin Tillman, James Vardaman, Theodore Bilbo, Thomas Dixon, and J. Thomas Heflin, to name a few—called Washington their insidious enemy. One descriptive label for Washington might be centrist coalition politics. The Tuskegee Machine had the middle and undecided majority of white and black people behind it. Washington was a rallying point for the southern moderates, the northern publicists and makers of opinion, and the thousands who read his autobiography or crowded into halls to hear him. Among blacks he had the businessmen solidly behind him, and even, as August Meier has shown, a majority of the Talented Tenth of professional men, so great was his power to reward and punish, to make or break careers. He had access to the wellsprings of philanthropy, political preferment, and other white sources of black opportunity. For blacks at the bottom of the ladder, Washington's program offered education, a self-help formula, and, importantly for a group demoralized by the white aggression of that period, a social philosophy that gave dignity and purpose to lives of daily toil.

It could be said with some justification that the Tuskegee Machine was a stationary machine, that it went nowhere. Because the machine was held together by the glue of self-interest, Washington was frequently disappointed by the inadequate response of his allies. The southern upper class did not effectively resist disfranchisement as he had hoped and never gave blacks the equal economic chance that he considered an integral part of the Atlanta Compromise. Washington's philanthropist-friends never stood up for equal opportunity in public education. Black businessmen frequently found their own vested interest in a captive market rather than a more open society. And Washington himself often took the view that whatever was good for Tuskegee and himself was good for the Negro.

To the charge that he accomplished nothing, it can only be imagined what Washington would have answered, since he did not have the years of hindsight and self-justification that some of his critics enjoyed. He would probably have stressed how much worse the southern racial reaction would have been without his coalition of moderates, his soothing syrup, and his practical message to blacks of self-improvement and progress along the lines of least resistance. Washington's power over his following, and hence his power to bring about change, have probably been exaggerated. It was the breadth rather than the depth of his coalition that was unique. Perhaps one Booker T. Washington was enough. But even today, in a very different society, Washington's autobiography is still in print. It still has some impalpable power to bridge the racial gap, to move new readers to take the first steps across the color line. Many of his ideas of self-help and racial solidarity still have currency in the black community. But he was an important leader because, like Frederick Douglass before him and Martin Luther King after him, he had the program and strategy and skill to influence the behavior of not only the Afro-American one-tenth, but the white nine-tenths of the American people. He was a political realist.

POSTSCRIPT

Did Booker T. Washington's Philosophy and Actions Betray the Interests of African Americans?

Discussions of race relations in the late nineteenth- and early twentieth-century United States invariably focus upon the ascendancy of Booker T. Washington, his apparent accommodation to existing patterns of racial segregation, and the conflicting traditions within black thought, epitomized by the clash between Washington and Du Bois. Seldom, however, is attention given to black nationalist thought in the "age of Booker T. Washington."

Black nationalism, centered on the concept of racial solidarity, has been a persistent theme in African American history and reached one of its most important stages of development between 1880 and 1920. In the late 1800s, Henry McNeal Turner and Edward Wilmot Blyden encouraged greater interest in the repatriation of black Americans to Africa, especially Liberia. This goal continued into the twentieth century and culminated in the "Back-to-Africa" program of Marcus Garvey and his Universal Negro Improvement Association. Interestingly, Booker T. Washington also exhibited nationalist sentiment by encouraging blacks to withdraw from white society, develop their own institutions and businesses, and engage in economic and moral uplift. Washington's nationalism concentrated on economic self-help and manifested itself in 1900 with the establishment of the National Negro Business League.

A thorough assessment of the protest and accommodationist views of black Americans is presented in August Meier, *Negro Thought in America, 1880–1915* (University of Michigan Press, 1963). See Rayford Logan, *The Betrayal of the Negro: From Rutherford B. Hayes to Woodrow Wilson* (Macmillan, 1965). By far the best studies of Booker T. Washington are two volumes by Louis R. Harlan: *Booker T. Washington: The Making of a Black Leader, 1856–1901* (Oxford University Press, 1972) and *Booker T. Washington: The Wizard of Tuskegee, 1901–1915* (Oxford University Press, 1983). In addition, Harlan has edited the 13-volume *Booker T. Washington Papers* (University of Illinois Press, 1972–1984). For assessments of two of Booker T. Washington's harshest critics, see David Levering Lewis, *W. E. B. Du Bois: Biography of a Race, 1868–1919* (Henry Holt, 1993) and *W. E. B Du Bois: The Fight for Equality and the American Century, 1919–1963* (Henry Holt, 2000), and Stephen R. Fox, *The Guardian of Boston: William Monroe Trotter* (Atheneum, 1970). John H. Bracey, Jr., August Meier, and Elliott Rudwick, *Black Nationalism in America* (Bobbs-Merrill, 1970), provide an invaluable collection of documents pertaining to black nationalism. See also Edwin S. Redkey, *Black Exodus: Black Nationalist and Back-to-Africa Movements, 1890–1910* (Yale University Press, 1969), and Hollis R. Lynch, *Edward Wilmot Blyden: Pan-Negro*

Patriot, 1832–1912 (Oxford University Press, 1967). Diverse views of Marcus Garvey, who credited Booker T. Washington with inspiring him to seek a leadership role on behalf of African Americans, are found in Edmund David Cronon, *Black Moses: The Story of Marcus Garvey and the Universal Negro Improvement Association* (University of Wisconsin Press, 1955); Tony Martin, *Race First: The Ideological and Organizational Struggles of Marcus Garvey and the UNIA* (Greenwood Press, 1976); and Judith Stein, *The World of Marcus Garvey: Race and Class in Modern Society* (Louisiana State University Press, 1986). Some of Garvey's own writings are collected in Amy Jacques-Garvey, ed., *Philosophy and Opinions of Marcus Garvey* (1925; Atheneum, 1969).

ISSUE 3

Was Early Twentieth-Century American Foreign Policy in the Caribbean Basin Dominated by Economic Concerns?

YES: Walter LaFeber, from *Inevitable Revolutions: The United States in Central America* (W. W. Norton, 1983)

NO: David Healy, from *Drive to Hegemony: The United States in the Caribbean, 1898–1917* (University of Wisconsin Press, 1988)

ISSUE SUMMARY

YES: Professor of history Walter LaFeber argues that the United States developed a foreign policy that deliberately made the Caribbean nations its economic dependents from the early nineteenth century on.

NO: Professor of history David Healy maintains that the two basic goals of American foreign policy in the Caribbean were to provide security against the German threat and to develop the economies of the Latin American nations, whose peoples were considered to be racially inferior.

Geographically, the Caribbean area runs from the tip of the Gulf of Mexico into the Caribbean Sea and includes two major sets of countries. First, the six Central American nations of Guatemala, Honduras, El Salvador, Nicaragua, Costa Rica, and Panama stretch along a narrow 300-mile strip between Mexico and Colombia, which separates the Pacific and Atlantic oceans. Second are a number of islands—Cuba, Haiti, the Dominican Republic, and Puerto Rico—which extend below Florida eastward into the Atlantic Ocean. Ironically, parts of Cuba, which has been a major enemy of the United States for the past 30 years, lie only 90 miles from Key West, Florida.

U.S. involvement in Central America was minimal until the mid-nineteenth century, when the acquisition of California and the subsequent discovery of gold there spurred interest in the building of a canal in Panama or Nicaragua to connect the two oceans. Worried about England's desire to build a similar canal, the United States had Great Britain sign the Clayton-Bulwer Treaty in 1850, which provided that neither country would seek exclusive control over an Isthmian route.

Ironically, America's first excursions into Nicaragua were by invitation. In 1855 the Liberals in Nicaragua grew tired of trying to unseat the Conservative president who had Guatemalan aid. They hired William Walker, a Tennessee-born soldier of fortune to fight the Conservatives. In a bizarre turn of events, Walker not only assembled an army and captured the capital, he also became Nicaragua's president in 1856. During his 10 months in office, Walker tried to impose Anglo-Saxon values on the unwilling Nicaraguans. An invasion financed by Peru, Britain, Cornelius Vanderbilt, and the rest of the Central American countries succeeded in overthrowing Walker. U.S. Marines escorted him out of the country in 1857. He attempted a comeback but was caught and executed in Honduras in 1860.

During the next four decades the United States became preoccupied with its own internal affairs. But by the turn of the twentieth century, three events brought the United States back to the Caribbean area—the Spanish-American War, the Panama Canal controversy, and the Roosevelt Corollary to the Monroe Doctrine. In 1898 U.S. soldiers liberated Cuba in a "splendid little war" with Spain and acquired Puerto Rico as an American territory. Five years later President Theodore Roosevelt supported a revolution in Panama to overthrow Colombian rule and proceeded to negotiate a treaty to build a canal 15 days after the new government of Panama had been created. Finally, in 1904 Roosevelt redefined the Monroe Doctrine. Worried that European countries might intervene in the Dominican Republic because of the money owed to European banks, Roosevelt declared that America should help "backward" states pay their bills. The United States took over the customs office of the Dominican Republic and used the revenues to pay off European bill collectors. The Roosevelt Corollary stated that the United States would actively intervene on behalf of the Central American nations. The "insurrectionary habit" brought U.S. Marines to the Dominican Republic in 1916. American troops were also sent to Haiti, Honduras, and Nicaragua.

Why did the United States constantly intervene in the affairs of the Caribbean nations during the first two decades of the twentieth century? In the following essays, Walter LaFeber argues that, given the nineteenth-century racial attitudes which considered all races other than white to be inferior, the United States easily justified its expansion across the continent. Therefore, says LaFeber, the United States adopted a foreign policy which deliberately made the Caribbean nations its *economic* dependents from the early nineteenth century on. David Healy disagrees with the theory of economic neodependency, stating that U.S. interventions were motivated by two factors: to stabilize the area by having American businesses help these radically backward Caribbean nations develop their resources and to provide security against a military threat from Germany.

YES

Walter LaFeber

Inevitable Revolutions

An Overview of the System

> *Central America is the most important place in the world for the United States today.*
>
> *U.S. Ambassador to the United Nations,*
> Jeane Kirkpatrick, 1981

> *What we see in Central America today would not be much different if Fidel Castro and the Soviet Union did not exist.*
>
> *U.S. Ambassador to Panama,*
> Ambler Moss, 1980

No area in the world is more tightly integrated into the United States political-economic system, and none—as President Ronald Reagan warned a joint session of Congress in April 1983—more vital for North American security, than Central America. Washington, D.C. is closer to El Salvador than to San Francisco. Nearly two-thirds of all U.S. trade and the nation's oil imports, as well as many strategic minerals, depend on the Caribbean sea lanes bordered by the five Central American nations.

North Americans have always treated the region differently from the remainder of Latin America. The five nations cover only a little more than one-hundredth of the Western Hemisphere's land area, contain a mere one-fortieth of its population, stretch only nine hundred miles north to south and (at the widest points) less than three hundred miles from ocean to ocean. But this compact region has been the target of a highly disproportionate amount of North American investment and—especially—military intervention. Every twentieth-century intervention by U.S. troops in the hemisphere has occurred in the Central American-Caribbean region. The unusual history of the area was captured by former Chilean President Eduardo Frei, who observed that the Central American states "to a man from the deep South [of the Americas] seem at times more remote than Europe." Frei's remark also implied that the largest South American nations (Argentina, Chile, Brazil) historically looked east to Europe, while the Central Americans have turned north to the United States.

No region in the world is in greater political and economic turmoil than Central America. And there are few areas about which North Americans are more ignorant. The following is a capsule view of the five nations which, over the past century, have become dependent on the U.S. system. Each is quite different from the other four, but all five share a dependence on the United States that is deeply rooted in history. They also share poverty and inequality that have spawned revolutions in the seventies and eighties. . . .

These five countries are changing before our eyes. Such instability, importance to U.S. security, and North American ignorance about them form a combustible mixture. One explosion has already rocked the hemisphere: the Nicaraguan revolution became the most significant political event in the Caribbean region since 1959 when Fidel Castro seized power in Cuba. Revolutionary movements have since appeared in every other Central American nation except Costa Rica, and even that democracy has not been safe from terrorism.

The United States has countered those revolutions with its military power. Washington's recent policy, this book argues, is historically consistent for two reasons: first, for more than a century (if not since 1790), North Americans have been staunchly antirevolutionary; and second, U.S. power has been the dominant outside (and often inside) force shaping the societies against which Central Americans have rebelled. The reasons for this struggle between the Goliaths and Davids of world power (or what former Guatemalan President Juan José Arévalo called "the Shark and the Sardines") lie deeply embedded in the history of U.S.-Central American relations. As U.S. Ambassador to Panama Ambler Moss phrased the problem in 1980, "What we see in Central America today would not be much different if Fidel Castro and the Soviet Union did not exist."

These two themes—the U.S. fear of revolution and the way the U.S. system ironically helped cause revolutions in Central America—form the basis of this book. Before that story is told in detail, however, a short overview introduces the two themes.

The Revolutions of the 1970s and 1770s

Washington officials have opposed radical change not because of pressure from public opinion. Throughout the twentieth century, the overwhelming number of North Americans could not have identified each of the five Central American nations on a map, let alone ticked off the region's sins that called for an application of U.S. force.

The United States consistently feared and fought such change because it was a status quo power. It wanted stability, benefited from the on-going system, and was therefore content to work with the military-oligarchy complex that ruled most of Central America from the 1820s to the 1980s. The world's leading revolutionary nation in the eighteenth century became the leading protector of the status quo in the twentieth century. Such protection was defensible when it meant defending the more equitable societies of Western Europe and Japan, but became questionable when it meant bolstering poverty and inequality in Central America.

How North Americans turned away from revolution toward defense of oligarchs is one of the central questions in U.S. diplomatic history. The process, outlined in Chapter 1, no doubt began with the peculiar nature of the revolution in 1776. It was radical in that it proclaimed the ideal of personal freedom. The power of the British mercantilist state, Thomas Jefferson and some of his colleagues declared, had to be more subordinate to individual interest. North Americans, especially if they were white and male, could moreover realize such an ideal in a society that was roughly equitable at its birth, and possessed a tremendous landed frontier containing rich soil and many minerals that could provide food and a steadily growing economy for its people.

Central Americans have expressed similar ideals of freedom, but the historical sources of those ideals—not to mention the geographical circumstances in which they could be realized—have been quite different from the North American. Fidel Castro quoted the Declaration of Independence and compared burning Cuban cane fields in 1958 to the Boston Tea Party of 1773. But his political program for achieving the Declaration's principles flowed from such native Cuban revolutionaries as José Martí, not from Thomas Jefferson.

The need of Cubans and Central Americans to find different means for achieving their version of a just society arose in large part from their long experience with North American capitalism. This capitalism has had a Jekyll and Hyde personality. U.S. citizens see it as having given them the highest standard of living and most open society in the world. Many Central Americans have increasingly associated capitalism with a brutal oligarchy-military complex that has been supported by U.S. policies—and armies. Capitalism, as they see it, has too often threatened the survival of many for the sake of freedom for a few. For example, Latin Americans bitterly observed that when the state moved its people for the sake of national policy (as in Cuba or Nicaragua), the United States condemned it as smacking of Communist tyranny. If, however, an oligarch forced hundreds of peasants off their land for the sake of his own profit, the United States accepted it as simply the way of the real world. . . .

For the United States, capitalism and military security went hand-in-hand. They have, since the nineteenth-century, formed two sides of the same policy in Central America. Early on, the enemy was Great Britain. After 1900 it became Germany. Only after World War I were those dangers replaced by a Soviet menace. Fencing out Communists (or British, or Germans) preserved the area for North American strategic interests and profits. That goal was not argued. The problem arose when Washington officials repeatedly had to choose which tactic best preserved power and profits: siding with the status quo for at least the short term, or taking a chance on radical change that might (or might not) lead to long-term stability. Given the political and economic pressures, that choice was predetermined. As former Secretary of State Dean Acheson observed, there is nothing wrong with short-term stability. "When you step on a banana peel you have to keep from falling on your tail, you don't want to be lurching all over the place all the time. Short-term stability is all right, isn't it? Under the circumstances." The "circumstances" Acheson alluded to were the revolutions that began to appear in the newly emerging countries during the 1950s.

When applied to Central America, Acheson's view missed a central tenet of the region's history: revolutions have served the functions of elections in the United States; that is, they became virtually the only method of transferring power and bringing about needed change. Acheson's short-term stability too often turned out to be Washington's method for ensuring that Central American oligarchs did not have to answer to their fellow citizens.

The revolutionaries of the 1770s thus had less and less to say to the revolutionaries of the 1970s and 1980s. The latter were more anticapitalist, pro-statist, and concerned much less with social stability than were the former. These differences appeared as the upheavals increased in number and intensity. . . . Revolutions in such areas as Central America were inevitable. The only choice was whether North Americans would work with those revolutionaries to achieve a more orderly and equitable society, or whether—as occurred in Guatemala and Nicaragua—Washington officials would try to cap the upheavals until the pressure built again to blow the societies apart with even greater force.

Neodependency: The U.S. System

Central American revolutions have thus not only been different from, but opposed to, most of the U.S. revolutionary tradition. This opposition can be explained historically. For in rebelling against their own governments, Central Americans have necessarily rebelled against the U.S. officials and entrepreneurs who over many decades made Central America a part of their own nation's system. Not that day-to-day control, in Washington's view, was necessary or desirable. Actually governing such racially different and politically turbulent nations as Guatemala or Honduras was one headache that U.S. officials tried to avoid at every turn. They instead sought informal control, and they finally obtained it through a system that can be described as "neodependency."

First outlined in the 1960s, the theory of "dependency" has been elaborated until it stands as the most important and provocative method of interpreting U.S.-Latin American relations. Dependency may be generally defined as a way of looking at Latin American development, not in isolation, but as part of an international system in which the leading powers (and since 1945, the United States in particular), have used their economic strength to make Latin American development dependent on—and subordinate to—the interests of those leading powers. This dependence, the theory runs, has stunted the Latins' economic growth by forcing their economies to rely on one or two main export crops or on minerals that are shipped off to the industrial nations. These few export crops, such as bananas or coffee, make a healthy domestic economy impossible, according to the theory, because their price depends on an international marketplace which the industrial powers, not Central America can control. Such export crops also blot up land that should be used to grow foodstuffs for local diets. Thus malnutrition, even starvation, grow with the profits of the relatively few producers of the export crops.

Dependency also skews Central American politics. The key export crops are controlled by foreign investors or local elites who depend on foreigners for capital, markets, and often for personal protection. In the words of a Chilean scholar, these foreign influences become a "kind of 'fifth column'" that distorts economic and political development without taking direct political control of the country. Thus dependency theory denies outright a cherished belief of many North Americans: that if they are allowed to invest and trade freely, the result will be a more prosperous and stable Central America. To the contrary, dependency theorists argue, such investment and trade has been pivotal in misshaping those nations' history until revolution appears to be the only instrument that can break the hammerlock held by the local oligarchy and foreign capitalists. Latin American development, in other words, has not been compatible with United States economic and strategic interests.

[The next section] outlines how Central America became dependent on the United States. But as the story unfolds, it becomes clear that the economic aspects of dependency theory are not sufficient to explain how the United States gained such control over the region. Other forms of power, including political and military, accompanied the economic. In Nicaragua from 1909 to 1912, for example, or in Guatemala during the 1954 crisis, or in El Salvador during the eighties, economic leverage proved incapable of reversing trends that North American officials despised and feared. Those officials then used military force to destroy the threats. The United States thus has intervened frequently with troops or covert operations to ensure that ties of dependency remained.

In this respect, U.S. foreign policy has sharply distinguished Central America and the Caribbean nations from the countries in South America. In the latter region, U.S. political threats have been rarer. Direct, overt military intervention has been virtually nonexistent. Central American nations, however, have received special attention. Washington officials relied primarily on their nation's immense economic power to dominate Central America since 1900 . . . but they also used military force to ensure that control. Hence the term neodependency to define that special relationship.

To return to the original theme of [this discussion], no region in the world is more tightly integrated into the United States economic and security system than Central America. That region, however, is being ripped apart by revolutions that have already begun in Nicaragua, El Salvador, and Guatemala, and threaten Honduras. Even Costa Rica, with the most equitable and democratic system in Central America, is unsettled. As the dominant power in the area for a century, the United States bears considerable responsibility for the conditions that burst into revolution. The U.S. system was not designed accidentally or without well-considered policies. It developed slowly between the 1820s and 1880s, then rapidly, reaching maturity in the 1940s and 1950s. It was based on principles that had worked, indeed on principles that made the United States the globe's greatest power: a confidence in capitalism, a willingness to use military force, a fear of foreign influence, and a dread of revolutionary instability.

The application of those principles to Central America has led to a massive revolutionary outbreak. This history of U.S.-Central American relations during the past 150 years attempts to explain why this occurred. . . .

T.R. and TAFT: Justifying Intervention

In 1898 an awesome North American force needed fewer than three months to crush the remnants of Spain's New World empire and then establish bases in territory as close as the Caribbean and as distant as the Philippines. In 1901 the United States forced the British to terminate the Clayton-Bulwer treaty so Washington could fully control the building and defense of an isthmian canal. That same year William McKinley was assassinated and Theodore Roosevelt became president of the United States.

The famed Rough Rider, who fought publicly if not brilliantly in Cuba during the 1898 war, believed as much as Blaine that the United States was the "natural protector"—and should be the main beneficiary—of Central American affairs. But Roosevelt's methods were characteristically more direct than Blaine's. Nor was he reluctant to use them on Latin Americas whom he derisively called "Dagoes" because, in his view, they were incapable of either governing themselves or—most important in T. R.'s hierarchy of values—maintaining order. The U.S. emergence as a world power and Roosevelt's ascendency to the White House were accompanied by a third historic event during the years from 1898 to 1901: the largest export of North American capital to that time. The country remained an international debtor until World War I, but the force of the new U.S. industrial and agricultural complexes was felt many years before. A large-scale capital market centered in New York City allowed further expansion and concentration of those complexes.

England's investments in Central America meanwhile peaked in 1913 at about $115 million. More than two-thirds of the money, however, was in Costa Rica and Guatemala. And of the total amount, about $75 million—almost wholly in Costa Rica and Guatemala—represented British railroad holdings. Another $40 million was invested in government bonds, most of which were worthless. U.S. investments in Central America, on the other hand, climbed rapidly from $21 million in 1897 to $41 million in 1908, and then to $93 million by the eve of World War I. These differed from the British not only in the rapidity of growth, but in the overwhelming amount (over 90 percent) that went into such direct investments as banana plantations and mining, rather than into government securities, and in the power—perhaps even a monopoly power—these monies were buying in Honduran and Nicaraguan politics. Not that the two British bastions were invulnerable. In Guatemala, U.S. railroad holdings amounted to $30 million between 1897 and 1914 until they rapidly closed ground on England's investment of slightly over $40 million. U.S. fruit companies alone nearly equalled Great Britain's entire investment in Costa Rica's economic enterprises.

No one understood these movements and their implications as well as Elihu Root, T. R.'s secretary of state between 1905 and 1909, the nation's premier corporate lawyer, and perhaps his generation's shrewdest analyst of the new corporate America. Returning from a trip through Latin America in 1906, Root told a convention of businessmen that during the past few years three centuries of that nation's history had suddenly closed. The country's indebtedness had given way to a "surplus of capital" that was "increasing with extraordinary rapidity." As this surplus searched throughout the world for markets to conquer and vast projects to build, the mantle of world empire was being passed: "As in their several ways England and France and Germany have stood, so we in our own way are beginning to stand and must continue to stand toward the industrial enterprise of the world."

The northern and southern hemispheres perfectly suited each other, Root observed. People to the south needed North American manufacturers and the latter needed the former's raw materials. Even the personalities complemented each other: "Where we accumulate, they spend. While we have less of the cheerful philosophy" which finds "happiness in the existing conditions of life," as the Latins do, "they have less of the inventive faculty which strives continually to increase the productive power of men." Root closed by putting it all in historical perspective: "Mr. Blaine was in advance of his time. . . . Now, however, the time has come; both North and South America have grown up to Blaine's policy."

In important respects Root's speech of 20 November 1906 resembled Frederick Jackson Turner's famous essay of 1893 on the closing of the North American frontier. Both men understood that three centuries of U.S. development had terminated during their lifetime and that a new phase of the nation's history had begun. Both revealed social and racial views which shaped the new era's policies. Both were highly nationalistic if not chauvinistic. Most important, both used history as a tool to rationalize the present and future: the dynamic new United States necessarily prepared itself to find fresh frontiers abroad to replace the closed frontier at home.

Unfortunately for Root's plans, internal revolts and external wars tormented Central America at the time. The upheavals and the consequent danger of European intervention posed special problems after 1903. For in that year Roosevelt helped Panama break away from Colombia and he then began to build the isthmian canal. In a private letter of 1905 Root drew the lesson: "The inevitable effect of our building the Canal must be to require us to police the surrounding premises. In the nature of things, trade and control, and the obligation to keep order which go with them, must come our way." The conclusion was unarguable.

It must be noted, however, that one of Root's assumptions was faulty. The Panama Canal was only an additional, if major, reason for injecting U.S. power into Central America. That power had actually begun moving into the region a half-century before. It could claim de facto political and military predominance years before canal construction began. And as Root himself argued in his 1906 speech, United States development, especially in the economic realm, foretold a new relationship with Latin America even if the canal were never built. The Panamanian passageway accelerated the growth of U.S. power in Central America. It also magnificently symbolized that power. But it did not create the power or the new relationship.

For many reasons, therefore—to ensure investments, secure the canal, act as a "natural protector," and, happily, replace the declining presence of the British—Roosevelt announced in 1905 that henceforth the United States would act as the policeman to maintain order in the hemisphere. He focused this Roosevelt Corollary to the Monroe Doctrine on the Caribbean area, where Santo Domingo was beset by revolutions and foreign creditors, but his declaration had wider meaning: "All that this country desires is that the other republics on this continent shall be happy and prosperous; and they cannot be happy and prosperous unless they maintain order within their boundaries and behave with a just regard for their obligations toward outsiders."

Perhaps Roosevelt's major gift to U.S. statecraft was his formulation of why revolutions were dangerous to his nation's interest, and the justification he then provided to use force, if necessary, to end them. But his Corollary meant more than merely making war for peace. It exemplified North American disdain for people who apparently wanted to wage revolts instead of working solid ten-hour days on the farm. Roosevelt saw such people as "small bandit nests of a wicked and inefficient type," and to U.S. Progressives such as T.R., the only sin greater than inefficiency was instability. A top U.S. naval official called the outbreaks "so-called revolutions" that "are nothing less than struggles between different crews of bandits for the possession of the customs houses—and the loot." A fellow officer agreed that only the civilized Monroe Doctrine held "a large part of this hemisphere in check against cosmic tendencies."

Of course that view completely reversed the meaning of the original Doctrine. Monroe and Adams had originally intended it to protect Latin American revolutions from outside (that is, European) interference. Eighty years later the power balance had shifted to the United States, and the Doctrine itself shifted to mean that Latin Americans should now be controlled by outside (that is, North American) intervention if necessary. Roosevelt justified such intervention as only an exercise of "police" power, but that term actually allowed U.S. presidents to intervene according to any criteria they were imaginative enough to devise. In the end they could talk about "civilization," and "self-determination," but their military and economic power was its own justification.

Roosevelt's successor, William Howard Taft, and Secretary of State Philander C. Knox hoped that T.R.'s military "Big Stick" could be replaced by the more subtle and constructive dollar. They held to the traditional North American belief in the power of capital for political healing. To bestow such blessings Knox thought it only proper that the United States seize other nations' customs revenues so they could not become the target of "devastating and unprincipled revolutions." To stabilize Central America—and to have U.S. investors do well while doing good—Taft and Knox searched for an all-encompassing legal right for intervention. The president bluntly told a Mexican diplomat that North Americans could "not be content until we have secured some formal right to compel the peace between those Central American Governments," and "have the right to knock their heads together until they should maintain peace between them." Such a general right was never discovered because legal experts in the State Department warned Knox that such a thing did not exist. Taft and Knox fell back on straight dollar diplomacy; that instrument, given their views of Central Americans, then led them to use force in the T.R. manner. As noted below, Knox soon relied upon what he termed "the moral value" of naval power.

To argue, therefore, that the United States intervened in Central America simply to stop revolutions and bestow the blessings of stability tells too little too simply. The Roosevelt Corollary and Taft's dollar diplomacy rested on views on history, the character of foreign peoples, and politics that anticipated attitudes held by North Americans throughout much of the twentieth century. These policies were applied by presidents who acted unilaterally and set historic precedents for the global application of U.S. power in later years.

North Americans seldom doubted that they could teach people to the south to act more civilized. The potential of U.S. power seemed unlimited, and as that power grew so did the confidence with which it was wielded. Brooks Adams, the grandson and great-grandson of presidents, and a brilliant eccentric who was a friend and adviser of Roosevelt, studied history deeply, then emerged to declare that the 1898 war was "the turning point in our history. . . . I do believe that we may dominate the world, as no nation has dominated it in recent time." In a personal letter, Adams spoke for his generation when he asserted that the years from 1900 to 1914 would "be looked back upon as the grand time. We shall, likely enough, be greater later, but it is the dawn which is always golden. The first taste of power is always the sweetest."

David Healy **NO**

Drive to Hegemony

After experiencing a heady victory in the Spanish-American War, the United States acquired a small but far-flung empire and embarked upon a more energetic course in foreign affairs. For the next generation its diplomatic efforts were focused principally on two regions, northern Latin America and the Far East. In both regions Washington sought to become a leading shaper of events and fount of influence, but with very different results. In spite of its pretentious Open Door policy, the United States repeatedly met with frustration and failure in its Far Eastern efforts; by 1917 it had little to show for them but an enduring rivalry with Japan and a Philippine colony already coming to be seen as a white elephant. In the Caribbean area, by contrast, it had established an effective regional hegemony.

The reasons for the nation's differing success rate in these areas are not hard to find, for they emerge clearly in even a superficial comparison of the two. First of all, in the Far East the United States was a latecomer to a long-standing rivalry involving a number of competitors: Great Britain, Russia, Germany, France, and the rising local power, Japan. Located halfway around the globe from the United States, the region was never regarded in Washington as vital, however intense the occasional burst of diplomatic involvement might become, and certainly no one at the time ever suggested that it had any bearing upon the security of the United States.

The Caribbean region, by contrast, was close to the United States and far from the other great powers. No other major power challenged United States hegemony there. Great Britain, with a large economic presence, the world's mightiest navy, and secure bases in Jamaica, Trinidad, the Lesser Antilles, British Guiana, and British Honduras, was best positioned to mount such a challenge but consciously refrained. Although Americans [The use of *American* to mean *from the United States* is widely accepted in much of the world. In Latin America, *North American* is the term most used to denote United States origin. Since there is no generally satisfactory term available, I have used both interchangeably.] long feared that Germany would pick up the gauntlet, no significant opposition to Washington's growing power came from Berlin. The region was of secondary or marginal importance to the other nations of real weight, and of primary importance only to the United States. If necessary, the Americans were ready to fight for their aims in the Caribbean, and the other powers knew it. Locked into their own European tensions, they found nothing in the area worth a war with a rising naval and industrial power. As continental tensions rose steadily, then exploded into general war in 1914, Europe was increasingly debarred from any meaningful power commitments in the New World.

In addition to being the only major power with a free hand in the Caribbean, the United States possessed other regional advantages. Again, these emerge plainly from a regional comparison. American ambitions in the Far East initially included hopes of economic penetration, particularly into the markets of China. While these were at that time not large, Europeans and Americans alike shared a mistaken conviction that China was on the brink of rapid westernization and economic development which would make it a large consumer of western manufactures. In practice, China's trade with the developed world was not only rather static but overwhelmingly dominated by the British, while Japan emerged as a formidable regional business rival. As a result, the American economic stake in the Far East never became very large.

Once more the Caribbean was different. The British were also well entrenched in Caribbean trade, investment, and shipping in 1898, but not so strongly as in the Far East, while North American enterprise made steady inroads from the late nineteenth century on. By 1917 United States economic influence in the Caribbean had passed that of Great Britain, particularly in the countries in which Washington was most interested. The First World War clinched the American advantage by closing off the supply of European goods and money. Yankee businessmen quickly moved in to fill the void, making gains which substantially survived the end of the war.

A final contrast is even more striking: that between the vastness of China and the relative smallness of the Caribbean states. Both were vulnerable and disorganized at the turn of the century, but the teeming population of China had for centuries passively absorbed a succession of conquerors. To use force effectively in China might require considerable and expensive efforts extended over years, and the problem was compounded by the number of great-power rivals to be considered. The Russo-Japanese War of 1904–1905 was a grim warning of the price which the unwary could be obliged to pay; the winners as well as the losers suffered scores of thousands of casualties and paid dearly in gold as well as blood.

The scale of the effort required in the Caribbean was drastically smaller. Unchallenged by major rivals, Washington could overawe each small state one to one, in most cases not even needing to use its forces to make its point. When the United States did commit troops to action, seldom as many as two thousand were involved, and never more than three. There were normally enough marines stationed in the region or available nearby on the mainland to handle even small local wars without much extra expenditure, and never were they very bloody—for the North Americans, at any rate. Divided into many small, weak states, the Caribbean region posed little resistance to a determined great-power drive for hegemony.

Given these strategic and economic advantages, the United States quickly became dominant in the Caribbean. This . . . is an account of that rise to dominance, which began in 1898 and was substantially completed by 1917. The pages that follow do not, however, deal with the entire Gulf-Caribbean region. Mexico, important as it was, and however intimately entangled with the United States, constitutes another story. Like Colombia and Venezuela, it was not a part of the central system of Caribbean control erected in this period by the United States, but rather an indicator of the limits of that system. These larger countries also felt the weight of Washington's power and, in Mexico's case especially, played host to a myriad of North American enterprises, but never passed wholly within the circle of North American hegemony. Thus while Mexico's story has much in common with those of its neighbors, it is different in kind and will not be told here. Also omitted are the Caribbean colonies of Great Britain, France, and the Netherlands, with which Washington made no effort to interfere. This . . . is about United States relations, official and unofficial, with the independent states of Central America and the Greater Antilles, and the former Spanish colonies which passed under United States control in 1898. It is about the techniques developed to exercise hegemony over the small sovereign states of the Caribbean, the reasons why North Americans desired such hegemony, and some of the effects which resulted from its establishment. . . .

Assumptions, Biases, and Preconceptions

As the twentieth century got under way, the United States stood poised to extend its interests far beyond the initial Caribbean stepping-stones of Cuba and Puerto Rico. Even as this process began, many of the nation's people and policy makers already harbored a set of shared assumptions which would condition their future actions in the area. These assumptions touched upon the relations between the powerful industrialized states and the weaker and less developed ones, the economic potential of the Caribbean region and the capabilities of its peoples, and the probability of a European threat to the region's security.

Such preconceptions did not necessarily originate in the United States; some were borrowed from European views and experience, while many were jointly held on both sides of the Atlantic. By 1900, the European powers had a long history of interaction with other societies in every part of the world, and had established an extensive set of behavioral norms, many of which were accepted in the United States as a matter of course. The Old World was still a world of empires, and the thirty years before 1900 had witnessed a massive advance of European colonialism across Africa and Southeast Asia. Europeans of the Victorian age tended to divide the peoples of the world into the civilized and the barbarous, and their nations into the progressive and the stagnant. They saw non-European peoples lacking modern industrial societies as not merely different, but inferior, and worse yet, obstructive. These peoples, they felt, had no right to stand in the way of the world's development; "civilization" needed their raw materials, their agricultural production, and the economic opportunities which they represented. . . .

This assumed need raised problems in dealing with preindustrial nations. This was especially true of those with exotic legal and commercial codes, those prone to political violence, and those whose magnates or governments failed to honor contracts with the outside world. Once European men and money had committed themselves to enterprises in such places, their home governments must be ready to protect their lives and property against local misbehavior. The Palmerston Circular, issued by the government of Great Britain in 1849, formally claimed the right to intervene for its citizens abroad either in their individual capacity or as members of corporate organizations. Other governments claimed the same right, and the diplomatic protection of citizens' economic activities abroad became an increasingly important function of foreign offices and their legations and consulates.

It was not always clear when a citizen or corporation had been wronged, of course; frequently the disputes were murky, with much to blame on both sides. Furthermore, the issue may have been formally decided after due process by the legal system of the host country, but the imperial powers refused to accept this as decisive. . . .

The borrowers soon learned the tactics of evasion. Some Latin American governments regularly defaulted on their loans, and most did so at least once. Almost all of them contracted new loans to repay the old, usually enlarging the total in order to have fresh funds in hand for current needs. Governments regularly pledged specific sources of revenue—most often customs collections or export taxes—to the service of existing debts, then used them for other purposes in violation of their promises. It was not long before the whole process of contracting such debts became a vicious game without rules, in which each side tried to take advantage of the other. By the turn of the century some semblance of order began to emerge, as the complex and sordid controversies of the past were increasingly settled by compromise. In such settlements the debtor government paid only an agreed fraction of the sometimes fantastic totals charged against them by the bondholders. Even in 1900, however, the whole field of Caribbean government loans was still dangerous to the uninitiated, and too often tarred with scandal. . . .

If belief in special enterprisers' rights under international law commanded a consensus in the United States, so did confidence that the Caribbean countries contained a rich field for enterprise. American travelers of the period almost invariably saw vast economic promise in the region. The genuinely fertile island of Cuba set the standard, while the lush foliage of the tropics suggested a similar productivity for most of the other areas. Thus Nicaragua, for example, was widely regarded as having equal possibilities. Speaking of that country, a traveler of the 1880s concluded: "Nature has blessed it with wonderful resources, and a few years of peace and industry would make the country prosperous without comparison. . . ." Some years later the navy's Admiral James G. Walker echoed the sentiment: "The country's natural resources are immense. Millions of acres of rich land . . . need but little development to yield enormous harvests." In 1906 the United States minister drew a dismal picture of the present state of the country, then went on to contrast this with its latent potential: "This lamentable picture is one of the most fertile, beautiful countries in tropical America, which would rapidly advance in wealth and population were there security of life or property." A half dozen years later, another transient Yankee saw the future prosperity of the land in the cultivation of sugar and rubber by foreign investors, once political stability should be restored. "For these people and for this country as much can be done as we did for Cuba," he wrote, "and without firing a shot." . . .

Almost invariably, each glowing forecast of future prosperity was accompanied by harsh criticisms of the current society of the country under discussion. Thus Nicaragua had heretofore failed to flourish because "so much attention has been paid to politics that little is left for anything else," and frequently recurring civil wars disrupted labor and production. Bad government was reputed to be almost universal. The same British diplomat who saw such material promise in all of the Central American states found in their rulers a major obstacle to development. "Their dishonest methods, total lack of justice, and their shiftiness make it almost useless to endeavor to deal with these Governments as with civilized nations," he declared. "Presidents, Ministers, Judges, police and all other Government or local officials appear to have but one object, namely, to extort and steal as much as possible during their term of office." Elihu Root dismissed the public life of Santo Domingo in a sentence: "Her politics are purely personal, and have been a continual struggle of this and that and the other man to secure ascendancy and power."

To these outside observers, the failure of government was closely associated with the defects of the population. Witness after witness testified that the Caribbean peoples were ignorant, lazy, backward, perhaps vicious. The London *Times* correspondent who gave such a favorable report of Santo Domingo's land and resources described the people as "easy-going and improvident," devoid of initiative or enterprise. When he asked a rural cultivator why he did not dig a ditch and irrigate his field, the man replied that if such a thing were necessary, God would have made it. Admiral Walker saw the Nicaraguans as "dreaming the years away" without past traditions or future ambitions to inspirit them. The American author of a 1910 travel book on Central America did not attempt to conceal his contempt for the people of that region: "Barbarism, enervated by certain civilized forms, without barbarism's vigor, tells all in a word. Scenes of disgust I might repeat to the point of nausea; utter lack of sanitation, of care of body as well as mind, expose a scrofulous people to all the tropical diseases. . . ." To this writer, Central America was not properly a part of the larger Latin American whole, for the South Americans were civilized and progressive, the Central Americans not so. They would be better called "Indo-Americans," he thought, to indicate their inferiority. . . .

The truth was that the American public of the early twentieth century expected to find inferior qualities in nonwhite peoples from tropical societies. Racism in the United States was older than the nation itself; Indians and blacks had suffered from the stigma of inequality since early colonial times. The legacies of the frontier and slavery had long since hardened into fixed attitudes, only superficially changed by the passing of Indian resistance or the episodes of the Civil War and Reconstruction. By the late nineteenth century the South was resubmerging its black population under grandfather clauses, Jim Crow legislation, and lynch law, while Indians were consigned to segregated "reservations" and forgotten. Even the newer European immigrants, flocking in from Southern and Eastern Europe and bringing different cultural backgrounds into the mainstream, were received with deep suspicion and scarcely concealed intimations of inferiority. The inequality of peoples was a pervasive idea in turn-of-the-century America; the Indians, mestizos, and blacks of the Caribbean could hope for little from United States public opinion.

The period entertained not only racial, but geographical biases. A widely read book entitled *The Control of the Tropics* appeared in 1898 with a large impact in both England and America. Written by an Englishman named Benjamin Kidd, its thesis centered on the allegation that the tropical peoples were always and everywhere incapable of self-government and economic development, and their societies were typically characterized by anarchy and bankruptcy. The roots of this alleged condition were not merely racial; white men of "high efficiency," living too long amid slack standards in an enervating climate, were themselves in danger of degeneration. Such men must return regularly to their homelands to renew their mental, moral, and physical vigor, or succumb in time to the universal tropical decay. If tropical areas were to be developed, therefore, they must be governed and managed by career executives and civil servants sent out from the vigorous societies of the north, and regularly replaced by new blood. Since the last great field for the world's economic growth lay in the tropics, Kidd declared, the matter was of more than theoretical importance, and scores of reviewers and readers in the United States agreed with him. . . .

Potentially rich, but peopled by inferior stocks and retarded by inimical tropical conditions, the future of the region lay primarily with outsiders: that was the message, implicit or explicit, received by public opinion in the United States. Yet a plethora of witnesses asserted their confidence in the area's future. Given even a modest degree of order and stability, they chorused, foreign business enterprise would soon be able to tap the varied riches awaiting its fulfilling hand. With economic development under way, a generalized prosperity would soon transform the lives, the institutions, perhaps even the nature of the local populations. For the benefits of economic growth would assuredly be mutual; the native peoples of the Caribbean would gain at least as much as the entrepreneurs who came from abroad to invest their money and talents. A rising level of wealth would bring peace, education, and progress to currently benighted areas, provided of course that the developers enjoyed a relatively free hand. Furthermore, the glowing prospects so often described were typically placed, not in the remote future, but in the next decade or sooner. The driving engine of this economic miracle was to lie primarily in tropical agriculture: the sugar, coffee, bananas, or tobacco in which foreign investors were already so interested. In addition some infrastructure would be needed, particularly in the form of railroads and public utilities, while mining and lumbering represented further fields of action. . . .

In the unsparing light of hindsight, it is easy to indict these prophets of progress and prosperity for their hypocrisy. After a century of partial and selective foreign development, the Caribbean region is not rich, but poor. While the enterprisers often made money, and local elites received a more modest share, their activities produced nothing like a generalized prosperity. On the contrary, a vast inequality of incomes left many in penury and most barely above the subsistence level. And in the long run, even the investors' profits were limited; most of the twentieth century has seen agricultural products exchange at a disadvantage with industrial goods, the terms of trade being largely controlled by the industrial and financial centers. World market surpluses of sugar, coffee, and other tropical staples have further driven prices down, so that only during major wars does a true agricultural prosperity bloom in the tropical world.

In the light of these facts, it is tempting to conclude that the claims and promises by which foreign enterprisers justified themselves in the early twentieth century were insincere and self-serving. Self-serving they certainly were, but not necessarily insincere. It is, after all, easiest to believe what is welcome; belief and self-interest typically run hand in hand. More seriously, the enterpriser of 1900 or 1915 had persuasive reasons to believe in the viability of an agriculturally based economic development. At that very time, Argentina was rapidly emerging as the most prosperous and "modern" of Latin American states, making a major success of selling wheat and beef to a hungry Europe. Since the bulk of Argentina's population sprang from recent European immigrants, the lesson seemed to be that the more efficient "races" could indeed wring wealth out of the soil, and that the process was inhibited elsewhere mainly by the deficiencies of the natives. Furthermore, Argentine economic development had been managed and financed to a notable extent from England, demonstrating the efficacy of foreign enterprise. With a fast-growing productive base, a solid infrastructure, and a relatively stable political system, Argentina was widely seen as a role model for all of the Latin America.

Closer to home, the enterprising Yankee had an even more compelling example of the possibilities of market agriculture. The United States itself had long flourished through the export of huge agricultural surpluses, which had played an essential role in financing nineteenth-century industrialization. Nor was this a phenomenon of the past; American food and fibers still dominated the world market, and their profitability had continued to spur the development of large sections of the nation. The Great Plains constituted the last great agricultural frontier, and in 1900 that region was just approaching full development. Within the memory of millions of living Americans, vast areas west of the Mississippi had been settled and broken to the plow. With startling speed, railroads were built, cities founded, churches, opera houses, universities created—an entire new society, comprising numerous states of the union, had appeared as if by magic in a few decades, quickly achieving American standards of wealth, productivity, and material consumption.

The undeniable fact was that united States economic development had historically been tightly linked to a varied and prosperous agriculture. Its modern industrial economy was built on a foundation of soil-based wealth; its citizens took it as a given that the one was a natural precondition for the other. What they had done at home, right up to the early twentieth century, they assumed they could do anywhere else where a reasonable resource base existed. They had little reason to doubt that a healthy economic development could spring from the export of agricultural surpluses to a world market, and every reason to have faith in the process.

In retrospect, of course, there are obvious flaws in this assumption. The relatively favorable terms of trade enjoyed by agricultural products at the beginning of the century were to disappear almost permanently after the First World War. A crop like sugar, considered as an enterprise, differed significantly from grain or meat, given sugar's special demand for cheap seasonal labor and its wildly fluctuating world price. Large-scale corporate farming by foreign businesses was hardly the same as the family farming which prevailed for so long in the United States. And nowhere in the Caribbean, except perhaps in Cuba, were there large tracts of land possessing anything like the incomparable richness of soil and climate which characterized the more prosperous farming areas of the United States. At the time, however, it appeared otherwise. The Great Plains, with their harsh climate, insect plagues, lack of trees, and inadequate rivers seemed the ultimate in nature's resistance to exploitation. Surely the nation which had brought such a region to productivity could repeat its success in the lush, warm valleys of the Caribbean, where the limitations of tropical soils were still imperfectly understood. Flush with surplus capital, confident of their new technology, and glorying in past success, it never occurred to Yankee enterprisers to doubt their ability to pluck riches from the neighboring lands to the south. Neither did they doubt that their success in this would bring the region progress and prosperity. What had happened so often at home was now to be duplicated abroad, they believed, and so did their contemporaries.

What American businessmen and policy makers feared in the Caribbean was not economic failure, but the challenge of their transatlantic rivals to United States control of the region. If they saw the principal barrier to Caribbean development in the supposed deficiencies of the native peoples, they were only slightly less concerned with the threat of European intervention in the area. France's invasion of Mexico in the 1860s, the French Panamá canal project of the 1880s, and the events leading to the Venezuelan crisis with England in the mid-1890s all mobilized long-standing fears in the United States that Europe's imperial rivalries might spill over into the Americans. As Richard Olney's "twenty-inch gun" note of 1895 had so dramatically stated, most Americans would regard such outside intervention in the hemisphere as disastrous, threatening United States security, prestige, and future economic growth. The Monroe Doctrine's dictum against the possibility had long expressed a central tenet of United States foreign policy, and commanded the most widespread popular support. . . .

In general, however, contemporary Americans were united in their opposition to European expansion in the New World, and after 1900 they came quickly to focus their strongest fears and suspicions, no longer on France or Great Britain, but on the rising power of imperial Germany. From the beginning of the twentieth century, this perceived "German threat" constituted one of the ongoing assumptions behind United States policies in the Caribbean.

Belief in a German threat to the Americas was growing rapidly even before Theodore Roosevelt became president in 1901, and it became pervasive in the policy-making circles of the Roosevelt administration. As early as 1898, Roosevelt himself believed that "of all the nations of Europe it seems to me that Germany is by far the most hostile to us." By 1901, he was certain that only a major naval building program could deter the kaiser's ambitions. "I find that the Germans regard our failure to go forward in building up the navy this year as a sign that our spasm of preparation, as they think it, has come to an end," he wrote,

> that we shall sink back, so that in a few years they will be in a position to take some step in the West Indies or South America which will make us either put up or shut up on the Monroe Doctrine; they counting upon their ability to trounce us if we try the former horn of the dilemma.

To an English correspondent, Roosevelt confided that "as things are now the Monroe Doctrine does not touch England . . . the only power that needs to be reminded of its existence is Germany." In particular, he feared the Germans would find ways to acquire the Dutch and Danish possessions in the Americas to use as bases for the insertion of their power. By 1905, however, the president felt that his firm stance, accompanied by a continuing program of naval expansion, had become an effective deterrent: "I think I succeeded in impressing on the Kaiser, quietly and unofficially . . . that the violation of the Monroe Doctrine by territorial aggrandizement on his part around the Caribbean meant war, not ultimately, but immediately, and without any delay." It was, however, a deterrent which required continual alertness and preparation, he thought. . . .

These fears of hostile German intentions were not confined to administration insiders, but were matters of common knowledge and objects of frequent discussion in the press. They outlived the end of the Roosevelt administration, to be reinvigorated by the events of the First World War. Why were Americans so sure that Germany's power was dangerous to them, and how accurate was their assumption?

Germany, like the United States, was a fast-rising industrial power and a relative newcomer to the imperial scramble for colonies. Also like the United States, it had recently entered the international competition to become a leading naval power. Its flamboyant kaiser, fond of military show and symbolism, talked altogether too freely at times of his grandiose ambitions. The Prussian military tradition dominated the new German Empire, and if its navy aimed to become one of the strongest in due time, the position of its army was already fixed at or near the top. This was, in short, a formidable, energetic state, which appeared both ambitious and menacing to powers with established claims. . . .

There were also reasons to tie a prospective German threat to the Caribbean. Admiral Alfred von Tirpitz, the powerful German naval chief, wished to acquire bases in the western hemisphere to match those already held by Great Britain and France. He thought of finding such bases on the coast of Brazil, where three hundred thousand German immigrants had settled in the recent past, or in the Galapagos Islands on the Pacific side of South America. He also talked, however, of gaining possession for Germany of the Dutch or Danish colonies in the Caribbean area and thereby gaining a base at Curaçao, Surinam, or the Virgin Islands, a possibility that worried American naval strategists.

Between 1897 and 1905, German naval staff officers elaborated a series of war plans involving an attack upon the east coast of the United States. Their original concept of a direct descent upon New York, Norfolk, Boston, or elsewhere was eventually modified to include the prior seizure of an advanced base in Puerto Rico or Cuba. Such a staging point would make an invasion less risky, and had the added advantage that its seizure would force the American fleet to come out and fight at a time and place chosen by the Germans. By 1901 the Army General Staff had joined the Admiralty Staff in joint planning, General Alfred von Schlieffen originally estimating that fifty thousand men would be required to take and hold Cuba. A later version of the plan substituted Puerto Rico for Cuba, and reduced the troop strength for its seizure to something over twelve thousand men. Finally, in 1906, the war operations plan was reduced to a mere theoretical exercise, as rising tensions in Europe made it too dangerous to consider committing Germany's entire naval strength to operations in another part of the world. The continued increase in United States naval strength also acted to discourage German planners, and in 1909 the German navy's Caribbean–South Atlantic squadron was discontinued.

While Germany's war plans were kept secret, some idea of their nature leaked through to the United States, where American naval leaders added a real fear of invasion to their earlier anti-German bias. Repeated rumors of the German General Staff's hostile activity confirmed Theodore Roosevelt in his belief in a Teutonic threat and his determination to keep the navy strong. Interestingly, his conviction in 1905 that he had succeeded in deterring the kaiser's ambitions through a policy of firmness and strength came reasonably close to the moment when Berlin itself ceased to consider an American adventure. By 1909 President William Howard Taft would call talk of German aggression in the hemisphere "absurd," and even the navy became less convinced that a clash was imminent.

By that time, however, Americans perceived another kind of threat, as Germany's economic penetration of Latin America and success in selling its exports there identified her as a leading trade rival. The large German immigration to South America and the prominent role of resident German businessmen in many Latin American cities reinforced the picture of a drive for economic domination. Such domination was achieved in fact only in tiny, poverty-stricken Haiti, where German merchants did control the great bulk of international trade. Elsewhere, however, the growth of United States trade outpaced that of its rivals, including Germany; rapid Latin American economic growth in the early twentieth century had in fact increased the exports of all the leading suppliers to the area, but none more than the United States.

Whether there really was a "German threat" to the United States or its Caribbean interests is still a matter of debate. H. H. Herwig and David Trask have argued that the intensive German war planning at the beginning of the century indicated a serious interest in naval and military circles in an aggressive war against the United States. Admiral von Tirpitz made no secret of his ambitions in the western hemisphere, and he had considerable influence over the impressionable kaiser. True, such a war now appears adventurist and dangerous, risking German power far from home for distinctly marginal purposes, and the Germans themselves eventually thought better of it. However, they long discounted American naval, and more especially military, strength on the assumption that the United States armed forces were weakened by indiscipline and inefficiency. Thus, according to this view, it was only the growing crisis in Europe itself that finally acted to cancel out Berlin's aspirations in the New World.

Melvin Small agrees that Americans long feared a German attack, but concludes that the decision makers in Berlin never seriously considered Latin American conquest or North American aggression. Whatever intellectual gymnastics the service leaders undertook, they did not reflect actual government policy, his argument implies. Certainly after 1903, he says, the kaiser's government hoped for good relations with the United States, not confrontation. All in all, Small believes, the "German threat" had been more apparent than real. Yet Small omits a close scrutiny of the period from 1898 to 1903, where lay the strongest indications of a hostile German purpose. On the other hand, no one has made much of a case for a German threat after 1906, even if one existed earlier. One is forced to conclude that the *continuation* of the fear of German designs in the hemisphere was ill founded, even as one concedes the sincerity of most of its prophets.

Justified or not, fear of Germany played a significant part in American thinking about the area as a vital security zone. Concern for the national security blended in turn with economic objectives, status ambition, and even reforming zeal to motivate a quest for United States hegemony. As they looked southward, Americans saw a potentially rich area awaiting development. They believed its resident peoples backward and inferior, incapable by themselves of achieving progress or material development. They feared that European rivals might challenge American power and policies in the region, and in particular that Germany would do so, perhaps go even further and unleash armed aggression against the United States. And they accepted a European-made concept of international law which upheld the rights and interests of foreign enterprisers in undeveloped countries. All of these assumptions, singly and together, encouraged Americans to feel that they should play a leading role in the Caribbean, in order to benefit themselves, develop the region, and forestall foreign threats. Most Americans soon came to see United States hegemony as practical, right, legally justified, and even necessary.

POSTSCRIPT

Was Early Twentieth-Century American Foreign Policy in the Caribbean Basin Dominated by Economic Concerns?

In *Drive to Hegemony,* Healy provides us with a sophisticated summary of the most recent scholarship. Yet, in a number of ways Healy supports the views of Samuel F. Bemis, which are developed in *Latin American Policy of the United States* (Harcourt, Brace & World, 1943). Both argue that U.S. foreign policy was primarily concerned with the German threat to the security in the Caribbean. Both recognize the importance of economic factors, yet maintain that American businesses would invest or trade in the Caribbean only when encouraged by the U.S. government.

Healy gives the economic argument a new twist when he says that it was understandable why so many Yankees believed that the Caribbean was ripe for economic development. Since the United States built its industrial revolution upon its agricultural export surpluses, the assumption was that the Latin American nations could do likewise. But Healy is not willing to call the North Americans "benevolent imperialists" as Bemis does. Instead, he recognizes that American policy makers considered their neighbors to be of "racially inferior" stock and used this to partially explain the lack of economic progress in the Caribbean.

LaFeber has a different perspective than Healy in his view of U.S. relations with Central America. "From the beginning," argues LaFeber, "North American leaders believed their new republic was fated to be dominant in Spanish-held Mexico, Central America, and, indeed, the regions beyond. . . . Capitalism and military security went hand in hand . . . and since the nineteenth century, formed two sides of the same policy in Central America." LaFeber's emphasis on economic forces determining our relationship in the Caribbean is hardly new. In 1934 Charles Beard and George H. E. Smith anticipated many of Bemis's arguments and presented a detailed account of the penetration of Latin America by big business in *The Idea of National Interest* (Macmillan, 1934). LaFeber's broadened definition of imperialism is also not a new concept. Over 30 years ago, William Appleman Williams, LaFeber's graduate school mentor, in *The Tragedy of American Diplomacy,* 2d rev., enlarged ed. (Delta, 1972), argued that the United States created an informal empire in Latin America, Asia, and later Europe via the penetration of American business interests.

What distinguishes LaFeber's analysis is his application of the economic theory of "neodependency" to describe U.S. relations in the Caribbean. First outlined in the 1960s by a number of radical economists, the theory of dependency argues that the United States has used its economic strength to make the development of Latin American countries economically dependent upon the United States. Highly controversial, this theory has been criticized by David Ray in "The Dependency Model of Latin America Underdevelopment: Three Basic Fallacies," *Journal of Interamerican Studies and World Affairs* (February 1973). Ray's critique is very general, but it very easily applies to LaFeber's use of the dependency theory in his discussion of U.S. policy in the Caribbean area. He argues that "the model claims that dependency is caused by the economics of capitalism." If this is true, how can Soviet economic imperialism in Eastern Europe be explained? These countries are economically dominated by Russia, a country that lacks a capitalist economic system. The dependency model also assumes "that private foreign investment is invariably exploitative and invariably detrimental to Latin American development." But not all foreign investments are bad. Although investments in extractive industries can distort a country's economy, investments in industries that seek to expand the domestic market may be beneficial to the Central American nation. Finally, the model assumes that these countries face only two choices: dependent capitalism or nondependent "popular revolutionary governments which open the way to socialism." Consider the examples of Cuba and Nicaragua today. To what extent are they less dependent upon the Soviet bloc trade than they previously had been on trade with the West? How vulnerable are they to Soviet pressures on political and economic issues? In short, "the dependency theorists," says Ray, "conceptualize dependency/nondependency as a dichotomous variable, rather than a continuous one."

Many fine monographic studies have appeared on this subject in the last 20 years. Good overviews of this research can be found in David M. Pletcher's "United States Relations with Latin America: Neighborliness and Exploitation," *American Historical Review* (February 1977) and Richard V. Salisbury's "Good Neighbors? The United States and Latin America in the Twentieth Century," in Gerald K. Haines and J. Samuel Walker, eds., *American Foreign Relations: A Historiographical Overview* (Greenwood Press, 1981).

In a review essay of David Healy's *Drive to Hegemony* in *Diplomatic History* (Summer 1990), David M. Pletcher provides an annotated bibliographical review of all the major works on this subject for the past 75 years. An accessible and acerbic critique of the Williams-LaFeber economic analysis of United States–Caribbean relations can be found in Arthur M. Schlesinger, Jr., *The Cycles of American History* (Houghton Mifflin, 1986).

ISSUE 4

Was Woodrow Wilson a Naive Idealist?

YES: Henry Kissinger, from *Diplomacy* (Simon & Schuster, 1994)

NO: William G. Carleton, from "A New Look at Woodrow Wilson," *The Virginia Quarterly Review* (Autumn 1962)

ISSUE SUMMARY

YES: Former national security adviser and political scholar Henry Kissinger characterizes President Woodrow Wilson as a high-minded idealist whose views have made it difficult for later presidents to develop a logical foreign policy based on national self-interest.

NO: William G. Carleton, who was a professor emeritus of history and political science, believed that Woodrow Wilson understood better than his nationalistic opponents the new international role that America would play in world affairs.

Historians have dealt with Woodrow Wilson rather strangely. The presidential polls conducted by historian Arthur Schlesinger in 1948 and 1962, as well as the 1983 Murray-Blessing poll, ranked Wilson among the top 10 presidents. As you will see when you read the "No" selection, historian William G. Carleton considers him to be the greatest twentieth-century president, only two notches below Thomas Jefferson and Abraham Lincoln. Yet, among his biographers, Wilson, for the most part, has been treated ungenerously. They carp at him for being naive, overly idealistic, too inflexible, rigid, uncompromising, formal, stiff, unkind, disloyal to friends, overcompromising, oratorical, preachy, messianic, and moralistic. It appears that, like many of his contemporaries, Wilson's biographers respect the man but do not like the person.

Why has Wilson been treated with a nagging pettiness by historians? Perhaps the reasons have to do with Wilson's own introspective personality and his lack of formal political experience. He was, along with Jefferson, and to some extent Theodore Roosevelt, our most intellectual president. He spent nearly 20 years as a history and political science teacher and scholar at Bryn Mawr College, Wesleyan University, and Princeton University, his alma mater. While his multivolume *History of the United States* now appears dated as it gathers dust on musty library shelves, Wilson's Ph.D. dissertation on congressional government, which he wrote as a graduate student at Johns Hopkins University, remains a classic statement of the weakness of leadership in the American constitutional system.

In addition to working many years as a college professor, Wilson served a short stint as a lawyer and spent eight distinguished years as president of Princeton University, which he turned into one of the outstanding universities in the country. He introduced the preceptorial system, widely copied today, which supplemented course lectures with discussion conferences led by young instructors, and he took the lead in reorganizing the university's curriculum.

Historians agree that no president, with the exception of Franklin Roosevelt and perhaps Ronald Reagan, performed the ceremonial role of the presidency as well as Wilson. His speeches rang with oratorical brilliance and substance. No wonder he abandoned the practice of Jefferson and his successors by delivering the president's annual State of the Union Address to Congress in person rather than in writing.

During his first four years, Wilson also fashioned an ambitious legislative program. Wilson's "New Freedom" pulled together conservative and progressive, rural and urban, and southern and northern Democrats. This coalition passed such measures as the Underwood/Simmons Tariff Act, the first bill to significantly lower tariff rates since the Civil War, and the Owens/Keating Child Labor Act. It was through Wilson's adroit maneuvering that the Federal Reserve System was established. This banking measure, the most significant in U.S. history, established a major federal agency, which regulates the money supply in the country to this day. Finally, President Wilson revealed his flexibility when he abandoned his initial policy of rigid and indiscriminate trust-busting for one of regulating big business through the creation of the Federal Trade Commission.

It is in his roles as commander in chief and chief diplomat that Wilson has received his greatest criticisms. In the first selection, scholar-diplomat Henry Kissinger argues that because Woodrow Wilson believed that America was a morally superior nation, his intermingling of power and principle made it difficult for future presidents to develop a foreign policy based on a coherent outline of national interest. In the second selection, Professor William Carleton gives a spirited defense of Wilson's foreign policies. He believes that narrow-minded nationalists, like Senator Henry Cabot Lodge, destroyed the international peace of the postwar world by blocking America's entrance into the League of Nations.

YES

Henry Kissinger

The Hinge: Theodore Roosevelt or Woodrow Wilson

Until early in this century, the isolationist tendency prevailed in American foreign policy. Then, two factors projected America into world affairs: its rapidly expanding power, and the gradual collapse of the international system centered on Europe. Two watershed presidencies marked this progression: Theodore Roosevelt's and Woodrow Wilson's. These men held the reins of government when world affairs were drawing a reluctant nation into their vortex. Both recognized that America had a crucial role to play in world affairs though they justified its emergence from isolation with opposite philosophies.

Roosevelt was a sophisticated analyst of the balance of power. He insisted on an international role for America because its national interest demanded it, and because a global balance of power was inconceivable to him without American participation. For Wilson, the justification of America's international role was messianic: America had an obligation, not to the balance of power, but to spread its principles throughout the world. During the Wilson Administration, America emerged as a key player in world affairs, proclaiming principles which, while reflecting the truisms of American thought, nonetheless marked a revolutionary departure for Old World diplomats. These principles held that peace depends on the spread of democracy, that states should be judged by the same ethical criteria as individuals, and that the national interest consists of adhering to a universal system of law.

To hardened veterans of a European diplomacy based on the balance of power, Wilson's views about the ultimately moral foundations of foreign policy appeared strange, even hypocritical. Yet Wilsonianism has survived while history has bypassed the reservations of his contemporaries. Wilson was the originator of the vision of a universal world organization, the League of Nations, which would keep the peace through collective security rather than alliances. Though Wilson could not convince his own country of its merit, the idea lived on. It is above all to the drumbeat of Wilsonian idealism that American foreign policy has marched since his watershed presidency, and continues to march to this day.

America's singular approach to international affairs did not develop all at once, or as the consequence of a solitary inspiration. In the early years of the Republic, American foreign policy was in fact a sophisticated reflection of the

American national interest, which was, simply, to fortify the new nation's independence. Since no European country was capable of posing an actual threat so long as it had to contend with rivals, the Founding Fathers showed themselves quite ready to manipulate the despised balance of power when it suited their needs; indeed, they could be extraordinarily skillful at maneuvering between France and Great Britain not only to preserve America's independence but to enlarge its frontiers. Because they really wanted neither side to win a decisive victory in the wars of the French Revolution, they declared neutrality. Jefferson defined the Napoleonic Wars as a contest between the tyrant on the land (France) and the tyrant of the ocean (England)—in other words, the parties in the European struggle were morally equivalent. Practicing an early form of nonalignment, the new nation discovered the benefit of neutrality as a bargaining tool, just as many an emerging nation has since.

At the same time, the United States did not carry its rejection of Old World ways to the point of forgoing territorial expansion. On the contrary, from the very beginning, the United States pursued expansion in the Americas with extraordinary singleness of purpose. After 1794, a series of treaties settled the borders with Canada and Florida in America's favor, opened the Mississippi River to American trade, and began to establish an American commercial interest in the British West Indies. This culminated in the Louisiana Purchase of 1803, which brought to the young country a huge, undefined territory west of the Mississippi River from France along with claims to Spanish territory in Florida and Texas—the foundation from which to develop into a great power. . . .

Though in fact the British Royal Navy protected America from depredations by European powers, American leaders did not perceive Great Britain as their country's protector. Throughout the nineteenth century, Great Britain was considered the greatest challenge to American interests, and the Royal Navy the most serious strategic threat. No wonder that, when America began to flex its muscles, it sought to expel Great Britain's influence from the Western Hemisphere, invoking the Monroe Doctrine which Great Britain had been so instrumental in encouraging.

. . . By 1902, Great Britain had abandoned its claim to a major role in Central America.

Supreme in the Western Hemisphere, the United States began to enter the wider arena of international affairs. America had grown into a world power almost despite itself. Expanding across the continent, it had established its preeminence all around its shores while insisting that it had no wish to conduct the foreign policy of a Great Power. At the end of the process, America found itself commanding the sort of power which made it a major international factor, no matter what its preferences. America's leaders might continue to insist that its basic foreign policy was to serve as a "beacon" for the rest of mankind, but there could be no denying that some of them were also becoming aware that America's power entitled it to be heard on the issues of the day, and that it did not need to wait until all of mankind had become democratic to make itself a part of the international system.

No one articulated this reasoning more trenchantly than Theodore Roosevelt. He was the first president to insist that it was America's duty to make its influence felt globally, and to relate America to the world in terms of a concept of national interest. Like his predecessors, Roosevelt was convinced of America's beneficent role in the world. But unlike them, Roosevelt held that America had real foreign policy interests that went far beyond its interest in remaining unentangled. Roosevelt started from the premise that the United States was a power like any other, not a singular incarnation of virtue. If its interests collided with those of other countries, America had the obligation to draw on its strength to prevail. . . .

For Roosevelt, muscular diplomacy in the Western Hemisphere was part of America's new global role. The two oceans were no longer wide enough to insulate America from the rest of the world. The United States had to become an actor on the international stage. Roosevelt said as much in a 1902 message to the Congress: "More and more, the increasing interdependence and complexity of international political and economic relations render it incumbent on all civilized and orderly powers to insist on the proper policing of the world."

Roosevelt commands a unique historical position in America's approach to international relations. No other president defined America's world role so completely in terms of national interest, or identified the national interest so comprehensively with the balance of power. Roosevelt shared the view of his countrymen, that America was the best hope for the world. But unlike most of them, he did not believe that it could preserve the peace or fulfill its destiny simply by practicing civic virtues. In his perception of the nature of world order, he was much closer to Palmerston or Disraeli than to Thomas Jefferson.

A great president must be an educator, bridging the gap between his people's future and its experience. Roosevelt taught an especially stern doctrine for a people brought up in the belief that peace is the normal condition among nations, that there is no difference between personal and public morality, and that America was safely insulated from the upheavals affecting the rest of the world. For Roosevelt rebutted each of these propositions. To him, international life meant struggle, and Darwin's theory of the survival of the fittest was a better guide to history than personal morality. In Roosevelt's view, the meek inherited the earth only if they were strong. To Roosevelt, America was not a cause but a great power—potentially the greatest. He hoped to be the president destined to usher his nation onto the world scene so that it might shape the twentieth century in the way Great Britain had dominated the nineteenth—as a country of vast strengths which had enlisted itself, with moderation and wisdom, to work on behalf of stability, peace, and progress.

. . . In a world regulated by power, Roosevelt believed that the natural order of things was reflected in the concept of "spheres of influence," which assigned preponderant influence over large regions to specific powers, for example, to the United States in the Western Hemisphere or to Great Britain on the Indian subcontinent. In 1908, Roosevelt acquiesced to the Japanese occupation of Korea because, to his way of thinking, Japanese-Korean relations had to be determined by the relative power of each country, not by the provisions of a treaty or by international law. . . .

With Roosevelt holding such European-style views, it was not surprising that he approached the global balance of power with a sophistication matched by no other American president and approached only by Richard Nixon. Roosevelt at first saw no need to engage America in the specifics of the European balance of power because he considered it more or less self-regulating. But he left little doubt that, if such a judgment were to prove wrong, he would urge America to engage itself to re-establish the equilibrium. Roosevelt gradually came to see Germany as a threat to the European balance and began to identify America's national interest with those of Great Britain and France. . . .

In one of history's ironies, America did in the end fulfill the leading role Roosevelt had envisioned for it, and within Roosevelt's lifetime, but it did so on behalf of principles Roosevelt derided, and under the guidance of a president whom Roosevelt despised. Woodrow Wilson was the embodiment of the tradition of American exceptionalism, and originated what would become the dominant intellectual school of American foreign policy—a school whose precepts Roosevelt considered at best irrelevant and at worst inimical to America's long-range interests. . . .

Wilson's was an astonishing achievement. Rejecting power politics, he knew how to move the American people. An academic who arrived in politics relatively late, he was elected due to a split in the Republican Party between Taft and Roosevelt. Wilson grasped that America's instinctive isolationism could be overcome only by an appeal to its belief in the exceptional nature of its ideals. Step by step, he took an isolationist country into war, after he had first demonstrated his Administration's devotion to peace by a passionate advocacy of neutrality. And he did so while abjuring any selfish national interests, and by affirming that America sought no other benefit than vindication of its principles.

In Wilson's first State of the Union Address, on December 2, 1913, he laid down the outline of what later came to be known as Wilsonianism. Universal law and not equilibrium, national trustworthiness and not national self-assertion were, in Wilson's view, the foundations of international order. Recommending the ratification of several treaties of arbitration, Wilson argued that binding arbitration, not force, should become the method for resolving international disputes:

> There is only one possible standard by which to determine controversies between the United States and other nations, and that is compounded of these two elements: Our own honor and our obligations to the peace of the world. A test so compounded ought easily to be made to govern both the establishment of new treaty obligations and the interpretation of those already assumed. . . .

America's influence, in Wilson's view, depended on its unselfishness; it had to preserve itself so that, in the end, it could step forward as a credible arbiter between the warring parties. Roosevelt had asserted that the war in Europe, and especially a German victory, would ultimately threaten American security. Wilson maintained that America was essentially disinterested, hence should emerge as mediator. Because of America's faith in values higher than the balance of power, the war in Europe now afforded it an extraordinary opportunity to proselytize for a new and better approach to international affairs.

Roosevelt ridiculed such ideas and accused Wilson of pandering to isolationist sentiments to help his re-election in 1916. In fact, the thrust of Wilson's policy was quite the opposite of isolationism. What Wilson was proclaiming was not America's withdrawal from the world but the universal applicability of its values and, in time, America's commitment to spreading them. Wilson restated what had become the conventional American wisdom since Jefferson, but put it in the service of a crusading ideology:

- America's special mission transcends day-to-day diplomacy and obliges it to serve as a beacon of liberty for the rest of mankind.
- The foreign policies of democracies are morally superior because the people are inherently peace-loving.
- Foreign policy should reflect the same moral standards as personal ethics.
- The state has no right to claim a separate morality for itself.

Wilson endowed these assertions of American moral exceptionalism with a universal dimension:

> Dread of the power of any other nation we are incapable of. We are not jealous of rivalry in the fields of commerce or of any other peaceful achievement. We mean to live our own lives as we will; but we mean also to let live. We are, indeed, a true friend to all the nations of the world, because we threaten none, covet the possessions of none, desire the overthrow of none.

No other nation has ever rested its claim to international leadership on its altruism. All other nations have sought to be judged by the compatibility of their national interests with those of other societies. Yet, from Woodrow Wilson through George Bush, American presidents have invoked their country's unselfishness as the crucial attribute of its leadership role. Neither Wilson nor his later disciples, through the present, have been willing to face the fact that, to foreign leaders imbued with less elevated maxims, America's claim to altruism evokes a certain aura of unpredictability; whereas the national interest can be calculated, altruism depends on the definition of its practitioner.

To Wilson, however, the altruistic nature of American society was proof of divine favor:

> It was as if in the Providence of God a continent had been kept unused and waiting for a peaceful people who loved liberty and the rights of men more than they loved anything else, to come and set up an unselfish commonwealth.

The claim that American goals represented providential dispensation implied a global role for America that would prove far more sweeping than any Roosevelt had ever imagined. For he had wanted no more than to improve the balance of power and to invest America's role in it with the importance commensurate with its growing strength. In Roosevelt's conception, America would have been one nation among many—more powerful than most and part of an elite group of great powers—but still subject to the historic ground rules of equilibrium.

Wilson moved America onto a plane entirely remote from such considerations. Disdaining the balance of power, he insisted that America's role was "not to prove . . . our selfishness, but our greatness." If that was true, America had no right to hoard its values for itself. As early as 1915, Wilson put forward the unprecedented doctrine that the security of America was inseparable from the security of *all* the rest of mankind. This implied that it was henceforth America's duty to oppose aggression *everywhere:*

> . . . because we demand unmolested development and the undisturbed government of our own lives upon our own principles of right and liberty, we resent, from whatever quarter it may come, the aggression we ourselves will not practice. We insist upon security in prosecuting our self-chosen lines of national development. We do more than that. We demand it also for others. We do not confine our enthusiasm for individual liberty and free national development to the incidents and movements of affairs which affect only ourselves. We feel it wherever there is a people that tries to walk in these difficult paths of independence and right.

Envisioning America as a beneficent global policeman, this foreshadowed the containment policy, which would be developed after the Second World War. . . .

Germany's announcement of unrestricted submarine warfare and its sinking of the *Lusitania* became the proximate cause of America's declaration of war. But Wilson did not justify America's entry into the war on the grounds of specific grievances. National interests were irrelevant; Belgium's violation and the balance of power had nothing to do with it. Rather, the war had a moral foundation, whose primary objective was a new and more just international order. "It is a fearful thing," Wilson reflected in the speech asking for a declaration of war,

> to lead this great peaceful people into war, into the most terrible and disastrous of all wars, civilization itself seeming to be in the balance. But right is more precious than peace, and we shall fight for the things which we have always carried nearest our hearts, for democracy, for the right of those who submit to authority to have a voice in their own governments, for the rights and liberties of small nations, for a universal dominion of right by such a concert of free peoples as shall bring peace and safety to all nations and make the world itself at last free.

In a war on behalf of such principles, there could be no compromise. Total victory was the only valid goal. Roosevelt would almost certainly have expressed America's war aims in political and strategic terms; Wilson, flaunting American disinterest, defined America's war aims in entirely moral categories. In Wilson's view, the war was not the consequence of clashing national interests pursued without restraint, but of Germany's unprovoked assault on the international order. More specifically, the true culprit was not the German nation, but the German Emperor himself. . . .

Wilson's historic achievement lies in his recognition that Americans cannot sustain major international engagements that are not justified by their moral faith. His downfall was in treating the tragedies of history as aberrations, or as due to the shortsightedness and the evil of individual leaders, and in his rejection of any objective basis for peace other than the force of public opinion and the worldwide spread of democratic institutions. In the process, he would ask the nations of Europe to undertake something for which they were neither philosophically nor historically prepared, and right after a war which had drained them of substance.

For 300 years, the European nations had based their world order on a balancing of national interests, and their foreign policies on a quest for security, treating every additional benefit as a bonus. Wilson asked the nations of Europe to base their foreign policy on moral convictions, leaving security to result incidentally, if at all. But Europe had no conceptual apparatus for such a disinterested policy, and it still remained to be seen whether America, having just emerged from a century of isolation, could sustain the permanent involvement in international affairs that Wilson's theories implied.

Wilson's appearance on the scene was a watershed for America, one of those rare examples of a leader who fundamentally alters the course of his country's history. Had Roosevelt or his ideas prevailed in 1912, the question of war aims would have been based on an inquiry into the nature of American national interest. Roosevelt would have rested America's entry into the war on the proposition—which he in fact advanced—that, unless America joined the Triple Entente, the Central Powers would win the war and, sooner or later, pose a threat to American security.

The American national interest, so defined, would, over time, have led America to adopt a global policy comparable to Great Britain's toward Continental Europe. For three centuries, British leaders had operated from the assumption that, if Europe's resources were marshaled by a single dominant power, that country would then have the resources to challenge Great Britain's command of the seas, and thus threaten its independence. Geopolitically, the United States, also an island off the shores of Eurasia, should, by the same reasoning, have felt obliged to resist the domination of Europe or Asia by any one power and, even more, the control of *both* continents by the *same* power. In these terms, it should have been the extent of Germany's geopolitical reach and not its moral transgressions that provided the principal *casus belli*.

However, such an Old World approach ran counter to the wellspring of American emotions being tapped by Wilson—as it does to this day. Not even Roosevelt could have managed the power politics he advocated, though he died convinced that he could have. At any rate, Roosevelt was no longer the president, and Wilson had made it clear, even before America entered the war, that he would resist any attempt to base the postwar order on established principles of international politics.

Wilson saw the causes of the war not only in the wickedness of the German leadership but in the European balance-of-power system as well. On January 22, 1917, he attacked the international order which had preceded the war as a system of "organized rivalries":

> The question upon which the whole future peace and policy of the world depends is this: Is the present war a struggle for a just and secure peace, or

> only for a new balance of power? . . There must be, not a balance of power, but a community of power; not organized rivalries, but an organized common peace.

What Wilson meant by "community of power" was an entirely new concept that later became known as "collective security" (though William Gladstone in Great Britain had put forward a stillborn variation of it in the course of 1880). Convinced that all the nations of the world had an equal interest in peace and would therefore unite to punish those who disturbed it, Wilson proposed to defend the international order by the moral consensus of the peace-loving:

> . . . this age is an age . . . which rejects the standards of national selfishness that once governed the counsels of nations and demands that they shall give way to a new order of things in which the only questions will be: "Is it right?" "Is it just?" "Is it in the interest of mankind?"

To institutionalize this consensus, Wilson put forward the League of Nations, a quintessentially American institution. Under the auspices of this world organization, power would yield to morality and the force of arms to the dictates of public opinion. Wilson kept emphasizing that, had the public been adequately informed, the war would never have occurred—ignoring the passionate demonstrations of joy and relief which had greeted the onset of war in *all* capitals, including those of democratic Great Britain and France. If the new theory was to work, in Wilson's view, at least two changes in international governance had to take place: first, the spread of democratic governments throughout the world, and, next, the elaboration of a "new and more wholesome diplomacy" based on "the same high code of honor that we demand of individuals."

In 1918, Wilson stated as a requirement of peace the hitherto unheard-of and breathtakingly ambitious goal of "the destruction of every arbitrary power anywhere that can separately, secretly and of its single choice disturb the peace of the world; or, if it cannot be presently destroyed, at the least its reduction to virtual impotence." A League of Nations so composed and animated by such attitudes would resolve crises without war, Wilson told the Peace Conference on February 14, 1919:

> . . . throughout this instrument [the League Covenant] we are depending primarily and chiefly upon one great force, and that is the moral force of the public opinion of the world—the cleansing and clarifying and compelling influences of publicity . . . so that those things that are destroyed by the light may be properly destroyed by the overwhelming light of the universal expression of the condemnation of the world.

The preservation of peace would no longer spring from the traditional calculus of power but from worldwide consensus backed up by a policing mechanism. A universal grouping of largely democratic nations would act as the "trustee of peace," and replace the old balance-of-power and alliance systems.

Such exalted sentiments had never before been put forward by any nation, let alone been implemented. Nevertheless, in the hands of American idealism they were turned into the common currency of national thinking on foreign policy. Every American president since Wilson has advanced variations of Wilson's theme. Domestic debates have more often dealt with the failure to fulfill Wilson's ideals (soon so commonplace that they were no longer even identified with him) than with whether they were in fact lending adequate guidance in meeting the occasionally brutal challenges of a turbulent world. For three generations, critics have savaged Wilson's analysis and conclusions; and yet, in all this time, Wilson's principles have remained the bedrock of American foreign-policy thinking.

And yet Wilson's intermingling of power and principle also set the stage for decades of ambivalence as the American conscience tried to reconcile its principles with its necessities. The basic premise of collective security was that all nations would view every threat to security in the same way *and* be prepared to run the same risks in resisting it. Not only had nothing like it ever actually occurred, nothing like it was destined to occur in the entire history of both the League of Nations and the United Nations. Only when a threat is truly overwhelming and genuinely affects all, or most, societies is such a consensus possible—as it was during the two world wars and, on a regional basis, in the Cold War. But in the vast majority of cases—and in nearly all of the difficult ones—the nations of the world tend to disagree either about the nature of the threat or about the type of sacrifice they are prepared to make to meet it. This was the case from Italy's aggressions against Abyssinia in 1935 to the Bosnian crisis in 1992. And when it has been a matter of achieving positive objectives or remedying perceived injustices, global consensus has proved even more difficult to achieve. Ironically, in the post–Cold War world, which has no overwhelming ideological or military threat and which pays more lip service to democracy than has any previous era, these difficulties have only increased.

Wilsonianism also accentuated another latent split in American thought on international affairs. Did America have any security interests it needed to defend regardless of the methods by which they were challenged? Or should America resist only changes which could fairly be described as illegal? Was it the fact or the method of international transformation that concerned America? Did America reject the principles of geopolitics altogether? Or did they need to be reinterpreted through the filter of American values? And if these should clash, which would prevail?

The implication of Wilsonianism has been that America resisted, above all, the method of change, and that it had no strategic interests worth defending if they were threatened by apparently legal methods. As late as the Gulf War, President Bush insisted that he was not so much defending vital oil supplies as resisting the principle of aggression. And during the Cold War, some of the domestic American debate concerned the question whether America, with all its failings, had a moral right to organize resistance to the Moscow threat.

Theodore Roosevelt would have had no doubt as to the answer to these questions. To assume that nations would perceive threats identically or be prepared to react to them uniformly represented a denial of everything he had ever stood for. Nor could he envision any world organization to which victim and aggressor could comfortably belong at the same time. In November 1918, he wrote in a letter:

> I am for such a League provided we don't expect too much from it. . . . I am not willing to play the part which even Aesop held up to derision when he wrote of how the wolves and the sheep agreed to disarm, and how the sheep as a guarantee of good faith sent away the watchdogs, and were then forthwith eaten by the wolves.

The following month, he wrote this to Senator Knox of Pennsylvania:

> The League of Nations may do a little good, but the more pompous it is and the more it pretends to do, the less it will really accomplish. The talk about it has a grimly humorous suggestion of the talk about the Holy Alliance a hundred years ago, which had as its main purpose the perpetual maintenance of peace. The Czar Alexander by the way, was the President Wilson of this particular movement a century ago.

In Roosevelt's estimation, only mystics, dreamers, and intellectuals held the view that peace was man's natural condition and that it could be maintained by disinterested consensus. To him, peace was inherently fragile and could be preserved only by eternal vigilance, by the arms of the strong, and by alliances among the like-minded.

But Roosevelt lived either a century too late or a century too early. His approach to international affairs died with him in 1919; no significant school of American thought on foreign policy has invoked him since. On the other hand, it is surely the measure of Wilson's intellectual triumph that even Richard Nixon, whose foreign policy in fact embodied many of Roosevelt's precepts, considered himself above all a disciple of Wilson's internationalism, and hung a portrait of the wartime president in the Cabinet Room.

The League of Nations failed to take hold in America because the country was not yet ready for so global a role. Nevertheless, Wilson's intellectual victory proved more seminal than any political triumph could have been. For, whenever America has faced the task of constructing a new world order, it has returned in one way or another to Woodrow Wilson's precepts. At the end of World War II, it helped build the United Nations on the same principles as those of the League, hoping to found peace on a concord of the victors. When this hope died, America waged the Cold War not as a conflict between two superpowers but as a moral struggle for democracy. When communism collapsed, the Wilsonian idea that the road to peace lay in collective security, coupled with the worldwide spread of democratic institutions, was adopted by administrations of both major American political parties.

In Wilsonianism was incarnate the central drama of America on the world stage: America's ideology has, in a sense, been revolutionary while, domestically, Americans have considered themselves satisfied with the *status quo*. Tending to turn foreign-policy issues into a struggle between good and evil, Americans have generally felt ill at ease with compromise, as they have with partial or inconclusive outcomes. The fact that America has shied away from seeking vast geopolitical transformations has often associated it with defense of the territorial, and sometimes the political, *status quo*. Trusting in the rule of law, it has found it difficult to reconcile its faith in peaceful change with the historical fact that almost all significant changes in history have involved violence and upheaval.

America found that it would have to implement its ideals in a world less blessed than its own and in concert with states possessed of narrower margins of survival, more limited objectives, and far less self-confidence. And yet America has persevered. The postwar world became largely America's creation, so that, in the end, it did come to play the role Wilson had envisioned for it—as a beacon to follow, and a hope to attain.

William G. Carleton **NO**

A New Look at Woodrow Wilson

All high-placed statesmen crave historical immortality. Woodrow Wilson craved it more than most. Thus far the fates have not been kind to Wilson; there is a reluctance to admit him to as great a place in history as he will have.

Congress has just gotten around to planning a national memorial for Wilson, several years after it had done this for Theodore Roosevelt and Franklin D. Roosevelt. Wilson is gradually being accepted as one of the nation's five or six greatest Presidents. However, the heroic mold of the man on the large stage of world history is still generally unrecognized.

There is a uniquely carping, hypercritical approach to Wilson. Much more than other historical figures he is being judged by personality traits, many of them distorted or even fancied. Wilson is not being measured by the yardstick used for other famous characters of history. There is a double standard at work here.

What are the common errors and misrepresentations with respect to Wilson? In what ways is he being judged more rigorously? What are the reasons for this? Why will Wilson eventually achieve giant stature in world history?

There are two criticisms of Wilson that go to the heart of his fame and place in history. One is an alleged inflexibility and intransigence, an inability to compromise. The other is that he had no real understanding of world politics, that he was a naïve idealist. Neither is true.

If Wilson were indeed as stubborn and adamant as he is often portrayed he would have been a bungler at his work, for the practice and art of politics consist in a feeling for the possible, a sense of timing, a capacity for give-and-take compromise. In reality, Wilson's leadership of his party and the legislative accomplishments of his first term were magnificent. His performance was brilliantly characterized by the very qualities he is said to have lacked: flexibility, accommodation, a sense of timing, and a willingness to compromise. In the struggles to win the Federal Reserve Act, the Clayton Anti-Trust Law, the Federal Trade Commission, and other major measures of his domestic program, Wilson repeatedly mediated between the agrarian liberals and the conservatives of his party, moving now a little to the left, now to the right, now back to the left. He learned by experience, cast aside pride of opinion, accepted and maneuvered for regulatory commissions after having warned of their danger during the campaign of 1912, and constantly acted as a catalyst of the opposing factions of his party and of shifting opinion.

The cautious way Wilson led the country to military preparedness and to war demonstrated resiliency and a sense of timing of a high order. At the Paris Conference Wilson impressed thoughtful observers with his skill as a negotiator; many European diplomats were surprised that an "amateur" could do so well. Here the criticism is not that Wilson was without compromise but that he compromised too much.

Actually, the charge that Wilson was incapable of compromise must stand or fall on his conduct during the fight in the Senate over the ratification of the League of Nations, particularly his refusal to give the word to the Democratic Senators from the South to vote for the Treaty with the Lodge Reservations, which, it is claimed, would have assured ratification. Wilson, say the critics, murdered his own brain child. It is Wilson, and not Lodge, who has now become the villain of this high tragedy.

Now, would a Wilsonian call to the Southerners to change their position have resulted in ratification? Can we really by sure? In order to give Southerners time to readjust to a new position, the call from the White House would have had to have been made several weeks before that final vote. During that time what would have prevented Lodge from hobbling the League with still more reservations? Would the mild reservationists, all Republicans, have prevented this? The record shows, I think, that in the final analysis the mild reservationists could always be bamboozled by Lodge in the name of party loyalty. As the fight on the League had progressed, the reservations had become more numerous and more crippling. Wilson, it seems, had come to feel that there simply was no appeasing Lodge.

During the Peace Conference, in response to the Senatorial Round Robin engineered by Lodge, Wilson had reopened the whole League question and obtained the inclusion of American "safeguards" he felt would satisfy Lodge. This had been done at great cost, for it had forced Wilson to abandon his position as a negotiator above the battles for national advantages and to become a suppliant for national concessions. This had resulted in his having to yield points in other parts of the Treaty to national-minded delegations from other countries. When Wilson returned from Paris with the completed Treaty, Lodge had "raised the ante," the Lodge Reservations requiring the consent of other signatory nations were attached to the Treaty, and these had multiplied and become more restrictive in nature as the months went by. Would not then a "final" yielding by Wilson have resulted in even stiffer reservations being added? Was not Lodge using the Reservations to effect not ratification but rejection, knowing that there was a point beyond which Wilson could not yield?

Wilson seems honestly to have believed that the Lodge Reservations emasculated the League. Those who read them for the first time will be surprised, I think, to discover how nationally self-centered they were. If taken seriously, they surely must have impaired the functioning of the League. However, Wilson was never opposed to clarifying or interpretative reservations which would not require the consent of the other signatories. Indeed, he himself wrote the Hitchcock Reservations.

Even had the League with the Lodge Reservations been ratified, how certain can we really be that this would have meant American entrance into the League? Under the Lodge Reservations, every signatory nation had to accept them before the United States could become a member. Would all the signatories have accepted every one of the fifteen Lodge Reservations? The United States had no monopoly on chauvinism, and would not other nations have interposed reservations of their own as a condition to their acceptance of the Lodge Reservations?

At Paris, Wilson had personally experienced great difficulty getting his own mild "reservations" incorporated into the Covenant. Now, at this late date, would Britain have accepted the Lodge Reservation on Irish self-determination? In all probability. Would Japan have accepted the Reservation on Shantung? This is more doubtful. Would the Latin American states have accepted the stronger Reservation on the Monroe Doctrine? This is also doubtful. Chile had already shown concern, and little Costa Rica had the temerity to ask for a definition of the Doctrine. Would the British Dominions have accepted the Reservation calling for one vote for the British Empire or six votes for the United States? Even Lord Grey, who earlier had predicted that the signatories would accept the Lodge Reservations, found that he could not guarantee acceptance by the Dominions, and Canada's President of the Privy Council and Acting Secretary for External Affairs, Newton W. Rowell, declared that if this Reservation were accepted by the other powers Canada would withdraw from the League.

By the spring of 1920, Wilson seems to have believed that making the League of Nations the issue in the campaign of 1920 would afford a better opportunity for American participation in an effective League than would further concessions to Lodge. To Wilson, converting the Presidential election into a solemn referendum on the League was a reality. For months, because of his illness, he had lived secluded in the White House, and the memories of his highly emotional reception in New York on his return from Paris and of the enthusiasm of the Western audiences during his last speaking trip burned vividly bright. He still believed that the American people, if given the chance, would vote for the League without emasculating reservations. Does this, then, make Wilson naïve? It is well to remember that in the spring of 1920 not even the most sanguine Republican envisaged the Republican sweep that would develop in the fall of that year.

If the strategy of Wilson in the spring of 1920 was of debatable wisdom, the motives of Lodge can no longer be open to doubt. After the landslide of 1920, which gave the Republicans the Presidency and an overwhelming majority in a Senate dominated by Lodge in foreign policy, the Treaty was never resurrected. The Lodge Reservations, representing months of gruelling legislative labor, were cavalierly jettisoned, and a separate peace was made with Germany.

What, then, becomes of the stock charge that Wilson was intolerant of opposition and incapable of bending? If the truth of this accusation must rest on Wilson's attitude during the Treaty fight, and I think it must, for he showed remarkable adaptability in other phases of his Presidency, then it must fall. The situation surrounding the Treaty fight was intricately tangled, and there is certainly as much evidence on the side of Wilson's forbearance as on the side of his obstinacy.

A far more serious charge against Wilson is that he had no realistic understanding of world politics, that he was an impractical idealist whose policies intensified rather than alleviated international problems. Now what American statesman of the period understood world politics better than Wilson—or indeed in any way as well as he? Elihu Root, with his arid legalism? Philander Knox, with his dollar diplomacy? Theodore Roosevelt or Henry Cabot Lodge? Roosevelt and Lodge had some feel for power politics, and they understood the traditional balance of power, at least until their emotions for a dictated Allied victory got the better of their judgment: but was either of them aware of the implications for world politics of the technological revolution in war and the disintegration of the old balance of power? And were not both of them blind to a new force in world politics just then rising to a place of importance—the anti-imperialist revolutions, which even before World War I were getting under way with the Mexican Revolution and the Chinese Revolution of Sun Yat-sen?

Wilson is charged with having no understanding of the balance of power, but who among world statesmen of the twentieth century better sated the classic doctrine of the traditional balance of power than Wilson in his famous Peace Without Victory speech? And was it not Theodore Roosevelt who derided him for stating it? With perfectly straight faces Wilson critics, and a good many historians, tell us that TR, who wanted to march to Berlin and saddle Germany with a harsh peace, and FDR, who sponsored unconditional surrender, "understood" the balance of power, but that Wilson, who fought to salvage a power balance by preserving Germany from partition, was a simple-simon in world politics—an illustration of the double standard at work in evaluating Wilson's place in history.

Wilson not only understood the old, but with amazing clarity he saw the new, elements in world politics. He recognized the emergence of the anti-imperialist revolutions and the importance of social politics in the international relations of the future. He recognized, too, the implications for future world politics of the technological revolution in war, of total war, and of the disintegration of the old balance of power—for World War I had decisively weakened the effective brakes on Japan in Asia, disrupted the Turkish Empire in the Middle East and the Austro-Hungarian Empire in Europe, and removed Russia as a make-weight for the foreseeable future. Wilson believed that a truncated Germany and an attempted French hegemony would only add to the chaos, but he saw too that merely preserving Germany as a power unit would not restore the old balance of power. To Wilson, even in its prime the traditional balance of power had worked only indifferently and collective security would have been preferable, but in his mind the revolutionary changes in the world of 1919 made a collective-security system indispensable.

Just what is realism in world politics? Is it not the ability to use purposefully many factors, even theoretically contradictory ones, and to use them not singly and consecutively but interdependently and simultaneously, shifting the emphasis as conditions change? If so, was not Wilson a very great realist in world politics? He used the old balance-of-power factors, as evidenced by his fight to save Germany as a power unit and his sponsoring of a tripartite alliance of the United States, Britain, and France to guarantee France from any German aggression until such time as collective security would become effective. But he labored to introduce into international relations the new collective-security factors to supplement and gradually supersede in importance the older factors, now increasingly outmoded by historical developments. To label as doctrinaire idealist one who envisaged world politics in so broad and flexible a way is to pervert the meaning of words. . . .

Ranking the Presidents has become a popular game, and even Presidents like to play it, notably Truman and Kennedy. In my own evaluation, I place Wilson along with Jefferson and Lincoln as the nation's three greatest Presidents, which makes Wilson our greatest twentieth-century President. If rated solely on the basis of long-range impact on international relations, Wilson is the most influential of all our Presidents.

What are the achievements which entitle Wilson to so high a place? Let us consider the major ones, although of course some of these are more important than others.

. . . [B]etter than any responsible statesman of his day, Wilson understood and sympathized with the anti-imperialist revolutions and their aspirations for basic internal reforms. He withdrew American support for the Bankers' Consortium in China, and the United States under Wilson was the first of the great powers to recognize the Revolution of Sun Yat-sen. Early in his term he had to wrestle with the Mexican Revolution. He saw the need for social reform; avoided the general war with Mexico that many American investors, Catholics, and professional patriots wanted; and by refusing to recognize the counter-revolution of Huerta and cutting Huerta off from trade and arms while allowing the flow of arms to Carranza, Villa, and Zapata, he made possible the overthrow of the counter-revolution and the triumph of the Revolution. What merciless criticism was heaped on Wilson for insisting that Latin Americans should be positively encouraged to institute reforms and develop democratic practices. Yet today Americans applaud their government's denial of Alliance-for-Progress funds to Latin American countries which refuse to undertake fundamental economic and social reforms and flout democracy.

. . . [C]onfronted with the stupendous and completely novel challenge of having to mobilize not only America's military strength but also its civilian resources and energies in America's first total war, the Wilson Administration set up a huge network of administrative agencies, exemplifying the highest imagination and creativity in the art of practical administration. FDR, in his New Deal and in his World War II agencies, was to borrow heavily from the Wilson innovations.

. . . Wilson's Fourteen Points and his other peace aims constituted war propaganda of perhaps unparalleled brilliance. They thrilled the world. They gave high purpose to the peoples of the Allied countries and stirred their war efforts. Directed over the heads of the governments to the enemy peoples themselves, they produced unrest, helped bring about the revolutions that overthrew the Sultan, the Hapsburgs, and the Hohenzollerns, and hastened the end of the war.

. . . [T]he Treaty of Versailles, of which Wilson was the chief architect, was a better peace than it would have been (considering, among other things, the imperialist secret treaties of the Allies) because of Wilson's labors for a just peace. The League of Nations was founded, and this was to be the forerunner of the United Nations. To the League was assigned the work of general disarmament. The mandate system of the League, designed to prepare colonial peoples for self-government and national independence, was a revolutionary step away from the old imperialism. The aspirations of many peoples in Europe for national independence were fulfilled. (If the disruption of the Austro-Hungarian Empire helped destroy the old balance of power, it must be said that in this particular situation Wilson's doctrine of national autonomy only exploited an existing fact in the interest of Allied victory, and even had there been no Wilsonian self-determination the nationalities of this area were already so well developed that they could not have been denied independence after the defeat of the Hapsburgs. Wilson's self-determination was to be a far more *creative* force among the colonial peoples than among the Europeans.) The Treaty restrained the chauvinism of the Italians, though not as much as Wilson would have liked. It prevented the truncating of Germany by preserving to her the Left Bank of the Rhine. The war-guilt clause and the enormous reparations saddled on Germany were mistakes, but Wilson succeeded in confining German responsibility to civilian damage and the expenses of Allied military pensions rather than the whole cost of the war; and had the United States ratified the Treaty and participated in post-war world affairs, as Wilson expected, the United States would have been in a position to join Britain in scaling down the actual reparations bill and in preventing any such adventure as the French seizure of the Ruhr in 1923, from which flowed Germany's disastrous inflation and the ugly forces of German nihilism. (There is poignancy in the broken Wilson's coming out of retirement momentarily in 1923 to denounce France for making "waste paper" of the Treaty of Versailles.) Finally, if Shantung was Wilson's Yalta, he paid the kind of price FDR paid and for precisely the same reason—the collapse of the balance of power in the immediate area involved.

. . . [T]he chief claim of Wilson to a superlative place in history—and it will not be denied him merely because he was turned down by the United States Senate—is that he, more than any other, formulated and articulated the ideology which was the polestar of the Western democracies in World War I, in World War II, and in the decades of Cold War against the Communists. Today, well past the middle of the twentieth century, the long-time program of America is still a Wilsonian program: international collective security, disarmament, the lowering of economic barriers between nations (as in America's support for the developing West European community today), anti-colonialism, self-determination of nations, and democratic social politics as an alternative to Communism. And this was the program critics of Wilson called "anachronistic," a mere "throwback" to nineteenth-century liberalism!

America today is still grappling with the same world problems Wilson grappled with in 1917, 1918, and 1919, and the programs and policies designed to meet them are still largely Wilsonian. But events since Wilson's time have made his solutions more and more prophetic and urgent. The sweep of the anti-imperialist revolutions propels us to wider self-determination and social politics. The elimination of space, the increasing interdependence of the world, the further disintegration of the balance of power in World War II, and the nuclear revolution in war compel us to more effective collective security and to arms control supervised by an agency of the United Nations.

There will be more unwillingness to identify Wilson with social politics abroad than with the other policies with which he is more clearly identified. Historians like to quote George L. Record's letter to Wilson in which he told Wilson that there was no longer any glory in merely standing for political democracy, that political democracy had arrived, that the great issues of the future would revolve around economic and social democracy. But Wilson stood in no need of advice on this score. Earlier than any other responsible statesman, Wilson had seen the significance of the Chinese Revolution of Sun Yat-sen and of the Mexican Revolution, and he had officially encouraged both. Wilson believed that economic and social reform was implicit in the doctrine of self-determination, especially when applied to the colonial peoples. He recognized, too, that the Bolshevist Revolution had given economic and social reform a new urgency in all parts of the world. He was also well aware that those who most opposed his program for a world settlement were the conservative and imperialist elements in Western Europe and Japan, that socialist and labor groups were his most effective supporters. He pondered deeply how closely and openly he could work with labor and socialist parties in Europe without cutting off necessary support at home. (This—how to use social democracy and the democratic left to counter Communism abroad and still carry American opinion—was to be a central problem for every discerning American statesman after 1945.) Months before he had received Record's letter, Wilson himself had expressed almost the same views as Record. In a long conversation with Professor Stockton Axson at the White House, Wilson acknowledged that his best support was coming from labor people, that they were in touch with world movements and were international-minded, that government ownership of some basic resources and industries was coming, even in the United States, and that it was by a program of social democracy that Communism could be defeated.

In 1918 two gigantic figures—Wilson and Lenin—faced each other and articulated the contesting ideologies which would shake the world during the century. Since then, the lesser leaders who have succeeded them have added little to the ideology of either side. We are now far enough into the century to see in what direction the world is headed, provided there is no third world war. It is not headed for Communist domination. It is not headed for an American hegemony. And it is not headed for a duality with half the world Communist and the other half capitalist. Instead, it is headed for a new pluralism. The emerging new national societies are adjusting their new industrialism to their own conditions and cultures; and their developing economies will be varying mixtures of privatism, collectivism, and welfarism. Even the Communist states differ from one another in conditions, cultures, stages of revolutionary development, and degrees of Marxist "orthodoxy" or "revisionism." And today, all national states, old and new, Communist and non-Communist, join the United Nations as a matter of course.

There will be "victory" for neither "side," but instead a world which has been historically affected by both. Lenin's international proletarian state failed to materialize, but the evolving economies of the underdeveloped peoples are being influenced by his collectivism. However, the facts that most of the emerging economies are mixed ones, that they are working themselves out within autonomous national frameworks, and that the multiplying national states are operating internationally through the United Nations all point to a world which will be closer to the vision of Wilson than to that of Lenin. For this reason Wilson is likely to become a world figure of heroic proportions, with an acknowledged impact on world history more direct and far-reaching than that of any other American.

POSTSCRIPT

Was Woodrow Wilson a Naive Idealist?

Henry Kissinger is particularly well suited to write a history of *Diplomacy* (Simon & Schuster, 1994). At Harvard he received a Ph.D. in political science and wrote a dissertation subsequently published as *A World Restored: Metternich, Castlereagh and the Problems of Peace, 1812–1822* (Houghton Mifflin, 1973). In it he admired how the major nations restored the balance of power in Europe once Napoleon was defeated. As President Nixon's chief assistant for national security affairs and later as Nixon's and then Ford's secretary of state in the 1970s, Kissinger became one of the nation's most active, visible, and controversial diplomats. He applied the "realistic" approach to American foreign policy that he had previously written about.

As an exponent of realism, Kissinger excoriates Wilson's handling of America's entrance into World War I and the subsequent negotiations of the peace treaty at Versailles. According to Kissinger, Wilson was reflective of an excessive moralism and naiveté, which Americans hold about the world even today. Rejecting the fact that the United States had a basic national interest in preserving the balance of power of Europe, Wilson told the American people that they were entering the war to "bring peace and safety to all nations and make the world itself at last free." Kissinger believes that Theodore Roosevelt, the realist, had a firmer handle on foreign policy than did Wilson, the idealist. But in the long run, Wilsonianism triumphed and has influenced every modern-day president's foreign policy.

Kissinger's critique of Wilson is similar to the realist critique of traditional American foreign policy put forth during the height of the cold war in the 1950s by journalist Walter Lippman and by political scientists Hans Morgenthau and Robert Endicott Osgood. Morgenthau and Osgood's study *Ideals and Self-Interest in America's Foreign Relations* (University of Chicago Press, 1953) established the realist/idealist dichotomy utilized by Kissinger. George F. Kennan, another "realistic" diplomat, advanced a similar criticism about what he called the "legalistic-moralistic" streak that could be found in American foreign policy; see *American Diplomacy, 1900–1950* (Mentor Books, 1951).

Scholars have criticized the realist approach to Wilson for a number of reasons. Some say that it is "unrealistic" to expect an American president to ask for a declaration of war to defend abstract principles such as the balance of power or our national interest. Presidents and other elected officials must have a moral reason if they expect the American public to support a foreign war in which American servicemen might be killed.

Many recent historians agree with David F. Trask that Wilson developed realistic and clearly articulated goals and coordinated his larger diplomatic aims with the use of force better than any other wartime U.S. president. See "Woodrow Wilson and the Reconciliation of Force and Diplomacy, 1917–1918," *Naval War College Review* (January/February 1975). Arthur S. Link, editor of *The Wilson Papers,* who has spent a lifetime writing about Wilson, follows a similar line of argument in his lectures delivered at Johns Hopkins University in 1956; see, for example, *Woodrow Wilson: Revolution, War, and Peace,* rev. ed. (Harlan Davidson, 1979). Finally, John Milton Cooper, Jr., in *The Warrior and the Priest: Woodrow Wilson and Theodore Roosevelt* (Harvard University Press, 1984), presents Wilson as the realist and Theodore Roosevelt as the idealist.

In the second selection William G. Carleton presents an impassioned defense of both Wilson's policies at Versailles as well as their implication for the future of American foreign policy. Carleton responds to the two main charges historians continue to level against Wilson: his inability to compromise and his naive idealism. Unlike Professor Thomas A. Bailey, who in *Woodrow Wilson and the Great Betrayal* (Macmillan, 1945) blames Wilson for failing to compromise with Senator Henry Cabot Lodge, Carleton excoriates the chairman of the Senate Foreign Relations Committee for adding "nationally self-centered" reservations that he knew would emasculate the League of Nations and most likely cause other nations to add reservations to the Treaty of Versailles. Wilson, says, Carleton, was a true realist when he rejected the Lodge reservations.

Nor was Wilson a naive idealist. "He recognized," says Carleton, "the emergence of the anti-imperialist revolutions . . . the importance of social politics in the international relations of the future . . . the implications for future world politics of the technological revolutions in war, of total war, and of the disintegration of the old balance of power." Carleton advanced many of the arguments that historians like Professors Trask and Link later used in defending Wilson's "higher realism."

Books continue to proliferate about Wilson. Critical from a realistic perspective are Jan Willem Schulte Nordholt, *Woodrow Wilson: A Life for World Peace* (University of California Press, 1991) and Lloyd E. Ambrosius, *Wilsonian Statecraft: Theory and Practice of Liberal Internationalism During World War I* (Scholarly Resources Books, 1991). Two older, mildly critical, well-written summaries are Daniel M. Smith's *The Great Departure: The United States and World War I, 1914–1920* (John Wiley, 1965) and Robert H. Ferrell, *Woodrow Wilson and World War I, 1917–1921* (Harper & Row, 1985).

Books sympathetic to Wilson include: Arthur Walworth, *Wilson and His Peacemakers: American Diplomacy at the Paris Peace Conference* (W. W. Norton, 1986) and Kendrick A. Clements, *The Presidency of Woodrow Wilson* (University Press of Kansas, 1992). See also the biography by August Heckscher, *Woodrow Wilson* (Scribners, 1991), and Thomas J. Knock, *To End All Wars: Woodrow Wilson and the Quest for a New World Order* (Oxford University Press, 1992).

On the Internet . . .

Internet Web sites containing historical material relevant to the subjects discussed in Part 2 can be reached through the McGraw-Hill history site.

http://www.mhhe.com/socscience/history/usa/link/linktop.htm

Prohibition

The National Archives offers visitors the chance to view "The Volstead Act and Related Prohibition Documents." Documents reproduced on the site include the amendments establishing and repealing Prohibition, photographs, and a memo pertaining to the investigation of a conspiracy to transport liquor during Prohibition.

http://www.archives.gov/

New Deal Network

Launched by the Frank and Eleanor Roosevelt Institute (FERI) in October 1996, the New Deal Network (NDN) is a research and teaching resource on the World Wide Web devoted to the public works and arts project of the New Deal. At the core of the NDN is a database of photographs, political cartoons, and texts (speeches, letters, and other historic documents from the New Deal period). Currently, there are over 20,000 items in this database.

http://newdeal.feri.org/index.htm

World War II Resources

This site links to primary source materials on the Web related to World War II, including original documents regarding all aspects of the war. You can see documents on Nazi-Soviet relations from the archives of the German Foreign Office, speeches of Franklin D. Roosevelt on foreign policy, and much more.

http://metalab.4NC.edu/pha

PART 2

From Prosperity Through the Great Depression and World War II, 1919–1945

In the 1920s, tensions rose between the values of the nation's rural past and the new social and moral values of modern America. There was controversy over whether the prohibition movement curbed drinking or whether it created a climate of lawlessness in the 1920s. In Dayton, Tennessee, modernists challenged the statute supported by the fundamentalist dominated state legislature, which forbade the teaching of evolution in the schools as a scientific explanation of the origins of the universe. A second Ku Klux Klan emerged—more nativist than racist—that was supported by fundamentalist and middle-class Protestants who feared the changing values and moral standards of America.

The onset of a more activist federal government accelerated with the Great Depression. With more than a quarter of the workforce unemployed, Franklin D. Roosevelt was elected on a promise to give Americans a "New Deal." Every sector of the economy was affected by the proliferation of the alphabet soup New Deal agencies. Big business, agriculture, and banking continued to receive their share of government handouts, but working-class Americans were also given government help with work-relief programs, social security benefits, and collective bargaining for labor unions. Historians continue to debate whether the New Deal measures ameliorated or prolonged the Great Depression.

The emergence of a conservative Congress and the impending world war killed the New Deal by 1939. With the fall of France to the Germans in the summer of 1940, FDR tried to abandon the traditional foreign policy of isolationism by aiding allies in Europe and Asia without becoming involved in the war. It didn't work. On December 7, 1941, the Japanese attacked Pearl Harbor and destroyed most of the Pacific fleet. It's been 64 years since the attack occurred, and historians still argue whether the president withheld information about the coming attack or whether FDR was completely caught off-guard. The result was unprecedented. From 1941 through the summer of 1945, the United States fought a two-front war in Europe and Asia.

- Was the Ku Klux Klan of the 1920s an Extremist Movement?
- Did the New Deal Prolong the Great Depression?
- Did President Roosevelt Deliberately Withhold Information About the Attack on Pearl Harbor from the American Commanders?

ISSUE 5

Was the Ku Klux Klan of the 1920s an Extremist Movement?

YES: David H. Bennett, from *The Party of Fear: From Nativist Movements to the New Right in American History* (University of North Carolina Press, 1988)

NO: Stanley Coben, from *Rebellion Against Victorianism: The Impetus for Cultural Change in 1920s America* (Oxford University Press, 1991)

ISSUE SUMMARY

YES: Professor of history David H. Bennett argues that the Ku Klux Klan of the 1920s was supported mainly by fundamentalist Protestants who were opposed to the changing values associated with the Catholic and Jewish immigrants.

NO: Professor of history Stanley Coben believes that local Klansmen were solid, middle-class citizens who were concerned about the decline in moral standards in their communities.

There have been three Ku Klux Klans in American history: (1) the Reconstruction Klan, which arose in the South at the end of the Civil War and whose primary purpose was to prevent the newly emancipated blacks from voting and attaining social and economic equality with whites; (2) the 1920s Klan, which had national appeal and emerged out of disillusionment with the aftermath of U.S. intervention in World War I and the changing social and economic values that had transformed America as a result of the full-scale Industrial Revolution; and (3) the modern Klan, which arose after World War II in the rural areas of the Deep South and (like the Reconstruction Klan) came about to prevent blacks from attaining the political and legal rights guaranteed by the passage of the civil rights legislation in the 1950s and 1960s.

The Klan of the 1920s was founded in 1915 by William J. Simmons, a Methodist circuit preacher, and 15 of his followers. For five years the resurrected Klan consisted of only 4,000 or 5,000 members in scattered Klans throughout Georgia and Alabama. On June 7, 1920, Simmons signed a contract with two clever salespersons, Edward Clarke and Elizabeth Tyler, who pioneered some of the most remarkable organizing and mass marketing techniques of the pro-business decade of the 1920s. The campaign was an immediate success. Between June 1920 and October 1921, 85,000 men joined the Klan. Total membership figures are difficult to ascertain, but somewhere between 3 and 5 million people joined the Klan. This means that one of every four Protestant males in America was a member of the Klan.

The 1920s Klan differed greatly from its predecessors and successors because it had wide-ranging influence in politics across the nation. The Klan was not merely a southern movement but a national movement that was strongest in the Midwest and Southwest. Politically, Klan members dominated state legislatures in Oklahoma, Texas, and Indiana, and city councils in such far-western places as El Paso, Texas; Denver, Colorado; Anaheim, California; and Tillamook, Oregon. The Klan of the 1920s was the most powerful right-wing movement of the decade.

While the 1920s Klan disliked blacks, it focused its attacks upon the Catholic and Jewish immigrants who had been coming to America since the 1890s. Klansmen particularly disliked Catholics, who constituted 36 percent of the nation's population in 1920. Catholics were accused of placing loyalty to the pope ahead of loyalty to the nation. If Catholics gained political control, the Klan asserted, separation of church and state would end, and freedoms of speech, press, and religious worship would also be abolished.

The Klan was also inspired by the xenophobic (fear of foreigners) atmosphere of the time. America's participation in World War I had ended in public disillusionment. The U.S. Senate reflected the country's dislike of all things foreign when it refused to ratify President Woodrow Wilson's Treaty of Versailles. Antiforeign feelings were also reflected in the passage of the 1921 and 1924 reform laws, which severely curtailed immigration from southern and eastern Europe and completely excluded Japanese and other oriental groups.

Most explanations for the fall of the 1920s Klan seem unsatisfactory. Greed may have been one cause. There was a lot of money involved—it has been estimated that as much as $75 million in Klan initiation fees and wardrobes ended up in the pockets of various Klan leaders—and everyone seemed to have their hand in the till. Moral hypocrisy also infiltrated the Klan. While many Klan members were afraid of the changing standards of morality and supported Klan politicians who preached law and order, the opposite was often the case. Third, the depression of the 1930s and World War II may have contributed to the Klan's fall by directing people's energies elsewhere.

Was the 1920s Ku Klux Klan an extremist organization? According to David H. Bennett in the following selection, the Klan was a traditional nativist organization supported mainly by fundamentalist Protestants who were opposed to the changing social and moral values of the 1920s associated with the Catholic and Jewish immigrants. In the second selection, Stanley Coben asserts that most Klansmen were ordinary white, middle-class Protestants who composed what he has described elsewhere as "the largest grassroots conservative . . . movement in American history."

David H. Bennett

YES

Traditional Nativism's Last Stand

Restating the Themes of Nativism

The Ku Klux Klan under Hiram Wesley Evans and associates offered a program reminiscent of its nativist progenitors, the Know Nothings and the APA. Klan papers and magazines, books and articles by Klan leaders, laid out the appeal of the new nativism.

One spokesman, Reverend E. H. Laugher, in *The Kall of the Klan of Kentucky.* explained that "the KKK is not a lodge or a society or a political party." Rather, it is a mass movement, "a crusade of American people who are beginning to realize that they have neglected their public and religious duty to stand up for Americanism." This meant remembering that America was discovered by Norsemen, colonized by Puritans, that the United States was "purely Anglo-Saxon and Nordic." It was essential to "preserve our racial purity," he insisted, to avoid "mongrelization." It was imperative to maintain separation of church and state because "the forces of Protestantism" were protectors of the "doctrine of Americanism." The Roman Catholic church, appealing to the polyglot peoples who threatened the good and pure society, must be blocked in its drive to dominate and destroy the great nation.

In *The Fiery Cross, The Kourier, The American Standard, Dawn, The Imperial Night-Hawk,* and other publications, Klan ideologists assaulted Catholics, Jews, and aliens. "Jesus was a Protestant," the faithful were told, he had "split with the priests" because he had truth and right on his side. The Roman Catholic church, laboring under "the growth of Popish despotism," was irreligious and un-American. In fact, the "Papacy's campaign against liberalism and freedom" made it a proper "ally of Mussolini's fascism," just as the church had been on the side of other autocracies since medieval times. In America, the "spirit of Bunker Hill and Valley Forge," that longing for democracy and individualism which informed the Revolution and the words of the Founding Fathers, was at odds with a "hierarchical Church, which, like an octopus, has stretched its tentacles into the very vitals of the body politic of the nation." The church's effort to undermine the public schools, to "reach out for the children of Protestantism," to "hit anywhere with any weapon" in an unscrupulous campaign to impose its will, meant that every Catholic in public life, from school board member to national politician, must be watched carefully. "Do you know," a Klan editorialist asked, "that eight states have Roman Catholic administrations, 690 public schools teach from the Roman Catholic catechism, sixty-two percent of all elected and appointed offices in the United States are now held by Catholics, who also are a majority of the teachers in many major city school systems?"

The threat of the church was everywhere. The "Romanized press" tried to propagandize a gullible public. Catholics evaded taxes as a matter of course, refusing to share the burdens of government, preferring to subsidize sinister schemes hatched by their prelates. The church used Jesuits to engage in "occult mental manipulations" and tried to "subjugate the Negro race through spiritual domination." The pope favored child labor, and because "20,000 ordained priests in America are vassals to this Imperial Monarch in Rome," the same could be expected of church leaders in the United States. Indeed, Catholics were in no sense trustworthy Americans; during the Great War, "German sentiment was the fruit of carefully prepared and skillfully disseminated Roman propaganda." But it would be wrong to conclude that the Klan was anti-Catholic, leaders insisted, because its arguments were "wholly and solely concentrated on being one hundred per cent American." In fact, one writer suggested, the Klan is "no more aimed at Roman Catholics than it would be aimed at Buddhists, Confucianists or Mohammedans, or anybody else who owes allegiance to any foreign person and/or religion."

Like the nineteenth-century nativists, Klan initiates were asked to protect America from the diabolical plans of Jesuits and other leaders of this un-American presence. From colonial days, anti-Catholicism had been a dominant theme in the history of these movements, a way of displacing fears and angers on alien intruders. In the 1920s, with Irish Catholics maintaining positions of prominence in urban and national politics, continuing to gain greater influence in a growing economy, Klan spokesmen returned to the old themes. The assault on the church was repeated in almost every Klan speech, article, and editorial. This modern Ku Klux Klan dressed its members in garb borrowed from the Reconstruction vigilante organization, but its real roots were in traditional nativism, stretching back much further in the American experience.

But to its attack on Catholicism, the modern Klan added an anti-Semitic element. The APA, emerging during the new immigration, had touched on this theme; Klan writers developed the argument. "Jews are everywhere a separate and distinct people, living apart from the great Gentile masses," said the author of *Klansmen: Guardians of Liberty*. But these people are not "home builders or tillers of the soil." Evans had made a similar argument in a speech at Dallas in December 1922: "The Jew produces nothing anywhere on the face of the earth. He does not till the soil. He does not create or manufacture anything for common use. He adds nothing to the sum of human welfare." Yet not only were Jews unproductive, Klan theoreticians insisted, they were un-American. They were not interested in integration: "No, not the Jew . . . he is different." These people, who "defied the melting pot for one thousand years," believed in their own superiority, in "Jewry Uber Alles." They hatched secret plans to advance their interests to "cause wars and to subjugate America." Certain conspiratorial Jews must be "absolutely and eternally" opposed when they plotted their "crimes and wrongs." They were nothing more than money-grubbing and immoral vultures, "moral lepers who gloat over human tragedy, rejoice in the downfall of the guileless and inexperienced." The unethical practices of Jewish businessmen—often seen as winners in the economic competition of the boom years—and the radical schemes of Jewish Marxists were considered equally repugnant, dangers to America. But so, too, was the cultural depravity of strategically placed "Semites" in the media. "Jew Movies Urge Sex and Vice," the Klan headline shouted like an echo from Ford's *Dearborn Independent;* "Jewish corruption in jazz" was a result of "their monopoly over popular songs." In the big cities, "ninety five per cent of bootleggers are Jews."

It was the Roaring Twenties, and as mores changed, as traditional social arrangements were overturned, as skirts went up and speakeasies flourished, as the movies and radio made their mark with Tin Pan Alley songs popularized by so many show business celebrities, the Klan found a way of identifying these disturbing developments in an antialien context, of standing up for America by assailing yet another band of un-Americans.

Still, the Jews were only one part of a larger alien problem in America. Again, like the Know Nothings and the patriotic fraternalists of the 1890s, these nativists were concerned with the threat they saw posed by all non-Anglo-Saxon immigrants and their descendants. Imperial Wizard Evans spoke of "the vast horde of immigrants who have reached our shores," these "Italian anarchists, Irish Catholic malcontents, Russian Jews, Finns, Letts, Lithuanians of the lowest class." Even after the Immigration Act of 1924, which Evans characterized as a "new era dawning for America" and took full credit for security—"typifying the influence exerted by our organization"—he warned that undesirables "are still bootlegged into the nation," still try to "flaunt our immigration laws." This "polyglotism" was intolerable, for many of the most recent immigrants from southern and eastern Europe and from Asia still could not read and write English. They were unfamiliar with American history and tradition, "were unaware that America is fundamentally an Anglo-Saxon achievement." And because these alien peoples "congregate in our great centers, our cities are a menace to democracy," they are "modern Sodoms and Gomorrahs." Is "Petrograd in its ruin and desolation a picture of New York in the future"? There was only one possible response. "America for the Americans," Evans exhorted, for if "this state of affairs continues, the American race is doomed to cultural destruction." In words that might have been lifted from a Know Nothing broadside, he continued: "Illiteracy, disease, insanity, and mental deficiency are still pouring in among us."

The "foreigners" were responsible for a host of social problems. Evans lectured on "our alien crime-plague" and Klan papers reported on alien thugs, Italian mobsters and rum runners, even a "Newark alien hiding whiskey in U.S. flag." The aliens threatened female virtue: "Foreign women sell their bodies for gain." They threatened the safety of American womanhood: "Women Are Struck Down by Foreign Mob," screamed one headline, "Aliens Poison Hoosier Women," said another. Some aliens were radicals: "Russians Would Make America Red, Peril is a Very Real One." Others would destroy the nation through political sabotage: "Use the Ballot, the Italian Ambassador Recommends, to

Advance the Interests of Italians' Native Land." And over all these perils loomed the threat of Irish Catholic party machine manipulators. Leaders of the church in America, most formidable of the foreign operatives, these "Irish Romanists in Tammany . . . lead the Jews, Poles, Italians, Germans, Czechs, Magyars"; it was a "vast army under command of the Irish Roman ward heelers." The only way to deal with the foreign devils, to safeguard our sacred institutions, was to re-Americanize the land. Evans announced: "Against us are all the forces of the mixed alliance composed of alienism, Romanism, hyphenism, Bolshevism and un-Americanism which aim to use this country as a dumping ground for the fermenting races of the Old World." But "we of the Klan are on the firing line . . . like the soldiers of the American Expeditionary Force in France, we stand up for America and take pride and joy in the wounds we receive . . . the Knights of the Ku Klux Klan have become the trustees under God for Protestant American nationalism."

The cause of the Klan, in the phrases of its spokesmen, could not have been more noble, more dangerous, or more urgent. But among those many American values that Klansmen were sworn to protect, one had particular urgency. This was the protection of "womanhood." In pursuing this goal, the Klan invoked memories of that long line of femininity's defenders who marched under the banners of nativism, back to the days of Maria Monk.

A Texas Klansman, author of *Religious and Patriotic Ideals of the Ku Klux Klan,* reminded initiates that they had sworn to "promote good works and thus protect the chastity of womanhood, the virtue of girlhood, the sanctity of the home." Spokesmen repeatedly used the term "chivalry" in describing the movement's principles. The role of women in the literature of the Klan was explicitly traditional. They were the moral arbiters of society, for "even in the midst of all the pressing duties of maternal care and home making, women have found time to keep the spiritual fire of the nation burning on the altar . . . women have been the conscience keepers of the race." But the role was not so traditional that women would be repressed, for it was "Rome Which Opposes the Advancement of Womanhood," said the headline, the Jesuits who favor policies pushing women into "semi-oriental seclusion." The Klan would preserve and protect women so they might aid in the shaping of American destiny; "the fate of the nation is in the hands of women." As one Klan newswriter put it, they can be "not only help meets but help mates." After all, the "very mentioning of the word 'woman' always arrests the attention of every true man. Whatever else the human heart may forget in the rough experiences of life, it cannot forget its mother."

The call to protect these fragile, sensitive, vulnerable women led to violence. Local Klans were accused of floggings, tar and featherings, and beatings in several states in the South, Southwest, and lower Midwest. The victims of the masked night riders often were alleged adulterers and wife-beaters, men said not to be supporting their families, men who had deserted their women. But the enemies of "pure womanhood" included sinners of both sexes. "Fallen women" were the targets in some rural bastions. Young women accused of prostitution or adultery were stripped naked, tarred, left half-conscious with their hair shorn. The sexual frustrations of these bands of white-robed small-townsmen, envious of the freedom exercised by millions of more liberated urbanites in the jazz age, finding perverse pleasure in this part of their crusade for morality, reveling in the projection of their anger and the displacement of their resentments of these symbolic villains, recalled the nunnery craze of the early nineteenth century.

In fact, another generation of nativists meant another resurgence of convent tales. *Dawn* [a major Klan paper in Chicago] offered "Convent Cruelties: The True Story of Ex-Nun Helen Jackson," advertising offprints of this sadomasochistic piece for many months after initial publication. Other Klan journals featured, among several exposés, "Behind Convent Walls" and "Roman Priest Alienates Innocent Women's Love."

Women who knew their role and understood their place were offered membership in affiliate groups open to "patriotic ladies." Simmons's Kamelai had been disbanded, but Hiram Evans introduced the Women of the Ku Klux Klan, an organization which absorbed such local groups as Ladies of the Invisible Empire in Louisiana and the Order of American Women in Texas. This new national organization established its own Imperial Palace, a pillared mansion in Little Rock, Arkansas. It sent its own kleagles [officials in the Klan] into the field, calling on Klansmen to influence wives and sisters to join. By fall 1924, when the Ku Klux Klan said its membership numbered in the millions, the women's auxiliary claimed a following of two hundred thousand. The initiates were not, as one anti-Klan writer suggested, "nativist amazons." They were expected to perform customary housewifely chores; they prepared food for Klan outings, picnics, and klambakes. In fact, their order was little more than the instrument of one man's authority. James Comer, Evans's early ally and grand dragon of the Arkansas Klan, bankrolled the Women of the Ku Klux Klan and controlled its activities. He forced the resignation of its imperial commander to install Robbie Gill, an initiate friend who would soon be his wife, as new leader. It was Commander Gill who told the Second Imperial Klonvocation: "God gave Adam Woman to be his comrade and counselor . . . Eve's name meant life, society, company. Adam was lord and master." Like earlier nativists, Klansmen never questioned the assumption of male dominance. The American dream they sought to protect had no room for sexual equality. But the image of threatened womanhood was essential to their own search for masculine validation, even as it had been in the days of *The Awful Disclosures of Maria Monk*. That had been another age in which economic growth and status anxiety served as a setting for the resurgence of the antialien crusade.

The attacks on Catholics and foreigners and the vows to protect imperiled American women tied the Ku Klux Klan to a long history of similar movements. It was traditional nativism's last stand. Its emergence in the 1920s raised questions to which contemporary journalists and academics offered a variety of answers.

Reporter Robert L. Duffus, author of a series of anti-Klan articles in the *World's Work,* argued that many recruits came from "the back counties of the south and lower midwest," where men carry guns, women are objects of the deference but also of exploitation, and the disappointed seek causes outside themselves. Professor Frank Tannenbaum, writing in 1924, agreed in part, seeing Klansmen as seekers after "artificial thrills" as a way of dealing with the boredom of small-town life, people ready to use coercion in defense of social status, people "losing their grip" in a world of change. But Tannenbaum also looked to recent events as a source of this mood of restlessness. The Great War aroused human passions, he suggested, the "hope of a new and beatific world after the defeat of the German evil." The Klan offered an explanation of why the war brought no "dawning of Utopia." It was the Catholic, the radical, the foreigner who was in league with the devil.

Later, scholars would embrace some of these views. Though not sharing pro-Klan journalist Stanley Frost's rosy vision of Klansmen as a knighthood of admirable reformers, they agreed that the Klan represented a response to the war, a zeal to cleanse and reform American society. The rise of fundamentalist fervor in the 1920s, which provided an additional setting for the Klan, was seen as another reaction to the war. Anti-Catholicism was in the air in many parts of the nation in these years. As with fundamentalism, the Klan's crusade for conformity to old values and old social arrangements was seen as a "characteristic response to a common disillusion."

The Ku Klux Klan, like the Red Scare, was given new life by the souring of the international crusade. Almost all students of the Klan have made this point. But the reason why the Klan grew in the 1920s had more to do with social and economic strains in a society experiencing almost unprecedented growth.

Those who joined were not, as Duffus suggested, only losers in the boom years. Along with poor farmers, blue-collar workers, mechanics, and day laborers some bankers, lawyers, doctors, ministers, and prosperous businessmen were recruited in different regions. There were communities in which political careers and professional success depended on membership. But the Klan appealed more to those who were not members of any elite. Imperial Wizard and Emperor Evans observed: "We are a movement of the plain people, very weak in the matter of culture, intellectual support and trained leadership. . . . We demand a return of power into the hands of the everyday, not highly cultured, not overly intellectualized but entirely unspoiled and not de-Americanized average citizens of the old stock." The Klan everywhere appealed to those who believed that their older vision of America was at risk. In the struggle to preserve enduring American values, the movement offered a sense of common purpose in service of a cause greater than self. It offered an idealism that had a magnetic pull for many. Its shrewd managers, interested in money, power, and influence for themselves, knew how to package the movement. But the popularity of the Klan, once it began to spread across the land, did not depend on the Clarkes and Tylers or their successors as marketing specialists and salesmen. Like the earlier nativist fraternities, it was rooted in a longing for order, in misty memories of some stable and happy past, in fears of what new perils modernity might bring, in the search for community in an age of flux.

The movement provided community. Local Klans sponsored Sunday dinners and square dances, basketball tournaments and rodeos, carnivals and circuses, fireworks displays featuring "electric fiery crosses," social events of all kinds. It was comforting to be in the Klan, and it could be fun. Klansmen also took care of each other. Businessmen placed ads for Klan Klothes Kleaned or

Krippled Kars Kured, expecting fraternal ties would result in new customers. Other activities offered bonding through unified action to clean up the community: boycotts of businesses run by "immoral men," committees to ferret out bootleggers and bars.

The communal ties seemed at one with religious conviction. The movement that defended Protestantism won the tacit endorsement of many clergymen, some who joined the order. Most nationally prominent church leaders stayed away from the Klan, and some Methodist, Presbyterian, and Episcopalian notables and publications even attacked it, but these assaults from influential cosmopolitans only served to underscore Evans's claims that his movement was the instrument of the mass of common people. The Klan made inroads in many Protestant communities, particularly among Southern Baptists and others influenced by fundamentalist concerns. A major part of the Protestant press remained silent on the issue, but many local church papers endorsed the goals of an organization that appealed for support in the name of old-time values and that old-time religion.

The Klan's growth was meteoric. In 1924, Stanley Frost reported that "some say it has six million members." Frost himself claimed only some 4.5 million in the movement. Robert Duffus put the number at 2.5 million in 1923. Other guesses ranged upward of 5 million. It was impossible to be certain; the Klan left only fragmentary local records and no national archives. But one modern scholar, using available data, estimated it had over 2 million recruits in 1924; another, in a careful review of conflicting claims, put it at over 2 million initiates across the years, with some 1.5 million at any one time. What is certain is that it had become a true mass movement, one of the major developments in the history of the 1920s, a great monument to the antialien impulse in America.

The Klan Across America

But it did not prosper equally in all sections of the country. In the Deep South, where the Klan was born, it exerted considerable influence in some states. Still, its membership never exceeded a quarter of a million. . . .

The Klan lasted longer in Indiana, home of its most powerful, most successful organization in the United States. The man who was instrumental in recruiting a quarter of a million knights statewide—almost forty thousand in Indianapolis—was Grand Dragon David D. Stephenson. Only thirty years old in 1921, Stephenson had been one of the four key state leaders helping Evans oust Simmons before the first national meeting in Atlanta. Rewarded with the organizing rights for twenty-three states in the North, this charismatic figure, who liked to compare himself to Napoleon, already was a successful coal dealer when he joined the Invisible Empire. But in the Klan, he would make a fortune in recruitment fees and build a reputation as a mesmerizing orator, the super salesman of the national Klan.

In Indiana, his order sponsored parades and athletic contests, field days and picnics. It offered community and festivity, but always in the name of protecting Protestant America from its enemies. In "Middletown," the Lynds found it had become a working-class movement and "tales against the Catholics ran like wild fire" through Muncie. Local Klansmen vowed they would unmask only "when and not until the Catholics take the prison walls down from the convents and nunneries." Anti-Catholic, anti-Semitic, antiblack rhetoric filled Stephenson's colorful speeches: the Klan stood for temperance and patriotism, the aliens were threatening traditional American values. This appeal was so successful that store owners soon put TWK [Trade with a Klansman] in their windows; the secrecy of the order could be violated with little fear of retaliation in a state in which hundreds of thousands were flocking to join the most popular movement in memory. In fact, so many initiates paid their kleck-token to Stephenson that it was estimated he made between $2 and $5 million in eighteen months. The grand dragon acquired a ninety-eight-foot yacht, which he kept on Lake Huron, a fleet of automobiles, a palatial suburban home, and elaborate offices in downtown Indianapolis. There, the mayor opposed "Steven" and his order until a Klansman named Edward Jackson won the Republican primary for governor in 1923. Now the Klan took control of the county party machinery. Jackson's subsequent election gave Stephenson and his movement state power unmatched by any other Klan.

A high point was reached with the fabled Konklave at Kokomo, when "200,000 men and women filled with love of country"—in the words of the *Fiery Cross* (Indiana State Edition)—gathered for the Klan's greatest single meeting. Tens of thousands of cars brought members from across Indiana and Ohio. Stephenson, attired in a sequined purple robe and escorted by his team of personal bodyguards, finally mounted the rostrum. He explained that he was late for the meeting because "the President of the United States kept me counselling upon matters of state." He proceeded to deliver a quintessentially nativist exhortation, filled with pleas for America and plans for vigilant opposition to the aliens. Always a riveting stump speaker, Stephenson was most respected for his organizational skills. But his Bonapartist complex and rumors for numerous sexual indiscretions and alcoholic binges soon led to conflicts with state and national Klan leaders. Evans turned against him, and he resigned as state grand dragon in September 1923. But D. C. Stephenson was not through. He marshaled support for a special state meeting the following May, in which his followers elected him once against their grand dragon, thus rejecting the authority of national headquarters. Stephenson continued to flout the hierarchical authority of the national Klan, staying in power during the election year of 1924, a time which marked the KKK's most significant impact in American politics. But by 1925, the Indiana chief was caught up in the scandal that ended in his prison sentence, a sordid affair that fatally wounded not only the Indiana Klan but the national movement as well. . . .

Although the Klan had suffered setbacks in Oklahoma, Texas, Colorado, Oregon, Illinois, and other states by early 1925, it still seemed a formidable national movement in the year after the election. Then came the Stephenson scandal in Indiana. The grand dragon was implicated in the death of a statehouse employee named Madge Oberholtzer. Although it was widely reported that he had known many attractive women in Indianapolis, D. C. Stephenson chose to lavish particular attention on Oberholtzer. She later testified that he compelled her to drink with him, finally forcing her at gunpoint to a train. In the private compartment he attacked and "sexually mutilated" her. Oberholtzer took a fatal overdose of drugs after this incident, but she lingered for weeks before her death; she had time to dictate the entire story to the prosecuting attorney, one of the new officials Stephenson could not control in Marion County. The revelations devastated the entire movement. The desperate grand dragon, on trial for murder, was abandoned by his former henchman, Governor Ed Jackson. Panicky Klan papers now assailed their leader. The *Indian Kourier* headline declared: "D. C. Stephenson Not a Klansman," and called him an "enemy of the order," reporting that he had been "repudiated by all true Knights of the Empire." Stephenson responded by revealing the contents of his "little black box," which contained records implicating many highly placed, Klan-backed officials as corrupters, providing evidence of their malfeasance of office. The movement did not recover in Indiana. While Stephenson languished in jail (he would not be released until 1956), the Klan found its political influence evaporating, its membership deserting by the thousands. Hypocrisy, greed, and dishonesty by the leadership was bad enough, but Stephenson's violation of the symbolic crusade for purity, chastity, womanhood, and temperance was too much. As the greatest of the state Klans dissolved, the national empire of the Ku Klux Klan began to crumble everywhere.

By late in the decade, the Klan was a shell of the powerful movement of 1923–24. Although thousands of hooded men marched in the last great parade down the boulevards of Washington in the summer of 1925, many more were abandoning the order. Al Smith's presidential candidacy in 1928 was the occasion for one final, convulsive anti-Catholic effort by the Invisible Empire, but Herbert Hoover's victory owed little to the Klan. In the 1930s, the shriveled movement receded from public view, and its remaining publicists turned away from Catholicism to communism when seeking the alien menace within. Hiram Wesley Evans, before he lost what had become the all but meaningless title of imperial wizard in 1939, even accepted the invitation of church leaders to attend the dedication of the Roman Catholic Cathedral, ironically built on the site of the old Imperial Headquarters in Atlanta. The old order was no more. By 1944, with the federal government pressing for the payment of back taxes on Klan profits from the prosperous 1920, remaining national officers officially disbanded the Ku Klux Klan.

Although small state and local organizations calling themselves Ku Klux Klan, using the terminology of the earlier movement, and dressing members in similar regalia would reemerge in the late 1940s to play occasional roles in anti-black and anti-civil rights violence up through the 1980s, the great Klan of the 1920s was long dead. It had faltered so quickly after the spectacular growth early in the decade for many reasons. It lacked a clear legislative agenda. It experienced heavy weather in the political struggles in several states, where adroit enemies could use its weaknesses to build support for their own interests. It was led, in many areas, by people who were the embodiment of precisely those qualities that Klan ideology asked initiates to oppose: heavy drinkers and swindlers, sexual exploiters and dishonest manipulators of the theme of patriotism. In the end, the movement that offered fraternity to men in tumultuous times, that provided a nativist response to the crisis of values troubling so many in the Roaring Twenties, could not endure the revelations of scandal, the lack of constancy, the confused policies of the leadership. Like its antialien progenitors, the Ku Klux Klan was a movement that symbolized a longing for order, a desire to displace anger and anxiety. With no programmatic reason for being, men would desert it if it ceased to fulfill its symbolic function. As major newspapers turned against it, as articulate figures in the ministry and education, as well as in public life, pointed to its hypocrisy and treated it with scathing contempt, the mass of members simply drifted away. As with the Red Scare, the patriotic activity of the 1890s, and the antialien excitement of the pre–Civil War years, nativism's last stand had a relatively short run.

Stanley Coben NO

The Guardians

The early twentieth-century assaults on Victorianism provoked a strong organized defense by fundamentalists, Prohibitionists, and various conservative and patriotic organizations. However, the huge nationwide Ku Klux Klan, with at least three million members, emerged as the most visible and powerful guardian of Victorianism during the 1920s.

Unlike the vigilante groups which had used the name Ku Klux Klan after the Civil War and during the mid-twentieth-century battles against integration, the Klan of the 1920s did not focus on protecting white supremacy in the South. At the height of the Klan's power in 1924, Southerners formed only 16 percent of its total membership. Over 40 percent of early twentieth-century Klan members lived in the three midwestern states of Indiana, Ohio, and Illinois. The Klan enrolled more members in Connecticut than in Mississippi, more in Oregon than in Louisiana, and more in New Jersey than in Alabama. Klan membership in Indianapolis was almost twice that in South Carolina and Mississippi combined.

Also, Klan members in the mid-1920s were not any more violent than other native, white, middle-class Protestant males. After the Klan organized nationally for maximum profit and political action in 1921, the organization expelled members and whole chapters charged with having taken part in vigilante activities. However, inconclusive newspaper and government investigations into the activities of a small minority of early Klansmen during 1921 gave the organization a violent image. The name Ku Klux Klan (adopted mainly because of the Klan's role in the immensely popular film, *The Birth of a Nation*), the Klan's secrecy, and the order's refusal to admit anyone except native white Protestant males contributed to this image, especially among blacks, Catholics, Jews, and champions of civil liberties.

The image of the Klan held by critics of the organization during the 1920s was affected too by the Klan's rhetoric. That rhetoric reflected still widely accepted Victorian ideas about a racial hierarchy and about the dangers to American society posed by Catholics, blacks, Jews, and Asians. These popular beliefs had assisted the passage of immigration-restriction acts and had helped to defeat the presidential bid of Al Smith. They already had led to nationwide segregation and to disenfranchisement of southern blacks. Therefore, almost nowhere that Klans-backed politicians won power did Klan racist rhetoric need to be transformed into legislation. Nowhere did Klansmen running for office need to advocate violence under any circumstance, even against blacks in the South.

The near absence of Klan violence against southern blacks was explained, in part, by a perceptive editorial in the Savannah, Georgia, *Tribune,* a black-owned newspaper which strongly supported Marcus Garvey's black nationalist Universal Negro Improvement Association and was outspoken about civil-rights violations. The *Tribune*'s editorial (whose conclusions were corroborated by other evidence), published July 13, 1922, stated:

> The evidence is that in the South the Ku Klux are not bothering with the Negroes. The naked truth is that when a band of lynchers sets out to kill a Negro they do not take the trouble to mask. They do not think it necessary to join a secret society, pay initiation fees and buy regalia when Negroes are the quarry.

A Georgia mob did not find it necessary to don masks before lynching Leo Frank in 1915, the year that the early twentieth-century Klan met to organize outside Atlanta.

The Klan's primary objectives consisted of guarding the major Victorian concepts and the interests these protected. The ideas of character, largely reserved for white Protestants, the home and family in which character was formed, and distinctly separate gender roles stood foremost among these concepts. A series of articles entitled "The Klansman's Criterion of Character," published weekly from March 1 to March 29, 1924, in the Klan's national newspaper *Searchlight,* illustrated what the Klan expected of its leaders as well as of its ordinary members.

Jesus provided the chief model for *Searchlight*'s definition of character: "He never compromised when dealing with the leaders of the Jews. He would not lie in order to save his own life." Jesus "was the unflinching, accomplishing, achieving Christ, because he was the purposeful, steadfast, determined Christ." Furthermore, Jesus accomplished his great mission on earth without the advantages enjoyed by members of the privileged business elites and the intelligentsia: "He controlled no centers of influence; He commanded neither learning nor wealth."

Searchlight implied that Klan members had undertaken the task of guarding, in the United States, Jesus' accomplishments:

> The Klan is engaged in a holy crusade against that which is corrupting and destroying the best in American life. The Klan is devoted to the holy mission of developing that which is right and clean and beneficent in our country. The Klan is active in its ministry of helpfulness and service. . . . Such enthusiastic devotion to right principles and the holy cause must characterize true Klansmen, if they are to be like Him whom they have accepted as their "Criterion of Character."

The "Kloran" of the "Knights of the Ku Klux Klan," the order's ritual book used to conduct all meetings and initiations, declared on its cover the order's dedication to "Karacter, Honor, Duty."

Every recent study that has examined the characteristics of klan members—in urban and rural communities of California, Colorado, Georgia, Indiana, Ohio, Oregon, Tennessee, Texas, and Utah—has found that Klansmen constituted a cross section of the local native white Protestant male population, except for the very top and bottom socioeconomic levels of that population. Virtually every Klan candidate for state and local office appealed to this constituency—Klan and non-Klan—with promises to reduce or eliminate those results of character defects which threatened the home and family: violations of Prohibition especially, but also drug abuse, prostitution, gambling, political corruption, traffic violations, and Sunday blue-law offenses.

As local Klan chapters, or Klaverns, prepared to sweep almost every political office in rural Fremont County, Colorado, the county's Klan leaders invited a national Klan lecturer, "Colonel" McKeever, to help bring out the Klan vote. Speaking to an overflow audience in the Canon City armory (1920 population of 4,551), the county's largest community, McKeever proclaimed a typical Klan message.

> The Klan stands for law enforcement; money and politics must cease to play a role [particularly in Prohibition enforcement] in our courts. The Klan stands for the American home; there is no sanctuary like a mother's heart, no altar like a mother's knee. The Klan stands for good men in office.

The Klan attempted to combat all "forces of evil which attack the American home." Threatening the "purity of women," claimed an editorial in the *Fiery Cross,* Indiana's Klan newspaper, were businessmen who employed female secretaries: "Everyone knows of instances where businessmen insist on dating secretaries and imply that should they refuse, their jobs are in danger." . . .

Klan membership held a strong attraction for large numbers of men who already belonged to secret white Protestant fraternal organizations. . . . The Klan offered a more blatant racism, anti-Catholicism, and anti-Semitism, as well as direct participation in politics to members of such societies as the Masons, Odd Fellows, and Knights of Pythias. Moreover, the basic objectives of these other orders resembled those of the Klan in respects more important than ritual and fraternity. The most recent and discerning historian of the Freemasons, Lynn Dumenil, summarized the fundamental Masonic aims: "Not only would America become homogeneous again, but the perpetuation of the values of native, Protestant Americans would be assured."

Kleagles received instructions to contact local ministers, fraternal lodge members, and potentially favorable newspaper editors upon entering a community. They were to ascertain the strongest needs of local white Protestants with the aid of these contacts and to begin enrolling members. . . .

The most thorough statistical analyses of Klan membership during the 1920s have been written by Christopher Cocoltchos, Leonard Moore, and Robert Goldberg. A clear pattern emerges from Cocoltchos's information about Orange County, California, Moore's study of Indiana, and Goldberg's analysis of the Colorado Klan. Other recent books and articles support their conclusions.

These studies of members' characteristics found that Klansmen represented a near cross section of the white Protestant male population in their communities. Everywhere, the Klan fought to overcome the power of business and professional elites, except in some small towns. Outside those towns, few members of these elites joined the Klan, and those who did tended to be the younger members who evidently believed that their ambitions could be best furthered by the Klan.

In these communities as a whole, Catholics, blacks, Jews, and recent immigrants formed a very small part of the population. The few exceptions were the black population of Indianapolis, which almost equaled the proportion of blacks in the country; the German Catholic population of Anaheim, California, which led the anti-Klan elite there; and the Mexican-American Catholic population of Orange County, which was thoroughly segregated when the Klan was organized and which the Klan consequently ignored altogether. The percentages of those minorities in these communities were insignificant compared with the proportions of these same minorities in major cities like New York, Chicago, Cleveland, and St. Louis, where native white Protestants constituted a minority of the residents (in some cases, less than one-quarter).

Klansmen were concentrated in middle white-collar positions and among small businessmen. Those who were blue-collar workers were overwhelmingly in skilled positions. Members belonged to all major Protestant denominations, but the Klan included very few members of fundamentalist sects. They attended services in Northern Methodist and Disciples of Christ churches especially. Klansmen generally had lived in their communities longer than nonmembers, usually at least ten years before they joined the order, yet they tended to be younger. Well over three-quarters of them were married. They belonged to more civil and fraternal organizations, particularly to the Masons. They possessed greater wealth, more property, and registered to vote in 1924 in much larger proportions than did nonmembers in their communities. Klansmen in the mid-1920s decidedly were not a fringe group of vigilantes; they were solid middle-class citizens and individuals of high Victorian character.

Indiana served as the focal point of Klan power in America. The Indiana Klan enrolled more members and a much larger proportion of the state population than did the Klaverns of any other state. The state capital, Indianapolis, was referred to by a leading historian of the Klan as the "Center of Klandom."

Information about Klan members' characteristics in three Indiana communities, representative of the states' large and small cities and of its rural town, illustrates the Klan's composition in Indiana. The three communities are Indianapolis, a major industrial and commercial city whose population in 1920 was 314,000; Richmond, an industrial city with a population of 27,000 in 1920; and Crown Point, a commercial township of 4,312, which served the surrounding farming area.

Individuals in high white-collar occupations among Indianapolis's Klan members equalled almost exactly the proportion of men with that status in the city as a whole. However, the Indianapolis Klan contained none of the high executives of the city's largest corporations—such as Van Camp, one of the largest food canning companies in the nation; Eli Lilly, a major pharmaceutical manufacturer; and the Stutz and Dusenburg motor-car companies. Disciples of Christ, Lutheran, and United Brethren ranked highest among the church affiliations of Indianapolis's Klansmen.

About 75 percent of Richmond's Klan members occupied white-collar or skilled-worker positions compared to 64 percent of non-Klansmen in such positions. However, non-Klansmen filled the city's highest white-collar jobs in considerably larger proportions than did Klansmen. The greatest differences between the Protestant church affiliations of Richmond's Klan members and those of Richmond's citizens as a whole lay in the much higher proportion of Klansmen who belonged to Presbyterian, United Brethren, Disciples of Christ, and Episcopal congregations.

The occupational profile of Crown Point's Klan members resembled that of Indianapolis and Richmond Knights. Moore found that "Crown Point's wealthiest citizens did not appear to play any role in the Klan." Sixty-one percent of Crown Point's church-member Knights belonged to Methodist, Lutheran, Presbyterian, or Disciples of Christ congregations.

In each of these three Indiana communities, Kleagles and local Klan organizers used vocal and written criticism of American Catholics, blacks, Jews, and recent immigrants as part of their recruiting rhetoric. However, Moore concluded that the Indiana Klan "did not employ violence as a strategy, and only a tiny fraction of the hooded order's membership ever engaged in violent or threatening acts."

The characteristics of Orange County Klansmen differed little from those of the Indiana members. For fast growing Anaheim, the county seat, Cocoltchos derived statistical information for Klan, non-Klan, and active anti-Klan residents. The latter included those who had joined the club devoted to defeating the Klan politically and also those who had signed both of the petitions opposing the Anaheim Klan.

A much higher proportion of Anaheim Klansmen held professional and administrative jobs than did non-Klansmen, but twice as high a percentage of active anti-Klansmen—who included the city's established business, professional and farming elite—occupied such positions as Klan members. Klansmen worked in trade, service, and skilled positions in greater proportions than did either of the other groups.

Over half the Anaheim Klansmen with a specific church affiliation belonged to Disciples of Christ and Northern Methodist congregations. Catholic was the largest single church affiliation among those actively opposed to the Klan—over 25 percent.

Cocoltchos also collected statistics for Anaheim Klan leaders and the anti-Klan elite, which led activities in the city directed against the Klan. His data proved very informative for an understanding of the Klan's conflicts with the Anaheim business and professional elite.

The anti-Klan elite of three hundred individuals overlapped to a very large extent Anaheim's traditional elite. The median age of the elite in 1924 was fifty-four years compared to forty-two-and-a-half years for Klan leaders. The median years of prior residence in Anaheim was thirty-and-a-half years for the elite and fifteen years for Klan leaders in 1924. Ninety percent of elite members belonged to civic clubs, while 72 percent of Klan leaders did.

Forty-five percent of the elite occupied professional and administrative positions compared to 27 percent of the Klan leaders. Half of the latter worked in the retail and wholesale trades. The median wealth of Klan leaders amounted to $7,460 compared to $36,534 for members of the anti-Klan elite. Seventy-two percent of Klansmen had already run for or held public office in 1924 compared to 55 percent of the elite. The Klan leaders, despite their role as prosperous community activists, faced a near united front of Anaheim's wealthy, well-entrenched business, professional, and large farmer elite.

In the smaller city of Fullerton, California, Klansmen differed from the non-Klan population largely in their much larger proportion of members working in service and skilled jobs. Klan members owned more property and acknowledged much greater median wealth. A significantly higher proportion of them were married, belonged to civic clubs, and voted in 1924. Klansmen belonged predominantly to Disciples of Christ, Northern Methodist, Episcopalian, and Northern Baptist churches.

Half of the Ku Klux Klan's members in Colorado lived in the capital and largest city, Denver. A much higher percentage of Denver's Klansmen worked in both high and middle white-collar occupations than did members of the male population as a whole. However, Goldberg found that "Denver's elite clubs listed only a handful of Klansmen among their members," and none belonged to the most prestigious social clubs, such as the Denver Club, the Denver Country Club, and the University Club. Only one Klan member was listed in Denver's Social Register. A much lower proportion of Klansmen than male citizens of Denver worked in skilled, semi-skilled, and unskilled labor jobs. Goldberg was unable to collect information about individual church membership, but over 70 percent of Denver's Disciples of Christ churches, 33 percent of its Methodist churches, and 25 percent of its Baptist churches actively supported the Klan.

A Kleagle did not arrive in Canon City, Colorado (with a population of 4,551 in 1920) and surrounding rural Fremont County until 1923. Of the Klan's members between 1924 and 1928, 40 percent occupied high or middle white-collar positions. Only 1.5 percent worked at unskilled jobs. One-quarter of Canon City's Klansmen belonged to the Masons as well. Klan-member ministers guided the town's Methodist and Baptist churches and the fundamentalist Church of Christ congregation.

These statistics bear out Leonard Moore's conclusions about the meaning of the latest books and articles about the Klan:

> Together, these recent works make it nearly impossible to interpret the 1920's Klan as an aberrant fringe group. . . . In-depth analysis of state and community Klans from different regions of the country make it

> clear . . . that the Klan was composed primarily of average citizens representing nearly all parts of America's white Protestant society. . . .

Leonard Moore summarized what he called the Klan's "basic message":

> The average white Protestant was under attack: his values and traditions were being undermined; his vision of America's national purpose and social order appeared threatened; and his ability to shape the course of public affairs seemed to have been diminished.

Basing its political activity upon this message and the failure of state and local elites to address it satisfactorily, the Klan won a high degree of political power and influence in the states of Alabama, California, Colorado, Georgia, Indiana, Kansas, Louisiana, Oklahoma, Oregon, and Texas. It took political control of hundreds of American cities and towns, including Akron, Atlanta, Birmingham, Dallas, Denver, El Paso, Evansville, Gary, Indianapolis, Little Rock, Oklahoma City, Portland, Oregon, Terre Haute, and Youngstown.

However, the powerful business elite of Richmond, Indiana, thwarted the Klan's political efforts. Richmond's major employers were International Harvester and the Pennsylvania Railroad. The successful anti-Klan forces were led by members of the Rotary Club, limited to representatives of the city's industrial corporations, top executives of its other businesses, and its most successful retail merchants. The Rotary received aid from the Kiwanis Club, dominated by small businessmen and city officials.

Explaining the Klan's near-total triumph in Indiana, Moore concluded that the state and local elites "stood nearly alone as a white Protestant social group unwilling to support the Klan." That group, he declared, surpassed Indiana's Catholics, blacks, and Jews as the order's chief opponents. When Indiana's Klan chapters sought political power, Moore found "their most powerful rivals were . . . the Rotary Club and the Chamber of Commerce, not the powerless or nonexistent ethnic minorities." When the Klan swept the state election of 1924, "the real victims were not the state's Catholics but the Republican . . . political establishment, which, almost overnight, found itself removed from power."

In Indianapolis, businessmen organized in the Chamber of Commerce and the Indiana Taxpayers' Association formed an important component of the Old Guard Republican establishment. School issues symbolized the conflict between the Old Guard and the Klan. Voters, led by the Klan, approved a series of school bond issues, meant to renovate dilapidated schools and to alleviate overcrowding in the city's elementary and high schools. The Chamber of Commerce and the Taxpayers' Associations organized a Citizen's League to hide their own opposition to all spending for schools, except for a segregated high school to educate the city's black children. The school board refused to appropriate funds for any other construction. In the school-board election of 1925, the Klan elected all five of its candidates to replace the five Citizen's League incumbents. A school construction program started soon afterward. Aided by voter mobilization for the school-board election, the Klan won virtually every city political office in 1925.

In Lake County, where Crown Point served as county seat, Moore concluded: "Prohibition enforcement and public corruption had a . . . preponderant influence on Klan political victories." Exports of liquor by Chicago criminal organizations had left Lake County soaked in alcohol and full of corruption. In the November 1924 elections, every Lake County candidate endorsed by the Klan—including those in Crown Point—won election. . . .

Starting in the mid-1920s, the Ku Klux Klan ebbed in numbers and in influence. The three chief reasons for this decline were the inability of the order to achieve its promises, the demoralization of members because of scandals involving Klan leaders and spokesmen (whom members expected to appear and act more honestly than their opponents), and counter-attacks by the ethnic and religious groups and business elites which held political control of the nation's major cities.

After an initial burst of enthusiasm for the Klan, when it gained control of city, county, and state governments, inexperienced Klan elected officials found their programs rendered ineffective by professional politicians. Therefore voters—including Klan members—who had supported the Klan were disappointed by the order's accomplishments.

For example, in Indiana, where the Klan elected its candidate for governor and won large majorities in both houses of the legislature in 1925, Klansmen enacted only one of their proposals into law. That measure, obliging all public schools to teach their students about the United States Constitution, obtained bipartisan support.

Other bills introduced by Klan legislators—such as legislation mandating daily Bible reading in Indiana's schools, forcing parochial schools to use the same textbooks as public schools, and compelling public schools to hire only public-school graduates as teachers—failed to pass. Legislators, especially in the state senate, and the Klan governor killed such measures rather than face the controversy that such blatant attacks on religious liberty would cause. The near certainty of adverse judicial decisions increased the reluctance of these politicians (particularly those who hoped to seek national office) to risk their careers.

Indiana Grand Dragon David C. Stephenson's crimes damaged the Klan most. Stephenson collected over a million dollars from Klansmen between 1922 and 1924. Most of this was used to support a most un-Klansmanlike lifestyle. He bought luxurious automobiles, an imposing suburban home, and a yacht on which he entertained numerous women. He also purchased a large liquor supply. Several times, his drinking binges brought him close to arrest by police.

In April 1925, Stephenson took one of his female companions, twenty-eight-year-old Madge Oberholtzer of Indianapolis, on an overnight train ride to Hammond, Indiana. During this trip, Stephenson repeatedly raped Oberholtzer. When they arrived in Hammond, she bought and swallowed a deadly poison.

It took effect during the return trip to Indianapolis, but Stephenson refused to let the suffering woman see a physician until they reached Indianapolis. By then it was too late.

Before Oberholtzer died, she gave police a full statement. The State of Indiana charged Stephenson with causing her suicide because he had forced her to lose "that which she held dearer than life—her chastity." Stephenson was indicted and convicted of kidnapping, rape, and second-degree murder. He received a sentence of life imprisonment.

Stephenson confidently expected a pardon from Indiana's Governor Ed Jackson, a Klansman. When Jackson refused his request, Stephenson offered to testify about the corruption of Jackson and other state and local Klan officials. As a result, Mayor John Duvall of Indianapolis went to prison for violating the Corrupt Practices Act—so did the county sheriff, its congressman, the city purchasing agent, and a large number of less important Klan officeholders. Based on Stephenson's testimony, a grand jury indicted Governor Jackson for bribery, but he escaped prison because the statute of limitations on his offenses had expired. Soon after these revelations Klan membership in Indiana began shrinking. Fewer than seven thousand members remained by 1928.

Stephenson's trial, well publicized by newspapers and magazines, distressed Klansmen throughout America. Their outrage increased when they learned about the crimes of Dr. John Galen Locke, Colorado's Grand Dragon and Denver's Exalted Cyclops. In January 1925, Locke arranged the kidnapping of Klan member Keith Boehm, a high-school student. Taken to Locke's office and threatened with castration unless he married his pregnant girlfriend, Boehm agreed to the marriage. Locke explained to the Denver *Post* that "When I learned of what happened . . . I meant to see to it that young Boehm, as a Klansman, should do the manly thing." The district attorney brought kidnapping and conspiracy charges against Locke. Luckily for Locke, Klan opponent Judge Ben B. Lindsay of the juvenile court disqualified himself from the case. Locke's attorney engineered changes of venue until the case landed before a Klansman judge who found technical reasons to dismiss it.

Then federal Treasury officials charged Locke with failing to report any income or to pay income taxes despite the fees he earned as a physician and from Klan initiation fees and commissions on the sale of Klan robes. Locke went to prison until Colorado's governor, who had been chosen by the Grand Dragon, established a fund to pay Locke's back taxes. Other Klansmen paid Locke's fine. Mass defections from Colorado's Klan began. Imperial Wizard Hiram Evans requested Locke's resignation, and Locke immediately complied.

In Anaheim, the politically defeated Chamber of Commerce and Rotary Club collected sufficient signatures on petitions late in 1924 to force recently elected Klan city council members into a recall election. Minor scandals and a failure to appreciably diminish Prohibition violations already had cost the Klan some support. Anaheim's Klan leader, Reverend Mr. Meyers, sought to renew Klan members' enthusiasm by bringing Protestant evangelist E. E. Bulgin to the city in January 1925 to conduct revival meetings. Bulgin arrived on January 11, set up his tent, and began the services.

A group of Anaheim's ministers sent Bulgin and local newspapers a letter inquiring whether he had been brought to Anaheim "for the express purpose of assisting in the re-election of the members of the city council whose removal is being sought because of their Klan affiliations." Bulgin proclaimed his neutrality concerning the election. At the following evening's revival meeting, however, Bulgin told his assembled flock that "the way to vote right and never make a mistake is to find out what side the ex-saloonkeepers, the bootleggers and the harlots are on and get on the other side." Bulgin's nightly meetings attracted large and enthusiastic audiences.

Representatives of the Chamber of Commerce and of the Rotary and the Lion's clubs of Anaheim contacted the Knights of Columbus and the Catholic Truth Society in many parts of the West, asking for information about Bulgin. An Okmulgee, Oklahoma, attorney replied that Bulgin's real specialty was selling stock in fictitious or worthless mining companies. In return, he had taken deeds to some citizens' homes. Telegrams from Eastland, Texas, and Lewiston, Idaho, stated that Bulgin had been chased out of those cities after being charged with fraud in numerous lawsuits. Two of Anaheim's newspapers printed these replies.

On February 3, 1925, almost 77 percent of Anaheim's voters—a larger proportion than the record turnout less than six months before that had elected the Klan councilmen—went to the polls. Every Klan-endorsed council member was recalled by a substantial margin.

The Ku Klux Klan paid dearly for its obvious role in reinvigorating Victorian racism and religious bigotry. Kenneth Jackson pointed out that "Relatively few reports of Klan-related violence between 1915 and 1924 are contained in the files of United States Department of Justice." However, in September 1923, the *Literary Digest,* a Klan opponent, published an article entitled "The Klan as a Victim of Mob Violence." The Indiana state *Fiery Cross* complained in 1924 that "The list of the outrages against Klansmen is so long that it would take weeks to compile even an incomplete list."

In dozens of cities—such as Fort Worth; San Antonio; Terre Haute; and Portland, Maine—Klan headquarters and meeting places were bombed and burned. After numerous warnings, the shop believed to be the publication headquarters of the Chicago Klan's journal, *Dawn,* was gutted by a bomb. An editorial in the *Fiery Cross* asked plaintively: Why does not anyone "ever read about halls of the Knights of Columbus being destroyed mysteriously?"

Catholics and blacks had threatened the Klan with violence. The editor of the *Catholic World,* published by the Paulist Fathers, warned early in 1923 that because of the Klan, Catholics "may be driven to self-defense, even to the extent of bloodshed." The equally staid *Bulletin* of the National Catholic Welfare Council declared:

> In this struggle for the supremacy of law and order over lawlessness and despotism, no quarter should be given those self-appointed patriots who distort and disgrace our Americanism and whose weapons are darkness, the mask, violence, intimidation and mob rule.

The Harlem-based radical black nationalist African Black Brotherhood proclaimed in its journal that "The nation-wide mobilization under the Christian cross and the Stars and Stripes of cracker America is plainly an act of war . . . , war of the cracker element of the white race against the whole Negro race." The Chicago *Defender,* the most widely read black newspaper in the United States, urged its readers in a front-page editorial to prepare to fight "against sons who now try to win by signs and robes what their fathers lost by fire and sword."

When the Klan began organizing in and around the nation's largest cities, members of the order soon discovered that white Protestant authority no longer prevailed throughout the land. In these cities Catholics, blacks, Jews, and recent immigrants formed a majority of the population—sometimes a very large majority.

Soon after Kleagles ventured into New York City, Irish Catholic Mayor John F. Hylan told his police commissioner in 1922: "I desire you to treat this group of racial and religious haters as you would the Reds and bomb throwers. Drive them out of our city." Two New York City grand juries commenced investigations of the Klan, and the New York City Council quickly passed legislation forcing associations not incorporated in New York to file membership lists. Klan members in New York and suburban Westchester County during the 1920s totalled about 16,000, less than Klan membership in Akron or Youngstown, Ohio.

Chicago's large Klan chapter did nothing to help enforce Prohibition laws. However, the West Suburban Ministers and Citizens Association organized to help enforce those laws in and around Chicago. Soon afterward, the association's leader, a minister, was found shot to death a block from Al Capone's headquarters in suburban Cicero. This warning ended private attempts to fight Prohibition offenses in Chicago.

The Chicago City Council appointed a five-man committee in December 1922 to investigate the Klan and then report back to the council. The five members were identified as Ald. Robert J. Mulcahy, Irish; Ald. Louis B. Henderson, black; Ald. U. S. Schwartz, Jewish; Ald. S. S. Walkowiak, Polish; and Ald. Oscar H. Olsen, Norwegian. Largely as a result of the committee's unanimous report, the city council resolved by a vote of fifty-six to two to rid Chicago's municipal payroll of Klansmen. The Illinois legislature also received the report and consequently passed a bill prohibiting the wearing of masks in public. The measure cleared the Illinois House of Representatives by a vote of 100 to 2, and the Illinois State Senate by 26 to 1. Illinois's Klansmen were thus forced to hold most of their parades, picnics, and other gatherings in Indiana and Ohio.

Boston's Mayor James Michael Curley barred Klan meetings in Boston, and the city council approved his order. He gave speeches before burning crosses and in an emotion-choked voice always proclaimed: "There it burns, the cross of hatred upon which Our Lord, Jesus Christ, was crucified—the cross of human avarice, and not the cross of love and charity. . . ." Homes and stores of suspected Klansmen in Boston were bombarded with bricks and stones.

On the outskirts of major cities, where the Klan sometimes dared to march or meet, the Knights received even worse treatment. Ten thousand Klansmen gathered near Carnegie, just outside Pittsburgh, on August 25, 1923, to witness an initiation featuring an address by Imperial Wizard Hiram Evans. When they tried to march back to the heavily Catholic, immigrant, and black town, however, a mob stood in their path. The Klansmen continued marching through a hail of rocks and bottles. Then a volley of shots rang out. One Klansman lay dead, a dozen others fell seriously wounded, and about a hundred more suffered minor injuries. The other Klan members turned and ran.

Commenting on the Carnegie massacre, the Washington *Star* declared that "Parades of the Klan, with its masked and hooded members, tend to create disorder and rioting." An editorial in the Washington *Post* stated that the paper agreed with the *New York Times* that "The Klan is merely reaping as it has sown."

Other Klan meetings were broken up by lethal shotgun blasts. In New York's suburban county of Queens, police ended a Memorial Day parade of 4,000 Klansmen by waving waiting cars through the whole parade line.

Hiram Evans summarized the Klan's plight when he stated in March 1926 that "The Nordic American today is a stranger in large parts of the land his fathers gave him. Moreover, he is a most unwelcome stranger, and one most spat upon."

Evans described accurately the result of the Klan's defense as Victorianism's essence. The most important social trends and the great social reform movements of the nineteenth and twentieth centuries had indeed left Klansmen strangers in most of the land their ancestors had settled.

POSTSCRIPT

Was the Ku Klux Klan of the 1920s an Extremist Movement?

Bennett places the 1920s Ku Klux Klan within the nativist tradition of American right-wing political movements. He argues that Klan ideology reasserted its hostility toward the Catholic and Jewish immigrants from southern and eastern Europe who had poured into America since the 1890s. He points out that Irish Catholics were associated with the saloons and the political bosses who controlled the machines in the large cities. In Bennett's view, the Klan was made up of Protestant fundamentalists who wished to reassert the traditional values of an earlier America.

Coben argues that many Klansmen were attracted to the Klan because they were legitimately concerned with the breakdown of traditional standards of morality and the increases in alcohol consumption and crime that they believed were occurring in their communities. Coben also argues that Klansmen were more often middle-class businessmen, small shopkeepers, and skilled workers who were fighting the well-to-do businessmen, the large farmers, and their allied Catholic, Jewish, and black ethnic groups for political control.

Recent scholarship on the 1920s Klan has focused on its grass-roots participation in local and state politics. Klansmen are viewed less as extremists and more as political pressure groups whose aims were to gain control of various local and state government offices. The best overview of this perspective is Shawn Lay, ed., *The Invisible Empire in the West: Toward a New Historical Appraisal of the Ku Klux Klan of the 1920s* (University of Illinois Press, 1992).

Indiana was at the heart of the second Klan and is the focus of much recent research. A good starting point is William E. Wilson's "That Long Hot Summer in Indiana," *American Heritage* (August 1965). M. William Lutholtz gives a well-researched but old-fashioned interpretative journalistic study of Indiana's amoral, opportunistic grand dragon in *Grand Dragon: D. C. Stephenson and the Ku Klux Klan in Indiana, 1921–1928* (University of North Carolina Press, 1991), while Leonard J. Moore, in *Citizen Klansmen: The Ku Klux Klan in Indiana, 1921–1928* (University of North Carolina Press, 1991), sees the Indiana group as concerned, middle-class citizens who challenged the local elites to clean up the political and immoral corruption in the state in order to reinforce traditional family values. Nancy MacLean, in *Behind the Mask of Chivalry: The Making of the Second Ku Klux Klan* (Oxford University Press, 1994), argues that the second Klan's lower middle class subverted traditional Republican values into a "reactionary populism" that bore a "family resemblance" to the movement Adolf Hitler rode to power in the 1930s.

ISSUE 6

Did the New Deal Prolong the Great Depression?

YES: Gary Dean Best, from *Pride, Prejudice, and Politics: Roosevelt Versus Recovery, 1933–1938* (Praeger, 1990)

NO: Roger Biles, from *A New Deal for the American People* (Northern Illinois University Press, 1991)

ISSUE SUMMARY

YES: Professor of history Gary Dean Best argues that Roosevelt established an antibusiness environment with the creation of the New Deal regulatory programs, which retarded the nation's economic recovery from the Great Depression until World War II.

NO: Professor of history Roger Biles contends that, in spite of its minimal reforms and non-revolutionary programs, the New Deal created a limited welfare state that implemented economic stabilizers to avert another depression.

The catastrophe triggered by the 1929 Wall Street debacle crippled the American economy, deflated the optimistic future most Americans assumed to be their birthright, and ripped apart the values by which the country's businesses, farms, and governments were run. During the next decade, the inertia of the Great Depression stifled their attempts to make ends meet.

The world depression of the 1930s began in the United States. The United States had suffered periodic economic setbacks—in 1873, 1893, 1907, and 1920—but those slumps had been limited and temporary. The omnipotence of American productivity, the ebullient American spirit, and the self-deluding thought "it can't happen here" blocked out any consideration of an economic collapse that might devastate the capitalist economy and threaten U.S. democratic government.

All aspects of American society trembled from successive jolts; there were 4 million unemployed people in 1930 and 9 million more by 1932. Those who had not lost their jobs took pay cuts or worked for scrip. There was no security for those whose savings were lost forever when banks failed or stocks declined.

Manufacturing halted, industry shut down, and farmers destroyed wheat, corn, and milk rather than sell them at a loss. Worse, there were millions of homeless Americans—refugees from the cities roaming the nation on freight trains, victims of the drought or the Dust Bowl seeking a new life farther west, and hobo children estranged from their parents.

Business and government leaders alike seemed immobilized by the economic giant that had fallen to its knees. Herbert Hoover, the incumbent president at the start of the Great Depression, attempted some relief programs. However, they were ineffective considering the magnitude of the unemployment, hunger, and distress.

As governor of New York, Franklin D. Roosevelt (who was elected president in 1932) had introduced some relief measures, such as industrial welfare and a comprehensive system of unemployment remedies, to alleviate the social and economic problems facing the citizens of the state. Yet his campaign did little to reassure his critics that he was more than a "Little Lord Fauntleroy" rich boy who wanted to be the president. In light of later developments, Roosevelt may have been the only presidential candidate to deliver more programs than he actually promised.

The first "hundred days" of the New Deal attempted to jump-start the economy with dozens of recovery and relief measures. On inauguration day, FDR told the nation "the only thing we have to fear is fear itself." A bank holiday was immediately declared. Congress passed the Emergency Banking Act, which pumped Federal Reserve notes into the major banks and stopped the wave of bank failures. Later banking acts separated commercial and investment institutions, and the Federal Deposit Insurance Corporation (FDIC) guaranteed people's savings from a loss of up to $2,500 in member banks. A number of relief agencies were set up that provided work for youth and able-bodied men on various state and local building projects. Finally the Tennessee Valley Administration (TVA) was created to provide electricity in rural areas not serviced by private power companies.

In 1935 the Supreme Court ended the First New Deal by declaring both the Agriculture Adjustment Administration and National Recovery Act unconstitutional. In response to critics on the left who felt that the New Deal was favoring the large banks, big agriculture, and big business, FDR shifted his approach in 1935. The Second New Deal created the Works Project Administration (WPA), which became the nation's largest employer in its eight years of operation. Social Security was passed, and the government guaranteed monthly stipends for the aged, the unemployed, and dependent children. Labor pressured the administration for a collective bargaining bill. The Wagner Act established a National Labor Relations Board to supervise industry-wide elections. The steel, coal, automobile and some garment industries were unionized as membership tripled from 3 million in 1933 to 9 million in 1939.

With the immediate crisis over, entrenched conservatives in Congress blocking new legislation and World War II looming, the New Deal ended by 1938. In the first selection, historian Gary Dean Best argues that with its swollen government agencies, promotion of cartels, confiscatory taxes, and dubious antitrust lawsuits, the New Deal prolonged the depression. But historian Roger Biles contends that, in spite of its minimal reform programs, the New Deal created a limited welfare state that implemented economic stabilizers to avert another depression.

YES

Gary Dean Best

Pride, Prejudice and Politics: Roosevelt Versus Recovery, 1933–1938

This book had its genesis in the fact that I have for a long time felt uncomfortable with the standard works written about Franklin Delano Roosevelt and the New Deal, and with the influence those works have exerted on others writing about and teaching U.S. history. Although I approach the subject from a very different perspective, Paul K. Conkin's preface to the second edition of *The New Deal* (1975) expressed many of my own misgivings about writings on the subject. Conkin wrote that "pervading even the most scholarly revelations was a monotonous, often almost reflexive, and in my estimation a very smug or superficial valuative perspective—approval, even glowing approval, of most enduring New Deal policies, or at least of the underlying goals that a sympathetic observer could always find behind policies and programs."

Studies of the New Deal such as Conkin described seemed to me to be examples of a genre relatively rare in U.S. historiography—that of "court histories." . . .

But, like most historians teaching courses dealing with the Roosevelt period, I was captive to the published works unless I was willing and able to devote the time to pursue extensive research in the period myself. After some years that became possible, and this book is the result.

My principal problem with Roosevelt and the New Deal was not over his specific reforms or his social programs, but with the failure of the United States to recover from the depression during the eight peacetime years that he and his policies governed the nation. I consider that failure tragic, not only for the 14.6 percent of the labor force that remained unemployed as late as 1940, and for the millions of others who subsisted on government welfare because of the prolonged depression, but also because of the image that the depression-plagued United States projected to the world at a crucial time in international affairs. In the late 1930s and early 1940s, when U.S. economic strength might have given pause to potential aggressors in the world, our economic weakness furnished encouragement to them instead.

From the standpoint, then, not only of our domestic history, but also of the tragic events and results of World War II, it has seemed to me that Roosevelt's failure to generate economic recovery during this critical period deserved more attention than historians have given it.

Most historians of the New Deal period leave the impression that the failure of the United States to recover during those eight years resulted from Roosevelt's unwillingness to embrace Keynesian spending. According to this thesis, recovery came during World War II because the war at last forced Roosevelt to spend at the level required all along for recovery. This, however, seemed to me more an advocacy of Keynes' theories by the historians involved that an explanation for the U.S. failure to recover during those years. Great Britain, for example, managed to recover by the late 1930s without recourse to deficit spending. By that time the United States was, by contrast, near the bottom of the list of industrial nations as measured in progress toward recovery, with most others having reached the predepression levels and many having exceeded them. The recovered countries represented a variety of economic systems, from state ownership to private enterprise. The common denominator in their success was not a reliance on deficit spending, but rather the stimulus they furnished to industrial enterprise.

What went wrong in the United States? Simplistic answers such as the reference to Keynesianism seemed to me only a means of avoiding a real answer to the question. A wise president, entering the White House in the midst of a crippling depression, should do everything possible to stimulate enterprise. In a free economy, economic recovery means *business* recovery. It follows, therefore, that a wise chief executive should do everything possible to create the conditions and psychology most conducive to business recovery—to encourage business to expand production, and lenders and investors to furnish the financing and capital that are required. An administration seeking economic recovery will do as little as possible that might inhibit recovery, will weigh all its actions with the necessity for economic recovery in mind, and will consult with competent business and financial leaders, as well as economists, to determine the best policies to follow. Such a president will seek to promote cooperation between the federal government and business, rather than conflict, and will seek to introduce as much consistency and stability as possible into government economic policies so that businessmen and investors can plan ahead. While obviously the destitute must be cared for, ultimately the most humane contribution a liberal government can make to the victims of a depression is the restoration of prosperity and the reemployment of the idle in genuine jobs.

In measuring the Roosevelt policies and programs during the New Deal years against such standards, I was struck by the air of unreality that hung over Washington in general and the White House in particular during this period. Business and financial leaders who questioned the wisdom of New Deal policies were disregarded and deprecated because of their "greed" and "self-interest," while economists and business academicians who persisted in calling attention to the collision between New Deal policies and simple economic realities were dismissed for their "orthodoxy." As one "orthodox" economist pointed out early in the New Deal years,

> economic realism . . . insists that policies aiming to promote recovery will, in fact, ratard recovery if and where they fail to take into account correctly of stubborn facts in the existing economic situation and of the arithmetic

> of business as it must be carried out in the economic situation we are trying to revive. The antithesis of this economic realism is the vaguely hopeful or optimistic idealism in the field of economic policy, as such, which feels that good intentions, enough cleverness, and the right appeal to the emotions of the people ought to insure good results in spite of inconvenient facts.

Those "inconvenient facts" dogged the New Deal throughout these years, only to be stubbornly resisted by a president whose pride, prejudices, and politics would rarely permit an accommodation with them.

Most studies of the New Deal years approach the period largely from the perspective of the New Dealers themselves. Critics and opponents of Roosevelt's policies and programs are given scant attention in such works except to point up the "reactionary" and "unenlightened" opposition with which Roosevelt was forced to contend in seeking to provide Americans with "a more abundant life." The few studies that have concentrated on critics and opponents of the New Deal in the business community have been by unsympathetic historians who have tended to distort the opposition to fit the caricature drawn by the New Dealers, so that they offer little to explain the impact of Roosevelt's policies in delaying recovery from the depression.

The issue of *why* businessmen and bankers were so critical of the New Deal has been for too long swept under the rug, together with the question of *how* Roosevelt and his advisers could possibly expect to produce an economic recovery while a state of war existed between his administration and the employers and investors who, alone, could produce such a recovery. Even a Keynesian response to economic depression is ultimately dependent on the positive reactions of businessmen and investors for its success, as Keynes well knew, and those reactions were not likely to be as widespread as necessary under such a state of warfare between government and business. Businessmen, bankers, and investors may have been "greedy" and "self-interested." They may have been guilty of wrong perceptions and unfounded fears. But they are also the ones, in a free economy, upon whose decisions and actions economic recovery must depend. To understand their opposition to the New Deal requires an immersion in the public and private comments of critics of Roosevelt's policies. The degree and nature of business, banking, and investor concern about the direction and consequences of New Deal policies can be gleaned from the hundreds of banking and business periodicals representative of every branch of U.S. business and finance in the 1930s, and from the letters and diaries of the New Deal's business and other critics during the decade.

Statistics are useful in understanding the history of any period, but particularly periods of economic growth or depression. Statistics for the Roosevelt years may easily be found in *Historical Statistics of the United States* published by the Bureau of the Census, U.S. Department of Commerce (1975). Some of the trauma of the depression years may be inferred from the fact that the population of the United States grew by over 17 million between 1920 and 1930, but by only about half of that (8.9 million) between 1930 and 1940.

Historical Statistics gives the figures . . . for unemployment, 1929–1940. These figures are, however, only estimates. The federal government did not monitor the number of unemployed during those years. Even so, these figures are shocking, indicating as they do that even after the war had begun in Europe, with the increased orders that it provided for U.S. mines, factories, and farms, unemployment remained at 14.6 percent.

One characteristic of the depression, to which attention was frequently called during the Roosevelt years, was the contrast between its effects on the durable goods and consumer goods industries. Between 1929 and 1933, expenditures on personal durable goods dropped by nearly 50 percent, and in 1938 they were still nearly 25 percent below the 1929 figures. Producers' durable goods suffered even more, failing by nearly two-thirds between 1929 and 1933, and remaining more than 50 percent below the 1929 figure in 1938. At the same time, expenditures on nondurable, or consumer, goods showed much less effect. Between 1929 and 1933 they fell only about 14.5 percent, and by 1938 they exceeded the 1929 level. These figures indicate that the worst effects of the depression, and resultant unemployment, were being felt in the durable goods industries. Roosevelt's policies, however, served mainly to stimulate the consumer goods industries where the depression and unemployment were far less seriously felt.

One consequence of Roosevelt's policies can be seen in the U.S. balance of trade during the New Deal years. By a variety of devices, Roosevelt drove up the prices of U.S. industrial and agricultural products, making it difficult for these goods to compete in the world market, and opening U.S. markets to cheaper foreign products. . . . With the exception of a $41 million deficit in 1888, these were the only deficits in U.S. trade for a century, from the 1870s to the 1970s.

. . . [W]hile suicides during the Roosevelt years remained about the same as during the Hoover years, the death rate by "accidental falls" increased significantly. In fact, according to *Historical Statistics,* the death rate by "accidental falls" was higher in the period 1934–1938 than at any other time between 1910 and 1970 (the years for which figures are given).

Interestingly, the number of persons arrested grew steadily during the depression years. In 1938 nearly twice as many (554,000) were arrested as in 1932 (278,000), and the number continued to increase until 1941. And, while the number of telephones declined after 1930 and did not regain the 1930 level until 1939, the number of households with radios increased steadily during the depression years. And Americans continued to travel. Even in the lowest year, 1933, 300,000 Americans visited foreign countries (down from 517,000 in 1929), while the number visiting national parks, monuments, and such, steadily increased during the depression—in 1938 nearly five times as many (16,331,000) did so as in 1929 (3,248,000).

Comparisons of the recovery of the United States with that of other nations may be found in the volumes of the League of Nations' *World Economic Survey* for the depression years. [A] table (from the volume of 1938/39) shows comparisons of unemployment rates. From this it can be seen that in 1929 the United States had the lowest unemployment rate of the countries listed; by 1932 the United States was midway on the list, with seven nations reporting higher unemployment rates and seven reporting lower unemployment. By mid-1938, however, after over five years of the New Deal, only three nations had higher unemployment rates, while twelve had lower unemployment. The United States, then, had lost ground in comparison with the other nations between 1932 and 1938.

The *World Economic Survey* for 1937/38 compared the levels of industrial production for 23 nations in 1937, expressed as a percentage of their industrial production in 1929. . . . It must be remembered that the figures for the United States reflect the level of industrial production reached just before the collapse of the economy later that year. Of the 22 other nations listed, 19 showed a higher rate of recovery in industrial production that the United States, while only 3 lagged behind. One of these, France, had followed policies similar to those of the New Deal in the United States. As the *World Economic Survey* put it, both the Roosevelt administration and the Blum government in France had "adopted far-reaching social and economic policies which combined recovery measures with measures of social reform." It added: "The consequent doubt regarding the prospects of profit and the uneasy relations between businessmen and the Government have in the opinion of many, been an important factor in delaying recovery," and the two countries had, "unlike the United Kingdom and Germany," failed to "regain the 1929 level of employment and production." The *World Economic Survey* the following year (1939) pointed out that industrial production in the United States had fallen from the 92.2 to 65 by June 1938, and hovered between 77 and 85 throughout 1939. Thus, by the end of 1938 the U.S. record was even sorrier than revealed by the [data].

Every survey of American historians consistently finds Franklin Delano Roosevelt ranked as one of this nation's greatest presidents. Certainly, exposure to even a sampling of the literature on Roosevelt and the New Deal can lead one to no other conclusion. Conventional wisdom has it that Roosevelt was an opportune choice to lead the United States through the midst of the Great Depression, that his cheerful and buoyant disposition uplifted the American spirit in the midst of despair and perhaps even forestalled a radical change in the direction of American politics toward the right or the left. Roosevelt's landslide reelection victory in 1936, and the congressional successes in 1934, are cited as evidence of the popularity of both the president and the New Deal among the American people. Polls by both Gallup and the Democratic National Committee early in the 1936 campaign, however, give a very different picture, and suggest that the electoral victories can be as accurately accounted for in terms of the vast outpourings of federal money in 1934 and 1936, and the inability or unwillingness of Landon to offer a genuine alternative to the New Deal in the latter year. To this must be added the fact that after early 1936 two of the most unpopular New Deal programs—the NRA and the AAA—had been removed as issues by the Supreme Court.

Conventional wisdom, in fact, suffers many setbacks when the Roosevelt years are examined from any other perspective than through a pro–New Deal

Prism—from the banking crisis of 1933 and the first inaugural address, through the reasons for the renewed downturn in 1937, to the end of the New Deal in 1937–1938. The American present has been ill-served by the inaccurate picture that has too often been presented of this chapter in the American past by biographers and historians. Roosevelt's achievements in alleviating the hardship of the depression are deservedly well known, his responsibility for prolonging the hardship is not. His role in providing long-overdue and sorely needed social and economic legislation is in every high school American history textbook, but the costs for the United States of his eight-year-long war against business recovery are mentioned in none.

Such textbooks (and those in college, too) frequently contain a chapter on the Great Depression, followed by one on the New Deal, the implication being that somewhere early in the second of the chapters the depression was ended by Roosevelt's policies. Only careful reading reveals that despite Roosevelt's immense labors to feed the unemployed, only modest recovery from the lowest depths of the depression was attained before the outbreak of World War II. Roosevelt, readers are told, was too old-fashioned, too conservative, to embrace the massive compensatory spending and unbalanced budgets that might have produced a Keynesian recovery sooner. But World War II, the books tell us, made such spending necessary and the recovery that might have occurred earlier was at last achieved.

Generations of Americans have been brought up on this version of the New Deal years. Other presidential administrations have been reevaluated over the years, and have risen or fallen in grace as a result, but not the Roosevelt administration. The conventional wisdom concerning the Roosevelt administration remains the product of the "court historians," assessments of the New Deal period that could not have been better written by the New Dealers themselves. The facts, however, are considerably at variance with this conventional wisdom concerning the course of the depression, the reasons for the delay of recovery, and the causes of the recovery when it came, finally, during World War II.

From the uncertainty among businessmen and investors about the new president-elect that aborted a promising upturn in the fall of 1932, to the panic over the prospect of inflationary policies that was a major factor in the banking crisis that virtually paralyzed the nation's economy by the date of his inauguration, Roosevelt's entry into the White House was not an auspicious beginning toward recovery. The prejudices that were to guide the policies and programs of the New Deal for the next six years were revealed in Roosevelt's inaugural address, although the message was largely overlooked until it had become more apparent in the actions of the administration later. It was an attitude of hostility toward business and finance, of contempt for the profit motive of capitalism, and of willingness to foment class antagonism for political benefit. This was not an attitude that was conducive to business recovery, and the programs and policies that would flow from those prejudices would prove, in fact, to be destructive of the possibility of recovery.

There followed the "hundred days," when Roosevelt rammed through Congress a variety of legislation that only depressed business confidence more. The new laws were served up on attractive platters, with tempting descriptions—truth in securities, aid for the farmer, industrial self-regulation—but when the covers were removed the contents were neither attractive nor did they match the labels. By broad grants of power to the executive branch of the government, the legislation passed regulation of the U.S. economy into the hands of New Dealers whose aim was not to promote recovery but to carry out their own agendas for radical change of the economic system even at the expense of delaying recovery. Thus, truth in securities turned to paralysis of the securities markets, aid for the farmer became a war against profits by processors of agricultural goods, and industrial self-regulation became government control and labor-management strife. International economic cooperation as a device for ending the depression was abandoned for an isolationist approach, and throughout 1933 the threat of inflation added further uncertainty for businessmen and investors.

The grant of such unprecedented peacetime authority to an American president aroused concern, but these after all were only "emergency" powers, to be given up once recovery was on its way. Or were they? Gradually the evidence accumulated that the Tugwells and the Brandeisians intended to institutionalize the "emergency" powers as permanent features of American economic life. By the end of 1933, opposition to the New Deal was already sizable. Business alternated between the paralysis of uncertainty and a modest "recovery" born of purchases and production inspired by fear of higher costs owing to inflation and the effects of the AAA and NRA. The implementation of the latter two agencies in the fall of 1933 brought a renewed downturn that improved only slightly during the winter and spring. A renewed legislative onslaught by the New Deal in the 1934 congress, combined with labor strife encouraged by the provisions of the NIRA, brought a new collapse of the economy in the fall of 1934, which lowered economic indices once again to near the lowest levels they had reached in the depression.

The pattern had been established. The war against business and finance was under way, and there would be neither retreat nor cessation. Roosevelt's pride and prejudices, and the perceived political advantages to be gained from the war, dictated that his administration must ever be on the offensive and never in retreat. But the administration suffered defeats, nevertheless, and embarrassment. The Supreme Court proved a formidable foe, striking down both the NRA and the AAA. Dire predictions from the administration about the implications for the economy of the loss of the NRA proved embarrassing when the economy began to show gradual improvement after its departure. But defeat did not mean retreat. Under the goading of Felix Frankfurter and his disciples, Roosevelt became even more extreme in his verbal and legislative assault against business. Their attempts to cooperate with the Roosevelt administration having been spurned, businessmen and bankers awakened to the existence of the war being waged upon them and moved into opposition. Roosevelt gloried in their opposition and escalated the war against them in the 1936 reelection campaign.

Reelected in 1936 on a tidal wave of government spending, and against a lackluster Republican campaigner who offered no alternative to the New Deal, Roosevelt appeared at the apogee of his power and prestige. His triumph was, however, to be short-lived, despite an enhanced Democratic majority in Congress. A combination of factors was about to bring the New Deal war against business to a stalemate and eventual retreat. One of these was his ill-advised attempt to pack the Supreme Court with subservient justices, which aroused so much opposition even in his own party that he lost control of the Democrat-controlled Congress. More important, perhaps, was the growing economic crisis that the Roosevelt administration faced in 1937, largely as a result of its own past policies. The massive spending of 1936, including the payment of the veterans' bonus, had generated a speculative recovery during that year from concern about inflationary consequences. Fears of a "boom" were increased as a result of the millions of dollars in dividends, bonuses, and pay raises dispensed by businesses late in 1936 as a result of the undistributed profits tax. The pay raises, especially, were passed on in the form of higher prices, as were the social security taxes that were imposed on businesses beginning with 1937. Labor disturbances, encouraged by the Wagner Labor Act and the Roosevelt alliance with John L. Lewis' Congress of Industrial Organizations in the 1936 campaign, added further to the wage-price spiral that threatened as 1937 unfolded. Massive liquidations of low-interest government bonds, and sagging prices of the bonds, fueled concern among bankers and economists, and within the Treasury, that a "boom" would imperil the credit of the federal government and the solvency of the nation's banks whose portfolios consisted mainly of low-interest government bonds.

In considering the two principal options for cooling the "boom"—raising interest rates or cutting federal spending—the Roosevelt administration chose to move toward a balanced budget. It was a cruel dilemma that the New Dealers faced. All knew that the economy had not yet recovered from the depression, yet they were faced with the necessity to apply brakes to an economy that was becoming overheated as a consequence of their policies. Moreover, the reduction in consumer purchasing power caused by the cuts in federal spending was occurring at the same time that purchasing power was already being eroded as a result of the higher prices that worried the administration. Private industry, it should have been obvious, could not "take up the slack," since the Roosevelt administration had done nothing to prepare for the transition from government to private spending that John Maynard Keynes and others had warned them was necessary. The New Dealers had been far too busy waging war against business to allow it the opportunity to prepare for any such transition.

In fact, far from confronting the emergency of 1937 by making long-overdue attempts to cooperate with business in generating recovery, Roosevelt was busy pressing a new legislative assault against them. Denied passage of his legislative package by Congress during its regular 1937 session, Roosevelt called a special session for November despite evidence that the economy had begun a new downturn. Even the collapse of the stock market, within days after his announcement of the special session, and the growing unemployment that soon followed, did not deter Roosevelt from his determination to drive the legislative assault through it. With the nation in the grips of a full-blown economic collapse, Roosevelt offered nothing to the special session but the package of antibusiness legislation it had turned down in the regular session. Once again he was rebuffed by Congress. The nation drifted, its economic indices falling, with its president unwilling to admit the severity of the situation or unable to come to grips with what it said about the bankruptcy of the New Deal policies and programs.

By early 1938, Roosevelt was faced with problems similar to those he had faced when he first entered the White House five years earlier, but without the political capital he had possessed earlier. In 1933 the Hoover administration could be blamed for the depression. In 1938 the American people blamed the Roosevelt administration for retarding recovery. Five years of failure could not be brushed aside. Five years of warfare against business and disregard of criticism and offers of cooperation had converted supporters of 1933 into cynics or opponents by 1938. Even now, however, pride, prejudice, and politics dominated Roosevelt, making it impossible for him to extend the needed olive branch to business. The best that he could offer in 1938 was a renewal of federal spending and more of the same New Deal that had brought the nation renewed misery. In the 1938 congressional session he continued to press for passage of the antibusiness legislation that had been rejected by both sessions of 1937.

But Congress was no longer the pliant body it had been in 1933, and in the 1938 congressional elections the people's reaction was registered when the Republicans gained 81 new seats in the House and 8 in the Senate—far more than even the most optimistic Republican had predicted. If the message was lost on Roosevelt, it was obvious to some in his administration, notably his new Secretary of Commerce Harry Hopkins and his Secretary of the Treasury Henry Morgenthau. Two of the earliest business-baiters in the circle of Roosevelt advisers, they now recognized the bankruptcy of that course and the necessity for the administration to at last strive for recovery by removing the obstacles to normal and profitable business operation that the New Deal had erected. This was not what Roosevelt wanted to hear, nor was it what his Frankfurter disciples wanted him to hear. These latter knew, as Hopkins and Morgenthau had learned earlier, just which Rooseveltian buttons could be pushed to trigger his antibusiness prejudices and spite. A battle raged within the New Deal between the Frankfurter radicals and the "new conservatives," Hopkins and Morgenthau, amid growing public suspicion that the former were not interested in economic recovery.

It was not a fair battle. Hopkins and Morgenthau knew how to play the game, including use of the press, and had too many allies. They did not hesitate to talk bluntly to Roosevelt, perhaps the bluntest talk he had heard since the death of Louis McHenry Howe. Moreover, Roosevelt could afford the loss of a Corcoran and/or a Cohen, against whom there was already a great deal of congressional opposition, but a break with both Hopkins and Morgenthau would have been devastating for an administration already on the defensive. Gradually the Frankfurter radicals moved into eclipse, along with their policies, to be replaced increasingly by recovery and preparedness advocates, including many from the business and financial world.

Conventional wisdom has it that the massive government spending of World War II finally brought a Keynesian recovery from the depression. Of more significance, in comparisons of the prewar and wartime economic policies of the Roosevelt administration, is the fact that the war against business that characterized the former was abandoned in the latter. Both the attitude and policies of the Roosevelt administration toward business during the New Deal years were reversed when the president found new, foreign enemies to engage his attention and energies. Antibusiness advisers were replaced by businessmen, pro-labor policies became pro-business policies, cooperation replaced confrontation in relations between the federal government and business, and even the increased spending of the war years "trickled down" rather than "bubbling up." Probably no American president since, perhaps, Thomas Jefferson ever so thoroughly repudiated the early policies of his administration as Roosevelt did between 1939 and 1942. This, and not the emphasis on spending alone, is the lesson that needs to be learned from Roosevelt's experience with the depression, and of the legacy of the New Deal economic policies.

The judgment of historians concerning Roosevelt's presidential stature is curiously at odds with that of contemporary observers. One wonders how scholars of the Roosevelt presidency are able so blithely to ignore the negative assessments of journalists, for example, of the stature of Raymond Clapper, Walter Lippmann, Dorothy Thompson, and Arthur Krock, to name only a few. Can their observations concerning Roosevelt's pettiness and spitefulness, their criticism of the obstacles to recovery created by his anticapitalist bias, and their genuine concern over his apparent grasp for dictatorial power be dismissed so cavalierly? Is there any other example in U.S. history of an incumbent president running for reelection against the open opposition of the two previous nominees of his own party? Will a public opinion poll ever again find 45 percent of its respondents foreseeing the likelihood of dictatorship arising from a president's policies? Will a future president ever act in such a fashion that the question will again even suggest itself to a pollster? One certainly hopes not.

Perhaps the positive assessment of Roosevelt by American historians rests upon a perceived liberalism of his administration. If so, one must wonder at their definition of liberalism. Surely a president who would pit class against class for political purposes, who was fundamentally hostile to the very basis of a free economy, who believed that his ends could justify very illiberal means, who was intolerant of criticism and critics, and who grasped for dictatorial power does not merit description as a liberal. Nor are the results of the Gallup poll mentioned above consistent with the actions of a liberal president. If the perception is based on Roosevelt's support for the less fortunate "one-third" of the nation, and his program of social legislation, then historians need to be reminded that such actions do not, in themselves, add up to liberalism, they having been used by an assortment of political realists and demagogues—of the left and the right—to gain and hold power.

There were certainly positive contributions under the New Deal, but they may not have outweighed the negative aspects of the period. The weight of the negative aspects would, moreover, have been much heavier except for the existence of a free and alert press, and for the actions of the Supreme Court and Congress in nullifying, modifying, and rejecting many of the New Deal measures. When one examines the full range of New Deal proposals and considers the implications of their passage in the original form, the outline emerges of a form of government alien to any definition of liberalism except that of the New Dealers themselves. Historians need to weigh more thoroughly and objectively the implications for the United States if Roosevelt's programs had been fully implemented. They need also to assess the costs in human misery of the delay in recovery, and of reduced U.S. influence abroad at a critical time in world affairs owing to its economic prostration. We can only speculate concerning the possible alteration of events from 1937 onward had the United States faced the world with the economic strength and military potential it might have displayed had wiser economic policies prevailed from 1933 to 1938. There is, in short, much about Roosevelt and the New Deal that historians need to reevaluate.

New Deal
↓
antibusiness → prolonged the depression
↓
WWII gained the recovery

Neg. outweight pos. aspects of New Deal

Roger Biles **NO**

A New Deal for the American People

At the close of the Hundred Days, Franklin D. Roosevelt said, "All of the proposals and all of the legislation since the fourth day of March have not been just a collection of haphazard schemes, but rather the orderly component parts of a connected and logical whole." Yet the president later described his approach quite differently. "Take a method and try it. If it fails admit it frankly and try another. But above all, try something." The impetus for New Deal legislation came from a variety of sources, and Roosevelt relied heavily at various times on an ideologically diverse group of aides and allies. His initiatives reflected the contributions of, among others, Robert Wagner, Rexford Tugwell, Raymond Moley, George Norris, Robert LaFollette, Henry Morgenthau, Marriner Eccles, Felix Frankfurter, Henry Wallace, Harry Hopkins, and Eleanor Roosevelt. An initial emphasis on recovery for agriculture and industry gave way within two years to a broader-based program for social reform; entente with the business community yielded to populist rhetoric and a more ambiguous economic program. Roosevelt suffered the opprobrium of both the conservatives, who vilified "that man" in the White House who was leading the country down the sordid road to socialism, and the radicals, who saw the Hyde Park aristocrat as a confidence man peddling piecemeal reform to forestall capitalism's demise. Out of so many contradictory and confusing circumstances, how does one make sense of the five years of legislative reform known as the New Deal? And what has been its impact on a half century of American life?[1]

A better understanding begins with the recognition that little of the New Deal was new, including the use of federal power to effect change. Nor, for all of Roosevelt's famed willingness to experiment, did New Deal programs usually originate from vernal ideas. Governmental aid to increase farmers' income, propounded in the late nineteenth century by the Populists, surfaced in Woodrow Wilson's farm credit acts. The prolonged debates over McNary-Haugenism in the 1920s kept the issue alive, and Herbert Hoover's Agricultural Marketing Act set the stage for further federal involvement. Centralized economic planning, as embodied in the National Industrial Recovery Act, flowed directly from the experiences of Wilson's War Industries Board; not surprisingly, Roosevelt chose Hugh Johnson, a veteran of the board, to head the National Recovery Administration. Well established in England and Germany before the First World War, social insurance appeared in a handful of states—notably Wisconsin—before the federal government became involved. Similarly, New Deal labor reform took its cues from the path-breaking work of state legislatures. Virtually alone in its originality, compensatory fiscal policy seemed revolutionary in the 1930s. Significantly, however, Roosevelt embraced deficit spending quite late after other disappointing economic policies and never to the extent Keynesian economists advised. Congress and the public supported the New Deal, in part, because of its origins in successful initiatives attempted earlier under different conditions.

Innovative or not, the New Deal clearly failed to restore economic prosperity. As late as 1938 unemployment stood at 19.1 percent and two years later at 14.6 percent. Only the Second World War, which generated massive industrial production, put the majority of the American people back to work. To be sure, partial economic recovery occurred. From a high of 13 million unemployed in 1933, the number under Roosevelt's administration fell to 11.4 million in 1934, 10.6 million in 1935, and 9 million in 1936. Farm income and manufacturing wages also rose, and as limited as these achievements may seem in retrospect, they provided sustenance for millions of people and hope for many more. Yet Roosevelt's resistance to Keynesian formulas for pump priming placed immutable barriers in the way of recovery that only war could demolish. At a time calling for drastic inflationary methods, Roosevelt introduced programs effecting the opposite result. The NRA restricted production, elevated prices, and reduced purchasing power, all of which were deflationary in effect. The Social Security Act's payroll taxes took money from consumers and out of circulation. The federal government's $4.43 billion deficit in fiscal year 1936, impressive as it seemed, was not so much greater than Hoover's $2.6 billion shortfall during his last year in office. As economist Robert Lekachman noted, "The 'great spender' was in his heart a true descendant of thrifty Dutch Calvinist forebears." It is not certain that the application of Keynesian formulas would have sufficed by the mid-1930s to restore prosperity, but the president's cautious deflationary policies clearly retarded recovery.[2]

Although New Deal economic policies came up short in the 1930s, they implanted several "stabilizers" that have been more successful in averting another such depression. The Securities and Exchange Act of 1934 established government supervision of the stock market, and the Wheeler-Rayburn Act allowed the Securities and Exchange Commission to do the same with public utilities. Severely embroiled in controversy when adopted, these measures have become mainstays of the American financial system. The Glass-Steagall Banking Act forced the separation of commercial and investment banking and broadened the powers of the Federal Reserve Board to change interest rates and limit loans for speculation. The creation of the Federal Deposit Insurance Corporation (FDIC) increased government supervision of state banks and significantly lowered the number of bank failures. Such safeguards restored confidence in the discredited banking system and established a firm economic foundation that performed well for decades thereafter.

The New Deal was also responsible for numerous other notable changes in American life. Section 7(a) of the NIRA, the Wagner Act, and the Fair Labor Standards Act transformed the relationship between workers and business and breathed life into a troubled labor movement on the verge of total extinction.

In the space of a decade government laws eliminated sweatshops, severely curtailed child labor, and established enforceable standards for hours, wages and working conditions. Further, federal action eliminated the vast majority of company towns in such industries as coal mining. Although Robert Wagner and Frances Perkins dragged Roosevelt into labor's corner, the New Deal made the unions a dynamic force in American society. Moreover, as Nelson Lichtenstein has noted, "by giving so much of the working class an institutional voice, the union movement provided one of the main political bulwarks of the Roosevelt Democratic party and became part of the social bedrock in which the New Deal welfare state was anchored."[3]

Roosevelt's avowed goal of "cradle-to-grave" security for the American people proved elusive, but his administration achieved unprecedented advances in the field of social welfare. In 1938 the president told Congress: "Government has a final responsibility for the well-being of its citizenship. If private co-operative endeavor fails to provide work for willing hands and relief for the unfortunate, those suffering hardship from no fault of their own have a right to call upon the Government for aid; and a government worthy of its name must make fitting response." The New Deal's safety net included low-cost housing; old-age pensions; unemployment insurance; and aid for dependent mothers and children, the disabled, the blind, and public health services. Sometimes disappointing because of limiting eligibility requirements and low benefit levels, these social welfare programs nevertheless firmly established the principle that the government had an obligation to assist the needy. As one scholar wrote of the New Deal, "More progress was made in public welfare and relief than in the three hundred years after this country was first settled."[4]

More and more government programs, inevitably resulting in an enlarged administrative apparatus and requiring additional revenue, added up to a much greater role for the national government in American life. Coming at a time when the only Washington bureaucracy most of the people encountered with any frequency was the U.S. Postal Service, the change seemed all the more remarkable. Although many New Deal programs were temporary emergency measures, others lingered long after the return of prosperity. Suddenly, the national government was supporting farmers, monitoring the economy, operating a welfare system, subsidizing housing, adjudicating labor disputes, managing natural resources, and providing electricity to a growing number of consumers. "What Roosevelt did in a period of a little over 12 years was to change the form of government," argued journalist Richard L. Strout. "Washington had been largely run by big business, by Wall Street. He brought the government to Washington." Not surprisingly, popular attitudes toward government also changed. No longer willing to accept economic deprivation and social dislocation as the vagaries of an uncertain existence, Americans tolerated—indeed, came to expect—the national government's involvement in the problems of everyday life. No longer did "government" mean just "city hall."[5]

The operation of the national government changed as well. For one thing, Roosevelt's strong leadership expanded presidential power, contributing to what historian Arthur Schlesinger, Jr., called the "imperial presidency." Whereas Americans had in previous years instinctively looked first to Capitol

Hill, after Roosevelt the White House took center stage in Washington. At the same time, Congress and the president looked at the nation differently. Traditionally attentive only to one group (big business), policymakers in Washington began responding to other constituencies such as labor, farmers, the unemployed, the aged, and to a lesser extent, women, blacks, and other disadvantaged groups. This new "broker state" became more accessible and acted on a growing number of problems, but equity did not always result. The ablest, richest, and most experienced groups fared best during the New Deal. NRA codes favored big business, and AAA benefits aided large landholders; blacks received relief and government jobs but not to the extent their circumstances merited. The long-term result, according to historian John Braeman, has been "a balkanized political system in which private interests scramble, largely successfully, to harness governmental authority and/or draw upon the public treasury to advance their private agendas."[6]

Another legacy of the New Deal has been the Roosevelt revolution in politics. Urbanization and immigration changed the American electorate, and a new generation of voters who resided in the cities during the Great Depression opted for Franklin D. Roosevelt and his party. Before the 1930s the Democrats of the northern big-city machines and the solid South uneasily coexisted and surrendered primacy to the unified Republican party. The New Deal coalition that elected Roosevelt united behind common economic interests. Both urban northerners and rural southerners, as well as blacks, women, and ethnic immigrants, found common cause in government action to shield them from an economic system gone haywire. By the end of the decade the increasing importance of the urban North in the Democratic party had already become apparent. After the economy recovered from the disastrous depression, members of the Roosevelt coalition shared fewer compelling interests. Beginning in the 1960s, tensions mounted within the party as such issues as race, patriotism, and abortion loomed larger. Even so, the Roosevelt coalition retained enough commitment to New Deal principles to keep the Democrats the nation's majority party into the 1980s.[7]

Yet for all the alterations in politics, government, and the economy, the New Deal fell far short of a revolution. The two-party system survived intact, and neither fascism, which attracted so many followers in European states suffering from the same international depression, nor communism attracted much of a following in the United States. Vital government institutions functioned without interruption and if the balance of powers shifted, the national dremained capitalistic; free enterprise and private ownership, not socialism, emerged from the 1930s. A limited welfare state changed the meld of the public and private but left them separate. Roosevelt could be likened to the British conservative Edmund Burke, who advocated measured change to offset drastic alterations—"reform to preserve." The New Deal's great achievement was the application of just enough change to preserve the American political economy.

Indications of Roosevelt's restraint emerged from the very beginning of the New Deal. Rather than assume extraordinary executive powers as Abraham Lincoln had done in the 1861 crisis, the president called Congress into special session. Whatever changes ensued would come through normal governmental activity. Roosevelt declined to assume direct control of the economy, leaving the nation's resources in the hands of private enterprise. Resisting the blandishments of radicals calling for the nationalization of the banks, he provided the means for their rehabilitation and ignored the call for national health insurance and federal contributions to Social Security retirement benefits. The creation of such regulatory agencies as the SEC confirmed his intention to revitalize rather than remake economic institutions. Repeatedly during his presidency Roosevelt responded to congressional pressure to enact bolder reforms, as in the case of the National Labor Relations Act, the Wagner-Steagall Housing Act, and the FDIC. The administration forwarded the NIRA only after Senator Hugo Black's recovery bill mandating 30-hour workweeks seemed on the verge of passage.

As impressive as New Deal relief and social welfare programs were, they never went as far as conditions demanded or many liberals recommended. Fluctuating congressional appropriations, oscillating economic conditions, and Roosevelt's own hesitancy to do too much violence to the federal budget left Harry Hopkins, Harold Ickes, and others only partially equipped to meet the staggering need. The president justified the creation of the costly WPA in 1935 by "ending this business of relief." Unskilled workers, who constituted the greatest number of WPA employees, obtained but 60 to 80 percent of the minimal family income as determined by the government. Roosevelt and Hopkins continued to emphasize work at less than existing wage scales so that the WPA or PWA never competed with free labor, and they allowed local authorities to modify pay rates. They also continued to make the critical distinction between the "deserving" and "undeserving" poor, making sure that government aided only the former. The New Deal never challenged the values underlying this distinction, instead seeking to provide for the growing number of "deserving" poor created by the Great Depression. Government assumed an expanded role in caring for the disadvantaged, but not at variance with existing societal norms regarding social welfare.

The New Deal effected no substantial redistribution of income. The Wealth Tax Act of 1935 (the famous soak-the-rich tax) produced scant revenue and affected very few taxpayers. Tax alterations in 1936 and 1937 imposed no additional burdens on the rich; the 1938 and 1939 tax laws actually removed a few. By the end of the 1930s less than 5 percent of Americans paid income taxes, and the share of taxes taken from personal and corporate income levies fell below the amount raised in the 1920s. The great change in American taxation policy came during World War II, when the number of income tax payers grew to 74 percent of the population. In 1942 Treasury Secretary Henry Morgenthau noted that "for the first time in our history, the income tax is becoming a people's tax." This the New Deal declined to do.[8]

Finally, the increased importance of the national government exerted remarkably little influence on local institutions. The New Deal seldom dictated and almost always deferred to state and local governments—encouraging, cajoling, bargaining, and wheedling to bring parochial interests in line with national objectives. As Harry Hopkins discovered, governors and mayors angled to obtain as many federal dollars as possible for their constituents but with no strings attached. Community control and local autonomy, conditions thought to be central to American democracy, remained strong, and Roosevelt understood the need for firm ties with politicians at all levels. In his study of the New Deal's impact on federalism, James T. Patterson concludes: "For all the supposed power of the New Deal, it was unable to impose all its guidelines on the autonomous forty-eight states. . . . What could the Roosevelt administration have done to ensure a more profound and lasting impression on state policy and politics? Very little."[9]

Liberal New Dealers longed for more sweeping change and lamented their inability to goad the president into additional action. They envisioned a wholesale purge of the Democratic party and the creation of a new organization embodying fully the principles of liberalism. They could not abide Roosevelt's toleration of the political conservatives and unethical bosses who composed part of the New Deal coalition. They sought racial equality, constraints upon the southern landholding class, and federal intrusion to curb the power of urban real estate interests on behalf of the inveterate poor. Yet to do these things would be to attempt changes well beyond the desires of most Americans. People pursuing remunerative jobs and the economic security of the middle class approved of government aiding the victims of an unfortunate economic crisis but had no interest in an economic system that would limit opportunity. The fear that the New Deal would lead to such thoroughgoing change explains the seemingly irrational hatred of Roosevelt by the economic elite. But, as historian Barry Karl has noted, "it was characteristic of Roosevelt's presidency that he never went as far as his detractors feared or his followers hoped."[10]

The New Deal achieved much that was good and left much undone. Roosevelt's programs were defined by the confluence of forces that circumscribed his admittedly limited reform agenda—hostile judiciary; powerful congressional opponents, some of whom entered into alliances of convenience with New Dealers and some of whom awaited the opportunity to build on their opposition; the political impotence of much of the populace; the pugnacious independence of local and state authorities; the strength of people's attachment to traditional values and institutions; and the basic conservatism of American culture. Obeisance to local custom and the decision to avoid tampering with the fabric of American society allowed much injustice to survive while shortchanging blacks, women, small farmers, and the "unworthy" poor. Those who criticized Franklin Roosevelt for an unwillingness to challenge racial, economic, and gender inequality misunderstood either the nature of his electoral mandate or the difference between reform and revolution—or both.

If the New Deal preserved more than it changed, that is understandable in a society whose people have consistently chosen freedom over equality. Americans traditionally have eschewed expanded government, no matter how efficiently managed or honestly administered, that imposed restraints on personal success—even though such limitations redressed legitimate grievances or righted imbalances. Parity, most Americans believed, should not be purchased with the loss of liberty. But although the American dream has always entailed individual success with a minimum of state interference, the profound shock of capitalism's near demise in the 1930s undermined numerous previously unquestioned beliefs. The inability of capitalism's "invisible hand" to stabilize the market and the failure of the private sector to restore prosperity enhanced the consideration of stronger executive leadership and centralized planning. Yet with the collapse of democratic governments and their replacement by totalitarian regimes, Americans were keenly sensitive to any threats to liberty. New Deal programs, frequently path breaking in their delivery of federal resources outside normal channels, also retained a strong commitment to local government and community control while promising only temporary disruptions prior to the return of economic stability. Reconciling the necessary authority at the federal level to meet nationwide crises with the local autonomy desirable to safeguard freedom has always been one of the salient challenges to American democracy. Even after New Deal refinements, the search for the proper balance continues.

Notes

1. Otis L. Graham Jr., and Meghan Robinson Wander, eds., *Franklin D. Roosevelt, His Life and Times: An Encyclopedic View* (Boston: G. K. Hall, 1985), p. 285 (first quotation); Harvard Sitkoff, "Introduction," in Sitkoff, *Fifty Years Later*, p. 5 (second quotation).
2. Richard S. Kirkendall, "The New Deal as Watershed: The Recent Literature," *Journal of American History* 54 (March 1968), p. 847 (quotation).
3. Graham and Wander, *Franklin D. Roosevelt, His Life and Times*, p. 228 (quotation).
4. Leuchtenburg, "The Achievement of the New Deal," p. 220 (first quotation); Patterson, *America's Struggle against Poverty, 1900–1980*, p. 56 (second quotation).
5. Louchheim, *The Making of the New Deal: The Insiders Speak*, p. 15 (quotation).
6. John Braeman, "The New Deal: The Collapse of the Liberal Consensus," *Canadian Review of American Studies* 20 (Summer 1989), p. 77.
7. David Burner, *The Politics of Provincialism: The Democratic Party in Transition, 1918–1932* (New York: Alfred A. Knopf, 1968).
8. Mark Leff, *The Limits of Symbolic Reform*, p. 287 (quotation).
9. James T. Patterson, *The New Deal and the States: Federalism in Transition* (Princeton: Princeton University Press, 1969), p. 202.
10. Barry D. Karl, *The Uneasy State: The United States from 1915 to 1945* (Chicago: University of Chicago Press, 1983), p. 124.

Tried to change gov.? get rid of two-party system FDR appealed to many

POSTSCRIPT

Did the New Deal Prolong the Great Depression?

Both Biles and Best agree that the New Deal concentrated a tremendous amount of power in the executive branch of the government. They also acknowledge that it was World War II—not the New Deal's reform programs—that pulled the United States out of the depression. But the two historians disagree with each other in their assumptions and assessments of the New Deal.

Best argues that the New Deal was radical in its anti-business assumptions. His conservative critique is similar to Jim Powell's *FDR's Folly: How Roosevelt and His New Deal Prolonged the Great Depression* (Crown Forum, 2003). Powell has been a senior fellow since 1988 at the Cato Institute in Washington, D.C., a well-known conservative and libertarian think tank that has produced a number of policymakers who have staffed the Reagan and two Bush presidential administrations. Powell argues that the New Deal itself with its short-sighted programs increased the size and power of the federal government, which prevented the country from ending the depression more quickly. Powell's critique is based on the conservative assumptions of the well-known free-market advocates Milton Friedman and Anna Jacobson Schwartz, who argue in *A Monetary History of the United States, 1867–1960* (Princeton University Press, 1963) that the Great Depression was a government failure, brought on primarily by Federal Reserve policies that abruptly cut the money supply. This view runs counter to those of Peter Temin, *Did Monetary Forces Cause the Depression?* (Norton, 1976), Michael A. Bernstein, *The Great Depression: Delayed Recovery and Economic Change in America* (Cambridge University Press, 1987), and the readable and lively account of John Kenneth Galbraith, *The Great Crash* (Houghton Mifflin, 1955), which argue that the crash exposed various structural weaknesses in the economy that caused the depression.

Both Best's and Powell's analysis can be faulted on several grounds. For example, they underestimate the enormity of the economic crisis facing the country on the eve of Roosevelt's inauguration. Bank failures were rampant, farmers declared "farm holidays" and destroyed crops to keep up prices, and an assassin tried to kill the president-elect in Miami. As Roosevelt often quipped, "People don't eat in the long run, they eat every day." His immediate response to the crisis was the "100 days" New Deal recovery programs.

Best and Powell agree with other liberal and radical New Deal analysts that it was World War II and not the New Deal that brought us out of the Great Depression. If this is true, didn't the recovery take place because of the enormous sums of money that the government pumped into the defense industries and the armed services that reduced the unemployment rate to almost 0 percent?

Historian Roger Biles argues that the New Deal was a non-revolution compared to the economic and political changes that were taking place in communist Russia, fascist Italy, and Nazi Germany. The New Deal, in his view, was not so new. Social insurance appeared earlier in several states, notably Wisconsin. The economic planning embodied in the National Industrial Recovery Act extends back to President Wilson's World War I War Industries Board. The use of the federal government to aid farmers was begun with President Wilson's Farm Credit Act and continued during the Harding, Collidge, and Hoover administrations.

Although the recovery doesn't come about until World War II, Biles admits that the New Deal changed the relationship between the federal government and the people. The New Deal stabilized the banking industry and stock exchange. It ameliorated the relationship of workers with business with its support of the Wagner Act and the Fair Standard Labor Act. Social Security provided a safety net for the aged, the unemployed, and the disabled. In politics, urbanization and immigration cemented a new Democratic coalition in 1936 with the conservative South around common economic interests until the 1980s when racial issues and the maturing of a new suburban middle class fractured the Democratic majority.

Biles' analysis basically agrees with the British historian Anthony J. Badger who argues in *The New Deal* (Hill and Wang, 1989) that the New Deal was a "holding operation" until the Second World War created the "political economy of modern America." Both Biles and Badger argue that once the immediate crisis of 1933 subsided, opposition to the New Deal came from big business, conservative congressmen, and local governments who resisted the increasing power of the federal government. As the Office of War Information told Roosevelt, the American people's post-war aspirations were "compounded largely of 1929 values and the economics of the 1920s, levend with a handover from the makeshift controls of the war."

The most recent annotated bibliography is Robert F. Himmelberg, *The Great Depression and the New Deal* (Greenwood Press, 2001). The conservative case with full bibliographical references is contained in Powell's *FDR's Folly.* See also Robert Eden's edited *The New Deal and Its Legacy: Critique and Reappraisal* (Greenwood Press, 1989). Two important collections of recent writings are David E. Hamilton, ed., *The New Deal* (Houghton Mifflin, 1999) and Colin Gordon, ed., *Major Problems in American History 1920–1945* (Houghton Mifflin, 1999). Finally Steve Fraser and Gary Gerstle edited a series of social and economic essays, which they present in *The Rise and Fall of the New Deal Order, 1930–1980* (Princeton University Press, 1989).

Out of vogue but still worth reading are the sympathetic studies of the New Deal by William Leuchtenburg, *Franklin D. Roosevelt and the New Deal* (Harper and Row, 1963) and his interpretative essays written over 30 years in *The FDR Years: On Roosevelt and His Legacy* (Columbia University Press, 1985). See also the beautifully written but never to be completed second and third volumes of Arthur M. Schlesinger, Jr.'s *The Coming of the New Deal* (Houghton Mifflin, 1959) and *The Politics of Upheaval* (Houghton Mifflin, 1960), which advances the interpretation of the first and second New Deal, found in most American history survey textbooks.

ISSUE 7

Did President Roosevelt Deliberately Withhold Information About the Attack on Pearl Harbor from the American Commanders?

YES: Robert A. Theobald, from *The Final Secret of Pearl Harbor: The Washington Contribution to the Japanese Attack* (Devin-Adair, 1954)

NO: Roberta Wohlstetter, from *Pearl Harbor: Warning and Decision* (Stanford University Press, 1967)

ISSUE SUMMARY

YES: Retired Rear Admiral Robert A. Theobald argues that President Franklin D. Roosevelt deliberately withheld information from the commanders at Pearl Harbor in order to encourage the Japanese to make a surprise attack on the weak U.S. Pacific Fleet.

NO: Historian Roberta Wohlstetter contends that even though naval intelligence broke the Japanese code, conflicting signals and the lack of a central agency coordinating U.S. intelligence information made it impossible to predict the Pearl Harbor attack.

In 1899 and 1900 Secretary of State John Hay enunciated two notes, known as the Open Door policy. The first pronouncement attempted to provide equal access to commercial rights in China for all nations. The second note called on all countries to respect China's "territorial and administrative" integrity. For the next 40 years the open door was restated by every president from Theodore Roosevelt to Franklin Roosevelt for two reasons: (1) to prevent China from being taken over by Japan, and (2) to preserve the balance of power in the world. The Open Door policy appeared to work during World War I and the 1920s.

The Nine-Power Treaty of 1922 restated the Open Door principles, and its signatories agreed to assist China in forming a stable government. Japan supported the agreements because the world economy was reasonably stable. But the worldwide depression had a major effect on the foreign policies of all nations. Japan decided that she wanted to extend her influence politically as well as economically in Asia. On the night of September 18, 1931, an explosion, probably staged by Japanese militarists, damaged the Japanese-controlled South Manchurian Railroad. Japanese troops not only overran Chinese troops stationed in South Manchuria but within five months established the puppet state of Manchukuo. When the League of Nations condemned Japan's actions, the Japanese gave their two-year's notice and withdrew from the league. A turn for the worse came for the Chinese on July 7, 1937, when a shooting incident at the Marco Polo Bridge between Chinese and Japanese troops led to a full-scale war on China's mainland. President Franklin Roosevelt took a strong verbal stand in a speech he delivered on October 5, 1937, demanding that nations stirring up "international anarchy" should be quarantined.

Roosevelt aided the Chinese with nonembargoed, nonmilitary goods when he found a loophole in the neutrality laws. Japan's goal to establish a "new order in East Asia" was furthered by the outbreak of World War II in Europe in the fall of 1939 and the ease with which the German army overran and defeated France the following spring. In September 1940 Japanese forces occupied northern French Indochina (later known as Vietnam). Although Roosevelt was unable to stop Japan's military expansionism, he did jar them with economic sanctions. When the Japanese occupied southern Indochina on July 25, 1941, Roosevelt again jolted the Japanese government by issuing an order freezing all Japanese assets in the United States, which created major problems. Japan had only 12 to 18 months of oil in reserves for military use. A military statement had developed in the war with China in part because the United States was funneling economic and military aid to her ally. Consequently, Japan sought an accommodation with the United States in the fall of 1941. Japan tried to negotiate two plans that would have resulted in a partial withdrawal from Indochina and the establishment of a coalition government in China proper that would be partially controlled by the Japanese and would take place once the war stopped. In return, America would resume trade with Japan prior to the July 26 freezing of Japanese assets.

Because American cryptologists had broken the Japanese diplomatic code for a second time in the summer of 1941, American policymakers knew that these were Japan's final proposals. Secretary of State Cordell Hull sent the Japanese a note on November 26 that restated America's Open Door policy and asked "the government of Japan [to] withdraw all military naval, air, and police forces from China and from Indochina." When Japan rejected the proposal both sides realized this meant war. Where or when was the question. Japan's surprise December 7 attack on Pearl Harbor provided the answer.

In the following selection, Robert A. Theobald argues that President Roosevelt deliberately withheld information from the Hawaiian army and naval commanders at Pearl Harbor in order to encourage the Japanese to make a surprise attack on the weak Pacific Fleet. In the second selection, Roberta Wohlstetter maintains that even though naval intelligence broke the Japanese code, conflicting signals made it impossible to predict the Pearl Harbor attack.

YES

Robert A. Theobald

The Final Secret of Pearl Harbor

Having been present at Pearl Harbor on December 7, 1941, and having appeared with Admiral Husband E. Kimmel when that officer testified before the Roberts Commission,[1] the author has ever since sought a full understanding of the background that made that day possible. For many years, he gathered and pieced together the available evidence which appeared to shed light upon the Washington happenings concerned with that attack. These studies produced very definite conclusions regarding the manner in which our country's strategy had been shaped to entice the Japanese to attack Pearl Harbor, and the efforts that have since been made to keep these facts from the knowledge of the American People.

For over three years, the thirty-nine-volume set which comprises the Record of Proceedings of all the Pearl Harbor Investigations has been available to the author. Serious study of these volumes has caused many revisions of errors in detail, but it has served to divest the writer's mind of all doubt regarding the soundness of his basic conclusions.

It is firmly believed that those in Washington who knew the facts, decided from the first that considerations of patriotism and loyalty to their wartime Commander-in-Chief required that a veil of secrecy should be drawn about the President's handling of the situation which culminated in the Pearl Harbor attack.

While there was great justification for this secrecy during the continuance of the war, the reasons for it no longer exist. The war is finished. President Roosevelt and his administration are now history. Dictates of patriotism requiring secrecy regarding a line of national conduct in order to preserve it for possible future repetition do not apply in this case because, in this atomic age, facilitating an enemy's surprise attack, as a method of initiating a war, is unthinkable. Our Pearl Harbor losses would preclude that course of action in the future without consideration of the increased destructiveness of present and future weapons. Finally, loyalty to their late President in the matter of Pearl Harbor would be better served today, if his friends would discard their policy of secrecy in favor of full publicity.

Another consideration which today strongly favors a complete understanding of the whole Pearl Harbor story, is the thought of justice to the professional reputations of the Hawaiian Commanders, Admiral Kimmel and General Short—a justice which is long overdue.

Throughout the war, maintenance of the national morale at the highest possible level demanded complete public confidence in the President and his principal military advisers. During that time, the public could not be given cause to assign a tithe of blame for the Pearl Harbor attack to Washington. And so, dating from the report of the Roberts Commission, most of the responsibility for Pearl Harbor has been placed upon the two Hawaiian Commanders. This carefully executed plan which diverted all suspicion from Washington contributed its full measure to the successful conduct of the war.

The time has come when full publicity should be given to the Washington contribution to the Pearl Harbor attack, in order that the judgment of the American people may assign to Admiral Kimmel and General Short no more than their just and proper share of the responsibility for that tragic day.

Manifestly, many readers will be reluctant to agree with the main conclusions which have been reached in this study. In recognition of this fact, the normal sequence of deductive reasoning is discarded in favor of the order used in a legal presentation. The case is stated at the outset, and the evidence is then marshalled and discussed. The reader is thus enabled to weigh each fact, as it is presented, against the conclusions, which have been firmly implanted in the mind of the author by the summation of these facts.

The sole purpose of the subject matter contained herein is a searching for the truth, and it is hoped that the absence of any ulterior motive is apparent throughout. Comments of a critical character concerning the official actions of officers frequently intersperse the pages which follow. No criticism of the officer is intended. Those officers were obeying orders, under circumstances which were professionally most trying to them. Such comments are necessary to a full understanding of the discussion of the moment, however, but there is no intention to impugn the motives of any individual. Patriotism and loyalty were the wellsprings of those motives. . . .

Main Deduction: President Roosevelt Circumvents American Pacifism

In the spring of 1940, Denmark, Norway, Holland, Belgium and France were conquered by Germany, and throughout the remainder of that year Great Britain's situation was so desperate that many expected her collapse early in the ensuing year. Fortunately, however, the Axis powers turned East in 1941 to conquer Greece and to attack Russia.

There is every reason to believe that when France was overcome President Roosevelt became convinced the United States must fight beside Great Britain, while the latter was still an active belligerent, or later sustain the fight alone, as the last democratic stronghold in a Nazi world. Never, however, had the country been less prepared for war, both psychologically and physically. Isolationism was a dominant philosophy throughout the land, and the armed forces were weak and consequently unready.

The United States not only had to become an active participant in democracy's fight as quickly as possible, but a people, completely united in support of the war effort, had to be brought into the arena. But, how could the country be made to fight? Only a cataclysmic happening could move Congress to enact a declaration of war; and that action would not guarantee that the nation's response would be the completely united support which victory has always demanded. This was the President's problem, and his solution was based upon the simple fact that, while it takes two to make a fight, either one may start it.

As the people of this country were so strongly opposed to war, one of the Axis powers must be forced to involve the United States, and in such a way as to arouse the American people to wholehearted belief in the necessity of fighting. This would require drastic action, and the decision was unquestionably a difficult one for the President to make.

In this connection, it should be remembered that Japan, Germany, and Italy signed the Tripartite Treaty on September 28, 1940, by which the three nations agreed to make common cause against any nation, not then a participant in the European war or the Sino-Japanese conflict, which attacked one of the signatories.

Thereafter, the fact that war with Japan meant war with Germany and Italy played an important part in President Roosevelt's diplomatic strategy. Throughout the approach to war and during the fighting, the primary U.S. objective was the defeat of Germany.

To implement the solution of his problem, the President: (1) instituted a successful campaign to correct the Nation's military unpreparedness; (2) offered Germany repeated provocations, by violations of neutrality and diplomatic usage; (3) applied ever-increasing diplomatic-economic pressure upon Japan, which reached its sustained climax on July 25, 1941, when the United States, Great Britain, and the Netherlands stopped their trade with Japan and subjected her to almost complete economic encirclement; (4) made mutual commitments with the British Prime Minister at Newfoundland in August, 1941, which promised mutual support in the event that the United States, Great Britain, or a third country not then at war were attacked by Japan in the Pacific; (5) terminated the Washington conference with the note of November 26, 1941, which gave Japan no choice but surrender or war; (6) retained a weak Pacific Fleet in Hawaiian waters, despite contrary naval advice, where it served only one diplomatic purpose, an invitation to a Japanese surprise attack; (7) furthered that surprise by causing the Hawaiian Commanders to be denied invaluable information from decoded Japanese dispatches [or "Magic"] concerning the rapid approach of the war and the strong probability that the attack would be directed at Pearl Harbor.

This denial of information was a vital feature of enticing a Japanese surprise attack upon Pearl Harbor. If Admiral Kimmel and General Short had been given the knowledge possessed by the Washington authorities, the Hawaiian Commands would have been alerted against an overseas attack. The Pacific Fleet would have kept the sea during the first days of December, 1941, until the issue of peace or war had been decided. With the highly effective Japanese espionage in Hawaii, this would have caused Tokyo to cancel the surprise attack.

The problem which faced Lincoln during March of 1861 was identical in principle—to unite the sentiment of the North behind the policy of compelling the seceded Southern states by force of arms to return to the Union. For a month after his inauguration, he made no move, and then South Carolina's insistent demands for the surrender of Fort Sumter gave him the answer to his problem. He refused to surrender the fort, and dispatched a fleet to reprovision it. South Carolina then fired the first shots of the Civil War. Pearl Harbor was President Roosevelt's Fort Sumter.

Diplomatically, President Roosevelt's strategy of forcing Japan to war by unremitting and ever-increasing diplomatic-economic pressure, and by simultaneously holding our Fleet in Hawaii as an invitation to a surprise attack, was a complete success. Militarily, our ship and personnel losses mark December 7, 1941 as the day of tragic defeat. One is forced to conclude that the anxiety to have Japan, beyond all possibility of dispute, commit the first act of war, caused the President and his civilian advisers to disregard the military advice which would somewhat have cushioned the blow. The President, before the event, probably envisaged a *Panay* incident[2] of somewhat larger proportions. Despite the fact that the attack laid the foundation for complete victory, a terrific price was paid, as the following account of the ship, plane, and personnel losses discloses.

The Pearl Harbor Losses: Facts and Figures

The Japanese clearly intended that their entire surprise attack should be delivered against military objectives. The first waves of the attack were delivered against the airfields on the Island of Oahu—Army, Navy, and Marine Corps—to reduce the air-borne opposition as much as possible. The main attacks began 15 minutes after these preliminary attacks, and were primarily directed against the capital ships in Pearl Harbor. Damage inflicted upon smaller vessels was clearly the incidental consequence of the main operation. Very few planes dropped their bombs upon the city of Honolulu. Three planes did so in the late phases of the attack, but their last-minute changes of course indicated that this was done because those particular pilots did not care to encounter the severe anti-aircraft fire that was then bursting over their main target area.

In December, 1941, the capital ships of the Pacific Fleet numbered twelve: 9 Battleships; 3 Carriers. Of these, eight Battleships but none of the Carriers were present in Pearl Harbor at the time of the Japanese attack: the Battleship *Colorado* was in the Bremerton Navy Yard; the Carrier *Enterprise* was in a Task Force returning from Wake; the *Lexington* was in a Task Force ferrying planes to Midway; the *Saratoga* was on the West Coast, having just completed a Navy Yard overhaul.

The results of the Japanese air attacks upon the U.S. Pacific Fleet in Pearl Harbor on December 7, 1941, were as follows:

Battleships:

Arizona: total loss, as her forward magazines blew up;

Oklahoma: total loss, capsized and sank in harbor—later raised solely to clear harbor of the obstruction and resunk off Oahu;

California, West Virginia: sank in upright position at their berths with quarterdecks awash—much later raised, repaired, and returned to active war service;

Nevada: beached while standing out of the harbor, to prevent sinking in deep water after extensive bomb damage—repaired and returned to active war service;

Pennsylvania, Maryland, and Tennessee: all received damage but of a less severe character.

Smaller Ships:

Cruisers: Helena, Honolulu, and *Raleigh* were all damaged, but were repaired and returned to active war service;

Destroyers: Two damaged beyond repair; two others damaged but repaired and returned to active war service;

Auxiliary Vessels: 1 Seaplane Tender, 1 Repair Ship, both severely damaged but repaired and returned to active war service;

Target Ship: Utah, former battleship, sank at her berth.

The Japanese attacks upon the various Oahu airfields resulted in the following U.S. plane losses: Navy 80; Army 97.

U.S. military personnel casualties were: Navy, including Marine Corps, 3077 officers and enlisted men killed, 876 wounded; Army, including the Army Air Corps, 226 officers and enlisted men killed, 396 wounded. Total: 4575.

The Japanese losses were 48 planes shot down and three midget submarines destroyed. These vessels displaced 45 tons and were of little, if any, military value.

The Final Summation

Review of the American Moves Which Led to the Japanese Attack

Our Main Deduction is that President Roosevelt forced Japan to war by unrelenting diplomatic-economic pressure, and enticed that country to initiate hostilities with a surprise attack by holding the Pacific Fleet in Hawaiian waters as an invitation to that attack.

The evidence shows how surely the President moved toward war after June, 1940. His conversation with Admiral Richardson in October, 1940, indicated his conviction that it would be impossible without a stunning incident to obtain a declaration of war from Congress.

Despite the conditions of undeclared war which existed in the Atlantic during the latter half of 1941, it had long been clear that Germany did not intend to contribute to the creation of a state of formal war between her and the United States. The Tripartite Treaty of September, 1940, however, supplied the President with the answer. Under that treaty, war with Japan meant war with Germany and Italy.

The highlights of the ever-increasing pressure upon Japan were:

1. the extension of financial and military aid to China in concert with Great Britain and the Netherlands, which began early in 1941;
2. the stoppage of Philippine exports to Japan by Executive Order on May 29, 1941;
3. the freezing of Japanese assets and the interdiction of all trade with Japan by the United States, Great Britain, and the Netherlands on July 25, 1941;
4. President Roosevelt's very frank statements of policy to Ambassador Nomura in their conference of August 17, 1941;
5. the termination of the Washington conference by the American note of November 26, 1941, which brought the war to the United States as the President so clearly intended it would.

That the Pearl Harbor attack was in accord with President Roosevelt's plans is attested by the following array of facts:

1. President Roosevelt and his military and naval advisers were well aware that Japan invariably started her wars with a surprise attack synchronized closely with her delivery of the Declaration of War;
2. In October, 1940, the President stated that, if war broke out in the Pacific, Japan would commit the overt act which would bring the United States into the war;
3. The Pacific Fleet, against contrary naval advice, was retained in Hawaii by order of the President for the alleged reason that the Fleet, so located, would exert a restrictive effect upon Japanese aggressions in the Far East;
4. The Fleet in Hawaii was neither powerful enough nor in the necessary strategic position to influence Japan's diplomatic decisions, which could only be accomplished by the stationing of an adequate naval force in Far Eastern waters;
5. Before that Fleet could operate at any distance from Pearl Harbor, its train (tankers, supply and repair vessels) would have had to be tremendously increased in strength—facts that would not escape the notice of the experienced Japanese spies in Hawaii;
6. President Roosevelt gave unmistakable evidence, in March, 1941, that he was not greatly concerned with the Pacific Fleet's effects upon Japanese diplomatic decisions, when he authorized the weakening of that Fleet, already inferior to that of Japan, by the detachment of 3 battleships, 1 aircraft carrier, 4 light cruisers, and 18 destroyers for duty in the Atlantic—a movement which would immediately be detected by Japanese espionage in Hawaii and Panama Canal Zone;
7. The successful crippling of the Pacific Fleet was the only surprise operation which promised the Japanese Navy sufficiently large results to justify the risk of heavy losses from land-based air attacks if the surprise failed;
8. Such an operation against the Fleet in Hawaii was attended with far greater chances of success, especially from the surprise standpoint, and far less risk of heavy losses than a similar attack against that Fleet based in U.S. West Coast ports;

9. The retention of the Fleet in Hawaii, especially after its reduction in strength in March, 1941, could serve only one possible purpose, an invitation to a surprise Japanese attack;
10. The denial to the Hawaiian Commanders of all knowledge of Magic was vital to the plan for enticing Japan to deliver a surprise attack upon the Fleet in Pearl Harbor, because, as late as Saturday, December 6, Admiral Kimmel could have caused that attack to be cancelled by taking his Fleet to sea and disappearing beyond land-based human ken.

Review of the Situation Known to Washington Before the Attack

From the beginning of the Washington conference in November, 1941, President Roosevelt and his advisers had repeated evidence that this was Japan's last and supreme effort to break the economic encirclement by peaceful means.

Throughout the negotiations, the Japanese secret dispatches stressed a "deadline date," after which "things were automatically going to happen."

Automatic events which were to follow the breakdown of such vital negotiations could only be acts of war, clear evidence that Japan intended to deliver a surprise attack to initiate the hostilities.

The fact that surprise was essential to the Japanese plans was repeatedly emphasized, on and after November 28, by the Tokyo dispatches and by telephone instructions to the two Ambassadors, cautioning them to keep alive the appearance of continuing negotiation.

Everyone familiar with Japanese military history knew that her first acts of war against China in 1894 and Russia in 1904 had been surprise attacks against the main fleets of those countries.

The only American Naval Force in the Pacific that was worth the risk of such an operation was the Fleet in Hawaiian waters.

The President and his military naval advisers well knew, on October 9, from the Tokyo dispatch to Honolulu of September 24, that Japan intended to plan a surprise air attack on the American Fleet in Pearl Harbor, and had daily evidence from the late decodes of certain Tokyo-Honolulu dispatches during the period, December 3–6 inclusive, that the planned attack was soon to occur.

On November 26, the recipients of Magic all had positive information from the Tokyo dispatch to Hong Kong of November 14 that Japan intended war with the United States and Great Britain if the Washington negotiations should fail.

The Tokyo dispatch to the Washington Embassy of November 28 definitely stated that the Japanese Government considered that the American note of the 26th had terminated all possibility of further negotiations.

The Tokyo-Berlin messages dated November 30 instructed the Japanese Ambassador to inform Hitler and von Ribbentrop that war between Japan and the Anglo-Saxon nations would come sooner than anyone expected.

The Japanese code-destruction messages of December 1 and 2 meant that war was extremely close at hand.

With the distribution of the Pilot Message at 3:00 P.M. on Saturday, December 6, the picture was complete for President Roosevelt and the other recipients of Magic, both in Washington and Manila. It said that the answer to the American note was about to arrive in the Embassy, that it was very lengthy, and that its delivery to the U.S. Government was to be especially timed. That timed delivery could only have meant that the answer was a Declaration of War, synchronized with a surprise attack. No other deduction was tenable.

The Saturday receipt of this definite information strongly supported the existing estimates in the War and Navy Departments, that the Japanese surprise attack would be delivered on a Sunday, and marked the morrow, Sunday, December 7, as the day. All this, beyond doubt, was known to President Roosevelt, General Marshall, and Admiral Stark at about 3:00 P.M. on that Saturday, Washington time, 21 hours before the next sunrise in Hawaii.

In obedience to the basic dictates of the Military Art, the information contained in the Pilot Message and the unmistakable implications thereof should have been transmitted to Admiral Kimmel and General Short at once. There was no military consideration that would warrant or tolerate an instant's delay in getting this word to those officers. There cannot be the slightest doubt that General Marshall and Admiral Stark would have had this done, if they had not been restrained from doing so by the orders of President Roosevelt. In the situation which then existed for them, no officer of even limited experience, if free to act, could possibly decide otherwise.

The fighting words in the selected passages of the 13-part message received on that same Saturday were merely additional evidence that this was a Declaration of War. The 14th part received early Sunday morning was further confirmation of that fact.

The 1:00 P.M. Washington delivery, ordered by the time-of-delivery dispatch, clearly indicated Pearl Harbor as the objective of the surprise attack, the final link in the long chain of evidence to that effect.

There Would Have Been No Pearl Harbor If Magic Had Not Been Denied to the Hawaiian Commanders

The recurrent fact of the true Pearl Harbor story has been the repeated withholding of information from Admiral Kimmel and General Short. If the War and Navy Departments had been free to follow the dictates of the Art of War, the following is the minimum of information and orders those officers would have received.

The Tokyo-Honolulu dispatches regarding the exact berthing of U.S. ships in Pearl Harbor and, in that connection, a reminder that Japan invariably started her wars with a surprise attack on the new enemy's Main Fleet; the dispatches concerning the Washington Conference and the deadline date after which things were automatically going to happen—evidence that this was Japan's last effort to solve U.S.-Japanese differences by peaceful means and the strong intimation of the surprise attack; the Tokyo-Hong Kong dispatch of November 14, which told of Japan's intentions to initiate war with the two Anglo-Saxon powers if the Washington negotiations failed; the Tokyo-Washington dispatch of November 28, which stated that the American note of November 26 had terminated those negotiations; the Pilot Message of December 6, which told that the Declaration of War was about to arrive in Washington, and that its delivery to the U.S. Government was to be especially timed, an essential feature for synchronizing the surprise attack with that delivery.

Not later than by November 28, the War and Navy Departments should have ordered the Hawaiian Commanders to place the Joint Army-Navy Coastal Frontier Defense Plans in effect, and to unify their Commands; the Navy Department should have ordered the mobilization of the Naval Establishment.

On November 28, the Chief of Naval Operations should have ordered Admiral Kimmel to recall the *Enterprise* from the Wake operation, and a few days later should have directed the cancellation of the contemplated sending of the *Lexington* to Midway.

. . . [N]ot one word of this information and none of the foregoing orders were sent to Hawaii.

General Marshall Looks Ahead, but Admiral Stark Lets the Cat Out of the Bag

Everything that happened in Washington on Saturday and Sunday, December 6 and 7, supports the belief that President Roosevelt had directed that no message be sent to the Hawaiian Commanders before noon on Sunday, Washington time.

General Marshall apparently appreciated that failure to act on the Declaration of War message and its timed delivery was going to be very difficult to explain on the witness stand when the future inevitable investigation into the incidents of those days took place. His avoidance of contact with the messages after the Pilot message until 11:25 on Sunday morning was unquestionably prompted by these thoughts. Otherwise, he would undoubtedly have been in his office by 8:00 A.M. on that fateful day.

Admiral Stark, on the other hand, did arrive in his office at 9:25 A.M. on Sunday, and at once accepted delivery of the full Declaration of War message. Against the advice of his assistants, he refused to inform Admiral Kimmel of its receipt. Forty minutes later, he knew that the 14-part message was to be delivered to the U.S. Government at 1:00 P.M., Washington time, which was 7:30 A.M., Hawaiian time, as was pointed out to him at once. Again, despite the urging of certain of his aides, he refused to send word to Admiral Kimmel.

Never before in recorded history had a field commander been denied information that his country would be at war in a matter of hours, and that everything pointed to a surprise attack upon his forces shortly after sunrise. No Naval Officer, on his own initiative, would ever make such a decision as Admiral Stark thus did.

That fact and Admiral Stark's decisions on that Sunday morning, even if they had not been supported by the wealth of earlier evidence, would reveal, beyond question, the basic truth of the Pearl Harbor story, namely that these Sunday messages and so many earlier ones, of vital import to Admiral Kimmel's exercise of his command, were not sent because Admiral Stark had orders from the President, which prohibited that action.

This deduction is fully supported by the Admiral's statement to the press in August, 1945, that all he did during the pre-Pearl Harbor days was done on order of higher authority, which can only mean President Roosevelt. The most arresting thing he did, during that time, was to withhold information from Admiral Kimmel.

President Roosevelt's Strategy Accomplishes Its Purpose

Thus, by holding a weak Pacific Fleet in Hawaii as an invitation to a surprise attack, and by denying the Commander of that Fleet the information which might cause him to render that attack impossible, President Roosevelt brought war to the United States on December 7, 1941. He took a fully aroused nation into the fight because none of its people suspected how the Japanese surprise attack fitted into their President's plans. Disastrous as it was from a naval standpoint, the Pearl Harbor attack proved to be the diplomatic prelude to the complete defeat of the Axis Powers.

As each reader will make up his own mind regarding the various questions raised by President Roosevelt's solution to his problem, nothing would be gained by an ethical analysis of that solution.

Notes

1. Admiral Kimmel had asked the author to act as his counsel before the Roberts Commission, but the Admiral was not allowed counsel. Nevertheless, although his status before the Commission was anomalous, the author did accompany the Admiral whenever the latter testified before that body, and late on the first day of that testimony was sworn as a witness. During the discussion connected with this swearing, the following exchange occurred:

   Justice Roberts: "So it is understood that you are not acting as counsel."
   Admiral Theobald: "No, sir."
   General McCoy: "The admiral is not on trial, of course."
   Justice Roberts: "No, this is not a trial of the admiral, in any sense."

   It has always been difficult to understand Justice Roberts' statement that Admiral Kimmel was not on trial. The Commission came into being to investigate the surprise attack upon the Fleet which he had commanded at the time, and it was generally recognized that the result of the inquiry would be the severe arraignments of Admiral Kimmel and General Short, which did constitute the principal findings of the Commission; findings which were given wide publicity at the earliest possible moment.
2. U.S.S. *Panay*, an American gunboat, sunk by Japanese bombing planes on the Yangtze River on December 12, 1937.

NO

Roberta Wohlstetter

Surprise

If our intelligence system and all our other channels of information failed to produce an accurate image of Japanese intentions and capabilities, it was not for want of the relevant materials. Never before have we had so complete an intelligence picture of the enemy. And perhaps never again will we have such a magnificent collection of sources at our disposal.

Retrospect

To review these sources briefly, an American cryptanalyst, Col. William F. Friedman, had broken the top-priority Japanese diplomatic code, which enabled us to listen to a large proportion of the privileged communications between Tokyo and the major Japanese embassies throughout the world. Not only did we know in advance how the Japanese ambassadors in Washington were advised, and how much they were instructed to say, but we also were listening to top-secret messages on the Tokyo-Berlin and Tokyo-Rome circuits, which gave us information vital for conduct of the war in the Atlantic and Europe. In the Far East this source provided minute details on movements connected with the Japanese program of expansion into Southeast Asia.

Besides the strictly diplomatic codes, our cryptanalysts also had some success in reading codes used by Japanese agents in major American and foreign ports. Those who were on the distribution list for MAGIC had access to much of what these agents were reporting to Tokyo and what Tokyo was demanding of them in the Panama Canal Zone, in cities along the east and west coasts of the Americas from northern Canada as far south as Brazil, and in ports throughout the Far East, including the Philippines and the Hawaiian Islands. They could determine what installations, what troop and ship movements, and what alert and defense measures were of interest to Tokyo at these points on the globe, as well as approximately how much correct information her agents were sending her.

Our naval leaders also had at their disposal the results of radio traffic analysis. While before the war our naval radio experts could not read the content of any Japanese naval or military coded messages, they were able to deduce from a study of intercepted ship call signs the composition and location of the Japanese Fleet units. After a change in call signs, they might lose sight of some units, and units that went into port in home waters were also lost because the ships in port used frequencies that our radios were unable to intercept. Most of the time, however, our traffic analysts had the various Japanese Fleet units accurately pinpointed on our naval maps.

Extremely competent on-the-spot economic and political analysis was furnished by Ambassador Grew and his staff in Tokyo. Ambassador Grew was himself a most sensitive and accurate observer, as evidenced by his dispatches to the State Department. His observations were supported and supplemented with military detail by frequent reports from American naval attachés and observers in key Far Eastern ports. Navy Intelligence had men with radio equipment located along the coast of China, for example, who reported the convoy movements toward Indochina. There were also naval observers stationed in various high-tension areas in Thailand and Indochina who could fill in the local outlines of Japanese political intrigue and military planning. In Tokyo and other Japanese cities, it is true, Japanese censorship grew more and more rigid during 1941, until Ambassador Grew felt it necessary to disclaim any responsibility for noting or reporting overt military evidence of an imminent outbreak of war. This careful Japanese censorship naturally cut down visual confirmation of the decoded information but very probably never achieved the opaqueness of Russia's Iron Curtain.

During this period the data and interpretations of British intelligence were also available to American officers in Washington and the Far East, though the British and Americans tended to distrust each other's privileged information.

In addition to secret sources, there were some excellent public ones. Foreign correspondents for *The New York Times, The Herald Tribune*, and *The Washington Post* were stationed in Tokyo and Shanghai and in Canberra, Australia. Their reporting as well as their predictions on the Japanese political scene were on a very high level. Frequently their access to news was more rapid and their judgment of its significance as reliable as that of our Intelligence officers. This was certainly the case for 1940 and most of 1941. For the last few weeks before the Pearl Harbor strike, however, the public newspaper accounts were not very useful. It was necessary to have secret information in order to know what was happening. Both Tokyo and Washington exercised very tight control over leaks during this crucial period, and the newsmen accordingly had to limit their accounts to speculation and notices of diplomatic meetings with no exact indication of the content of the diplomatic exchanges.

The Japanese press was another important public source. During 1941 it proclaimed with increasing shrillness the Japanese government's determination to pursue its program of expansion into Southeast Asia and the desire of the military to clear the Far East of British and American colonial exploitation. This particular source was rife with explicit signals of aggressive intent.

Finally, an essential part of the intelligence picture for 1941 was both public and privileged information on American policy and activities in the Far East. During the year the pattern of action and interaction between the Japanese and American governments grew more and more complex. At the last, it became especially important for anyone charged with the responsibility of ordering an alert to know what moves the American government was going to make with respect to Japan, as well as to try to guess what Japan's next move would be, since Japan's next move would respond in part to ours. Unfortunately our military leaders, and especially our Intelligence officers, were sometimes as surprised as the Japanese at the moves of the White House and the State Department. They usually had more orderly anticipations about Japanese policy and conduct than they had about America's. On the other hand, it was also true that State Department and White House officials were handicapped in judging Japanese intentions and estimates of risk by an inadequate picture of our own military vulnerability.

All of the public and private sources of information mentioned were available to America's political and military leaders in 1941. It is only fair to remark, however, that no single person or agency ever had at any given moment all the signals existing in this vast information network. The signals lay scattered in a number of different agencies; some were decoded, some were not; some traveled through rapid channels of communication, some were blocked by technical or procedural delays; some never reached a center of decision. But it is legitimate to review again the general sort of picture that emerged during the first week of December from the signals readily at hand. Anyone close to President Roosevelt was likely to have before him the following significant fragments.

There was first of all a picture of gathering troop and ship movements down the China coast and into Indochina. The large dimensions of this movement to the south were established publicly and visually as well as by analysis of ship call signs. Two changes in Japanese naval call signs—one on November 1 and another on December 1—had also been evaluated by Naval Intelligence as extremely unusual and as signs of major preparations for some sort of Japanese offensive. The two changes had interfered with the speed of American radio traffic analysis. Thousands of interceptions after December 1 were necessary before the new call signs could be read. Partly for this reason American radio analysts disagreed about the locations of the Japanese carriers. One group held that all the carriers were near Japan because they had not been able to identify a carrier call sign since the middle of November. Another group believed that they had located one carrier division in the Marshalls. The probability seemed to be that the carriers, wherever they were, had gone into radio silence; and past experience led the analysts to believe that they were therefore in waters near the Japanese homeland, where they could communicate with each other on wavelengths that we could not intercept. However, our inability to locate the carriers exactly, combined with the two changes in call signs, was itself a danger signal.

Our best secret source, MAGIC, was confirming the aggressive intentions of the new military cabinet in Tokyo, which had replaced the last moderate cabinet on October 17. In particular, MAGIC provided details of some of the preparations for the move into Southeast Asia. Running counter to this were increased troop shipments to the Manchurian border in October. (The intelligence picture is never clear-cut.) But withdrawals had begun toward the end of that month. MAGIC also carried explicit instructions to the Japanese ambassadors in Washington to pursue diplomatic negotiations with the United States with increasing energy, but at the same time it announced a deadline for the favorable conclusion of the negotiations, first for November 25, later postponed until November 29. In case of diplomatic failure by that date, the Japanese ambassadors were told, Japanese patience would be exhausted, Japan was determined to pursue her Greater East Asia policy, and on November 29 "things" would automatically begin to happen.

On November 26 Secretary Hull rejected Japan's latest bid for American approval of her policies in China and Indochina. MAGIC had repeatedly characterized this Japanese overture as the "last," and it now revealed the ambassadors' reaction of consternation and despair over the American refusal and also their country's characterization of the American Ten Point Note as an "ultimatum."

On the basis of this collection of signals, Army and Navy Intelligence experts in Washington tentatively placed D-day *for the Japanese Southeastern campaign* during the week end of November 30, and when this failed to materialize, during the week end of December 7. They also compiled an accurate list of probable British and Dutch targets and included the Philippines and Guam as possible American targets.

Also available in this mass of information, but long forgotten, was a rumor reported by Ambassador Grew in January, 1941. It came from what was regarded as a not-very-reliable source, the Peruvian embassy, and stated that the Japanese were preparing a surprise air attack on Pearl Harbor. Curiously the date of the report is coincident roughly with what we now know to have been the date of inception of Yamamoto's plan; but the coincidence is fairly pure. The rumor was traced to a Japanese cook in the Embassy who had been reading a novel that began with an attack on Pearl Harbor. Consequently everyone concerned, including Ambassador Grew, labeled the rumor as quite fantastic and the plan as absurdly impossible. American judgment was consistent with Japanese judgment at this time, since Yamamoto's plan was in direct contradiction to Japanese naval tactical doctrine.

Perspective

On the basis of this rapid recapitulation of the highlights in the signal picture, it is apparent that our decisionmakers had at hand an impressive amount of information on the enemy. They did not have the complete list of targets, since none of the last-minute estimates included Pearl Harbor. They did not know the exact hour and date for opening the attack. They did not have an accurate knowledge of Japanese capabilities or of Japanese ability to accept very high risks. The crucial question then, we repeat, is, If we could enumerate accurately the British and Dutch targets and give credence to a Japanese attack against them either on November 30 or December 7, why were we not expecting a specific danger to *ourselves?* And by the word "expecting," we mean expecting in the sense of taking specific alert actions to meet the contingencies of attack by land, sea, or air.

There are several answers to this question. . . . First of all, it is much easier *after* the event to sort the relevant from the irrelevant signals. After the event, of course, a signal is always crystal clear; we can now see what disaster it was signaling, since the disaster has occurred. But before the event it is obscure and pregnant with conflicting meanings. It comes to the observer embedded in an atmosphere of "noise," i.e., in the company of all sorts of information that is useless and irrelevant for predicting the particular disaster. For example, in Washington, Pearl Harbor signals were competing with a vast number of signals from the European theater. These European signals announced danger more frequently and more specifically than any coming from the Far East. The Far Eastern signals were also arriving at a center of decision where they had to compete with the prevailing belief that an unprotected offensive force acts as a deterrent rather than a target. In Honolulu they were competing not with signals from the European theater, but rather with a large number of signals announcing Japanese intentions and preparations to attack Soviet Russia rather than to move southward; here they were also competing with expectations of local sabotage prepared by previous alert situations.

In short, we failed to anticipate Pearl Harbor not for want of the relevant materials, but because of a plethora of irrelevant ones. Much of the appearance of wanton neglect that emerged in various investigations of the disaster resulted from the unconscious suppression of vast congeries of signs pointing in every direction except Pearl Harbor. It was difficult later to recall these signs since they had led nowhere. Signals that are characterized today as absolutely unequivocal warnings of surprise air attack on Pearl Harbor become, on analysis in the context of December, 1941, not merely ambiguous but occasionally inconsistent with such an attack. To recall one of the most controversial and publicized examples, the winds code, both General Short and Admiral Kimmel testified that if they had had this information, they would have been prepared on the morning of December 7 for an air attack from without. The messages establishing the winds code are often described in the Pearl Harbor literature as Tokyo's declaration of war against America. If they indeed amounted to such a declaration, obviously the failure to inform Honolulu of this vital news would have been criminal negligence. On examination, however, the messages proved to be instructions for code communication after normal commercial channels had been cut. In one message the recipient was instructed on receipt of an execute to destroy all remaining codes in his possession. In another version the recipient was warned that the execute would be sent out "when relations are becoming dangerous" between Japan and three other countries. There was a different code term for each country: England, America, and the Soviet Union.

There is no evidence that an authentic execute of either message was ever intercepted by the United States before December 7. The message ordering code destruction was in any case superseded by a much more explicit codedestruction order from Tokyo that was intercepted on December 2 and translated on December 3. After December 2, the receipt of a winds-code execute for code destruction would therefore have added nothing new to our information, and code destruction in itself cannot be taken as an unambiguous substitute for a formal declaration of war. During the first week of December the United States ordered all American consulates in the Far East to destroy all American codes, yet no one has attempted to prove that this order was equivalent to an American declaration of war against Japan. As for the other winds-code message, provided an execute had been received warning that relations were dangerous between Japan and the United States, there would still have been no way on the basis of this signal alone to determine whether Tokyo was signaling Japanese intent to attack the United States or Japanese fear of an American surprise attack (in reprisal for Japanese aggressive moves against American allies in the Far East). It was only after the event that "dangerous relations" could be interpreted as "surprise air attack on Pearl Harbor."

There is a difference, then, between having a signal available somewhere in the heap of irrelevancies, and perceiving it as a warning; and there is also a difference between perceiving it as a warning, and acting or getting action on it. These distinctions, simple as they are, illuminate the obscurity shrouding this moment in history.

Many instances of these distinctions have been examined in the course of this study. We shall recall a few of the most dramatic now. To illustrate the difference between having and perceiving a signal, let us [look at] Colonel Fielder. . . . Though he was an untrained and inexperienced Intelligence officer, he headed Army Intelligence at Pearl Harbor at the time of the attack. He had been on the job for only four months, and he regarded as quite satisfactory his sources of information and his contacts with the Navy locally and with Army Intelligence in Washington. Evidently he was unaware that Army Intelligence in Washington was not allowed to send him any "action" or policy information, and he was therefore not especially concerned about trying to read beyond the obvious meaning of any given communication that came under his eyes. Colonel Bratton, head of Army Far Eastern Intelligence in Washington, however, had a somewhat more realistic view of the extent of Colonial Fielder's knowledge. At the end of November, Colonel Bratton had learned about the winds-code setup and was also apprised that the naval traffic analysis unit under Commander Rochefort in Honolulu was monitoring 24 hours a day for an execute. He was understandably worried about the lack of communication between this unit and Colonel Fielder's office, and by December 5 he finally felt that the matter was urgent enough to warrant sending a message directly to Colonel Fielder about the winds code. Now any information on the winds code, since it belonged to the highest classification of secret information, and since it was therefore automatically evaluated as "action" information, could not be sent through normal G-2 channels. Colonel Bratton had to figure out another way to get the information to Colonel Fielder. He sent this message: "Contact Commander Rochefort immediately thru Commandant Fourteenth Naval District regarding broadcasts from Tokyo reference weather." Signal Corps records establish that Colonel Fielder received this message. How did he react to it? He filed it. According to his testimony in 1945, it made no impression on him and he did not attempt to see Rochefort. He could not sense any urgency behind the lines because he was not expecting immediate trouble, and his expectations determined what he read. A warning signal was available to him, but he did not perceive it.

Colonel Fielder's lack of experience may make this example seem to be an exception. So let us recall the performance of Captain Wilkinson, the naval officer who headed the Office of Naval Intelligence in Washington in the fall of 1941 and who is unanimously acclaimed for a distinguished and brilliant career. His treatment of a now-famous Pearl Harbor signal does not sound much different in the telling. After the event, the signal in question was labeled "the bomb-plot message." It originated in Tokyo on September 24 and was sent to an agent in Honolulu. It requested the agent to divide Pearl Harbor into five areas and to make his future reports on ships in harbor with reference to those areas. Tokyo was especially interested in the locations of battleships, destroyers, and carriers, and also in any information on the mooring of more than one ship at a single dock.

This message was decoded and translated on October 9 and shortly thereafter distributed to Army, Navy, and State Department recipients of MAGIC. Commander Kramer, a naval expert on MAGIC, had marked the message with an asterisk, signifying that he thought it to be of particular interest. But what was its interest? Both he and Wilkinson agreed that it illustrated the "nicety" of Japanese intelligence, the incredible zeal and efficiency with which they collected detail. The division into areas was interpreted as a device for shortening the reports. Admiral Stark was similarly impressed with Japanese efficiency, and no one felt it necessary to forward the message to Admiral Kimmel. No one read into it a specific danger to ships anchored in Pearl Harbor. At the time, this was a reasonable estimate, since somewhat similar requests for information were going to Japanese agents in Panama, Vancouver, Portland, San Diego, San Francisco, and other places. It should be observed, however, that the estimate was reasonable only on the basis of a very rough check on the quantity of espionage messages passing between Tokyo and these American ports. No one in Far Eastern Intelligence had subjected the messages to any more refined analysis. An observer assigned to such a job would have been able to record an increase in the frequency and specificity of Tokyo's requests concerning Manila and Pearl Harbor in the last weeks before the outbreak of war, and he would have noted that Tokyo was not displaying the same interest in other American ports. These observations, while not significant in isolation, might have been useful in the general signal picture.

There is no need, however, to confine our examples to Intelligence personnel. Indeed, the crucial areas where the signals failed to communicate a warning were in the operational branches of the armed services. Let us take Admiral Kimmel and his reaction to the information that the Japanese were destroying most of their codes in major Far Eastern consulates and also in London and Washington. Since the Pearl Harbor attack, this information has frequently been characterized by military experts who were not stationed in Honolulu as an "unmistakable tip-off." As Admiral Ingersoll explained at the congressional hearings, with the lucidity characteristic of statements after the event:

> If you rupture diplomatic negotiations you do not necessarily have to burn your codes. The diplomats go home and they can pack up their codes with their dolls and take them home. Also, when you rupture diplomatic negotiations, you do not rupture consular relations. The consuls stay on.
>
> Now, in this particular set of dispatches that did not mean a rupture of diplomatic negotiations, it meant war, and that information was sent out to the fleets as soon as we got it. . . .[1]

The phrase "it meant war" was, of course, pretty vague; war in Manila, Hong Kong, Singapore, and Batavia is not war 5000 miles away in Pearl Harbor. Before the event, for Admiral Kimmel, code burning in major Japanese consulates in the Far East may have "meant war," but it did not signal danger of an air attack on Pearl Harbor. In the first place, the information that he received was not the original MAGIC. He learned from Washington that Japanese consulates were burning "almost all" of their codes, not all of them, and Honolulu was not included on the list. He knew from a local source that the Japanese consulate in Honolulu was burning secret papers (not necessarily codes), and this back yard burning had happened three or four times during the year. In July, 1941, Kimmel had been informed that the Japanese consulates in lands neighboring Indochina had destroyed codes, and he interpreted the code burning in December as a similar attempt to protect codes in case the Americans or their British and Dutch allies tried to seize the consulates in reprisal for the southern advance. This also was a reasonable interpretation at the time, though not an especially keen one.

Indeed, at the time there was a good deal of evidence available to support all the wrong interpretations of last-minute signals, and the interpretations appeared wrong only *after* the event. There was, for example, a good deal of evidence to support the hypothesis that Japan would attack the Soviet Union from the east while the Russian Army was heavily engaged in the west. Admiral Turner, head of Navy War Plans in Washington, was an enthusiastic adherent of this view and argued the high probability of a Japanese attack on Russia up until the last week in November, when he had to concede that most of Japan's men and supplies were moving south. Richard Sorge, the expert Soviet spy who had direct access to the Japanese Cabinet, had correctly predicted the southern move as early as July, 1941, but even he was deeply alarmed during September and early October by the large number of troop movements to the Manchurian border. He feared that his July advice to the Soviet Union had been in error, and his alarm ultimately led to his capture on October 14. For at this time he increased his radio messages to Moscow to the point where it was possible for the Japanese police to pinpoint the source of the broadcasts.

It is important to emphasize here that most of the men that we have cited in our examples, such as Captain Wilkinson and Admirals Turner and Kimmel—these men and their colleagues who were involved in the Pearl Harbor disaster—were as efficient and loyal a group of men as one could find. Some of them were exceptionally able and dedicated. The fact of surprise at Pearl Harbor has never been persuasively explained by accusing the participants, individually or in groups, of conspiracy or negligence or stupidity. What these examples illustrate is rather the very human tendency to pay attention to the signals that support current expectations about enemy behavior. If no one is listening for signals of an attack against a highly improbable target, then it is very difficult for the signals to be heard.

For every signal that came into the information net in 1941 there were usually several plausible alternative explanations, and it is not surprising that our observers and analysts were inclined to select the explanations that fitted the popular hypotheses. They sometimes set down new contradictory evidence side by side with existing hypotheses, and they also sometimes held two contradictory beliefs at the same time. We have seen this happen in G-2 estimates for the fall of 1941. Apparently human beings have a stubborn attachment to old beliefs and an equally stubborn resistance to new material that will upset them.

Besides the tendency to select whatever was in accord with one's expectations, there were many other blocks to perception that prevented our analysts from making the correct interpretation. We have just mentioned the masses of conflicting evidence that supported alternative and equally reasonable hypotheses. This is the phenomenon of noise in which a signal is embedded. Even at its normal level, noise presents problems in distraction; but in addition to the natural clatter of useless information and competing signals, in 1941 a number of factors combined to raise the usual noise level. First of all, it had been raised, especially in Honolulu, by the background of previous alert situations and false alarms. Earlier alerts, as we have seen, had centered attention on local sabotage and on signals supporting the hypothesis of a probable Japanese attack on Russia. Second, in both Honolulu and Washington, individual reactions to danger had been numbed, or at least dulled, by the continuous international tension.

A third factor that served to increase the natural noise level was the positive effort made by the enemy to keep the relevant signals quiet. The Japanese security system was an important and successful block to perception. It was able to keep the strictest cloak of secrecy around the Pearl Harbor attack and to limit knowledge only to those closely associated with the details of military and naval planning. In the Japanese Cabinet only the Navy Minister and the Army Minister (who was also Prime Minister) knew of the plan before the task force left its final port of departure.

In addition to keeping certain signals quiet, the enemy tried to create noise, and sent false signals into our information system by carrying on elaborate "spoofs." False radio traffic made us believe that certain ships were maneuvering near the mainland of Japan. The Japanese also sent to individual commanders false war plans for Chinese targets, which were changed only at the last moment to bring them into line with the Southeastern movement.

A fifth barrier to accurate perception was the fact that the relevant signals were subject to change, often very sudden change. This was true even of the so-called static intelligence, which included data on capabilities and the composition of military forces. In the case of our 1941 estimates of the infeasibility of torpedo attacks in the shallow waters of Pearl Harbor, or the underestimation of the range and performance of the Japanese Zero, the changes happened too quickly to appear in an intelligence estimate.

Sixth, our own security system sometimes prevented the communication of signals. It confronted our officers with the problem of trying to keep information from the enemy without keeping it from each other, and, as in the case of MAGIC, they were not always successful. As we have seen, only a very few key individuals saw these secret messages, and they saw them only briefly. They had no opportunity or time to make a critical review of the material, and each one assumed that others who had seen it would arrive at identical interpretations. Exactly who those "others" were was not quite clear to any recipient.

Admiral Stark, for example, thought Admiral Kimmel was reading all of MAGIC. Those who were not on the list of recipients, but who had learned somehow of the existence of the decodes, were sure that they contained military as well as diplomatic information and believed that the contents were much fuller and more precise than they actually were. The effect of carefully limiting the reading and discussion of MAGIC, which was certainly necessary to safeguard the secret of our knowledge of the code, was thus to reduce this group of signals to the point where they were scarcely heard.

To these barriers of noise and security we must add the fact that the necessarily precarious character of intelligence information and predictions was reflected in the wording of instructions to take action. The warning messages were somewhat vague and ambiguous. Enemy moves are often subject to reversal on short notice, and this was true for the Japanese. They had plans for canceling their attacks on American possessions in the Pacific up to 24 hours before the time set for attack. A full alert in the Hawaiian Islands, for example, was one condition that might have caused the Pearl Harbor task force to return to Japan on December 5 or 6. The fact that intelligence predictions must be based on moves that are almost always reversible makes understandable the reluctance of the intelligence analyst to make bold assertions. Even if he is willing to risk his reputation on a firm prediction of attack at a definite time and place, no commander will in turn lightly risk the penalties and costs of a full alert. In December, 1941, a full alert required shooting down any unidentified aircraft sighted over the Hawaiian Islands. Yet this might have been interpreted by Japan as the first overt act. At least that was one consideration that influenced General Short to order his lowest degree of alert. While the cautious phrasing in the messages to the theater is certainly understandable, it nevertheless constituted another block on the road to perception. The sentences in the final theater warnings—"A surprise aggressive move in any direction is a possibility" and "Japanese future action unpredictable but hostile action possible at any moment"—could scarcely have been expected to inform the theater commanders of any change in their strategic situation.

Last but not least we must also mention the blocks to perception and communication inherent in any large bureaucratic organization, and those that stemmed from intraservice and interservice rivalries. The most glaring example of rivalry in the Pearl Harbor case was that between Naval War Plans and Naval Intelligence. A general prejudice against intellectuals and specialists, not confined to the military but unfortunately widely held in America, also made it difficult for intelligence experts to be heard. McCollum, Bratton, Sadtler, and a few others who felt that the signal picture was ominous enough to warrant more urgent warnings had no power to influence decision. The Far Eastern code analysts, for example, were believed to be too immersed in the "Oriental point of view." Low budgets for American Intelligence departments reflected the low prestige of this activity, whereas in England, Germany, and Japan, 1941 budgets reached a height that was regarded by the American Congress as quite beyond reason.

In view of all these limitations to perception and communication, is the fact of surprise at Pearl Harbor, then, really so surprising? Even with these limitations explicitly recognized, there remains the step between perception and action. Let us assume that the first hurdle has been crossed: An available signal has been perceived as an indication of imminent danger. Then how do we resolve the next questions: What specific danger is the signal trying to communicate, and what specific action or preparation should follow?

On November 27, General MacArthur had received a war warning very similar to the one received by General Short in Honolulu. MacArthur's response had been promptly translated into orders designed to protect his bombers from possible air attack from Formosan land bases. But the orders were carried out very slowly. By December 8, Philippine time, only half of the bombers ordered to the south had left the Manila area, and reconnaissance over Formosa had not been undertaken. There was no sense of urgency in preparing for a Japanese air attack, partly because our intelligence estimates had calculated that the Japanese aircraft did not have sufficient range to bomb Manila from Formosa.

The information that Pearl Harbor had been attacked arrived at Manila early in the morning of December 8, giving the Philippine forces some 9 or 10 hours to prepare for an attack. But did an air attack on Pearl Harbor necessarily mean that the Japanese would strike from the air at the Philippines? Did they have enough equipment to mount both air attacks successfully? Would they come from Formosa or from carriers? Intelligence had indicated that they would have to come from carriers, yet the carriers were evidently off Hawaii. MacArthur's headquarters also pointed out that there had been no formal declaration of war against Japan by the United States. Therefore approval could not be granted for a counterattack on Formosan bases. Furthermore there were technical disagreements among airmen as to whether a counterattack should be mounted without advance photographic reconnaissance. While Brereton was arranging permission to undertake photographic reconnaissance, there was further disagreement about what to do with the aircraft in the meantime. Should they be sent aloft or should they be dispersed to avoid destruction in case the Japanese reached the airfields? When the Japanese bombers arrived shortly after noon, they found all the American aircraft wingtip to wingtip on the ground. Even the signal of an actual attack on Pearl Harbor was not an unambiguous signal of an attack on the Philippines, and it did not make clear what response was best.

Note

1. *Hearings*, Part 9, p. 4226.

POSTSCRIPT

Did President Roosevelt Deliberately Withhold Information About the Attack on Pearl Harbor from the American Commanders?

Theobald was an eyewitness to the Pearl Harbor attack. In his selection, he defends his former boss, Admiral Husband E. Kimmel of the U.S. Pacific Fleet, from responsibility for the fleet's lack of preparation prior to Japan's surprise attack. Theobald argues that President Roosevelt and his chief military aides deliberately withheld from Kimmel information that they had received from intelligence intercepts going to Japanese diplomats that the Japanese navy was going to attack Pearl Harbor on December 7. Why would Roosevelt do such a thing? Because, says Theobald, Roosevelt wanted to enter the war against Germany and Japan, but he could not mobilize a reluctant public for war unless the United States was attacked first. Disastrous as it was from a naval standpoint, says Theobald, "the Pearl Harbor attack proved to be the diplomatic prelude to the complete defeat of the Axis Powers."

Theobald wrote *The Final Secret of Pearl Harbor* in the 1950s at the height of the battle between the internationist historians, who defended Roosevelt's policies toward Germany and Japan, and the revisionists, who believed that Roosevelt unnecessarily and deliberately deceived the American public by enticing the Japanese to attack Pearl Harbor. Both groups held different assumptions about the nature of America's foreign policy before World War II. Internationalists believed that Germany and Japan constituted threats to world peace and the overall balance of power and that they had to be defeated with or without active U.S. participation in the war. Revisionist historians believed that Germany and Japan did not threaten America's security even if they controlled Europe and Asia. For the best defenses of President Roosevelt's foreign policies, see Robert Dallek, *Franklin Roosevelt and American Foreign Policy, 1932–1945* (Oxford University Press, 1979) and Waldo H. Heinrichs, *Threshold of War: Franklin D. Roosevelt and American Entry Into World War II* (Oxford University Press, 1988). Early revisionist studies of Roosevelt are summarized in Harry Elmer Barnes, ed., *Perpetual War for Perpetual Peace: A Critical Examination of the Foreign Policy of Franklin D. Roosevelt and Its Aftermath* (Caxton, 1953). Later criticisms include John T. Toland, *Infamy: Pearl Harbor and Its Aftermath* (Doubleday, 1982) and *Wind Over Sand: The Diplomacy of Franklin Roosevelt* (University of Georgia Press, 1988).

Theobald's account raises a number of questions. Did Roosevelt shift 3 battleships, 1 aircraft carrier, 4 light cruisers, and 18 destroyers for duty in mention)?

Or was Roosevelt, who knew that their intelligence agents would be aware of the maneuvers, trying to entice the Japanese to attack Pearl Harbor? What about Theobald's charge that the commanders at Pearl Harbor were deliberately denied information about Japan's plans so that the Japanese Navy would be tempted to attack the fleet? If this is true, why wasn't Roosevelt tried as a war criminal (after his death)? Furthermore, if the president wanted to use the attack to get America into the war, why would he destroy most of his Pacific task force? Perhaps Gordon W. Prange is correct to reject revisionist historians in his massive, well-documented account *At Dawn We Slept: The Untold Story of Pearl Harbor* (McGraw-Hill, 1981). Prange faults the commanders at Pearl Harbor: Lieutenant General Walter C. Short, for example, was so obsessed with sabotage that ammunition was not available when the attack came. Short also failed to use radar and ignored Washington's orders to undertake reconnaissance.

Although most revisionists will disagree with her, Wohlstetter's analysis of the decision-making process provides an alternative to both the revisionist conspiratorial views of Roosevelt and his staunchest defenders. Wohlstetter makes several telling points. First, the intelligence community was organizationally divided between army and navy intelligence units in Washington, D.C., and Hawaii, so there was no systematic analysis of the decrypted diplomatic messages collectively known as MAGIC by the War Department's Signal Intelligence Service (SIS). Second, because of the abundance of information from public and private sources as well as from diplomatic intelligence intercepts, it was difficult to sort through the noise level and separate relevant materials from irrelevant materials. Third, the Japanese themselves provided misleading signals so that American observers would think the fleet was home—near the Marshall Islands. Fourth, even though President Roosevelt knew that war was coming with Japan, he thought the attack might be against Russia in Siberia, with its oil reserves, or in Southeast Asia against the British and Dutch possessions, especially Indonesia, with its important supply of rubber. Finally, Wohlstetter contends that even with an eight-hour warning, America's leaders in the Philippines were immobilized by bureaucratic indecisiveness and that Japanese planes destroyed most of the American aircraft at Clark Field because the planes were not moved to hidden areas.

The starting points for further study on Pearl Harbor are Hans Trefouse, *Pearl Harbor: The Continuing Controversy* (Krieger, 1982) and Akira Iriye, *Pearl Harbor and the Coming of the Pacific War: A Brief History With Documents and Essays* (St. Martin's Press, LLC, 1999). On Pearl Harbor itself see Gordon Prange, *Pearl Harbor: The Verdict of History* (McGraw-Hill, 1986). A trenchant analysis with a comprehensive bibliography of the whole period is Justus D. Doenecke and John E. Wiltz, *From Isolation to War: 1931–1941,* 2d ed. (Harlan Davidson, 1991). For a discussion of early interpretations, see Wayne S. Cole, "American Entry Into World War II: A Historiographical Appraisal," *Mississippi Valley Historical Review* (March 1957). For a more recent evaluation, see J. Gary Clifford, "Both Ends of the Telescope: New Perspectives on F.D.R. and American Entry Into World War II," *Diplomatic History* (Spring 1989).

On the Internet . . .

Internet Web sites containing historical material relevant to the subjects discussed in this chapter can be reached through the McGraw-Hill history site.

http://www.mhhe.com/socscience/history/usa/link/linktop.htm

Cold War Hot Links

This page contains links to Web pages on the Cold War that a variety of people have created. They run the entire spectrum of political thought and provide some interesting views on the Cold War and the state of national security.

http://www.stmartin.edu/~dprice/cold.war.html

American Studies Web: Economy Politics Resources

This American Studies Web site provides numerous links to organizations, online journals, and general professional and scholarly sites related to the U.S. economy and contemporary politics. Some sites offer up-to-the-minute information.

http://www.georgetown.edu/crossroads

PART 3

American High, 1945–1963

World War II ended in 1945. But the peace that everyone hoped for never came. By 1947, a "Cold War" between the Western powers and the Russians was in full swing. The Russians had drawn an "iron curtain" around eastern Europe, and the Americans had provided economic and military assistance to western Europe via the Truman Doctrine and Marshall Plan. In 1949, President Truman put the knife into our traditional isolationist foreign policy with the entrance of the United States into the North Atlantic Treaty Organization (NATO). Shortly thereafter, the Russians exploded an atomic bomb, the Chinese communists won the civil war, and in the summer of 1950, American soldiers were fighting a hot war of "containment" against communist expansion in Korea.

Meanwhile, a second red scare took place when it was discovered that communists had infiltrated the State and Treasury Departments of the U.S. government, as well as the atomic bomb development site at Los Alamos, New Mexico. Several high-profile trials of former State Department official Alger Hiss and communists Julius and Ethel Rosenberg captured the public's attention. By the early 1950s, state and local government agencies were overreacting by banning subversive books from local libraries and administering loyalty oaths to teachers. On a national level, left-leaning government workers who were not communists often lost their jobs, and a generation of China experts accused of selling out China to the communists lost their jobs, which set back our China policy for two decades. Senator Joseph McCarthy's investigations into government finally overreached in 1954 when the Wisconsin senator's committee held televised hearings investigating communist subversion in the army.

Americans were not only anxious about their lives in the 1950s; paradoxically, they had become the most affluent generation in history. Middle-class white Americans had moved to the new "Levittown" suburbs, while Presidents Truman, Eisenhower, and Kennedy managed an economy whose major problem was keeping inflation under control.

On November 22, 1963, America was shocked when President John F. Kennedy was assassinated while riding in an open car passing Dealey Plaza in Dallas, Texas, on a campaign stop. From a twenty-first century perspective, the death of Kennedy marked the end of the American high.

- Was the United States Responsible for the Cold War?
- Did Communism Threaten America's Internal Security After World War II?
- Did Lee Harvey Oswald Kill President Kennedy by Himself?

ISSUE 8

Was the United States Responsible for the Cold War?

YES: Thomas G. Paterson, from *Meeting the Communist Threat: Truman to Reagan* (Oxford University Press, 1988)

NO: John Lewis Gaddis, from *Russia, the Soviet Union, and the United States: An Interpretive History*, 2d ed. (McGraw-Hill, 1990)

ISSUE SUMMARY

YES: Professor of history Thomas G. Paterson argues that the Truman administration exaggerated the Soviet threat after World War II because the United States had expansionist political and economic global needs.

NO: Professor of history John Lewis Gaddis argues that the power vacuum that existed in Europe at the end of World War II exaggerated and made almost inevitable a clash between the democratic, capitalist United States and the totalitarian, communist USSR.

Historians are unable to agree on exactly when the cold war began. This is because of the rocky relationship that existed between the United States and the Soviet Union since World War I. The Wilson administration became upset when the communist government declared its neutrality in the war and pulled Russia out of the allied coalition. The Russian leader V. I. Lenin resented the allied intervention in Siberia from 1918 to 1920 because he believed that the pretext for rescuing Czech troops was an excuse to undermine Russia's communist government. The relationship between the two countries improved in 1933 after President Franklin D. Roosevelt accorded diplomatic recognition to the communist government. In the late 1930s the relationship soured once again. Russia, unable to negotiate a security treaty with France, signed a nonaggression pact with Germany on August 23, 1939. This allowed Adolf Hitler to attack Poland in early September and Soviet leader Joseph Stalin to attack Finland and take over the Baltic states Latvia, Lithuania, and Estonia. In September 1939, as World War II was breaking out in Europe, the United States—like the USSR—was officially neutral. But the Roosevelt administration pushed modifications of the neutrality laws through Congress, which enabled significant amounts of economic and military assistance to be extended to England and France. In one of history's great ironies, Stalin, who distrusted everyone, ignored British prime minister Winston Churchill's warnings and was caught completely off guard when Hitler occupied the Balkans and then launched his surprise attack against the Russians in June 1941. By November, lend-lease was extended to the Russians, who would receive a total of $11 billion by the end of the war.

The wartime coalition of the United States, Great Britain, and the USSR was an odd combination. Their common goal—defeat Hitler—temporarily submerged political differences. During the war the United States actually sided with Russia against Great Britain over the appropriate military strategy. Russia and the United States wanted a second front established in France.

As the military victory in Europe became clear, political differences began to crack open the alliance. A number of wartime conferences were held to coordinate military strategy; to establish political and economic international agencies, such as the United Nations and the International Monetary Fund; and to plan the reestablishment of governments in Eastern and Western Europe. Differences developed over the structure of the United Nations; the composition of the Polish and other Eastern European governments; and the boundaries, reparations, and occupational questions surrounding postwar Germany.

The military situation dominated the Yalta Conference in February 1945. Since the atomic bomb had not yet been tested, the United States thought that a landed invasion of the Japanese mainland would be necessary to win the war. At this time Russia and Japan were neutral toward each other. Stalin promised that three months after the war in Europe ended he would invade Japan. In return Roosevelt promised Stalin the territories and sphere of influence Russia held in Asia prior to 1905, which she had lost in a war with Japan.

Sole possession of the atomic bomb by the United States loomed in the background as the two powers failed to settle their differences after the war. Secretary of State James Byrnes hoped that the bomb would make the Russians more "manageable" in Europe, but atomic diplomacy was never really practiced. Nor were attempts at economic coercion successful.

By 1946 the cold war had begun. In February Stalin gave a speech declaring that communism and capitalism were incompatible and that future wars were inevitable. The next month, at a commencement address with President Harry S. Truman at his side, Churchill declared that an "iron curtain" had descended over Eastern Europe. In May 1946 the allies refused to send any more industrial equipment to the Russian zone in Germany.

Who started the cold war? Was it inevitable, or should one side take more of the blame? In the following selection, Thomas G. Paterson argues that the Truman administration exaggerated the Soviet threat to world peace after World War II because the United States had its own expansionist, political, and economic global needs. In the second selection, John Lewis Gaddis asserts that the power vacuum that existed in Europe at the end of World War II exaggerated ideological, political, and economic differences and made a clash between the United States and the USSR almost inevitable.

Thomas G. Paterson

YES

Harry S Truman, American Power, and the Soviet Threat

President Harry S Truman and his Secretary of State Dean Acheson, Henry A. Kissinger once remarked, "ushered in the most creative period in the history of American foreign policy." Presidents from Eisenhower to Reagan have exalted Truman for his decisiveness and success in launching the Truman Doctrine, the Marshall Plan, and NATO [North Atlantic Treaty Organization], and for staring the Soviets down in Berlin during those hair-trigger days of the blockade and airlift. John F. Kennedy and Lyndon B. Johnson invoked memories of Truman and the containment doctrine again and again to explain American intervention in Vietnam. Jimmy Carter has written in his memoirs that Truman had served as his model—that he studied Truman's career more than that of any other president and came to admire greatly his courage, honesty, and willingness "to be unpopular if he believed his actions were the best for the country." Some historians have gone so far as to claim that Truman saved humankind from World War III. On the other hand, he has drawn a diverse set of critics. The diplomat and analyst George F. Kennan, the journalist Walter Lippmann, the political scientist Hans Morgenthau, politicians of the left and right, like Henry A. Wallace and Robert A. Taft, and many historians have questioned Truman's penchant for his quick, simple answer, blunt, careless rhetoric, and facile analogies, his moralism that obscured the complexity of causation, his militarization of American foreign policy, his impatience with diplomacy itself, and his exaggeration of the Soviet threat. . . .

Because of America's unusual postwar power, the Truman Administration could expand the United States sphere of influence beyond the Western Hemisphere and also intervene to protect American interests. But this begs a key question: Why did President Truman think it necessary to project American power abroad, to pursue an activist, global foreign policy unprecedented in United States history? The answer has several parts. First, Americans drew lessons from their experience in the 1930s. While indulging in their so-called "isolationism," they had watched economic depression spawn political extremism, which in turn, produced aggression and war. Never again, they vowed. No more appeasement with totalitarians, no more Munichs. "Red Fascism" became a popular phrase to express this American idea. The message seemed evident: To prevent a reincarnation of the 1930s, the United States would have to use its vast power to fight economic instability abroad. Americans felt compelled to project their power, second, because they feared, in the peace-and-prosperity thinking of the time, economic doom stemming from an economic sickness abroad that might spread to the United States, and from American dependency on overseas supplies of raw materials. To aid Europeans and other people would not only help them, but also sustain a high American standard of living and gain political friends, as in the case of Italy, where American foreign aid and advice influenced national elections and brought defeat to the left. The American fear of postwar shortages of petroleum also encouraged the Truman Administration to penetrate Middle Eastern oil in a major way. In Saudi Arabia, for example, Americans built and operated the strategically important Dhahran Airport and dominated that nation's oil resources.

Another reason why Truman projected American power so boldly derived from new strategic thinking. Because of the advent of the air age, travel across the world was shortened in time. Strategists spoke of the shrinkage of the globe. Places once deemed beyond American curiosity or interest now loomed important. Airplanes could travel great distances to deliver bombs. Powerful as it was, then, the United States also appeared vulnerable, especially to air attack. As General Carl A. Spaatz emphasized: "As top dog, America becomes target No. 1." He went on to argue that fast aircraft left no warning time for the United States. "The Pearl Harbor of a future war might well be Chicago, or Detroit, or even Washington." To prevent such an occurrence, American leaders worked to acquire overseas bases in both the Pacific and Atlantic, thereby denying a potential enemy an attack route to the Western Hemisphere. Forward bases would also permit the United States to conduct offensive operations more effectively. The American strategic frontier had to be pushed outward. Thus the United States took the former Japanese-controlled Pacific islands of the Carolines, Marshalls, and Marianas, maintained garrisons in Germany and Japan, and sent military missions to Iran, Turkey, Greece, Saudi Arabia, China, and to fourteen Latin American states. The joint Chiefs of Staff and Department of State lists of desired foreign bases, and of sites where air transit rights were sought, included such far-flung spots as Algeria, India, French Indochina, New Zealand, Iceland, and the Azores. When asked where the American Navy would float, Navy Secretary James Forrestal replied: "Wherever there is a sea." Today we may take the presumption of a global American presence for granted, but in Truman's day it was new, even radical thinking, especially after the "isolationist" 1930s.

These several explanations for American globalism suggest that the United States would have been an expansionist power whether or not the obstructionist Soviets were lurking about. That is, America's own needs—ideological, political, economic, strategic—encouraged such a projection of power. As the influential National Security Council Paper No. 68 (NSC-68) noted in April 1950, the "overall policy" of the United States was "designed to foster a world environment in which the American system can survive and flourish." This policy "we would probably pursue even if there were no Soviet threat."

Americans, of course, did perceive a Soviet threat. Thus we turn to yet another explanation for the United States' dramatic extension of power early in the Cold War: to contain the Soviets. The Soviets unsettled Americans in so many ways. Their harsh Communist dogma and propagandistic slogans were not only monotonous; they also seemed threatening because of their call for world revolution and for the demise of capitalism. In the United Nations the Soviets cast vetoes and even on occasion walked out of the organization. At international conferences their "*nyets*" stung American ears. When they negotiated, the Soviets annoyed their interlocuters by repeating the same point over and over again, delaying meetings, or abruptly shifting positions. Truman labeled them "pigheaded," and Dean Acheson thought them so coarse and insulting that he once allowed that they were not "housebroken."

The Soviet Union, moreover, had territorial ambitions, grabbing parts of Poland, Rumania, and Finland, and demanding parts of Turkey. In Eastern Europe, with their Red Army positioned to intimidate, the Soviets quickly manhandled the Poles and Rumanians. Communists in 1947 and 1948 seized power in Hungary and Czechoslovakia. Some Americans predicted that the Soviet military would roll across Western Europe. In general, Truman officials pictured the Soviet Union as an implaccable foe to an open world, an opportunistic nation that would probe for weak spots, exploit economic misery, snuff out individual freedom, and thwart self-determination. Americans thought the worst, some claiming that a Soviet-inspired international conspiracy insured perennial hostility and a creeping aggression aimed at American interests. To Truman and his advisers, the Soviets stood as the world's bully, and the very existence of this menacing bear necessitated an activist American foreign policy and an exertion of American power as a "counterforce."

But Truman officials exaggerated the Soviet threat, imagining an adversary that never measured up to the galloping monster so often depicted by alarmist Americans. Even if the Soviets intended to dominate the world, or just Western Europe, they lacked the capabilities to do so. The Soviets had no foreign aid to dispense; outside Russia Communist parties were minorities; the Soviet economy was seriously crippled by the war; and the Soviet military suffered significant weaknesses. The Soviets lacked a modern navy, a strategic air force, the atomic bomb, and air defenses. Their wrecked economy could not support or supply an army in the field for very long, and their technology was antiquated. Their ground forces lacked motorized transportation, adequate equipment, and troop morale. A Soviet *blitzkrieg* invasion of Western Europe had little chance of success and would have proven suicidal for the Soviets, for even if they managed to gain temporary control of Western Europe by a military thrust, they could not strike the United States. So they would have to assume defensive positions and await crushing American attacks, probably including atomic bombings of Soviet Russia itself—plans for which existed.

Other evidence also suggests that a Soviet military threat to Western Europe was more myth than reality. The Soviet Union demobilized its forces after the war, dropping to about 2.9 million personnel in 1948. Many of its 175 divisions were under-strength, and large numbers of them were engaged in occupation duties, resisting challenges to Soviet authority in Eastern Europe. American intelligence sources reported as well that the Soviets could not count on troops of the occupied countries, which were quite unreliable, if not rebellious. At most, the Soviets had 700,000 to 800,000 troops available for an attack against the West. To resist such an attack, the West had about 800,000 troops, or approximate parity. For these reasons, top American leaders did not expect a Soviet onslaught against Western Europe. They and their intelligence sources emphasized Soviet military and economic weaknesses, not strengths, Soviet hesitancy, not boldness.

Why then did Americans so fear the Soviets? Why did the Central Intelligence Agency, the Joint Chiefs of Staff, and the President exaggerate the Soviet threat? The first explanation is that their intelligence estimates were just that—estimates. The American intelligence community was still in a state of infancy, hardly the well-developed system it would become in the 1950s and 1960s. So Americans lacked complete assurance that their figures on Soviet force deployment or armaments were accurate or close to the mark. When leaders do not know, they tend to assume the worst of an adversary's intentions and capabilities, or to think that the Soviets might miscalculate, sparking a war they did not want. In a chaotic world, the conception of a single, inexorably aggressive adversary also brought a comforting sense of knowing and consistency.

Truman officials also exaggerated the Soviet threat in order "to extricate the United States from commitments and restraints that were no longer considered desirable." For example, they loudly chastised the Soviets for violating the Yalta agreements; yet Truman and his advisers knew the Yalta provisions were at best vague and open to differing interpretations. But, more, they purposefully misrepresented the Yalta agreement on the vital question of the composition of the Polish government. In so doing, they hoped to decrease the high degree of Communist participation that the Yalta conferees had insured when they stated that the new Polish regime would be formed by reorganizing the provisional Lublin (Communist) government. Through charges of Soviet malfeasance Washington sought to justify its own retreat from Yalta, such as its abandonment of the $20 billion reparations figure for Germany (half of which was supposed to go to the Soviet Union).

Another reason for the exaggeration: Truman liked things in black and white, as his aide Clark Clifford noted. Nuances, ambiguities, and counterevidence were often discounted to satisfy the President's preference for the simpler answer or his pre-conceived notions of Soviet aggressiveness. In mid-1946, for example, the Joint Chiefs of Staff deleted from a report to Truman a section that stressed Soviet weaknesses. American leaders also exaggerated the Soviet threat because it was useful in galvanizing and unifying American public opinion for an abandonment of recent and still lingering "isolationism" and support for an expansive foreign policy. Kennan quoted a colleague as saying that "if it [Soviet threat] had never existed, we would have had to invent it, to create a sense of urgency we need to bring us to the point of decisive action." The military particularly overplayed the Soviet threat in order to persuade Congress to endorse larger defense budgets. This happened in 1948–49 with the creation of the North Atlantic Treaty Organization. NATO was established not to halt a Soviet military attack, because none was anticipated, but to give Europeans a psychological boost—a "will to resist." American officials believed that the European Recovery Program would falter unless there was a "sense of security" to buttress it. They nurtured apprehension, too, that some European nations might lean toward neutralism unless they were brought together under a security umbrella. NATO also seemed essential to help members resist internal subversion. The exaggerated, popular view that NATO was formed to deter a Soviet invasion of Western Europe by conventional forces stems, in part, from Truman's faulty recollection in his published memoirs.

Still another explanation for why Americans exaggerated the Soviet threat is found in their attention since the Bolshevik Revolution of 1917 to the utopian Communist goal of world revolution, confusing goals with actual behavior. Thus Americans believed that the sinister Soviets and their Communist allies would exploit postwar economic, social, and political disorder, not through a direct military thrust, but rather through covert subversion. The recovery of Germany and Japan became necessary, then, to deny the Communists political opportunities to thwart American plans for the integration of these former enemies into an American system of trade and defense. And because economic instability troubled so much of Eurasia, Communist gains through subversion might deny the United States strategic raw materials.

Why dwell on this question of the American exaggeration of the Soviet threat? Because it over-simplified international realities by under-estimating local conditions that might thwart Soviet/Communist successes and by over-estimating the Soviet ability to act. Because it encouraged the Soviets to fear encirclement and to enlarge their military establishment, thereby contributing to a dangerous weapons race. Because it led to indiscriminate globalism. Because it put a damper on diplomacy; American officials were hesitant to negotiate with an opponent variously described as malevolent, deceitful, and inhuman. They especially did not warm to negotiations when some critics were ready to cry that diplomacy, which could produce compromises, was evidence in itself of softness toward Communism.

Exaggeration of the threat also led Americans to misinterpret events and in so doing to prompt the Soviets to make decisions contrary to American wishes. For example, the Soviet presence in Eastern Europe, once considered a simple question of the Soviets' building an iron curtain or bloc after the war, is now seen by historians in more complex terms. The Soviets did not seem to have a master plan for the region and followed different policies in different countries. Poland and Rumania were subjugated right away; Yugoslavia, on the other hand, was an independent Communist state led by Josip Tito, who broke dramatically with Stalin in 1948; Hungary conducted elections in the fall of 1945 (the Communists got only 17 percent of the vote) and did not suffer a Communist coup until 1947; in Czechoslovakia, free elections in May 1946 produced a non-Communist government that functioned until 1948; Finland, although under Soviet scrutiny, affirmed its independence. The Soviets did not have a firm grip on Eastern Europe before 1948—a prime reason why many American leaders believed the Soviets harbored weaknesses.

American policies were designed to roll the Soviets back. The United States reconstruction loan policy, encouragement of dissident groups, and appeal for free elections alarmed Moscow, contributing to a Soviet push to secure the area. The issue of free elections illustrates the point. Such a call was consistent with cherished American principle. But in the context of Eastern

Europe and the Cold War, problems arose. First, Americans conspicuously followed a double standard which foreigners noted time and again; that is, if the principle of free elections really mattered, why not hold such elections in the United States' sphere of influence in Latin America, where an unsavory lot of dictators ruled? Second, free elections would have produced victories for anti-Soviet groups. Such results could only unsettle the Soviets and invite them to intervene to protect their interests in neighboring states—just as the United States had intervened in Cuba and Mexico in the twentieth century when hostile groups assumed power. In Hungary, for example, it was the non-Communist leader Ferenc Nagy who delayed elections in late 1946 because he knew the Communist Party would lose badly, thereby possibly triggering a repressive Soviet response. And, third, the United States had so little influence in Eastern Europe that it had no way of insuring free elections—no way of backing up its demands with power.

Walter Lippmann, among others, thought that the United States should tame its meddling in the region and make the best out of a bad arrangement of power. "I do believe," he said in 1947, "we shall have to recognize the principle of boundaries of spheres of influence which either side will not cross and have to proceed on the old principle that a good fence makes good neighbors." Kennan shared this view, as did one State Department official who argued that the United States was incapable of becoming a successful watchdog in Eastern Europe. American "barkings, growlings, snappings, and occasional bitings," Cloyce K. Huston prophesized, would only irritate the Soviets without reducing their power. Better still, argued some analysts, if the United States tempered its ventures into European affairs, then the Soviets, surely less alarmed, might tolerate more openness. But the United States did not stay out. Americans tried to project their power into a region where they had little chance of succeeding, but had substantial opportunity to irritate and alarm the always suspicious Soviets. In this way, it has been suggested, the United States itself helped pull down the iron curtain.

Another example of the exaggeration of the Soviet threat at work is found in the Truman Doctrine of 1947. Greece was beset by civil war, and the British could no longer fund a war against Communist-led insurgents who had a considerable non-Communist following. On March 12, Truman enunciated a universal doctrine: It "must be the policy of the United States to support free peoples who are resisting attempted subjugation by armed minorities or by outside pressures." Although he never mentioned the Soviet Union by name, his juxtaposition of words like "democratic" and "totalitarian" and his references to Eastern Europe made the menace to Greece appear to be the Soviets. But there was and is no evidence of Soviet involvement in the Greek civil war. In fact, the Soviets had urged both the Greek Communists and their allies the Yugoslavs to stop the fighting for fear that the conflict would draw the United States into the Mediterranean. And the Greek Communists were strong nationalists. The United States nonetheless intervened in a major way in Greek affairs, becoming responsible for right-wing repression and a military establishment that plagued Greek politics through much of its postwar history. As for Turkey, official Washington did not expect the Soviet Union to strike militarily against that bordering nation. The Soviets were too weak in 1947 to undertake such a major operation, and they were asking for joint control of the Dardanelles largely for defense, for security. Then why did the President, in the Truman Doctrine speech, suggest that Turkey was imminently threatened? American strategists worried that Russia's long-term objective was the subjugation of its neighbor. But they also wished to exploit an opportunity to enhance the American military position in the Mediterranean region and in a state bordering the Soviet Union. The Greek crisis and the Truman Doctrine speech provided an appropriate environment to build up an American military presence in the Eastern Mediterranean for use against the Soviets should the unwanted war ever come.

Truman's alarmist language further fixed the mistaken idea in the American mind that the Soviets were unrelenting aggressors intent upon undermining peace, and that the United States, almost alone, had to meet them everywhere. Truman's exaggerations and his commitment to the containment doctrine did not go unchallenged. Secretary Marshall himself was startled by the President's muscular anti-communist rhetoric, and he questioned the wisdom of overstating the case. The Soviet specialist Llewellyn Thompson urged "caution" in swinging too far toward "outright opposition to Russia. . . ." Walter Lippmann, in reacting to both Truman's speech and George F. Kennan's now famous "Mr. 'X'" article in the July 1947 issue of the journal *Foreign Affairs,* labeled containment a "strategic monstrosity," because it made no distinctions between important or vital and not-so-important or peripheral areas. Because American power was not omnipresent, Lippmann further argued, the "policy can be implemented only by recruiting, subsidizing and supporting a heterogeneous array of satellites, clients, dependents and puppets." He also criticized the containment doctrine for placing more emphasis on confrontation than on diplomacy.

Truman himself came to see that there were dangers in stating imprecise, universal doctrines. He became boxed by his own rhetoric. When Mao Zedong's forces claimed victory in 1949 over Jiang's regime, conservative Republicans, angry Democrats, and various McCarthyites pilloried the President for letting China "fall." China lost itself, he retorted. But his critics pressed the point: if containment was to be applied everywhere, as the President had said in the Truman Doctrine, why not China? Truman appeared inconsistent, when, in fact, in the case of China, he was ultimately prudent in cutting American losses where the United States proved incapable of reaching its goals. Unable to disarm his detractors on this issue, Truman stood vulnerable in the early 1950s to political demagogues who fueled McCarthyism. The long-term consequences in this example have been grave. Democrats believed they could never lose "another China"—never permit Communists or Marxists, whether or not linked to Moscow, to assume power abroad. President John F. Kennedy later said, for example, that he could not withdraw from Vietnam because that might be perceived as "another China" and spark charges that he was soft on Communism. America, in fact, could not bring itself to open diplomatic relations with the People's Republic of China until 1979.

Jiang's collapse joined the Soviet explosion of an atomic bomb, the formation of the German Democratic Republic (East Germany), and the

Sino-Soviet Friendship Treaty to arouse American feeling in late 1949 and early 1950 that the Soviet threat had dramatically escalated. Although Kennan told his State Department colleagues that such feeling was "largely of our own making" rather than an accurate accounting of Soviet actions, the composers of NSC-68 preferred to dwell on a more dangerous Soviet menace in extreme rhetoric not usually found in a secret report. But because the April 1950 document was aimed at President Truman, we can certainly understand why its language was hyperbolic. The fanatical and militant Soviets, concluded NSC-68, were seeking to impose "absolute authority over the rest of the world." America had to frustrate the global "design" of the "evil men" of the Kremlin, who were unrelentingly bent on "piecemeal aggression" against the "free world" through military force, infiltration, and intimidation. The report called for a huge American and allied military build-up and nuclear arms development.

NSC-68, most scholars agree, was a flawed, even amateurish document. It assumed a Communist monolith that did not exist, drew alarmist conclusions based upon vague and inaccurate information about Soviet capabilities, made grand, unsubstantiated claims about Soviet intentions, glossed over the presence of many non-democratic countries in the "free world," and recommended against negotiations with Moscow at the very time the Soviets were advancing toward a policy of "peaceful co-existence." One State Department expert on the Soviet Union, Charles E. Bohlen, although generally happy with the report's conclusions, faulted NSC-68 for assuming a Soviet plot for world conquest—for "oversimplifying the problem." No, he advised, the Soviets sought foremostly to maintain their regime and to extend it abroad "to the degree that is possible without serious risk to the internal regime." In short, there were limits to Soviet behavior. But few were listening to such cautionary voices. NSC-68 became American dogma, especially when the outbreak of the Korean War in June of 1950 sanctified it as a prophetic "we told you so."

The story of Truman's foreign policy is basically an accounting of how the United States, because of its own expansionism and exaggeration of the Soviet threat, became a global power. Truman projected American power after the Second World War to rehabilitate Western Europe, secure new allies, guarantee strategic and economic links, and block Communist or Soviet influence. He firmly implanted the image of the Soviets as relentless, worldwide transgressors with whom it is futile to negotiate. Through his exaggeration of the Soviet threat, Truman made it very likely that the United States would continue to practice global interventionism years after he left the White House.

John Lewis Gaddis

NO

The Origins of the Cold War: 1945–1953

It is, of course, a truism that coalitions tend not to survive their enemies' defeat. Certainly during World War II most observers of the international scene had expected differences eventually to arise among the victors. The hope had been, though, that a sufficiently strong framework of common interests—whether the United Nations or some mutually acceptable agreement on spheres of influence—would develop that could keep these differences within reasonable limits. This did not happen. Although both sides sought security, although neither side wanted a new war, disagreements over how to achieve those goals proved too great to overcome. With a rapidity that dismayed policymakers in both Washington and Moscow, allies shortly before united against the Axis found themselves in a confrontation with each other that would determine the shape of the postwar era. Russian-American relations, once a problem of rarely more than peripheral concern for the two countries involved, now became an object of rapt attention and anxiety for the entire world.

It is no simple matter to explain how national leaders in the United States and the Soviet Union came to hold such dissimilar concepts of postwar security. There did exist, in the history of the two countries' encounters with one another, an ample basis for mutual distrust. But there were also strong motives for cooperation, not the least of which was that, had they been able to act in concert, Russians and Americans might have achieved something close to absolute security in an insecure world. Their failure to do so may be attributed, ultimately, to irreconcilable differences in four critical areas: perceptions of history, ideology, technology, and personality.

Clearly the divergent historical experiences of the two countries conditioned their respective views of how best to attain security. The Russians tended to think of security in terms of space—not a surprising attitude, considering the frequency with which their country had been invaded, or the way in which they had used distance to defeat their adversaries. That such a concept

From RUSSIA, THE SOVIET UNION, AND THE UNITED STATES: AN INTERPRETATIVE HISTORY, 1990, pp. 175–193.

might be outmoded in an age of atomic weapons and long-range bombers appears not to have occurred to Stalin; Hitler's defeat brought no alteration in his determination to control as much territory along the periphery of the Soviet Union as possible. "He regarded as sure only whatever he held in his fist," the Yugoslav Communist Milovan Djilas has written. "Everything beyond the control of his police was a potential enemy."

Americans, on the other hand, tended to see security in institutional terms: conditioned by their own atypical historical experience, they assumed that if representative governments could be established as widely as possible, together with a collective security organization capable of resolving differences between them, peace would be assured. That such governments might not always harbor peaceful intentions toward their neighbors, that the United Nations, in the absence of great power agreement, might lack the means of settling disputes, occurred to only a few informed observers. The general public, upon whose support foreign policy ultimately depended, tended to accept Cordell Hull's vision of a postwar world in which "there will no longer be need for spheres of influence, for alliances, for balance of power, or any of the special arrangements through which, in the unhappy past, the nations sought to safeguard their security or to promote their interests."

There was, of course, room for compromising these conflicting viewpoints. Neither the United States nor its British ally had been prepared wholly to abandon spheres of influence as a means of achieving their own postwar security; both accepted the premise that the USSR was entitled to have friendly countries along its borders. The great difficulty was that, unlike the expansion of American and British influence into Western Europe and the Mediterranean, the Soviet Union's gains took place without the approval of most of the governments and most of the people in the areas involved. The Anglo-Americans simply did not find it necessary, in the same measure as did the Russians, to ensure their own security by depriving people within their sphere of influence of the right to self-determination. Given Western convictions that only the diffusion of democratic institutions could guarantee peace, given Hitler's all-too-vivid precedent, Moscow's imposition of influence in Eastern Europe seemed ominous, whatever its motives. Stalin found himself able to implement his vision of security only by appearing to violate that of the West. The result was to create for the Soviet Union new sources of hostility and, ultimately, insecurity in the world.

Ideological differences constituted a second source of antagonism. Stalin had deliberately downplayed the Soviet commitment to communism during the war, even to the point of abolishing the Comintern in 1943. Some Americans concluded that the Russians had abandoned that ideology altogether, if on no other grounds than that a nation that fought Germans so effectively could not be all bad. The European communist movement remained very much the instrument of Soviet policy, however, and the Russians used it to facilitate their projection of influence into Eastern Europe. This development raised fears in the West that Soviet collaboration against the Axis had been nothing but a marriage of convenience and that, victory having been achieved, the Kremlin was now embarking upon a renewed crusade for world revolution.

This was, it now appears, a mistaken view. Stalin had always placed the security of the Soviet state above the interests of international communism; it had been the former, not the latter, that had motivated his expansion into Eastern Europe. Far from encouraging communists outside the Soviet Union to seize power, Stalin initially advised restraint, especially in his dealings with such movements in France, Italy, Greece, and China. But the Soviet leader's caution was not all that clear in the West. Faced with the sudden intrusion of Russian power into Europe, faced with a revival of anticapitalist rhetoric among communists throughout the world, faced with painful evidence from the recent past of what happened when dictators' rhetoric was not taken seriously, observers in both Western Europe and the United States jumped to the conclusion that Stalin, like Hitler, had insatiable ambitions, and would not stop until contained.

Technological differences created a third source of tension. The United States alone emerged from World War II with an industrial plant superior to what it had possessed before that conflict started; the Soviet Union, in turn, had come out of the war with its land ravaged, much of its industry destroyed, and some twenty million of its citizens dead. The resulting disparity of power caused some Americans to exaggerate their ability to influence events in the rest of the world; it simultaneously produced in the Russians deep feelings of inferiority and vulnerability.

This problem manifested itself most obviously with regard to reconstruction. Stalin had hoped to repair war damage with the help of Lend-Lease and a postwar loan from the United States; his conviction that Americans would soon be facing a postwar depression led him to believe—drawing on clear Leninist principles—that Washington would have no choice but to provide such aid as a means of generating foreign markets for surplus products. His surprise was great when the United States passed up the economic benefits it would have derived from granting a loan in favor of the political concessions it hoped to obtain by withholding it. Nor would Washington allow the use of Lend-Lease for reconstruction; to compound the offense, the Truman administration also cut off, in 1946, the flow of reparations from the American zone in Germany. Whether more generous policies on these matters would have produced better relations with the Soviet Union is impossible to prove—certainly the Russians were never in such need of aid as to be willing to make major political concessions in order to get it. There is no doubt, though, that they bitterly resented their exclusion from these "fruits" of Western technology.

Another "fruit" of Western technology that impressed the Russians was, of course, the atomic bomb. Although Soviet leaders carefully avoided signs of concern about this new weapon, they did secretly accelerate their own bomb development project while simultaneously calling for the abolition of all such weapons of mass destruction. After much debate within the government, the United States, in the summer of 1946, proposed the Baruch Plan, which would have transferred control of all fissionable materials to the United Nations. In fact, however, neither the Russians nor the Americans had sufficient faith in the world organization to entrust their security completely to it. Washington at no point was willing to surrender its bombs until the control system had gone into effect, while Moscow was unwilling to accept the inspection provisions which would allow the plan to operate. Both sides had concluded by 1947 that they would find greater security in an arms race than in an unproven system of international control.

Finally, accidents of personality made it more difficult than it might otherwise have been to achieve a mutually agreeable settlement. The Russians perceived in the transition from Roosevelt to Truman an abrupt shift from an attitude of cooperation to one of confrontation. "The policy pursued by the US ruling circles after the death of Franklin D. Roosevelt," the official history of Soviet foreign policy asserts, "amounted to renunciation of dependable and mutually beneficial cooperation with the Soviet Union, a cooperation that was so effective . . . in the period of joint struggle against the nazi aggressors." In fact, though, Roosevelt's policy had been firmer than Stalin realized; Truman's was not as uncompromising as his rhetoric suggested. What was different was style: where Roosevelt had sought to woo the Soviet leader by meeting his demands wherever possible, the new chief executive, like a good poker player, tried to deal from positions of rhetorical, if not actual, strength. His tough talk was designed to facilitate, not impede, negotiations—any appearance of weakness, he thought, would only encourage the Russians to ask for more.

What Truman failed to take into account was the possibility that Stalin might also be bluffing. Given the history of Western intervention to crush Bolshevism, given the Soviet Union's ruined economy and weakened population, and given the atomic bomb's unexpected confirmation of American technological superiority, it seems likely that the aging Soviet dictator was as frightened of the West as the West was of him. Truman's tough rhetoric, together with Hiroshima's example, may well have reinforced Stalin's conviction that if *he* showed any signs of weakness, all would be lost. Both leaders had learned too well the lesson of the 1930s: that appeasement never pays. Prospects for an amicable resolution of differences suffered accordingly.

There was nothing in this set of circumstances that made the Cold War inevitable—few things ever are inevitable in history. But a situation such as existed in Europe in 1945, with two great powers separated only by a power vacuum, seemed almost predestined to produce hostility, whether either side willed it or not. As a result, the United States, the Soviet Union, and much of the rest of the world as well would have to suffer through that prolonged period of insecurity that observers at the time, and historians since, have called the "Cold War."

The evolution of United States policy toward the Soviet Union between 1945 and 1947 can be seen as a three-stage process of relating national interests to national capabilities. From V-J Day through early 1946, there existed genuine confusion in Washington as to both Soviet intentions and appropriate methods for dealing with them. Coordination between power and policy was, as a result, minimal. By the spring of 1946, a consensus had developed favoring resistance to further Soviet expansion, but little had been done to determine what resources would be necessary to accomplish that goal or to differentiate between areas of primary and secondary concern. It was not until 1947 that there began to emerge an approach to the Soviet Union that bore some reasonable relationship to American capabilities for projecting influence in the world.

There appeared to be no lack of power available to the United States for the purpose of ordering the postwar environment as it saw fit, but the task of transforming technological superiority into political influence proved frustratingly difficult. Secretary of State James F. Byrnes had hoped to trade reconstruction assistance and a commitment to the international control of atomic energy for Soviet concessions on such outstanding issues as implementation of the Yalta Declaration on Liberated Europe, peace treaties with former German satellites, and, ultimately, a final resolution of the German question itself. But the Russians maintained a posture of ostentatious unconcern about the atomic bomb, nor would they yield on significant issues to obtain reconstruction assistance. Congressional skepticism about Moscow's intentions ensured that any loan would carry a political price far beyond what the Russians would willingly pay, while public opinion pushed Truman into a decision to seek United Nations control of atomic energy before Byrnes had made any attempt to extract Soviet concessions in return. Economic and technological superiority thus won the United States surprisingly few practical benefits in its early postwar dealings with the USSR.

In Washington, moreover, there still existed a substantial number of officials who viewed Soviet hostility as the product of misunderstandings and who expected that, with restraint on both sides, a mutually satisfactory resolution of differences might still occur. It is significant that as late as November, 1945, a State Department representative could rebuke the Joint Chiefs of Staff for confidentially suggesting that the wartime alliance might not survive victory. "We must always bear in mind," a Department memorandum noted the following month, "that because of the differences between the economic and political systems [of the United States and the Soviet Union], the conduct of our relations requires more patience and diligence than with other countries." Despite his tough rhetoric, President Truman shared this view. Disagreements with the Russians were to be expected once the common bond of military necessity had been removed, he told his advisers; in time, they would disappear because "Stalin was a fine man who wanted to do the right thing."

But events made this position increasingly difficult to sustain. The Russians remained adamant in their determination to exclude Western influence from Eastern Europe and the Balkans, while a continued Soviet presence in Iran and Manchuria raised fears that Moscow might try to impose control over those territories as well. Russian interest in the eastern Mediterranean seemed to be growing, with demands for trusteeships over former Italian colonies, boundary rectifications at Turkey's expense, and a revision of the Montreux Convention governing passage through the Dardanelles. And in February, 1946, news of Soviet atomic espionage became public for the first time with the revelation that the Canadian government had arrested a group of Russian agents for trying to steal information about the bomb. That same month, Stalin in his first major postwar foreign policy speech stressed the incompatibility between communism and capitalism, implying that future wars were inevitable until the world economic system was restructured along Soviet lines.

It was at this point that there arrived at the State Department a dispatch from George F. Kennan, now *chargé d'affaires* at the American embassy in Moscow, which did much to clarify official thinking regarding Soviet behavior. Russian hostility toward the West, Kennan argued, stemmed chiefly from the internal necessities of the Stalinist regime: the Soviet dictator required a hostile outside world in order to justify his own autocratic rule. Marxism provided Soviet leaders with

> justification for their instinctive fear of the outside world, for the dictatorship without which they did not know how to rule, for cruelties they did not dare not to inflict, for sacrifices they felt bound to demand. . . . Today they cannot dispense with it. It is the fig leaf of their moral and intellectual respectability.

It followed that Stalin was, by nature, incapable of being reassured. "Nothing short of complete disarmament, delivery of our air and naval forces to Russia and resigning of the powers of government to American Communists would even dent this problem," Kennan noted in a subsequent dispatch, "and even then Moscow would smell a trap and would continue to harbor the most baleful misgivings." The solution, Kennan suggested, was to strengthen Western institutions in order to render them invulnerable to the Soviet challenge while simultaneously awaiting the eventual mellowing of the Soviet regime.

There was little in Kennan's analysis that he and other career Soviet expertshad not been saying for some time. What was new was Washington's receptivity to the message, a condition brought about both by frustration over Soviet behavior and by growing public and Congressional resistance to further concessions. In contrast to its earlier optimism about relations with Moscow, the State Department now endorsed Kennan's analysis as "the most probable explanation of present Soviet policies and attitudes." The United States, it concluded, should demonstrate to the Kremlin, "in the first instance by diplomatic means and in the last analysis by military force if necessary that the present course of its foreign policy can only lead to disaster for the Soviet Union."

The spring and summer of 1946 did see a noticeable toughening of United States policy toward the Soviet Union. In early March, Truman lent public sanction to Winston Churchill's strongly anti-Soviet "iron curtain" speech by appearing on the platform with him at Fulton, Missouri. That same month, Secretary of State Byrnes insisted on placing the issue of Iran before the United Nations, even after the Russians had agreed to withdraw their troops from that country. The termination of German reparations shipments came in May; three months later, Byrnes publicly committed the United States to support German rehabilitation, with or without the Russians. In July, Truman endorsed the continued presence of American troops in southern Korea on the grounds that that country constituted "an ideological battleground upon which our whole success in Asia may depend." Soviet pressure on Turkey for bases produced a decision in August to maintain an American naval force indefinitely in the eastern Mediterranean. In September, White House aide Clark Clifford submitted a report to the president, prepared after consultation with top military and diplomatic advisers, arguing that "this government should be prepared . . . to resist vigorously and successfully any efforts of the U.S.S.R. to expand into areas vital to American security."

But these policies were decided upon without precise assessments as to whether the means existed to carry them out. The atomic bomb was of little use for such purposes, given the strong inhibitions American officials felt about brandishing their new weapon in peacetime and given the limited number of bombs and properly equipped bombers available, if war came. Nor could the administration hold out the prospect of economic aid as a means of inducing more cooperative Soviet behavior, in the face of continued Congressional reluctance to appropriate funds for such purposes. Such conventional military power as the United States possessed was rapidly melting away under the pressures of demobilization, and although most Americans supported firmer policies toward the Soviet Union, the election of an economy-minded, Republican-controlled Congress in November suggested that few were prepared to assume the burdens, in the form of high taxes and military manpower levels, such policies would require.

Shortly thereafter a severe economic crisis, the product of remaining wartime dislocations and an unusually harsh winter, hit Western Europe. This development caused the British to announce their intention, in February, 1947, of terminating economic and military aid to Greece and Turkey, countries that had, up to that point, been regarded as within London's sphere of responsibility. It also raised the longer-range but even more frightening prospect that economic conditions in Western Europe generally might deteriorate to the point that communist parties there could seize power through coups or even free elections. Suddenly the whole European balance of power, which the United States had gone to war to restore, seemed once again in peril.

This situation, which appeared so to threaten European stability, was one the Russians had done little if anything to instigate; it was rather the product primarily of internal conditions within the countries involved. But there was little doubt of Moscow's ability to exploit the European economic crisis if nothing was done to alleviate it. And action was taken, with such energy and dispatch that the fifteen weeks between late February and early June, 1947, have come to be regarded as a great moment in the history of American diplomacy, a rare instance in which "the government of the United States operat[ed] at its very finest, efficiently and effectively."

Such plaudits may be too generous. Certainly the language Truman used to justify aid to Greece and Turkey ("at the present moment in world history nearly every nation must choose between alternative ways of life. . . . I believe that it must be the policy of the United States to support free peoples who are resisting attempted subjugation by armed minorities or by outside pressures") represented a projection of rhetoric far beyond either the administration's intentions or capabilities. Whatever its usefulness in prying funds out of a parsimonious Congress, the sweeping language of the "Truman Doctrine" would cause problems later on as the president and his foreign policy advisers sought to clarify distinctions between vital and peripheral interests in the world. That such distinctions were important became apparent with the announcement in June, 1947, of the Marshall Plan, an ambitious initiative that reflected, far more than did the Truman Doctrine, the careful calibration of ends to means characteristic of the administration's policy during this period.

The European Recovery Program, to use its official title, proposed spending some $17 billion for economic assistance to the non-communist nations of Europe over the next four years. (Aid was offered to the Soviet Union and its East European satellites as well, but with the expectation, which proved to be correct, that Moscow would turn it down.) It was a plan directed, not against Soviet military attack, a contingency United States officials considered remote, but against the economic malaise that had sapped self-confidence among European allies, rendering them vulnerable to internal communist takeovers. It involved no direct military commitments; rather, its architects assumed, much as had advocates of the "arsenal of democracy" concept before World War II, that the United States could most efficiently help restore the balance of power in Europe by contributing its technology and raw materials, but not its manpower. It represented a deliberate decision to focus American energies on the recovery of Europe at the expense of commitments elsewhere: it is significant that the spring of 1947 also saw the Truman administration move toward liquidating its remaining responsibilities in China and Korea. What took place in Washington during the famous "fifteen weeks," then, was not so much a proliferation of commitments as a reordering of priorities, executed with a sharp awareness of what the United States would have to accept in the world and what, given limited resources, it could realistically expect to change.

Unfortunately, rhetoric again obscured the point, this time by way of a mysterious article, entitled "The Sources of Soviet Conduct," which appeared in the July, 1947, issue of *Foreign Affairs*. Attributed only to a "Mr. X," it advanced the notion that

> the main element of any United States policy toward the Soviet Union must be that of a long-term, patient but firm and vigilant containment of Russian expansive tendencies. . . . Soviet pressure against the free institutions of the Western world is something that can be contained by the adroit and vigilant application of counter-force at a series of constantly shifting geographical and political points, corresponding to the shifts and maneuvers of Soviet policy.

Then, as now, nothing remained secret for very long, and word soon leaked out that "Mr. X" had been none other than Kennan, who had recently become head of the State Department's new Policy Planning Staff. This information gave the "X" article something of the character of an official document, and it quickly came to be seen as the definitive expression of administration policy toward the Soviet Union.

In fact, Kennan had not intended his article as a comprehensive prescription for future action; it was, rather, an elaboration of the analysis of Soviet behavior he had submitted in his February, 1946, telegram to the State Department. Such policy recommendations as Kennan did include reflected only in the most approximate and incomplete way the range of his thinking on Soviet-American relations. The article implied an automatic commitment to resist Russian expansionism wherever it occurred; there was in it little sense of the administration's preoccupation with limited means and of the consequent need to distinguish between primary and secondary interests. Nor did the piece make it clear that economic rather than military methods were to be employed as the chief instrument of containment. The safest generalization that can be made about the "X" article is that, like the Truman Doctrine, it was an outstanding demonstration of the obfuscatory potential of imprecise prose. It was not an accurate description of the policies the United States was, at that moment, in the process of implementing.

Kennan provided a much clearer explanation of what he meant by "containment" in a secret review of the world situation prepared for Secretary of State George C. Marshall in November, 1947. Soviet efforts to fill power vacuums left by German and Japanese defeats had largely been halted, Kennan argued, but this accomplishment had dangerously strained American resources: "The program of aid to Europe which we are now proposing to undertake will probably be the last major effort of this nature which our people could, or should, make. . . . It is clearly unwise for us to continue the attempt to carry alone, or largely singlehanded, the opposition to Soviet expansion." Further dispersal of resources could be avoided only by identifying clearly those parts of the world upon whose defense American security depended. Aside from the Western Hemisphere, Kennan's list included only non-communist Europe, the Middle East, and Japan. In China there was little the West could do, although there were as well "definite limitations on both the military and economic capabilities of the Russians in that area." Since Korea was "not of decisive strategic importance to us, our main task is to extricate ourselves without too great a loss of prestige." All in all, Kennan concluded, "our best answer is to strengthen in every way local forces of resistance, and persuade others to bear a greater part of the burden of opposing communism."

"Containment," then, involved no indiscriminate projection of commitments around the world: it was, instead, a policy precise in its identification of American interests, specific in its assessment of threats to those interests, frugal in its calculation of means required to ward off those threats, vague only in its public presentation. But this very vagueness would, in time, corrupt the concept, for where gaps between policy and rhetoric exist, it is often easier to bring the former into line with the latter than the other way around. The eventual consequence would be the promulgation of policies under the rubric of " containment" far removed from what that doctrine had been originally intended to mean.

Despite its limited character, the vigor of the American response to Soviet postwar probes apparently caught Stalin by surprise. His response was to try to strengthen further the security of his own regime; first by increasing safeguards against Western influences inside the Soviet Union; second, by tightening control over Russia's East European satellites; and finally by working to ensure central direction of the international communist movement. By a perverse kind of logic, each of these moves backfired, as did a much earlier Soviet initiative whose existence only came to light at this point—the establishment, in the United States during the 1930s, of a major espionage network directed from Moscow. The result, in each of these cases, was to produce consequences that only made it more difficult for Stalin to obtain the kind of security he sought.

Soviet leaders had always faced a dilemma regarding contacts with the West. Such associations might carry substantial benefits—certainly this had been true of collaboration with Great Britain and the United States during World War II. But there were also costs, not the least of which was the possibility that prolonged exposure to Western ideas and institutions might erode the still vulnerable base of the Soviet regime. It is an indication of the seriousness with which Stalin viewed this problem that he shipped hundreds of thousands of returning prisoners-of-war off to labor camps in 1945, much to the horror of Americans who had forcibly repatriated many of them at the Russians' request. By 1947, Moscow's campaign against Western influence had extended to literature, music, history, economics, and even genetics. As a result, Soviet prestige suffered throughout the world; the effect of these policies on science, and, in turn, on the advancement of Russian military capabilities, can only be guessed at.

Even more striking in its impact on the West, though, was Stalin's harsh effort to consolidate his control over Eastern Europe. Subservience to Moscow, not ideological uniformity, had been the chief Soviet priority in that area until 1947, but in June of that year the Russians imposed a communist-dominated government in Hungary, a country in which relatively free elections had been held in the fall of 1945. "I think it's an outrage," President Truman told a press conference on June 5. "The Hungarian situation is a terrible one." In February, 1948, the Communist Party of Czechoslovakia overthrew the duly-constituted government of that country—an event that produced the death, by either murder or suicide, of the popular Czech foreign minister, Jan Masaryk. It would be difficult to exaggerate the impact of this development in theWest, where guilty consciences still existed over what had been done to the Czechs at Munich ten years before. One immediate effect was to ensure Congressional passage of the Marshall Plan; another was to provoke Britain, France, and the Benelux countries into forming the Western Union, the first step toward a joint defensive alliance among the non-communist nations of Europe. There also followed the stimulation of something approaching a war scare in the United States, an administration request for Universal Military Training and the reinstitution of the draft, and a public condemnation by Truman of the Soviet Union as the "one nation [that] has not only refused to cooperate in the establishment of a just and honorable peace, but—even worse—has actively sought to prevent it."

Meanwhile, attempts to resolve the question of divided Germany had produced no results, despite protracted and tedious negotiations. In February, 1948, the three Western occupying powers, plus the Benelux countries, met in London and decided to move toward formation of an independent West German state. Stalin's response, after initial hesitation, was to impose a blockade on land access to Berlin, which the World War II settlement had left a hundred miles inside the Soviet zone. The Berlin crisis brought the United States and the Soviet Union as close to war as they would come during the early postwar years. Truman was determined that Western forces would stay in the beleaguered city, however untenable their military position there, and to reinforce this policy he ostentatiously transferred to British bases three squadrons of B-29 bombers. No atomic bombs accompanied these planes, nor were they even equipped to carry them. But this visible reminder of American nuclear superiority may well have deterred the Russians from interfering with air access to Berlin, and through this means the United States and its allies were able to keep their sectors of the city supplied for almost a year. Stalin finally agreed to lift the blockade in May, 1949, but not before repeating the dubious distinction he had achieved in the Russo-Finnish War a decade earlier: of appearing to be brutal and incompetent at the same time.

The Berlin blockade had two important consequences, both of which were detrimental from the Soviet point of view. It provided the impetus necessary to transform the Western Union into the North Atlantic Treaty Organization, a defensive alliance linking the United States, Canada, and ten Western European nations, established in April, 1949. Simultaneously, the blockade lessened prospects for a settlement of the German problem in collaboration with the Russians; the result was to accelerate implementation of the London program, a goal accomplished with the formation, in September, 1949, of the Federal Republic of Germany.

POSTSCRIPT

Was the United States Responsible for the Cold War?

Paterson's selection contains most of the arguments advanced by the revisionist critics of America's cold war policies: Truman's diplomatic style was blunt and impetuous, and he tended to oversimplify complex issues into black and white alternatives. Paterson believes that the Truman administration exaggerated the Russian threat to the balance of power in Europe. It is not clear whether this was a deliberate miscalculation or whether the Truman administration misperceived the motive behind the "iron curtain" that Russia drew around Eastern Europe. The author maintains that Stalin was more concerned with Russia's security needs than with world conquest.

Gaddis is much less critical than Paterson of America's postwar policy. He believes that the United States and Russia would inevitably clash once the common enemy—Hitler—was defeated because the two countries had fundamentally different political and economic systems. Gaddis maintains that for nearly two years there was confusion and uncertainty in the United States' foreign policy in Europe. Truman, he says, did not reverse Roosevelt's policy. His manner was more blunt and, consequently, he showed less patience in dealing with Stalin.

Gaddis acknowledges revisionist criticisms that the Americans misperceived Stalin's attempts to control Eastern Europe. The Soviet premier used expansionist rhetoric when he was primarily concerned about protecting Russia from another invasion. By early 1946 both sides were pursuing policies that would lead to an impasse.

In his book *We Now Know: Rethinking Cold War History* (Oxford University Press, 1997), Gaddis argues more strongly than he has in his previous works that Stalin was primarily responsible for the cold war. Based upon newly discovered, partially opened Soviet archival materials, Gaddis describes Stalin, Khrushchev, and even Chairman Mao as prisoners of a peculiar world view: "Aging Ponce de Leons in search of an ideological fountain of youth."

Students who wish to study the cold war in greater detail should consult *Containment: Documents on American Policy and Strategy, 1945–1950* edited by Thomas H. Etzold and John Lewis Gaddis (Columbia University Press, 1978). Another comprehensive work is Melvyn P. Leffler, *A Preponderance of Power: National Security, the Truman Administration, and the Cold War* (Stanford University Press, 1992). The two best readers to excerpt the various viewpoints on the cold war are Thomas G. Paterson and Robert J. McMahon, eds., *The Origins of the Cold War,* 3rd ed. (D. C. Heath, 1991) and Melvyn P. Leffler and David S. Painter, eds., *Origins of the Cold War: An International History* (Routledge, 1994). Finally, David Reynolds has edited a series of essays in *The Origins of the Cold War: International Perspectives* (Yale University Press, 1994).

ISSUE 9

Did Communism Threaten America's Internal Security After World War II?

YES: John Earl Haynes and Harvey Klehr, from *Venona: Decoding Soviet Espionage in America* (Yale University Press, 1999)

NO: Richard M. Fried, from *Nightmare in Red: The McCarthy Era in Perspective* (Oxford University Press, 1990)

ISSUE SUMMARY

YES: History professors John Earl Haynes and Harvey Klehr argue that army code-breakers during World War II's "Venona Project" uncovered a disturbing number of high-ranking U.S. government officials who seriously damaged American interests by passing sensitive information to the Soviet Union.

NO: Professor of history Richard M. Fried argues that the early 1950s were a "nightmare in red" during which American citizens had their First and Fifth Amendment rights suspended when a host of national and state investigating committees searched for Communists in government agencies, Hollywood, labor unions, foundations, universities, public schools, and even public libraries.

The 1917 triumph of the Bolshevik revolution in Russia and the ensuing spread of revolution to other parts of Eastern Europe and Germany inspired American radicals that the revolution was near. It also led to a wave of anti-Bolshevik hysteria. In the fall of 1919 two groups of radicals—one native-born, the other foreign-born—formed the Communist and Communist Labor Parties. Ultimately they would merge, yet between them they contained only 25,000 to 40,000 members.

The popular "front" policy, which lasted from 1935 to 1939, was the most successful venture undertaken by American Communists. The chief aim of the American Communists became not to increase party membership but to infiltrate progressive organizations. They achieved their greatest successes in the labor movement, which badly needed union organizers. As a consequence Communists controlled several major unions, such as the West Coast longshoremen and the electrical workers, and attained key offices in the powerful

United Autoworkers. Many American novelists, screenwriters, and actors also joined communist front organizations, such as the League of American Writers, and the Theatre Collective produced "proletarian" plays.

In the 1930s and 1940s the American Communist Party's major success was its ability to establish a conspiratorial underground in Washington. The release of the Venona intercepts of American intelligence during World War II indicates that some 349 American citizens and residents had a covert relationship with Soviet intelligence agencies.

During the war the Federal Bureau of Investigation (FBI) and Office of Strategic Services (OSS) conducted security clearances that permitted Communist supporters to work at high-level jobs if they met the qualifications. This changed in February 1947. In order to impress the Republicans that he wished to attack communism at home, President Harry S. Truman issued an executive order that inaugurated a comprehensive investigation of the loyalty of all government employees by the FBI and the Civil Service Commission.

Truman's loyalty program temporarily protected him from charges that he was "soft" on communism. His ability to ward off attacks on his soft containment policy against communism ran out in his second term. Alger Hiss, a high-level state department official, was convicted in 1949 of lying about his membership in the Ware Communist cell group. In September Truman announced to the American public that the Russians had successfully tested an atomic bomb. Shortly thereafter the Chinese Communists secured control over all of China when their nationalist opponents retreated to the island of Taiwan. Then on June 24, 1950, North Korea crossed the "containment" line at the 38th parallel and attacked South Korea.

The Republican response to these events was swift, critical, and partisan. Before his conviction, Hiss had been thoroughly investigated by the House Un-American Activities Committee. Had he led President Franklin D. Roosevelt and others to a sell-out of the Eastern European countries at the Yalta Conference in February 1945? Who lost China? Did liberal and leftist state department officials stationed in China give a pro-Communist slant to U.S. foreign policies in Asia?

Within this atmosphere Truman's attempt to forge a bipartisan policy to counter internal subversion of government agencies by Communists received a mortal blow when Senator Joseph A. McCarthy of Wisconsin publicly identified 205 cases of individuals who appeared to be either card-carrying members or loyal to the Communist Party.

How legitimate was the second great red scare? Did communism threaten America's internal security in the cold war era? In the following selections, John Earl Haynes and Harvey Klehr contend that a sizeable number of highlevel government officials had passed sensitive information to Russian intelligence, while Richard M. Fried argues that the 1950s became a "red nightmare" when state and national government agencies overreacted in their search for Communists, violating citizens' rights of free speech and a defense against self-incrimination under the First and Fifth Amendments.

John Earl Haynes and Harvey Klehr

YES

Venona and the Cold War

The Venona Project began because Carter Clarke did not trust Joseph Stalin. Colonel Clarke was chief of the U.S. Army's Special Branch, part of the War Department's Military Intelligence Division, and in 1943 its officers heard vague rumors of secret German-Soviet peace negotiations. With the vivid example of the August 1939 Nazi-Soviet Pact in mind, Clarke feared that a separate peace between Moscow and Berlin would allow Nazi Germany to concentrate its formidable war machine against the United States and Great Britain. Clarke thought he had a way to find out whether such negotiations were under way.

Clarke's Special Branch supervised the Signal Intelligence Service, the Army's elite group of code-breakers and the predecessor of the National Security Agency. In February 1943 Clarke ordered the service to establish a small program to examine ciphered Soviet diplomatic cablegrams. Since the beginning of World War II in 1939, the federal government had collected copies of international cables leaving and entering the United States. If the cipher used in the Soviet cables could be broken, Clarke believed, the private exchanges between Soviet diplomats in the United States and their superiors in Moscow would show whether Stalin was seriously pursuing a separate peace.

The coded Soviet cables, however, proved to be far more difficult to read than Clarke had expected. American code-breakers discovered that the Soviet Union was using a complex two-part ciphering system involving a "one-time pad" code that in theory was unbreakable. The Venona code-breakers, however, combined acute intellectual analysis with painstaking examination of thousands of coded telegraphic cables to spot a Soviet procedural error that opened the cipher to attack. But by the time they had rendered the first messages into readable text in 1946, the war was over and Clarke's initial goal was moot. Nor did the messages show evidence of a Soviet quest for a separate peace. What they did demonstrate, however, stunned American officials. Messages thought to be between Soviet diplomats at the Soviet consulate in New York and the People's Commissariat of Foreign Affairs in Moscow turned out to be cables between professional intelligence field officers and Gen. Pavel Fitin, head of the foreign intelligence directorate of the KGB in Moscow. Espionage, not diplomacy, was the subject of these cables. One of the first cables rendered into coherent text was a 1944 message from KGB officers in New York showing that the Soviet Union had infiltrated America's most secret enterprise, the atomic bomb project.

By 1948 the accumulating evidence from other decoded Venona cables showed that the Soviets had recruited spies in virtually every major American government agency of military or diplomatic importance. American authorities learned that since 1942 the United States had been the target of a Soviet espionage onslaught involving dozens of professional Soviet intelligence officers and hundreds of Americans, many of whom were members of the American Communist party (CPUSA). The deciphered cables of the Venona Project identify 349 citizens, immigrants, and permanent residents of the United States who had had a covert relationship with Soviet intelligence agencies. Further, American cryptanalysts in the Venona Project deciphered only a fraction of the Soviet intelligence traffic, so it was only logical to conclude that many additional agents were discussed in the thousands of unread messages. Some were identified from other sources, such as defectors' testimony and the confessions of Soviet spies.

The deciphered Venona messages also showed that a disturbing number of high-ranking U.S. government officials consciously maintained a clandestine relationship with Soviet intelligence agencies and had passed extraordinarily sensitive information to the Soviet Union that had seriously damaged American interests. Harry White—the second most powerful official in the U.S. Treasury Department, one of the most influential officials in the government, and part of the American delegation at the founding of the United Nations—had advised the KGB about how American diplomatic strategy could be frustrated. A trusted personal assistant to President Franklin Roosevelt, Lauchlin Currie, warned the KGB that the FBI had started an investigation of one of the Soviets' key American agents, Gregory Silvermaster. This warning allowed Silvermaster, who headed a highly productive espionage ring, to escape detection and continue spying. Maurice Halperin, the head of a research section of the Office of Strategic Services (OSS), then America's chief intelligence arm, turned over hundreds of pages of secret American diplomatic cables to the KGB. William Perl, a brilliant young government aeronautical scientist, provided the Soviets with the results of the highly secret tests and design experiments for American jet engines and jet aircraft. His betrayal assisted the Soviet Union in quickly overcoming the American technological lead in the development of jets. In the Korean War, U.S. military leaders expected the Air Force to dominate the skies, on the assumption that the Soviet aircraft used by North Korea and Communist China would be no match for American aircraft. They were shocked when Soviet MiG-15 jet fighters not only flew rings around U.S. propeller-driven aircraft but were conspicuously superior to the first generation of American jets as well. Only the hurried deployment of America's newest jet fighter, the F-86 Saber, allowed the United States to match the technological capabilities of the MiG-15. The Air Force prevailed, owing more to the skill of American pilots than to the design of American aircraft.

And then there were the atomic spies. From within the Manhattan Project two physicists, Klaus Fuchs and Theodore Hall, and one technician, David Greenglass, transmitted the complex formula for extracting bomb-grade uranium from ordinary uranium, the technical plans for production facilities, and the engineering principles for the "implosion" technique. The latter process made possible an atomic bomb using plutonium, a substance much easier to manufacture than bomb-grade uranium.

The betrayal of American atomic secrets to the Soviets allowed the Soviet Union to develop atomic weapons several years sooner and at a substantially lower cost than it otherwise would have. Joseph Stalin's knowledge that espionage assured the Soviet Union of quickly breaking the American atomic monopoly emboldened his diplomatic strategy in his early Cold War clashes with the United States. It is doubtful that Stalin, rarely a risk-taker, would have supplied the military wherewithal and authorized North Korea to invade South Korea in 1950 had the Soviet Union not exploded an atomic bomb in 1949. Otherwise Stalin might have feared that President Harry Truman would stanch any North Korean invasion by threatening to use atomic weapons. After all, as soon as the atomic bomb had been developed, Truman had not hesitated to use it twice to end the war with Japan. But in 1950, with Stalin in possession of the atomic bomb, Truman was deterred from using atomic weapons in Korea, even in the late summer when initially unprepared American forces were driven back into the tip of Korea and in danger of being pushed into the sea, and then again in the winter when Communist Chinese forces entered the war in massive numbers. The killing and maiming of hundreds of thousands of soldiers and civilians on both sides of the war in Korea might have been averted had the Soviets not been able to parry the American atomic threat.

Early Soviet possession of the atomic bomb had an important psychological consequence. When the Soviet Union exploded a nuclear device in 1949, ordinary Americans as well as the nation's leaders realized that a cruel despot, Joseph Stalin, had just gained the power to destroy cities at will. This perception colored the early Cold War with the hues of apocalypse. Though the Cold War never lost the potential of becoming a civilization-destroying conflict, Stalin's death in March 1953 noticeably relaxed Soviet-American tensions. With less successful espionage, the Soviet Union might not have developed the bomb until after Stalin's death, and the early Cold War might have proceeded on a far less frightening path.

Venona decryptions identified most of the Soviet spies uncovered by American counterintelligence between 1948 and the mid-1950s. The skill and perseverance of the Venona code-breakers led the U.S. Federal Bureau of Investigation (FBI) and British counterintelligence (MI5) to the atomic spy Klaus Fuchs. Venona documents unmistakably identified Julius Rosenberg as the head of a Soviet spy ring and David Greenglass, his brother-in-law, as a Soviet source at the secret atomic bomb facility at Los Alamos, New Mexico. Leads from decrypted telegrams exposed the senior British diplomat Donald Maclean as a major spy in the British embassy in Washington and precipitated his flight to the Soviet Union, along with his fellow diplomat and spy Guy Burgess. The arrest and prosecution of such spies as Judith Coplon, Robert Soblen, and Jack Soble was possible because American intelligence was able to read Soviet reports about their activities. The charges by the former Soviet spy Elizabeth Bentley that several dozen mid-level government officials, mostly secret Communists, had assisted Soviet intelligence were corroborated in Venona documents and assured American authorities of her veracity.

With the advent of the Cold War, however, the spies clearly identified in the Venona decryptions were the least of the problem. Coplon, Rosenberg, Greenglass, Fuchs, Soble, and Soblen were prosecuted, and the rest were eased out of the government or otherwise neutralized as threats to national security. But that still left a security nightmare. Of the 349 Americans the deciphered Venona cables revealed as having covert ties to Soviet intelligence agencies, less than half could be identified by their real names and nearly two hundred remained hidden behind cover names. American officials assumed that some of the latter surely were still working in sensitive positions. Had they been promoted and moved into policy-making jobs? Had Muse, the unidentified female agent in the OSS, succeeded in transferring to the State Department or the Central Intelligence Agency (CIA), the successor to the OSS? What of Source No. 19, who had been senior enough to meet privately with Churchill and Roosevelt at the Trident Conference? Was the unidentified KGB source Bibi working for one of America's foreign assistance agencies? Was Donald, the unidentified Navy captain who was a GRU (Soviet military intelligence) source, still in uniform, perhaps by this time holding the rank of admiral? And what of the two unidentified atomic spies Quantum and Pers? They had given Stalin the secrets of the uranium and plutonium bomb: were they now passing on the secrets of the even more destructive hydrogen bomb? And how about Dodger, Godmother, and Fakir? Deciphered Venona messages showed that all three had provided the KGB with information on American diplomats who specialized in Soviet matters. Fakir was himself being considered for an assignment representing the United States in Moscow. Which of the American foreign service officers who were also Soviet specialists were traitors? How could Americans successfully negotiate with the Soviet Union when the American negotiating team included someone working for the other side? Western Europe, clearly, would be the chief battleground of the Cold War. To lose there was to lose all: the task of rebuilding stable democracies in postwar Europe and forging the NATO military alliance was America's chief diplomatic challenge. Yet Venona showed that the KGB had Mole, the appropriate cover name of a Soviet source inside the Washington establishment who had passed on to Moscow high-level American diplomatic policy guidance on Europe. When American officials met to discuss sensitive matters dealing with France, Britain, Italy, or Germany, was Mole present and working to frustrate American goals? Stalin's espionage offensive had not only uncovered American secrets, it had also undermined the mutual trust that American officials had for each other.

The Truman administration had expected the end of World War II to allow the dismantling of the massive military machine created to defeat Nazi Germany and Imperial Japan. The government slashed military budgets, turned weapons factories over to civilian production, ended conscription, and returned millions of soldiers to civilian life. So, too, the wartime intelligence and security apparatus was demobilized. Anticipating only limited need for foreign intelligence and stating that he wanted no American Gestapo, President Truman abolished America's chief intelligence agency, the Office of Strategic

Services. With the coming of peace, emergency wartime rules for security vetting of many government employees lapsed or were ignored.

In late 1945 and in 1946, the White House had reacted with a mixture of indifference and skepticism to FBI reports indicating significant Soviet espionage activity in the United States. Truman administration officials even whitewashed evidence pointing to the theft of American classified documents in the 1945 *Amerasia* case because they did not wish to put at risk the continuation of the wartime Soviet-American alliance and wanted to avoid the political embarrassment of a security scandal. By early 1947, however, this indifference ended. The accumulation of information from defectors such as Elizabeth Bentley and Igor Gouzenko, along with the Venona decryptions, made senior Truman administration officials realize that reports of Soviet spying constituted more than FBI paranoia. No government could operate successfully if it ignored the challenge to its integrity that Stalin's espionage offensive represented. In addition, the White House sensed that there was sufficient substance to the emerging picture of a massive Soviet espionage campaign, one assisted by American Communists, that the Truman administration was vulnerable to Republican charges of having ignored a serious threat to American security. President Truman reversed course and in March 1947 issued a sweeping executive order establishing a comprehensive security vetting program for U.S. government employees. He also created the Central Intelligence Agency, a stronger and larger version of the OSS, which he had abolished just two years earlier. In 1948 the Truman administration followed up these acts by indicting the leaders of the CPUSA under the sedition sections of the 1940 Smith Act. While the Venona Project and the decrypted messages themselves remained secret, the substance of the messages with the names of scores of Americans who had assisted Soviet espionage circulated among American military and civilian security officials. From the security officials the information went to senior executive-branch political appointees and members of Congress. They, in turn, passed it on to journalists and commentators, who conveyed the alarming news to the general public.

Americans' Understanding of Soviet and Communist Espionage

During the early Cold War, in the late 1940s and early 1950s, every few months newspaper headlines trumpeted the exposure of yet another network of Communists who had infiltrated an American laboratory, labor union, or government agency. Americans worried that a Communist fifth column, more loyal to the Soviet Union than to the United States, had moved into their institutions. By the mid-1950s, following the trials and convictions for espionage-related crimes of Alger Hiss, a senior diplomat, and Julius and Ethel Rosenberg for atomic spying, there was a widespread public consensus on three points: that Soviet espionage was serious, that American Communists assisted the Soviets, and that several senior government officials had betrayed the United States. The deciphered Venona messages provide a solid factual basis for this consensus. But the government did not release the Venona decryptions to the public, and it successfully disguised the source of its information about Soviet espionage. This decision denied the public the incontestable evidence afforded by the messages of the Soviet Union's own spies. Since the information about Soviet espionage and American Communist participation derived largely from the testimony of defectors and a mass of circumstantial evidence, the public's belief in those reports rested on faith in the integrity of government security officials. These sources are inherently more ambiguous than the hard evidence of the Venona messages, and this ambiguity had unfortunate consequences for American politics and Americans' understanding of their own history.

The decision to keep Venona secret from the public, and to restrict knowledge of it even within the government, was made essentially by senior Army officers in consultation with the FBI and the CIA. Aside from the Venona code-breakers, only a limited number of military intelligence officers, FBI agents, and CIA officials knew of the project. The CIA in fact was not made an active partner in Venona until 1952 and did not receive copies of the deciphered messages until 1953. The evidence is not entirely clear, but it appears that Army Chief of Staff Omar Bradley, mindful of the White House's tendency to leak politically sensitive information, decided to deny President Truman direct knowledge of the Venona Project. The president was informed about the substance of the Venona messages as it came to him through FBI and Justice Department memorandums on espionage investigations and CIA reports on intelligence matters. He was not told that much of this information derived from reading Soviet cable traffic. This omission is important because Truman was mistrustful of J. Edgar Hoover, the head of the FBI, and suspected that the reports of Soviet espionage were exaggerated for political purposes. Had he been aware of Venona, and known that Soviet cables confirmed the testimony of Elizabeth Bentley and Whittaker Chambers, it is unlikely that his aides would have considered undertaking a campaign to discredit Bentley and indict Chambers for perjury, or would have allowed themselves to be taken in by the disinformation being spread by the American Communist party and Alger Hiss's partisans that Chambers had at one time been committed to an insane asylum.

There were sensible reasons . . . for the decision to keep Venona a highly compartmentalized secret within the government. In retrospect, however, the negative consequences of this policy are glaring. Had Venona been made public, it is unlikely there would have been a forty-year campaign to prove that the Rosenbergs were innocent. The Venona messages clearly display Julius Rosenberg's role as the leader of a productive ring of Soviet spies. Nor would there have been any basis for doubting his involvement in atomic espionage, because the deciphered messages document his recruitment of his brother-in-law, David Greenglass, as a spy. It is also unlikely, had the messages been made public or even circulated more widely within the government than they did, that Ethel Rosenberg would have been executed. The Venona messages do not throw her guilt in doubt; indeed, they confirm that she was a participant in her husband's espionage and in the recruitment of her brother for atomic espionage. But they suggest that she was essentially an accessory to her husband's activity, having knowledge of it and assisting him but not acting as a principal.

Had they been introduced at the Rosenberg trial, the Venona messages would have confirmed Ethel's guilt but also reduced the importance of her role.

Further, the Venona messages, if made public, would have made Julius Rosenberg's execution less likely. When Julius Rosenberg faced trial, only two Soviet atomic spies were known: David Greenglass, whom Rosenberg had recruited and run as a source, and Klaus Fuchs. Fuchs, however, was in England, so Greenglass was the only Soviet atomic spy in the media spotlight in the United States. Greenglass's confession left Julius Rosenberg as the target of public outrage at atomic espionage. That prosecutors would ask for and get the death penalty under those circumstances is not surprising.

In addition to Fuchs and Greenglass, however, the Venona messages identify three other Soviet sources within the Manhattan Project. The messages show that Theodore Hall, a young physicist at Los Alamos, was a far more valuable source than Greenglass, a machinist. Hall withstood FBI interrogation, and the government had no direct evidence of his crimes except the Venona messages, which because of their secrecy could not be used in court; he therefore escaped prosecution. The real identities of the sources Fogel and Quantum are not known, but the information they turned over to the Soviets suggests that Quantum was a scientist of some standing and that Fogel was either a scientist or an engineer. Both were probably more valuable sources than David Greenglass. Had Venona been made public, Greenglass would have shared the stage with three other atomic spies and not just with Fuchs, and all three would have appeared to have done more damage to American security than he. With Greenglass's role diminished, that of his recruiter, Julius Rosenberg, would have been reduced as well. Rosenberg would assuredly have been convicted, but his penalty might well have been life in prison rather than execution.

There were broader consequences, as well, of the decision to keep Venona secret. The overlapping issues of Communists in government, Soviet espionage, and the loyalty of American Communists quickly became a partisan battleground. Led by Republican senator Joseph McCarthy of Wisconsin, some conservatives and partisan Republicans launched a comprehensive attack on the loyalties of the Roosevelt and Truman administrations. Some painted the entire New Deal as a disguised Communist plot and depicted Dean Acheson, Truman's secretary of state, and George C. Marshall, the Army chief of staff under Roosevelt and secretary of state and secretary of defense under Truman, as participants, in Senator McCarthy's words, in "a conspiracy on a scale so immense as to dwarf any previous such venture in the history of man. A conspiracy of infamy so black that, when it is finally exposed, its principals shall be forever deserving of the maledictions of all honest men." There is no basis in Venona for implicating Acheson or Marshall in a Communist conspiracy, but because the deciphered Venona messages were classified and unknown to the public, demagogues such as McCarthy had the opportunity to mix together accurate information about betrayal by men such as Harry White and Alger Hiss with falsehoods about Acheson and Marshall that served partisan political goals.

A number of liberals and radicals pointed to the excesses of McCarthy's charges as justification for rejecting the allegations altogether. Anticommunism further lost credibility in the late 1960s when critics of U.S. involvement in the Vietnam War blamed it for America's ill-fated participation. By the 1980s many commentators, and perhaps most academic historians, had concluded that Soviet espionage had been minor, that few American Communists had assisted the Soviets, and that no high officials had betrayed the United States. Many history texts depicted America in the late 1940s and 1950s as a "nightmare in red" during which Americans were "sweat-drenched in fear" of a figment of their own paranoid imaginations. As for American Communists, they were widely portrayed as having no connection with espionage. One influential book asserted emphatically, "There is no documentation in the public record of a direct connection between the American Communist Party and espionage during the entire postwar period."

Consequently, Communists were depicted as innocent victims of an irrational and oppressive American government. In this sinister but widely accepted portrait of America in the 1940s and 1950s, an idealistic New Dealer (Alger Hiss) was thrown into prison on the perjured testimony of a mentally sick anti-Communist fanatic (Whittaker Chambers), innocent progressives (the Rosenbergs) were sent to the electric chair on trumped-up charges of espionage laced with anti-Semitism, and dozens of blameless civil servants had their careers ruined by the smears of a professional anti-Communist (Elizabeth Bentley). According to this version of events, one government official (Harry White) was killed by a heart attack brought on by Bentley's lies, and another (Laurence Duggan, a senior diplomat) was driven to suicide by more of Chambers's malignant falsehoods. Similarly, in many textbooks President Truman's executive order denying government employment to those who posed security risks, and other laws aimed at espionage and Communist subversion, were and still are described not as having been motivated by a real concern for American security (since the existence of any serious espionage or subversion was denied) but instead as consciously antidemocratic attacks on basic freedoms. As one commentator wrote, "The statute books groaned under several seasons of legislation designed to outlaw dissent."

Despite its central role in the history of American counterintelligence, the Venona Project remained among the most tightly held government secrets. By the time the project shut down, it had decrypted nearly three thousand messages sent between the Soviet Union and its embassies and consulates around the world. Remarkably, although rumors and a few snippets of information about the project had become public in the 1980s, the actual texts and the enormous import of the messages remained secret until 1995. The U.S. government often has been successful in keeping secrets in the short term, but over a longer period secrets, particularly newsworthy ones, have proven to be very difficult for the government to keep. It is all the more amazing, then, how little got out about the Venona Project in the fifty-three years before it was made public.

Unfortunately, the success of government secrecy in this case has seriously distorted our understanding of post–World War II history. Hundreds of books and thousands of essays on McCarthyism, the federal loyalty security program, Soviet espionage, American communism, and the early Cold War have perpetuated many myths that have given Americans a warped view of the nation's history in the 1930s, 1940s, and 1950s. The information that these messages reveal substantially revises the basis for understanding the early history of the Cold War and of America's concern with Soviet espionage and Communist subversion.

In the late 1970s the FBI began releasing material from its hitherto secret files as a consequence of the passage of the Freedom of Information Act (FOIA). Although this act opened some files to public scrutiny, it has not as yet provided access to the full range of FBI investigative records. The enormous backlog of FOIA requests has led to lengthy delays in releasing documents; it is not uncommon to wait more than five years to receive material. Capricious and zealous enforcement of regulations exempting some material from release frequently has elicited useless documents consisting of occasional phrases interspersed with long sections of redacted (blacked-out) text. And, of course, even the unexpurgated FBI files show only what the FBI learned about Soviet espionage and are only part of the story. Even given these hindrances, however, each year more files are opened, and the growing body of FBI documentation has significantly enhanced the opportunity for a reconstruction of what actually happened.

The collapse of the Union of Soviet Socialist Republics in 1991 led to the opening of Soviet archives that had never been examined by independent scholars. The historically rich documentation first made available in Moscow's archives in 1992 has resulted in an outpouring of new historical writing, as these records allow a far more complete and accurate understanding of central events of the twentieth century. But many archives in Russia are open only in part, and some are still closed. In particular, the archives of the foreign intelligence operations of Soviet military intelligence and those of the foreign intelligence arm of the KGB are not open to researchers. Given the institutional continuity between the former Soviet intelligence agencies and their current Russian successors, the opening of these archives is not anticipated anytime soon. However, Soviet intelligence agencies had cooperated with other Soviet institutions, whose newly opened archives therefore hold some intelligence-related material and provide a back door into the still-closed intelligence archives.

But the most significant source of fresh insight into Soviet espionage in the United States comes from the decoded messages produced by the Venona Project. These documents, after all, constitute a portion of the materials that are still locked up in Russian intelligence archives. Not only do the Venona files supply information in their own right, but because of their inherent reliability they also provide a touchstone for judging the credibility of other sources, such as defectors' testimony and FBI investigative files.

Stalin's Espionage Assault on the United States

Through most of the twentieth century, governments of powerful nations have conducted intelligence operations of some sort during both peace and war. None, however, used espionage as an instrument of state policy as extensively as did the Soviet Union under Joseph Stalin. In the late 1920s and 1930s, Stalin directed most of the resources of Soviet intelligence at nearby targets in Europe and Asia. America was still distant from Stalin's immediate concerns, the threat to Soviet goals posed by Nazi Germany and Imperial Japan. This perception changed, however, after the United States entered the world war in December 1941. Stalin realized that once Germany and Japan were defeated, the world would be left with only three powers able to project their influence across the globe: the Soviet Union, Great Britain, and the United States. And of these, the strongest would be the United States. With that in mind, Stalin's intelligence agencies shifted their focus toward America.

The Soviet Union, Great Britain, and the United States formed a military alliance in early 1942 to defeat Nazi Germany and its allies. The Soviet Union quickly became a major recipient of American military (Lend-Lease) aid, second only to Great Britain; it eventually received more than nine billion dollars. As part of the aid arrangements, the United States invited the Soviets to greatly expand their diplomatic staffs and to establish special offices to facilitate aid arrangements. Thousands of Soviet military officers, engineers, and technicians entered the United States to review what aid was available and choose which machinery, weapons, vehicles (nearly 400,000 American trucks went to the Soviet Union), aircraft, and other matériel would most assist the Soviet war effort. Soviet personnel had to be trained to maintain the American equipment, manuals had to be translated into Russian, shipments to the Soviet Union had to be inspected to ensure that what was ordered had been delivered, properly loaded, and dispatched on the right ships. Entire Soviet naval crews arrived for training to take over American combat and cargo ships to be handed over to the Soviet Union.

Scores of Soviet intelligence officers of the KGB (the chief Soviet foreign intelligence and security agency), the GRU (the Soviet military intelligence agency), and the Naval GRU (the Soviet naval intelligence agency) were among the Soviet personnel arriving in America. These intelligence officers pursued two missions. One, security, was only indirectly connected with the United States. The internal security arm of the KGB employed several hundred thousand full-time personnel, assisted by several million part-time informants, to ensure the political loyalty of Soviet citizens. When the Soviets sent thousands of their citizens to the United States to assist with the Lend-Lease arrangement, they sent this internal security apparatus as well. A significant portion of the Venona messages deciphered by American code-breakers reported on this task. The messages show that every Soviet cargo ship that arrived at an American port to pick up Lend-Lease supplies had in its crew at least one, often two, and sometimes three informants who reported either to the KGB or to the Naval GRU. Their task was not to spy on Americans but to watch the Soviet merchant seamen for signs of political dissidence and potential defection. Some of the messages show Soviet security officers tracking down merchant seamen who had jumped ship, kidnapping them, and spiriting themback aboard Soviet ships in disregard of American law. Similarly, other messages discuss informants, recruited or planted by the KGB in every Soviet office in the United States, whose task was to report signs of ideological deviation or potential defection among Soviet personnel.

A second mission of these Soviet intelligence officers, however, was espionage against the United States. . . . The deciphered Venona cables do more than reveal the remarkable success that the Soviet Union had in recruiting spies and gaining access to many important U.S. government agencies and laboratories dealing with secret information. They expose beyond cavil the American Communist party as an auxiliary of the intelligence agencies of the Soviet Union. While not every Soviet spy was a Communist, most were. And while not every American Communist was a spy, hundreds were. The CPUSA itself worked closely with Soviet intelligence agencies to facilitate their espionage. Party leaders were not only aware of the liaison; they actively worked to assist the relationship.

Information from the Venona decryptions underlay the policies of U.S. government officials in their approach to the issue of domestic communism. The investigations and prosecutions of American Communists undertaken by the federal government in the late 1940s and early 1950s were premised on an assumption that the CPUSA had assisted Soviet espionage. This view contributed to the Truman administration's executive order in 1947, reinforced in the early 1950s under the Eisenhower administration, that U.S. government employees be subjected to loyalty and security investigations. The understanding also lay behind the 1948 decision by Truman's attorney general to prosecute the leaders of the CPUSA under the sedition sections of the Smith Act. It was an explicit assumption behind congressional investigations of domestic communism in the late 1940s and 1950s, and it permeated public attitudes toward domestic communism.

The Soviet Union's unrestrained espionage against the United States from 1942 to 1945 was of the type that a nation directs at an enemy state. By the late 1940s the evidence provided by Venona of the massive size and intense hostility of Soviet intelligence operations caused both American counterintelligence professionals and high-level policy-makers to conclude that Stalin had already launched a covert attack on the United States. In their minds, the Soviet espionage offensive indicated that the Cold War had begun not after World War II but many years earlier.

NO

Richard M. Fried

"Bitter Days": The Heyday of Anti-Communism

Even independent of [Joseph] McCarthy, the years 1950–1954 marked the climax of anti-communism in American life. The Korean stalemate generated both a bruising debate over containment and a sourness in national politics. Korea's sapping effect and a series of minor scandals heightened the Democratic Party's anemia. In addition, the 1950 congressional campaign, revealing McCarthyism's apparent sway over the voters and encouraging the GOP's right wing, signaled that anti-communism occupied the core of American political culture. "These," said liberal commentator Elmer Davis in January 1951, "are bitter days—full of envy, hatred, malice, and all uncharitableness."

Critics of these trends in American politics had scant power or spirit. Outside government, foes of anti-Communist excesses moved cautiously lest they be redbaited and rarely took effective countermeasures. Liberals seldom strayed from the safety of the anti-Communist consensus. Radicals met the hostility of the dominant political forces in Cold War America and fared poorly. In government, anti-communism ruled. Senate resistance to McCarthy was scattered and weak. In the House, HUAC [House Un-American Activities Committee] did much as it pleased. [President Harry S.] Truman upheld civil liberties with occasional eloquence, but he remained on the defensive, and his Justice Department often seemed locked in near-alliance with the Right in Congress. [Dwight D.] Eisenhower, when not appeasing the McCarthyites, appeared at times no more able to curb them than had Truman.

Even at his peak, McCarthy was not the sole anti-Communist paladin, though he cultivated that impression. As McCarthyism in its broader sense outlived the personal defeat of McCarthy himself, so, in its prime, it exceeded his reach. Its strength owed much to the wide acceptance, even by McCarthy's critics, of the era's anti-Communist premises. Along with McCarthy, they made the first half of the 1950s the acme of noisy anti-communism and of the ills to which it gave birth.

Soon after the 1950 campaign, skirmishing over the Communist issue renewed in earnest. In December Senator Pat McCarran joined the hunt for subversives by creating the Senate Internal Security Subcommittee (SISS). As chairman of that panel (and the parent Judiciary Committee), the crusty Nevada Democrat packed it with such like-minded colleagues as Democrats

James Eastland and Willis Smith and Republicans Homer Ferguson and William Jenner. While McCarthy darted about unpredictably, McCarran moved glacially but steadily to his objective, crushing opposition.

McCarran's panel spotlighted themes that McCarthy had raised giving them a more sympathetic hearing than had the Tydings Committee. In February 1951, federal agents swooped down on a barn in Lee, Massachusetts, seized the dead files of the Institute of Pacific Relations (IPR) and trucked them under guard to Washington. After sifting this haul, a SISS subcommittee opened an extended probe of the IPR, which led to a new inquest on "who lost China" and resulted in renewed loyalty and security proceedings, dismissals from the State Department and prosecution—all to McCarthy's greater, reflected glory.

The subcommittee acquired a reputation—more cultivated than deserved—for honoring due process. SISS was punctilious on some points: evidence was formally introduced (when an excerpt was read, the full text was put in the record); hearings were exhaustive (over 5,000 pages); witnesses were heard in executive session before they named names in public; their credentials and the relevance of their testimony were set forth; and some outward courtesies were extended.

The fairness was only skin-deep, however. Witnesses were badgered about obscure events from years back and about nuances of aging reports. Diplomat John Carter Vincent was even asked if he had plans to move to Sarasota, Florida. When he termed it a most "curious" question, counsel could only suggest that perhaps the Florida Chamber of Commerce had taken an interest. The subcommittee strove to ensnare witnesses in perjury. One China Hand called the sessions "generally Dostoyevskian attacks not only on a man's mind but also his memory." To have predicted Jiang's decline or Mao's rise was interpreted as both premeditating and helping to cause that outcome.

A product of the internationalist do-goodery of YMCA leaders in the 1920s, the IPR sought to promote peace and understanding in the Pacific. It had both national branches in countries interested in the Pacific and an international secretariat. Well funded by corporations and foundations in its palmier days, the IPR had more pedigree than power. McCarran's subcommittee insisted that IPR's publications pushed the Communist line on China. Louis Budenz testified that the Kremlin had assigned Owen Lattimore the job of giving the IPR journal, *Pacific Affairs,* a Party-line tilt. Budenz claimed that when he was in the Party, he received "official communications" describing Lattimore (and several China Hands) as Communists.

McCarran's panel spent a year grilling Lattimore, other IPR officials, and various China experts and diplomats as it tried to knit a fabric of conspiracy out of its evidence and presuppositions. McCarran claimed that, but for the machinations of the coterie that ran IPR, "China today would be free and a bulwark against the further advance of the Red hordes into the Far East." He charged that the IPR-USSR connection had led to infiltration of the government by persons aligned with the Soviets, of faculties by Red professors, and of textbooks by pro-Communist ideas. He called Lattimore "a conscious and articulate instrument of the Soviet conspiracy."

The hearings revealed naiveté about communism, showed that IPR principals had access to important officials during the war, and turned up levels of maneuvering that sullied IPR's reputation for scholarly detachment. Proven or accused Reds did associate with the IPR and may well have sought leverage through it. There were tendentious claims in IPR publications, as in one author's simplistic dichotomy of Mao's "democratic China" and Jiang's "feudal China." Lattimore was a more partisan editor of *Pacific Affairs* than he conceded. However, in political scientist Earl Latham's measured assessment, the hearings "show something less than subversive conspiracy in the making of foreign policy, and something more than quiet routine." Nor was it proven that IPR had much influence over policy. Perhaps the China Hands had been naive to think that a reoriented policy might prevent China's Communists from falling "by default" under Soviet control and thus might maintain American leverage. Yet those who argued that unblinking support of Jiang could have prevented China's "loss" were more naive still.

Unable to prove, in scholarly terms, its thesis of a successful pro-Communist conspiracy against China, SISS could still carry it politically. The loyalty-security program helped enforce it. New charges, however stale, motivated the State Department Loyalty-Security Board to reexamine old cases of suspected employees, even if they had been previously cleared. Moreover, nudged by the Right, Truman toughened the loyalty standard in April 1951, putting a heavier burden of proof on the accused. Thus under Hiram Bingham, a Republican conservative, the Loyalty Review Board ordered new inquiries in cases decided under the old standard. . . .

The purge of the China Hands had long-term impact. American attitudes toward China remained frozen for two decades. Battered by McCarthyite attacks, the State Department's Far Eastern Division assumed a conservative bunkerlike mentality. Selected by President John F. Kennedy to shake the division up, Assistant Secretary of State Averell Harriman found it "a disaster area filled with human wreckage." Personnel who did not bear wounds from previous battles were chosen to handle Asian problems. Vincent's successor on the China desk was an impeccably conservative diplomat whose experience lay in Europe. JFK named an ambassador to South Vietnam whose prior work had been with NATO. In the 1950s, the field of Asian studies felt the blindfold of conformity as the momentum of U.S. foreign policy carried the country toward the vortex of Vietnam.

The IPR Investigation was but one of many inquiries during the early 1950s that delved into Communist activities. The Eighty-first Congress spawned 24 probes of communism; the Eighty-second, 34; and the Eighty-third, 51. HUAC busily sought new triumphs. In 1953, 185 of the 221 Republican Congressmen asked to serve on it. But HUAC faced the problem all monopolies meet when competitors pour into the market. Besides McCarran and McCarthy, a Senate labor subcommittee probed Red influences in labor unions, two committees combed the U.N. Secretariat for Communists, and others dipped an oar in when the occasion arose.

In part HUAC met the competition with strenuous travel. Hearings often bore titles like "Communist Activities in the Chicago Area"—or Los Angeles,

Detroit, or Hawaii. The Detroit hearings got a musician fired, a college student expelled, and UAW Local 600 taken over by the national union. In 1956 two Fisher Body employees were called before a HUAC hearing in St. Louis. When angry fellow workers chalked such slogans as "Russia has no Fifth amendment" on auto bodies and staged a work stoppage, the two men were suspended. The impact of junketing congressional probers was often felt in such local fallout rather than in federal punishments (though many witnesses were cited for contempt of Congress). That indeed was the point. A witness might use the Fifth Amendment to avoid perjury charges, but appearing before a committee of Congress left him open to local sanctions.

Lawmakers fretted over communism in the labor movement. The presence of left-wing unionists in a defense plant offered a frequent pretext for congressional excursions. HUAC addressed the issue often; McCarthy, occasionally; House and Senate labor subcommittees paid close heed. The liberal anti-Communist Hubert Humphrey held an inquiry designed both to meet the problem and to protect clean unions from scattershot redbaiting. Lest unions be handled too softly, in 1952 Pat McCarran, Herman Welker, and John Marshall Butler conceived the formidably labeled "Task Force Investigating Communist Domination of Certain Labor Organizations."

Attacks on radical union leadership from both within and without the labor movement proliferated in the early 1950s. During 1952 hearings in Chicago, HUAC jousted with negotiators for the Communist-led United Electrical Workers just as they mounted a strike against International Harvester. In 1953 McCarthy's subcommittee also bedeviled UE locals in New York and Massachusetts. Such hearings often led to firings and encouraged or counterpointed raids by rival unions. They hastened the decline of the left wing of the labor movement.

The UE was beset on all sides. When the anti-communist International United Electrical Workers Union (IUE), led by James Carey, was founded, Truman Administration officials intoned blessings. The Atomic Energy Commission pressured employers like General Electric to freeze out the UE; IUE literature warned that plants represented by the UE would lose defense contracts. The CIO lavishly funded Carey's war with the UE. Three days before a 1950 election to decide control of a Pittsburgh area local, the vocal anti-Communist Judge Michael Musmanno arrived at a plant gate to campaign for the IUE. Bedecked in naval uniform, he was convoyed by a detachment of National Guardsmen, bayonets fixed and flags unfurled. Many local Catholic clergy urged their flocks to vote for the IUE on the basis of anti-communism. Carey's union won a narrow victory.

These labor wars sometimes produced odd bedfellows. Carey criticized McCarthy, but the latter's 1953 Boston hearings helped the IUE keep control of key GE plants in the area. GE management declared before the hearings that it would fire workers who admitted they were Reds; it would suspend those who declined to testify and, if they did not subsequently answer the charges, would dismiss them. Thus besieged, the UE often settled labor disputes on a take-what-it-could basis.

Where left-wing unions maintained reputations for effective bargaining, anti-communism had limited effect. The UE's tactical surrender of its youthful militancy probably eroded its rank-and-file support more than did any redbaiting. Yet the Longshoremen's Union, despite Smith Act prosecutions against its leaders in Hawaii and the effort to deport Harry Bridges, kept control of West Coast docks. (Indeed, having come to tolerate Bridges by the 1950s, business leaders had lost enthusiasm for persecuting him.) Similarly, the Mine, Mill and Smelter Workers Union held onto some strongholds despite recurrent redbaiting. Weaker leftist unions like the United Public Workers or the Fur and Leather Workers succumbed to raiding and harassment.

In an era when mainline labor was cautious, organizing initiatives often did originate with more radical unions and so fell prey to anti-Communist attack. In 1953 a CIO retail workers' union, some of whose organizers were Communists, struck stores in Port Arthur, Texas. A commission of inquiry named by Governor Allen Shivers (then seeking reelection) found "clear and present danger" of Communist sway over Texas labor. Shivers claimed he had foiled a Communist-led union's "well-laid plans to spread its tentacles all along the Gulf Coast and eventually into *your* community." Other Southern organizing drives succumbed to redbaiting too.

By the 1950s, labor's assertiveness had waned; where it persisted, it met defeat; and new organizing drives were few. Internal dissent—indeed, debate—was virtually stilled. Its momentum sapped and its membership reduced by over a third, the CIO merged with the AFL in a 1955 "shotgun wedding." Having won a place within the American consensus, labor paid a dear price to keep it.

Conservatives feared Communist influence in the nation's schools as well as in its factories. The influence of the "Reducators" and of subversive ideas that ranged, in various investigators' minds, from outright communism to "progressive education" perennially intrigued legislators at the state and national levels.

The Communists' long-running control of the New York Teachers Union alarmed the Senate Internal Security Subcommittee. Previously, the 1940–41 Rapp-Coudert inquiry had led to the dismissal of a number of New York City teachers. In 1949 the Board of Education began a new purge. From 1950 to early 1953, twenty-four teachers were fired and thirty-four resigned under investigation. By one estimate, over three hundred New York City teachers lost their jobs in the 1950s. SISS thus served to reinforce local activities with its 1952–53 hearings in New York City. The refusal by Teachers Union leaders to testify about their affiliations established grounds for their dismissal under Section 903 of the city charter.

Ultimately, the probers failed in their aim to expose Marxist-Leninist propagandizing in Gotham's classrooms. Bella Dodd, a former Communist and Teachers Union leader, claimed that Communist teachers who knew Party dogma "cannot help but slant their teaching in that direction." A Queens College professor said he knew a score of students whom the Communists had "ruined" and turned into "misfits." Yet aside from a few parents' complaints and "one case where I think we could prove it," the city's school superintendent had no evidence of indoctrination. Though Communists had obviously acquired great leverage in the Teachers Union, SISS located its best case of university subversion in a book about *China*.

HUAC quizzed educators too, but its scrutiny of the movie industry earned higher returns when it resumed its inquiry into Hollywood in 1951. By then the Hollywood Ten* were in prison, the film industry's opposition to HUAC was shattered, and the blacklist was growing. Fear washed through the movie lots. The economic distress visited on Hollywood by the growth of television further frazzled nerves. Said one witness, the renewed assault was "like taking a pot shot at a wounded animal." When subpoenaed, actress Gale Sondergaard asked the Screen Actors Guild for help, its board rebuffed her, likening her criticism of HUAC to the Communist line. The Screen Directors Guild made its members take a loyalty oath.

Yet few secrets were left to ferret out: the identity of Hollywood's Communists had long ceased to be a mystery. Early in the 1951 hearings, Congressman Francis Walter even asked why it was "material . . . to have the names of people when we already know them?" For HUAC, getting new information had become secondary to conducting ceremonies of exposure and penitence. Would the witness "name names" or not?

Of 110 witnesses subpoenaed in 1951, 58 admitted having had Party involvements. Some cogently explained why they had since disowned communism. Budd Schulberg recalled that while he was writing *What Makes Sammy Run,* the Party told him to submit an outline, confer with its literary authorities, and heed its artistic canons. *The Daily Worker* received his book favorably, but after being updated on Party aesthetics, the reviewer wrote a second piece thrashing the novel. One screenwriter recalled how the Party line on a studio painters' strike shifted perplexingly in 1945: we "could walk through the picket lines in February, and not in June."

Witnesses seeking to steer between punishment and fingering co-workers faced tearing ethical choices. Naming known Reds or those previously named might stave off harm, but this ploy was tinged with moral bankruptcy. Some soured ex-Communists did resist giving names, not wanting, in actor Larry Parks's phrase, to "crawl through the mud to be an informer." Some named each other; some said little, ducking quickly behind the Fifth Amendment. Others told all. The 155 names that writer Martin Berkeley gave set a record. Others gabbed freely. Parrying with humor the oft-asked question—would he defend America against the Soviets?—actor Will Geer, already middle-aged, cheerfully agreed to fight in his way: growing vegetables and entertaining the wounded. The idea of people his vintage shouldering arms amused him; wars "would be negotiated immediately."

In this as in all inquiries, witnesses trod a path set with snares. The courts disallowed the Hollywood Ten's use of the First Amendment to avoid testifying, so a witness's only protection was the Fifth Amendment guarantee against self-incrimination. Even this route crossed minefields. *Blau v. U.S.* (1950) ruled that one might plead the Fifth legitimately to the question of Party membership. However, the 1950 case of *Rogers v. U.S.* dictated caution: one had to invoke the

* [The Hollywood Ten were members of the film industry who refused to testify before Congress in 1947 about communist infiltration of the industry.—Ed.]

Fifth at the outset, not in the middle, of a line of questions inching toward incrimination. Having testified that she herself held a Party office, the court ruled, Jane Rogers had waived her Fifth Amendment privilege and could not then refuse to testify about others.

HUAC tried to quick-march Fifth-takers into pitfalls. One gambit was a logical fork: if answering would incriminate him, a witness might use the Fifth; but if innocent, he could not honestly do so. Thus, the committee held, the witness was either guilty or lying—even though the courts did not accept this presumption of guilt. However, a new odious category, the "Fifth-Amendment Communist," was born. Such witnesses, whether teachers, actors, or others, rarely hung onto their jobs.

Legal precedent also demanded care in testifying about associations. One witness pled the Fifth in response to the question of whether he was a member of the American Automobile Association. HUAC members enjoyed asking if witnesses belonged to the Ku Klux Klan, hoping to nettle them into breaking a string of refusals to answer. On their part, witnesses devised novel defenses like the so-called "diminished Fifth." A witness resorting to the "slightly diminished Fifth" would deny present CP membership but refuse to open up his past or that of others; those using the "fully diminished Fifth," on the other hand, testified about their own pasts but no one else's. (The "augmented Fifth" was like the slightly diminished Fifth, but the witness also disclaimed any sympathy for communism.)

The question of whether to testify freely or take the Fifth convulsed the higher precincts of American arts and letters. Writer Lillian Hellman, subpoenaed in 1952, took the bold step of writing HUAC's chairman that she would take the Fifth only if asked to talk about others. She realized that by answering questions about herself, she waived her privilege and was subject to a contempt citation, but better that than to "bring bad trouble" to innocent people. She simply would not cut her conscience "to fit this year's fashions." When she testified, she did invoke the Fifth but scored a coup with her eloquent letter and managed to avoid a contempt citation. In 1956 the playwright Arthur Miller also refused to discuss other people but, unlike Hellman, did not take the Fifth. (His contempt citation was later overturned.)

Art came to mirror politics. Miller had previously written *The Crucible,* whose hero welcomed death rather than implicate others in the seventeenth-century Salem witch trials. Admirers stressed the play's relevance to modern witch-hunts. In contrast, Elia Kazan, who had named names, directed the smash movie *On the Waterfront,* whose hero (Marlon Brando), implored by a fighting priest (Karl Malden) to speak out, agreed to inform against criminals in a longshoremen's union. None of these works dealt with communism, but their pertinence to current political issues was not lost. Among the arbiters of American culture, these moral choices prompted heated debate, which still reverberated in the 1980s.

The issues were not only philosophical. The sanctions were real. Noncooperative witnesses were blacklisted, their careers in Hollywood shattered. Many drifted into other lines of work. Many became exiles, moving to Europe,

Mexico, or New York. Some suffered writer's block. Some families endured steady FBI surveillance and such vexations as sharply increased life insurance premiums (for an assertedly dangerous occupation). Being blacklisted so dispirited several actors that their health was impaired, and premature death resulted. Comedian Philip Loeb, blacklisted and unemployable, his family destroyed, committed suicide in 1955.

Even though several hundred members of the entertainment industry forfeited their livelihoods after HUAC appearances, the studios, networks, producers, and the committee itself did not admit publicly that a blacklist existed. (Privately, some were candid. "Pal, you're dead," a soused producer told writer Millard Lampell. "They told me that I couldn't touch you with a barge pole.") In this shadow world, performers and writers wondered if their talents had indeed eroded. Had one's voice sharpened, one's humor dulled?

For blacklisting to work, HUAC's hammer needed an anvil. It was duly provided by other groups who willingly punished hostile or reluctant witnesses. American Legion publications spread the word about movies whose credits were fouled by subversion; Legionnaires (and other local true believers) could pressure theatre owners, if necessary, by trooping down to the Bijou to picket offending films. The mere threat of such forces soon choked off the supply of objectionable pictures at the source. Indeed, Hollywood, responding to broad hints from HUAC and to its own reading of the political climate, began making anti-Communist potboilers. These low-budget "B" pictures did poorly at the box office. They provided insurance, not profits.

Though entertainment industry moguls justified screening employees' politics by citing the threat from amateur censors, usually professional blacklisters made the system work. Blacklisting opened up business vistas on the Right. In 1950 American Business Consultants, founded by three ex-FBI agents, published *Red Channels,* a compendium listing 151 entertainers and their Communist-front links. *Counterattack,* an ABC publication started in 1947, periodically offered the same type of information. In 1953 an employee left ABC to establish Aware, Inc., which sold a similar service. Companies in show biz subscribed to these countersubversive finding aids and paid to have the names of those they might hire for a show or series checked against "the files." Aware charged five dollars to vet a name for the first time, two dollars for rechecks. It became habit for Hollywood, radio and TV networks, advertisers, and stage producers (though blacklisting had its weakest hold on Broadway) not to employ entertainers whose names cropped up in such files.

A few found ways to evade total proscription. Writers could sometimes submit work under pseudonyms. Studios asked some writers on the blacklist to doctor ailing scripts authored by others. The blacklisted writers received no screen credits and were paid a pittance, but at least they were working. Ostracized actors did not have this option. Said comedian Zero Mostel: "I am a man of a thousand faces, all of them blacklisted." A TV producer once called a talent agent to ask, "Who have you got like John Garfield?" He had Garfield himself, the agent exclaimed; but, of course, the blacklisted Garfield was taboo.

Unlike actors, blacklisted writers could also find work in television, which devoured new scripts ravenously. As in film, some used assumed names. Others worked through "fronts" (whence came the title of Woody Allen's 1976 movie). They wrote, but someone else put his name to the script (and might demand up to half of the income). Mistaken-identity plot twists worthy of a Restoration comedy resulted. One writer using a pseudonym wrote a script that he was asked, under a second pseudonym, to revise. Millard Lampell submitted a script under a phony name; the producers insisted that the script's writer appear for consultation; told that he was away and unavailable, they went for a quick fix: they asked Lampell to rewrite his own (unacknowledged) script.

The obverse of blacklisting was "clearance." Desperate actors or writers could seek absolution from a member of the anti-Communist industry. Often, not surprisingly, the person to see was one who had played a part in creating the blacklist. Roy Brewer, the chief of the International Alliance of Theatrical Stage Employees, had redbaited the leftist craft guilds, but helped rehabilitate blacklistees, as did several conservative newspaper columnists. The American Legion, which issued lists of Hollywood's undesirables, also certified innocence or repentance. A listee might get by with writing a letter to the Legion. Or he might be made to list suspect organizations he had joined and to tell why he joined, when he quit, who invited him in, and whom he had enticed. Thus the written route to clearance might also require naming names.

To regain grace, some sinners had to repent publicly, express robust patriotism in a speech or article, or confess to having been duped into supporting leftist causes. Typically, a blacklistee had to be willing to tell all to the FBI or to HUAC. Even liberal anti-Communists were "graylisted," and some had to write clearance letters. Humphrey Bogart had bought trouble by protesting the 1947 HUAC hearings against the Hollywood Ten. In his article, "I'm No Communist," he admitted he had been a "dope" in politics. Actor John Garfield, whose appearance before HUAC sent his career and life into a tailspin, was at the time of his death about to publish an article titled "I Was a Sucker for a Left Hook."

Like teachers and entertainers, charitable foundations also triggered the suspicion of congressional anti-Communists. These products of capitalism plowed back into society some of the vast wealth of their Robber Baron founders, but conservatives found their philanthropic tastes too radical. In 1952 a special House committee led by Georgia conservative Eugene Cox inquired into the policies of tax-exempt foundations. Did not "these creatures of the capitalist system," asked Cox, seek to "bring the system into disrepute" and to assume "a socialistic leaning"? . . .

How deeply did anti-communism gouge the social and political terrain of the 1950s? With dissent defined as dangerous, the range of political debate obviously was crimped. The number of times that books were labeled dangerous, thoughts were scourged as harmful, and speakers and performers were rejected as outside the pale multiplied. Anti-Communist extremism and accompanying pressures toward conformity had impact in such areas as artistic expression, the labor movement, the cause of civil rights, and the status of minorities in American life.

For some denizens of the Right, threats of Communist influence materialized almost anywhere. For instance, Illinois American Legionnaires warned that the Girl Scouts were being spoonfed subversive doctrines. Jack Lait and Lee Mortimer's yellow-journalistic *U.S.A. Confidential* warned parents against the emerging threat of rock and roll. It bred dope use, interracialism, and sex orgies. "We know that many platter-spinners are hopheads. Many others are Reds, left-wingers, or hecklers of social convention." Not every absurdity owed life to the vigilantes, however. A jittery Hollywood studio cancelled a movie based on Longfellow's "Hiawatha" for fear it would be viewed as "Communist peace propaganda."

Books and ideas remained vulnerable. It is true that the militant Indiana woman who abhorred *Robin Hood's* subversive rob-from-the-rich-and-give-to the-poor message failed to get it banned from school libraries. Other locales were less lucky. A committee of women appointed by the school board of Sapulpa, Oklahoma, had more success. The board burned those books that it classified as dealing improperly with socialism or sex. A spokesman claimed that only five or six "volumes of no consequence" were destroyed. A librarian in Bartlesville, Oklahoma, was fired for subscribing to the *New Republic, Nation,* and *Negro Digest.* The use of UNESCO [United Nations Educational, Scientific, and Cultural Organization] materials in the Los Angeles schools became a hot issue in 1952. A new school board and superintendent were elected with a mandate to remove such books from school libraries.

Local sanctions against unpopular artists and speakers often were effective. In August 1950, a New Hampshire resort hotel banned a talk by Owen Lattimore after guests, apparently riled by protests of the Daughters of the American Revolution and others, remonstrated. Often local veterans—the American Legion and Catholic War Veterans—initiated pressures. The commander of an American Legion Post in Omaha protested a local production of a play whose author, Garson Kanin, was listed in *Red Channels.* A founder of *Red Channels* warned an American Legion anti-subversive seminar in Peoria, Illinois, that Arthur Miller's *Death of a Salesman,* soon to appear locally, was "a Communist dominated play." Jaycees and Legionnaires failed to get the theatre to cancel the play, but the boycott they mounted sharply curbed the size of the audience.

Libraries often became focal points of cultural anxieties. Not every confrontation ended like those in Los Angeles or Sapulpa, but librarians felt they were under the gun. "I just put a book that is complained about away for a while," said one public librarian. Occasionally, books were burned. "Did you ever try to burn a book?" asked another librarian. "It's *very* difficult." One-third of a group of librarians sampled in the late 1950s reported having removed "controversial" items from their shelves. One-fifth said they habitually avoided buying such books.

Academics, too, were scared. Many college and university social scientists polled in 1955 confessed to reining in their political views and activities. Twenty-seven percent had "wondered" whether a political opinion they had expressed might affect their job security or promotion; 40 percent had worried that a student might pass on "a warped version of what you have said and lead to false ideas about your political views." Twenty-two percent had at times "refrained from expressing an opinion or participating in some activity in order not to embarrass" their institution. Nine percent had "toned down" recent writing to avoid controversy. One teacher said he never expressed his own opinion in class. "I express the recognized and acknowledged point of view." Some instructors no longer assigned *The Communist Manifesto.*

About a hundred professors actually lost jobs, but an even greater number of frightened faculty trimmed their sails against the storm. Episodes far short of dismissal could also have a chilling effect. An economist at a Southern school addressed a business group, his talk, titled "Know Your Enemy," assessed Soviet resources and strengths. He was denounced to his president as a Communist. Another professor was assailed for advocating a lower tariff on oranges. "If I'd said potatoes, I wouldn't have been accused unless I had said it in Idaho." Some teachers got in mild trouble for such acts as assigning Robert and Helen Lynds' classic sociological study, *Middletown,* in class or listing the Kinsey reports on human sexuality as recommended reading. A professor once sent students to a public library to read works by Marx because his college's library had too few copies. Librarians logged the students' names.

The precise effect of all this professed anxiety was fuzzy. Many liberals claimed that Americans had been cowed into silence, that even honest anti-Communist dissent had been stilled, and that basic freedoms of thought, expression, and association had languished. The worriers trotted out appropriate comparisons: the witch trials in Salem, the Reign of Terror in France, the Alien and Sedition Acts, Know-Nothingism, and the Palmer raids. Justice William O. Douglas warned of "The Black Silence of Fear." Prominent foreigners like Bertrand Russell and Graham Greene decried the pall of fear they observed in America. On July 4, 1951, a *Madison Capital-Times* reporter asked passersby to sign a paper containing the Bill of Rights and parts of the Declaration of Independence. Out of 112, only one would do so. President Truman cited the episode to show McCarthyism's dire effects. McCarthy retorted that Truman owed an apology to the people of Wisconsin in view of that paper's Communist-line policies. Some McCarthy allies upheld the wisdom of refusing to sign any statement promiscuously offered.

McCarthy's defenders ridiculed the more outlandish laments for vanished liberties. A New York rabbi who blamed "McCarthyism" for the current spree of college "panty raids" offered a case in point. Conservative journalist Eugene Lyons was amused by an ACLU spokesman, his tonsils flaring in close-up on television, arguing "that in America no one any longer dares open his mouth." Such talk, said Lyons, led to "hysteria over hysteria." In their apologia for McCarthy, William F. Buckley and L. Brent Bozell snickered at such silliness. They found it odd that, in a time when left-of-center ideas were supposedly being crushed, liberals seemed to monopolize symposia sponsored by the major universities, even in McCarthy's home state, and that Archibald MacLeish and Bernard De Voto, two of those who condemned the enervating climate of fear, had still managed to garner two National Book Awards and a Pulitzer Prize. To Buckley and Bozell, the only conformity present was a proper one—a consensus that communism was evil and must be fought wholeheartedly.

But did such an argument miss the point? The successes enjoyed by prominent, secure liberals were one thing; far more numerous were the cases of those less visible and secure who lost entertainment and lecture bookings, chances to review books, teaching posts, even assembly-line jobs. The fight over the Communist menace had gone far beyond roistering debate or asserting the right of those who disagree with a set of views not to patronize them. People, a great number of whom had committed no crime, were made to suffer.

POSTSCRIPT

Did Communism Threaten America's Internal Security After World War II?

The "Venona Transcripts" represent only one set of sources depicting the Soviet spy apparatus in the United States. The Venona papers were not released to the public until 1995. Haynes and Klehr have also collaborated on two documentary collections based on the archives of the American Communist Party, which had been stored for decades in Moscow and were opened to foreign researchers in 1992. See *The Secret World of American Communism* (Yale University Press, 1995) and *The Soviet World of American Communism* (Yale University Press, 1998), both of which contain useful collections of translated Russian documents, which are virtually impossible to access. Haynes and Klehr's work also substantiates charges made by Allen Weinstein and his translator, former KGB agent Alexander Vassiliev, in *The Haunted Wood: Soviet Espionage in America—The Stalin Era* (Random House, 1999).

According to Fried, 24 teachers from New York City were fired and 34 resigned while under investigation between 1950 and early 1953. According to one estimate, over 300 teachers in the city lost their jobs because of their political beliefs. Similar dismissals also took place in public universities and colleges across the country. Book burnings were rare, but many public libraries discarded pro-Communist books or put them in storage. In Bartlesville, Oklahoma, in 1950, librarian Ruth Brown was fired from her job after 30 years ostensibly for circulating magazines like *The New Republic* and *The Nation,* which were deemed subversive. Actually, many agree that she was fired for supporting civil rights activism, a fact that the American Library Association left out in defending her. See Louise S. Robinson, *The Dismissal of Miss Ruth Brown: Civil Rights, Censorship, and the American Library* (University of Oklahoma Press, 2000).

Four books represent a good starting point for students: M. J. Heale, *American Anticommunism: Combating the Enemy Within, 1830–1970* (Johns Hopkins University Press, 1990) extends Americans' fears of subversion back to the Jackson years; Ellen Schrecker, *The Age of McCarthyism: A Brief History With Documents* (Bedford Books, 1994) blames both parties for the excesses of the anti-Communist assault against radicals who were fighting against status quo race relations in the 1930s and 1940s; John Earl Haynes, *Red Scare or Red Menace? American Communism and Anticommunism in the Cold War Era* (Ivan R. Dee, 1996), which argues that anticommunism was a reasonable response to a real threat; and Richard Gid Powers, *Not Without Honor: The History of American Anticommunism* (Free Press, 1995), which portrays anticommunism as a mainstream political movement with many variations.

ISSUE 10

Did Lee Harvey Oswald Kill President Kennedy by Himself?

YES: President's Commission on the Assassination of President John F. Kennedy, from *The Warren Report: Report of the President's Commission on the Assassination of President John F. Kennedy* (September 24, 1964)

NO: Michael L. Kurtz, from *Crime of the Century: The Kennedy Assassination From a Historian's Perspective,* 2d ed. (University of Tennessee Press, 1993)

ISSUE SUMMARY

YES: The President's Commission on the Assassination of President John F. Kennedy argues that Lee Harvey Oswald was the sole assassin of President Kennedy and that he was not part of any organized conspiracy, domestic or foreign.

NO: Professor of history Michael L. Kurtz argues that the Warren Commission ignored evidence of Oswald's connections with organized criminals and with pro-Castro and anti-Castro supporters, as well as forensic evidence that points to multiple assassins.

On November 22, 1963, at 12:30 p.m., President John F. Kennedy was shot while riding in a motorcade with his wife, Jacqueline, and Governor and Mrs. John Connally through the western end of downtown Dallas, Texas. After Secret Service agent Roy Kellerman noticed that the president was shot, he ordered the car to proceed as quickly as possible to Parkland Hospital. At one o'clock the president was pronounced dead. A stunned nation mourned for five days. Yet nearly 40 years later many questions remain unanswered. Did Lee Harvey Oswald kill President Kennedy? How many shots were fired? Was there a second or third shooter? Was Oswald set up, or was he part of a grand conspiracy? Did Jack Ruby kill Oswald on the way to his arraignment because he was distraught over the president's death or because he was ordered by the Mafia to kill Oswald?

A belief in conspiracies has been a common thread throughout American history. "The script has become familiar," according to professor of history

Robert Alan Goldberg. "Individuals and groups, acting in secret, move and shape recent American history. Driven by a lust for power and wealth, they practice deceit, subterfuge, and even assassination brazenly executed. Nothing is random or the matter of coincidence."

Popular views on American foreign policy, for example, are strewn with conspiracies. Here is a partial list: munitions makers led America into World War I; President Franklin D. Roosevelt deliberately exposed the fleet at Pearl Harbor to a Japanese attack in order to get the United States into World War II; Roosevelt sold out Eastern Europe to the Soviets at the Yalta Conference because he was pro-Russian; the Communists infiltrated the State Department and foreign service, which permitted the Communists to take over China in 1949; and the "seven sisters"—the big oil companies—deliberately curtailed the flow of oil in 1974 in order to jack up gasoline prices.

Assassinations—the overthrow of an opponent through murder—are not as common in American politics as they have been in other countries. Only four presidents have been assassinated in the United States—Abraham Lincoln, James Garfield, William McKinley and John F. Kennedy. All the assassins were identified as white males who were somewhat delusional or, at best, loners promoting a cause. The best known is John Wilkes Booth, a famous actor who killed Lincoln because the president had destroyed slavery and the Old South. Garfield was murdered by a disappointed office seeker, McKinley by an anarchist, and Kennedy supposedly by a disgruntled Marxist.

The Lincoln and Kennedy assassinations are unique because the deaths of both presidents are linked with conspiracies. Most Lincoln scholars reject the theory that Secretary of War Edward Stanton plotted with Booth to kill the president. But the Kennedy assassination has produced an enormous quantity of literature, if not all of first-rate quality, arguing that Kennedy was the victim of a conspiracy.

In the following selection, the President's Commission on the Assassination of President John F. Kennedy rejects the view that Lee Harvey Oswald was involved with any other person or group in a conspiracy to assassinate the president. The commission denies that Oswald was a foreign agent or was encouraged by any foreign government to kill the president. Nor was Oswald "an agent, employee, or informant of the FBI, CIA or any other governmental agency." In short, Oswald fit the profile of the brooding lone gunmen who killed Garfield and McKinley and set the tone for Arthur Bremmer, Squeaky Frome, and John Hinkley, who tried to kill presidential candidate George Wallace and Presidents Gerald Ford and Ronald Reagan, respectively.

In the second selection, Michael L. Kurtz questions the conclusions of the *Warren Report.* He argues that forensic evidence points to a possible second or third killer located at the grassy knoll in front of the motorcade in addition to the assassin who fired shots from the sixth floor of the Texas School Book Depository Building. Kurtz also contends that Oswald had connections with minor organized crime figures and with both pro-Castro and anti-Castro plotters, supporting the existence of a conspiracy.

President's Commission on the Assassination of President John F. Kennedy **YES**

The Warren Report

The Commission has . . . reached certain conclusions based on all the available evidence. No limitations have been placed on the Commission's inquiry; it has conducted its own investigation, and all Government agencies have fully discharged their responsibility to cooperate with the Commission in its investigation. These conclusions represent the reasoned judgment of all members of the Commission and are presented after an investigation which has satisfied the Commission that it: has ascertained the truth concerning the assassination of President Kennedy to the extent that a prolonged and thorough search makes this possible.

1. The shots which killed President Kennedy and wounded Governor Connally-were fired from the sixth floor window at the southeast corner of the Texas School Book Depository. This determination is based upon the following:

(a) Witnesses at the scene of the assassination saw a rifle being fired from the sixth floor window of the Depository Building, and some witnesses saw a rifle in the window immediately after the shots were fired.
(b) The nearly whole bullet found on Governor Connally's stretcher at Parkland Memorial Hospital and the two bullet fragments found in the front seat of the Presidential limousine were fired from the 6.5-millimeter Mannlicher-Carcano rifle found on the sixth floor of the Depository Building to the exclusion of all other weapons.
(c) The three used cartridge cases found near the window on the sixth floor at the southeast corner of the building were fired from the same rifle which fired the above-described bullet and fragments, to the exclusion of all other weapons.
(d) The windshield in the Presidential limousine was struck by a bullet fragment on the inside surface of the glass, but was not penetrated.
(e) The nature of the bullet wounds suffered by President Kennedy and Governor Connally and the location of the car at the time of the shots establish that the bullets were fired from above and behind the Presidential limousine, striking the President and the Governor as follows:
    (1) President Kennedy was first struck by a bullet which entered at the back of his neck and exited through the lower front

From President's Commission on the Assassination of President John F. Kennedy, *The Warren Report: Report of the President s Commission on the Assassination of President John F. Kennedy* (September 24, 1964). Washington, D.C.: U.S. Government Printing Office, 1964.

portion of his neck, causing a wound which would not necessarily have been lethal. The President was struck a second time by a bullet which entered the right-rear portion of his head, causing a massive and fatal wound.

(2) Governor Connally was struck by a bullet which entered on the right side of his back and traveled downward through the right side of his chest, exiting below his right nipple. This bullet then passed through his right wrist and entered his left thigh where it caused a superficial wound.

(f) There is no credible evidence that the shots were fired from the Triple Underpass, ahead of the motorcade, or from any other location.

2. The weight of the evidence indicates that there were three shots fired.

3. Although it is not necessary to any essential findings of the Commission to determine just which shot hit Governor Connally, there is very persuasive evidence from the experts to indicate that the same bullet which pierced the President's throat also caused Governor Connally's wounds. However, Governor Connally's testimony and certain other factors have given rise to some difference of opinion as to this probability but there is no question in the mind of any member of the Commission that all the shots which caused the President's and Governor Connally's wounds were fired from the sixth floor window of the Texas School Book Depository.

4. The shots which killed President Kennedy and wounded Governor Connally were fired by Lee Harvey Oswald. This conclusion is based upon the following:

(a) The Mannlicher-Carcano 6.5-millimeter Italian rifle from which the shots were fired was owned by and in the possession of Oswald.

(b) Oswald carried this rifle into the Depository Building on the morning of November 22, 1963.

(c) Oswald, at the time of the assassination, was present at the window from which the shots were fired.

(d) Shortly after the assassination, the Mannlicher-Carcano rifle belonging to Oswald was found partially hidden between some cartons on the sixth floor and the improvised paper bag in which Oswald brought the rifle to the Depository was found close by the window from which the shots were fired.

(e) Based on testimony of the experts and their analysis of films of the assassination, the Commission has concluded that a rifleman of Lee Harvey Oswald's capabilities could have fired the shots from the rifle used in the assassination within the elapsed time of the shooting. The Commission has concluded further that Oswald possessed the capability with a rifle which enabled him to commit the assassination.

(f) Oswald lied to the police after his arrest concerning important substantive matters.

(g) Oswald had attempted to kill Maj. Gen. Edwin A. Walker (Resigned, U.S. Army) on April 10, 1963, thereby demonstrating his disposition to take human life.

5. Oswald killed Dallas Police Patrolman J. D. Tippit approximately 45 minutes after the assassination. This conclusion upholds the finding that Oswald fired the shots which killed President Kennedy and wounded Governor Connally and is supported by the following:

(a) Two eyewitnesses saw the Tippit shooting and seven eyewitnesses heard the shots and saw the gunman leave the scene with revolver in hand. These nine eyewitnesses positively identified Lee Harvey Oswald as the man they saw.
(b) The cartridge cases found at the scene of the shooting were fired from the revolver in the possession of Oswald at the time of his arrest to the exclusion of all other weapons.
(c) The revolver in Oswald's possession at the time of his arrest was purchased by and belonged to Oswald.
(d) Oswald's jacket was found along the path of flight taken by the gunman as he fled from the scene of the killing.

6. Within 80 minutes of the assassination and 35 minutes of the Tippit killing Oswald resisted arrest at the theatre by attempting to shoot another Dallas police officer.

7. The Commission has reached the following conclusions concerning Oswald's interrogation and detention by the Dallas police:

(a) Except for the force required to effect his arrest, Oswald was not subjected to any physical coercion by any law enforcement officials. He was advised that he could not be compelled to give any information and that any statements made by him might be used against him in court. He was advised of his right to counsel. He was given the opportunity to obtain counsel of his own choice and was offered legal assistance by the Dallas Bar Association, which he rejected at that time.
(b) Newspaper, radio, and television reporters were allowed uninhibited access to the area through which Oswald had to pass when he was moved from his cell to the interrogation room and other sections of the building, thereby subjecting Oswald to harassment and creating chaotic conditions which were not conducive to orderly interrogation or the protection of the rights of the prisoner.
(c) The numerous statements, sometimes erroneous, made to the press by various local law enforcement officials, during this period of confusion and disorder in the police station, would have presented serious obstacles to the obtaining of a fair trial for Oswald. To the extent that the information was erroneous or misleading, it helped to create doubts, speculations, and fears in the mind of the public which might otherwise not have arisen.

8. The Commission has reached the following conclusions concerning the killing of Oswald by Jack Ruby on November 24, 1963:

(a) Ruby entered the basement of the Dallas Police Department shortly after 11:17 a.m. and killed Lee Harvey Oswald at 11:21 a.m.

(b) Although the evidence on Ruby's means of entry is not conclusive, the weight of the evidence indicates that he walked down the ramp leading from Main Street to the basement of the police department.
(c) There is no evidence to support the rumor that Ruby may have been assisted by any members of the Dallas Police Department in the killing of Oswald.
(d) The Dallas Police Department's decision to transfer Oswald to the county jail in full public view was unsound. The arrangements made by the police department on Sunday morning, only a few hours before the attempted transfer, were inadequate. Of critical importance was the fact that news media representatives and others were not excluded from the basement even after the police were notified of threats to Oswald's life. These deficiencies contributed to the death of Lee Harvey Oswald.

9. The Commission has found no evidence that either Lee Harvey Oswald or Jack Ruby was part of any conspiracy, domestic or foreign, to assassinate President Kennedy. The reasons for this conclusion are:

(a) The Commission has found no evidence that anyone assisted Oswald in planning or carrying out the assassination. In this connection it has thoroughly investigated, among other factors, the circumstances surrounding the planning of the motorcade route through Dallas, the hiring of Oswald by the Texas School Book Depository Co. on October 15, 1963, the method by which the rifle was brought into the building, the placing of cartons of books at the window, Oswald's escape from the building, and the testimony of eyewitnesses to the shooting.
(b) The Commission has found no evidence that Oswald was involved with any person or group in a conspiracy to assassinate the President, although it has thoroughly investigated, in addition to other possible leads, all facets of Oswald's associations, finances, and personal habits, particularly during the period following his return from the Soviet Union in June 1962.
(c) The Commission has found no evidence to show that Oswald was employed, persuaded, or encouraged by any foreign government to assassinate President Kennedy or that he was an agent of any foreign government, although the Commission has reviewed the circumstances surrounding Oswald's defection to the Soviet Union, his life there from October of 1959 to June of 1962 so far as it can be reconstructed, his known contacts with the Fair Play for Cuba Committee and his visits to the Cuban and Soviet Embassies in Mexico City during his trip to Mexico from September 26 to October 3, 1963, and his known contacts with the Soviet Embassy in the United States.
(d) The Commission has explored all attempts of Oswald to identify himself with various political groups, including the Communist Party, U.S.A., the Fair Play for Cuba Committee, and the Socialist Workers Party, and has been unable to find any evidence that the contacts which he initiated were related to Oswald's subsequent assassination of the President.

(e) All of the evidence before the Commission established that there was nothing to support the speculation that Oswald was an agent, employee, or informant of the FBI, the CIA, or any other governmental agency. It has thoroughly investigated Oswald's relationships prior to the assassination with all agencies of the U.S. Government. All contacts with Oswald by any of these agencies were made in the regular exercise of their different responsibilities.
(f) No direct or indirect relationship between Lee Harvey Oswald and Jack Ruby has been discovered by the Commission, nor has it been able to find any credible evidence that either knew the other, although a thorough investigation was made of the many rumors and speculations of such a relationship.
(g) The Commission has found no evidence that Jack Ruby acted with any other person in the killing of Lee Harvey Oswald.
(h) After careful investigation the Commission has found no credible evidence either that Ruby and Officer Tippit, who was killed by Oswald, knew each other or that Oswald and Tippit knew each other.

Because of the difficulty of proving negatives to a certainty the possibility of others being involved with either Oswald or Ruby cannot be established categorically, but if there is any such evidence it has been beyond the reach of all the investigative agencies and resources of the United States and has not come to the attention of this Commission.

10. In its entire investigation the Commission has found no evidence of conspiracy, subversion, or disloyalty to the U.S. Government by any Federal, State, or local official.

11. On the basis of the evidence before the Commission it concludes that Oswald acted alone. Therefore, to determine the motives for the assassination of President Kennedy, one must look to the assassin himself. Clues to Oswald's motives can be found in his family history, his education or lack of it, his acts, his writings, and the recollections of those who had close contacts with him throughout his life. The Commission has presented with this report all of the background information bearing on motivation which it could discover. Thus, others may study Lee Oswald's life and arrive at their own conclusions as to his possible motives.

The Commission could not make any definitive determination of Oswald's motives. It has endeavored to isolate factors which contributed to his character and which might have influenced his decision to assassinate President Kennedy. These factors were:

(a) His deep-rooted resentment of all authority which was expressed in a hostility toward every society in which he lived;
(b) His inability to enter into meaningful relationships with people, and a continuous pattern of rejecting his environment in favor of new surroundings;
(c) His urge to try to find a place in history and despair at times over failures in his various undertakings;
(d) His capacity for violence as evidenced by his attempt to kill General Walker;

(e) His avowed commitment to Marxism and communism, as he understood the terms and developed his own interpretation of them; this was expressed by his antagonism toward the United States, by his defection to the Soviet Union, by his failure to be reconciled with life in the United States even after his disenchantment with the Soviet Union, and by his efforts, though frustrated, to go to Cuba.

Each of these contributed to his capacity to risk all in cruel and irresponsible actions.

12. The Commission recognizes that the varied responsibilities of the President require that he make frequent trips to all parts of the United States and abroad. Consistent with their high responsibilities Presidents can never be protected from every potential threat. The Secret Service's difficulty in meeting its protective responsibility varies with the activities and the nature of the occupant of the Office of President and his willingness to conform to plans for his safety. In appraising the performance of the Secret Service it should be understood that it has to do its work within such limitations. Nevertheless, the Commission believes that recommendations for improvements in Presidential protection are compelled by the facts disclosed in this investigation.

(a) The complexities of the Presidency have increased so rapidly in recent years that the Secret Service has not been able to develop or to secure adequate resources of personnel and facilities to fulfill its important assignment. This situation should be promptly remedied.
(b) The Commission has concluded that the criteria and procedures of the Secret Service designed to identify and protect against persons considered threats to the President, were not adequate prior to the assassination.
    (1) The Protective Research Section of the Secret Service, which is responsible for its preventive work, lacked sufficient trained personnel and the mechanical and technical assistance needed to fulfill its responsibility.
    (2) Prior to the assassination the Secret Service's criteria dealt with direct threats against the President. Although the Secret Service treated the direct threats against the President adequately, it failed to recognize the necessity of identifying other potential sources of danger to his security. The Secret Service did not develop adequate and specific criteria defining those persons or groups who might present a danger to the President. In effect, the Secret Service largely relied upon other Federal or State agencies to supply the information necessary for it to fulfill its preventive responsibilities, although it did ask for information about direct threats to the President.

(c) The Commission has concluded that there was insufficient liaison and coordination of information between the Secret Service and other Federal agencies necessarily concerned with Presidential protection. Although the FBI, in the normal exercise of its responsibility, had secured considerable information about Lee Harvey Oswald, it had no official responsibility, under the Secret Service criteria existing at the time of the President's trip to Dallas, to refer to the Secret Service the information it had about Oswald. The Commission has concluded, however, that the FBI took an unduly restrictive view of its role in preventive intelligence work prior to the assassination. A more carefully coordinated treatment of the Oswald case by the FBI might well have resulted in bringing Oswald's activities to the attention of the Secret Service.

(d) The Commission has concluded that some of the advance preparations in Dallas made by the Secret Service, such as the detailed security measures taken at Love Field and the Trade Mart, were thorough and well executed. In other respects, however, the Commission has concluded that the advance preparations for the President's trip were deficient.

  (1) Although the Secret Service is compelled to rely to a great extent on local law enforcement officials, its procedures at the time of the Dallas trip did not call for well-defined instructions as to the respective responsibilities of the police officials and others assisting in the protection of the President.

  (2) The procedures relied upon by the Secret Service for detecting the presence of an assassin located in a building along a motorcade route were inadequate. At the time of the trip to Dallas, the Secret Service as a matter of practice did not investigate, or cause to be checked, any building located along the motorcade route to be taken by the President. The responsibility for observing windows in these buildings during the motorcade was divided between local police personnel stationed on the streets to regulate crowds and Secret Service agents riding in the motorcade. Based on its investigation the Commission has concluded that these arrangements during the trip to Dallas were clearly not sufficient.

(e) The configuration of the Presidential car and the seating arrangements of the Secret Service agents in the car did not afford the Secret Service agents the opportunity they should have had to be of immediate assistance to the President at the first sign of danger.

(f) Within these limitations, however, the Commission finds that the agents most immediately responsible for the President's safety reacted promptly at the time the shots were fired from the Texas School Book Depository Building.

NO

Michael L. Kurtz

Some Questions

When a historian investigates a past event, he usually begins by asking questions about that event. Innumerable questions about the Kennedy assassination have been raised. Some of them are worth considering, for they touch upon the most critical features of the assassination mysteries. The available evidence does not permit definitive answers to all those questions, but they do deserve attention.

1. Who killed President Kennedy?

This, of course, remains the central mystery in the entire assassination saga. Unfortunately, we do not know the answer. That more than one individual fired shots at the president cannot seriously be doubted. Their identities, however, are unknown.

2. Did Lee Harvey Oswald fire any of the shots?

The evidence against Oswald is impressive: the discovery of his rifle bearing his palmprint on the sixth floor of the Book Depository building; the testimony of eyewitness Howard Brennan; Oswald's prints on the cartons and paper sack at the window; the discovery of three cartridge cases from his rifle by the window; the discovery of two bullet fragments fired from his rifle in the limousine; his departure from the building soon after the shooting.

On the other side of the coin, the evidence in Oswald's favor is equally impressive: eyewitness identification of him on the second floor of the Depository building fifteen minutes before the assassination and two minutes after it; the lack of his prints on the outside of the rifle; the questions as to whether the cartridge cases had actually been fired from the rifle during the assassination; the extremely difficult feat of marksmanship an assassin firing from the window faced; the lack of corroboration for Brennan's contradictory and confused identification.

3. How did Lee Harvey Oswald escape the scene of the assassination?

There is no evidence to support the claim of the Warren Commission that Oswald walked out through the front door of the Book Depository building at 12:33. With the exception of the bus transfer allegedly found in Oswald's pocket, neither is there any evidence to support the commission's claim that Oswald caught a bus and a taxi. Replete with contradictions, the testimony of Mary Bledsoe and William Whaley hardly prove that the bus and taxi ride took place.

In contrast, the eyewitness and photographic evidence strongly supports Deputy Sheriff Roger Craig's testimony that he saw Oswald run from the rear of the building about fifteen minutes after the assassination and enter a station wagon driven by a dark-skinned man. Eyewitness Helen Monaghan saw Oswald in an upper floor of the building five to ten minutes after the shots. Eyewitnesses Helen Forrest and James Pennington corroborated Craig's story, for they, too, saw Oswald flee the building and enter the station wagon. While not conclusive, this evidence very solidly supports the conspiracy theory.

4. Was Oswald's gun fired at President Kennedy and Governor Connally?

The fact that two large bullet fragments, ballistically proven traceable to Oswald's rifle, were found in the front seat of the presidential limousine supplies very strong evidence that the rifle was fired once, although the possibility that the fragments were planted in the car cannot be disproven.

No other evidence proves that the rifle was fired more than once. Even if they could be proven beyond question to have been fired from Oswald's rifle, the three empty cartridge cases found on the floor by the sixth-floor window of the Depository building provide no indication that they were fired from the weapon on 22 November 1963. Obviously, the possibility exists that they were fired previously and dropped there to implicate Oswald. Even if the rifle was one of the assassination weapons, there is no proof that Oswald fired it.

5. Are the backyard photographs of Oswald holding a rifle authentic?

Because of several apparent discrepancies between the man pictured in the photographs and known pictures of the real Oswald, many Warren Commission critics questioned the authenticity of the backyard photographs. The panel of photographic experts appointed by the House Select Committee did exhaustive tests on the photographs and negatives and concluded that they were authentic.

For all of the commotion about the photographs, their relevance to the assassination is obscure. They were taken in April 1963, seven months before the assassination. Photographs of Oswald holding a weapon at that time hardly prove or disprove that he discharged that weapon seven months later.

6. How many shots were fired?

The Warren Commission based its three-shot theory primarily on the three cartridge cases, and the House Committee based its four-shot theory primarily on the Dallas police tape. The earwitnesses provide little assistance, for their accounts of the number of shots range from none to seven. Nor do the wounds on Kennedy and Connally provide an answer. Connally's wounds could have been caused by as few as one and as many as three shots, while Kennedy's may have been caused by from two to four shots. The bulk of the evidence points to four shots, three from the rear and one from the front.

7. How many shots struck President Kennedy?

On the surface, the two bullet wounds in the rear of Kennedy's body and the two in front suggest four as the answer to the question. However, the possibility that the two front holes were exit wounds for the rear holes demands close analysis. The rear holes of entrance in the head and back are positive evidence of two shots. As we have seen, the huge, gaping wound in the right front of the president's head could not simply have been an exit hole from one of Oswald's bullets. Almost certainly, it was also an entrance wound caused by a "dum-dum" or exploding bullet fired from the Grassy Knoll. The front wound in Kennedy's throat was probably *not* caused by a separate bullet. The answer, therefore, is at least three.

8. What caused the tiny bullet hole in President Kennedy's throat?

The Warren Commission's and House Committee's claim that this hole was the exit hole for the bullet that entered Kennedy's back is not supported by the evidence. The wound in the president's throat was round, clean, and encircled by a ring of bruising. Moreover, it was extremely small, smaller than the diameter of most bullets. The Forensic Pathology Panel's assertion that the buttoned collar of Kennedy's shirt caused his skin to stretch taut, thus resulting in a small exit wound, appears erroneous. Ordinarily, bullets exiting through taut skin cause large exit wounds because the bullets push tissue and matter through the skin causing it to explode outward, much as a paper bag filled with air will expand and rupture in an uneven, jagged manner as the air rushes out.

If the throat wound were an entrance wound, as some critics have charged, there would have to be some evidence of its path through the body. Since there is none, this explanation can likewise be discounted.

The most plausible explanation for the wound is that it was caused by a fragment of bone or bullet from the head shot. No hole in the neck is visible in enlargements of individual frames of the Zapruder film and in other visual records. This virtually eliminates both the exit and entrance wound theories. The most reasonable explanation, then, is that a fragment was forced through the skull cavity by the tremendous cranial pressure of the head shot and exited through the president's neck.

9. Was Bullet 399 a genuine assassination bullet?

The overwhelming weight of the evidence indicates that Bullet 399 played no role in the Kennedy assassination. The bullet's almost intact condition precludes it as the cause of Governor Connally's wounds. The removal of bullet fragments from the governor's wrist, the extensive damage to his rib and wrist, and the wounds ballistics tests results all argue persuasively against Bullet 399 as having caused any of Connally's injuries.

A bullet was discovered on a hospital stretcher that had no connection with the assassination. Darrell Tomlinson and O. P. Wright, the only two witnesses who saw the bullet on the stretcher, refused to believe that Bullet 399 was the one they saw. Nor would the two Secret Service officials who handled the stretcher bullet agree that Bullet 399 was the one they handled.

Although Bullet 399 was fired from Oswald's rifle, there is no evidence whatsoever to suggest that it caused any of the wounds on Kennedy and Connally. The Warren Commission and the House Committee assumed that Bullet 399 was the infamous single bullet, primarily because it could be traced to Oswald's rifle. Both bodies, however, failed to investigate the possibility that the bullet was planted in order to implicate Oswald.

It is possible that Bullet 399 entered Kennedy's back, penetrated only a couple of inches into the body, and did not exit—later falling out during external cardiac massage. This, in fact, was the original impression of the autopsy pathologists. If this is the case, we do not know how it wound up on a hospital stretcher that had no connection with the assassination.

Because of the incomplete information available, we still do not know when Bullet 399 was fired or how it came into the possession of the FBI as an item of ballistic evidence.

10. Did an assassin fire shots from the Grassy Knoll?

Yes. The huge, gaping hole in the right front of President Kennedy's head was almost certainly caused by an exploding bullet fired from the knoll. The rapid backward and leftward movement of Kennedy's head, as well as the backward and leftward spray of brain tissue, skull bone, and blood are very strong indicators of a shot from the right front. Assuming that it is authentic, the acoustical tape actually recorded the sound of a knoll shot.

Eye and earwitness testimony furnishes further evidence of a shot from the knoll. Almost three-quarters of the witnesses who testified heard shots from the knoll during the shooting, and three people saw a flash of light there. Five witnesses smelled gunpowder in the knoll area. A witness saw a man fleeing the knoll immediately after the shooting, and two law enforcement officials encountered phony "Secret Service" men in the parking lot behind the knoll within minutes after the gunfire.

11. If a shot came from the Grassy Knoll, why was no physical evidence of it discovered?

The answer to this question, so frequently asked by defenders of the *Warren-Report,* is as simple as it is obvious. Common sense should be sufficient to explain that anyone taking the risk of killing the President of the United States would also have taken the precautions necessary to avoid leaving physical evidence of his guilt. The peculiar part of this aspect of the assassination case is not the lack of physical evidence on the knoll, but the plethora of evidence scattered all over the sixth floor of the Book Depository building. The two government investigations insist that Lee Harvey Oswald did not even bother to pick up the three cartridge cases and paper bag near the sixth-floor window but, in the process of descending the building stairs, paused for the refreshment of a Coke before departing the building.

An assassin with even the slightest concern with making a successful escape would hardly have selected the sixth floor of the Depository Building for his firing site. He would have been trapped on an upper floor of the building. His only means of escape would have been to descend six flights of stairs and then weave his way through the crowd of spectators and police to freedom.

The Grassy Knoll, on the other hand, provided a natural and ideal sniper's position. The six-foot-high wooden fence and the abundance of shrubbery concealed him from the crowd, yet gave him an undisturbed line of fire at the president. The parking lot right behind the knoll gave him quick access to a getaway vehicle.

12. *Who were the "Secret Service" men encountered on the knoll right after the shots?*

We know that they were not genuine Secret Service agents since all agents remained with the motorcade during its dash to Parkland Hospital. The men who flashed "Secret Service" credentials to Officer Smith and Constable Weizman, therefore, were imposters, and their identities have never been discovered. It need hardly be mentioned that the Warren Commission made no attempt to investigate this obviously serious matter.

13. *Who were the three "tramps" arrested in the railroad yards behind the Grassy Knoll?*

The theory that two of the three men were E. Howard Hunt and Frank Sturgis may be dismissed as unwarranted speculation. However, their true identities have never been determined. The Dallas police must have had some reason for arresting them but destroyed the records of the arrest. It is unlikely that the police would have suspended their search for the president's assassin to look for vagrants. However, as with so many other aspects of this case, the incomplete evidence does not permit an answer to the question.

14. *Were two men seen together on an upper floor of the Texas School Book Depository building?*

Yes. Witnesses Carolyn Walther, Richard Carr, Ruby Henderson, Arnold Rowland, and Johnny L. Powell saw two men, one of them dark-complected, together on the sixth floor. The Hughes and Bronson films of the assassination apparently show two men near the sixth-floor window.

15. *Why did the Secret Service fail to respond to the initial gunshots and attempt to protect President Kennedy?*

The Zapruder and other films and photographs of the assassination clearly reveal the utter lack of response by Secret Service agents Roy Kellerman and James Greer, who were in the front seat of the presidential limousine. After the first two shots, Greer actually slowed the vehicle to less than five miles an hour. Kellerman merely sat in the front seat, seemingly oblivious to the shooting. In contrast, Secret Service Agent Rufus Youngblood responded instantly to the first shot, and before the head shots were fired, had covered Vice-President Lyndon Johnson with his body.

Trained to react instantaneously, as in the attempted assassinations of President Gerald Ford by Lynette Fromme and Sara Jane Moore and of President Ronald Reagan by John Warnock Hinckley, the Secret Service agents assigned to protect President Kennedy simply neglected their duty. The reason for their neglect remains one of the more intriguing mysteries of the assassination.

16. *Why have so many important witnesses in the assassination case met strange deaths?*

It is true that certain key individuals in the Kennedy assassination case have met with sudden death under rather unusual circumstances. Among these are Lee Harvey Oswald, David Ferrie, and Jimmy Hoffa. Oswald was gunned down by Jack Ruby in the presence of seventy armed policemen. Ferrie died of natural causes after typing two suicide notes. Hoffa mysteriously disappeared.

The deaths of these and other persons connected with the case have prompted some assassination researchers to speculate that certain sinister forces responsible for Kennedy's murder are responsible for these deaths. However, there is no concrete evidence linking any of the deaths with the assassination itself. Unless such evidence is produced, all attempts to establish such a connection must remain in the realm of conjecture.

17. *Was a paper bag found on the floor by the sixth-floor window?*

The *Warren Report* claims that it was. However, the bag was not photographed in place, and Dallas law enforcement officers Luke Mooney, Roger Craig, and Gerald Hill, the first three policemen to reach the "sniper's nest," testified that they did *not* see the 38-inch-long sack, which, according to the *Report,* lay only two feet from the window. Three officers who arrived later remember seeing a bag there.

Once again, we are faced with conflicting evidence, and the reader has to decide for himself which appears more reliable.

18. *Were all the eyewitnesses to the assassination interviewed?*

No. Incredibly, the Dallas police did not seal off Dealey Plaza right after the assassination. They permitted traffic to proceed on Elm Street, just as if nothing had happened there. Over half the eyewitnesses simply left and went home without ever being questioned. Many inmates in the Dallas County Jail watched the motorcade from their prison cells. Even though these men literally constituted a captive audience, none was ever interrogated.

19. Did the Dallas police mishandle the physical evidence?

Yes. The paper bag allegedly found near the sixth-floor window was not photographed in place. The three empty cartridge cases were placed in an envelope, with no indication of the precise location in which each case was found. The police mishandled the book cartons around the window so badly that while only three of Oswald's prints were found on the nineteen cartons, twenty-four prints of policemen were found. The police permitted the press to enter the Depository building shortly after the discovery of the rifle. Before a thorough search of the building had taken place, the press roamed all over it, conceivably destroying evidence. The Dallas police neglected to mark and seal each item of physical evidence, e. g., the rifle, the revolver, the cartridge cases, thus separating each from the others. Instead, they put all the evidence in a large box, an action that resulted in their needlessly touching each other. The police, moreover, gave the Warren Commission three separate and contradictory versions of the transcription of the police radio calls at the time of the assassination. The Dallas police also produced four different, contradictory versions of the way in which the boxes by the window were stacked.

20. Why did the authorities change the motorcade route?

The original route, published in the *Dallas Morning-News* on 22 November 1963, called for the motorcade to proceed directly on Main Street through the triple underpass, *without* making the cumbersome turns onto Houston and Elm streets. The motorcade, however, did make the turn onto Elm, so it could take the Elm Street ramp to Stemmons Freeway. This was not the most direct route to President Kennedy's destination, the Trade Mart building. It would have been quicker and safer for the caravan to go straight on Main Street to Industrial Boulevard, where the Trade Mart is located. We do not know why the change was made.

21. Why did Officer Tippit stop Oswald?

It is difficult to accept the Warren Commission's claim that Tippit stopped Oswald because Oswald fitted the description of the suspect in the Kennedy assassination. That description was so general that it could have described thousands of individuals. Since Tippit had a view only of Oswald's rear, one wonders how he could have matched him with the suspect. Furthermore, if Tippit really suspected Oswald, he almost surely would have drawn his revolver against such a dangerous suspect. Yet, according to the commission's star eyewitness, Helen Markham, Tippit not only made no attempt to make the arrest of a lifetime, he engaged him in friendly conversation.

Neither the Warren Commission nor the House Select Committee on Assassinations tried to explore the unusual circumstances surrounding Tippit's presence in the area. Almost every other police officer in Dallas was ordered to proceed to Dealey Plaza, Parkland Hospital, or Love Field Airport. Tippit alone received instructions to remain where he was, in the residential Oak Cliffs section, where no suspicion of criminal activity had been raised. The police dispatcher also ordered Tippit to "be at large for any emergency that comes in," most unusual instructions, since the primary duty of all policemen is to "be at large" for emergencies.

22. Did Oswald murder J. D. Tippit?

The evidence against Oswald is strong. Eyewitness Helen Markham identified-Oswald as the murderer. The House Select Committee located another eyewitness, Jack Tatum, who also identified Oswald as the killer. Six other witnesses saw Oswald fleeing the murder scene, and four cartridge cases fired from Oswald's revolver were found at the scene.

On the other hand, eyewitnesses Aquila Clemmons and Frank Wright saw two men kill Tippit. A witness, questioned by the FBI but never called before the Warren Commission, saw a man who did not resemble Oswald kill Tippit. The bullets removed from Tippit's body were too mutilated to permit identification of them with Oswald's revolver. Moreover, the cartridge cases and the bullets did not match, the cases coming from different manufacturers than the bullets.

Clearly, the proper channel for resolving this conflicting evidence was a court of law, but Oswald's death made this impossible. As noted, neither the commission nor the committee conducted its inquiry under the adversary process to help settle such issues. The question, therefore, must remain unanswered.

23. Why was Officer Tippit patrolling an area outside his assigned district when he was shot?

Only J. D. Tippit could answer that question, and he is dead. At 12:45 P.M., fifteen minutes after the assassination, the Dallas police dispatcher ordered Tippit to proceed to the "central Oak Cliffs area," which is outside his regularly assigned district. The original Dallas police version of the police tape contains no reference to Tippit. The second version, transcribed five months later, contains the order to Tippit. J. D. Tippit was the only policeman in Dallas who was given instructions to patrol a quiet residential area, where no crime had been committed. Every available police officer was ordered to proceed immediately to Dealey Plaza or to Parkland Hospital. The last known location of Officer Tippit was Lancaster and Eighth, about eight blocks from the murder scene. Tippit reported this location at 12:54, twenty-one minutes before he was shot. The Warren Commission would have us believe that Tippit was so careful and methodical in his duties that it took him twenty-one minutes to travel eight blocks. This is a speed of about two miles an hour, slower than a normal walking pace. Obviously, this is yet another matter requiring further investigation.

24. Why did it take Oswald thirty minutes to run from the scene of the Tippit murder to the Texas theater only five blocks away?

Officer Tippit was killed at 1:15 P.M. and Oswald ran into the Texas Theater at 1:45. Clearly, it did not take him a half-hour to run five blocks. Neither the Warren Commission nor the House Select Committee produced any evidence to indicate what Oswald did during that time span.

25. How many shots were fired at Officer Tippit?

The official Tippit autopsy report states that four bullets were recovered from Tippit's body. Four bullets now form part of the physical evidence in the case. Yet, as with so many other parts of the Kennedy assassination, some of the circumstances underlying the discovery of this evidence appear strange and indeed mysterious.

The original Dallas police inventory of evidence turned over to the FBI lists "bullet [*sic*] recovered from body of Officer J. D. Tippit." The other three bullets did not turn up until four months after the murder, when they were discovered in a file cabinet at Dallas police headquarters (the same cabinet that contained the tape?).

On 11 December 1963, Secret Service agents Edward Moore and Forrest Sorrels reported their conversation with Dallas medical examiner Dr. Earl Rose: "only three of the four bullets penetrated into Tippit's body. The fourth apparently hit a button on the officer's coat. . . . When the examination [autopsy] was performed, three bullets were removed from the body and turned over to the Police Crime Lab." The police homicide report confirms this. According to that report, Tippit was shot "once in the right temple, once in the right side of the chest, and once in center of stomach." The actual autopsy, however, states that three bullets struck Tippit in the chest and one struck him in the head. A letter from J. Edgar Hoover to J. Lee Rankin notifies the commission that the FBI did not receive the "three [*sic*] bullets until late March 1964, four months after the assassination. Yet Secret Service agents Moore and Sorrels reported on 11 December, only three weeks after the murder, that the bullets "are now in the possession of the FBI."

The obvious contradictions in the evidence leave unanswered the questions of whether three or four shots struck Tippit and what happened to the bullets. Considering the fact that three of the bullets were Remingtons and one was a Winchester, while two of the cartridge cases found at the Tippit murder scene were Remingtons and two were Winchesters, it is not unreasonable to conclude that the Tippit murder requires clarification.

26. Why did Jack Ruby kill Lee Harvey Oswald?

The Warren Commission's claim that Ruby wanted to spare Mrs. Kennedy the personal ordeal of a trial seems flimsy. When Earl Warren interviewed Ruby in the Dallas jail, Ruby pleaded with the chief justice to let him testify in Washington, where he would tell the real story behind the whole assassination controversy. Inexplicably, Warren denied Ruby's request.

While it is possible to imagine numerous motives for Ruby's act, there is no reliable, independent evidence to substantiate such speculation. Whatever Ruby's reasons, they remain unknown.

27. How did Ruby gain access to the heavily guarded basement of Dallas police headquarters?

The House Select Committee on Assassinations uncovered evidence that indicated the likelihood that a Dallas police officer assisted Ruby in entering the basement.

The fact that Ruby managed to walk past seventy armed law enforcement officials and gun down Oswald obviously raises suspicions of a conspiracy in this murder. The available evidence, however, does not permit a conclusive determination either of the nature or extent of that conspiracy.

28. Did Jack Ruby and Lee Harvey Oswald know each other?

Over a dozen reliable witnesses claim to have seen the two men together during the four months prior to the assassination. Six separate eyewitnesses saw Ruby and Oswald in Ruby's Carousel Club in November 1963. Those witnesses included three employees and three patrons of the club. The author has interviewed a journalist who saw a photograph of Ruby and Oswald together.

The other witnesses included a lady who saw Ruby and Oswald together in New Orleans in the summer of 1963. While the FBI dismissed her account, Ruby, in fact, did visit New Orleans during that period.

Again, the evidence is not conclusive, but it does strongly suggest that Ruby and Oswald may very well have known each other before the assassination.

29. Did the Dallas police violate Lee Harvey Oswald's legal rights while they held him in custody?

Despite the Warren Commission's disclaimer, the answer is a decided affirmative. At his midnight press conference on 22 November, Oswald told newsmen that he was "not allowed legal representation" and requested "someone to come forward to give me legal assistance." The Dallas police chief, Jesse Curry, admitted that "we were violating every principle of interrogation." . . . [T]he police lineups appeared rigged to make identification of Oswald almost certain. He was the only suspect with a bruised and cut face and with disheveled clothing. He was dressed differently from the other men in the lineup. He was put in a lineup with three teenagers. At least one witness was persuaded by the police to sign an affidavit identifying Oswald *before* he viewed the lineup. The search warrant authorizing the search of Oswald's room did not specify the objects being sought by the police.

30. Did Oswald drive an automobile?

The Warren Commission claims that he did not, but there is substantial evidence to the contrary. Albert Bogard, a Dallas new car salesman, swore that he took Oswald for a test drive of a car less than two weeks before the assassination. Edith Whitworth and Gertrude Hunter saw Oswald driving a blue 1957 Ford about two weeks before the assassination. One of the lodgers in Oswald's rooming house at 1026 North Beckley Avenue let him drive his blue Ford sedan. Two service station operators recalled Oswald's driving a car and having it serviced. Journalists attempting to trace Oswald's route from Laredo, Mexico, to Dallas interviewed numerous service station operators, cafe owners, and other proprietors who recalled Oswald's stopping at their establishments.

31. With whom did Oswald associate during his stay in New Orleans in the spring and summer of 1963?

Although the Warren Commission concluded that Oswald's Marxist, pro-Castro views led him to various activities promoting those views, it failed to demonstrate that Oswald contacted even one individual of similar views during his New Orleans stay. The evidence, in fact, demonstrated that *all* of Oswald's known associations were with individuals of right-wing persuasion. The author's extensive research into this topic has produced much new evidence of Lee Harvey Oswald's right-wing activities in New Orleans.

On numerous occasions, Oswald associated with Guy Bannister, an ex-FBI official and a private investigator. Militantly anti-Castro and rabidly segregationist, Bannister was well known in the New Orleans area for his extremist views. Twice, Bannister and Oswald visited the campus of Louisiana State University in New Orleans and engaged students in heated discussions of federal racial policies. During these discussions, Oswald vehemently attacked the civil rights policies of the Kennedy administration.

Another right-wing extremist with whom Oswald associated was David William Ferrie. A defrocked Eastern Orthodox priest, an expert pilot, a research chemist, and a sexual deviate, Ferrie also actively participated in anti-Castro organizations and smuggled supplies to anti-Castro rebels in Cuba. Once, Ferrie and Oswald attended a party, where they discussed the desirability of a *coup d'état* against the Kennedy administration. On another occasion, Oswald and Ferrie were seen at Ponchartrain Beach, a New Orleans amusement park. Oswald and Ferrie also frequented the Napoleon House bar, a popular hangout for college students. There they often debated Kennedy's foreign policy with the students. Accompanied by two "Latins," Ferrie and Oswald were observed in Baton Rouge, where they openly denounced Kennedy's foreign and domestic policies.

One of the most significant eyewitness observations was of Ferrie, Oswald, and numerous Cubans, all dressed in military fatigues and carrying automatic rifles, conducting what appeared to be a "military training maneuver." This event took place near Bedico Creek, a swampy inland body of water near Lake Ponchartrain, about fifty miles north of New Orleans. This occurred in early September 1963, two months after the final government raid on anti-Castro guerrilla camps in the United States.

The night of 22 November, David Ferrie drove 250 miles from New Orleans to Galveston, Texas, in a blinding thunderstorm. At Galveston, Ferrie received and made several long-distance telephone calls. The following day, he drove to Houston, then Alexandria, Louisiana, and then to Hammond, where he spent the night in the dormitory room of a friend who was a student at a local college. Then he returned to New Orleans, where he underwent questioning by the FBI. Shortly after the assassination, Ferrie deposited over seven thousand dollars in his bank account, even though he did not have a steady job.

Obviously, these New Orleans activities of Oswald's warrant further investigation. The House Select Committee on Assassinations appreciated the significance of Oswald's New Orleans activities but failed to investigate them properly. Instead, it devoted much attention to such irrelevant matters as Ferrie's tenuous link to Carlos Marcello and the bookmaking activities of Oswald's uncle.

What relationship these matters have to the assassination of President Kennedy is unclear. As we have seen, the evidence does not permit a definitive statement about Oswald's role in the Kennedy murder. As far as David Ferrie and Guy Bannister are concerned, there is no evidence at all to link them to the crime. The New Orleans evidence, however, does demonstrate that Oswald's public image as a pro-Castro Marxist was a facade masking the anti-Castro and anti-Communist agitator beneath.

32. How significant was the Garrison investigation?

In February 1967, New Orleans District Attorney Jim Garrison announced that his office was investigating the assassination. This sensational news aroused a storm of controversy and publicity. The Garrison investigation resulted in the arrest and trial of New Orleans businessman Clay Shaw for conspiracy to murder John F. Kennedy. The 1969 trial resulted in Shaw's acquittal.

During the two-year investigation, Garrison made many irresponsible statements about the FBI, CIA, and other government agencies and about assassins firing from manholes and escaping through underground sewers. However, he did reveal the large extent to which the federal government had suppressed evidence about the assassination, demonstrated the relationship between Oswald and Bannister and Ferrie, and brought out much new information about the Zapruder film, the Kennedy autopsy, and ballistics evidence.

33. Did Oswald work for an intelligence agency of the United States government?

No. The evidence clearly shows that Oswald had no direct relationship with United States intelligence. After his defection to the Soviet Union, both the FBI and CIA maintained dossiers on Oswald, but these files contain no information pertinent to the assassination. Those writers who have suggested that Oswald's sojourn in the U.S.S.R., his trip to Mexico City, or his contacts with FBI Agent James Hosty proved significant to the assassination have failed to substantiate their theories.

34. Was an imposter buried in Lee Harvey Oswald's grave?

Differences of up to three inches in reports of Oswald's height, plus minor variations in the reports of certain physical marks on Oswald's body (wrist scars, mastoidectomy scar, etc.) have led some critics, most notably Michael Eddowes, a British investigator, to call for a disinterrment of Oswald's coffin and an exhumation autopsy on the body in it.

Eddowes's theory that while he was in the Soviet Union, Oswald was eliminated by the KGB and his place taken by a trained imposter is far-fetched. Oswald lived with his wife for over a year after they left the U.S.S.R. Oswald's mother, brother, and other relatives all saw him and had close contact with him and did not notice anything unusual about him.

35. Is vital evidence in the Kennedy assassination missing from the National Archives collection of assassination materials?

Numerous items of critical significance are indeed missing: the president's brain, tissue slides of his wounds, several autopsy photographs and X-rays, some bullet fragments originally tested by the FBI, and miscellaneous documents and other materials. The lack of these materials obviously presents a formidable obstacle to any attempt to answer some of the key questions about the assassination. Why they are missing is not known.

36. Why did the FBI and CIA withhold information from the Warren Commission?

As far as the FBI is concerned, it seems that the main reason was J. Edgar Hoover's precipitous decision that there was no assassination conspiracy and his almost paranoid desire not to tarnish the bureau's public image. Hoover tried to dissuade Lyndon Johnson from appointing a presidential commission to investigate the assassination, but Johnson bowed to public pressure. One of Hoover's top assistants, William Sullivan, stated that Hoover regarded the Warren Commission as an adversary and even periodically leaked information to the press to force the commission to conduct its inquiry along the lines of the already completed FBI report. The acting attorney general Nicholas deB. Katzenbach, testified that if the FBI had come across evidence of a conspiracy, "what would have happened to that information, God only knows." The 125,000 pages of FBI assassination files, many of them marked by Hoover himself, contain much information that the bureau never shared with the commission.

The CIA, too, failed to share all of its information with the Warren Commission. But its refusal to do so stemmed from the nature of the agency itself. The purpose of the CIA is to gather intelligence, a function that requires secrecy. The agency investigated the assassination only as it related to foreign activities. It appointed Richard Helms as its liaison with the Warren Commission, and Helms gave the commission only information that did not compromise the CIA's extensive network of agents. It is true that the CIA did not inform the Warren Commission about various matters, but in almost all instances, the information withheld had only an indirect connection with the assassination.

37. *In his book* Best Evidence, *David Lifton asserted that the body of President Kennedy was altered to conceal evidence of shots from the front. How valid is Lifton's theory?*

In his book, Lifton asserted that an unidentified group of conspirators planned, executed, and concealed the assassination of President Kennedy. Even though the Zapruder film and certain other evidence indicated gunfire from the Grassy Knoll, the "best evidence" in the case and the evidence that would be given the most credence in a court of law was the official autopsy. Therefore, the conspirators altered the body of President Kennedy to make it appear he had been shot from behind.

When the president was rushed into the emergency room at Parkland Hospital, the doctors noticed a tiny hole in the throat. They all believed that this hole was clearly a wound of entrance, as the remarks to the press by the Parkland physicians indicated. Furthermore, the Dallas doctors stated, both in their written medical reports and in their testimony before the Warren Commission, that there was a very large wound of exit in the rear of the president's head. These observations were substantiated by those of laboratory and X-ray technicians, photographers, and physicians at Bethesda Naval Hospital who saw the body before the autopsy began.

To assure the success of their scheme, the plotters had to change the nature of the wounds on the body in order to make it appear that it contained only evidence of rear-entry wounds. The conspirators, therefore, carried out an elaborate plot of what Lifton calls "deception and disguise," a fantastic plot that entailed altering the body of John Kennedy.

From interviews with witnesses at Bethesda and from other sources, Lifton concludes that the body was removed from its bronze coffin while the presidential party was aboard Air Force One on the trip from Dallas to Washington. As the television cameras focused on the removal of the bronze coffin from the plane, the conspirators put the body in a helicopter and flew it to Bethesda. There they arranged various means, including two ambulances, to deceive the official party awaiting the arrival of the bronze coffin.

As this deception took place, his body was altered to give it the appearance of having been struck from the rear. The conspirators removed the brain and "reconstructed" the skull, eradicating all signs of the massive exit hole in the back of the head. They also placed small entrance holes in the upper back and in the rear of the head. When the actual autopsy was performed, the pathologists inspected a body that gave the appearance of being hit twice from behind. Lifton quotes the Sibert-O'Neill FBI autopsy report that "surgery of the head area" had been performed prior to the start of the postmortem. This, Lifton believes, was the alteration done on the original head wounds.

David Lifton's theory is not only novel, but it presents a startling account of an assassination plot conceived, executed, and disguised by the executive branch of the federal government. David Lifton has a reputation as one of the most thorough assassination researchers. His work is well documented and displays a careful attention to detail. For these reasons, and because of the sensational nature of Lifton's theory, an analysis of his main points will now be presented.

The documentary record substantiates Lifton's contention that medical descriptions of the Kennedy head wounds vary widely. Most of the Dallas doctors did testify that they saw a large exit wound in the back of the head, whereas the autopsy describes a small entrance wound in the back of the head and a large exit wound to the front. Lifton, however, ignored the fact that not all the Dallas doctors saw a large wound in the rear of the head. Dr. Charles Baxter stated that he saw a wound in the "temporal parietal plate of bone" in the side of the head. Dr. Adolph Giesecke noted the absence of skull from the top of the head to the ear, and from the browline to the back of the head. Dr. Kenneth Salyer observed a wound of the right temporal region on the side of the head. And Dr. Marion Jenkins mentioned "a great laceration of the right side of the head." Lifton quoted only those Dallas physicians who saw the large hole in the rear of the head and thus presented a misleading impression to his readers.

More significantly, Lifton ignored a vital aspect of the evidence. Throughout the emergency room treatment, President Kennedy lay on his back, with the back of his head resting on the mattress of the emergency cart. As Dr. Malcolm Perry told the Warren Commission, "He was lying supine [on his back] on the emergency cart." At no time was he turned over. If there was one point on which all the Dallas doctors agreed, it was that they never saw the president's back, including the rear of his head.

During the twenty minutes in which they worked to save President Kennedy's life, the Parkland physicians did not even attempt to treat the head wound. Their efforts at resuscitation centered on the tracheotomy and on closed chest massage. Busy with these emergency measures, the doctors did not examine the head wound closely. During the time in which they were in the emergency room, the Dallas doctors glanced at the head wound and saw blood and brain tissue oozing out and two large flaps of scalp covering much of the hair and exposing the cranial cavity. They did not see the head after it was cleaned, and they took no measurements to record the exact nature of the wounds. As one of the Dallas physicians remarked to the author, the reason he and his colleagues mentioned a large wound in the rear of the head is that from their brief glances at the head, it looked like a rear wound. However, after seeing the Zapruder film and the autopsy drawings, he was perfectly satisfied that the would was indeed in the right front of the head.

Another omission in Lifton's theory is his belief that the conspirators inflicted wounds on the body over six hours after the assassination. Although he claims to have read widely in textbooks on forensic pathology, Lifton apparently did not notice one of the most elementary principles of autopsy procedure: damage inflicted on a body after death is easily distinguishable from that inflicted on a living body. If the conspirators had reconstructed Kennedy's skull and produced two entrance wounds on the body, the Bethesda pathologists would have recognized the postmortem changes. By the time of the autopsy, the body was in the beginning stages of rigor mortis and exhibited signs of livor mortis and algor mortis (three of the stages a corpse undergoes after death). Any damage inflicted on that body would have displayed definite pathological signs of alteration, and the entrance wounds in the back and the head would not have shown microscopic indications of "coagulation necrosis," since the blood had long since ceased circulating.

Lifton claims that John Kennedy was shot in the front of the head by gunfire from the Grassy Knoll, thus causing the large exit wound in the rear observed by the Dallas doctors. Yet he fails to account for the fact that no one at Dallas or Bethesda saw an entrance wound in the front of the head. If the Dallas doctors were so observant as to see an exit wound in the rear of the head while the president lay face-up on the cart, why did they not see the entrance wound also?

Instead of the contradictory recollections of the Dallas doctors, we possess-the objective evidence of the Zapruder film. Frames Z314–335 clearly depict the very large wound on the right front side of John Kennedy's head. The film also shows that the rear of the head remains intact throughout the assassination. Lifton argues that the CIA must have "doctored" the film to produce a false image. In addition to producing no evidence whatsoever to support this speculation, Lifton ignored the fact that the film graphically shows the violent backward movement of the head, hardly evidence of a rear-entering shot.

The autopsy X-rays and photographs depict the entrance holes in the back and in the rear of the head and also the huge, gaping wound in the right front of the head. According to Lifton, the photographs and X-rays were taken after the reconstruction of the body, so they would corroborate the autopsy findings. As we have seen, the photographs and X-rays do not provide irrefutable evidence of wounds inflicted only from the rear. The very large wound on the right side of the head depicted in these visual records could have been made by the explosion of a "dum-dum" bullet fired from the right front. In addition, through dental identification and precise comparisons of certain anatomical features, experts hired by the House Select Committee on Assassinations positively identified the X-rays and photographs as authentic and the body depicted in them as that of John F. Kennedy. If the skull were "reconstructed," as Lifton claims, the X-rays would not contain the anatomical features essential to proper authentication.

In his work, Lifton quotes extensively from the FBI agents present at the autopsy and from laboratory technicians. FBI Agents Sibert and O'Neill, for example, stated that "surgery of the head area" had been performed prior to the autopsy. To Lifton, this is proof that the conspirators had reconstructed the skull. In fact, the Sibert-O'Neill report was written by the agents the day after the autopsy. It is neither a verbatim record of the proceedings nor a detailed medical recounting of the events that took place. The laboratory technicians and other witnesses to the autopsy provided widely divergent accounts of the wounds. By quoting only those that supported his thesis, Lifton provided a very misleading account to his readers, as he did with the Dallas doctors.

Another of Lifton's arguments is that during the autopsy, Dr. Humes removed the brain from the cranial vault without recourse to the surgical procedures normally required. To Lifton, this was evidence that the brain had been removed prior to the autopsy by the conspirators in order to alter it. This argument has little basis. The autopsy protocol, as well as the testimony of the pathologists, attest to the enormous damage done to the head. The skull was shattered. Almost three-quarters of the right half of the brain had been blown out of the head. When Dr. Humes began his examination of the head, pieces of the skull came apart in his hands, vivid testimony to the explosive impact of the bullet. All of the damage to the head that Lifton details as unusual can be explained as the result of an exploding bullet literally blowing the head apart.

Lifton believes that the autopsy photographs showing the large, gaping wound in the right front of President Kennedy's head were deliberately altered to make the wound appear as an exit wound. That it was an exit wound is precisely what the autopsy pathologists believed and what all subsequent medical inspections of the photographs concluded. However, the wound is not necessarily one of exit. An exploding bullet fired from the right front could have caused that wound. In the first volume of the House Select Committee on Assassinations hearings on the murder of Martin Luther King, drawings made from autopsy photographs of Dr. King clearly show a huge hole almost four inches long and two inches wide on the lower right side of the face, just above the jaw. According to the committee's Forensic Pathology Panel, this huge wound in Dr. King's face was an *entrance* wound caused by the explosion of a soft-nosed 30.06 bullet. Dr. Michael Baden, the chairman of the panel, told the committee that "the injuries seen on Dr. King with the bursting explosive-like injury to the face" were "entirely consistent" with an entrance wound of an exploding bullet.

David Lifton's theory, as sensational as it may appear, simply does not stand verified by the objective evidence. As detailed here, the autopsy left much room for criticism, and the fact that certain items of the medical evidence are missing obviously raises suspicions of a possible cover-up. The questions surrounding the death of President Kennedy are numerous, many of them still unanswered. Those posed by David Lifton, however, do not fall into this category.

POSTSCRIPT

Did Lee Harvey Oswald Kill President Kennedy by Himself?

Since the Kennedy assassination, more than 3,000 books, articles, fictional films, documentaries, plays, television programs, and newsletters on the subject have been released. One book that summarizes and critically analyzes the literature, provides an interpretation of the assassination, and contains an extensive bibliographical listing is Robert Alan Goldberg, *Enemies Within: The Culture of Conspiracy in Modern America* (Yale University Press, 2001). Also see Bob Callahan, *Who Shot JFK? A Guide to the Major Conspiracy Theories* (Simon & Schuster, 1993), which features pointed and humorous illustrations by Mark Zingarelli in addition to a lively text that provides welcome relief from themore sober accounts.

Could a single bullet have wounded Governor Connally *and* killed Kennedy? Dennis Brio supports the single-bullet theory in a series of articles in the May and October 1992 issues of the *Journal of the American Medical Association*. Critics' dissenting letters appear in the October 1992 issue, and John Lattimer responds in the March 1993 issue. The single-bullet theory is also supported by Gerald Posner in chapter 14 of *Case Closed: Lee Harvey Oswald and the Assassination of JFK* (Random House, 1993). Posner's argument relies upon computer enhancements of the Zapruder film (the only one to record the entire shooting) by Michael West and the Failure Analysis Associates, a firm specializing in computer reconstruction for lawsuits. But John Nichols, a forensic pathologist, and Charles Wilber, a forensic scientist, have conducted studies that indicate that major bullet no. 399 could not have inflicted all the damage to Connally. See their presentations in the video *Reasonable Doubt: The Single Bullet Theory* (White Star Productions, 1988).

Conspiracy theories about the Kennedy assassination abound. Organized crime might have played a part for a number of reasons. For example, Attorney General Robert Kennedy, the president's brother, had been investigating alleged racketeering in Jimmy Hoffa's Teamster's Union, which he began doing for a Senate committee in the 1950s. Also, John H. Davis, in *The Kennedy Contract: The Mafia Plot to Assassinate the President* (Harper Paperbacks, 1993) and *Mafia Kingfish: Carlos Marcello and the Assassination of John F. Kennedy* (McGraw-Hill, 1989), contends that New Orleans Mafia chieftain Carlos Marcello ordered a hit on the president because Kennedy had reneged on his promise to go easy on organized crime after the Mob delivered the deciding vote from Illinois from the west side of Chicago in the close presidential election of 1960.

On the Internet . . .

Internet Web sites containing historical material relevant to the subjects discussed in this part can be reached through the McGraw-Hill history site.

http://www.mhhe.com/socscience/history/usa/link/linktop.htm

Civil Rights: A Status Report

Kevin Hollaway is the author of this detailed history of black civil rights, from the discovery of the New World to the present. In his own words, "It is not my intent to complain about the present state of Black America, nor to provide excuses. My intent is [to] provide an unbiased picture of Black American history; something that is often missing from many classrooms in America."

http://home.earthlink.net/~civilrightsreport/

The History Place Presents: The Vietnam War

This page of History Place offers comprehensive timelines of U.S. involvement in the Vietnam conflict from 1945 to 1975, with quotes and analysis. You can also jump to specific events and topics, such as the Tet Offensive, the Geneva Conference, and the Pentagon Papers.

http://www.historyplace.com/unitedstates/vietnam

The National Women's History Project

The National Women's History Project is a nonprofit organization dedicated to recognizing and celebrating the diverse and historic accomplishments of women by providing information and educational material and programs.

http://www.nwhp.org

Sallie Bingham Center for Women's History and Culture

The Sallie Bingham Center for Women's History and Culture is an integral part of Duke University's Special Collections Library, which houses a broad range of rare and unique primary source material. This page offers links to online collections, archives, and bibliographies on women's history.

http://odyssey.lib.duke.edu/women/

PART 4

From Liberation Through Watergate, 1963–1974

The 1960s were an incredibly tumultuous decade. The civil rights movement reached its highest point with the passage of the Civil Rights Act of 1964, which outlawed segregation. In 1965, President Johnson signed the Voting Rights Act, which enabled blacks to vote in large numbers in the deep southern states for the first time since the 1890s. Much of the publicity of the civil rights revolution centered around Martin Luther King, Jr., a conservative militant with a relationship with both the black and white communities. Was King's leadership essential to the movement, or would the success of local grass-roots activism have achieved similar results?

President Johnson attempted to match his success in civil rights with an economic recovery program for the "other" Americans who were left out of the New Deal reforms of the 1930s. The "Great Society" programs legislation passed in the overwhelming liberal Democratic Congress between 1964 and 1966. How successful were these programs?

Johnson's successor was President Richard Nixon, a lifetime controversial president whose successes and failures continue to be overshadowed by the Watergate scandal that forced him to resign. Was Nixon the implementer of Johnson's programs, or did he really want to kill the Great Society by allowing Congress to self-destruct?

The second half of the 1960s was dominated by Vietnam. Was Johnson's escalation of the war in 1965 inevitable, or could he have found a way out?

Perhaps the most significant reform movement of the 1970s was the Women's Liberation Movement. Did the protesters go too far and create a culture that destroyed marriage, devalued traditional homemaking, and encouraged sexual promiscuity? Or did they pave the way for women to compete with men in the job market as physicians, lawyers, and business executives?

ISSUE 11

Was Martin Luther King, Jr.'s Leadership Essential to the Success of the Civil Rights Revolution?

YES: Adam Fairclough, from "Martin Luther King, Jr. and the Quest for Nonviolent Social Change," *Phylon* (Spring 1986)

NO: Clayborne Carson, from "Martin Luther King, Jr.: Charismatic Leadership in a Mass Struggle," *Journal of American History* (September 1987)

ISSUE SUMMARY

YES: Professor of history Adam Fairclough argues that Martin Luther King, Jr., was a pragmatic reformer who organized nonviolent direct-action protests in strategically targeted local communities, which provoked violence from his opponents, gaining publicity and sympathy for the civil rights movement.

NO: Professor of history Clayborne Carson concludes that the civil rights struggle would have followed a similar course of development even if King had never lived because its successes depended upon mass activism, not the actions of a single leader.

The modern civil rights movement goes back to the Reconstruction era (1865–1877), when blacks were granted freedom, citizenship, and voting rights. By the end of the nineteenth century, however, black Americans had been legally segregated in public facilities, which included schools, parks, swimming pools, and municipal and state offices. At the same time the southern states had disenfranchised blacks or intimidated them into not voting. The black middle class, led by Booker T. Washington, had accepted legal segregation as a trade-off for limited economic opportunities in their segregated communities.

The black community entered the twentieth century determined to regain its rights as American citizens. During the opening years of the twentieth century, a group of northern black professionals, led by its most prominent intellectual W. E. B Du Bois, joined with white progressives and formed the National Association for the Advancement of Colored People (NAACP). The main objective of the NAACP was to eradicate the accomodationist policies of Booker T. Washington and the acceptance of segregation through the "separate but equal principle," which the Supreme Court had written into the legal system. This was accomplished in 1896 when the Court ruled in *Plessy v. Ferguson* that segregating blacks and whites into separate railroad cars was permissible provided both facilities were equal.

Realizing that no civil rights legislation could pass through the committee chaired in Congress by southern white conservatives, the NAACP decided to attack the separate but equal principle established in the *Plessy* case through the courts. The concept of separate but equal was challenged in a series of court cases in which it was argued that segregation violated the equal protection clause of the Fourteenth Amendment.

The legal system moves very slowly, but protest movements often speed up changes. As early as the 1930s blacks picketed stores in Harlem when they were refused service. In 1947 there were protests at Palisades Amusement Park in northern New Jersey when blacks were not allowed to purchase tickets to the swimming pool.

The first big step in the nonviolence resistance phase of the civil rights movement came in 1956 with the Montgomery Bus Boycott. On December 1, 1955, Rosa Parks, a middle-aged black seamstress, refused to give up her seat to a white passenger as required by Alabama law. E. B. Nixon, an officer with the allblack Brotherhood of Sleeping Car Porters and local head of the NAACP, bailed his friend and fellow worker Parks out of jail. She then gave Nixon permission to use her arrest to mount a one-day bus boycott.

On the day of the boycott Nixon asked Martin Luther King, Jr., a 27-year-old son of a prominent Atlanta minister and a newcomer to Montgomery, to deliver the keynote address at a mass rally of the Montgomery Improvement Association (MIA). King appeared an unlikely candidate to challenge the status quo on race relations. He grew up comfortably, was middle class, was educated at the black Atlanta University complex, and received a master's degree at Crozier Theological Seminary at Boston University. Though King had never been politically active before, he delivered a memorable address to an overflow audience at a local Baptist church.

The Montgomery Bus Boycott led to a Supreme Court ruling that declared unconstitutional a Montgomery ordinance that required segregated city buses. The boycott provided a number of lessons for civil rights leaders. First, it made many black southerners more assertive in their demands for full citizenship in spite of a white backlash of bomb threats and Ku Klux Klan (KKK) rallies. Second, it propelled King into the spotlight. Third, it captured the attention of the nation's news media and gained sympathetic coverage of its causes. Finally, the boycott produced a new set of tactics, which speeded up the pace of desegregation for the black community.

In the selections that follow, Adam Fairclough demonstrates the importance of King's leadership to the civil rights movement, while Clayborne Carson plays down the mythical image of King, arguing that King is a product of a movement that would have occurred even if King had never lived.

Adam Fairclough

YES

Martin Luther King, Jr. and the Quest for Nonviolent Social Change

The Alabama cities of Birmingham and Selma have given their names to the most effective campaigns of nonviolent protest in recent history. The Birmingham demonstrations paved the way for the 1964 Civil Rights Act, which swept away segregation in public accommodations. The Selma protests of 1965 engendered the Voting Rights Act, a measure that cut away the political basis of white supremacy by ending the disfranchisement of blacks. Together, this legislation amounted to a "Second Reconstruction" of the South, restoring to black Southerners rights that had been formally granted after the Civil War but stripped away after the Compromise of 1877.

Understanding of this historical breakthrough, however, is far from perfect. It is beyond doubt that the man who led the Birmingham and Selma protests, Martin Luther King, Jr., made a mighty contribution. But more needs to be known about the dynamics of social change in the 1960s and about the political world in which King and his followers operated. King's biography, much of it hagiographic in character, has tended to simplify these dynamics and neglect the wider political context. There has been inadequate appreciation, too, of the hard-headed calculation that entered into King's strategy, the political sophistication of his advisers, and the importance of his organizational base, the Southern Christian Leadership Conference (SCLC). Nevertheless, some historians and political scientists have begun to analyze critically the campaigns of nonviolent direct action undertaken by King and SCLC. Implicitly or explicitly, their work has cast doubt on many commonly held assumptions about the civil rights movement and raised important questions. Why, if most whites disapproved of it so strongly, could nonviolent protest succeed in generating political support for the civil rights movement? Was nonviolent direct action a means of persuasion, or did it depend for its effectiveness upon pressure and coercion? To what extent, if any, did King seek deliberately to provoke violence by whites? How much support did King's tactics command among blacks? Did he create a truly "mass" movement, or were his victories achieved in spite of limited backing? This essay explores the evolution, execution, and political impact of King's methods in an attempt to explain the dynamics of nonviolent direct action.

From MARTIN LUTHER KING, JR. AND THE QUEST FOR NONVIOLENT SOCIAL CHANGE, vol. 47, no. 1, Spring 1986, pp. 1–15.

In the most systematic study of King's techniques to date, political scientist David J. Garrow argued that the evolution of King's strategy fell into two phases. During the first, from his emergence as a leader in 1956 to the Albany protests of 1961–62, King conceived of direct action as a means of persuading Southern whites of the moral injustice of segregation and discrimination. When the Albany campaign failed, however, King abandoned this approach as unrealistic and, according to Garrow, adopted a strategy of "nonviolent coercion." Instead of trying to convince their adversaries of the rightness of their goals, King and SCLC sought to pressure the federal government into curbing white supremacists through legislation. Implemented with great success in Birmingham and Selma, this new strategy mobilized Northern public opinion behind the civil rights movement through dramatic confrontations that publicized segregationist violence. Since it invited violent opposition, this strategy, Garrow believes, "bordered on nonviolent provocation."

Garrow is not alone in detecting a distinct shift from persuasion to coercion in the way King conducted nonviolent direct action, with the coercive elements very much to the fore by the time of the 1963 Birmingham campaign. Elliott M. Zashin earlier had advanced a similar argument in his study, *Civil Disobedience and Democracy* (1972). Their experience in the deep South, Zashin contended, convinced most black activists that nonviolent protest had virtually no effect on white racists: its only value lay in its utility as a pressure tactic. By 1964, few entertained the notion that direct action could change the values of the adversary. King, Zashin believed, came to a similar conclusion and although, for reasons of diplomacy, he downplayed the coercive nature of his tactics, SCLC's leader "clearly . . . recognized the pressure involved in direct action." As he admitted in his celebrated "Letter From Birmingham City Jail," nonviolent protest sought to "create such a crisis and foster such a tension that a community which has constantly refused to negotiate is forced to confront the issue."

Before examining this argument, it is necessary to recognize that the historical analysis of King's thought presents a number of problems. First, King never expounded his theory of nonviolence in a systematic way, nor did he record a detailed account of his tactics. In addition, many of his books, articles and speeches were partly or wholly "ghosted," and it is not always easy to determine exactly what King did write. Third it must be borne in mind that King's writings and speeches were public statements designed to persuade and convince, and many of them were tailored to white audiences. Finally, King did not live in an intellectual vacuum: he had a wide circle of friends, colleagues and advisers with whom he debated tactics and strategy. His thinking was never fixed and rigid. Indeed, it would be astonishing if King's perception of the world remained static in view of the turbulent era in which he lived. Without doubt, he became more hard-headed and politically astute as a result of age and experience. In "Letter From Birmingham City Jail," for example, he expressed profound disappointment that the civil rights movement had failed to attract more support from white Southerners. There is no reason to suppose that this disillusionment was insincere.

It is doubtful, however, that King's strategy underwent a basic shift in emphasis of the kind posited by Zashin and Garrow. There is little evidence that King ever believed that nonviolent protest functioned solely, or even mainly, as a form of moral persuasion. Quite the contrary; in his earliest public writings he equated nonviolence with struggle and resistance organized through a militant mass movement. Philosophically and in practice, he explicitly rejected the notion that oppressed groups could overcome their subjection through ethical appeals and rational argument; they also needed an effective form of pressure. The assertion that King failed to appreciate the necessity for "black power" is simply erroneous. "A mass movement exercising nonviolence," he wrote in 1957, "is an object lesson in power under discipline." Having recently led a successful year-long economic boycott supported by 50,000 black people, he surely knew what he was talking about. A *New York Times* profile in March, 1956 noted that King stressed the Hegelian concept of "struggle as a law of growth," and that he regarded the bus boycott "as just one aspect of a world-wide revolt of oppressed peoples."

The intentions of the people who created SCLC underline this point. Bayard Rustin, Stanley Levison and Ella Baker were seasoned political activists who moved in the circles of the New York Left. Steeped in Marxist and socialist ideas, they regarded nonviolent direct action in political, not moral, terms. "The basic conception of SCLC," said Baker, "was that it would capitalize on what was developed in Montgomery in terms of mass action." In Levison's words, the subject was "to reproduce that pattern of mass action, underscore mass, in other cities and communities." It is unlikely that King viewed SCLC in any other way.

To emphasize King's political realism is not to deny his underlying idealism. For him, nonviolence was an ethical imperative, and his commitment to it was absolute and consistent. Moreover, he did sometimes imply that nonviolent protest worked partly through persuasion, by "awakening a sense of moral shame in the opponent." Nonviolent resisters, he explained, touched the hearts and consciences of their adversaries, converting oppressors into friends. But the significance of such statements should not be exaggerated. He admitted that "when the underprivileged demand freedom, the privileged first react with bitterness and resistance;" nonviolence could not change the "heart" of the oppressor until the social structure that perpetuated injustice and false ideology had been destroyed. His verbal characterizations of nonviolence must also be read in context. In sermons, for example, he frequently likened nonviolence to a kind of supranatural power—a "Soul Force" that could defeat physical force. Of course, such descriptions were not meant to be taken literally: King was simplifying complex ideas and communicating them in a way that black Southerners—poorly educated, politically inexperienced, but imbued with a deep religious sensibility—could grasp easily. King's belief that some adversaries might still be touched by the suffering and goodwill of nonviolent resisters was genuine, although in Bayard Rustin's opinion it "was often very confusing—and frustrating—to his followers." But this belief was marginal to his strategy of protest. When King spoke of "converting" oppressors, he was thinking of a long-term historical process rather than an immediate personal response.

There was, therefore, an underlying continuity in King's conception of nonviolent direct action. It envisaged a mass movement opposed to white supremacy and which operated primarily through direct pressure. It assumed that racism was a Southern anachronism and that a growing majority of whites sympathized with the goal of integration and equality. It regarded the federal government as a potential ally, and it believed that the nonviolent protesters attracted support if their opponents responded with violence. The notion of a pre-1963 "persuasive" strategy aimed at winning over Southern whites and a post-1963 "coercive" strategy designed to provoke federal intervention is misleading. King consistently followed the two-pronged strategy of exerting pressure on Southern whites and seeking to involve the federal government.

Federal involvement comprised a crucial element in SCLC's strategy as early as 1961, when King called upon President Kennedy to issue a "Second Emancipation Proclamation"—an Executive Order banning segregation and discrimination. King was not alone, of course, in appreciating the importance of federal action: with the election of a Democratic President whose platform included a strong civil-rights plank, black leaders sensed a golden opportunity to mobilize federal support for their goals. They knew that political considerations made Kennedy reluctant to meddle in the South's "local" affairs. But the daring Freedom Rides of May–August 1961 demonstrated that nonviolent protest could spur the government to action, even against its will, by creating a crisis of law and order to which it had to respond.

SCLC's protests in Albany, Georgia, represented King's first major effort to implement the two-pronged strategy outlined above. On the one hand he exerted pressure on local whites, through demonstrations, sit-ins and economic boycotts, to negotiate over the demands of blacks. On the other hand, by creating a serious local crisis and generating public concern, he tried to induce the federal government to intervene in some way. That he failed on both counts does not mean that the strategy was unsound or that it differed in essentials from the one successfully pursued in Birmingham. King failed in Albany for tactical reasons, notably inadequate planning and poor choice of target, rather than over-reliance on "nonviolent persuasion." The significance of Birmingham is not that King finally discovered the necessity for pressure, but that he at last discovered how to make that pressure effective.

If the strategy was clear, the tactics had to be developed and refined through trial and error and the experience of others. From the founding of SCLC in 1957 to the Birmingham campaign of 1963, King was speculating, experimenting and learning, attempting to adapt a theory that both to political realities and to the practical considerations that constrained black Southerners.

King learned two vital tactical lessons during these years. The first was that he would have to make do with limited numbers. SCLC's architects had anticipated that the Montgomery bus boycott would spark a wave of similar protests throughout the South. For a variety of reasons, however, this did not happen. Many blacks were skeptical of boycotts. More radical tactics like sit-ins and demonstrations evoked still deeper misgivings: they set back orderly progress; they alienated white moderates and provoked a "backlash;" they were wasteful and ineffective. Jail often spelt economic disaster, and individuals thought twice about volunteering for arrest if their families might suffer as a consequence. True, the sit-in movement of 1960 showed that students and young people, free from the economic burdens and family responsibilities that constrained their elders, would willingly act as "foot soldiers" in direct action campaigns. The sit-ins also demonstrated how direct action itself tended to promote unity and support among blacks, rendering the conservatism of older leaders less troublesome. Even so, the number of "foot soldiers" was limited; the concept, much in vogue in 1960–1964, of a "nonviolent army" that would steamroll the opposition through sheer weight of numbers turned out to be unrealistic. Albany taught King that no more than 5 percent of a given black population could be persuaded to volunteer for jail. He learned to frame his tactics accordingly.

The second tactical lesson was that, to quote Bayard Rustin, "protest becomes an effective tactic to the degree that it elicits brutality and oppression from the power structure." The government's conduct during the Freedom Rides—intervening in Alabama, where Klan mobs had been permitted to run amok, but adopting a "hands-off" policy towards Mississippi, where the police had kept order and carried out "peaceful" arrests—sent a coded but clear message to Southern segregationists; federal intervention could be avoided if the authorities kept violence in check. Albany's Chief of Police, Lauri Pritchett, applied this lesson with intelligence and skill, out-maneuvering the protesters. First, he trained his men to arrest demonstrators courteously and without unnecessary force. "For a period of four to five months," he reported to the city commission, "members of the Albany Police Department was [*sic*] indoctrinated to this plan of nonviolence. . . . At each roll call [they] were lectured and shown films on how to conduct themselves." Second, anticipating a "jail-in," Pritchett secured ample prison space in the surrounding counties. Finally, to protect the City's legal flank he charged demonstrators with such offenses as breach of the peace and unlawful assembly rather than with violation of the segregation laws. His plan worked to perfection: blacks went to jail by the thousands—King himself went three times—but the City adamantly refused to negotiate and the federal government did virtually nothing.

However much King and SCLC deplored Pritchett's self-serving definition of "nonviolence," they had to accept that victory had eluded them. Clearly, SCLC needed to be much more careful in its choice of target. In Birmingham, King elected to confront an adversary with a clear record of brutality, gambling on a violent response which, publicized by a violence-fixated press, would galvanize public opinion and jolt the federal government into action. In 1951 the reporter Carl Rowan had described Birmingham as "the world's most race-conscious city . . . a city of gross tensions, a city where the color line is drawn in every conceivable place [and where] Eugene "Bull" Connor, white-supremacist police commissioner, sees that no man, white or black, crosses the line." Connor was still police commissioner in 1963, and SCLC calculated that this man, notorious for his Klan connections and violence toward blacks, would react to nonviolent protests in a manner very different from Pritchett's. It disclaimed any intent to "provoke" violence. Nevertheless, as local black leader Fred Shuttlesworth put it, "the idea of facing 'Bull' Connor was the thing." Acting as predicted by SCLC, Connor's response to the protests of early May—the mass arrest of children, the use of fire-hoses and police-dogs—was publicized the world over.

But did the protests really achieve anything? The desegregation agreement which King won with the help of federal mediators has often been denigrated. One of the most widely read texts on black history describes it as "token concessions that were later not carried out." At the time, Southern whites argued that orderly change was already on the way; the protests merely hindered that process. It is surely no coincidence, however, that the first small steps in the direction of desegregation occurred precisely when King's campaign climaxed. Few blacks believed that the city's businessmen would have accepted desegregation but for the double pressure of the demonstrations and the economic boycott of downtown stores. Conservative blacks like A. G. Gaston, who had initially opposed direct action, changed their minds when they saw that the white merchants were bending: "The demonstrations gave us a wedge we never had before to use at the bargaining table." Narrow as it was, the agreement of May 10, 1963, represented the city's first substantive break with its white supremacist past. In the most thorough available study of the negotiations, historian Robert Corley concluded that "the end of segregation was dramatically hastened because King and his demonstrators threatened chaos in a city whose leaders were now desperate for order."

What of its impact on federal policy: did Birmingham produce the Civil Rights Act, as King and Shuttlesworth liked to claim? Garrow thinks not, pointing to the gap between SCLC's protests and the introduction of the Bill, as well as the long delay in its becoming law. He suggests that the lack of a clear goal in Birmingham, plus the black rioting of early May, might explain why there was "no widespread national outcry, no vocal reaction by the nation's clergy, and no immediate move by the administration to propose salutary legislation." Birmingham, he concludes, was far less successful than SCLC's later campaign in Selma.

Comparisons between Birmingham and Selma, however, must be treated with caution. It is true, as Garrow notes, that Birmingham produced a relatively muted response from Congress; Selma prompted nearly two hundred sympathetic speeches, Birmingham a mere seventeen. But a simple statistical comparison is misleading for the political context in 1963 was very different from that of 1965. Congressmen were far more wary about speaking out on civil rights in 1963. Most regarded it as a sure "vote-loser," and Northern Democrats were anxious to avoid a damaging intra-party dispute that would redound to the benefit of the Republican party. But in 1965, with the Republicans routed in the elections of the previous year, Northern Democrats felt politically less inhibited. In addition, by 1965 the nation had become more accustomed to the idea that the government should combat racial discrimination; far fewer people still maintained that the South's racial problems could be solved through local, voluntary action. Finally, by 1965 the civil rights movement enjoyed greater legitimacy and respectability. To compare the Congressional response to Birmingham with the reaction to Selma two years later is to compare like with unlike.

The impact of Birmingham should not be judged by its effect on Congress: the initiative for the Civil Rights Bill came from the Executive, not the Legislative branch. And by all accounts, SCLC's protests were pivotal in persuading the Kennedy administration to abandon its executive-action strategy in favor of legislation. Robert Kennedy was the driving force behind the Bill. For two years he had tried to deal with each racial crisis on an ad hoc basis. However, Birmingham convinced him that crises would recur, with increasing frequency and magnitude, unless the government adopted a more radical approach. According to Edwin Guthman, who served under Attorney General Kennedy, the violence in Birmingham "convinced the President and Bob that stronger federal civil rights laws were needed."

Did the rioting in Birmingham detract from the effectiveness of SCLC's campaign? SCLC did everything possible to minimize the likelihood of counterviolence by blacks. But King and his advisers realized that the Kennedy administration was not simply responding to the moral outrage evoked by Connor's tactics; it was far more perturbed by the threat of chaos and bloodshed. Birmingham raised the specter of retaliation by blacks and the prospect of a violent revolt by them, leading to uncontrollable racial warfare, began to haunt John and Robert Kennedy. Much as he deplored violence by his followers, King consciously exploited this anxiety for the sake of furthering his goals. In "Letter From Birmingham City Jail" he buttressed his appeal for support by whites by warning that without major concessions "millions of Negroes will . . . seek solace in black-nationalist ideologies—a development that would inevitably lead to a frightening racial nightmare." Thus did he redefine nonviolence as an alternative to, or defense against, violence by blacks. This argument reached its target: the Civil Rights Bill was in large measure designed to get blacks off the streets, to obviate the threat of violence, and to strengthen the influence of "responsible" black leaders.

In Birmingham, King broke the political logjam and delivered a hammer-blow against white supremacy. Mass movements did not come made-to-order, however; their success hinged upon sound planning, intelligent leadership, and a fortuitous situation. King had the advantage in Birmingham of a strong local base created by Fred Shuttlesworth, meticulous planning by Wyatt Walker, and a civic elite that was amenable to change. His next campaign, in St. Augustine, Florida (March–July 1964), went awry because the local movement was weak, the planning poor, and opposition by whites intransigent. Largely ineffective, the St. Augustine protests also suffered from lack of clarity in goals; because of this confusion, SCLC's tactics tended to cancel out each other. It is easy to see why King targeted St. Augustine. Heavily dependent on the tourist industry, the city's economy could be seriously damaged by demonstrations. Second, SCLC's chances of engineering a dramatic confrontation were excellent: Northern Florida was Ku Klux Klan country. A branch had been organized in the St. Augustine area in the summer of 1936, and it had close ties with the city and county police. From King's point of view, the Klan presence made St. Augustine doubly attractive. Demonstrations would flush the Klan into the open, thus compelling the state authorities or, failing these, the federal government to suppress it. The nature of SCLC's strategy was evident from its use of the night march. Adopted at the instance of Hosea Williams, who had pioneered this tactic in Savannah, the night march invited attack. The resulting Klan violence showed the police in their true colors, exposing the inadequacy of local law enforcement.

By publicizing the Klan menace King did succeed, with help from U.S. District Judge Bryan Simpson, in making Governor Farris Bryant crack down on white troublemakers. The strategy of forcing the Klan out of the woodwork, however, hampered the achievement of desegregation, SCLC's publicly stated goal. Moreover, in light of the imminent passage of the Civil Rights Bill, SCLC's demonstrations against segregated motels and restaurants seemed pointless. King reasoned that when whites accepted desegregation under legal compulsion they could avoid making any admission that blacks were not treated fairly. "This is morally wrong," he insisted. "We want them to admit that segregation is evil and take it upon themselves to rid this city of it." Yet it made little difference in practice if they abandoned segregation under the pressure of direct action rather than the compulsion of the law, and in any event, the Civil Rights Act, backed up by legal action from the NAACP Legal Defense Fund, desegregated St. Augustine's public accommodations.

In the Selma campaign (January–April 1965), everything went right. The local movement, built up by The Student Nonviolent Coordinating Committee (SNCC), was solidly entrenched. The strategy of the protests had been carefully thought out by James Bevel. SCLC's preparatory staff work was thorough. Above all, the campaign had a single clear, attainable goal—federal voting rights legislation—to which both the target and the tactics were directly relevant. With justice, Selma has been singled out as the most effective application of nonviolent direct action in the history of the civil rights movement.

The notes which he penned in Selma jail give a fascinating insight into King's tactics. In detailed written instructions to Andrew Young, SCLC's executive director, King orchestrated the protests from his cell with masterly finesse. Perhaps the most telling lines were those chiding Young for cancelling a demonstration in response to a favorable court decision. "Please don't be too soft," he wrote his lieutenant. "We have the offensive. It was a mistake not to march today. In a crisis we must have a sense of drama. . . . We may accept the restraining order as a partial victory, but we can't stop." Not until SCLC triggered the violent confrontation of March 7—"Bloody Sunday"—did King feel his goal securely within reach.

The efficacy of King's tactics at Selma flowed from the fact that, to quote Zashin, "people were shocked by the segregationists' violence, not because the self-suffering of the demonstrators was saliently impressive." Garrow came to the same conclusion, adding that the non-controversial nature of SCLC's goal, the right to vote, and the complete absence of violence by blacks both helped to make the campaign a success.

The fact that SCLC designed its tactics to elicit violence might appear callous and irresponsible. Yet the assertion that SCLC deliberately "provoked" violence by whites has to be qualified. If their nonviolent efforts to secure basic Constitutional rights met with violence from racist whites, King argued, then law, logic and morality required society to punish the perpetrators of violence, not condemn its victims. It might seem paradoxical that King invited racist violence but denied in any sense provoking it. But he could also argue that violence was intrinsic to white supremacy and that nonviolent protesters merely brought that violence to the public's attention. In some notes he prepared for a press conference, he anticipated the question "Does your movement depend on violence?" by writing, "When you give witness to an evil you do not cause that evil but you oppose it so it can be cured." The violence of March 7, he added, "brought into every home the terror and brutality that Negroes face every day."

Nevertheless, SCLC's tactics exposed King to the charge that he manipulated local blacks, offering his followers as targets for the aggression of whites. Although undeniably manipulative, nobody could justifiably accuse SCLC of disguising to its followers the dangers they faced. "There can be no remission of sin without the shedding of blood," wrote King. SCLC's claim to leadership rested on the fact that its staff shared the same risks as the rank-and-file demonstrators. Thus King came under the sharpest criticism when he seemed to be avoiding the perils that he asked his followers to brave.

By staging its protests in carefully contrived, highly publicized situations, SCLC tried to evoke violence by whites while keeping casualties to a minimum. The news media played a crucial, if unwitting, role in this strategy. "The presence of reporters," wrote Paul Good, "not only publicized their cause but also acted as a deterrent in places where officials feared bad publicity." Television crews and photographers had an especially inhibiting effect; as Bayard Rustin put it, "Businessmen and chambers of commerce across the South dreaded the cameras." Even in Birmingham, and to some extent in Selma as well, extensive press coverage caused law enforcement officials to proceed with caution. As another of King's advisers, Stanley Levison, pointed out, "the fact that the demonstrations focused public attention from all over the country . . . restrained even the most vicious elements from moving out too freely." When the police did resort to violence, they usually stopped short of lethal force; in all of SCLC's demonstrations in the South, only two deaths resulted from police attacks. SCLC realized moreover, that the news value of racist violence depended as much on the ability of the press to report it as on the gravity of the violence itself. Snarling German Shepherds, gushing fire-hoses, and club-wielding state troopers could have a greater impact on the public consciousness than murders and bombings if reporters and film crews were present at the scene. Nonviolent protest, wrote King, "dramatized the essential meaning of the conflict and in magnified strokes made clear who was the evildoer and who was the undeserving victim." SCLC tried to evoke dramatic violence rather than deadly violence, and King, as August Meier pointed out in 1965, constantly retreated "from situations that might result in the deaths of his followers."

Despite his enormous popularity and prestige, King learned never to take support of blacks for granted. Leadership and tactics, not numbers, were the key ingredients in King's successes. In the teeming cities of the North, one-twentieth of the black population amounted to a small army. The potential for nonviolent direct action seemed immense. If the team that had organized Selma were turned loose on Chicago, Andrew Young speculated, SCLC would have numbers enough—perhaps 100,000—to bring the city to a standstill. The sheer power of numbers in the North was "awesome," he thought. "I tremble to think what might happen if it is not organized and disciplined in the interests of positive social change." Even as Young spoke, a devastating riot was unfolding in Los Angeles, which, after five days of violence, left thirty-one blacks and three whites dead. On the heels of the Watts riot King, previously so cautious about leaving the South, insisted that SCLC move North and move fast; "The present mood dictates that we cannot wait." Thus it was with a mixture of self-confidence and pessimistic urgency that SCLC embarked on its first Northern campaign.

The anticipated numbers, however, failed to materialize. Chicago had a black population of a million, but it stayed on the sidelines. Barely 50,000 people attended the biggest mass rally: King's demonstrations attracted, at most, twenty-five hundred, at least half of whom were white. King, it has been argued, was out of tune with the mood, culture, and problems of the Northern ghetto. The product of a cocooned middle-class environment, he was not attuned to the cynicism and defeatism that so often prevailed among the black urban poor. His bourgeois emphasis on thrift and self-help obscured him to the realities of their plight; his goal of integration (expressed in Chicago by the demand for "open housing") was marginal, at best, to their immediate concerns. There is a scintilla of truth in this argument. Yet there were many sound reasons for attacking housing segregation, the most visible and far-reaching expression of white racism. Exposure to the Chicago slums, moreover, soon brought home to King the poverty and degradation of the urban ghetto, rapidly disabusing him of his more simplistic assumptions about the efficacy of "bootstrap" economics.

The fact remained, nevertheless, that only a tiny minority acted on King's message. By 1966, in fact, King was becoming increasingly isolated as an advocate of nonviolent direct action. The concept of independent action by blacks in opposition to the white majority—a concept popularized by SNCC's slogan, "Black Power"—was fast gaining ground among intellectuals and activists. But the opposite strategy of seeking political change in coalition with whites was also winning converts. Articulated most persuasively by Bayard Rustin, the coalition strategy envisaged little role for nonviolent direct action on the grounds that economic problems simply were not susceptible to marches and demonstrations. Indeed, Rustin argued that in the post-Watts era, with rioting and repression feeding off each other, direct action had become counterproductive, alienating whites and "breeding despair and impotence" among blacks. Reflecting on SCLC's decline from the perspective of the mid-1970s, Rustin concluded that King persisted in the tactics of protest long after their usefulness had been exhausted.

The disturbed political climate of the late 1960s made doubtful the success of any strategy of blacks. King assessed "Black Power" as a confused, impractical doctrine, and he deplored its connotations of violence and separatism. Yet Rustin's coalitionism struck him as only slightly less unrealistic. In practice, it boiled down to giving blanket support to the Johnson administration—a line rendered both morally repugnant and politically futile by Johnson's growing obsession with the war in Vietnam. The defeat of the 1966 Civil Rights Bill and the Republicans gains in the November elections signalled the disintegration of the informal, bi-partisan "coalition of conscience" which had sustained the civil rights movement in 1963–65. King accurately sensed that it would be impossible—and, in light of the conservatism and hawkishness of most trade unions, undesirable—to resurrect it. Yet he could offer no alternative strategy with any conviction. Indeed, political trends plus his own experiences in Chicago persuaded him that he had badly underestimated the force of white racism. Blacks were not confronting a regional minority but a national majority. It was a shattering conclusion and it drove him to despair.

During the last two years of his life, King was torn between his old faith in the capacity of liberal democracy for enlightened reform, and a Marxian view of the state as an engine of capitalist exploitation. That he became more radical is certain; the need for a thoroughgoing redistribution of wealth and power was a consistent theme of his public and private statements. Occasionally, in his darkest moments, he feared that America was drifting irreversibly toward facsism. Yet King could never forget that the federal government had been his ally. He wanted to believe the current reactionary trend was a passing phase, the irrational spin-off of rioting and war. Although shaken by Chicago and alienated from the President, he convinced himself that public opinion was malleable and the government still susceptible to the right kind of pressure. Nonviolent protest could still work, he insisted to his somewhat skeptical staff. "If it hasn't worked in the North, it just hasn't been tried enough."

King's last project, the "Poor People's Campaign," is sometimes described as revolutionary. To some it recalled the "nonviolent army" idea of the early 1960s. King himself spoke of "class struggle" and threatened massive civil disobedience on a scale that could bring Washington to a grinding halt. Behind the radical rhetoric, however, the strategy and tactics of the campaign closely resembled the pattern of Birmingham and Selma. Although he spoke of creating a new radical coalition, the groups King looked to for support were, by and large, the same that had comprised the "coalition of conscience" in the earlier period. He envisaged a "Selma-like movement" which, if "powerful enough, dramatic enough, and morally appealing enough," would mobilize "the churches, labor, liberals, intellectuals," as well as the new breed of "Black Power" militants and "New Left" white radicals. Far from raising a "nonviolent army," King planned to bring only three thousand demonstrators to Washington—about the number who had gone to jail in Birmingham and Selma. "We aren't going to close down the Pentagon," he told SCLC's board of directors. "Anybody talking about closing down the Pentagon is just talking foolishness. We can't close down Capitol Hill." The aim was not to "coerce" the federal government, but to generate a sympathetic response from the people of the nation. King's demands were moderate, he believed, and he wanted to promote consensus, not conflict.

Had he lived, King might well have achieved at least a partial success. The political situation in 1968 was volatile and fluid; the election of Richard Nixon, and the years of "benign neglect," was not a foregone conclusion. Perhaps King would have cancelled or postponed the Poor People's Campaign, reasoning that a Hubert Humphrey or Robert Kennedy presidency would give him more room for maneuver. In terms of influence and accomplishment, King outstripped all other black leaders and would-be leaders. His capacity to adapt to rapidly changing circumstances would surely have been tested to the limit, but a healthy and astute pragmatism had always been part of his outlook. "I am still searching myself," he told his staff. "I don't have all the answers, and I certainly have no claim to omniscience." There was no magic formula for social change; the dynamics of direct action could only be discovered in struggle, in resistance, even in defeat.

Clayborne Carson

NO

Martin Luther King, Jr.: Charismatic Leadership in a Mass Struggle

The legislation to establish Martin Luther King, Jr.'s birthday as a federal holiday provided official recognition of King's greatness, but it remains the responsibility of those of us who study and carry on King's work to define his historical significance. Rather than engaging in officially approved nostalgia, our remembrance of King should reflect the reality of his complex and multifaceted life. Biographers, theologians, political scientists, sociologists, social psychologists, and historians have given us a sizable literature of King's place in Afro-American protest tradition, his role in the modern black freedom struggle, and his electic ideas regarding nonviolent activism. Although King scholars may benefit from and may stimulate the popular interest in King generated by the national holiday, many will find themselves uneasy participants in annual observances to honor an innocuous, carefully cultivated image of King as a black heroic figure.

The King depicted in serious scholarly works is far too interesting to be encased in such a didactic legend. King was a controversial leader who challenged authority and who once applauded what he called "creative maladjusted nonconformity." He should not be transformed into a simplistic image designed to offend no one—a black counterpart to the static, heroic myths that have embalmed George Washington as the Father of His Country and Abraham Lincoln as the Great Emancipator.

One aspect of the emerging King myth has been the depiction of him in the mass media, not only as the preeminent leader of the civil rights movement, but also as the initiator and sole indispensible element in the southern black struggles of the 1950s and 1960s. As in other historical myths, a Great Man is seen as the decisive factor in the process of social change, and the unique qualities of a leader are used to explain major historical events. The King myth departs from historical reality because it attributes too much to King's exceptional qualities as a leader and too little to the impersonal, large-scale social factors that made it possible for King to display his singular abilities on a national stage. Because the myth emphasizes the individual at the expense of the black movement, it not only exaggerates King's historical importance but also distorts his actual, considerable contribution to the movement.

A major example of this distortion has been the tendency to see King as a charismatic figure who single-handedly directed the course of the civil rights movement through the force of his oratory. The charismatic label however, does not adequately define King's role in the southern black struggle. The term *charisma* has traditionally been used to describe the godlike, magical qualities possessed by certain leaders. Connotations of the term have changed, of course, over the years. In our more secular age, it has lost many of its religious connotations and now refers to a wide range of leadership styles that involve the capacity to inspire—usually through oratory—emotional bonds between leaders and followers. Arguing that King was not a charismatic leader, in the broadest sense of the term, becomes somewhat akin to arguing that he was not a Christian, but emphasis on King's charisma obscures other important aspects of his role in the black movement. To be sure, King's oratory was exceptional and many people saw King as a divinely inspired leader, but King did not receive and did not want the kind of unquestioning support that is often associated with charismatic leaders. Movement activists instead saw him as the most prominent among many outstanding movement strategists, tacticians, ideologues, and institutional leaders.

King undoubtedly recognized that charisma was one of many leadership qualities at his disposal, but he also recognized that charisma was not a sufficient basis for leadership in a modem political movement enlisting numerous self-reliant leaders. Moreover, he rejected aspects of the charismatic model that conflicted with his sense of his own limitations. Rather than exhibiting unwavering confidence in his power and wisdom, King was a leader full of self-doubts, keenly aware of his own limitations and human weaknesses. He was at times reluctant to take on the responsibilities suddenly and unexpectedly thrust upon him. During the Montgomery bus boycott, for example, when he worried about threats to his life and to the lives of his wife and child, he was overcome with fear rather than confident and secure in his leadership role. He was able to carry on only after acquiring an enduring understanding of his dependence on a personal God who promised never to leave him alone.

Moreover, emphasis on King's charisma conveys the misleading notion of a movement held together by spellbinding speeches and blind faith rather than by a complex blend of rational and emotional bonds. King's charisma did not place him above criticism. Indeed, he was never able to gain mass support for his notion of nonviolent struggle as a way of life, rather than simply a tactic. Instead of viewing himself as the embodiment of widely held Afro-American racial views, he willingly risked his popularity among blacks through his steadfast advocacy of nonviolent strategies to achieve radical social change.

He was a profound and provocative public speaker as well as an emotionally powerful one. Only those unfamiliar with the Afro-American clergy would assume that his oratorical skills were unique, but King set himself apart from other black preachers through his use of traditional black Christian idiom to advocate unconventional political ideas. Early in his life King became disillusioned with the unbridled emotionalism associated with his father's religious fundamentalism, and, as a thirteen year old, he questioned the bodily resurrection of Jesus in his Sunday school class. His subsequent search for an intellectually satisifying religious faith conflicted with the emphasis on emotional expressiveness that pervades evangelical religion. His preaching manner was rooted in the traditions of the black church, while his subject matter, which often reflected his wide-ranging philosophical interests, distinguished him from other preachers who relied on rhetorical devices that manipulated the emotions of the listeners. King used charisma as a tool for mobilizing black communities, but he always used it in the context of other forms of intellectual and political leadership suited to a movement containing many strong leaders.

Recently, scholars have begun to examine the black struggle as a locally based mass movement, rather than simply a reform movement led by national civil rights leaders. The new orientation in scholarship indicates that King's role was different from that suggested in King-centered biographies and journalistic accounts. King was certainly not the only significant leader of the civil rights movement, for sustained protest movements arose in many southern communities in which King had little or no direct involvement.

In Montgomery, for example, local black leaders such as E. D. Nixon, Rosa Parks, and Jo Ann Robinson started the bus boycott before King became the leader of the Montgomery Improvement Association. Thus, although King inspired blacks in Montgomery and black residents recognized that they were fortunate to have such a spokesperson, talented local leaders other than King played decisive roles in initiating and sustaining the boycott movement.

Similarly, the black students who initiated the 1960 lunch counter sit-ins admired King, but they did not wait for him to act before launching their own movement. The sit-in leaders who founded the Student Nonviolent Coordinating Committee (SNCC) became increasingly critical of King's leadership style, linking it to the feelings of dependency that often characterize the followers of charismatic leaders. The essence of SNCC's approach to community organizing was to instill in local residents the confidence that they could lead their own struggles. A SNCC organizer failed if local residents became dependent on his or her presence; as the organizers put it, their job was to work themselves out of a job. Though King influenced the struggles that took place in the Black Belt regions of Mississippi, Alabama, and Georgia, those movements were also guided by self-reliant local leaders who occasionally called on King's oratorical skills to galvanize black protestors at mass meetings while refusing to depend on his presence.

If King had never lived, the black struggle would have followed a course of development similar to the one it did. The Montgomery bus boycott would have occurred, because King did not initiate it. Black students probably would have rebelled—even without King as a role model—for they had sources of tactical and ideological inspiration besides King. Mass activism in southern cities and voting rights efforts in the deep South were outgrowths of large-scale social and political forces, rather than simply consequences of the actions of a single leader. Though perhaps not as quickly and certainly not as peacefully nor with as universal a significance, the black movement would probably have achieved its major legislative victories without King's leadership, for the southern Jim Crow system was a regional anachronism, and the forces that undermined it were inexorable.

To what extent, then, did King's presence affect the movement? Answering that question requires us to look beyond the usual portrayal of the black struggle. Rather than seeing an amorphous mass of discontented blacks acting out strategies determined by a small group of leaders, we would recognize King as a major example of the local black leadership that emerged as black communities mobilized for sustained struggles. If not as dominant a figure as sometimes portrayed, the historical King was nevertheless a remarkable leader who acquired the respect and support of self-confident, grass-roots leaders, some of whom possessed charismatic qualities of their own. Directing attention to the other leaders who initiated and emerged from those struggles should not detract from our conception of King's historical significance; such movement-oriented research reveals King as a leader who stood out in a forest of tall trees.

King's major public speeches—particularly the "I Have a Dream" speech—have received much attention, but his exemplary qualities were also displayed in countless strategy sessions with other activists and in meetings with government officials. King's success as a leader was based on his intellectual and moral cogency and his skill as a conciliator among movement activists who refused to be simply King's "followers" or "lieutenants."

The success of the black movement required the mobilization of black communities as well as the transformation of attitudes in the surrounding society, and King's wide range of skills and attributes prepared him to meet the internal as well as the external demands of the movement. King understood the black world from a privileged position, having grown up in a stable family within a major black urban community; yet he also learned how to speak persuasively to the surrounding white world. Alone among the major civil rights leaders of his time, King could not only articulate black concerns to white audiences, but could also mobilize blacks through his day-to-day involvement in black community institutions and through his access to the regional institutional network of the black church. His advocacy of nonviolent activism gave the black movement invaluable positive press coverage, but his effectiveness as a protest leader derived mainly from his ability to mobilize black community resources.

Analyses of the southern movement that emphasize its nonrational aspects and expressive functions over its political character explain the black struggle as an emotional outburst by discontented blacks, rather than recognizing that the movement's strength and durability came from its mobilization of black community institutions, financial resources, and grass-roots leaders. The values of southern blacks were profoundly and permanently transformed not only by King, but also by involvement in sustained protest activity and community-organizing efforts, through thousands of mass meetings, workshops, citizenship classes, freedom schools, and informal discussions. Rather than merely accepting guidance from above, southern blacks were resocialized as a result of their movement experiences.

Although the literature of the black struggle has traditionally paid little attention to the intellectual content of black politics, movement activists of the 1960s made a profound, though often ignored, contribution to political thinking. King may have been born with rare potential, but his most significant leadership attributes were related to his immersion in, and contribution to, the intellectual ferment that has always been an essential part of Afro-American freedom struggles. Those who have written about King have too often assumed that his most important ideas were derived from outside the black struggle—from his academic training, his philosophical readings, or his acquaintance with Gandhian ideas. Scholars are only beginning to recognize the extent to which his attitudes and those of many other activists, white and black, were transformed through their involvement in a movement in which ideas disseminated from the bottom up as well as from the top down.

Although my assessment of King's role in the black struggles of his time reduces him to human scale, it also increases the possibility that others may recognize his qualities in themselves. Idolizing King lessens one's ability to exhibit some of his best attributes or, worse, encourages one to become a debunker, emphasizing King's flaws in order to lessen the inclination to exhibit his virtues. King himself undoubtedly feared that some who admired him would place too much faith in his ability to offer guidance and to overcome resistance, for he often publicly acknowledged his own limitations and mortality. Near the end of his life, King expressed his certainty that black people would reach the Promised Land whether or not he was with them. His faith was based on an awareness of the qualities that he knew he shared with all people. When he suggested his own epitaph, he asked not to be remembered for his exceptional achievements—his Nobel Prize and other awards, his academic accomplishments; instead, he wanted to be remembered for giving his life to serve others, for trying to be right on the war question, for trying to feed the hungry and clothe the naked, for trying to love and serve humanity. "I want you to say that I tried to love and serve humanity." Those aspects of King's life did not require charisma or other superhuman abilities.

If King were alive today, he would doubtless encourage those who celebrate his life to recognize their responsibility to struggle as he did for a more just and peaceful world. He would prefer that the black movement be remembered not only as the scene of his own achievements, but also as a setting that brought out extraordinary qualities in many people. If he were to return, his oratory would be unsettling and intellectually challenging rather than remembered diction and cadences. He would probably be the unpopular social critic he was on the eve of the Poor People's Campaign rather than the object of national homage he became after his death. His basic message would be the same as it was when he was alive, for he did not bend with the changing political winds. He would talk of ending poverty and war and of building a just social order that would avoid the pitfalls of competitive capitalism and repressive communism. He would give scant comfort to those who condition their activism upon the appearance of another King, for he recognized the extent to which he was a product of the movement that called him to leadership.

The notion that appearances by Great Men (or Great Women) are necessary preconditions for the emergence of major movements for social change reflects not only a poor understanding of history, but also a pessimistic view of the possibilities for future social change. Waiting for the Messiah is a human weakness that is unlikely to be rewarded more than once in a millennium. Studies of King's life offer support for an alternative optimistic belief that ordinary people can collectively improve their lives. Such studies demonstrate the capacity of social movements to transform participants for the better and to create leaders worthy of their followers.

POSTSCRIPT

Was Martin Luther King, Jr.'s Leadership Essential to the Success of the Civil Rights Revolution?

Fairclough delivers an important portrait of King. He challenges not only the mythical views about King but also the portraits that a number of his biographers have written. First of all, he places King within the context of the dynamics of the social changes of the 1960s. Fairclough disagrees with those who see King primarily as a great orator and a symbolic leader of the movement. He argues that King was a flexible and practical revolutionary who understood that power, not moral suasion, lay at the heart of the civil rights protest movements. Consequently, Fairclough disputes David J. Garrow's contention in *Bearing the Cross: Martin Luther King, Jr. and the Southern Christian Leadership Conference* (Morrow/Avon, 1999) that King's belief about nonviolence was originally viewed as a form of moral suasion. When the demonstrations failed to convert white southerners or even attract white moderates, says Garrow, King finally realized that mass protests would only work as a pressure tactic that was needed to evoke a violent response from the oppressors.

Fairclough denies that King ever made such an ideological shift. King, in his view, was a realist who understood that nonviolence was a tactic used in a struggle to achieve power. While he may have been disappointed that only a few white southerners converted to the movement, the Montgomery Bus Boycott of 1956 was only the first phase of a worldwide revolt of oppressed people.

Carson might seem to underestimate the uniqueness of King. He admits that King could speak persuasively to the white community and at the same time "mobilize black community resources." These ideas were first articulated by the historian August Meier, who described King as a conservative militant in his widely reprinted article "On the Role of Martin Luther King," *New Politics* (Winter 1965). King not only bridged the black and white power structures, but he also acted as a broker between the more militant protest groups, such as the Student Nonviolent Coordinating Committee (SNCC) and the more conservative, legal-oriented NAACP.

The literature on King is enormous. An interpretive short biography is Adam Fairclough, *Martin Luther King, Jr.* (University of Georgia Press, 1995). Older interpretations are nicely summarized in C. Eric Lincoln, ed., *Martin Luther King, Jr.: A Profile* (Hill & Wang, 1970), which includes Meier's classic essay. Peter J. Albert and Ronald Hoffman have edited a more recent symposium, *We Shall Overcome: Martin Luther King, Jr. and the Black Freedom Struggle* (Da Capo Press, 1990). Stephen B. Oates, *Let the Trumpet Sound: The Life of Martin Luther King, Jr.* (Harper & Row, 1982) uses King's papers but is mainly descriptive. Also see Oates, "Trumpet of Conscience: A Portrait of Martin Luther King, Jr.," *American History Illustrated* (April 1988); David Garrow, "Martin Luther King, Jr. and the Cross of Leadership," *Peace and Change* (Fall 1987); and "The Intellectual Development of Martin Luther King, Jr.: Influences and Commentaries," *Union Seminary Quarterly* (vol. 40, 1986), pp. 5–20. A well-written early biography is David L. Lewis, *King: A Critical Biography* (Praeger, 1970). See also Lewis's "Martin Luther King, Jr. and the Promise of Nonviolent Populism," in John Hope Franklin and August Meier, eds., *Black Leaders of the Twentieth Century* (University of Illinois Press, 1982). Two volumes that defy description are Taylor Branch's sprawling *Parting the Waters* (Simon & Schuster, 1988) and *Pillar of Fire* (Simon & Schuster, 1998), which takes the reader through the King years up to 1965. A third volume has yet to be published.

The literature of the civil rights movement is also enormous. Two of the best overviews written for students are John A. Salmond, *My Mind Set on Freedom: A History of the Civil Rights Movement, 1954–1968* (Ivan R. Dee, 1997), a survey in the American Ways series; and Peter B. Levy, *The Civil Rights Movement* (Greenwood Press, 1998), which is part of the Greenwood Press Guides to Historic Events of the Twentieth Century series. Two excellent collections of essays are Charles W. Eagles, ed., *The Civil Rights Movement in America* (University Press of Mississippi, 1986), a symposium held at the University of Mississippi in 1985 among several of the most important civil rights historians, and Paul Winters, ed., *The Civil Rights Movement* (Greenhaven Press, 2000), which contains a number of useful topical articles. Three more detailed studies are Jack M. Bloom's theoretical *Class, Race, and the Civil Rights Movement* (Indiana University Press, 1987); Harvard Sitkoff, *The Struggle for Black Equality, 1954–1992,* rev. ed. (Hill & Wang, 1993); and David R. Goldfield, *Black, White, and Southern: Race Relations and Southern Culture, 1940 to the Present* (Louisiana State University Press, 1990). The best film series on the civil rights movement is Henry Hampton's 14-hour *Eyes on the Prize: America's Civil Rights Years, 1954–1965.* Two excellent primary source anthologies came from this series: Clayborne Carson et al., eds., *Eyes on the Prize: Civil Rights Reader* (Penguin Books, 1991) and Henry Hampton and Steve Fayer, eds., *Voice of Freedom: An Oral History of the Civil Rights Movement From the 1950s Through the 1980s* (Bantam Books, 1990).

Local studies that de-emphasize the national movement covered so well by the contemporary press and most American history texts include William Chafe, *Civilities and Civil Rights: Greensboro, North Carolina, and the Black Struggle for Freedom* (Oxford University Press, 1981), which castigates the white moderates for using southern charm to avoid the racial divide; Adam Fairclough, *Race and Democracy: The Civil Rights Struggle in Louisiana, 1915–1972* (University of Georgia Press, 1995); Charles M. Payne, *I've Got the Light of Freedom: The Organizing Tradition and the Mississippi Freedom Struggle* (University of California Press, 1995); and John Dittmer, *Local People: The Struggle for Civil Rights in Mississippi* (University of Illinois, 1994).

ISSUE 12

Was America's Escalation of the War in Vietnam Inevitable?

YES: Brian VanDeMark, from *Into the Quagmire: Lyndon Johnson and the Escalation of the Vietnam War* (Oxford University Press, 1991)

NO: H. R. McMaster, from *Dereliction of Duty: Lyndon Johnson, Robert McNamara, the Joint Chiefs of Staff, and the Lies That Led to Vietnam* (HarperCollins, 1997)

ISSUE SUMMARY

YES: Professor of history Brian VanDeMark argues that President Lyndon Johnson failed to question the viability of increasing U.S. involvement in the Vietnam War because he was a prisoner of America's global containment policy.

NO: H. R. McMaster, an active-duty army tanker, maintains that the Vietnam disaster was not inevitable but a uniquely human failure whose responsibility was shared by President Johnson and his principal advisers.

At the end of World War II, imperialism was coming to a close in Asia. Japan's defeat spelled the end of its control over China, Korea, and the countries of Southeast Asia. Attempts by the European nations to reestablish their empires were doomed. Anti-imperialist movements emerged all over Asia and Africa, often producing chaos.

The United States faced a dilemma. America was a nation conceived in revolution and was sympathetic to the struggles of Third World nations. But the United States was afraid that many of the revolutionary leaders were Communists who would place their countries under the control of the expanding empire of the Soviet Union. By the late 1940s the Truman administration decided that it was necessary to stop the spread of communism. The policy that resulted was known as *containment.*

Vietnam provided a test of the containment doctrine in Asia. Vietnam had been a French protectorate from 1885 until Japan took control of it during World War II. Shortly before the war ended, the Japanese gave Vietnam its independence, but the French were determined to reestablish their influence in the area. Conflicts emerged between the French-led nationalist forces of South Vietnam and the Communist-dominated provisional government of the Democratic Republic of Vietnam (DRV), which was established in Hanoi in August 1945. Ho Chi Minh was the president of the DRV. An avowed Communist since the 1920s, Ho had also become the major nationalist figure in Vietnam. As the leader of the anti-imperialist movement against French and Japanese colonialism for over 30 years, Ho managed to tie together the communist and nationalist movements in Vietnam.

A full-scale war broke out in 1946 between the communist government of North Vietnam and the French-dominated country of South Vietnam. After the Communists defeated the French at the battle of Dien Bien Phu in May 1954, the latter decided to pull out. At the Geneva Conference that summer, Vietnam was divided at the 17th parallel, pending elections.

The United States became directly involved in Vietnam after the French withdrew. In 1955 the Republican president Dwight D. Eisenhower refused to recognize the Geneva Accord but supported the establishment of the South Vietnamese government. In 1956 South Vietnam's leader, Ngo Dinh Diem, with U.S. approval, refused to hold elections, which would have provided a unified government for Vietnam in accordance with the Geneva Agreement. The Communists in the north responded by again taking up the armed struggle. The war continued for another 19 years.

Both President Eisenhower and his successor, John F. Kennedy, were anxious to prevent South Vietnam from being taken over by the Communists, so economic assistance and military aid were provided. Kennedy's successor, Lyndon Johnson, changed the character of American policy in Vietnam by escalating the air war and increasing the number of ground forces from 21,000 in 1965 to a full fighting force of 550,000 at its peak in 1968.

The next president, Richard Nixon, adopted a new policy of "Vietnamization" of the war. Military aid to South Vietnam was increased to ensure the defeat of the Communists. At the same time, American troops were gradually withdrawn from Vietnam. South Vietnamese president Thieu recognized the weakness of his own position without the support of U.S. troops. He reluctantly signed the Paris Accords in January 1973 only after being told by Secretary of State Henry Kissinger that the United States would sign them alone. Once U.S. soldiers were withdrawn, Thieu's regime was doomed. In spring 1975 a full-scale war broke out, and the South Vietnamese government collapsed.

In the following selection, Brian VanDeMark argues that President Johnson failed to question the viability of increasing U.S. involvement in Vietnam because he was a prisoner of America's global containment policy and because he did not want his opponents to accuse him of being soft on communism. In the second selection, H. R. McMaster argues that the Vietnam disaster was not inevitable but a uniquely human failure whose responsibility was shared by Johnson and his civilian and military advisers.

YES

Brian VanDeMark

Into the Quagmire

Vietnam divided America more deeply and painfully than any event since the Civil War. It split political leaders and ordinary people alike in profound and lasting ways. Whatever the conflicting judgments about this controversial war—and there are many—Vietnam undeniably stands as the greatest tragedy of twentieth-century U.S. foreign relations.

America's involvement in Vietnam has, as a result, attracted much critical scrutiny, frequently addressed to the question, "Who was guilty?"—"Who led the United States into this tragedy?" A more enlightening question, it seems, is "How and why did this tragedy occur?" The study of Vietnam should be a search for explanation and understanding, rather than for scapegoats.

Focusing on one important period in this long and complicated story—the brief but critical months from November 1964 to July 1965, when America crossed the threshold from limited to large-scale war in Vietnam—helps to answer that question. For the crucial decisions of this period resulted from the interplay of longstanding ideological attitudes, diplomatic assumptions and political pressures with decisive contemporaneous events in America and Vietnam.

Victory in World War II produced a sea change in America's perception of its role in world affairs. Political leaders of both parties embraced a sweepingly new vision of the United States as the defender against the perceived threat of monolithic communist expansion everywhere in the world. This vision of American power and purpose, shaped at the start of the Cold War, grew increasingly rigid over the years. By 1964–1965, it had become an ironbound and unshakable dogma, a received faith which policymakers unquestionably accepted—even though the circumstances which had fostered its creation had changed dramatically amid diffused authority and power among communist states and nationalist upheaval in the colonial world.

Policymakers' blind devotion to this static Cold War vision led America into misfortune in Vietnam. Lacking the critical perspective and sensibility to reappraise basic tenets of U.S. foreign policy in the light of changed events and local circumstances, policymakers failed to perceive Vietnamese realities accurately and thus to gauge American interests in the area prudently. Policymakers, as a consequence, misread an indigenous, communist-led nationalist movement as part of a larger, centrally directed challenge to world order and stability; tied American fortunes to a non-communist regime of slim popular legitimacy and effectiveness; and intervened militarily in the region far out of proportion to U.S. security requirements.

An arrogant and stubborn faith in America's power to shape the course of foreign events compounded the dangers sown by ideological rigidity. Policymakers in 1964–1965 shared a common postwar conviction that the United States not only should, but could, control political conditions in South Vietnam, as elsewhere throughout much of the world. This conviction had led Washington to intervene progressively deeper in South Vietnamese affairs over the years. And when—despite Washington's increasing exertions—Saigon's political situation declined precipitously during 1964–1965, this conviction prompted policymakers to escalate the war against Hanoi, in the belief that America could stimulate political order in South Vietnam through the application of military force against North Vietnam.

Domestic political pressures exerted an equally powerful, if less obvious, influence over the course of U.S. involvement in Vietnam. The fall of China in 1949 and the ugly McCarthyism it aroused embittered American foreign policy for a generation. By crippling President Truman's political fortunes, it taught his Democratic successors, John Kennedy and Lyndon Johnson [LBJ], a strong and sobering lesson: that another "loss" to communism in East Asia risked renewed and devastating attacks from the right. This fear of reawakened McCarthyism remained a paramount concern as policymakers pondered what course to follow as conditions in South Vietnam deteriorated rapidly in 1964–1965.

Enduring traditions of ideological rigidity, diplomatic arrogance, and political vulnerability heavily influenced the way policymakers approached decisions in Vietnam in 1964–1965. Understanding the decisions of this period fully, however, also requires close attention to contemporary developments in America and South Vietnam. These years marked a tumultuous time in both countries, which affected the course of events in subtle but significant ways.

Policymakers in 1964–1965 lived in a period of extraordinary domestic political upheaval sparked by the civil rights movement. It is difficult to overstate the impact of this upheaval on American politics in the mid-1960s. During 1964–1965, the United States—particularly the American South—experienced profound and long overdue change in the economic, political, and social rights of blacks. This change, consciously embraced by the liberal administration of Lyndon Johnson, engendered sharp political hostility among conservative southern whites and their deputies in Congress—hostility which the politically astute Johnson sensed could spill over into the realm of foreign affairs, where angry civil rights opponents could exact their revenge should LBJ stumble and "lose" a crumbling South Vietnam. This danger, reinforced by the memory of McCarthyism, stirred deep political fears in Johnson, together with an abiding aversion to failure in Vietnam.

LBJ feared defeat in South Vietnam, but he craved success and glory at home. A forceful, driving President of boundless ambition, Johnson sought to harness the political momentum created by the civil rights movement to enact a far-reaching domestic reform agenda under the rubric of the Great Society. LBJ would achieve the greatness he sought by leading America toward justice and opportunity for all its citizens, through his historic legislative program.

Johnson's domestic aspirations fundamentally conflicted with his uneasy involvement in Vietnam. An experienced and perceptive politician, LBJ knew his domestic reforms required the sustained focus and cooperation of Congress. He also knew a larger war in Vietnam jeopardized these reforms by drawing away political attention and economic resources. America's increasing military intervention in 1964–1965 cast this tension between Vietnam and the Great Society into sharp relief.

Johnson saw his predicament clearly. But he failed to resolve it for fear that acknowledging the growing extent and cost of the war would thwart his domestic reforms, while pursuing a course of withdrawal risked political ruin. LBJ, instead, chose to obscure the magnitude of his dilemma by obscuring America's deepening involvement as South Vietnam began to fail. That grave compromise of candor opened the way to Johnson's eventual downfall.

Events in South Vietnam during 1964–1965 proved equally fateful. A historically weak and divided land, South Vietnam's deeply rooted ethnic, political, and religious turmoil intensified sharply in the winter of 1964–1965. This mounting turmoil, combined with increased communist military attacks, pushed Saigon to the brink of political collapse.

South Vietnam's accelerating crisis alarmed American policymakers, driving them to deepen U.S. involvement considerably in an effort to arrest Saigon's political failure. Abandoning the concept of stability in the South *before* escalation against the North, policymakers now embraced the concept of stability *through* escalation, in the desperate hope that military action against Hanoi would prompt a stubbornly elusive political order in Saigon.

This shift triggered swift and ominous consequences scarcely anticipated by its architects. Policymakers soon confronted intense military, political, and bureaucratic pressures to widen the war. Unsettled by these largely unforeseen pressures, policymakers reacted confusedly and defensively. Rational men, they struggled to control increasingly irrational forces. But their reaction only clouded their attention to basic assumptions and ultimate costs as the war rapidly spun out of control in the spring and summer of 1965. In their desperation to make Vietnam policy work amid this rising tide of war pressures, they thus failed ever to question whether it could work—or at what ultimate price. Their failure recalls the warning of a prescient political scientist, who years before had cautioned against those policymakers with "an infinite capacity for making ends of [their] means."

The decisions of 1964–1965 bespeak a larger and deeper failure as well. Throughout this period—as, indeed, throughout the course of America's Vietnam involvement—U.S. policymakers strove principally to create a viable noncommunist regime in South Vietnam. For many years and at great effort and cost, Washington had endeavored to achieve political stability and competence in Saigon. Despite these efforts, South Vietnam's political disarray persisted and deepened, until, in 1965, America intervened with massive military force to avert its total collapse.

Few policymakers in 1964–1965 paused to mull this telling fact, to ponder its implications about Saigon's viability as a political entity. The failure to reexamine this and other fundamental premises of U.S. policy—chief among them Vietnam's importance to American national interests and Washington's ability to forge political order through military power—proved a costly and tragic lapse of statesmanship. . . .

The legacy of Vietnam, like the war itself, remains a difficult and painful subject for Americans. As passions subside and time bestows greater perspective, Americans still struggle to understand Vietnam's meaning and lessons for the country. They still wonder how the United States found itself ensnared in an ambiguous, costly, and divisive war, and how it can avoid repeating such an ordeal in the future.

The experience of Lyndon Johnson and his advisers during the decisive years 1964–1965 offers much insight into those questions. For their decisions, which fundamentally transformed U.S. participation in the war, both reflected and defined much of the larger history of America's Vietnam involvement.

Their decisions may also, one hopes, yield kernels of wisdom for the future; the past, after all, can teach us lessons. But history's lessons, as Vietnam showed, are themselves dependent on each generation's knowledge and understanding of the past. So it proved for 1960s policymakers, whose ignorance and misperception of Southeast Asian history, culture, and politics pulled America progressively deeper into the war. LBJ, [Secretary of State Dean] Rusk, [Robert] McNamara, [McGeorge] Bundy, [Ambassador Maxwell] Taylor—most of their generation, in fact—mistakenly viewed Vietnam through the simplistic ideological prism of the Cold War. They perceived a deeply complex and ambiguous regional struggle as a grave challenge to world order and stability, fomented by communist China acting through its local surrogate, North Vietnam.

This perception, given their mixture of memories—the West's capitulation to Hitler at Munich, Stalin's postwar truculence, Mao's belligerent rhetoric—appears altogether understandable in retrospect. But it also proved deeply flawed and oblivious to abiding historical realities. Constrained by their memories and ideology, American policymakers neglected the subtle but enduring force of nationalism in Southeast Asia. Powerful and decisive currents—the deep and historic tension between Vietnam and China; regional friction among the Indochinese states of Vietnam, Laos, and Cambodia; and, above all, Hanoi's fanatical will to unification—went unnoticed or unweighed because they failed to fit Washington's worldview. Although it is true, as Secretary of State Rusk once said, that "one cannot escape one's experience," Rusk and his fellow policymakers seriously erred by falling uncritical prisoners of their experience.

Another shared experience plagued 1960s policymakers like a ghost: the ominous specter of McCarthyism. This frightful political memory haunted LBJ and his Democratic colleagues like a barely suppressed demon in the national psyche. Barely ten years removed from the traumatic "loss" of China and its devastating domestic repercussions, Johnson and his advisers remembered its consequences vividly and shuddered at a similar fate in Vietnam. They talked about this only privately, but then with genuine and palpable fear. Defense Secretary McNamara, in a guarded moment, confided to a newsman in the spring of 1965 that U.S. disengagement from South Vietnam threatened "a disastrous political fight that could . . . freeze American political debate and even affect political freedom."

Such fears resonated deeply in policymakers' minds. Nothing, it seemed, could be worse than the "loss" of Vietnam—not even an intensifying stalemate secured at increasing military and political risk. For a President determined to fulfill liberalism's postwar agenda, Truman's ordeal in China seemed a powerfully forbidding lesson. It hung over LBJ in Vietnam like a dark shadow he could not shake, an agony he would not repeat.

McCarthyism's long shadow into the mid-1960s underscores a persistent and troubling phenomenon of postwar American politics: the peculiar vulnerability besetting liberal Presidents thrust into the maelstrom of world politics. In America's postwar political climate—dominated by the culture of anti-communism—Democratic leaders from Truman to Kennedy to Johnson remained acutely sensitive to the domestic repercussions of foreign policy failure. This fear of right-wing reaction sharply inhibited liberals like LBJ, narrowing what they considered their range of politically acceptable options, while diminishing their willingness to disengage from untenable foreign commitments. Thus, when Johnson did confront the bitter choice between defeat in Vietnam and fighting a major, inconclusive war, he reluctantly chose the second because he could not tolerate the domestic consequences of the first. Committed to fulfilling the Great Society, fearful of resurgent McCarthyism, and afraid that disengagement meant sacrificing the former to the latter, LBJ perceived least political danger in holding on.

But if Johnson resigned never to "lose" South Vietnam, he also resigned never to sacrifice his cherished Great Society in the process. LBJ's determination, however understandable, nonetheless led him deliberately and seriously to obscure the nature and cost of America's deepening involvement in the war during 1964–1965. This decision bought Johnson the short-term political maneuverability he wanted, but at a costly long-term political price. As LBJ's credibility on the war subsequently eroded, public confidence in his leadership slowly but irretrievably evaporated. And this, more than any other factor, is what finally drove Johnson from the White House.

It also tarnished the presidency and damaged popular faith in American government for more than a decade. Trapped between deeply conflicting pressures, LBJ never shared his dilemma with the public. Johnson would not, or felt he dare not, trust his problems with the American people. LBJ's decision, however human, tragically undermined the reciprocal faith between President and public indispensable to effective governance in a democracy. Just as tragically, it fostered a pattern of presidential behavior which led his successor, Richard Nixon, to eventual ruin amid even greater popular political alienation.

Time slowly healed most of these wounds to the American political process, while reconfirming the fundamental importance of presidential credibility in a democracy. Johnson's Vietnam travail underscored the necessity of public trust and support to presidential success. Without them, as LBJ painfully discovered, Presidents are doomed to disaster.

Johnson, in retrospect, might have handled his domestic dilemma more forthrightly. An equally serious dilemma, however, remained always beyond his—or Washington's—power to mend: the root problem of political disarray in South Vietnam. The perennial absence of stable and responsive government in Saigon troubled Washington policymakers profoundly; they understood, only too well, its pivotal importance to the war effort and to the social and economic reforms essential to the country's survival. Over and over again, American officials stressed the necessity of political cooperation to their embattled South Vietnamese allies. But to no avail. As one top American in Saigon later lamented, "[Y]ou could tell them all 'you've got to get together [and stop] this haggling and fighting among yourselves,' but how do you make them do it?" he said. "How do you make them do it?"

Washington, alas, could not. As Ambassador Taylor conceded early in the war, "[You] cannot order good government. You can't get it by fiat." This stubborn but telling truth eventually came to haunt Taylor and others. South Vietnam never marshaled the political will necessary to create an effective and enduring government; it never produced leaders addressing the aspirations and thus attracting the allegiance of the South Vietnamese people. Increasing levels of U.S. troops and firepower, moreover, never offset this fundamental debility. America, as a consequence, built its massive military effort on a foundation of political quicksand.

The causes of this elemental flaw lay deeply imbedded in the social and political history of the region. Neither before nor after 1954 was South Vietnam ever really a nation in spirit. Divided by profound ethnic and religious cleavages dating back centuries and perpetuated under French colonial rule, the people of South Vietnam never developed a common political identity. Instead, political factionalism and rivalry always held sway. The result: a chronic and fatal political disorder.

Saigon's fundamental weakness bore anguished witness to the limits of U.S. power. South Vietnam's shortcomings taught a proud and mighty nation that it could not save a people in spite of themselves—that American power, in the last analysis, offered no viable substitute for indigenous political resolve. Without this basic ingredient, as Saigon's turbulent history demonstrated, Washington's most dedicated and strenuous efforts will prove extremely vulnerable, if not futile.

This is not a happy or popular lesson. But it is a wise and prudent one, attuned to the imperfect realities of an imperfect world. One of America's sagest diplomats, George Kennan, understood and articulated this lesson well when he observed: "When it comes to helping people to resist Communist pressures, . . . no assistance . . . can be effective unless the people themselves have a very high degree of determination and a willingness to help themselves. The moment they begin to place the bulk of the burden on us," Kennan warned, "the whole situation is lost." This, tragically, is precisely what befell America in South Vietnam during 1964–1965. Hereafter, as perhaps always before—*external* U.S. economic, military, and political support provided the vital elements of stability and strength in South Vietnam. Without that *external* support, as events following America's long-delayed withdrawal in 1973 showed, South Vietnam's government quickly failed.

Washington's effort to forge political order through military power spawned another tragedy as well. It ignited unexpected pressures which quickly overwhelmed U.S. policymakers, and pulled them ever deeper into the war. LBJ and his advisers began bombing North Vietnam in early 1965 in a desperate attempt to spur political resolve in South Vietnam. But their effort boomeranged wildly. Rather than stabilizing the situation, it instead unleashed forces that soon put Johnson at the mercy of circumstances, a hostage to the war's accelerating momentum. LBJ, as a result, began steering with an ever looser hand. By the summer of 1965, President Johnson found himself not the controller of events but largely controlled by them. He had lost the political leader's "continual struggle," in the words of Henry Kissinger, "to rescue an element of choice from the pressure of circumstance."

LBJ's experience speaks powerfully across the years. With each Vietnam decision, Johnson's vulnerability to military pressure and bureaucratic momentum intensified sharply. Each step generated demands for another, even bigger step—which LBJ found increasingly difficult to resist. His predicament confirmed George Ball's admonition that war is a fiercely unpredictable force, often generating its own inexorable momentum.

Johnson sensed this danger almost intuitively. He quickly grasped the dilemma and difficulties confronting him in Vietnam. But LBJ lacked the inner strength—the security and self-confidence—to overrule the counsel of his inherited advisers.

Most of those advisers, on the other hand—especially McGeorge Bundy and Robert McNamara—failed to anticipate such perils. Imbued with an overweening faith in their ability to "manage" crises and "control" escalation, Bundy and McNamara, along with Maxwell Taylor, first pushed military action against the North as a lever to force political improvement in the South. But bombing did not rectify Saigon's political problems; it only exacerbated them, while igniting turbulent military pressures that rapidly overwhelmed these advisers' confident calculations.

These advisers' preoccupation with technique, with the application of power, characterized much of America's approach to the Vietnam War. Bundy and McNamara epitomized a postwar generation confident in the exercise and efficacy of U.S. power. Despite the dark and troubled history of European intervention in Indochina, these men stubbornly refused to equate America's situation in the mid-1960s to France's earlier ordeal. To them, the United States possessed limitless ability, wisdom, and virtue; it would therefore prevail where other western powers had failed.

This arrogance born of power led policymakers to ignore manifest dangers, to persist in the face of ever darkening circumstances. Like figures in Greek tragedy, pride compelled these supremely confident men further into disaster. They succumbed to the affliction common to great powers throughout the ages—the dangerous "self-esteem engendered by power," as the political philosopher Hans Morgenthau once wrote, "which equates power and virtue, [and] in the process loses all sense of moral and political proportion."

Tradition, as well as personality, nurtured such thinking. For in many ways, America's military intervention in Vietnam represented the logical fulfillment of a policy and outlook axiomatically accepted by U.S. policymakers for nearly two decades—the doctrine of global containment. Fashioned at the outset of the Cold War, global containment extended American interests and obligations across vast new areas of the world in defense against perceived monolithic communist expansion. It remained the lodestar of America foreign policy, moreover, even as the constellation of international forces shifted dramatically amid diffused authority and power among communist states and nationalist upheaval in the post-colonial world.

Vietnam exposed the limitations and contradictions of this static doctrine in a world of flux. It also revealed the dangers and flaws of an undiscriminating, universalist policy which perceptive critics of global containment, such as the eminent journalist Walter Lippmann, had anticipated from the beginning. As Lippmann warned about global containment in 1947:

> Satellite states and puppet governments are not good material out of which to construct unassailable barriers [for American defense]. A diplomatic war conducted as this policy demands, that is to say conducted indirectly, means that we must stake our own security and the peace of the world upon satellites, puppets, clients, agents about whom we can know very little. Frequently they will act for their own reasons, and on their own judgments, presenting us with accomplished facts that we did not intend, and with crises for which we are unready. The "unassailable barriers" will present us with an unending series of insoluble dilemmas. We shall have either to disown our puppets, which would be tantamount to appeasement and defeat and loss of face, or must support them at an incalculable cost. . . .

Here lay the heart of America's Vietnam troubles. Driven by unquestioning allegiance to an ossified and extravagant doctrine, Washington officials plunged deeply into a struggle which itself dramatized the changed realities and complexities of the postwar world. Their action teaches both the importance of re-examining premises as circumstances change and the costly consequences of failing to recognize and adapt to them.

Vietnam represented a failure not just of American foreign policy but also of American statesmanship. For once drawn into the war, LBJ and his advisers quickly sensed Vietnam's immense difficulties and dangers—Saigon's congenital political problems, the war's spiraling military costs, the remote likelihood of victory—and plunged in deeper nonetheless. In their determination to preserve America's international credibility and protect their domestic political standing, they continued down an ever costlier path.

That path proved a distressing, multifaceted paradox. Fearing injury to the perception of American power, diminished faith in U.S. resolve, and a conservative political firestorm, policymakers rigidly pursued a course which ultimately injured the substance of American power by consuming exorbitant lives and resources, shook allied confidence in U.S. strategic judgment, and shattered liberalism's political unity and vigor by polarizing and paralyzing American society.

Herein lies Vietnam's most painful but pressing lesson. Statesmanship requires judgment, sensibility, and, above all, wisdom in foreign affairs—the wisdom to calculate national interests prudently and to balance commitments with effective power. It requires that most difficult task of political leaders: "to distinguish between what is desireable and what is possible, . . . between what is desireable and what is essential."

This is important in peace; it is indispensable in war. As the great tutor of statesmen, Carl von Clausewitz, wrote, "Since war is not an act of senseless passion but is controlled by its political object, the value of this object must determine the sacrifices to be made for it in *magnitude* and also in *duration.* Once the expenditure of effort exceeds the value of the political object," Clausewitz admonished, "the object must be renounced. . . ." His maxim, in hindsight, seems painfully relevant to a war which, as even America's military commander in Vietnam, General William Westmoreland, concluded, "the vital security of the United States was not and possibly could not be clearly demonstrated and understood. . . ."

LBJ and his advisers failed to heed this fundamental principle of statesmanship. They failed to weigh American costs in Vietnam against Vietnam's relative importance to American national interests and its effect on overall American power. Compelled by events in Vietnam and, especially, coercive political pressures at home, they deepened an unsound, peripheral commitment and pursued manifestly unpromising and immensely costly objectives. Their failure of statesmanship, then, proved a failure of judgment and, above all, of proportion.

H. R. McMaster

NO

Dereliction of Duty

The Americanization of the Vietnam War between 1963 and 1965 was the product of an unusual interaction of personalities and circumstances. The escalation of U.S. military intervention grew out of a complicated chain of events and a complex web of decisions that slowly transformed the conflict in Vietnam into an American war.

Much of the literature on Vietnam has argued that the "Cold War mentality" put such pressure on President Johnson that the Americanization of the war was inevitable. The imperative to contain Communism was an important factor in Vietnam policy, but neither American entry into the war nor the manner in which the war was conducted was inevitable. The United States went to war in Vietnam in a manner unique in American history. Vietnam was not forced on the United States by a tidal wave of Cold War ideology. It slunk in on cat's feet.

Between November 1963 and July 1965, LBJ made the critical decisions that took the United States into war almost without realizing it. The decisions, and the way in which he made them, profoundly affected the way the United States fought in Vietnam. Although impersonal forces, such as the ideological imperative of containing Communism, the bureaucratic structure, and institutional priorities, influenced the president's Vietnam decisions, those decisions depended primarily on his character, his motivations, and his relationships with his principal advisers.

Most investigations of how the United States entered the war have devoted little attention to the crucial developments which shaped LBJ's approach to Vietnam and set conditions for a gradual intervention. The first of several "turning points" in the American escalation comprised the near-contemporaneous assassinations of Ngo Dinh Diem and John F. Kennedy. The legacy of the Kennedy administration included an expanded commitment to South Vietnam as an "experiment" in countering Communist insurgencies and a deep distrust of the military that manifested itself in the appointment of officers who would prove supportive of the administration's policies. After November 1963 the United States confronted what in many ways was a new war in South Vietnam. Having deposed the government of Ngo Dinh Diem and his brother Nhu, and having supported actions that led to their deaths, Washington assumed responsibility for the new South Vietnamese leaders. Intensified Viet Cong activity added impetus to U.S. deliberations, leading Johnson and his advisers to conclude that the situation in South Vietnam demanded action beyond military advice and support. Next, in the spring of 1964, the Johnson administration adopted graduated pressure as its strategic concept for the Vietnam War. Rooted in Maxwell Taylor's national security strategy of flexible response, graduated pressure evolved over the next year, becoming the blueprint for the deepening American commitment to maintaining South Vietnam's independence. Then, in August 1964, in response to the Gulf of Tonkin incident, the United States crossed the threshold of direct American military action against North Vietnam.

The Gulf of Tonkin resolution gave the president carte blanche for escalating the war. During the ostensibly benign "holding period" from September 1964 to February 1965, LBJ was preoccupied with his domestic political agenda, and McNamara built consensus behind graduated pressure. In early 1965 the president raised U.S. intervention to a higher level again, deciding on February 9 to begin a systematic program of limited air strikes on targets in North Vietnam and, on February 26, to commit U.S. ground forces to the South. Last, in March 1965, he quietly gave U.S. ground forces the mission of "killing Viet Cong." That series of decisions, none in itself tantamount to a clearly discernable decision to go to war, nevertheless transformed America's commitment in Vietnam.

Viewed together, those decisions might create the impression of a deliberate determination on the part of the Johnson administration to go to war. On the contrary, the president did not want to go to war in Vietnam and was not planning to do so. Indeed, as early as May 1964, LBJ seemed to realize that an American war in Vietnam would be a costly failure. He confided to McGeorge Bundy, " . . . looks like to me that we're getting into another Korea. It just worries the hell out of me. I don't see what we can ever hope to get out of this." It was, Johnson observed, "the biggest damn mess that I ever saw. . . . It's damn easy to get into a war, but . . . it's going to be harder to ever extricate yourself if you get in." Despite his recognition that the situation in Vietnam demanded that he consider alternative courses of action and make a difficult decision, LBJ sought to avoid or to postpone indefinitely an explicit choice between war and disengagement from South Vietnam. In the ensuing months, however, each decision he made moved the United States closer to war, although he seemed not to recognize that fact.

The president's fixation on short-term political goals, combined with his character and the personalities of his principal civilian and military advisers, rendered the administration incapable of dealing adequately with the complexities of the situation in Vietnam. LBJ's advisory system was structured to achieve consensus and to prevent potentially damaging leaks. Profoundly insecure and distrustful of anyone but his closest civilian advisers, the president viewed the JCS [Joint Chiefs of Staff] with suspicion. When the situation in Vietnam seemed to demand military action, Johnson did not turn to his military advisers to determine how to solve the problem. He turned instead to his civilian advisers to determine how to postpone a decision. The relationship between the president, the secretary of defense, and the Joint Chiefs led to the curious situation in which the nation went to war without the benefit of effective military advice from the organization having the statutory responsibility to be the nation's "principal military advisers."

What Johnson feared most in 1964 was losing his chance to win the presidency in his own right. He saw Vietnam principally as a danger to that goal. After the election, he feared that an American military response to the deteriorating situation in Vietnam would jeopardize chances that his Great Society would pass through Congress. The Great Society was to be Lyndon Johnson's great domestic political legacy, and he could not tolerate the risk of its failure. McNamara would help the president first protect his electoral chances and then pass the Great Society by offering a strategy for Vietnam that appeared cheap and could be conducted with minimal public and congressional attention. McNamara's strategy of graduated pressure permitted Johnson to pursue his objective of not losing the war in Vietnam while postponing the "day of reckoning" and keeping the whole question out of public debate all the while.

McNamara was confident in his ability to satisfy the president's needs. He believed fervently that nuclear weapons and the Cold War international political environment had made traditional military experience and thinking not only irrelevant, but often dangerous for contemporary policy. Accordingly, Mc Namara, along with systems analysts and other civilian members of his own department and the Department of State, developed his own strategy for Vietnam. Bolstered by what he regarded as a personal triumph during the Cuban missile crisis, McNamara drew heavily on that experience and applied it to Vietnam. Based on the assumption that carefully controlled and sharply limited military actions were reversible, and therefore could be carried out at minimal risk and cost, graduated pressure allowed McNamara and Johnson to avoid confronting many of the possible consequences of military action.

Johnson and McNamara succeeded in creating the illusion that the decisions to attack North Vietnam were alternatives to war rather than war itself. Graduated pressure defined military action as a form of communication, the object of which was to affect the enemy's calculation of interests and dissuade him from a particular activity. Because the favored means of communication (bombing fixed installations and economic targets) were not appropriate for the mobile forces of the Viet Cong, who lacked an infrastructure and whose strength in the South was political as well as military, McNamara and his colleagues pointed to the infiltration of men and supplies into South Vietnam as proof that the source and center of the enemy's power in Vietnam lay north of the seventeenth parallel, and specifically in Hanoi. Their definition of the enemy's source of strength was derived from that strategy rather than from a critical examination of the full reality in South Vietnam—and turned out to be inaccurate.

Graduated pressure was fundamentally flawed in other ways. The strategy ignored the uncertainty of war and the unpredictable psychology of an activity that involves killing, death, and destruction. To the North Vietnamese, military action, involving as it did attacks on their forces and bombing of their territory, was not simply a means of communication. Human sacrifices in war evoke strong emotions, creating a dynamic that defies systems analysis quantification. Once the United States crossed the threshold of war against North Vietnam with covert raids and the Gulf of Tonkin "reprisals," the future course of events depended not only on decisions made in Washington but also on enemy responses and actions that were unpredictable. McNamara, however, viewed the war as another business management problem that, he assumed, would ultimately succumb to his reasoned judgment and others' rational calculations. He and his assistants thought that they could predict with great precision what amount of force applied in Vietnam would achieve the results they desired and they believed that they could control that force with great precision from halfway around the world. There were compelling contemporaneous arguments that graduated pressure would not affect Hanoi's will sufficiently to convince the North to desist from its support of the South, and that such a strategy would probably lead to an escalation of the war. Others expressed doubts about the utility of attacking North Vietnam by air to win a conflict in South Vietnam. Nevertheless, McNamara refused to consider the consequences of his recommendations and forged ahead oblivious of the human and psychological complexities of war.

Despite their recognition that graduated pressure was fundamentally flawed, the JCS were unable to articulate effectively either their objections or alternatives. Interservice rivalry was a significant impediment. Although differing perspectives were understandable given the Chiefs' long experience in their own services and their need to protect the interests of their services, the president's principal military advisers were obligated by law to render their best advice. The Chiefs' failure to do so, and their willingness to present single-service remedies to a complex military problem, prevented them from developing a comprehensive estimate of the situation or from thinking effectively about strategy.

When it became clear to the Chiefs that they were to have little influence on the policy-making process, they failed to confront the president with their objections to McNamara's approach to the war. Instead they attempted to work within that strategy in order to remove over time the limitations to further action. Unable to develop a strategic alternative to graduated pressure, the Chiefs became fixated on means by which the war could be conducted and pressed for an escalation of the war by degrees. They hoped that graduated pressure would evolve over time into a fundamentally different strategy, more in keeping with their belief in the necessity of greater force and its more resolute application. In so doing, they gave tacit approval to graduated pressure during the critical period in which the president escalated the war. They did not recommend the total force they believed would ultimately be required in Vietnam and accepted a strategy they knew would lead to a large but inadequate commitment of troops, for an extended period of time, with little hope for success.

McNamara and Lyndon Johnson were far from disappointed with the joint Chiefs' failings. Because his priorities were domestic, Johnson had little use for military advice that recommended actions inconsistent with those priorities. McNamara and his assistants in the Department of Defense, on the other hand, were arrogant. They disparaged military advice because they thought that their intelligence and analytical methods could compensate for their lack of military experience and education. Indeed military experience seemed to them a liability because military officers took too narrow a view and based their advice on antiquated notions of war. Geopolitical and technological changes of the last fifteen years, they believed, had rendered advice based on military experience irrelevant and, in fact, dangerous. McNamara's disregard for military experience and for history left him to draw principally on his staff in the Department of Defense and led him to conclude that his only real experience with the planning and direction of military force, the Cuban missile crisis, was the most relevant analogy to Vietnam.

While they slowly deepened American military involvement in Vietnam, Johnson and McNamara pushed the Chiefs further away from the decision-making process. There was no meaningful structure through which the Chiefs could voice their views—even the chairman was not a reliable conduit. NSC meetings were strictly *pro forma* affairs in which the president endeavored to build consensus for decisions already made. Johnson continued Kennedy's practice of meeting with small groups of his most trusted advisers. Indeed he made his most important decisions at the Tuesday lunch meetings in which Rusk, McGeorge Bundy, and McNamara were the only regular participants. The president and McNamara shifted responsibility for real planning away from the JCS to ad hoc committees composed principally of civilian analysts and attorneys, whose main goal was to obtain a consensus consistent with the president's pursuit of the middle ground between disengagement and war. The products of those efforts carried the undeserved credibility of proposals that had been agreed on by all departments and were therefore hard to oppose. McNamara and Johnson endeavored to get the advice they wanted by placing conditions and qualifications on questions that they asked the Chiefs. When the Chiefs' advice was not consistent with his own recommendations, McNamara, with the aid of the chairman of the Joint Chiefs of Staff, lied in meetings of the National Security Council about the Chiefs' views.

Rather than advice McNamara and Johnson extracted from the JCS acquiescence and silent support for decisions already made. Even as they relegated the Chiefs to a peripheral position in the policy-making process, they were careful to preserve the facade of consultation to prevent the JCS from opposing the administration's policies either openly or behind the scenes. As American involvement in the war escalated, Johnson's vulnerability to disaffected senior military officers increased because he was purposely deceiving the Congress and the public about the nature of the American military effort in Vietnam. The president and the secretary of defense deliberately obscured the nature of decisions made and left undefined the limits that they envisioned on the use of force. They indicated to the Chiefs that they would take actions that they never intended to pursue. McNamara and his assistants, who considered communication the purpose of military action, kept the nature of their objective from the JCS, who viewed "winning" as the only viable goal in war. Finally, Johnson appealed directly to them, referring to himself as the "coach" and them as "his team." To dampen their calls for further action, Lyndon Johnson attempted to generate sympathy from the JCS for the great pressures that he was feeling from those who opposed escalation.

The ultimate test of the Chiefs' loyalty came in July 1965. The administration's lies to the American public had grown in magnitude as the American military effort in Vietnam escalated. The president's plan of deception depended on tacit approval or silence from the JCS. LBJ had misrepresented the mission of U.S. ground forces in Vietnam, distorted the views of the Chiefs to lend credibility to his decision against mobilization, grossly understated the numbers of troops General Westmoreland had requested, and lied to the Congress about the monetary cost of actions already approved and of those awaiting final decision. The Chiefs did not disappoint the president. In the days before the president made his duplicitous public announcement concerning Westmoreland's request, the Chiefs, with the exception of commandant of the Marine Corps Greene, withheld from congressmen their estimates of the amount of force that would be needed in Vietnam. As he had during the Gulf of Tonkin hearings, Wheeler lent his support to the president's deception of Congress. The "five silent men" on the Joint Chiefs made possible the way the United States went to war in Vietnam.

Several factors kept the Chiefs from challenging the president's subterfuges. The professional code of the military officer prohibits him or her from engaging in political activity. Actions that could have undermined the administration's credibility and derailed its Vietnam policy could not have been undertaken lightly. The Chiefs felt loyalty to their commander in chief. The Truman-MacArthur controversy during the Korean War had warned the Chiefs about the dangers of overstepping the bounds of civilian control. Loyalty to their services also weighed against opposing the president and the secretary of defense. Harold Johnson, for example, decided against resignation because he thought he had to remain in office to protect the Army's interests as best he could. Admiral McDonald and Marine Corps Commandant Greene compromised their views on Vietnam in exchange for concessions to their respective services. Greene achieved a dramatic expansion of the Marine Corps, and McDonald ensured that the Navy retained control of Pacific Command. None of the Chiefs had sworn an oath to his service, however. They had all sworn, rather, to "support and defend the Constitution of the United States."

General Greene recalled that direct requests by congressmen for his assessment put him in a difficult situation. The president was lying, and he expected the Chiefs to lie as well or, at least, to withhold the whole truth. Although the president should not have placed the Chiefs in that position, the flag officers should not have tolerated it when he had.

Because the Constitution locates civilian control of the military in Congress as well as in the executive branch, the Chiefs could not have been justified in deceiving the peoples' representatives about Vietnam. Wheeler in particular allowed his duty to the president to overwhelm his obligations under the Constitution. As cadets are taught at the United States Military Academy, the JCS relationship with the Congress is challenging and demands that military officers possess a strong character and keen intellect. While the Chiefs must present Congress with their best advice based on their professional experience and education, they must be careful not to undermine their credibility by crossing the line between advice and advocacy of service interests.

Maxwell Taylor had a profound influence on the nature of the civil-military relationship during the escalation of American involvement in Vietnam. In contrast to Army Chief of Staff George C. Marshall, who, at the start of World War II, recognized the need for the JCS to suppress service parochialism to provide advice consistent with national interests, Taylor exacerbated service differences to help McNamara and Johnson keep the Chiefs divided and, thus, marginal to the policy process. Taylor recommended men for appointment to the JCS who were less likely than their predecessors to challenge the direction of the administration's military policy, even when they knew that that policy was fundamentally flawed. Taylor's behavior is perhaps best explained by his close personal friendship with the Kennedy family; McNamara; and, later, Johnson. In contrast again to Marshall, who thought it important to keep a professional distance from President Franklin Roosevelt, Taylor abandoned an earlier view similar to Marshall's in favor of a belief that the JCS and the president should enjoy "an intimate, easy relationship, born of friendship and mutual regard."

The way in which the United States went to war in the period between November 1963 and July 1965 had, not surprisingly, a profound influence on the conduct of the war and on its outcome. Because Vietnam policy decisions were made based on domestic political expediency, and because the president was intent on forging a consensus position behind what he believed was a middle policy, the administration deliberately avoided clarifying its policy objectives and postponed discussing the level of force that the president was willing to commit to the effort. Indeed, because the president was seeking domestic political consensus, members of the administration believed that ambiguity in the objectives for fighting in Vietnam was a strength rather than a weakness. Determined to prevent dissent from the JCS, the administration concealed its development of "fall-back" objectives.

Over time the maintenance of U.S. credibility quietly supplanted the stated policy objective of a free and independent South Vietnam. The principal civilian planners had determined that to guarantee American credibility, it was not necessary to win in Vietnam. That conclusion, combined with the belief that the use of force was merely another form of diplomatic communication, directed the military effort in the South at achieving stalemate rather than victory. Those charged with planning the war believed that it would be possible to preserve American credibility even if the United States armed forces withdrew from the South, after a show of force against the North and in the South in which American forces were "bloodied." After the United States became committed to war, however, and more American soldiers, airmen, and Marines had died in the conflict, it would become impossible simply to disengage and declare America's credibility intact, a fact that should have been foreseen. The Chiefs sensed the shift in objectives, but did not challenge directly the views of civilian planners in that connection. McNamara and Johnson recognized that, once committed to war, the JCS would not agree to an objective other than imposing a solution on the enemy consistent with U.S. interests. The JCS deliberately avoided clarifying the objective as well. As a result, when the United States went to war, the JCS pursued objectives different from those of the president. When the Chiefs requested permission to apply force consistent with their conception of U.S. objectives, the president and McNamara, based on their goals and domestic political constraints, rejected JCS requests, or granted them only in part. The result was that the JCS and McNamara became fixated on the means rather than on the ends, and on the manner in which the war was conducted instead of a military strategy that could connect military actions to achievable policy goals.

Because forthright communication between top civilian and military officials in the Johnson administration was never developed, there was no reconciliation of McNamara's intention to limit the American military effort sharply and the Chiefs' assessment that the United States could not possibly win under such conditions. If they had attempted to reconcile those positions, they could not have helped but recognize the futility of the American war effort.

The Joint Chiefs of Staff became accomplices in the president's deception and focused on a tactical task, killing the enemy. General Westmoreland's "strategy" of attrition in South Vietnam, was, in essence, the absence of a strategy. The result was military activity (bombing North Vietnam and killing the enemy in South Vietnam) that did not aim to achieve a clearly defined objective. It was unclear how quantitative measures by which McNamara interpreted the success and failure of the use of military force were contributing to an end of the war. As American casualties mounted and the futility of the strategy became apparent, the American public lost faith in the effort. The Chiefs did not request the number of troops they believed necessary to impose a military solution in South Vietnam until after the Tet offensive in 1968. By that time, however, the president was besieged by opposition to the war and was unable even to consider the request. LBJ, who had gone to such great lengths to ensure a crushing defeat over Barry Goldwater in 1964, declared that he was withdrawing from the race for his party's presidential nomination.

Johnson thought that he would be able to control the U.S. involvement in Vietnam. That belief, based on the strategy of graduated pressure and McNamara's confident assurances, proved in dramatic fashion to be false. If the president was surprised by the consequences of his decisions between November 1963 and July 1965, he should not have been so. He had disregarded the advice he did not want to hear in favor of a policy based on the pursuit of his own political fortunes and his beloved domestic programs.

The war in Vietnam was not lost in the field, nor was it lost on the front pages of the *New York Times* or on the college campuses. It was lost in Washington, D.C., even before Americans assumed sole responsibility for the fighting in 1965 and before they realized the country was at war; indeed, even before the first American units were deployed. The disaster in Vietnam was not the result of impersonal forces but a uniquely human failure, the responsibility for which was shared by President Johnson and his principal military and civilian advisers. The failings were many and reinforcing: arrogance, weakness, lying in the pursuit of self-interest, and, above all, the abdication of responsibility to the American people.

POSTSCRIPT

Was America's Escalation of the War in Vietnam Inevitable?

The book from which VanDeMark's selection was excerpted is a detailed study of the circumstances surrounding the decisions that President Lyndon Johnson made to increase America's presence in Vietnam via the bombing raids of North Vietnam in February 1965 and the introduction of ground troops the following July. VanDeMark agrees with McMaster that Johnson did not consult the Joint Chiefs of Staff about the wisdom of escalating the war. In fact, Johnson's decisions of "graduated pressure" were made in increments by the civilian advisers surrounding Secretary of Defense Robert McNamara. The policy, if it can be called such, was to prevent the National Liberation Front and its Viet Cong army from taking over South Vietnam. Each service branch fought its own war without coordinating with one another or with the government of South Vietnam. In VanDeMark's view, U.S. intervention was doomed to failure because South Vietnam was an artificial and very corrupt nation-state created by the French and later supported by the Americans. It was unfortunate that the nationalist revolution was tied up with the Communists led by Ho Chi Minh, who had been fighting French colonialism and Japanese imperialism since the 1920s—unlike Korea and Malaysia, which had alternative, noncommunist, nationalist movements.

Why did Johnson plunge "into the quagmire"? For one thing, Johnson remembered how previous democratic presidents Franklin D. Roosevelt and Harry S. Truman had been charged with being soft on communism and accused of losing Eastern Europe to the Russians after the Second World War and China to the Communists in the Chinese Civil War in 1949. In addition, both presidents were charged by Senator Joseph McCarthy and others of harboring Communists in U.S. government agencies. If Johnson was tough in Vietnam, he could stop communist aggression. At the same time, he could ensure that his Great Society social programs of Medicare and job retraining, as well as the impending civil rights legislation, would be passed by Congress.

As an army officer who fought in the Persian Gulf War, McMaster offers a unique perspective on the decision-making processes used by government policymakers. McMaster spares no one in his critique of what he considers the flawed Vietnam policy of "graduated pressure." He says that McNamara, bolstered by the success of America during the Cuban Missile Crisis, believed that the traditional methods of fighting wars were obsolete. Johnson believed in McNamara's approach, and the president's own need for consensus in the decision-making process kept the Joint Chiefs of Staff out of the loop.

Unlike other military historians, who generally absolve the military from responsibility for the strategy employed during the war, McMaster argues that the Joint Chiefs of Staff were responsible for not standing up to Johnson and telling him that his military strategy was seriously flawed. McMaster's views are not as new as some reviewers of his book seem to think. Bruce Palmer, Jr., in *The Twenty-Five Year War: America's Military Role in Vietnam* (University Press of Kentucky, 1984), and Harry G. Summers, Jr., in *On Strategy: A Critical Analysis of the Vietnam War* (Presidio Press, 1982), also see a flawed strategy of war. Summers argues that Johnson should have asked Congress for a declaration of war and fought a conventional war against North Vietnam.

One scholar has claimed that over 7,000 books about the Vietnam War have been published. The starting point for the current issue is Lloyd Gardner and Ted Gittinger, eds., *Vietnam: The Early Decisions* (University of Texas Press, 1997). See also Larry Berman, *Planning a Tragedy: The Americanization of the War in Vietnam* (W. W. Norton, 1982) and *Lyndon Johnson's War* (W. W. Norton, 1989); David Halberstam, *The Best and the Brightest* (Random House, 1972); and Lloyd C. Gardner, *Pay Any Price: Lyndon Johnson and the Wars for Vietnam* (Ivan R. Dee, 1995). Primary sources can be found in the U.S. Department of State's two-volume *Foreign Relations of the United States, 1964–1968: Vietnam* (Government Printing Office, 1996) and in the relevant sections of one of the most useful collections of primary sources and essays, *Major Problems in the History of the Vietnam War,* 2d ed., by Robert J. McMahon (Houghton Mifflin, 2000).

The bureaucratic perspective can be found in a series of essays by George C. Herring entitled *LBJ and Vietnam: A Different Kind of War* (University of Texas Press, 1995). Herring is also the author of the widely used text *America's Longest War: the United States and Vietnam* (Alfred A. Knopf, 1986). A brilliant article often found in anthologies is by historian and former policymaker James C. Thomson, Jr., "How Could Vietnam Happen? An Autopsy," *The Atlantic Monthly* (April 1968). An interesting comparison of the 1954 Dien Bien Phu and 1965 U.S. escalation decisions is Fred I. Greenstein and John P. Burke, "The Dynamics of Presidential Reality Testing: Evidence From Two Vietnam Decisions," *Political Science Quarterly* (Winter 1989–1990). A nice review essay on Vietnam's impact on today's military thinking is Michael C. Desch's "Wounded Warriors and the Lessons of Vietnam," *Orbis* (Summer 1998).

ISSUE 13

Has the Women's Liberation Movement Been Harmful to American Women?

YES: F. Carolyn Graglia, from *Domestic Tranquility: A Brief Against Feminism* (Spence, 1998)

NO: Sara M. Evans, from "American Women in the Twentieth Century," in Harvard Sitkoff, ed., *Perspectives on Modern America: Making Sense of the Twentieth Century* (Oxford University Press, 2001)

ISSUE SUMMARY

YES: Writer and lecturer F. Carolyn Graglia argues that women should stay at home and practice the values of "true motherhood" because contemporary feminists have discredited marriage, devalued traditional homemaking, and encouraged sexual promiscuity.

NO: According to Professor Sara M. Evans, despite class, racial, religious, ethnic and regional differences, women in America experienced major transformations in their private and public lives in the twentieth century.

In 1961, President John F. Kennedy established the Commission on the Status of Women to examine "the prejudice and outmoded customs that act as barriers to the full realization of women's basic rights." Two years later, Betty Friedan, a closet leftist from suburban Rockland County, New York, wrote about the growing malaise of the suburban housewife in her best-seller *The Feminist Mystique* (W.W. Norton, 1963).

The roots of Friedan's "feminine mystique" go back much earlier than the post–World War II "baby boom" generation of suburban America. Women historians have traced the origins of the modern family to the early nineteenth century. As the nation became more stable politically, the roles of men, women, and children became segmented in ways that still exist today. Dad went to work, the kids went to school, and Mom stayed home. Women's magazines, gift books, and the religious literature of the period ascribed to these women a role that Professor Barbara Welter has called the "Cult of True

Womanhood." She describes the ideal woman as upholding four virtues—piety, purity, submissiveness, and domesticity.

In nineteenth-century America, most middle-class white women stayed home. Those who entered the workforce as teachers or became reformers were usually extending the values of the Cult of True Womanhood to the outside world. This was true of the women reformers in the Second Great Awakening and the peace, temperance, and abolitionist movements before the Civil War. The first real challenge to the traditional values system occurred when a handful of women showed up at Seneca Falls, New York, in 1848 to sign the Women's Declaration of Rights.

It soon became clear that if they were going to pass reform laws, women would have to obtain the right to vote. After an intense struggle, the Nineteenth Amendment was ratified on August 26, 1920. Once the women's movement obtained the vote, there was no agreement on future goals. The problems of the Great Depression and World War II overrode women's issues.

World War II brought about major changes for working women. Six million women entered the labor force for the first time, many of whom were married. "The proportion of women in the labor force," writes Lois Banner, "increased from 25 percent in 1940 to 36 percent in 1945. This increase was greater than that of the previous four decades combined." Many women moved into high-paying, traditionally men's jobs as policewomen, firefighters, and precision toolmakers. Steel and auto companies that converted over to wartime production made sure that lighter tools were made for women to use on the assembly lines. The federal government also erected federal childcare facilities.

When the war ended in 1945, many of these women lost their nontraditional jobs. The federal day-care program was eliminated, and the government told women to go home even though a 1944 study by the Women's Bureau concluded that 80 percent of working women wanted to continue in their jobs after the war.

Most history texts emphasize that women did return home, moved to the suburbs, and created a baby boom generation, which reversed the downward size of families in the years from 1946 to 1964. What is lost in this description is the fact that after 1947 the number of working women again began to rise, reaching 31 percent in 1951. Twenty-two years later, at the height of the women's liberation movement, it reached 42 percent.

When Friedan wrote *The Feminine Mystique* in 1963, both working-class and middle-class college-educated women experienced discrimination in the marketplace. When women worked, they were expected to become teachers, nurses, secretaries, and airline stewardesses—the lowest-paying jobs in the workforce. In the turbulent 1960s, this situation was no longer accepted.

In the following selection, F. Carolyn Graglia defends the traditional role of women in contemporary America. Women, she contends, should stay at home and practice the values of "true womanhood." Contemporary feminists, she argues, have devalued traditional homemaking, encouraged sexual promiscuity, and discredited marriage as a career for women. In the second selection, Sara M. Evans argues that in spite of class, racial, religious, ethnic, and regional differences, women in America experienced major transformations in their private and public lives in the twentieth century.

YES

F. Carolyn Graglia

Domestic Tranquility

Introduction

Since the late 1960s, feminists have very successfully waged war against the traditional family, in which husbands are the principal breadwinners and wives are primarily homemakers. This war's immediate purpose has been to undermine the homemaker's position within both her family and society in order to drive her into the work force. Its long-term goal is to create a society in which women behave as much like men as possible, devoting as much time and energy to the pursuit of a career as men do, so that women will eventually hold equal political and economic power with men. . . .

Feminists have used a variety of methods to achieve their goal. They have promoted a sexual revolution that encouraged women to mimic male sexual promiscuity. They have supported the enactment of no-fault divorce laws that have undermined housewives' social and economic security. And they obtained the application of affirmative action requirements to women as a class, gaining educational and job preferences for women and undermining the ability of men who are victimized by this discrimination to function as family breadwinners.

A crucial weapon in feminism's arsenal has been the status degradation of the housewife's role. From the journalistic attacks of Betty Friedan and Gloria Steinem to Jessie Bernard's sociological writings, all branches of feminism are united in the conviction that a woman can find identity and fulfillment only in a career. The housewife, feminists agree, was properly characterized by Simone de Beauvoir and Betty Friedan as a "parasite," a being something less than human, living her life without using her adult capabilities or intelligence, and lacking any real purpose in devoting herself to children, husband, and home.

Operating on the twin assumptions that equality means sameness (that is, men and women cannot be equals unless they do the same things) and that most differences between the sexes are culturally imposed, contemporary feminism has undertaken its own cultural impositions. Revealing their totalitarian belief that they know best how others should live and their totalitarian willingness to force others to conform to their dogma, feminists have sought to modify our social institutions in order to create an androgynous society in which male and female roles are as identical as possible. The results of the feminist juggernaut now engulf us. By almost all indicia of well-being, the institution of the American family has become significantly less healthy than it was thirty years ago.

Certainly, feminism is not alone responsible for our families' sufferings. As Charles Murray details in *Losing Ground,* President Lyndon Johnson's Great Society programs, for example, have often hurt families, particularly black families, and these programs were supported by a large constituency beyond the women's movement. What distinguishes the women's movement, however, is the fact that, despite the pro-family motives it sometimes ascribes to itself, it has actively sought the traditional family's destruction. In its avowed aims and the programs it promotes, the movement has adopted Kate Millett's goal, set forth in her *Sexual Politics,* in which she endorses Friedrich Engels's conclusion that "the family, as that term is presently understood, must go"; "a kind fate," she remarks, in "view of the institution's history." This goal has never changed: feminists view traditional nuclear families as inconsistent with feminism's commitment to women's independence and sexual freedom.

Emerging as a revitalized movement in the 1960s, feminism reflected women's social discontent, which had arisen in response to the decline of the male breadwinner ethic and to the perception—heralded in Philip Wylie's 1940s castigation of the evil "mom"—that Western society does not value highly the roles of wife and mother. Women's dissatisfactions, nevertheless, have often been aggravated rather than alleviated by the feminist reaction. To mitigate their discontent, feminists argued, women should pattern their lives after men's, engaging in casual sexual intercourse on the same terms as sexually predatory males and making the same career commitments as men. In pursuit of these objectives, feminists have fought unceasingly for the ready availability of legal abortion and consistently derogated both motherhood and the worth of full-time homemakers. Feminism's sexual teachings have been less consistent, ranging from its early and enthusiastic embrace of the sexual revolution to a significant backlash against female sexual promiscuity, which has led some feminists to urge women to abandon heterosexual sexual intercourse altogether.

Contemporary feminism has been remarkably successful in bringing about the institutionalization in our society of the two beliefs underlying its offensive: denial of the social worth of traditional homemakers and rejection of traditional sexual morality. The consequences have been pernicious and enduring. General societal assent to these beliefs has profoundly distorted men's perceptions of their relationships with and obligations to women, women's perceptions of their own needs, and the way in which women make decisions about their lives.

Traditional Homemaking Devalued

The first prong of contemporary feminism's offensive has been to convince society that a woman's full-time commitment to cultivating her marriage and rearing her children is an unworthy endeavor. Women, assert feminists, should treat marriage and children as relatively independent appendages to their life of full-time involvement in the workplace. To live what feminists assure her is the only life worthy of respect, a woman must devote the vast bulk of her time and energy to market production, at the expense of marriage and children. Children, she is told, are better cared for by surrogates, and marriage, as these feminists perceive it, neither deserves nor requires much attention; indeed, the very idea of a woman's "cultivating" her marriage seems ludicrous. Thus spurred on by the women's movement, many women have sought to become male clones.

But some feminists have appeared to modify the feminist message; voices—supposedly of moderation—have argued that women really are different from men. In this they are surely right: there are fundamental differences between the average man and woman, and it is appropriate to take account of these differences when making decisions both in our individual lives and with respect to social issues. Yet the new feminist voices have not conceded that acknowledged differences between the sexes are grounds for reexamining women's flight from home into workplace. Instead, these new voices have argued only that these differences require modification of the terms under which women undertake to reconstruct their lives in accordance with the blueprint designed by so-called early radicals. The edifice erected by radical feminism is to remain intact, subject only to some redecorating. The foundation of this edifice is still the destruction of the traditional family. Feminism has acquiesced in women's desire to bear children (an activity some of the early radicals discouraged). But it continues steadfast in its assumption that, after some period of maternity leave, daily care of those children is properly the domain of institutions and paid employees. The yearnings manifested in women's palpable desire for children should largely be sated, the new voices tell us, by the act of serving as a birth canal and then spending so-called quality time with the child before and after a full day's work.

Any mother, in this view, may happily consign to surrogates most of the remaining aspects of her role, assured that doing so will impose no hardship or loss on either mother or child. To those women whose natures make them less suited to striving in the workplace than concentrating on husband, children, and home, this feminist diktat denies the happiness and contentment they could have found within the domestic arena. In the world formed by contemporary feminism, these women will have status and respect only if they force themselves to take up roles in the workplace they suspect are not most deserving of their attention. Relegated to the periphery of their lives are the home and personal relationships with husband and children that they sense merit their central concern.

Inherent in the feminist argument is an extraordinary contradiction. Feminists deny, on the one hand, that the dimension of female sexuality which engenders women's yearning for children can also make it appropriate and satisfying for a woman to devote herself to domestic endeavors and provide her children's full-time care. On the other hand, they plead the fact of sexual difference to justify campaigns to modify workplaces in order to correct the effects of male influence and alleged biases. Only after such modifications, claim feminists, can women's nurturing attributes and other female qualities be adequately expressed in and truly influence the workplace. Manifestations of these female qualities, feminists argue, should and can occur in the workplace once it has been modified to blunt the substantial impact of male aggression and competitiveness and take account of women's special requirements.

Having launched its movement claiming the right of women—a right allegedly denied them previously—to enter the workplace on an *equal* basis with men, feminism then escalated its demands by arguing that female differences require numerous changes in the workplace. Women, in this view, are insufficiently feminine to find satisfaction in rearing their own children but too feminine to compete on an equal basis with men. Thus, having taken women out of their homes and settled them in the workplace, feminists have sought to reconstruct workplaces to create "feminist playpens" that are conducive to female qualities of sensitivity, caring, and empathy. Through this exercise in self-contradiction, contemporary feminism has endeavored to remove the woman from her home and role of providing daily care to her children—the quintessential place and activity for most effectively expressing her feminine, nurturing attributes.

The qualities that are the most likely to make women good mothers are thus redeployed away from their children and into workplaces that must be restructured to accommodate them. The irony is twofold. Children—the ones who could benefit most from the attentions of those mothers who do possess these womanly qualities—are deprived of those attentions and left only with the hope of finding adequate replacement for their loss. Moreover, the occupations in which these qualities are now to find expression either do not require them for optimal job performance (often they are not conducive to professional success) or were long ago recognized as women's occupations—as in the field of nursing, for example—in which nurturing abilities do enhance job performance.

Traditional Sexual Morality Traduced

The second prong of contemporary feminism's offensive has been to encourage women to ape male sexual patterns and engage in promiscuous sexual intercourse as freely as men. Initially, feminists were among the most dedicated supporters of the sexual revolution, viewing female participation in casual sexual activity as an unmistakable declaration of female equality with males. The women in our society who acted upon the teachings of feminist sexual revolutionaries have suffered greatly. They are victims of the highest abortion rate in the Western world. More than one in five Americans is now infected with a viral sexually transmitted disease which at best can be controlled but not cured and is often chronic. Sexually transmitted diseases, both viral and bacterial, disproportionately affect women because, showing fewer symptoms, they often go untreated for a longer time. These diseases also lead to pelvic infections that cause infertility in 100,000 to 150,000 women each year.

The sexual revolution feminists have promoted rests on an assumption that an act of sexual intercourse involves nothing but a pleasurable physical sensation, possessing no symbolic meaning and no moral dimension. This is an understanding of sexuality that bears more than a slight resemblance to sex as depicted in pornography: physical sexual acts without emotional involvement. In addition to the physical harm caused by increased sexual promiscuity, the denial that sexual intercourse has symbolic importance within a framework of moral accountability corrupts the nature of the sex act. Such denial necessarily makes sexual intercourse a trivial event, compromising the act's ability to fulfill its most important function after procreation. This function is to bridge the gap between males and females who often seem separated by so many differences, both biological and emotional, that they feel scarcely capable of understanding or communicating with each other.

Because of the urgency of sexual desire, especially in the male, it is through sexual contact that men and women can most easily come together. Defining the nature of sexual intercourse in terms informed by its procreative potentialities makes the act a spiritually meaningful event of overwhelming importance. A sexual encounter so defined is imbued with the significance conferred by its connection with a promise of immortality through procreation, whether that connection is a present possibility, a remembrance of children already borne, or simply an acknowledgment of the reality and truth of the promise. Such a sex act can serve as the physical meeting ground on which, by accepting and affirming each other through their bodies' physical unity, men and women can begin to construct an enduring emotional unity. The sexual encounter cannot perform its function when it is viewed as a trivial event of moral indifference with no purpose or meaning other than producing a physical sensation through the friction of bodily parts.

The feminist sexual perspective deprives the sex act of the spiritual meaningfulness that can make it the binding force upon which man and woman can construct a lasting marital relationship. The morally indifferent sexuality championed by the sexual revolution substitutes the sex without emotions that characterizes pornography for the sex of a committed, loving relationship that satisfies women's longing for romance and connection. But this is not the only damage to relationships between men and women that follows from feminism's determination to promote an androgynous society by convincing men and women that they are virtually fungible. Sexual equivalency, feminists believe, requires that women not only engage in casual sexual intercourse as freely as men, but also that women mimic male behavior by becoming equally assertive in initiating sexual encounters and in their activity throughout the encounter. With this sexual prescription, feminists mock the essence of conjugal sexuality that is at the foundation of traditional marriage.

Marriage as a Woman's Career Discredited

Even academic feminists who are considered "moderates" endorse doctrines most inimical to the homemaker. Thus, Professor Elizabeth Fox-Genovese, regarded as a moderate in Women's Studies, tells us that marriage can no longer be a viable career for women. But if marriage cannot be a woman's career, then despite feminist avowals of favoring choice in this matter, homemaking cannot be a woman's goal, and surrogate child-rearing must be her child's destiny. Contrary to feminist claims, society's barriers are not strung tightly to inhibit women's career choices. Because of feminism's very successful efforts, society encourages women to pursue careers, while stigmatizing and preventing their devotion to child-rearing and domesticity.

It was precisely upon the conclusion that marriage cannot be a viable career for women that *Time* magazine rested its Fall 1990 special issue on "Women: The Road Ahead," a survey of contemporary women's lives. While noting that the "cozy, limited roles of the past are still clearly remembered, sometimes fondly," during the past thirty years "all that was orthodox has become negotiable." One thing negotiated away has been the economic security of the homemaker, and *Time* advised young women that "the job of full-time homemaker may be the riskiest profession to choose" because "the advent of no-fault and equitable-distribution divorce laws" reflect, in the words of one judge, the fact that "[s]ociety no longer believes that a husband should support his wife."

No-fault divorce laws did not, however, result from an edict of the gods or some force of nature, but from sustained political efforts, particularly by the feminist movement. As a cornerstone of their drive to make women exchange home for workplace, and thereby secure their independence from men, the availability of no-fault divorce (like the availability of abortion) was sacrosanct to the movement. *Time* shed crocodile tears for displaced homemakers, for it made clear that women must canter down the road ahead with the spur of no-fault divorce urging them into the workplace. Of all *Time*'s recommendations for ameliorating women's lot, divorce reform—the most crying need in our country today—was not among them. Whatever hardships may be endured by women who would resist a divorce, *Time*'s allegiance, like that of most feminists, is clearly to the divorce-seekers who, it was pleased to note, will not be hindered in their pursuit of self-realization by the barriers to divorce that their own mothers had faced.

These barriers to divorce which had impeded their own parents, however, had usually benefited these young women by helping to preserve their parents' marriage. A five-year study of children in divorcing families disclosed that "the overwhelming majority preferred the unhappy marriage to the divorce," and many of them, "despite the unhappiness of their parents, were in fact relatively happy and considered their situation neither better nor worse than that of other families around them." A follow-up study after ten years demonstrated that children experienced the trauma of their parents' divorce as more serious and long-lasting than any researchers had anticipated. *Time* so readily acquiesced in the disadvantaging of homemakers and the disruption of children's lives because the feminist ideological parameters within which it operates have excluded marriage as a *proper* career choice. Removing the obstacles to making it a *viable* choice would, therefore, be an undesirable subversion of feminist goals.

That *Time* would have women trot forward on life's journey constrained by the blinders of feminist ideology is evident from its failure to question any feminist notion, no matter how silly, or to explore solutions incompatible with the ideology's script. One of the silliest notions *Time* left unexamined was that young women want "good careers, good marriages and two or three kids, and they don't want the children to be raised by strangers." The supposed realism of this expectation lay in the new woman's attitude that "I don't want to work 70 hours a week, but I want to be vice president, and *you* have to change." But even if thirty hours were cut from that seventy-hour workweek, the new woman would still be working the normal full-time week, her children would still be raised by surrogates, and the norm would continue to be the feminist version of child-rearing that *Time* itself described unflatteringly as "less a preoccupation than an improvisation."

The illusion that a woman can achieve career success without sacrificing the daily personal care of her children—and except among the very wealthy, most of her leisure as well—went unquestioned by *Time*. It did note, however, the dissatisfaction expressed by Eastern European and Russian women who had experienced as a matter of government policy the same liberation from home and children that our feminists have undertaken to bestow upon Western women. In what *Time* described as "a curious reversal of Western feminism's emphasis on careers for women," the new female leaders of Eastern Europe would like "to reverse the communist diktat that all women have to work." Women have "dreamed," said the Polish Minister of Culture and Arts, "of reaching the point where we have the choice to stay home" that communism had taken away. But blinded by its feminist bias, *Time* could only find it "curious" that women would choose to stay at home; apparently beyond the pale of respectability was any argument that it would serve Western women's interest to retain the choice that contemporary feminism—filling in the West the role of communism in the East—has sought to deny them.

Now was its feminist bias shaken by the attitudes of Japanese women, most of whom, *Time* noted, reject "equality" with men, choosing to cease work after the birth of a first child and later resuming a part-time career or pursuing hobbies or community work. The picture painted was that of the 1950s American suburban housewife reviled by Betty Friedan, except that the American has enjoyed a higher standard of living (particularly a much larger home) than has the Japanese. In Japan, *Time* observed, being "a housewife is nothing to be ashamed of." Dishonoring the housewife's role was a goal, it might have added, that Japanese feminists can, in time, accomplish if they emulate their American counterparts.

Japanese wives have broad responsibilities, commented *Time,* because most husbands leave their salaries and children entirely in wives' hands; freed from drudgery by modern appliances, housewives can "pursue their interests in a carefree manner, while men have to worry about supporting their wives and children." Typically, a Japanese wife controls household finances, giving her husband a cash allowance, the size of which, apparently, dissatisfies one-half of the men. Acknowledging that Japanese wives take the leadership in most homes, one husband observed that "[t]hings go best when the husband is swimming in the palm of his wife's hand." A home is well-managed, said one wife, "if you make your men feel that they're in control when they are in front of others, while in reality you're in control." It seems like a good arrangement to me.

Instead of inquiring whether a similar carefree existence might appeal to some American women, *Time* looked forward to the day when marriage would no longer be a career for Japanese women, as their men took over household and child-rearing chores, enabling wives to join husbands in the workplace. It was noted, however, that a major impediment to this goal, which would have to be corrected, was the fact that Japanese day-care centers usually run for only eight hours a day. Thus, *Time* made clear that its overriding concern was simply promoting the presence of women in the work force. This presence is seen as a good *per se,* without any *pro forma* talk about the economic necessity of a second income and without any question raised as to whether it is in children's interest to spend any amount of time—much less in excess of eight hours a day—in communal care. . . .

The Awakened Brünnhilde

. . . Those who would defend anti-feminist traditionalism today are like heretics fighting a regnant Inquisition. To become a homemaker, a woman may need the courage of a heretic. This is one reason that the defense of traditional women is often grounded in religious teachings, for the heretic's courage usually rests on faith. The source of courage I offer is the conviction, based on my own experience, that contemporary feminism's stereotypical caricature of the housewife did not reflect reality when Friedan popularized it, does not reflect reality today, and need not govern reality.

Feminists claimed a woman can find identity and fulfillment only in a career; they are wrong. They claimed a woman can, in that popular expression, "have it all"; they are wrong—she can have only some. The experience of being a mother at home is a different experience from being a full-time market producer who is also a mother. A woman can have one or the other experience, but not both at the same time. Combining a career with motherhood requires a woman to compromise by diminishing her commitment and exertions with respect to one role or the other, or usually, to both. Rarely, if ever, can a woman adequately perform in a full-time career if she diminishes her commitment to it sufficiently to replicate the experience of being a mother at home.

Women were *never* told they could *not* choose to make the compromises required to combine these roles; within the memory of all living today there were always some women who did so choose. But by successfully degrading the housewife's role, contemporary feminism undertook to force this choice upon all women. I declined to make the compromises necessary to combine a career with motherhood because I did not want to become like Andrea Dworkin's spiritual virgin. I did not want to keep my being intact, as Dworkin puts it, so that I could continue to pursue career success. Such pursuit would have required me to hold too much of myself aloof from husband and children: the invisible "wedge-shaped core of darkness" that Virginia Woolf described as being oneself would have to be too large, and not enough of me would have been left over for them.

I feared that if I cultivated that "wedge-shaped core of darkness" within myself enough to maintain a successful career, I would be consumed by that career, and that thus desiccated, too little of me would remain to flesh out my roles as wife and mother. Giving most of myself to the market seemed less appropriate and attractive than reserving myself for my family. Reinforcing this decision was my experience that when a woman lives too much in her mind, she finds it increasingly difficult to live through her body. Her nurturing ties to her children become attenuated; her physical relationship with her husband becomes hollow and perfunctory. Certainly in my case, Dr. James C. Neely spoke the truth in *Gender: The Myth of Equality:* "With too much emphasis on intellect, a woman becomes 'too into her head' to function in a sexual, motherly way, destroying by the process of thought the process of feeling her sexuality."

Virginia Woolf never compromised her market achievements with motherhood; nor did the Brontë sisters, Jane Austen, or George Eliot. Nor did Helen Frankenthaler who, at the time she was acknowledged to be the most prominent living female artist, said in an interview: "We all make different compromises. And, no, I don't regret not having children. Given my painting, children could have suffered. A mother must make her children come first: young children are helpless. Well, paintings are objects but they're also helpless." I agree with her; that is precisely how I felt about the briefs I wrote for clients. Those briefs were, to me, like helpless children; in writing them, I first learned the meaning of complete devotion. I stopped writing them because I believed they would have been masters too jealous of my husband and my children.

Society never rebuked these women for refusing to compromise their literary and artistic achievements. Neither should it rebuke other kinds of women for refusing to compromise their own artistry of motherhood and domesticity. Some women may agree that the reality I depict rings truer to them than the feminist depiction. This conviction may help them find the courage of a heretic. Some others, both men and women, may see enough truth in the reality I depict that they will come to regret society's acquiescence in the status degradation of the housewife. They may then accept the currently unfashionable notion that society should respect and support women who adopt the anti-feminist perspective.

It is in society's interest to begin to pull apart the double-bind web spun by feminism and so order itself as not to inhibit any woman who *could* be an awakened Brünnhilde. Delighted and contented women will certainly do less harm—and probably more good—to society than frenzied and despairing ones. This is not to suggest that society should interfere with a woman's decision to follow the feminist script and adopt any form of spiritual virginity that suits her. But neither should society continue to validate destruction of the women's pact by the contemporary feminists who sought to make us all follow their script. We should now begin to dismantle our regime that discourages and disadvantages the traditional woman who rejects feminist spiritual virginity and seeks instead the very different delight and contentment that she believes best suits her.

Sara M. Evans

NO

American Women in the Twentieth Century

In 1900, our foremothers predicted that the twentieth century would be the "century of the child." It might be more accurate, however, to call it the "century of women." Among the many dramatic changes in American society, it is hard to find an example more striking than the changes in women's lives on every level.

At the beginning of the twentieth century, women were challenging the confines of an ideology that relegated them to the private realm of domesticity. Despite the reality that thousands of women could be found in factories, offices, and fields—not to mention in a wide variety of political and reform activities—those ideas still held powerful sway both in law and in dominant notions of propriety. Over the course of the twentieth century, however, women in America emerged fully (though still not equally) into all aspects of public life—politics, labor force participation, professions, mass media, and popular culture. As they did so, they experienced a transformation in the fundamental parameters of their private lives as well—marriage, family, fertility, and sexuality. In complex ways, women transformed the landscapes of both public and private life so that at century's end we are left with a deeply puzzling conundrum about just what we mean by the terms *public* and *private.*

Women, of course, are part of every other social group. Deeply divided by race, class, religion, ethnicity, and region, they don't always identify with one another, and as a result women's collective identity—their sense of solidarity as women—has waxed and waned. Twice in this century, however, there has been a massive wave of activism focused on women's rights. We can trace the surges of change in women's status that accompanied each of these, one at the beginning and another near the end of the century.

Changes in women's lives were certainly driven by large structural forces such as the emergence of the postindustrial service economy, rising levels of education, and the exigencies of two world wars. Yet they have also been due to women's own self-organized activism in two great waves and in numerous ripples in between. In some instances women fought for the right to participate in public life. In other instances, already present in public spaces, they struggled for equity. As a result of these struggles, American political and public life has undergone a series of fundamental transformations. Not only are women in different places at the end of the century then they were at the beginning, but also all Americans enter a new century shaped by the complexities of women's journey.

1900—Dawn of the Twentieth Century

At the beginning of the twentieth century, women's lives were defined primarily by their marital status, linked to race and class. If we take a snapshot (understanding that we are capturing a moment in a dynamic process of change), the normative adult woman—both statistically and in the images that pervaded popular culture—was married, middle class, and white. On average, women lived to 48.3 years; they married around age 22 and bore approximately four children. The vast majority of households consisted of male-headed married couples and their children.

In 1900 women's legal standing was fundamentally governed by their marital status. They had very few rights.

- A married woman had no separate legal identity from that of her husband.
- She had no right to control of her reproduction (even conveying information about contraception, for example, was illegal); and no right to sue or be sued, since she had no separate standing in court.
- She had no right to own property in her own name or to pursue a career of her choice.
- Women could not vote, serve on juries, or hold public office. According to the Supreme Court, Women were not "persons" under the Fourteenth Amendment to the Constitution that guarantees equal protection under the law.

These realities reflected an underlying ideology about women and men that allocated the public realms of work and politics to men and defined the proper place of women in society as fundamentally domestic. Confined to the realm of the home, women's duty to society lay in raising virtuous sons (future citizens) and dutiful daughters (future mothers). Over the course of the nineteenth century, however, women had pushed at the boundaries of their domestic assignment, both by choice and by necessity. They invented forms of politics outside the electoral arena by forming voluntary associations and building institutions in response to unmet social needs. In the 1830s, when women like Sarah and Angelina Grimké began to speak publicly against slavery, the mere appearance of a woman as a public speaker was considered scandalous. By 1900, however, women appeared in all manner of public settings, setting the stage for change in the twentieth century.

Signs of Change

A closer look at women's status in 1900 reveals trends that signal imminent change particularly in the areas of education, labor force participation, and sexuality. The coexistence of new possibilities alongside ongoing restrictions and discrimination laid the groundwork for challenges to the norms of female subordination.

Education Women in 1900 had achieved a high degree of literacy. In fact, more girls than boys actually graduated from high school, probably because boys had access to many jobs that did not require significant education. When it came to higher education, however, women were seriously disadvantaged. They were overtly excluded from most professional education: only about 5 percent of medical students were women, and women's exclusion from legal education shows up in the fact that in 1920 only 1.4 percent of lawyers in the United States were female.

It is crucial to note, however, that in 1900 women constituted about 30 percent of students in colleges and universities, including schools for the growing female professions of nursing, teaching, librarianship, and social work. In the long run, this was a potent mix, as thousands of middle-class women embraced the opportunity to pursue higher education, which in turn generated new expectations. Education was a crucial force in creating the key leadership as well as a highly skilled constituency for the feminist mobilizations at either end of the century.

Labor Force Participation In 1900, though wage labor was defined as a fundamentally male prerogative, women could be found in many parts of the labor force. Women's work outside the home, however, was framed by their marital status and overt discrimination based on race as well as sex.

- Approximately one in five women worked outside the home, a figure that was sharply distinguished by race: 41 percent nonwhite; 17 percent white.
- The average working woman was single and under age 25.
- Only 11 percent of married women worked outside the home (up to 15% by 1940), though the proportion among black women (26%) was considerably higher because discrimination against black men made it much harder for blacks to secure a livable income from a single wage.
- Available occupations were sharply limited. Most women who worked for wages served as domestics, farm laborers, unskilled factory operatives, or teachers. In fact, one in three women employed in nonagricultural pursuits worked in domestic service.
- Some new female-dominated professions, such as nursing, social work, and librarianship, were emerging. In addition, the feminization of clerical work, linked to the new technology of the typewriter and the record-keeping needs of growing corporate bureaucracies, signaled a dramatic trend that made the "working girl" increasingly respectable. By 1920 the proportion of women engaged in clerical work (25.6%) had surpassed the number in manufacturing (23.8), domestic service (18.2%), and agriculture (12.9%).

Sexuality and the Body Late Victorians presumed (if they thought about it at all) that female sexuality should be confined entirely to marriage. Compared with today, there was very little premarital sex, and women were understood not to have much in the way of sexual desire. It was illegal to transmit information about contraception, though women clearly conveyed it anyway through networks of rumor and gossip. Within the dominant middle class even the simplest acknowledgments of female sexuality were suppressed into euphemism and other forms of denial. Body parts could not be named in polite company, so chicken "legs" and "breast," for example, became "dark meat" and "white meat." Female attire covered women's bodies with clothing that revealed some shape but very little skin.

Yet, as the twentieth century dawned with its emerging consumer culture, sexuality could no longer be so easily contained. Popular culture included vaudeville, dance halls, and a growing variety of public amusements (such as the brand-new movie theaters). In the past, women who frequented such places risked having a "bad reputation." Yet the growing popularity of public amusements within the "respectable middle class" was beginning to challenge such perceptions.

Women's bodies were also finding new visibility in athletics. In the wildly popular arenas of public competition such as baseball and boxing, athletics were virtually synonymous with masculinity. And yet women were beginning to play lawn tennis, field hockey, and gymnastics. Some even rode bicycles.

Race, Class, and Gender Ideals Within the gender ideology of the urban middle class that emerged over the course of the nineteenth century, the "good woman" (and her antithesis) took on distinct characteristics associated with race and class. "Good" (white, Protestant, middle class) women embodied private virtues. They were chaste, domestic, pious, and submissive. "Bad" women were "low class"—immigrants, racial minorities—presumed to be promiscuous, bad mothers, and improper housewives largely on the basis of their presence in previously male-only public spaces (factories, saloons, dance halls). Such perceptions multiplied in the case of southern black women subjected to a regime of racial/sexual domination that included the constant threat of rape and the public humiliations of segregation. Yet, the denigration of lower-class and minority women on the basis of their presence in public was getting harder to sustain as growing numbers of supposedly "respectable" women showed up in the same, or similar, spaces.

The First Wave

This brief sketch of women's condition at the beginning of the century points to several forces for change that would bear fruit in the first few decades. The growth in women's education, their move into a wide variety of reform efforts as well as professions, laid the groundwork for a massive suffrage movement that demanded the most basic right of citizenship for women. The claim of citizenship was in many ways a deeply radical challenge to the ideology of separate spheres for men and women. It asserted the right of the individual woman to stand in direct relation to the state rather than to be represented through the participation of her husband or father. The growing power of the women's suffrage movement rested both on women's collective consciousness, born in female associations, and on increased individualism among women in an urbanizing industrializing economy.

While a small but crucial number of upper-middle-class women attended college, where they developed a transformed awareness of their own potential as women both individually and collectively, working-class immigrant and African-American women experienced both individualism and collectivity in very different ways. Forced to work outside the home in the least-skilled, lowest paying jobs, both they and their employers presumed that women's labor force participation was temporary. Unions objected to their presence and blocked them from apprenticeship and access to skilled jobs. Despite these obstacles, when wage-earning women organized their own unions, often in alliance with middle-class reformers, they exhibited awesome courage and militancy. In the garment district of New York, for example, the "uprising of the twenty thousand" in 1909 confounded the garment industry and led to a new kind of industrial unionism.

By 1910, middle-class white reformers had formed increasingly effective alliances with black and working-class women around the issue of women's suffrage. The massive mobilization of American women in the decade before the Nineteenth Amendment was ratified in 1920 included rallies of thousands of "working girls" and the organization of numerous African-American women's suffrage clubs. Shared exclusion from the individual right of civic participation symbolized their common womanhood. Following their victory, leaders of the National American Woman Suffrage Association joyfully dismantled their organization and reassembled as the newly formed League of Women Voters. Their new task, as they defined it, was to train women to exercise their individual citizenship rights.

Such a reorientation seemed congruent with the popular culture of the 1920s, which emphasized individual pleasures along with individual rights. The development of a consumer economy, emphasizing pleasure and using sexuality to sell, offered women other paths out of submissive domesticity and into more assertive forms of individualism, paths that did not require solidarity, indeed undermined it. The female subculture that relied on a singular definition of "woman" eroded. Female reform efforts remained a powerful force in American politics—laying much of the groundwork for the emergence of a welfare state—but a broad-based movement for women's rights no longer existed after 1920. The pace of change in areas like education and labor force participation also reached a plateau and remained relatively unchanged for several decades after 1920. Modern women were individuals. And "feminism" became an epithet.

The loss of female solidarity meant that women's organizations in subsequent decades drew on narrow constituencies with very different priorities. Professional women, lonely pioneers in many fields, felt the continuing sting of discrimination and sought to eradicate the last vestiges of legal discrimination with an Equal Rights Amendment (ERA). The National Women's Party, one of the leading organizations in the struggle, first proposed the ERA in 1923 for the vote. But they were opposed by former allies, social reformers who feared that the protections for working women, which they had won during the Progressive era, would be lost. Though fiercely opposed to the ERA, reformers continued to advocate a stronger role for government in responding to social welfare. Many of them—with leaders like Eleanor Roosevelt—assumed key positions in the 1930s and shaped the political agenda known as the New Deal. In particular, their influence on the Social Security Act laid the foundations of the welfare state. Even among female reformers, however, alliances across racial lines remained rare and fraught with difficulty. As the progressive female reform tradition shaped an emergent welfare state, African-American voices remained muted, the needs of working women with children unaddressed.

The Second Wave

By mid-century the conditions for another surge of activism were under way. During the Second World War women joined the labor force in unprecedented numbers. Most significant, perhaps, married women and women over age 35 became normative among working women by 1950. Yet cold war culture, in the aftermath of World War II, reasserted traditional gender roles. The effort to contain women within the confines of the "feminine mystique" (as Betty Friedan later labeled this ideology), however, obscured but did not prevent rising activism among different constituencies of women. Under the cover of popular images of domesticity, women were rapidly changing their patterns of labor force and civic participation, initiating social movements for civil rights and world peace, and flooding into institutions of higher education.

The President's Commission on the Status of Women, established in 1961, put women's issues back on the national political agenda by recruiting a network of powerful women to develop a set of shared goals. They issued a report in 1963, the same year that Friedan published The Feminine Mystique. That report documented in meticulous detail the ongoing realities of discrimination in employment and in wages, numerous legal disabilities such as married women's lack of access to credit, and the growing problems of working mothers without adequate child care. In 1964, Title VII of the Civil Rights Act gave women their most powerful legal weapon against employment discrimination. An opponent of civil rights introduced Title VII, and many members of Congress treated it as a joke. But Title VII passed because the small number of women then in Congress fiercely and effectively defended the need to prohibit discrimination on the basis of "sex" as well as race, religion, and national origin.

The second wave emerged simultaneously among professional women and a younger cohort of social activists. Professionals, with the leadership of women in labor unions, government leaders, and intellectuals like Friedan, created the National Organization for Women (NOW) in 1966 to demand enforcement of laws like Title VII. A second branch of feminist activism emerged from younger women in the civil rights movement and the student new left. Civil rights offered a model of activism, an egalitarian and visionary language, an opportunity to develop political skills, and role models of courageous female leaders. Young women broke away in 1967 to form consciousness-raising groups and build on the legacy of the movements that had trained them.

The slogan, "the personal is political," became the ideological pivot of the second wave of American feminism. It drove a variety of challenges to gendered relations of power, whether embodied in public policy or in the most intimate personal relationships. The force of this direct assault on the public/private dichotomy has left deep marks on American politics, American society, and the feminist movement itself. Issues like domestic violence, child care, abortion, and sexual harassment have become central to the American political agenda, exposing deep divisions in American society that are not easily subject to the give-and-take compromises of political horse-trading.

From 1968 to 1975, the "Women's Liberation Movement," using the techniques of consciousness-raising in small groups, grew explosively. The synergy between different branches of feminist activism made the 1970s a very dynamic era. Feminist policymakers dubbed the years 1968 to 1975 "the golden years" because of their success in courtrooms and legislatures. These included the Equal Rights Amendment, which passed Congress in 1972 and went to the states; the 1973 Supreme Court decision legalizing abortion (*Roe* v. *Wade*); Title IX of the Higher Education Act, which opened intercollegiate athletics to women; the Women's Equity Education Act; and the Equal Credit Opportunity Act.

Women formed caucuses and organizations in most professional associations and in the labor movement. By the mid-1970s there were feminist organizations representing a broad range of racial groups as well—African-American women, Chicanas and Hispanic women, Asian-American women, Native American women. Women also built new organizations among clerical workers to challenge the devaluation and limited opportunities of traditional women's work.

With their new strength, women challenged barriers to the professions (law, medicine), to ordination within mainstream Protestant and Jewish denominations, and to the full range of traditionally male blue-collar occupations, from carpenters to firefighters and police. They filed thousands of complaints of discrimination, mounted hundreds of lawsuits, and also built thousands of new institutions—day-care centers, shelters for battered women, bookstores, coffeehouses, and many others. The new feminism drew on women's stories to rethink the most intimate personal aspects of womanhood including abortion rights, sexual autonomy, rape, domestic violence, and lesbian rights.

The second wave of feminism also changed the American language both through its own publications (of which there were hundreds, the largest of them being *Ms.*, first published in 1972) and through pressure on commercial publishing houses and mass media. New words entered the American lexicon—"Ms.," "firefighter," "sexism"—while uses of the generic masculine (mankind, brotherhood, policeman) suddenly seemed exclusive. In Women's Studies programs, which grew rapidly in the early 1970s, young scholars rethought the paradigms of their disciplines and initiated new branches of knowledge.

The second wave provoked a strong reaction, of course, revealing not only male hostility but also deep fissures among women themselves. Antifeminism became a strong political force by the late 1970s with the mobilization of Phyllis Schlafley's Stop-ERA and antiabortion forces. In the face of widespread cultural anxiety about equality for women and changing gender roles, the Equal Rights Amendment stalled after 1975 and went down to defeat in 1982 despite an extension of the deadline for ratification. Antifeminism drew on the insecurities of a declining economy in the wake of the Vietnam War and on the growing political power of the New Right which made cultural issues (abortion, the ERA, "family values," and homophobia) central. The 1980s, framed by the hostile political climate of the Reagan administration, nourished a growing backlash against feminism in the media, the popular culture, and public policy. As public spending shifted away from social programs and toward the military, female poverty increased sharply. The Reagan boom after 1983 did not touch the poorest, disproportionately female and racial minority, segments of the population.

At the same time, the 1980s witnessed the continued growth of women's presence in positions of public authority: Supreme Court justice, astronaut, arctic explorer, military officer, truck driver, carpenter, Olympic star, bishop, rabbi. Mainstream religious denominations began to rewrite liturgies and hymnbooks to make them more "inclusive." Despite regular announcements of the "death" of feminism, it would be more accurate to say that in the 1980s feminism entered the mainstream with new levels of community activism, sophisticated political fundraisers like EMILY's List, and broad political alliances on issues like comparable worth. Experimental "counterinstitutions" started in the 1970s (battered women's shelters, health clinics, bookstores, etc.) survived by adopting more institutionalized procedures, professionalized staff, and state funding. Women's Studies took on the trappings of an academic discipline.

Feminism was broad, diffuse, and of many minds in the 1980s. Legal and cultural issues grew more complex. Feminist theorists wrestled with the realities of differences such as race, class, age, and sexual preference, asking themselves whether the category "woman" could withstand such an analysis. The multifaceted activities that embraced the label "feminist"—policy activism, research think tanks, literary theory, music, art, spirituality—signaled the fact that the women's movement had lost some cohesiveness.

The testimony of Anita Hill during the 1991 hearings on the nomination of Clarence Thomas to the Supreme Court, however, catalyzed a new round of national conversation, complicated by the deep fissures of race and sex. The sight of a genteel black woman being grilled by a committee of white men who made light of this "sexual harassment crap" mobilized thousands of women to run for office and contribute to campaigns. In 1992 an unprecedented number of women were elected to public office.

2000—Dawn of a New Millennium

If we return to our original categories to describe women's situation at the end of the twentieth century, the contrast with 1900 could hardly be more dramatic. The average woman now can expect to live 79.7 years (65% longer than her great-grandmother in 1900), marry at age 24.5, and bear only about two children (if any at all). There are now decades in women's lives—both before and after the years of childbearing and child care—which earlier generations never experienced. As a result of the second wave of women's rights activism in the final decades of the twentieth century, in politics and law, labor force participation, education, and sexuality women live in a truly different world. Yet, in each instance equity remains an elusive goal, suggesting the need for continued and revitalized activism in the twenty-first century.

Politics and Law

No longer defined by their marital status, women enjoy virtually the full range of formal legal rights. In addition to winning the right to vote in 1920, they achieved equal pay (for the same work) in 1963 and guarantees against discrimination in housing and employment in 1964 (Title VII of the Civil Rights Act). Since 1970 women have won the right to a separate legal identity; privacy rights regarding reproduction and bodily integrity; and rights to sue for discrimination in employment, to work when pregnant, to equal education, and to equal access to athletics. Whole new bodies of law have developed since the 1970s on issues like domestic violence and sexual harassment. Nonetheless, the failure of the Equal Rights Amendment (ERA) in 1982 means that women still have no constitutional guarantee of equality.

In the last twenty-five years we have also seen a dramatic growth in the numbers of female elected officials. In 1997 there were 60 women in Congress (11.2%)—14 of them women of color; 81 statewide executive officials (25%); 1,597 state legislators (21.5%); and 203 mayors of cities with population over 30,000 (20.6%). There are two women on the Supreme Court, 30 female circuit court judges (18.6%), and 107 female district court judges (17.2%).

Education

At the end of the twentieth century, 88 percent of young women ages 25 to 34 are high-school graduates. The transformations in primary and secondary education for girls cannot be captured in graduation numbers, however. They also reside in the admission of girls to shop and other vocational classes (and boys to cooking and sewing courses), in girls' participation in athletics, in curricula that—at least sometimes—emphasize women's achievements in the past, and in school counselors who no longer single-mindedly socialize girls for domesticity and/or nonskilled stereotypically female jobs.

In the arena of higher education women are closing in on equity. Today, 54 percent of all bachelor of arts degrees go to women; 25 percent of women aged 25 to 34 are college graduates. Most striking, the proportion of women in professional schools is now between 36 and 43 percent. The revolution of the late twenteeth century is evident in these figures, as most of the change occurred in the last three decades. Compare current numbers with those of 1960, when the proportion of women in law school was 2 percent (today 43%); medicine 6 percent (today 38%); MBA programs 4 percent (today 36%); Ph.D. programs 11 percent (today 39%), and dentistry 1 percent (today 38%).

Labor Force Participation

In stark contrast to a century ago, more than 61 percent of all women are in the labor force, including two-thirds of women with preschoolers and three-fourths of women with school-age children. Though African-American women continue to work at a higher rate than average (76% overall), the gap is clearly shrinking as the patterns that they pioneered are becoming the norm. With overt discrimination now outlawed, women practice virtually every occupation on the spectrum from blue collar to professional.

Yet alongside change, older patterns persist. Women remain concentrated in female-dominated, low-paid service occupations despite their presence in many professions and in traditionally male blue-collar occupations such as construction or truck driving. Although the exceptions are highly visible (tracked in the popular media frequently as interesting and unusual phenomena), 70 percent of women work either in the services industry (health and education) or in wholesale or retail trade. Women's median weekly earnings are still only 75 percent those of men—though there has been a dramatic gain since 1970 when they were 62.2 percent. (Note, however, that this change represents a combined gain for women of 17% and a 3% decline for men.)

Sexuality, Fertility, and Marriage

The late twentieth century has witnessed a sharp increase in single motherhood even as overall fertility has declined. One birth in three is to an unmarried woman; in 1970, that proportion was only one in ten. Sixty-nine percent of children live with two parents; 23.5 percent with mother only (for African Americans this is 52%).

Some of this single parenthood is due to divorce, something that was relatively rare in 1900 and today affects nearly one in every two marriages. The divorce rate seems to have peaked in 1980, however, and has declined somewhat since that time (in 1980 there were 5.2 divorces/1,000 population; today there are 4.4). Single motherhood is not the source of shame that it was in 1900, but it remains highly correlated with poverty.

If female sexuality was suppressed in 1900 (even though incompletely), at the end of the century sexual references and images saturate American culture. It was not until the 1930s that birth control became legal in most states. In 1961 the birth control pill introduced the possibility of radically separating sexual experience from the likelihood of procreation. Then in 1973, the Supreme Court's Roe v. Wade decision legalized abortion. Today, premarital sex is common, even normative. According to the Alan Guttmacher Institute, in the early 1990s 56 percent of women and 73 percent of men had sex by age 18.

As dramatic, homosexuality has become an open subject of public discourse, and lesbians—once completely hidden, even to one another—are creating new public spaces and organizations, fields of intellectual inquiry and theory, and families that rely on voluntary ties in the absence of any legal sanction. Lesbians have been a major constituency and source of leadership in the second feminist wave. Twenty years of visibility, however, is just a beginning. American society remains deeply, and emotionally, divided on the issue of homosexuality. Opposition to gay rights marks a key issue for the religious right, and open violence against lesbians and gay men continues.

Race and Class

The second wave grew directly from and modeled itself on the civil rights movement in the 1950s and 1960s. That movement, itself, relied heavily on the grass-roots (if relatively invisible) leadership of African-American women. In the last decades of the century, the voices of minority women have become increasingly distinct and powerful. Diversity among women, as in the society at large, has taken on new dimensions with a surge of immigration since the 1960s from Southeast Asia, East Africa, Central America, and other parts of the Third World. Predictions based on immigration and fertility suggest that by the middle of the next century whites will be only half the U.S. population. Women of color will become the new norm. Women remain deeply divided on racial grounds, but race is no longer defined as black and white.

Challenges to traditional conceptions of gender have also shaken the previous consensus on what constitutes a "good woman" (except perhaps to the right-wing traditionalists who still hold to a set of ideals quite similar to those that dominated American culture a century ago). Yet discomfort with women's move into public life is still widespread, and race and class stigmas remain. The massive growth of a welfare system whose clients are disproportionately women and children combines racial and gender stereotypes to create a new category of "bad women": single, minority, poor mothers. And wherever women appear in previously male-dominated environments, they remain suspect. In particular, the sharply polarized emotional response to Hillary Rodham Clinton during her time as first lady illustrates the undercurrent of anger at powerful, professional women. Radio talk shows have filled thousands of hours with hosts and callers venting their hostility toward this woman who, in their view, did not stay "in her place." But, of course, that is the open question at century's end: just what is "woman's place"?

Conclusion

This brief discussion of women in the twentieth century does not trace a smooth arc from the beginning of the century to the end. It is not simply about "progress" toward "equality." But it is, indeed, about a kind of sea change with unanticipated consequences and with dramatic acceleration in the last thirty years.

In the nineteenth century women created much of what today we call civil society. In the twentieth century they used that layer of society—which lies between formal governmental structures and private familial life—in an amazing variety of ways to reshape the landscape of American life. Virtually all of the public spaces previously presumed to belong properly to men—paid labor, higher education, electoral politics and public office, athletics—now incorporate a large and visible proportion of women. This theme of participation in public life, and the concomitant politicization of issues previously considered personal, runs through the entire century.

Such spectacular shifts have clearly been driven by large structural forces: the emergence of a postindustrial service economy, rising levels of education, two cataclysmic world wars, global power and national wealth on a level never imagined, changing patterns of marriage, fertility, and longevity. Yet the most dramatic changes can clearly be traced in equal measure to two large waves of women's activism.

The suffrage movement, by the 1910s, involved hundreds of thousands of women, branching out both tactically with the use of massive public parades and street corner speeches (females occupying public, political spaces) and in composition as it reached out to working women, immigrants, and minorities. That movement won for women the fundamental right of citizenship, the right to vote. And the Progressive movement on which it built laid the groundwork and provided many key players for the subsequent emergence of the welfare state. The impact of the second wave shows up in the astonishing acceleration of change in the last three decades of the century.

Each of these waves continued to surge forward in the decades after cresting. But each was also followed by a period in which the multiplicity of women's voices reasserted itself along with debates over the real meaning of equality. And each left much work undone for subsequent generations that face new issues and new dilemmas.

In the twenty-first century women will have choices that have never before been available, but they will not be easy. The twentieth century challenged our very definitions of male and female. Many of the signs of manhood and womanhood no longer function effectively. Work is no longer a manly prerogative and responsibility. Families are no longer constituted around a male breadwinner, a wife, and their children. More often they are two-income households (same or different sexes) or single-parent households. Large numbers of single men and women live alone. Yet "family values" have become a political code for attacks on welfare mothers, homosexuals, and nontraditional families (which, in fact, far outnumbered traditional ones). In the absence of significant societal or governmental support for women's traditional responsibilities, women assume a double burden. They participate in the labor force almost to the same degree as men, and yet work outside the home is still organized as though workers had wives to take care of household work, child care, and the myriad details of private life. Work outside the home makes few accommodations to the demands and priorities of family life.

The pioneering work of the twentieth century—as women made their way into hostile, male-dominated public spaces—remains unfinished. Most of the barriers have been broken at least once. But equity remains a distant goal. Achieving that goal is complicated by the fact that for the moment women are not a highly unified group. The contemporary struggles within feminism to deal with the differences among women are the essential precursor to any future social movement that claims to speak for women as a group. The very meanings of masculinity and femininity and their multiple cultural and symbolic references are now overtly contested throughout the popular culture.

Another legacy of the feminist movement that proclaimed that "the personal is political" is an unresolved ambiguity about just where the boundary between the personal and the political properly lies, and the dilemmas resulting from politicizing private life. At the end of the century, Americans faced a constitutional crisis rooted in the strange career of personal politics. For an entire year virtually everyone in the United States was riveted by the scandal concerning President Clinton, Monica Lewinsky, Kenneth Starr, and the American Congress. Behaviors that once would have been considered purely private (and gone unremarked by political reporters, for example) became the basis for impeachment. Who defended the distinction between public and private and who assaulted it? The tables seem to have turned with a vengeance as the right wing pried into intimate details about the president's sexual activities in a consensual relationship while the liberals (including feminist leaders) protested. The politicization of private life is indeed a double-edged sword. This should be no surprise, as conservative backlash since the 1970s has evidanced a clear willingness to use the power of the state to enforce its vision of proper private relationships on issues such as abortion, homosexuality, divorce, prayer in the schools, and the content of textbooks.

The recent history of feminism calls to our attention a number of dimensions in this crisis that should not go unnoticed. First, there have always been many members of society (racial and sexual minorities, welfare recipients, and women, to name only the most obvious) whose private behaviors have been scrutinized and regulated by those in power. By forcing these issues into public debate and evolving laws that might protect such groups (for example laws against sexual harassment) feminists have also removed the cover of silence that protected powerful men from public scrutiny for their private behaviors. That such laws were subsequently used in a campaign to unseat a president whose election was directly due to the votes of politically mobilized women resonates with irony.

Women's solidarity has waxed and waned across the twentieth century. It will certainly continue to do so in the twenty-first. The next wave of feminist activism will no doubt take a shape we cannot envision, just as no one at the dawn of the twentieth century could have imagined the battles that awaited them. That there will be another wave, however, is a safe prediction, given the unfinished agendas of the last century and the still unforeseen contradictions that future changes will create. The next wave will shape the new century.

Bibliography

William H. Chafe, *The American Woman: Her Changing Social, Economic, and Political Roles, 1920–1970* (New York: Oxford University Press, 1972), laid the groundwork for subsequent studies of twentieth-century women. Peter Filene examines the implications of changing definitions of womanliness and manliness on both sexes in *Him/Her Self: Sex Roles in Modern America*, 2nd ed. (Baltimore: Johns Hopkins University Press, 1986). Sara M. Evans, *Born for Liberty: A History of Women in America*, 2nd ed. (New York: Free Press, 1996) provides a general overview of women in American history.

The "first wave" of women's rights activism in the twentieth century is chronicled by Nancy F. Cott, *The Grounding of Modern Feminism* (New Haven, Conn.: Yale University Press, 1987), and Mari Jo Buhle and Paul Buhle, eds., *The Concise History of Woman Suffrage: Selections from the Classic Work of Stanton, Anthony, Gage, and Harper* (Urbana: University of Illinois Press, 1978). On women's role in the New Deal see Susan Ware, *Beyond Suffrage: Women in the New Deal* (Cambridge, Mass.: Harvard University Press, 1981). The critical eras of the 1940s and the cold war are examined in Susan Hartmann, *The Homefront and Beyond: American Women in the 1940s* (Boston: Twayne Publishers, 1982) and Elaine Tyler May, *Homeward Bound: American Families in the Cold War Era*

(New York: Basic Books, 1988). There is a growing literature on the "second wave" of feminism. Some starting points would be Sara Evans, *Personal Politics: The Roots of Women's Liberation in the Civil Rights Movement and the New Left* (New York: Vintage, 1980); Alice Echols, *Daring to Be Bad: Radical Feminism in America, 1967–1975* (Minneapolis: University of Minnesota Press, 1989); and Donald Mathews and Jane De Hart, *Sex, Gender, and the Politics of ERA* (New York: Oxford University Press, 1990).

For more depth on the history of sexuality see John D'Emilio and Estelle B. Freedman, *Intimate Matters: A History of Sexuality in America* (New York: Harper & Row, 1988); on education see Barbara Solomon, *In the Company of Educated Women: A History of Women and Higher Education in America* (New Haven, Conn.: Yale University Press, 1985); on women in the labor force see Julia Blackwelder, *Now Hiring: The Feminization of Work in the United States: 1900–1995* (College Station: Texas A&M University Press, 1997. Some excellent starting points on racial minority and immigrant ethnic women include Vicki L. Ruíz, *From Out of the Shadows: Mexican Women in Twentieth-Century America* (New York: Oxford University Press, 1999); on African-American women see Jacqueline Jones, *Labor of Love, Labor of Sorrow: Black Women, Work, and the Family from Slavery to the Present* (New York: Basic Books, 1985), and on Chinese women Judy Yung, *Unbound Feet: A Social History of Chinese Women in San Francisco* (Barkeley: University of California Press, 1995); Donna Gabaccia, *From the Other Side: Women, Gender, and Immigrant Life in the U.S., 1920–1990* (Bloomington: Indiana University Press, 1994),

For the most recent descriptions of women's status in all aspects of American life, see the series sponsored by the Women's Research and Education Institute in Washington, D.C., *The American Woman* (New York: W. W. Norton). This series has been updated biannually from its inception in 1987.

POSTSCRIPT

Has the Women's Liberation Movement Been Harmful to American Women?

F. Carolyn Graglia's critique of contemporary feminism is a throwback to women of the late nineteenth and early twentieth century who opposed the women social workers and suffragettes who entered the man's world. Her book is a modern restatement of Barbara Welter's classic and widely reprinted article, "The Cult of True Womanhood," *American Quarterly* (Summer 1996).

Graglia argues that contemporary feminism ignores women's primary role in raising the children and preserving the moral character of the family. She blames contemporary feminism along with the Great Society's social programs for promoting a sexual revolution that has destroyed the American family by fostering sexually transmitted diseases and a high divorce rate.

Historian Sara M. Evans takes a long-range view of the women's liberation movement. By comparing the political, legal, and domestic situation of women in 1900 with today, Evans charts the successes and failures that were achieved by the two waves of feminist protest movements in the twentieth century.

At the beginning of the twentieth century, a number of middle-class women from elite colleges in the northeast were in the vanguard of a number of progressive reform movements—temperance, anti-prostitution, child labor, and settlement houses. Working in tandem with the daughters of first-generation immigrants employed in the garment industry, the early feminists realized that laws affecting women could be passed only if women had the right to vote. The suffragettes overcame the arguments of male and female antisuffragists who associated women voters with divorce, promiscuity, and neglect of children and husbands with the ratification of the Nineteenth Amendment in 1920.

The women's movement stalled between the two wars for a variety of reasons: Women pursued their own individual freedom in a consumer-oriented society in the 1920s, and the Great Depression of the 1930s placed the economic survival of the nation at the forefront. But the Second World War had long-range effects on women. Minorities—African Americans and Hispanics—worked for over 3 years in factory jobs traditionally reserved for white males at high wages. So did married white females, often in their thirties. Although the majority of these women returned to the home or took more traditional low-paying "women's" jobs after the war, the consciousness of the changing role of women during the Second World War would reappear during the 1960s.

Evans points out the two streams that formed the women's liberation movement from the mid-1960s. First were the professional women like Betty Freidan, who created the National Organization for Women (NOW) in 1966, who worked with women leaders in labor unions, government, and consciousness-raising groups to demand enforcement of Title VII of the 1965 Civil Rights Act, which banned discrimination in employment and wages. A second wing of feminist activists came from the civil rights and anti-war new left protest groups from the elite universities. Many of these women felt like second-class citizens in these movements and decided they had their own issues that they had to deal with.

Evans dubbed the years 1968 to 1975 "the golden years" because of the following successes: "Passage of the Equal Rights Amendment in Congress in 1972; the 1973 Supreme Court decision (*Roe* v. *Wade*) legalizing abortion; Title IX of the Higher Education Act which opened intercollegiate athletics to women; the Women's Equity Education Act; and the Equal Credit Opportunity Act."

Evans points out that the women's movement suffered a "backlash" in the 1980s as America became much more conservative. The new right blamed the increases in divorce, single parenthood, out-of-wedlock births, abortions, and open homosexuality on the cultural values of the 1960s. But by the beginning of the twenty-first century, middle-class women made substantial gains in the professions compared with 1960: Law school today 43 percent, 1960 2 percent; medicine today 38 percent, 1960 6 percent; MBA programs today 35 percent, 1960 4 percent; dentistry today 38 percent, 1960 1 percent; and Ph.D. programs today 39 percent, 1960 11 percent. Working-class women, however, have been much less successful in breaking into traditional blue collar jobs such as truck driving and construction.

Both the antifeminist Graglia and to a much less extent the pro-feminist Evans have been critiqued by moderate feminists like Elizabeth Fox-Genovese and Cathy Young, who contend that contemporary feminists have not spoken to the concerns of married women, especially women from poor to lower-middle-class families who must work in order to help support the family. Fox-Genovese's *Feminism Is Not the Story of My Life: How Today's Feminist Elite Have Lost Touch With the Real Concerns of Women* (Doubleday, 1996) is peppered with interviews of white, African American, and Hispanic Americans of different classes and gives a more complex picture of the problems women face today. Young, author of *Cease Fire! Why Women and Men Must Join Forces to Achieve True Equality* (Free Press, 1999), asserts that Graglia denies the real discrimination women faced in the job market in the 1950s. Furthermore, Graglia's critique of the sexual revolution is an attempt to restore a view of female sexuality as essentially submissive.

In 1998 Harvard University Press reprinted Betty Friedan's two later books—*The Second Stage* and *It Changed My Life*, both with new introductions with suggestions for the twenty-first century—which are critical of some of the directions that the women's movement took.

Important books and articles by activists with a historical perspective include Sara Evans, *Personal Politics: The Roots of Women's Liberation in the Civil Rights Movement and the New Left* (Vintage, 1979). This book is nicely summarized in "Sources of the Second Wave: The Rebirth of Feminism," in Alexander Bloom, ed., *Long Time Gone: Sixties America Then and Now* (Oxford, 2001). For a general overview of women's history, see Evans, *Born for Liberty: A History of*

Women in America, 2nd ed. (Free Press, 1996), and Roger Adelson's "*Interview with Sara Margaret Evans*," *The Historian* (vol. 63, Fall 2000); Donna Gabaccia, *From the Other Side: Women, Gender and Immigrant Life in the U.S., 1920–1990* (Indiana University Press, 1994); and John D'Emilio and Estelle B. Freedman, *Intimate Matters: A History of Sexuality in America* (Harper & Row, 1988).

Review essays from various journals reflect the continuous battle over the importance of the women's movement. The neo-conservative magazine *Commentary* is constantly critical of feminism. See Elizabeth Kristol, "The Sexual Revolution" (April 1996) and Elizabeth Powers, "Back to Basics" (March 1999). Also critical is Daphne Patai, "Will the Real Feminists in Academe Stand Up," *The Chronicle of Higher Education* (October 6, 2000 pp. B6–9). Sympathetic to the movement is Christine Stansell, "Girlie Interrupted: The Generational Progress of Feminism," *The New Republic* (January 15, 2001); Andrew Hacker, "How Are Women Doing," *The New York Review of Books* (Fall 2000). See also Jo Freeman, "The Women's Liberation Movement: Its Origins, Structure, Activities, and Ideas," in Jo Freeman, ed., *Women: A Feminist Perspective*, 3rd ed. (Mayfield, 1984); Estelle B. Freedman, *No Turning Back: The History of Feminism and the Future of Women* (Balantine, 2001); and Susan Brownmiller, *In Our Time: Memoir of a Revolution* (Dial Press, 2000).

The best starting point is Ruth Rosen, *The World Split Open: How the Modern Woman's Movement Changed America* (Viking, 2000), written by a former Berkley activist for her students who were born in the 1980s.

Books that deal with the impact of the movement on specific groups include Johnnetta B. Cole and Beverly Gray-Sheftall, *Gender Talk: The Struggle for Women's Equality in African American Communities* (Balantine, 2003); Jacqueline Jones, *Labor of Love, Labor of Sorrow: Black Women, Work, and the Family from Slavery to the Present* (Basic Books, 1985); Vicki L. Ruiz, *From out of the Shadows: Mexican Women in Twentieth-Century Books* (April 11, 2002); and Kim France's review of Phyllis Chesler, *Letters to a Young Feminist* (Four Walls Eight Windows, 1998) in *The New York Times Book Review* (April 26, 1998 pp. 10–11).

ISSUE 14

Was Richard Nixon America's Last Liberal President?

YES: Joan Hoff-Wilson, from "Richard M. Nixon: The Corporate Presidency," in Fred I. Greenstein, ed., *Leadership in the Modern Presidency* (Harvard University Press, 1988)

NO: Bruce J. Schulman, from *The Seventies: The Great Shift in American Culture, Society, and Politics* (The Free Press/Simon & Schuster, 2001)

ISSUE SUMMARY

YES: According to professor of history Joan Hoff-Wilson, the Nixon presidency reorganized the executive branch and portions of the federal bureaucracy and implemented domestic reforms in civil rights, welfare, and economic planning, despite its limited foreign policy successes and the Watergate scandal.

NO: According to Professor Bruce J. Schulman, Richard Nixon was the first conservative president of the post–World War II era who undermined the Great Society legislative program of President Lyndon Baines Johnson and built a new Republican majority coalition of white, northern, blue-collar workers, and southern and sunbelt conservatives.

Richard Milhous Nixon was born in Yorba Linda in Orange County, California, on January 9, 1913. When he was nine, his family moved to Whittier, California. He attended Whittier College, where he excelled at student politics and debating. He earned a tuition-paid scholarship to Duke University Law School and graduated third out of a class of 25 in 1937. He returned to Whittier and for several years worked with the town's oldest law firm.

Nixon had hopes of joining a bigger law firm, but World War II intervened. He joined the navy as a lieutenant, junior grade, where he served in a Naval Transport Unit in the South Pacific for the duration of the war. Before his discharge from active duty, Republicans asked him to run for a seat in California's 12th congressional district in the House of Representatives. He won the primary and defeated Jerry Vorhees, a New Deal Democratic incumbent, in the general election of 1946. In that year, the Republicans gained control of Congress for the first time since 1930.

During Nixon's campaign against Vorhees, he accused Vorhees of accepting money from a communist-dominated political action committee. This tactic, known as "red-baiting," was effective in the late 1940s and early 1950s because the American public had become frightened of the communist menace. In 1950, Nixon utilized similar tactics in running for the U.S. Senate against Congresswoman Helen Gahaghan Douglas. He won easily.

Young, energetic, a vigorous campaign orator, and a senator from the second largest state in the Union with impeccable anticommunist credentials, Nixon was chosen by liberal Republicans to become General Dwight D. Eisenhower's running mate in the 1952 presidential election. In the election, Eisenhower and Nixon overwhelmed the Democrats. Nixon became the second-youngest vice president in U.S. history and actively used the office to further his political ambitions.

The 1960 presidential campaign was one of the closest in modern times. Nixon, who was considered young for high political office at that time, lost to an even younger Democratic senator from Massachusetts, John F. Kennedy. Out of 68 million votes cast, less than 113,000 votes separated the two candidates.

In 1962, Nixon was persuaded to seek the governorship of California on the premise that he needed a power boost to keep his presidential hopes alive for 1964. Apparently, Nixon was out of touch with state politics. Governor Pat Brown defeated him by 300,000 votes.

Nixon then left for New York City and became a partner with a big-time Wall Street legal firm. He continued to speak at Republican dinners, and he supported Barry Goldwater of Arizona for the presidency in March 1968. After Goldwater's decisive defeat by Lyndon B. Johnson, Nixon's political fortunes revived yet again. In March 1965, Johnson announced that he was not going to run again for the presidency. Nixon took advantage of the opening and won the Republican nomination.

During the 1968 presidential campaign, Nixon positioned himself between Democratic Vice President Hubert Humphrey, the liberal defender of the Great Society programs, and the conservative, law-and-order, third-party challenger Governor George Wallace of Alabama. Nixon stressed a more moderate brand of law and order and stated that he had a secret plan to end the war in Vietnam. He barely edged Humphrey in the popular vote, but Nixon received 301 electoral votes to 191 for Humphrey. Wallace received nearly 10 million popular votes and 46 electoral college votes.

This background brings us to Nixon's presidency. Was Nixon an effective president? In the following sections, Joan Hoff-Wilson argues that Nixon achieved a number of domestic policy successes in the areas of civil rights, welfare, and economic planning, and in the reorganization of the executive branch and some federal agencies. But Professor Bruce J. Schulman disagrees. He believes that President Nixon was the first conservative president of the post–World War II era who undermined the Great Society legislative programs of Lyndon Baines Johnson and built a new Republican majority coalition of northern white blue-collar workers and southern white conservatives and sunbelt space-age employees and its retirement communities.

YES

Joan Hoff-Wilson

Richard M. Nixon: The Corporate Presidency

Richard Milhous Nixon became president of the United States at a critical juncture in American history. Following World War II there was a general agreement between popular and elite opinion on two things: the effectiveness of most New Deal domestic policies and the necessity of most Cold War foreign policies. During the 1960s, however, these two crucial postwar consensual constructs began to break down; and the war in Indochina, with its disruptive impact on the nation's political economy, hastened their disintegration. By 1968 the traditional bipartisan, Cold War approach to the conduct of foreign affairs had been seriously undermined. Similarly, the "bigger and better" New Deal approach to the modern welfare state had reached a point of diminishing returns, even among liberals.

In 1968, when Richard Nixon finally captured the highest office in the land, he inherited not only Lyndon Johnson's Vietnam war but also LBJ's Great Society. This transfer of power occurred at the very moment when both endeavors had lost substantial support among the public at large and, most important, among a significant number of the elite group of decision makers and leaders of opinion across the country. On previous occasions when such a breakdown had occurred within policy- and opinion-making circles—before the Civil and Spanish American Wars and in the early years of the Great Depression—domestic or foreign upheavals had followed. Beginning in the 1960s the country experienced a similar series of failed presidents reminiscent of those in the unstable 1840s and 1850s, 1890s, and 1920s.

In various ways all the presidents in these transitional periods failed as crisis managers, often because they refused to take risks. Nixon, in contrast, "[couldn't] understand people who won't take risks." His proclivity for risk taking was not emphasized by scholars, journalists, and psychologists until after he was forced to resign as president. "I am not necessarily a respecter of the status quo," Nixon told Stuart Alsop in 1958; "I am a chance taker." Although this statement was made primarily in reference to foreign affairs, Nixon's entire political career has been characterized by a series of personal and professional crises and risky political policies. It is therefore not surprising that as president he rationalized many of his major foreign and domestic initiatives

Reprinted by permission of the publisher from "Richard M. Nixon: The Corporate Presidency" by Joan Hoff-Wilson in LEADERSHIP IN THE MODERN PRESIDENCY, edited by Fred I. Greenstein, pp. 164–167, 189–198, Cambridge, Mass.: Harvard University. Notes omitted.

as crises (or at least as intolerable impasses) that could be resolved only by dramatic and sometimes drastic measures.

A breakdown in either the foreign or domestic policy consensus offers both opportunity and danger to any incumbent president. Nixon had more opportunity for risk-taking changes at home and abroad during his first administration than he would have had if elected in 1960 because of the disruptive impact of war and domestic reforms during the intervening eight years. Also, he inherited a wartime presidency, with all its temporarily enhanced extralegal powers. Although the Cold War in general has permanently increased the potential for constitutional violations by presidents, only those in the midst of a full-scale war (whether declared or undeclared) have exercised with impunity what Garry Wills has called "semi-constitutional" actions. Although Nixon was a wartime president for all but twenty months of his five and one-half years in office, he found that impunity for constitutional violations was not automatically accorded a president engaged in an undeclared, unsatisfying, and seemingly endless war. In fact, he is not usually even thought of, or referred to, as a wartime president.

Periods of war and reform have usually alternated in the United States, but in the 1960s they burgeoned simultaneously, hastening the breakdown of consensus that was so evident by the time of the 1968 election. This unusual situation transformed Nixon's largely unexamined and rather commonplace management views into more rigid and controversial ones. It also reinforced his natural predilection to bring about change through executive fiat. Thus a historical accident accounts in part for many of Nixon's unilateral administrative actions during his first term and for the events leading to his disgrace and resignation during his second.

The first few months in the Oval Office are often intoxicating, and a new president can use them in a variety of ways. But during the socioeconomic confusion and conflict of the late 1960s and early 1970s, some of the newly appointed Republican policy managers (generalists) and the frustrated holdover Democratic policy specialists (experts) in the bureaucracy unexpectedly came together and began to consider dramatic policy changes at home and abroad. Complex interactions between these very different groups produced several significant shifts in domestic and foreign affairs during the spring and summer of 1969. A radical welfare plan and dramatic foreign policy initiatives took shape.

The country had elected only one other Republican president since the onset of FDR's reform administrations thirty-six years earlier. Consequently, Nixon faced not only unprecedented opportunities for changing domestic policy as a result of the breakdown in the New Deal consensus, but also the traditional problems of presidential governance, exacerbated in this instance by bureaucratic pockets of resistance from an unusual number of holdover Democrats. Such resistance was not new, but its magnitude was particularly threatening to a distrusted (and distrustful) Republican president who did not control either house of Congress. Nixon's organizational recommendations for containing the bureaucracy disturbed his political opponents and the liberal press as much as, if not more than, their doubts about the motivation behind many of his substantive and innovative suggestions on other domestic issues such as welfare and the environment.

Because much of the press and both houses of Congress were suspicious of him, Nixon naturally viewed administrative action as one way of obtaining significant domestic reform. Moreover, some of his initial accomplishments in administratively redirecting U.S. foreign policy ultimately led him to rely more on administrative actions at home than he might have otherwise. In any case, this approach drew criticism from those who already distrusted his policies and priorities. Nixon's covert and overt expansion and prolongation of the war during this period reinforced existing suspicions about his personality and political ethics. In this sense, liberal paranoia about his domestic programs fueled Nixon's paranoia about liberal opposition to the war, and vice versa. By 1972, Nixon's success in effecting structural and substantive change in foreign policy through the exercise of unilateral executive power increasingly led him to think that he could use the same preemptive administrative approach to resolve remaining domestic problems, especially following his landslide electoral victory. . . .

Foreign Policy Scorecard

It was clearly in Nixon's psychic and political self-interest to end the war in Vietnam as soon as possible. Although he came to office committed to negotiate a quick settlement, he ended up prolonging the conflict. As a result, he could never build the domestic consensus he needed to continue the escalated air and ground war (even with dramatically reduced U.S. troop involvement) and to ensure passage of some of his domestic programs. For Nixon (and Kissinger) Vietnam became a symbol of influence in the Third World that, in turn, was but one part of their geopolitical approach to international relations. Thus the war in Southeast Asia had to be settled as soon as possible so as not to endanger other elements of Nixonian diplomatic and domestic policy.

Instead, the president allowed his secretary of state to become egocentrically involved in secret negotiations with the North Vietnamese from August 4, 1969, to January 25, 1972 (when they were made public). As a result, the terms finally reached in 1973 were only marginally better than those rejected in 1969. The advantage gained from Hanoi's agreement to allow President Nguyen Van Thieu to remain in power in return for allowing North Vietnamese troops to remain in South Vietnam can hardly offset the additional loss of twenty thousand American lives during this three-year-period—especially given the inherent weaknesses of the Saigon government by 1973. On the tenth anniversary of the peace treaty ending the war in Vietnam, Nixon admitted to me that "Kissinger believed more in the power of negotiation than I did." He also said that he "would not have temporized as long" with the negotiating process had he not been "needlessly" concerned with what the Soviets and Chinese might think if the United States pulled out of Vietnam precipitately. Because Nixon saw no way in 1969 to end the war quickly except through overt massive bombing attacks, which the public demonstrated in 1970 and 1971 it would not tolerate, there was neither peace nor honor in

Vietnam by the time that war was finally concluded on January 27, 1973; and in the interim he made matters worse by secretly bombing Cambodia.

The delayed ending to the war in Vietnam not only cast a shadow on all Nixon's other foreign policy efforts but also established secrecy, wiretapping, and capricious personal diplomacy as standard operational procedures in the conduct of foreign policy that ultimately carried over into domestic affairs. Despite often duplicitous and arbitrary actions, even Nixon's strongest critics often credit him with an unusual number of foreign policy successes.

Although fewer of his foreign policy decisions were reached in a crisis atmosphere than his domestic ones, Nixon's diplomatic legacy is weaker than he and many others have maintained. For example, the pursuit of "peace and honor" in Vietnam failed; his Middle Eastern policy because of Kissinger's shuttling ended up more show than substance; his Third World policy (outside of Vietnam and attempts to undermine the government of Allende in Chile) were nearly nonexistent; détente with the USSR soon foundered under his successors; and the Nixon Doctrine has not prevented use of U.S. troops abroad. Only rapprochement with China remains untarnished by time because it laid the foundation for recognition, even though he failed to achieve a "two China" policy in the United Nations. This summary is not meant to discredit Richard Nixon as a foreign policy expert both during and after his presidency. It is a reminder that the lasting and positive results of his diplomacy may be fading faster than some aspects of his domestic policies.

Outflanking Liberals on Domestic Reform

Presidents traditionally achieve their domestic objectives through legislation, appeals in the mass media, and administrative actions. During his first administration Nixon offered Congress extensive domestic legislation, most of which aimed at redistributing federal power away from Congress and the bureaucracy. When he encountered difficulty obtaining passage of these programs, he resorted more and more to reform by administrative fiat, especially at the beginning of his second term. All Nixonian domestic reforms were rhetorically linked under the rubric of the New Federalism. Most competed for attention with his well-known interest in foreign affairs. Most involved a degree of the boldness he thought necessary for a successful presidency. Most increased federal regulation of nondistributive public policies. Most were made possible in part because he was a wartime Republican president who took advantage of acting in the Disraeli tradition of enlightened conservatism. Most offended liberals (as well as many conservatives), especially when it came to implementing certain controversial policies with legislation. Many were also undertaken in a crisis atmosphere, which on occasion was manufactured by individual members of Nixon's staff to ensure his attention and action.

In some instances, as political scientist Paul J. Halpern has noted, Nixon's long-standing liberal opponents in Congress "never even bothered to get the facts straight" about these legislative and administrative innovations; the very people who, according to Daniel Moynihan, formed the "natural constituency" for most of Nixon's domestic policies refused to support his programs. It may well have been that many liberals simply could not believe that Nixon would ever do the right thing except for the wrong reason. Thus they seldom took the time to try to determine whether any of his efforts to make the 1970s a decade of reform were legitimate, however politically motivated. Additionally, such partisan opposition made Nixon all the more willing to reorganize the executive branch of government with or without congressional approval.

My own interviews with Nixon and his own (and others') recent attempts to rehabilitate his reputation indicate that Nixon thinks he will outlive the obloquy of Watergate because of his foreign policy initiatives—not because of his domestic policies. Ultimately, however, domestic reform and his attempts at comprehensive reorganization of the executive branch may become the standard by which the Nixon presidency is judged.

Environmental Policy

Although Nixon's aides cite his environmental legislation as one of his major domestic achievements, it was not high on his personal list of federal priorities, despite polls showing its growing importance as a national issue. White House central files released in 1986 clearly reveal that John Ehrlichman was initially instrumental in shaping the president's views on environmental matters and conveying a sense of crisis about them. Most ideas were filtered through him to Nixon. In fact Ehrlichman, whose particular expertise was in land-use policies, has been described by one forest conservation specialist as "the most effective environmentalist since Gifford Pinchot." Ehrlichman and John Whitaker put Nixon ahead of Congress on environmental issues, especially with respect to his use of the permit authority in the Refuse Act of 1899 to begin to clean up water supplies before Congress passed any "comprehensive water pollution enforcement plan."

"Just keep me out of trouble on environmental issues," Nixon reportedly told Ehrlichman. This proved impossible because Congress ignored Nixon's recommended ceilings when it finally passed (over his veto) the Federal Water Pollution Control Act amendments of 1972. Both Ehrlichman and Whitaker agreed then and later that it was "budget-busting" legislation designed to embarrass the president on a popular issue in an election year. Statistics later showed that the money appropriated could not be spent fast enough to achieve the legislation's stated goals. The actual annual expenditures in the first years after passage approximated those originally proposed by Nixon's staff.

Revamping Welfare

Throughout the 1968 presidential campaign Nixon's own views on welfare remained highly unfocused. But once in the Oval Office he set an unexpectedly fast pace on the issue. On January 15, 1969, he demanded an investigation by top aides into a newspaper allegation of corruption in New York City's Human Resources Administration. Nixon's extraordinary welfare legislation originated in a very circuitous fashion with two low-level Democratic holdovers from the Johnson administration, Worth Bateman and James Lyday. These two bureaucrats fortuitously exercised more influence on Robert Finch,

Nixon's first secretary of health, education and welfare, than they had been able to on John W. Gardner and Wilbur J. Cohn, Johnson's two appointees. Finch was primarily responsible for obtaining Nixon's approval of what eventually became known as the Family Assistance Program (FAP).

If FAP had succeeded in Congress it would have changed the emphasis of American welfare from providing services to providing income; thus it would have replaced the Aid to Families with Dependent Children (AFDC) program, whose payments varied widely from state to state. FAP called for anywhere from $1,600 (initially proposed in 1969) to $2,500 (proposed in 1971) for a family of four. States were expected to supplement this amount, and in addition all ablebodied heads of recipient families (except mothers with preschool children) would be required to "accept work or training." However, if a parent refused to accept work or training, only his or her payment would be withheld. In essence, FAP unconditionally guaranteed children an annual income and would have tripled the number of children then being aided by AFDC.

A fundamental switch from services to income payments proved to be too much for congressional liberals and conservatives alike, and they formed a strange alliance to vote it down. Ironically, FAP's final defeat in the Senate led to some very impressive examples of incremental legislation that might not have been passed had it not been for the original boldness of FAP. For example, Supplementary Security Income, approved on October 17, 1972, constituted a guaranteed annual income for the aged, blind, and disabled.

The demise of FAP also led Nixon to support uniform application of the food stamp program across the United States, better health insurance programs for low-income families, and an automatic cost-of-living adjustment for Social Security recipients to help them cope with inflation. In every budget for which his administration was responsible—that is, from fiscal 1971 through fiscal 1975—spending on all human resource programs exceeded spending for defense for the first time since World War II. A sevenfold increase in funding for social services under Nixon made him (not Johnson) the "last of the big spenders" on domestic programs.

Reluctant Civil Rights Achievements

Perhaps the domestic area in which Watergate has most dimmed or skewed our memories of the Nixon years is civil rights. We naturally tend to remember that during his presidency Nixon deliberately violated the civil rights of some of those who opposed his policies or were suspected of leaking information. Nixon has always correctly denied that he was a conservative on civil rights, and indeed his record on this issue, as on so many others, reveals as much political expediency as it does philosophical commitment. By 1968 there was strong southern support for his candidacy. Consequently, during his campaign he implied that if elected he would slow down enforcement of federal school desegregation policies.

Enforcement had already been painfully sluggish since the 1954 *Brown v. Board of Education* decision. By 1968 only 20 percent of black children in the South attended predominantly white schools, and none of this progress had occurred under Eisenhower or Kennedy. Moreover, the most dramatic improvement under Johnson's administration did not take place until 1968, because HEW deadlines for desegregating southern schools had been postponed four times since the passage of the 1964 Civil Rights Act. By the spring of 1968, however, a few lower court rulings, and finally the Supreme Court decision in *Green v. Board of Education,* no longer allowed any president the luxury of arguing that freedom-of-choice plans were adequate for rooting out racial discrimination, or that de facto segregation caused by residential patterns was not as unconstitutional as *de jure* segregation brought about by state or local laws.

Despite the real national crisis that existed over school desegregation, Nixon was not prepared to go beyond what he thought the decision in *Brown* had mandated, because he believed that de facto segregation could not be ended through busing or cutting off funds from school districts. Nine days after Nixon's inauguration, his administration had to decide whether to honor an HEW-initiated cutoff of funds to five southern school districts, originally scheduled to take place in the fall of 1968 but delayed until January 29, 1969. On that day Secretary Finch confirmed the cutoff but also announced that the school districts could claim funds retroactively if they complied with HEW guidelines within sixty days. This offer represented a change from the most recent set of HEW guidelines, developed in March 1968, which Johnson had never formally endorsed by signing.

At the heart of the debate over various HEW guidelines in the last half of the 1960s were two issues: whether the intent of the Civil Rights Act of 1964 had been simply to provide freedom of choice or actually to compel integration in schools; and whether freedom-of-choice agreements negotiated by HEW or lawsuits brought by the Department of Justice were the most effective ways of achieving desegregation. Under the Johnson administration the HEW approach, based on bringing recalcitrant school districts into compliance by cutting off federal funding, had prevailed. Nixon, on the other hand, argued in his First Inaugural that the "laws have caught up with our consciences" and insisted that it was now necessary "to give life to what is in the law." Accordingly, he changed the emphasis in the enforcement of school desegregation from HEW compliance agreements to Justice Department actions—a legal procedure that proved very controversial in 1969 and 1970, but one that is standard now.

Nixon has been justifiably criticized by civil rights advocates for employing delaying tactics in the South, and particularly for not endorsing busing to enforce school desegregation in the North after the April 20, 1971, Supreme Court decision in *Swann v. Charlotte-Mecklenburg Board of Education.* Despite the bitter battle in Congress and between Congress and the executive branch after *Swann,* the Nixon administration's statistical record on school desegregation is impressive. In 1968, 68 percent of all black children in the South and 40 percent in the nation as a whole attended all-black schools. By the end of 1972, 8 percent of southern black children attended all-black schools, and a little less than 12 percent nationwide. A comparison of budget outlays is equally revealing. President Nixon spent $911 million on civil rights activities, including $75 million for civil rights enforcement in fiscal 1969. The Nixon administration's budget for fiscal 1973 called for $2.6 billion in total civil rights outlays, of which $602 million was earmarked for enforcement through a substantially strengthened Equal Employment Opportunity Commission. Nixon supported the civil rights goals of American Indians and women with less reluctance than he did school desegregation because these groups did not pose a major political problem for him and he had no similar legal reservations about how the law should be applied to them.

Mixing Economics and Politics

Nixon spent an inordinate amount of time on domestic and foreign economic matters. Nowhere did he appear to reverse himself more on views he had held before becoming president (or at least on views others attributed to him), and nowhere was his aprincipled pragmatism more evident. Nixon's failure to obtain more revenue through tax reform legislation in 1969, together with rising unemployment and inflation rates in 1970, precipitated an effort (in response to a perceived crisis) to balance U.S. domestic concerns through wage and price controls and international ones through devaluation of the dollar. This vehicle was the New Economic Policy, dramatically announced on August 15, 1971, at the end of a secret Camp David meeting with sixteen economic advisers. Largely as a result of Treasury Secretary Connally's influence, Nixon agreed that if foreign countries continued to demand ever-increasing amounts of gold for the U.S. dollars they held, the United States would go off the gold standard but would at the same time impose wage and price controls to curb inflation. The NEP perfectly reflected the "grand gesture" Connally thought the president should make on economic problems, and the August 15 television broadcast dramatized economic issues that most Americans, seldom anticipating longrange consequences, found boring.

When he was not trying to preempt Congress on regulatory issues, Nixon proposed deregulation based on free-market assumptions that were more traditionally in keeping with conservative Republicanism. The administration ended the draft in the name of economic freedom and recommended deregulation of the production of food crops, tariff and other barriers to international trade, and interest rates paid by various financial institutions. Except for wage and price controls and the devaluation of the dollar, none of these actions was justified in the name of crisis management. In general, however, political considerations made Nixon more liberal on domestic economic matters, confounding both his supporters and his opponents.

Nixon attributes his interest in international economics to the encouragement of John Foster Dulles and his desire as vice-president in the 1950s to create a Foreign Economic Council. Failing in this, he has said that his travels abroad in the 1950s only confirmed his belief that foreign leaders understood economics better than did American leaders, and he was determined to remedy this situation as president. Nixon faced two obstacles in this effort: Kissinger (because "international economics was not Henry's bag"), and State Department officials who saw "economic policy as government to government," which limited their diplomatic view of the world and made themso suspicious or cynical (or both) about the private sector that they refused to promote international commerce to the degree that Nixon thought they should. "Unlike the ignoramuses I encountered among economic officers at various embassies in the 1950s and 1960s," Nixon told me, "I wanted to bring economics to the foreign service."

Because of Nixon's own interest in and knowledge of international trade, he attempted as president to rationalize the formulation of foreign economic policy. After 1962, when he was out of public office and practicing law in New York, he had specialized in international economics and multinational corporations—definitely not Henry Kissinger's areas of expertise. In part because they were not a "team" on foreign economic policy and in part because Nixon bypassed the NSC almost entirely in formulating his New Economic Policy, Nixon relied not on his national security adviser but on other free-thinking outsiders when formulating foreign economic policy.

Next to John Connally, Nixon was most impressed with the economic views of Peter G. Peterson, who, after starting out in 1971 as a White House adviser on international economic affairs, became secretary of commerce in January 1972. Although Connally and Peterson appeared to agree on such early foreign economic initiatives as the NEP and the "get tough" policy toward Third World countries that nationalized U.S. companies abroad, as secretary of commerce Peterson ultimately proved much more sophisticated and sensitive than the secretary of the treasury about the United States' changed economic role in the world. In a December 27, 1971, position paper defending Nixon's NEP, Peterson remarked that the new global situation in which the United States found itself demanded "shared leadership, shared responsibility, and shared burdens. . . . The reform of the international monetary systems," he said, must fully recognize and be solidly rooted in "the growing reality of a genuinely interdependent and increasingly competitive world economy whose goal is mutual, shared prosperity—not artificial, temporary advantage." At no point did Peterson believe, as Connally apparently did, that "the simple realignment of exchange rates" would adequately address the economic realignment problems facing the international economy.

In 1971 Nixon succeeded in establishing an entirely new cabinet-level Council on International Economic Policy (CIEP), headed by Peterson. This was not so much a reorganization of functions as it was an alternative to fill an existing void in the federal structure and to provide "clear top-level focus on international economic issues and to achieve consistency between international and domestic economic policy." For a variety of reasons—not the least of which was Kissinger's general lack of interest in, and disdain for, the unglamorous aspects of international economics—the CIEP faltered and finally failed after Nixon left office. Its demise seems to have been hastened by Kissinger's recommendation to the Congressional Commission on Organization of Foreign Policy that it be eliminated, despite the fact that others, including Peterson, testified on its behalf. The CIEP was subsequently merged with the Office of the Special Trade Representative.

Even with Nixon's impressive foreign and domestic record, it cannot be said that he would have succeeded as a managerial or administrative president had Watergate not occurred. Entrenched federal bureaucracies are not easily controlled or divested of power even with the best policy-oriented management strategies. That his foreign policy management seems more successful is also no surprise: diplomatic bureaucracies are smaller, more responsive, and easier to control than their domestic counterparts. Moreover, public concern (except for Vietnam) remained minimal as usual, and individual presidential foreign policy initiatives are more likely to be remembered and to appear effective than domestic ones. Nonetheless, the real importance of Nixon's presidency may well come to rest not on Watergate or foreign policy, but on his attempts to restructure the executive branch along functional lines, to bring order to the federal bureaucracy, and to achieve lasting domestic reform. The degree to which those Nixonian administrative tactics that were legal and ethical (and most of them were) became consciously or unconsciously the model for his successors in the Oval Office will determine his final place in history.

Although Nixon's corporate presidency remains publicly discredited, much of it has been privately preserved. Perhaps this is an indication that in exceptional cases presidential effectiveness can transcend popular (and scholarly) disapproval. What Nixon lacked in charisma and honesty, he may in the long run make up for with his phoenixlike ability to survive disaster. Nixon has repeatedly said: "No politician is dead until he admits it." It is perhaps an ironic commentary on the state of the modern presidency that Richard Nixon's management style and substantive foreign and domestic achievements look better and better when compared with those of his immediate successors in the Oval Office.

NO

Bruce J. Schulman

"Down to the Nut-Cutting": The Nixon Presidency and American Public Life

. . . Nixon's ambitious and cunning policy agenda would poison American politics and fragment American society. His presidency, often deliberately, sometimes unintentionally, drilled a deep well of cynicism about national politics—about the possibilities for community and communication, about the capacity of government to address the nation's needs, about the dignity and necessity of public service itself. In the process, Nixon shifted the balance of power in American politics and the terms of debate in American culture. . . .

Tricky Dick

. . . Nixon's resentments persisted as well: his crude disregard for Jews, his contempt for African Americans, his hatred of the press. But most of all he hated the establishment, for its wealth and connections, its intellectual and cultural hauteur, its exclusiveness. "In this period of our history, the leaders and the educated class are decadent," President Nixon instructed his chief of staff, H. R. Haldeman. The educated become "brighter in the head, but weaker in the spine." The nation's elite, in Nixon's mind, no longer possessed any character. Nixon would prove it to them, and prove it in the most cunning of ways.

Nixon's presidency presented more than just a fascinating, and baffling, psychological profile. It even accomplished more than the unprecedented abuse of power Americans have too narrowly labeled "Watergate." His administration also posed a crucial historical problem about the evolution of contemporary American politics and public policy. Was Nixon the last of the liberals, or the first of the conservatives? Did his domestic presidency mark the last gasp of postwar liberalism—of energetic, activist government? Or did it mark the onset of a new, more cautious era—of small government, fiscal conservatism, diverting resources and initiative from the public to the private sector?

In some ways, Nixon did seem like the last interventionist liberal. He doubled the budgets for the National Endowment for the Arts (NEA) and the National Endowment for the Humanities (NEH). He proposed a guaranteed income for all Americans, signed the nation's principal environmental protection laws, and expanded affirmative action for racial minorities. Under Nixon's watch, the regulatory state swelled; federal agencies began monitoring nearly every aspect of American life. The Nixon administration created the Occupational Health and Safety Administration and instituted the first peacetime wage and price controls in U.S. history.

Nixon even conceded that "I am now a Keynesian in economics." He embraced the idea that a humming economy was the responsibility of the federal government and that the White House should actively intervene in economic affairs, carefully calibrating the policy controls, to ensure robust growth and low unemployment. Nixon even dispensed with the gold standard, that most reassuring symbol of conservative fiscal orthodoxy.

By the middle of his first term, Nixon's seeming unwillingness to crush liberalism and disband social programs angered many committed conservatives. Patrick Buchanan, the president's in-house right-wing fire-eater, warned that conservatives felt Nixon had betrayed them. "They are the niggers of the Nixon administration," Buchanan fumed in a scathing seven-page memo.

On the other hand, the Nixon era seemed to initiate a new, more conservative era in American politics. Nixon intervened on behalf of southern school districts, supporting efforts to curtail busing and slow the pace of school desegregation. He attacked the Warren Court, replacing such liberal icons as Abe Fortas and Earl Warren with Warren Burger and William Rehnquist (and even unsuccessfully attempted to appoint two southern conservatives to the Supreme Court). He dismantled, or at least attempted to eliminate, the principal agencies of 1960s liberalism, such as the Office of Economic Opportunity (which ran Lyndon Johnson's war on poverty) and the legal services program. While he signed the popular legislation restricting air and water pollution, Nixon also established procedures for economic cost-benefit review of all environmental regulations. And he made it clear that officials should scrap or water down any pollution control that might slow the economy or antagonize business.

Nixon also pioneered what came to be called devolution—transferring authority from the federal government to state and local governments and from the public sector to the private sphere. Through a complicated series of initiatives—a combination of block grants, revenue sharing, and the like—Nixon consigned to the states policy areas that had been the responsibility of the federal government. He also took problems and programs that had been thought to require public attention and shifted them to business and the private sector. Indeed, when Nixon left office in August 1974, CBS Evening News commentator Rod MacLeish described devolution as Nixon's major achievement. "As president," MacLeish told a national television audience, "Mr. Nixon made serious policy efforts to disburse responsibility as well as money for the alleviation of our domestic problems."

By the end of his first term, Nixon had embraced small government as his campaign theme. Concluding that cutting government could become a winning strategy, Nixon declared in his second inaugural address that "government must learn to take less from people so that people can do more for themselves." Reversing John F. Kennedy's famous call for collective sacrifice,

Nixon instructed, "In our own lives, let each of us ask—not just what will government do for me, but what can I do for myself?"

Faced with such a contradictory record, Nixon watchers have been tempted to split the difference. But Nixon the president did more than combine economic liberalism with social conservatism. He was no mere transitional president, a passage from one era to another that embraced elements of both, although many scholars have portrayed him as such. Others have dismissed Nixon as nothing more than opportunistic, swaying with the prevailing political winds. Primarily interested in foreign affairs, Nixon viewed domestic policy as a nuisance; he would do anything so long as it would not cost him votes.

Splitting the difference, however, mistakes not only Nixon's character, but his presidency's decisive influence on American political culture. Although Nixon was both a transitional president and an opportunist, those assessments miss his historical significance—the ways that the man (the psychological puzzle) and the policies (the historical problem) intertwined.

Not for nothing did Nixon earn the nickname Tricky Dick. Nixon was indeed the first of the conservatives. He fooled many observers, then and now, because he pursued this conservative agenda—this assault on public life—in a particularly devious sort of way. Unlike Barry Goldwater before him and Ronald Reagan after him, Nixon never took on big government directly. He rarely assailed the liberal establishment he so furiously hated and so openly resented. He did not attack liberal programs or the agencies and political networks that undergirded them. Rather, he subtly, cunningly undermined them. Nixon wanted to destroy the liberal establishment by stripping it of its bases of support and its sources of funds. . . .

Toward a Guaranteed Income?

Of all Richard Nixon's domestic policies, the most celebrated and the most controversial proposal never actually materialized: the Family Assistance Plan (FAP). In August 1969, Nixon appeared before the nation with a radical scheme, a far-reaching program the federal government had never before even contemplated—a minimum guaranteed income for every American family. Nixon proposed to abolish the existing welfare system with its labyrinthine series of benefits: AFDC (Aid to Families with Dependent Children), food stamps, housing subsidies, furniture grants. Nixon also promised to eliminate the army of social workers who ran the system and the mountains of paperwork they produced—to get rid of all that and simply replace it with direct cash grants to the poor.

"We face an urban crisis, a social crisis—and at the same time, a crisis of confidence in the capacity of government to do its job," Nixon explained when he announced the program. "Our states and cities find themselves sinking in a welfare quagmire, as case loads increase, as costs escalate, and as the welfare system stagnates enterprise and perpetuates dependency." The system, he complained, "created an incentive for fathers to desert their families," it spawned grossly unequal variations in benefits levels, it forced poor children to begin "life in an atmosphere of handout and dependency."

An ominous "welfare crisis" loomed by the time Nixon took command of the war on poverty. Between 1960 and 1975 the number of relief recipients doubled, from 7 to 14 million people. Including in-kind assistance—food stamps, Medicaid, public housing—more than 24 million Americans received means-tested benefits by the end of the Nixon years. By highlighting the problems of poverty, Lyndon Johnson's Great Society and the agencies it created had focused attention on the impoverished. Daniel Patrick Moynihan, the former Kennedy-Johnson poverty warrior who ran Nixon's Urban Affairs Council, became especially concerned with the explosion of AFDC costs in New York City. Although the economy hummed and unemployment had actually decreased, New York's welfare caseload had tripled in only five years. Moynihan and Nixon became convinced (wrongly) that New York's troubles portended the imminent collapse of the national welfare system.

Most observers, across the American political spectrum, agreed that something had to be done about welfare. On the far left, welfare radicals like the National Welfare Rights Organization (NWRO) sought to empower the poor. A group representing mostly single mothers, the NWRO encouraged poor people to apply for public assistance—to demand welfare as a right, not to accept it reluctantly and shamefully. And in fact, the vast expansion in caseloads during the 1960s stemmed not from growing numbers of people eligible for welfare but from a huge increase in the number of already eligible poor people who applied for welfare. In 1960, only about one-third of the Americans eligible for welfare actually received it; by the early 1970s, the figure had climbed to 90 percent, thanks in part to the agitation of advocates like the NWRO.

At the other end of the spectrum, free market economist Milton Friedman, a leading conservative guru, promoted his plan for a negative income tax. The grab-bag of welfare programs, Friedman asserted, served only the interests of the legislators who enacted them and the bureaucrats who administered them. Poverty resulted not from failed institutions, broken homes, or the legacy of slavery, but from a pure and simple shortage of cash. Government could cure poverty by dispensing money directly to the needy through the tax system; Americans earning less than an established minimum would receive money from the Internal Revenue Service (IRS) just as those above the threshold paid in their taxes. The negative income tax would allow poor citizens to purchase the goods and services they needed rather than the ones their congressmen and social workers insisted they should have.

Friedman was no great ally of public assistance, and he wanted to get government out of the welfare business. That sentiment appealed to Nixon. "Nixon didn't like welfare workers," his aide Martin Anderson recalled in a television documentary. A shift to cash grants would undermine the entire welfare establishment, circumventing the bureaucrats, the psychologists, and the social workers.

Nixon embraced the radical analyses of Friedman and the NWRO, rejecting the proposals for moderate, incremental welfare reform circulating on Capitol Hill and within the social service agencies. He would replace the entire

AFDC system with a national minimum standard, available to the welfare poor and working poor alike. "What I am proposing," Nixon announced, "is that the Federal Government build a foundation under the income of every American family with dependent children that cannot care for itself—and wherever in America that family may live." A federal minimum would support all such families, intact or "broken," working or on welfare. The program would include work incentives (to encourage earnings, benefits would be reduced by only fifty cents for every dollar earned) and work requirements (every recipient except mothers of preschool children would have to accept employment or job training). "A guaranteed income," Nixon explained, distinguishing his plan from rival proposals, "establishes a right without any responsibilities. Family assistance recognizes a need and establishes a responsibility."

Nixon seemingly pressed for a liberal goal: one that would expand welfare and extend benefits to millions of working poor. A guaranteed income for all Americans truly aimed to unite the fractured nation, to make every citizen a member of a national community with national standards. Assistance for every family seemed to envision everyone as part of the same national family. But however extravagant the hopes of FAP supporters, Nixon's guaranteed income plan pursued an authentically conservative objective. Nixon sought to dismantle the welfare system and the agencies and programs that administered it, eliminate the social workers who ran them, and starve the liberal networks they nourished.

Certainly Nixon cared more about undercutting his liberal opposition than about putting FAP into effect. While analysts disagreed then and today about Nixon's commitment to welfare reform, he certainly made little effort to secure its passage. Despite Moynihan's urging that he spend political capital to secure congressional approval, the president remained on the sidelines, allowing his most far-reaching policy proposal to wither and die.

And expire it did. Congressional Democrats and their liberal allies denounced Nixon's guaranteed minimum as too low. Demanding a much higher income floor—roughly four times the level Nixon offered—the NWRO urged supporters to "Zap FAP." The NWRO also encouraged Americans to "Live Like a Dog" on the proposed budget, which they computed to just nineteen cents a meal per person. Mainstream liberal organizations like the National Association for the Advancement of Colored People, the American Friends Service Committee, and the Methodist church also denounced Nixon's plan. Meanwhile, conservatives opposed FAP because it would extend public assistance to millions more Americans and add billions of dollars to the federal budget.

Representative Wilbur Mills (D, Arkansas), chairman of the Ways and Means Committee, steered FAP through the House, adding sweeteners for the states that offered low benefits. But the Senate Finance Committee, largely controlled by southern and rural legislators, buried the plan. Nixon resubmitted FAP three times but never worked to secure its passage. In 1972, when Democratic presidential candidate George McGovern announced his own proposed "demogrant" of a thousand dollars for every man, woman, and child in the United States, the FAP passed into oblivion. The very idea of replacing the welfare system with cash grants became the stuff of derisive jokes.

Denounced by both left and right, FAP ended up on the ash heap of history, but it was no failure for Richard Nixon. By introducing the guaranteed income program, Nixon divided his opponents and torpedoed more generous proposals for welfare reform. His apparent boldness in meeting the welfare crisis insulated Nixon from criticism; no one could claim that he fiddled while New York and other cities burned (or at least went broke). At the same time, the president's solicitude for the working poor, antipathy to the welfare bureaucracy, and stringent work requirements appealed to blue-collar voters and appeased the Republican right wing. Even in defeat, Nixon had pulled off a remarkable tactical victory.

The Silent Majority

Nixon's indirect, underhanded strategy with regard to welfare, environmental protection, housing, and the arts represented more than a career politician's cunning or a pathological liar's need to be devious. Every one of these maneuvers advanced Nixon's larger political objective: his ambition to transform American politics by creating a new majority coalition in the United States.

Nixon had long envisioned such a realignment. His 1968 campaign had hinged on winning over two sets of voters that normally remained loyal Democrats but appeared ready to switch parties. First, Nixon targeted white southerners. By hinting he would slow the pace of desegregation, Nixon's "southern strategy" drew Dixie's yellow-dog Democrats and prosperous new migrants to the metropolitan South into the emerging Republican majority. Second, Nixon went after blue-collar northerners—white ethnics who for generations had voted their pocketbooks and supported liberal Democrats, but had recently become alarmed about the social issues—crime, drugs, loose morals, streets filled with antiwar protestors and black militants.

In 1968, white southerners seemed ripe for this strategy. Many had opposed the civil rights revolution and resented the northern liberals they felt had imposed on them an odious second Reconstruction. In 1964, many southerners had abandoned the Democrats—the "Party of the Fathers"—and cast votes for Senator Barry Goldwater, and outspoken opponent of the Civil Rights Act. Goldwater won five Deep South states.

Nixon certainly welcomed the votes of disgruntled segregationists. The campaign enlisted South Carolina senator Strom Thurmond, the former Dixiecrat leader and recent convert to the GOP, to rally white southerners. Thurmond promised that Nixon would support local control of public schools. Nixon even hired a Thurmond protégé to coordinate his campaign in the South and bombarded the region with advertisements warning against wasted votes for Alabama governor George Wallace, the hero of massive resistance running a third-party campaign for president.

Still, in 1968 Nixon carefully chose not to tread in Thurmond or Goldwater's footsteps. The campaign recognized that Wallace had locked up the Deep South. Nixon understood that overt racial appeals for the Wallace vote would alienate moderates, and even many conservatives, in the burgeoning suburbs of the metropolitan South. So Nixon largely conceded the segregationist, rural

Deep South that Goldwater had won and constructed a plurality connecting the Sunbelt with blue-collar Rustbelt neighborhoods.

In a very close race, Nixon's strategists focused on middle-class white voters in the industrializing subdivisions of the peripheral South. The population of the South's major metropolises, Nixon recognized, had doubled or even tripled in the 1950s and 1960s. New suburbs were crowded with professionals and skilled workers from outside the South and young families who had come of age after the *Brown* decision and found massive resistance self-defeating.

In September 1968, Nixon launched a campaign swing through Dixie in Charlotte, North Carolina. There, he addressed a polite, well-dressed, middle class crowd. He made his familiar stump appeal to forgotten Americans, never even mentioning race. Pressed later by an interviewer, he staked out a middle ground, affirming support for *Brown* but criticizing the Democrats and the courts for pushing too hard, too fast. Nixon cleverly laid out a moderate approach, neither championing minority rights like Hubert Humphrey nor defending segregation and states' rights like Goldwater and Wallace. He simultaneously endorsed local desegregation efforts—the nominally color-blind freedom-of-choice plans that had enrolled a few black students in formerly all-black schools across the South and Southwest—and opposed openly race-conscious remedies like busing that threatened dramatic changes in the status quo.

That strategy appealed to crucial swing voters in the 1968 election, helping the Republican standard-bearer win Virginia, the Carolinas, Florida, Tennessee, and Kentucky. Nixon's southern strategy offered more than a short-term political prize. It was premised on the fundamental demographic and political shifts that would continue throughout the Seventies and would give a new shape to American life.

A young political consultant named Kevin Phillips diagnosed this power shift in a series of position papers for the Nixon campaign and in a 1969 book, *The Emerging Republican Majority.* Phillips identified a new locus of power in national politics, a region he called the Sunbelt that connected the booming subdivisions of the metropolitan South, the sun country of Florida and southern California, and the desert Southwest. Phillips described the Sunbelt's conservative leanings and its potential as the foundation for a political realignment. The "huge postwar white middle class push to the Florida-California sun country" seemed to be forging a new political era. "The persons most drawn to the new sun culture are the pleasure-seekers, the bored, the ambitious, the space-age technicians and the retired—a super-slice of the rootless, socially mobile group known as the American middle class." The region's politics, he concluded, "is bound to cast a lengthening national shadow."

Nixon and his top advisers recognized the growing influence of the Sunbelt South in national politics. Shortly after becoming president, Nixon changed his voting residence from New York to Florida. "The time has come," he declared in 1970, "to stop kicking the South around." He detected not only the rise of the Sunbelt but the growing influence of a Sunbelt mind-set in American life generally. The South and Southwest seemed to embody a new set of cultural attitudes about race, taxation, defense, government spending, and social mores—Sunbelt attitudes that might eventually spread into the suburbs and working-class neighborhoods of the old North.

In August 1970, while vacationing in San Clemente, Pat Buchanan alerted Nixon to *The Real Majority,* a political manual for the coming decade by Richard M. Scammon and Ben J. Wattenberg. Hoping to revive their own party, these two disaffected Democrats mapped the political landscape in Nixonian terms. The voter in the center, they asserted, the key to assembling a winning coalition, was a "47 year old Catholic housewife in Dayton, Ohio whose husband is a machinist." Since the 1930s, she and her blue-collar husband had always voted Democratic. According to Scammon and Wattenberg, they had voted their pocketbooks, looking to liberal Democrats for strong unions, high wages, cheap mortgages, and college loans for their children. But now, at the end of the 1960s, they might defect to the Republicans and vote conservative on social issues. "To know that the lady in Dayton is afraid to walk the streets alone at night," Scammon and Wattenberg explained, "to know that she has a mixed view about blacks and civil rights because before moving to the suburbs she lived in a neighborhood that became all black, to know that her brother-in-law is a policeman, to know that she does not have the money to move if her new neighborhood deteriorates, to know that she is deeply distressed that her son is going to a community junior college where LSD was found on campus—to know all this is the beginning of contemporary political wisdom."

The book thrilled Nixon. If he did nothing to deny blue-collar workers their fat pay envelopes and hit hard on rioters, protesters, and drugs, he could forge a new conservative majority. "P [the president] talked about Real Majority and need to get that thinking over to all our people," Haldeman reported. "Wants to hit pornography, dope, bad kids." Nixon himself asserted that the Republicans needed to "preempt the Social Issue in order to get the Democrats on the defensive. We should aim our strategy primarily at disaffected Democrats, a blue-collar workers, and at working-class white ethnics. We should," the president concluded, "set out to capture the vote of the forty-seven-year-old Dayton housewife."

Nixon made wooing these voters—Americans he famously named the Silent Majority in a 1969 speech—the subject of concerted effort. Indeed for several years, Nixon envisioned creating a new political party—he usually called it the Independent Conservative party—to foster a wholesale realignment of American politics. This new party would unite white southerners, the Silent Majority, and traditionally Republican rural and suburban conservatives around social issues. It would ostracize the socially liberal, economically conservative eastern establishment—Wall Street and business Republicans like Nelson Rockefeller who had long dominated Republican party affairs—and attack liberal Democrats for playing so heavily to "the fashionable, but unrepresentative constituencies of the young, the poor, the racial minorities, and the students."

Nixon envisioned a new party that would appeal to the "Okie from Muskogee," the hero of Merle Haggard's 1969 country and western hit. "I'm proud to be an Okie from Muskogee," Haggard declared, "a place where even squares can have a ball." Nixon admired Haggard's anthem as the authentic voice of the Silent Majority; Haggard's Oklahoma town honored the values of millions of worried, disgruntled Americans. "We don't smoke marijuana in

Muskogee," the singer explained. "We don't take our trips on LSD. We don't burn our draft cards down on Main Street. We like livin' right and bein' free." The song so impressed the president that Nixon invited Haggard to perform at the White House.

To build this new political agenda, Nixon not only inflamed the Silent Majority about social issues and appealed to the national pride of working Americans. He also took a number of concrete steps. First, he reached out to organized labor. Recognizing the social conservatism and deep-rooted patriotism of union Democrats, Nixon believed he could pry their votes away from the party of FDR. After National Guardsmen shot and killed antiwar marchers at Kent State University, 150,000 hard hats paraded for flag and country down New York's Broadway. Outraged that New York's liberal mayor had dropped the flag on city hall to half-staff in honor of the slain antiwar protesters, the construction workers denounced (and even beat up a handful of) hippies and student radicals, defended the war in Vietnam, and supported their president in the White House. Nixon deeply appreciated the construction workers' show of support, and the march reinforced his determination to incorporate labor into his New American Majority. The president offered generous loopholes for organized labor in his wage and price controls, horrifying Wall Street and business interests.

Second, Nixon named Texas governor John Connally, a former protégé of Lyndon Johnson, as his secretary of the treasury. By naming Connally to his cabinet and grooming him as his successor, Nixon hoped to entice conservative southern Democrats into his new majority. The president also understood that Connally would happily dispense with Republican economic orthodoxy and keep working people happy about their paychecks while Nixon stung the Democrats on social issues.

Nixon also valued Connally's Lone Star state charisma. Henry Kissinger thought that "there was no American public figure Nixon held in such awe. Connally's swaggering self-assurance," Kissinger reflected, "fulfilled Nixon's image of how a leader should act; he found it possible to emulate this conduct only in marginal comments on memoranda, never face to face." And Nixon never denigrated Connally behind his back, "a boon not granted to many."

In August 1971, under Connally's leadership, Nixon reversed field on economic policies. He adopted wage and price controls to cool inflation, a series of tax cuts to stimulate the economy in time for the 1972 elections, and he closed the gold window and allowed the dollar to float against other currencies, ending the Bretton Woods monetary system that had stabilized the international currency markets since World War II.

His mission accomplished, Connally returned to his native Texas in 1972 and took control of "Democrats for Nixon." The president imagined Connally as his natural successor. "By structuring it right," Haldeman recalled Nixon's ruminations in his diary, "we could develop a new majority party. Under a new name. Get control of the Congress without an election, simply by realignment, and make a truly historic change in the entire American political structure." From this coalition, with Nixon and Connally as "the strong men," Connally "clearly would emerge as the candidate for the new party in '76, and the P would strongly back him in that."

As the 1972 election approached, Nixon made little use of traditional party labels, touting his connections to Democrats like Connally and downplaying his own Republican affiliation. "Use the new American Majority," he told Haldeman, "not Republican majority." Nixon would seek the "election of Congressman and Senators who will support the P[resident], not who are Republicans."

Nixon even trumpeted his frequent escapes to La Casa Pacifica, his seaside retreat in San Clemente, California, as an assault on the establishment. Appealing to his new conservative majority, Nixon instructed his staff to tout his San Clemente home as the "Western White House." White House communications director Herb Klein informed reporters that the "San Clemente operation gives Westerners a symbolic share in the business of government. . . ." It proved that "Government is not an exclusively Eastern institution."

Nixon recognized by 1971 that the center of the American political spectrum had shifted toward the right. The archetypal Dayton housewife and her machinist husband were becoming fed up with liberals, bureaucracy, and big government. Many of them had moved to southern California, the outskirts of Houston, the suburbs of Charlotte and Atlanta. Increasingly these one-time loyal Democrats and millions of others like them believed that government programs helped only other people, not themselves. "We've had enough social programs: forced integration, education, housing," Nixon told his chief of staff as the 1972 election approached. "People don't want more on welfare. They don't want to help the working poor, and our mood has to be harder on this, not softer."

Nixon instructed his staff to adopt a tougher, more openly conservative stance. Attorney General John Mitchell launched a furious attack against black militants and student protesters in *Women's Wear Daily.* Mitchell tore into "these stupid kids" on college campuses and "the professors are just as bad if not worse. They don't know anything. Nor do these stupid bastards who are ruining our educational institutions." This country, Mitchell warned, "is going so far right you are not even going to recognize it." Nixon applauded his attorney general's hard line. "John—Good Job," he wrote. "Don't back off."

Nixon's strategy paid rich dividends in November 1972. He won reelection by a landslide over Democratic challenger George McGovern, in the process assembling the new majority of his fondest political dreams. Both organized labor and the white South went heavily for Nixon in 1972.

After winning reelection, Nixon decided to promote what he called a conservative revolution. "Now I planned to give expression to the more conservative values and beliefs of the New Majority throughout the country," Nixon recalled in his memoirs, "and use my power to put some teeth in my new American Revolution." Sounding his new conservative theme, Nixon declared in his second inaugural address, "Let us remember that America was not built by government but by people; not by welfare, but by work."

Still, the president understood that although Americans opposed expansive government in principle, in practice they demanded many specific public programs. Nixon understood, as he put it in a cabinet meeting, that "government spending is a lousy issue. People are for spending." The only way to slash popular programs was to portray cuts as "the only way to avoid inflation and higher taxes. . . . You never win," the president explained, "on the question of screwing up rich kids. You have to hit on higher taxes. You never debate the programs. By cutting the budget back, we are avoiding more taxes, and that's the line we have to use."

The budget thus became the instrument of Nixon's conservative revolution. The president set stringent targets for the fiscal year ending June 1973; to reach them, he refused to spend more than $12 billion that the Congress had already appropriated. This infuriated the Congress, which soon would debate whether these "impoundments" merited impeachment.

The impoundments were just the beginning. Having sundered the liberal policy networks and collapsed the liberal electoral coalition, Nixon next aimed to slash domestic spending. In February 1973, he proposed a shocking budget for the 1974 fiscal year, featuring deep cuts in government programs. Nixon proposed to eliminate urban renewal, impacted-area aid for school districts near military bases, hospital construction grants, soil management payments to farmers, and the Rural Electrification Administration. He slashed spending on milk for schoolchildren, mental health facilities, compensatory education for poor students. He meant to reverse the Great Society, calling for the abolition of the Office of Economic Opportunity, the vanguard of Lyndon Johnson's war on poverty.

Nixon would see neither his new American revolution nor his new majority politics through to completion. By the time he unveiled his rightward shift and his harsh budgets, the nation had become obsessed with the unfolding story of scandal in the White House. But, oddly, Nixon's personal failures—a scandal so large that he would become the first (and thus far only) president driven from office—would only aid his larger agenda. In trusting too much in government," Nixon intoned, "we have asked more of it than we can deliver." The time has come to turn away from activist government and replace it with "a new feeling of self-discipline.

In retrospect, most observers have read Nixon's declaration ironically; Watergate certainly proved that Americans had trusted too much in Nixon's government. But although the scandals brought down a Republican conservative and helped to elect the only Democratic president of the era, their principal effect was to discredit government itself. Watergate only intensified Americans' alienation from public life: their contempt for the secrecy, inefficiency, and failures of "big government.". . .

In fact, Watergate impressed many contemporary observers as a bizarre series of events presided over by a singular villain; it had been "historic but irrelevant." A year after Nixon left office, CBS News correspondent Bruce Morton concluded that "the fact is Watergate didn't change much." A decade later, many pundits echoed Morton's assessment. "Most experts," the *Los Angeles Times* reported on the tenth anniversary of Nixon's ouster, "find no evidence that the traumatic ousting of a U.S. President has caused any basic change in public attitudes about either the American system of government or the persons who occupy public positions." Sure, public confidence in government waned after Watergate, but it had been declining since the race riots and antiwar protests of the mid-1960s.

Still, Nixon's presidency, and its dramatic end, nourished a profound unease with a direction that American life had taken. And the scandal's most conspicuous and enduring effect ironically realized some of Richard Nixon's most grandiose objectives. Watergate gave a boost to conservatism and conservative Republican politicians. That effect did not immediately appear; in the first blip after Nixon's ruin, the Republicans took a bath as the Democrats won big in the 1974 midterm elections. In 1976, enough resentment persisted that Gerald Ford, Nixon's pardoner, narrowly lost the presidency to an unknown whose platform consisted of a fairly convincing promise that he would never lie to the American people.

But the general trends bolstered conservatives. The ultimate lesson of Watergate remained "you can't trust the government." The scandal reinforced a generalized antigovernment passion whose main effect worked against Democrats and liberals and for Republicans and conservatives. Even President Jimmy Carter represented a more conservative faction of the Democratic party: southern, fiscally responsible, suspicious of labor unions and government regulation.

When convicted felon and former attorney general John Mitchell left Washington, reporters mocked his earlier prediction. "In the next ten years," Mitchell had prophesied, "this country will go so far to the right you won't recognize it." Reporters shook their heads, but John Mitchell would have the last laugh.

And perhaps his chief would enjoy it. In retirement, Nixon would witness his enemies in disarray, their conception of government as the instrument of national purpose discredited, their vision of an inclusive national community debased. . . .

POSTSCRIPT

Was Richard Nixon America's Last Liberal President?

Joan Hoff-Wilson is one of the few professional historians to render a positive evaluation of President Nixon. She places him in the context of the late 1960s and early 1970s, when support for big government, New Deal, Great Society programs had dimmed, and the bipartisan, anticommunist foreign policy consensus had been shattered by the Vietnam War. She gives him high marks for vertically restructuring the executive branch of the government and for attempting a similar reorganization of the federal bureaucracy.

Unlike most defenders of Nixon, Hoff-Wilson considers Nixon's greatest achievement to be domestic. Although Nixon was a conservative, the welfare state grew during his presidency. In the area of civil rights, between 1968 and 1972, affirmative action programs were implemented, and schools with all black children in the southern states declined from 68 percent to 8 percent. Even on such Democratic staples as welfare, the environment, and economic planning, Nixon outflanked the liberals.

Hoff-Wilson has fleshed out her ideas in much greater detail in *Nixon Reconsidered* (Basic Books, 1994). British conservative cabinet minister and historian Jonathan Aitken has also written a favorable and more panoramic view of the former president entitled *Nixon: A Life* (Regnery Gateway, 1993).

Historian Stephen E. Ambrose's three-volume biography on Nixon (Simon & Schuster, 1987–1991) also substantiates Hoff-Wilson's emphasis on Nixon's domestic successes. Ambrose's evaluation is even more remarkable because he was a liberal historian who campaigned for George McGovern in 1972 and had to be talked into writing a Nixon biography by his publisher. In domestic policy, Ambrose told *The Washington Post* on November 26, 1989, Nixon "was proposing things in '73 and '74 he couldn't even make the front pages with—national health insurance for all, a greatly expanded student loan operation, and energy and environmental programs." With regard to foreign policy, both Ambrose and Aitken disagree with Hoff-Wilson; they consider Nixon's foreign policy substantial and far-sighted. In the second volume of his biography, *Nixon: The Triumph of a Politician, 1962–1972* (Simon & Schuster, 1989), Ambrose concludes that the president was "without peer in foreign relations where 'profound pragmatic' vision endowed him with the potential to become a great world statesman."

Professor Bruce Schulman disagrees with historians like Hoff-Wilson who see Nixon as the last liberal or with others who view him as a mere political opportunist. Schulman makes a strong case that Nixon pretended to support liberal measures in his first term such as increased national funding for the arts and humanities, enforcement of environmental laws, more public housing and a guaranteed annual income for poverty-ridden citizens. But as Schulman points out, many of these programs would be passed to private agencies or state and local governments through the use of block grants and revenue-sharing mechanisms. In the case of Family Assistance Program, Schulman believes Nixon expected Congress to kill the idea because it was too extreme for conservatives and didn't guarantee enough income to appease the radicals.

Schulman makes a strong case that Nixon spent the 1968 and 1972 presidential campaigns building a new conservative Republican majority. An avid reader, Nixon absorbed the ideas of Kevin Phillips, *The Emerging Republican Majority* (1969) and Richard M. Scammon and Ben J. Wattenberg's *The Real Majority* (1970). These authors suggested that the president could fashion a majority coalition of white southern Democratic conservatives, who disliked the civil rights acts; northern blue-collar workers who were more concerned about riots, increased crime, and use of illegal drugs than economic issues; and finally, migrants to the sunbelt states of Florida, Arizona, and southern California who retired or worked in space-age technological industries. Critics like veteran *The Washington Post* columnist David Broder disagree with this analysis. Because Nixon was obsessed with his reelection campaign in 1972, the president funneled all the money into his personal reelection campaign organization known as CREEP and defunded the money that the Republican National Committee could have used to support state and local candidates. The result was a 49-state electoral college victory for Nixon over his anti-war Democratic opponent George McGovern while the Democrats maintained strong majorities in the House of Representatives and the United States Senate. Had Nixon expended his political capital on state and local races, perhaps the Watergate burglary might not have happened. For Broder's comments, see the PBS 3-hour production on *Nixon: The American Experience* (1991) available on videotape or DVD.

Schulman believes that Watergate did not reinforce the belief that the system worked to curb an abuse of presidential power. Instead, it reinforced the negative attitude toward government that the American public had experienced with Lyndon Johnson's credibility gap in managing the Vietnam War. Nixon's former attorney general and campaign manager John Mitchell had it right in 1974 when he told a group of disbelieving reporters: "In the next ten years, this country will go so far to the right you won't recognize it." Reporters shook their heads but Reagan was elected for two terms in the 1980s, and in 1994, the Republicans swept the Democrats out of the House and controlled both houses of Congress for the first time since 1946.

In addition to the books mentioned, students should begin their research with Melvin Small's *The Presidency of Richard Nixon* (1999), a fair and balanced study in the University Press of Kansas' American Presidency series complete with footnotes and bibliography. David Greenberg has a fascinating study of *Nixon's Shadow: The History of an Image* (Norton, 2003), which chronicles the life and career of his images in search of the real Nixon. Jeff Hay has edited a series of secondary interpretations of *Richard Nixon* (2001) in the Greenhaven Press series on *Presidents and Their Decisions*. Interestingly, Hay neglects the domestic side, which Professor Hoff-Wilson claims were Nixon's major successes. This gap is filled by Allen J. Matusow's critical *Nixon's Economy: Booms, Busts, Dollars & Votes* (University of Kansas Press, 1998). Other biographies worth consulting include the liberal historian Herbert Parmet's panoramic *Richard Nixon and His America* (Little, Brown, 1990), the first to be based on Nixon's pre-presidential papers. Less thoroughly researched in primary sources but more insightful is *The New York Times* reporter Tom Wicker's *One of Us: Richard Nixon and the American Dream* (Random House, 1991).

In order to gain a real feel for the Nixon years, you should consult contemporary or primary accounts. Nixon himself orchestrated his own rehabilitation in *RN: The Memoirs of Richard Nixon* (Grosset & Dunlop, 1978); *The Real War* (Warner Books, 1980); *Real Peace* (Little, Brown, 1984); *No More Vietnams* (Arbor House, 1985); and *In the Arena: A Memoir of Victory, Defeat and Renewal* (Simon & Schuster, 1990). Nixon's own accounts should be compared with former national security adviser Henry Kissinger's memoirs *White House Years* (Little, Brown, 1979). *The Haldeman Diaries: Inside the Nixon White House* (Putnam, 1994), which is the subject of Kutler's review essay, is essential for any undertaking of Nixon. Haldeman's account fleshes out the daily tensions of life in the Nixon White House and adds important details to the Nixon and Kissinger accounts. Other primary accounts include Kenneth W. Thompson, ed., *The Nixon Presidency: Twenty-Two Intimate Perspectives of Richard M. Nixon, Portraits of American Presidents series,* vol. 6 (University Press of America, 1987), which contains a series of discussions with former officials of the Nixon administration conducted by the White Burkett Miller Center for the Study of Public Affairs at the University of Virginia.

Three of the best review essays on the new historiography about America's thirty seventh president are "Theodore Draper: Nixon, Haldeman, and History," *The New York Review of Books* (July 14, 1994); Sydney Blumenthal, "The Longest Campaign," *The New Yorker* (August 8, 1994); and Stanley I. Kutler, "Et tu, Bob?" *The Nation* (August 22–29, 1994), a critical review of *The Haldeman Diaries* that also contains a CD version, available on Sony Imagesoft, which contains 60 percent more of the original text than the book, as well as home movies, photos, and biographical information on the Nixon staff.

Researchers who want a first-hand glimpse of Nixon should take a trip to the National Archives and listen to some of the 4,000 hours of tape, many of which have been declassified and released earlier than the papers of other presidents because of the Watergate scandal. Stanley I. Kutler has edited some of them in *The Abuse of Power: The New Nixon Tapes* (Touchstone Books, 1998). Nixon's view can be compared with Haldeman's *Diaries* as well as *The Kissinger Transcripts* (New Press, 1998), edited by William Burr. Nixon's presidential papers, after several court suits, have also ended up in the National Archives. A sample of some of these papers can be found in Bruce Oudes, ed., *From the President: Richard Nixon's Secret Files* (Harper & Row, 1989).

On the Internet . . .

Internet Web sites containing historical material relevant to the subjects discussed in this part can be reached through the McGraw-Hill history site.

http://www.mhhe.com/socscience/history/usa/link/linktop.htm

American Immigration Resources on the Internet

This site contains many links to American immigration resources on the Internet. It includes a site on children's immigration issues, the Immigration and Naturalization Service home page, and a forum on immigration.

http://www.immigration-usa.com/resource.html

National Council for Science and the Environment

The National Council for Science and the Environment (NCSE) has been working since 1990 to improve the scientific basis for environmental decision making. NCSE is supported by almost 500 academic, scientific, environmental, and business organizations.

http://www.cnie.org

PART 5

Postindustrial America and the End of the Cold War, 1974–2005

The last quarter of the twentieth century continued America's fluctuations between affluence and anxiety. The 1970s was a decade of political corruption and the forced resignation of a president, high unemployment, 21 percent interest rates for cars and houses, and a two-hour wait at gasoline stations to fill a car for the outrageous sum of $2.00 per gallon.

President Ronald Reagan entered the White House with a conservative domestic agenda and a hard-line foreign policy. In his first term, he promoted a military budget of $1.5 trillion over a 5-year period and was the first president since Truman who refused to meet the Soviet leader. Did Reagan cause the arms race, hoping to bankrupt the Russians, or was he lucky that reformist Mikhail Gorbachev became the General Secretary of the Soviet Politburo?

The Civil Rights Acts of 1964 and 1965, which ended legal discrimination against blacks, also spurred passage of the non-discriminatory Immigration Reform Act of 1965. But similar to all laws, the act had unintended consequences. By the 1980s, millions of immigrants were pouring in from Latin American and Asian countries. This did not include the indeterminant number of illegals who crossed the Mexican border. Should America restrict these immigrants because they are primarily non-white groups who created a series of fragmented multicultural ethnic enclaves that lack a common culture? Or are these immigrants merely the latest stream who have historically populated the country and keep America's economy strong because they work harder and take jobs that native-born Americans reject?

A final problem that Americans must deal with is the state of the global environment. Is the biophysical basis of our economies, such as the atmospheric pollution affecting global climate, habitat destruction, and species extinction, so negative that it is irreversible in the long run? Or has the doomsday scenario for the earth been exaggerated because known resources are not finite, can be exploited more efficiently, and can be substituted?

- Did President Reagan Win the Cold War?
- Should America Remain a Nation of Immigrants?
- Environmentalism: Is the Earth Out of Balance?

ISSUE 15

Did President Reagan Win the Cold War?

YES: John Lewis Gaddis, from *The United States and the End of the Cold War: Implications, Reconsiderations, Provocations* (Oxford University Press, 1992)

NO: Daniel Deudney and G. John Ikenberry, from "Who Won the Cold War?" *Foreign Policy* (Summer 1992)

ISSUE SUMMARY

YES: Professor of history John Lewis Gaddis argues that President Reagan combined a policy of militancy and operational pragmatism to bring about the most significant improvement in Soviet-American relations since the end of World War II.

NO: Professors of political science Daniel Deudney and G. John Ikenberry contend that the cold war ended only when Soviet President Gorbachev accepted Western liberal values and the need for global cooperation.

The term *cold war* was first coined by the American financial whiz and presidential adviser Bernard Baruch in 1947. Cold war refers to the extended but restricted conflict that existed between the United States and the Soviet Union from the end of World War II in 1945 until 1990. Looking back, it appears that the conflicting values and goals of a democratic/capitalist United States and a communist Soviet Union reinforced this state of affairs between the two countries. Basically, the cold war ended when the Soviet Union gave up its control over the Eastern European nations and ceased to be a unified country itself.

The Nazi invasion of Russia in June 1941 and the Japanese attack on America's Pacific outposts in December united the United States and the Soviet Union against the Axis powers during World War II. Nevertheless, complications ensued during the top-level allied discussions to coordinate war strategy. The first meeting between the big three—U.S. president Franklin Roosevelt, British prime minister Winston Churchill, and Soviet premier Joseph Stalin—took place in Teheran in 1943 followed by another at Yalta in February 1945. These high-level negotiations were held under the assumption that wartime harmony among Britain, the United States, and the Soviet Union would continue; that Stalin, Churchill, and Roosevelt would lead the postwar world as they had conducted the war; and that the details of the general policies and agreements would be resolved at a less pressing time.

But none of these premises were fulfilled. By the time the Potsdam Conference (to discuss possible action against Japan) took place in July 1945, Churchill had been defeated in a parliamentary election, Roosevelt had died, and President Harry S. Truman had been thrust, unprepared, into his place. Of the big three, only Stalin remained as a symbol of continuity. Details about the promises at Teheran and Yalta faded into the background. Power politics, nuclear weapons, and mutual fears and distrust replaced the reasonably harmonious working relationships of the three big powers during World War II.

By 1947 the Truman administration had adopted a conscious policy of containment toward the Russians. This meant maintaining the status quo in Europe through various U.S. assistance programs. The NATO alliance of 1949 completed the shift of U.S. policy away from its pre–World War II isolationist policy and toward a commitment to the defense of Western Europe.

In the 1960s the largest problem facing the two superpowers was controlling the spread of nuclear weapons. The first attempt at arms control took place in the 1950s. After Stalin died in 1953, the Eisenhower administration made an "open-skies" proposal. This was rejected by the Russians, who felt (correctly) that they were behind the Americans in the arms race. In the summer of 1962 Soviet premier Nikita Khrushchev attempted to redress the balance of power by secretly installing missiles in Cuba that could be employed to launch nuclear attacks against U.S. cities. This sparked the Cuban Missile Crisis, the high point of the cold war, which brought both nations to the brink of nuclear war before the Russians agreed to withdraw the missiles.

During the Leonid Brezhnev–Richard Nixon years, the policy of *détente* (relaxation of tensions) resulted in a series of summit meetings. Most important was the SALT I agreement, which outlawed national antiballistic missile defenses and placed a five-year moratorium on the building of new strategic ballistic missiles.

Soviet-American relations took a turn for the worse when the Soviets invaded Afghanistan in December 1979. In response, President Jimmy Carter postponed presenting SALT II to the Senate and imposed an American boycott of the 1980 Olympic Games, which were held in Moscow.

Détente remained dead during President Ronald Reagan's first administration. Reagan not only promoted a military budget of $1.5 trillion over a five-year period, he also was the first president since Truman to refuse to meet the Soviet leader. Major changes, however, took place during Reagan's second administration. In the following selections, John Lewis Gaddis argues that President Reagan combined a policy of militancy and operational pragmatism to bring about significant improvements in Soviet-American relations, while Daniel Deudney and G. John Ikenberry credit Soviet president Mikhail Gorbachev with ending the cold war because he accepted Western liberal values and the need for global cooperation.

John Lewis Gaddis **YES**

The Unexpected Ronald Reagan

The task of the historian is, very largely, one of explaining how we got from where we were to where we are today. To say that the Reagan administration's policy toward the Soviet Union is going to pose special challenges to historians is to understate the matter: rarely has there been a greater gap between the expectations held for an administration at the beginning of its term and the results it actually produced. The last thing one would have anticipated at the time Ronald Reagan took office in 1981 was that he would use his eight years in the White House to bring about the most significant improvement in Soviet-American relations since the end of World War II. I am not at all sure that President Reagan himself foresaw this result. And yet, that is precisely what happened, with—admittedly—a good deal of help from Mikhail Gorbachev.

The question of how this happened and to what extent it was the product of accident or of conscious design is going to preoccupy scholars for years to come. The observations that follow are a rough first attempt to grapple with that question. Because we lack access to the archives or even very much memoir material as yet, what I will have to say is of necessity preliminary, incomplete, and almost certainly in several places dead wrong. Those are the hazards of working with contemporary history, though; if historians are not willing to run these risks, political scientists and journalists surely will. That prospect in itself provides ample justification for plunging ahead.

The Hard-Liner

. . . President Reagan in March, 1983, made his most memorable pronouncement on the Soviet Union: condemning the tendency of his critics to hold both sides responsible for the nuclear arms race, he denounced the U.S.S.R. as an "evil empire" and as "the focus of evil in the modern world." Two weeks later, the President surprised even his closest associates by calling for a long-term research and development program to create defense against attacks by strategic missiles, with a view, ultimately, to "rendering these nuclear weapons impotent and obsolete." The Strategic Defense Initiative was the most fundamental challenge to existing orthodoxies on arms control since negotiations on that subject had begun with the Russians almost three decades earlier. Once again it called into question the President's seriousness in seeking an end to—or even a significant moderation of—the strategic arms race.

Anyone who listened to the "evil empire" speech or who considered the implications of "Star Wars" might well have concluded that Reagan saw the Soviet-American relationship as an elemental confrontation between virtue and wickedness that would allow neither negotiation nor conciliation in any form; his tone seemed more appropriate to a medieval crusade than to a revival of containment. Certainly there were those within his administration who held such views, and their influence, for a time, was considerable. But to see the President's policies solely in terms of his rhetoric, it is now clear, would have been quite wrong.

For President Reagan appears to have understood—or to have quickly learned—the dangers of basing foreign policy solely on ideology: he combined militancy with a surprising degree of operational pragmatism and a shrewd sense of timing. To the astonishment of his own hard-line supporters, what appeared to be an enthusiastic return to the Cold War in fact turned out to be a more solidly based approach to detente than anything the Nixon, Ford, or Carter administrations had been able to accomplish.

The Negotiator

There had always been a certain ambivalence in the Reagan administration's image of the Soviet Union. On the one hand, dire warnings about Moscow's growing military strength suggested an almost Spenglerian gloom [reflecting the theory of philosopher Oswald Spengler, which holds that all major cultures grow, mature, and decay in a natural cycle] about the future: time, it appeared, was on the Russians' side. But mixed with this pessimism was a strong sense of self-confidence, growing out of the ascendancy of conservatism within the United States and an increasing enthusiasm for capitalism overseas, that assumed the unworkability of Marxism as a form of political, social, and economic organization: "The West won't contain communism, it will transcend communism," the President predicted in May, 1981. "It won't bother to . . . denounce it, it will dismiss it as some bizarre chapter in human history whose last pages are even now being written." By this logic, the Soviet Union had already reached the apex of its strength as a world power, and time in fact was on the side of the West.

Events proved the optimism to have been more justified than the pessimism, for over the next four years the Soviet Union would undergo one of the most rapid erosions both of internal self-confidence and external influence in modern history; that this happened just as Moscow's long and costly military buildup should have begun to pay political dividends made the situation all the more frustrating for the Russians. It may have been luck for President Reagan to have come into office at a peak in the fortunes of the Soviet Union and at a trough in those of the United States: things would almost certainly have improved regardless of who entered the White House in 1981. But it took more than luck to recognize what was happening, and to capitalize on it to the extent that the Reagan administration did.

Indications of Soviet decline took several forms. The occupation of Afghanistan had produced only a bloody Vietnam-like stalemate, with Soviet troops unable to suppress the rebellion, or to protect themselves and their clients, or to withdraw. In Poland a long history of economic mismanagement had produced, in the form of the Solidarity trade union, a rare phenomenon within the Soviet bloc: a true workers' movement. Soviet ineffectiveness became apparent in the Middle East in 1982 when the Russians were unable to provide any significant help to the Palestinian Liberation Organization during the Israeli invasion of Lebanon; even more embarrassing, Israeli pilots using American-built fighters shot down over eighty Soviet-supplied Syrian jets without a single loss of their own. Meanwhile, the Soviet domestic economy which [former Soviet premier Nikita] Khrushchev had once predicted would overtake that of the United States, had in fact stagnated during the early 1980s, Japan by some indices actually overtook the U.S.S.R. as the world's second largest producer of goods and services, and even China, a nation with four times the population of the Soviet Union, now became an agricultural exporter at a time when Moscow still required food imports from the West to feed its own people.

What all of this meant was that the Soviet Union's appeal as a model for Third World political and economic development—once formidable—had virtually disappeared, indeed as Moscow's military presence in those regions grew during the late 1970s, the Russians increasingly came to be seen, not as liberators, but as latter-day imperialists themselves. The Reagan administration moved swiftly to take advantage of this situation by funneling military assistance—sometimes openly sometimes covertly—to rebel groups (or "freedom fighters," as the President insisted on calling them) seeking to overthrow Soviet-backed regimes in Afghanistan, Angola, Ethiopia, Cambodia, and Nicaragua; in October, 1983, to huge domestic acclaim but with dubious legality Reagan even ordered the direct use of American military forces to overthrow an unpopular Marxist government on the tiny Caribbean island of Grenada. The Reagan Doctrine, as this strategy became known, sought to exploit vulnerabilities the Russians had created for themselves in the Third World: this latter-day effort to "roll back" Soviet influence would, in time, produce impressive results at minimum cost and risk to the United States.

Compounding the Soviet Union's external difficulties was a long vacuum in internal leadership occasioned by [President Leonid] Brezhnev's slow enfeeblement and eventual death in November, 1982; by the installation as his successor of an already-ill Yuri Andropov, who himself died in February 1984; and by the installation of his equally geriatric successor, Konstantin Chernenko. At a time when a group of strong Western leaders had emerged—including not just President Reagan but also Prime Minister Margaret Thatcher in Great Britain, President François Mitterrand in France, and Chancellor Helmut Kohl in West Germany—this apparent inability to entrust leadership to anyone other than party stalwarts on their deathbeds was a severe commentary on what the sclerotic Soviet system had become. "We could go no further without hitting the end," one Russian later recalled of Chernenko's brief reign. "Here was the General Secretary of the party who is also the Chairman of the Presidium of the

Supreme Soviet, the embodiment of our country, the personification of the party and he could barely stand up."

There was no disagreement within the Reagan administration about the desirability under these circumstances, of pressing the Russians hard. Unlike several of their predecessors, the President and his advisers did not see containment as requiring the application of sticks and carrots in equal proportion; wielders of sticks definitely predominated among them. But there were important differences over what the purpose of wielding the sticks was to be.

Some advisers, like [Secretary of Defense Casper] Weinberger, [Assistant Secretary of Defense for International Security Policy Richard] Perle, and [chief Soviet specialist on the National Security Council Richard] Pipes, saw the situation as a historic opportunity to exhaust the Soviet system. Noting that the Soviet economy was already stretched to the limit, they advocated taking advantage of American technological superiority to engage the Russians in an arms race of indefinite duration and indeterminate cost. Others, including Nitze, the Joint Chiefs of Staff, career Foreign Service officer Jack Matlock, who succeeded Pipes as chief Soviet expert at the NSC, and—most important—[Secretary of State Alexander M.] Haig's replacement after June, 1982, the unflamboyant but steady George Shultz, endorsed the principle of "negotiation from strength": the purpose of accumulating military hardware was not to debilitate the other side, but to convince it to negotiate.

The key question, of course, was what President Reagan's position would be. Despite his rhetoric, he had been careful not to rule out talks with the Russians once the proper conditions had been met: even while complaining, in his first press conference, about the Soviet propensity to lie, cheat, and steal, he had also noted that "when we can, . . . we should start negotiations on the basis of trying to effect an actual reduction in the numbers of nuclear weapons. That would be real arms reduction." But most observers—and probably many of his own advisers—assumed that when the President endorsed negotiations leading toward the "reduction," as opposed to the "limitation," of strategic arms, or the "zero option" in the INF [intermediate-range nuclear forces] talks, or the Strategic Defense Initiative, he was really seeking to avoid negotiations by setting minimal demands above the maximum concessions the Russians could afford to make. He was looking for a way they believed, to gain credit for cooperativeness with both domestic and allied constituencies without actually having to give up anything.

That would turn out to be a gross misjudgment of President Reagan, who may have had cynical advisers but was not cynical himself. It would become apparent with the passage of time that when the Chief Executive talked about "reducing" strategic missiles he meant precisely that; the appeal of the "zero option" was that it really would get rid of intermediate-range nuclear forces; the Strategic Defense Initiative might in fact, just as the President had said, make nuclear weapons "impotent and obsolete." A simple and straightforward man, Reagan took the principle of "negotiation from strength" literally: once one had built strength, one negotiated.

The first indications that the President might be interested in something other than an indefinite arms race began to appear in the spring and summer of

1983. Widespread criticism of his "evil empire" speech apparently shook him: although his view of the Soviet system itself did not change, Reagan was careful, after that point, to use more restrained language in characterizing it. Clear evidence of the President's new moderation came with the Korean airliner incident of September, 1983. Despite his outrage, Reagan did not respond—as one might have expected him to—by reviving his "evil empire" rhetoric; instead he insisted that arms control negotiations would continue, and in a remarkably conciliatory television address early in 1984 he announced that the United States was "in its strongest position in years to establish a constructive and realistic working relationship with the Soviet Union." The President concluded this address by speculating on how a typical Soviet couple—Ivan and Anya—might find that they had much in common with a typical American couple—Jim and Sally: "They might even have decided that they were all going to get together for dinner some evening soon."

It was possible to construct self-serving motives for this startling shift in tone. With a presidential campaign under way the White House was sensitive to Democratic charges that Reagan was the only postwar president not to have met with a Soviet leader while in office. Certainly it was to the advantage of the United States in its relations with Western Europe to look as reasonable as possible in the face of Soviet intransigence. But events would show that the President's interest in an improved relationship was based on more than just electoral politics or the needs of the alliance: it was only the unfortunate tendency of Soviet leaders to die upon taking office that was depriving the American Chief Executive—himself a spry septuagenarian—of a partner with whom to negotiate.

By the end of September, 1984—and to the dismay of Democratic partisans who saw Republicans snatching the "peace" issue from them—a contrite Soviet Foreign Minister Andrei Gromyko had made the pilgrimage to Washington to re-establish contacts with the Reagan administration. Shortly after Reagan's landslide re-election over Walter Mondale in November, the United States and the Soviet Union announced that a new set of arms control negotiations would begin early the following year, linking together discussions on START [Strategic Arms Reduction Talks], INF, and weapons in space. And in December, a hitherto obscure member of the Soviet Politburo, Mikhail Gorbachev, announced while visiting Great Britain that the U.S.S.R. was prepared to seek "radical solutions" looking toward a ban on nuclear missiles altogether. Three months later, Konstantin Chernenko, the last in a series of feeble and unimaginative Soviet leaders, expired, and Gorbachev—a man who was in no way feeble and unimaginative—became the General Secretary of the Communist Party of the Soviet Union. Nothing would ever be quite the same again.

Reagan and Gorbachev

Several years after Gorbachev had come to power, George F. Kennan was asked in a television interview how so unconventional a Soviet leader could have risen to the top in a system that placed such a premium on conformity. Kennan's reply reflected the perplexity American experts on Soviet affairs have felt in seeking to account for the Gorbachev phenomenon: "I really cannot explain it." It seemed most improbable that a regime so lacking in the capacity for innovation, self-evaluation, or even minimally effective public relations should suddenly produce a leader who excelled in all of these qualities; even more remarkable was the fact that Gorbachev saw himself as a revolutionary—a breed not seen in Russia for decades—determined, as he put it, "to get out of the quagmire of conservatism, and to break the inertia of stagnation."

Whatever the circumstances that led to it, the accession of Gorbachev reversed almost overnight the pattern of the preceding four years: after March, 1985, it was the Soviet Union that seized the initiative in relations with the West. It did so in a way that was both reassuring and unnerving at the same time: by becoming so determinedly cooperative as to convince some supporters of containment in the United States and Western Europe—uneasy in the absence of the intransigence to which they had become accustomed—that the Russians were now seeking to defeat that strategy by depriving it, with sinister cleverness, of an object to be contained.

President Reagan, in contrast, welcomed the fresh breezes emanating from Moscow and moved quickly to establish a personal relationship with the new Soviet leader. Within four days of Gorbachev's taking power, the President was characterizing the Russians as "in a different frame of mind than they've been in the past. . . . [T]hey, I believe, are really going to try and, with us, negotiate a reduction in armaments." And within four months, the White House was announcing that Reagan would meet Gorbachev at Geneva in November for the first Soviet-American summit since 1979.

The Geneva summit, like so many before it, was long on symbolism and short on substance. The two leaders appeared to get along well with one another: they behaved, as one Reagan adviser later put it, "like a couple of fellows who had run into each other at the club and discovered that they had a lot in common." The President agreed to discuss deep cuts in strategic weapons and improved verification, but he made it clear that he was not prepared to forgo development of the Strategic Defense Initiative in order to get them. His reason—which Gorbachev may not have taken seriously until this point—had to do with his determination to retain SDI as a means ultimately of rendering nuclear weapons obsolete. The President's stubbornness on this point precluded progress, at least for the moment, on what was coming to be called the "grand compromise": Paul Nitze's idea of accepting limits on SDI in return for sweeping reductions in strategic missiles. But it did leave the way open for an alert Gorbachev, detecting the President's personal enthusiasm for nuclear abolition, to surprise the world in January, 1986, with his own plan for accomplishing that objective: a Soviet-American agreement to rid the world of nuclear weapons altogether by the year 2000.

It was easy to question Gorbachev's motives in making so radical a proposal in so public a manner with no advance warning. Certainly any discussion of even reducing—much less abolishing—nuclear arsenals would raise difficult questions for American allies, where an abhorrence of nuclear weapons continued to coexist uneasily alongside the conviction that only their presence could deter superior Soviet conventional forces. Nor was the Gorbachev proposal clear on how Russians and Americans could ever impose abolition, even if they themselves agreed to it, on other nuclear and non-nuclear powers. Still, the line between rhetoric and conviction is a thin one: the first Reagan-Gorbachev summit may not only have created a personal bond between the two leaders; it may also have sharpened a vague but growing sense in the minds of both men that, despite all the difficulties in constructing an alternative, an indefinite continuation of life under nuclear threat was not a tolerable condition for either of their countries, and that their own energies might very well be directed toward overcoming that situation.

That both Reagan and Gorbachev were thinking along these lines became clear at their second meeting, the most extraordinary Soviet-American summit of the postwar era, held on very short notice at Reykjavik, Iceland, in October, 1986. The months that preceded Reykjavik had seen little tangible progress toward arms control; there had also developed, in August, an unpleasant skirmish between intelligence agencies on both sides as the KGB, in apparent retaliation for the FBI's highly publicized arrest of a Soviet United Nations official in New York on espionage charges, set up, seized, and held *USNEWS* correspondent Nicholas Daniloff on trumped-up accusations for just under a month. It was a sobering reminder that the Soviet-American relationship existed at several different levels, and that cordiality in one did not rule out the possibility of confrontation in others. The Daniloff affair also brought opportunity though, for in the course of negotiations to settle it Gorbachev proposed a quick "preliminary" summit, to be held within two weeks, to try to break the stalemate in negotiations over intermediate-range nuclear forces in Europe, the aspect of arms control where progress at a more formal summit seemed likely. Reagan immediately agreed.

But when the President and his advisers arrived at Reykjavik, they found that Gorbachev had much more grandiose proposals in mind. These included not only an endorsement of 50 percent cuts in Soviet and American strategic weapons across the board, but also agreement not to demand the inclusion of British and French nuclear weapons in these calculations—a concession that removed a major stumbling block to START—and acceptance in principle of Reagan's 1981 "zero option" for intermediate-range nuclear forces, all in return for an American commitment not to undermine SALT I's ban on strategic defenses for the next ten years. Impressed by the scope of these concessions, the American side quickly put together a compromise that would have cut ballistic missiles to zero within a decade in return for the right, after that time, to deploy strategic defenses against the bomber and cruise missile forces that would be left. Gorbachev immediately countered by proposing the abolition of *all* nuclear weapons within ten years, thus moving his original deadline from the year 2000 to 1996. President Reagan is said to have replied: "*All* nuclear weapons? Well, Mikhail, that's exactly what I've been talking about all along. . . . That's always been my goal."

A series of events set in motion by a Soviet diplomat's arrest on a New York subway platform and by the reciprocal framing of an American journalist in Moscow had wound up with the two most powerful men in the world agreeing—for the moment, and to the astonishment of their aides—on the abolition of all nuclear weapons within ten years. But the moment did not last. Gorbachev went on to insist, as a condition for nuclear abolition, upon a ban on the laboratory testing of SDI, which Reagan immediately interpreted as an effort to kill strategic defense altogether. Because the ABM treaty does allow for some laboratory testing, the differences between the two positions were not all that great. But in the hothouse atmosphere of this cold-climate summit no one explored such details, and the meeting broke up in disarray, acrimony, and mutual disappointment.

It was probably just as well. The sweeping agreements contemplated at Reykjavik grew out of hasty improvisation and high-level posturing, not careful thought. They suffered from all the deficiencies of Gorbachev's unilateral proposal for nuclear abolition earlier in the year; they also revealed how susceptible the leaders of the United States and the Soviet Union had become to each other's amplitudinous rhetoric. It was as if Reagan and Gorbachev had been trying desperately to outbid the other in a gigantic but surrealistic auction, with the diaphanous prospect of a nuclear-free world somehow on the block. . . .

Negotiations on arms control continued in the year that followed Reykjavik, however, with both sides edging toward the long-awaited "grand compromise" that would defer SDI in return for progress toward a START agreement. Reagan and Gorbachev did sign an intermediate-range nuclear forces treaty in Washington in December, 1987, which for the first time provided that Russians and Americans would actually dismantle and destroy—literally before each other's eyes—an entire category of nuclear missiles. There followed a triumphal Reagan visit to Moscow in May, 1988, featuring the unusual sight of a Soviet general secretary and an American president strolling amiably through Red Square, greeting tourists and bouncing babies in front of Lenin's tomb, while their respective military aides—each carrying the codes needed to launch nuclear missiles at each other's territory—stood discreetly in the background. Gorbachev made an equally triumphal visit to New York in December, 1988, to address the United Nations General Assembly: there he announced a *unilateral* Soviet cut of some 500,000 ground troops, a major step toward moving arms control into the realm of conventional forces.

When, on the same day Gorbachev spoke in New York, a disastrous earthquake killed some 25,000 Soviet Armenians, the outpouring of aid from the United States and other Western countries was unprecedented since the days of Lend Lease. One had the eerie feeling, watching anguished television reports from the rubble that had been the cities of Leninakan and Stipak—the breakdown of emergency services, the coffins stacked like logs in city parks, the mass burials—that one had glimpsed, on a small scale, something of what a nuclear war might actually be like. The images suggested just how vulnerable both super-powers remained after almost a half-century of trying to minimize vulnerabilities. They thereby reinforced what had become almost a ritual incantation pronounced by both Reagan and Gorbachev at each of their now-frequent summits: "A nuclear war cannot be won and must never be fought."

But as the Reagan administration prepared to leave office the following month, in an elegaic mood very different from the grim militancy with which it had assumed its responsibilities eight years earlier, the actual prospect of a nuclear holocaust seemed more remote than at any point since the Soviet-American nuclear rivalry had begun. Accidents, to be sure, could always happen. Irrationality though blessedly rare since 1945, could never be ruled out. There was reason for optimism, though, in the fact that as George Bush entered the White House early in 1989, the point at issue no longer seemed to be "how to fight the Cold War" at all, but rather "is the Cold War over?"

Ronald Reagan and the End of the Cold War

The record of the Reagan years suggests the need to avoid the common error of trying to predict outcomes from attributes. There is no question that the President and his advisers came into office with an ideological view of the world that appeared to allow for no compromise with the Russians; but ideology has a way of evolving to accommodate reality especially in the hands of skillful political leadership. Indeed a good working definition of leadership might be just this—the ability to accommodate ideology to practical reality—and by that standard, Reagan's achievements in relations with the Soviet Union will certainly compare favorably with, and perhaps even surpass, those of Richard Nixon and Henry Kissinger.

Did President Reagan intend for things to come out this way? That question is, of course, more difficult to determine, given our lack of access to the archives. But a careful reading of the public record would, I think, show that the President was expressing hopes for an improvement in Soviet-American relations from the moment he entered the White House, and that he began shifting American policy in that direction as early as the first months of 1983, almost two years before Mikhail Gorbachev came to power. Gorbachev's extraordinary receptiveness to such initiatives—as distinct from the literally moribund responses of his predecessors—greatly accelerated the improvement in relations, but it would be a mistake to credit him solely with the responsibility for what happened: Ronald Reagan deserves a great deal of the credit as well.

Critics have raised the question, though, of whether President Reagan was responsible for, or even aware of, the direction administration policy was taking. This argument is, I think, both incorrect and unfair. Reagan's opponents have been quick enough to hold him personally responsible for the failures of his administration; they should be equally prepared to acknowledge his successes. And there are points, even with the limited sources now available, where we can see that the President himself had a decisive impact upon the course of events. They include, among others: the Strategic Defense Initiative, which may have had its problems as a missile shield but which certainly worked in unsettling the Russians; endorsement of the "zero option" in the INF talks and real reductions in START, the rapidity with which the President entered into, and thereby legitimized, serious negotiations with Gorbachev once he came into office; and, most remarkably of all, his eagerness to contemplate alternatives to the nuclear arms race in a way no previous president had been willing to do.

Now, it may be objected that these were simple, unsophisticated, and, as people are given to saying these days, imperfectly "nuanced" ideas. I would not argue with that proposition. But it is important to remember that while complexity, sophistication, and nuance may be prerequisites for intellectual leadership, they are not necessarily so for political leadership, and can at times actually get in the way. President Reagan generally meant precisely what he said: when he came out in favor of negotiations from strength, or for strategic arms reductions as opposed to limitations, or even for making nuclear weapons ultimately irrelevant and obsolete, he did not do so in the "killer amendment" spirit favored by geopolitical sophisticates on the right; the President may have been conservative but he was never devious. The lesson here ought to be to beware of excessive convolution and subtlety in strategy, for sometimes simple-mindedness wins out, especially if it occurs in high places.

Finally President Reagan also understood something that many geopolitical sophisticates on the left have not understood: that although toughness may or may not be a prerequisite for successful negotiations with the Russians—there are arguments for both propositions—it is absolutely essential if the American people are to lend their support, over time, to what has been negotiated. Others may have seen in the doctrine of "negotiation from strength" a way of avoiding negotiations altogether, but it now seems clear that the President saw in that approach the means of constructing a domestic political base without which agreements with the Russians would almost certainly have foundered, as indeed many of them did in the 1970s. For unless one can sustain domestic support—and one does not do that by appearing weak—then it is hardly likely that whatever one has arranged with any adversary will actually come to anything.

There is one last irony to all of this: it is that it fell to Ronald Reagan to preside over the belated but decisive success of the strategy of containment George F. Kennan had first proposed more than four decades earlier. For what were Gorbachev's reforms if not the long-delayed "mellowing" of Soviet society that Kennan had said would take place with the passage of time? The Stalinist system that had required outside adversaries to justify its own existence now seemed at last to have passed from the scene; Gorbachev appeared to have concluded that the Soviet Union could continue to be a great power in world affairs only through the introduction of something approximating a market economy, democratic political institutions, official accountability, and respect for the rule of law at home. And that, in turn, suggested an even more remarkable conclusion: that the very survival of the ideology Lenin had imposed on Russia in 1917 now required infiltration—perhaps even subversion—by precisely the ideology the great revolutionary had sworn to overthrow.

I have some reason to suspect that Professor Kennan is not entirely comfortable with the suggestion that Ronald Reagan successfully completed the execution of the strategy he originated. But as Kennan the historian would be the first to acknowledge, history is full of ironies, and this one, surely, will not rank among the least of them.

Daniel Deudney and
G. John Ikenberry

NO

Who Won the Cold War?

The end of the Cold War marks the most important historical divide in half a century. The magnitude of those developments has ushered in a wide-ranging debate over the reasons for its end—a debate that is likely to be as protracted, controversial, and politically significant as that over the Cold War's origins. The emerging debate over why the Cold War ended is of more than historical interest: At stake is the vindication and legitimation of an entire world view and foreign policy orientation.

In thinking about the Cold War's conclusion, it is vital to distinguish between the domestic origins of the crisis in Soviet communism and the external forces that influenced its timing and intensity, as well as the direction of the Soviet response. Undoubtedly, the ultimate cause of the Cold War's outcome lies in the failure of the Soviet system itself. At most, outside forces hastened and intensified the crisis. However, it was not inevitable that the Soviet Union would respond to this crisis as it did in the late 1980s—with domestic liberalization and foreign policy accommodation. After all, many Western experts expected that the USSR would respond to such a crisis with renewed repression at home and aggression abroad, as it had in the past.

At that fluid historic juncture, the complex matrix of pressures, opportunities, and attractions from the outside world influenced the direction of Soviet change, particularly in its foreign policy. The Soviets' field of vision was dominated by the West, the United States, and recent American foreign policy. Having spent more than 45 years attempting to influence the Soviet Union, Americans are now attempting to gauge the weight of their country's impact and, thus, the track record of U.S. policies.

In assessing the rest of the world's impact on Soviet change, a remarkably simplistic and self-serving conventional wisdom has emerged in the United States. This new conventional wisdom, the "Reagan victory school," holds that President Ronald Reagan's military and ideological assertiveness during the 1980s played the lead role in the collapse of Soviet communism and the "taming" of its foreign policy. In that view the Reagan administration's ideological counter-offensive and military buildup delivered the knock-out punch to a system that was internally bankrupt and on the ropes. The Reagan Right's perspective is an ideologically pointed version of the more broadly held conventional wisdom on the end of the Cold War that emphasizes the success of the "peace-through-strength" strategy manifest in four decades of Western containment. After decades of waging a costly "twilight struggle," the West now celebrates the triumph of its military and ideological resolve.

The Reagan victory school and the broader peace-through-strength perspectives are, however, misleading and incomplete—both in their interpretation of events in the 1980s and in their understanding of deeper forces that led to the end of the Cold War. It is important to reconsider the emerging conventional wisdom before it truly becomes an article of faith on Cold War history and comes to distort the thinking of policymakers in America and elsewhere.

The collapse of the Cold War caught almost everyone, particularly hardliners, by surprise. Conservatives and most analysts in the U.S. national security establishment believed that the Soviet-U.S. struggle was a permanent feature of international relations. As former National Security Council adviser Zbigniew Brzezinski put it in 1986, "the American-Soviet contest is not some temporary aberration but a historical rivalry that will long endure." And to many hardliners, Soviet victory was far more likely than Soviet collapse. Many ringing predictions now echo as embarrassments.

The Cold War's end was a baby that arrived unexpectedly, but a long line of those claiming paternity has quickly formed. A parade of former Reagan administration officials and advocates has forthrightly asserted that Reagan's hardline policies were the decisive trigger for reorienting Soviet foreign policy and for the demise of communism. As former Pentagon officials like Caspar Weinberger and Richard Perle, columnist George Will, neoconservative thinker Irving Kristol, and other proponents of the Reagan victory school have argued, a combination of military and ideological pressures gave the Soviets little choice but to abandon expansionism abroad and repression at home. In that view, the Reagan military buildup foreclosed Soviet military options while pushing the Soviet economy to the breaking point. Reagan partisans stress that his dramatic "Star Wars" initiative put the Soviets on notice that the next phase of the arms race would be waged in areas where the West held a decisive technological edge.

Reagan and his administration's military initiatives, however, played a far different and more complicated role in inducing Soviet change than the Reagan victory school asserts. For every "hardening" there was a "softening": Reagan's rhetoric of the "Evil Empire" was matched by his vigorous anti-nuclearism; the military buildup in the West was matched by the resurgence of a large popular peace movement; and the Reagan Doctrine's toughening of containment was matched by major deviations from containment in East-West economic relations. Moreover, over the longer term, the strength marshaled in containment was matched by mutual weakness in the face of nuclear weapons, and efforts to engage the USSR were as important as efforts to contain it.

The Irony of Ronald Reagan

Perhaps the greatest anomaly of the Reagan victory school is the "Great Communicator" himself. The Reagan Right ignores that his anti-nuclearism was as strong as his anticommunism. Reagan's personal convictions on nuclear weapons were profoundly at odds with the beliefs of most in his administration. Staffed by officials who considered nuclear weapons a useful instrument of statecraft and who were openly disdainful of the moral critique of nuclear weapons articulated by the arms control community and the peace movement, the administration pursued the hardest line on nuclear policy and the Soviet Union in the postwar era. Then vice president George Bush's observation that nuclear weapons would be fired as a warning shot and Deputy Under Secretary of Defense T. K. Jones's widely quoted view that nuclear war was survivable captured the reigning ethos within the Reagan administration.

In contrast, there is abundant evidence that Reagan himself felt a deep antipathy for nuclear weapons and viewed their abolition to be a realistic and desirable goal. Reagan's call in his famous March 1983 "Star Wars" speech for a program to make nuclear weapons impotent and obsolete was viewed as cynical by many, but actually it expressed Reagan's heartfelt views, views that he came to act upon. As *Washington Post* reporter Lou Cannon's 1991 biography points out, Reagan was deeply disturbed by nuclear deterrence and attracted to abolitionist solutions. "I know I speak for people everywhere when I say our dream is to see the day when nuclear weapons will be banished from the face of the earth," Reagan said in November 1983. Whereas the Right saw anti-nuclearism as a threat to American military spending and the legitimacy of an important foreign policy tool, or as propaganda for domestic consumption, Reagan sincerely believed it. Reagan's anti-nuclearism was not just a personal sentiment. It surfaced at decisive junctures to affect Soviet perceptions of American policy. Sovietologist and strategic analyst Michael MccGwire has argued persuasively that Reagan's anti-nuclearism decisively influenced Soviet-U.S. relations during the early Gorbachev years.

Contrary to the conventional wisdom, the defense buildup did not produce Soviet capitulation. The initial Soviet response to the Reagan administration's buildup and belligerent rhetoric was to accelerate production of offensive weapons, both strategic and conventional. That impasse was broken not by Soviet capitulation but by an extraordinary convergence by Reagan and Mikhail Gorbachev on a vision of mutual nuclear vulnerability and disarmament. On the Soviet side, the dominance of the hardline response to the newly assertive America was thrown into question in early 1985 when Gorbachev became general secretary of the Communist party after the death of Konstantin Chernenko. Without a background in foreign affairs, Gorbachev was eager to assess American intentions directly and put his stamp on Soviet security policy. Reagan's strong antinuclear views expressed at the November 1985 Geneva summit were decisive in convincing Gorbachev that it was possible to work with the West in halting the nuclear arms race. The arms control diplomacy of the later Reagan years was successful because, as *Washington Post* journalist Don Oberdorfer has detailed in *The Turn: From the Cold War to a New Era* (1991), Secretary of State George Shultz picked up on Reagan's strong convictions and deftly side-stepped hard-line opposition to agreements. In fact, Schultz's success at linking presidential unease about nuclear weapons to Soviet overtures in the face of rightwing opposition provides a sharp contrast with John Foster Dulles's refusal to act on President Dwight Eisenhower's nuclear doubts and the opportunities presented by Nikita Khrushchev's détente overtures.

Reagan's commitment to anti-nuclearism and its potential for transforming the U.S-Soviet confrontation was more graphically demonstrated at the October 1986 Reykjavik summit when Reagan and Gorbachev came close to agreeing on a comprehensive program of global denuclearization that was far bolder than any seriously entertained by American strategists since the Baruch Plan of 1946. The sharp contrast between Reagan's and Gorbachev's shared skepticism toward nuclear weapons on the one hand, and the Washington security establishment's consensus on the other, was showcased in former secretary of defense James Schlesinger's scathing accusation that Reagan was engaged in "casual utopianism." But Reagan's anomalous anti-nuclearism provided the crucial signal to Gorbachev that bold initiatives would be reciprocated rather than exploited. Reagan's anti-nuclearism was more important than his administration's military buildup in catalyzing the end of the Cold War.

Neither anti-nuclearism nor its embrace by Reagan have received the credit they deserve for producing the Soviet-U.S. reconciliation. Reagan's accomplishment in this regard has been met with silence from all sides. Conservatives, not sharing Reagan's anti-nuclearism, have emphasized the role of traditional military strength. The popular peace movement, while holding deeply antinuclear views, was viscerally suspicious of Reagan. The establishment arms control community also found Reagan and his motives suspect, and his attack on deterrence conflicted with their desire to stabilize deterrence and establish their credentials as sober participants in security policy making. Reagan's radical anti-nuclearism should sustain his reputation as the ultimate Washington outsider.

The central role of Reagan's and Gorbachev's anti-nuclearism throws new light on the 1987 Treaty on Intermediate-range Nuclear Forces, the first genuine disarmament treaty of the nuclear era. The conventional wisdom emphasizes that this agreement was the fruit of a hard-line negotiating posture and the U.S. military buildup. Yet the superpowers' settlement on the "zero option" was not a vindication of the hard-line strategy. The zero option was originally fashioned by hardliners for propaganda purposes, and many backed off as its implementation became likely. The impasse the hard line created was transcended by the surprising Reagan-Gorbachev convergence against nuclear arms.

The Reagan victory school also overstates the overall impact of American and Western policy on the Soviet Union during the 1980s. The Reagan administration's posture was both evolving and inconsistent. Though loudly proclaiming its intention to go beyond the previous containment policies that were deemed too soft, the reality of Reagan's policies fell short. As Sovietologists Gail Lapidus and Alexander Dallin observed in a 1989 *Bulletin of the Atomic Scientists* article, the policies were "marked to the end by numerous zigzags and reversals, bureaucratic conflicts, and incoherence." Although rollback had long been a cherished goal of the Republican party's right wing, Reagan was unwilling and unable to implement it.

The hard-line tendencies of the Reagan administration were offset in two ways. First, and most important, Reagan's tough talk fueled a large peace movement in the United States and Western Europe in the 1980s, a movement that put significant political pressure upon Western governments to pursue farreaching arms control proposals. That mobilization of Western opinion created a political climate in which the rhetoric and posture of the early Reagan administration was a significant political liability. By the 1984 U.S. presidential election, the administration had embraced arms control goals that it had previously ridiculed. Reagan's own anti-nuclearism matched that rising public concern, and Reagan emerged as the spokesman for comprehensive denuclearization. Paradoxically, Reagan administration policies substantially triggered the popular revolt against the nuclear hardline, and then Reagan came to pursue the popular agenda more successfully than any other postwar president.

Second, the Reagan administration's hard-line policies were also undercut by powerful Western interests that favored East-West economic ties. In the early months of Reagan's administration, the grain embargo imposed by President Jimmy Carter after the 1979 Soviet invasion of Afghanistan was lifted in order to keep the Republican party's promises to Midwestern farmers. Likewise, in 1981 the Reagan administration did little to challenge Soviet control of Eastern Europe after Moscow pressured Warsaw to suppress the independent Polish trade union Solidarity, in part because Poland might have defaulted on multibillion dollar loans made by Western banks. Also, despite strenuous opposition by the Reagan administration, the NATO allies pushed ahead with a natural gas pipeline linking the Soviet Union with Western Europe. That a project creating substantial economic interdependence could proceed during the worst period of Soviet-U.S. relations in the 1980s demonstrates the failure of the Reagan administration to present an unambiguous hard line toward the Soviet Union. More generally, NATO allies and the vocal European peace movement moderated and buffered hardline American tendencies.

In sum, the views of the Reagan victory school are flawed because they neglect powerful crosscurrents in the West during the 1980s. The conventional wisdom simplifies a complex story and ignores those aspects of Reagan administration policy inconsistent with the hardline rationale. Moreover, the Western "face" toward the Soviet Union did not consist exclusively of Reagan administration policies, but encompassed countervailing tendencies from the Western public, other governments, and economic interest groups.

Whether Reagan is seen as the consummate hardliner or the prophet of anti-nuclearism, one should not exaggerate the influence of his administration, or of other short-term forces. Within the Washington beltway, debates about postwar military and foreign policy would suggest that Western strategy fluctuated wildly, but in fact the basic thrust of Western policy toward the USSR remained remarkably consistent. Arguments from the New Right notwithstanding, Reagan's containment strategy was not that different from those of his predecessors. Indeed, the broader peace-through-strength perspective sees the Cold War's finale as the product of a long-term policy, applied over the decades.

In any case, although containment certainly played an important role in blocking Soviet expansionism, it cannot explain either the end of the Cold War or the direction of Soviet policy responses. The West's relationship with the Soviet Union was not limited to containment, but included important elements of mutual vulnerability and engagement. The Cold War's end was not simply a result of Western strength but of mutual weakness and intentional engagement as well.

Most dramatically, the mutual vulnerability created by nuclear weapons overshadowed containment. Nuclear weapons forced the United States and the Soviet Union to eschew war and the serious threat of war as tools of diplomacy and created imperatives for the cooperative regulation of nuclear capability. Both countries tried to fashion nuclear explosives into useful instruments of policy, but they came to the realization—as the joint Soviet-American statement issued from the 1985 Geneva summit put it—that "nuclear war cannot be won and must never be fought." Both countries slowly but surely came to view nuclear weapons as a common threat that must be regulated jointly. Not just containment, but also the overwhelming and common nuclear threat brought the Soviets to the negotiating table. In the shadow of nuclear destruction, common purpose defused traditional antagonisms.

A second error of the peace-through-strength perspective is the failure to recognize that the West offered an increasingly benign face to the communist world. Traditionally, the Soviets' Marxist-Leninist doctrine held that the capitalist West was inevitably hostile and aggressive, an expectation reinforced by the aggression of capitalist, fascist Germany. Since World War II, the Soviets' principal adversaries had been democratic capitalist states. Slowly but surely Soviet doctrine acknowledged that the West's behavior did not follow Leninist expectations, but was instead increasingly pacific and cooperative. The Soviet willingness to abandon the Brezhnev Doctrine in the late 1980s in favor of the "Sinatra Doctrine"—under which any East European country could sing, "I did it my way"—suggests a radical transformation in the prevailing Soviet perception of threat from the West. In 1990, the Soviet acceptance of the de facto absorption of communist East Germany into West Germany involved the same calculation with even higher stakes. In accepting the German reunification, despite that country's past aggression, Gorbachev acted on the assumption that the Western system was fundamentally pacific. As Russian foreign minister Andrei Kozyrev noted subsequently, that Western countries are pluralistic democracies "practically rules out the pursuance of an aggressive foreign policy." Thus the Cold War ended despite the assertiveness of Western hardliners, rather than because of it.

The War of Ideas

The second front of the Cold War, according to the Reagan victory school, was ideological. Reagan spearheaded a Western ideological offensive that dealt the USSR a death blow. For the Right, driving home the image of the Evil Empire was a decisive stroke rather than a rhetorical flourish. Ideological warfare was such a key front in the Cold War because the Soviet Union was, at its core, an ideological creation. According to the Reagan Right, the supreme vulnerability of the Soviet Union to ideological assault was greatly underappreciated by Western leaders and publics. In that view, the Cold War was won by the West's uncompromising assertion of the superiority of its values and its complete denial of the moral legitimacy of the Soviet system during the 1980s. Western military strength could prevent defeat, but only ideological breakthrough could bring victory.

Underlying that interpretation is a deeply ideological philosophy of politics and history. The Reagan Right tended to view politics as a war of ideas, an orientation that generated a particularly polemical type of politics. As writer Sidney Blumenthal has pointed out, many of the leading figures in the neoconservative movement since the 1960s came to conservatism after having begun their political careers as Marxists or socialists. That perspective sees the Soviet Union as primarily an ideological artifact, and therefore sees struggle with it in particularly ideological terms. The neoconservatives believe, like Lenin, that "ideas are more fatal than guns."

Convinced that Bolshevism was quintessentially an ideological phenomenon, activists of the New Right were contemptuous of Western efforts to accommodate Soviet needs, moderate Soviet aims, and integrate the USSR into the international system as a "normal" great power. In their view, the *realpolitik* strategy urged by George Kennan, Walter Lippmann, and Hans Morgenthau was based on a misunderstanding of the Soviet Union. It provided an incomplete roadmap for waging the Cold War, and guaranteed that it would never be won. A particular villain for the New Right was Secretary of State Henry Kissinger, whose program of détente implied, in their view, a "moral equivalence" between the West and the Soviet Union that amounted to unilateral ideological disarmament. Even more benighted were liberal attempts to engage and co-opt the Soviet Union in hopes that the two systems could ultimately reconcile. The New Right's view of politics was strikingly globalist in its assumption that the world had shrunk too much for two such different systems to survive, and that the contest was too tightly engaged for containment or Iron Curtains to work. As James Burnham, the ex-communist prophet of New Right anticommunism, insisted in the early postwar years, the smallness of our "one world" demanded a strategy of "rollback" for American survival.

The end of the Cold War indeed marked an ideological triumph for the West, but not of the sort fancied by the Reagan victory school. Ideology played a far different and more complicated role in inducing Soviet change than the Reagan school allows. As with the military sphere, the Reagan school presents an incomplete picture of Western ideological influence, ignoring the emergence of ideological common ground in stimulating Soviet change.

The ideological legitimacy of the Soviet system collapsed in the eyes of its own citizens not because of an assault by Western ex-leftists, but because of the appeal of Western affluence and permissiveness. The puritanical austerity of Bolshevism's "New Soviet Man" held far less appeal than the "bourgeois decadence" of the West. For the peoples of the USSR and Eastern Europe, it was not so much abstract liberal principles but rather the Western way of life—the material and cultural manifestations of the West's freedoms—that subverted the Soviet vision. Western popular culture—exemplified in rock and roll, television, film, and blue jeans—seduced the communist world far more effectively than ideological sermons by anticommunist activists. As journalist William Echikson noted in his 1990 book *Lighting the Night: Revolution in Eastern Europe*, "instead of listening to the liturgy of Marx and Lenin, generations of would-be socialists tuned into the Rolling Stones and the Beatles."

If Western popular culture and permissiveness helped subvert communist legitimacy, it is a development of profound irony. Domestically, the New Right battled precisely those cultural forms that had such global appeal. V. I. Lenin's most potent ideological foils were John Lennon and Paul McCartney, not Adam Smith and Thomas Jefferson. The Right fought a two-front war against communism abroad and hedonism and consumerism at home. Had it not lost the latter struggle, the West may not have won the former.

The Reagan victory school argues that ideological assertiveness precipitated the end of the Cold War. While it is true that right-wing American intellectuals were assertive toward the Soviet Union, other Western activists and intellectuals were building links with highly placed reformist intellectuals there. The Reagan victory school narrative ignores that Gorbachev's reform program was based upon "new thinking"—a body of ideas developed by globalist thinkers cooperating across the East-West divide. The key themes of new thinking—the common threat of nuclear destruction, the need for strong international institutions, and the importance of ecological sustainability—built upon the cosmopolitanism of the Marxist tradition and officially replaced the Communist party's class-conflict doctrine during the Gorbachev period.

It is widely recognized that a major source of Gorbachev's new thinking was his close aide and speechwriter, Georgi Shakhnazarov. A former president of the Soviet political science association, Shakhnazarov worked extensively with Western globalists, particularly the New York-based group known as the World Order Models Project. Gorbachev's speeches and policy statements were replete with the language and ideas of globalism. The Cold War ended not with Soviet ideological capitulation to Reagan's anticommunism but rather with a Soviet embrace of globalist themes promoted by a network of liberal internationalists. Those intellectual influences were greatest with the state elite, who had greater access to the West and from whom the reforms originated.

Regardless of how one judges the impact of the ideological struggles during the Reagan years, it is implausible to focus solely on recent developments without accounting for longer-term shifts in underlying forces, particularly the widening gap between Western and Soviet economic performance. Over the long haul, the West's ideological appeal was based on the increasingly superior performance of the Western economic system. Although contrary to the expectation of Marx and Lenin, the robustness of capitalism in the West was increasingly acknowledged by Soviet analysts. Likewise, Soviet elites were increasingly troubled by their economy's comparative decline.

The Reagan victory school argues that the renewed emphasis on free-market principles championed by Reagan and then British prime minister Margaret Thatcher led to a global move toward market deregulation and privatization that the Soviets desired to follow. By rekindling the beacon of laissez-faire capitalism, Reagan illuminated the path of economic reform, thus vanquishing communism.

That view is misleading in two respects. First, it was West European social democracy rather than America's more free-wheeling capitalism that attracted Soviet reformers. Gorbachev wanted his reforms to emulate the Swedish model.

His vision was not of laissez-faire capitalism but of a social democratic welfare state. Second, the Right's triumphalism in the economic sphere is ironic. The West's robust economies owe much of their relative stability and health to two generations of Keynesian intervention and government involvement that the Right opposed at every step. As with Western popular culture, the Right opposed tendencies in the West that proved vital in the West's victory.

There is almost universal agreement that the root cause of the Cold War's abrupt end was the grave domestic failure of Soviet communism. However, the Soviet response to this crisis—accommodation and liberalization rather than aggression and repression—was significantly influenced by outside pressures and opportunities, many from the West. As historians and analysts attempt to explain how recent U.S. foreign policy helped end the Cold War, a view giving most of the credit to Reagan-era assertiveness and Western strength has become the new conventional wisdom. Both the Reagan victory school and the peace-through-strength perspective on Western containment assign a central role in ending the Cold War to Western resolve and power. The lesson for American foreign policy being drawn from those events is that military strength and ideological warfare were the West's decisive assets in fighting the Cold War.

The new conventional wisdom, in both its variants, is seriously misleading. Operating over the last decade, Ronald Reagan's personal anti-nuclearism, rather than his administration's hardline, catalyzed the accommodations to end the Cold War. His administration's effort to go beyond containment and on the offensive was muddled, counter-balanced, and unsuccessful. Operating over the long term, containment helped thwart Soviet expansionism but cannot account for the Soviet domestic failure, the end of East-West struggle, or the direction of the USSR'S reorientation. Contrary to the hard-line version, nuclear weapons were decisive in abandoning the conflict by creating common interests.

On the ideological front, the new conventional wisdom is also flawed. The conservatives' anticommunism was far less important in delegitimating the Soviet system than were that system's internal failures and the attraction of precisely the Western "permissive culture" abhorred by the Right. In addition, Gorbachev's attempts to reform communism in the late-1980s were less an ideological capitulation than a reflection of philosophical convergence on the globalist norms championed by liberal internationalists. And the West was more appealing not because of its laissez-faire purity, but because of the success of Keynesian and social welfare innovations whose use the Right resisted.

Behind the debate over who "won" the Cold War are competing images of the forces shaping recent history. Containment, strength, and confrontation—the trinity enshrined in conventional thinking on Western foreign policy's role in ending the Cold War—obscure the nature of these momentous changes. Engagement and interdependence, rather than containment, are the ruling trends of the age. Mutual vulnerability, not strength, drives security politics. Accommodation and integration, not confrontation, are the motors of change.

That such encouraging trends were established and deepened even as the Cold War raged demonstrates the considerable continuity underlying the West's support today for reform in the post-Soviet transition. Those trends also expose as one-sided and self-serving the New Right's attempt to take credit for the success of forces that, in truth, they opposed. In the end, Reagan partisans have been far more successful in claiming victory in the Cold War than they were in achieving it.

POSTSCRIPT

Did President Reagan Win the Cold War?

Now that the cold war is over, historians must assess why it ended so suddenly and unexpectedly. Did President Reagan's military buildup in the 1980s force the Russians into economic bankruptcy? Gaddis gives Reagan high marks for ending the cold war. By combining a policy of militancy and operational pragmatism, says Gaddis, Reagan brought about the most significant improvement in Soviet-American relations since the end of World War II. Deudney and Ikenberry disagree. In their view the cold war ended only when the Russians saw the need for international cooperation in order to end the arms race, prevent a nuclear holocaust, and liberalize their economy. It was Western global ideas and not the hard-line containment policy of the early Reagan administration that caused Gorbachev to abandon traditional Russian communism, according to Deudney and Ikenberry.

Gaddis has established himself as the leading diplomatic historian of the cold war period. His assessment of Reagan's relations with the Soviet Union is balanced and probably more generous than that of most contemporary analysts. It is also very useful because it so succinctly describes the unexpected shift from a hard-line policy to one of détente. Gaddis admits that not even Reagan could have foreseen the total collapse of communism and the Soviet empire. While he allows that Reagan was not a profound thinker, Gaddis credits him with the leadership skills to overcome any prior ideological biases toward the Soviet Union and to take advantage of Gorbachev's offer to end the arms race. While many of the president's hard-liners could not believe that the collapse of the Soviet Union was for real, Reagan was consistent in his view that the American arms buildup in the early 1980s was for the purpose of ending the arms race. Reagan, says Gaddis, accomplished this goal.

Deudney and Ikenberry give less credit to Reagan than to global influences in ending the cold war. In their view, Gorbachev softened his hard-line foreign policy and abandoned orthodox Marxist economic programs because he was influenced by Western European cosmopolitans who were concerned about the "common threat of nuclear destruction, the need for strong international institutions, and the importance of ecological sustainability." Deudney and Ikenberry agree that Reagan became more accommodating toward the Russians in 1983, but they maintain that the cold war's end "was not simply a result of Western strength but of mutual weakness and intentional engagement as well."

There is a considerable bibliography assessing the Reagan administration. Three *Washington Post* reporters have provided an early liberal and critical assessment of Reagan. Lou Cannon's *President Reagan: The Role of a Lifetime*

(Simon & Schuster, 1991) is a perceptive account of a reporter who has closely followed Reagan since he was governor of California. Haynes Johnson's *Sleepwalking Through History: America in the Reagan Years* (W. W. Norton, 1991) is more critical than Cannon's biography, but it is a readable account of Reagan's presidency. Don Oberdorfer, a former Moscow correspondent for the *Washington Post,* has written *The Turn: From the Cold War to a New Era: The United States and the Soviet Union, 1983–1990* (Poseidon Press, 1991). Oberdorfer credits Secretary of State George Schultz with Reagan's turnaround from a hard-line to a détente approach to foreign policy. Historian Michael R. Beschloss and *Time* magazine foreign correspondent Strobe Talbott interviewed Gorbachev for *At the Highest Levels: The Inside Story of the End of the Cold War* (Little, Brown, 1993), which carries the story from 1987 through the Bush administration.

Early evaluations of Reagan by historians and political scientists are useful, although any works written before 1991 are likely to be dated in their prognostications because of the collapse of the Soviet Union. Historian Michael Schaller, in *Reckoning With Reagan: America and Its President in the 1980s* (Oxford University Press, 1992), argues that Reagan created an illusion of national strength at the very time it was declining. Political scientist Coral Bell analyzes the disparity between Reagan's declaratory and operational policies in *The Reagan Paradox: U.S. Foreign Policy in the 1980s* (Rutgers University Press, 1989). A number of symposiums on the Reagan presidency have been published. Two of the best are David E. Kyvig, ed., *Reagan and the World* (Greenwood Press, 1990) and Dilys M. Hill, Raymond A. Moore, and Phil Williams, eds., *The Reagan Presidency: An Incomplete Revolution?* (St. Martin's Press, 1990), which contains primarily discussions of domestic policy.

Not all scholars are critical of Reagan. Some of his academic and intellectual supporters include British professor David Mervin, in the admiring portrait *Ronald Reagan and the American Presidency* (Longman, 1990), and Patrick Glynn, in *Closing Pandora's Box: Arms Races, Arms Control, and the History of the Cold War* (Basic Books, 1992). A number of conservative magazines have published articles arguing that American foreign policy hard-liners won the cold war. Two of the most articulate essays written from this viewpoint are Arch Puddington, "The Anti–Cold War Brigade," *Commentary* (August 1990) and Owen Harries, "The Cold War and the Intellectuals," *Commentary* (October 1991).

Books on the end of the cold war will continue to proliferate. Michael J. Hogan has edited the earliest views of the major historians in *The End of the Cold War: Its Meaning and Implications* (Cambridge University Press, 1992). Michael Howard reviews five books on the end of the cold war in "Winning the Peace: How Both Kennan and Gorbachev Were Right," *Times Literary Supplement* (January 8, 1993).

ISSUE 16

Should America Remain a Nation of Immigrants?

YES: Tamar Jacoby, from "Too Many Immigrants?" *Commentary* (April 2002)

NO: Patrick J. Buchanan, from *The Death of the West: How Dying Populations and Immigrant Invasions Imperil Our Country and Civilization* (Thomas Dunne Books, 2002)

ISSUE SUMMARY

YES: Social scientist Tamar Jacoby maintains that the newest immigrants keep America's economy strong because they work harder and take jobs that native-born Americans reject.

NO: Syndicated columnist Patrick J. Buchanan argues that America is no longer a nation because immigrants from Mexico and other Third World Latin American and Asian countries have turned America into a series of fragmented multicultural ethnic enclaves that lack a common culture.

Historians of immigration tend to divide the forces that encouraged voluntary migrations from one country to another into push and pull factors. Historically, the major reason why people left their native countries was the breakdown of feudalism and the subsequent rise of a commercially oriented economy. Peasants were pushed off the feudal estates of which they had been a part for generations. In addition, religious and political persecution for dissenting groups and the lack of economic opportunities for many middle-class émigrés also contributed to the migrations from Europe to the New World.

America was attractive to settlers long before the American Revolution took place. While the United States may not have been completely devoid of feudal traditions, immigrants perceived the United States as a country with a fluid social structure where opportunities abounded for everyone. By the mid-nineteenth century, the Industrial Revolution had provided opportunities for jobs in a nation that had always experienced chronic labor shortages.

There were four major periods of migration to the United States: 1607–1830, 1830–1890, 1890–1925, and 1968 to the present. In the seventeenth and eighteenth centuries, the white settlers came primarily, though not entirely, from the British Isles. They were joined by millions of African slaves. Both groups lived in proximity to several hundred thousand Native Americans. In those years the cultural values of Americans were a combination of what history professor Gary Nash has referred to as "red, white, and black." In the 30 years before the Civil War, a second phase began when immigrants came from other countries in northern and western Europe as well as China. Two European groups dominated. Large numbers of Irish Catholics emigrated in the 1850s because of the potato famine. Religious and political factors were as instrumental as economic factors in pushing the Germans to America. Chinese immigrants were also encouraged to come during the middle and later decades of the nineteenth century in order to help build the western portion of America's first transcontinental railroad and to work in low-paying service industries like laundries and restaurants.

By 1890 a third period of immigration had begun. Attracted by the unskilled jobs provided by the Industrial Revolution and the cheap transportation costs of fast-traveling, steam-powered ocean vessels, immigrants poured in at a rate of close to 1 million a year from Italy, Greece, Russia, and other countries of southern and eastern Europe. This flood continued until the early 1920s, when fears of a foreign takeover led Congress to pass legislation restricting the number of immigrants into the United States to 150,000 per year.

For the next 40 years America was ethnically frozen. The restriction laws of the 1920s favored northern and western European groups and were biased against southern and eastern Europeans. The depression of the 1930s, World War II in the 1940s, and minimal changes in the immigration laws of the 1950s kept migrations to the United States at a minimum level.

In the 1960s the immigration laws were drastically revised. The civil rights acts of 1964 and 1965, which ended legal discrimination against African Americans, were also the impetus for immigration reform. The 1965 Immigration Act represented a turning point in U.S. history. But it had unintended consequences. In conjunction with the 1990 Immigration Act, discrimination against non-European nations was abolished and preferences were given to family-based migrants over refugees and those with special skills. Immigrants from Latin American and Asian countries have dominated the fourth wave of migration and have used the loophole in the legislation to bring into the country "immediate relatives," such as spouses, children, and parents of American citizens who are exempt from the numerical ceilings of the immigration laws.

Should the United States allow the current flow of immigrants into the country to continue? In the following selection, Tamar Jacoby asserts that the newest immigrants keep America's economy strong because they work harder and take jobs that native-born workers reject. Jacoby also maintains that the newest immigrants will assimilate into mainstream culture as earlier generations did once the immigration laws provide permanence and stability. In the second selection, Patrick J. Buchanan argues that the new immigrants from Mexico, other parts of Latin America, and Asia who have been entering America since 1968 are destroying the core culture of the United States.

Tamar Jacoby

YES

Too Many Immigrants?

Of all the issues Americans have had to rethink in the wake of September 11, few seem more baffling than immigration. As polls taken in the following weeks confirmed, the attacks dramatically heightened people's fear of foreigners—not just Muslim foreigners, all foreigners. In one survey, fully two-thirds of the respondents said they wanted to stop any immigration until the war against terror was over. In Congress, the once marginal Immigration Reform Caucus quadrupled in size virtually overnight, and a roster of sweeping new proposals came to the fore: a six-month moratorium on all visas, shutting the door to foreign students, even militarizing our borders with troops and tanks.

In the end, none of these ideas came close to getting through Congress. On the issue of security, Republicans and Democrats, law-enforcement professionals and civilians alike agreed early on that it was critical to distinguish terrorists from immigrants—and that it was possible to protect the country without isolating it.

The Bush administration and Congress soon came up with similar plans based on the idea that the best defense was to intercept unwanted visitors before they reached the U.S.—when they applied for visas in their home country, were preparing to board a plane, or were first packing a lethal cargo shipment. A bipartisan bill now making its way through Congress calls for better screening of visa applications, enhanced intelligence-sharing among federal agencies, new tamper-proof travel documents with biometric data, and better tracking of the few hundred thousand foreign students already in the U.S.

But the security debate is only one front in a broader struggle over immigration. There is no question that our present policy is defective, and immigration opponents are hoping that the attacks will precipitate an all-out fight about overhauling it. Yet even if the goal is only to secure our borders, Americans are up against some fairly intractable realities.

In the aftermath of September 11, for example, there have been calls for tracking not just foreign students but all foreigners already in the country. This is not an unreasonable idea; but it would be next to impossible to implement. Even monitoring the entry and exit of visitors, as the Immigration and Naturalization Service (INS) has been charged with doing, has turned out to be a logistical nightmare—we are talking about a *half-billion* entries and probably an equal number of exits a year. (Of the total, incidentally, by far the largest number are Canadian and Mexican daily commuters, a third are Americans, and only a tiny percentage—fewer than a million a year—are immigrants seeking to make a new life in the U.S.) If collecting this information is difficult, analyzing and acting on it are a distant dream. As for the foreign-born population as a whole, it now stands at 28 million and growing, with illegal aliens alone estimated at between seven and eight million. It would take years just to identify them, much less find a way to track them all.

To this, the more implacable immigration opponents respond that if we cannot keep track of those already here, we should simply deport them. At the very least, others say, we should move to reduce radically the number we admit from now on, or impose a five- or ten-year moratorium. In the months since September 11, a variety of more and less extreme restrictionists have come together in a loose coalition to push forward such ideas. Although the movement has so far made little headway in Washington, it has become increasingly vocal, gaining a wide audience for its views, and has found a forceful, nationally known spokesman in the former presidential candidate and best-selling author Patrick J. Buchanan.

The coalition itself is a motley assemblage of bedfellows: liberals worried about the impact of large-scale immigration on population growth and the environment, conservatives exercised about porous borders and the shattering of America's common culture, plus a sizable contingent of outright racial demagogues. The best known organization pushing for restriction is the Federation for Immigration Reform, or FAIR, which provided much of the intellectual ammunition for the last big anti-immigration campaign, in the mid-1990's.

FAIR is still the richest and most powerful of the restrictionist groups. In the months since the attacks, a consortium it leads has spent some $300,000 on inflammatory TV ads in Western states where the 2002 mid-term elections will bring immigration issues to the fore; over pictures of the nineteen hijackers, the spots argue that the only way to keep America safe is to reduce immigration severely. But FAIR no longer dominates the debate as it once did, and newer groups are springing up around it.

On one flank are grassroots cells. Scrappier and more populist than FAIR, some consist of no more than an individual with a web page or radio show who has managed to accumulate a regional following; other local organizations have amassed enough strength to influence the politics of their states, particularly in California. On the other flank, and at the national level, FAIR is increasingly being eclipsed by younger, more media-savvy groups like the Center for Immigration Studies (CIS) in Washington and the writers associated with the website VDARE, both of which aim at swaying elite opinion in New York and Washington.

Different groups in the coalition focus on different issues, and each has its own style and way of presenting itself. One organization, Project USA, has devoted itself to putting up roadside billboards—nearly 100 so far, in a dozen states—with provocative messages like, "Tired of sitting in traffic? Every day, another 8,000 immigrants arrive. Every day!!" Those in the more respectable factions spend much energy distancing themselves from the more militant or fanatical, and even those with roughly the same mandate can seem, or sound, very different.

Consider CIS and VDARE. Created in 1985 as a fact-finding arm of FAIR, CIS is today arguably better known and more widely quoted than its parent. The group's executive director, Mark Krikorian, has made himself all but indispensable to anyone interested in immigration issues, sending out daily electronic compendiums of relevant news stories culled from the national press. His organization publishes scholarly papers on every aspect of the issue by a wide circle of respected academic researchers, many of whom would eschew any association with, say, FAIR's exclusionary politics. Along with his director of research, Steven Camarota, Krikorian is also a regular on Capitol Hill, where his restrained, informative testimony is influential with a broad array of elected officials.

VDARE, by contrast, wears its political views on its sleeve—and they are deliberately provocative. Founded a few years ago by the journalist Peter Brimelow, a senior editor at *Forbes* and the author of the best-selling *Alien Nation: Common Sense About America's Immigration Disaster* (1995), VDARE is named after Virginia Dare, "the first English child born in the New World." Kidnapped as an infant and never seen again, Virginia Dare is thought to have eventually married into a local Indian tribe, or to have been killed by it—almost equally unfortunate possibilities in the minds of VDARE's writers, who make no secret of their concern about the way America's original Anglo-Saxon stock is being transformed by immigration.

The overall strength of today's restrictionist movement is hard to gauge. But there is no question that recent developments—both September 11 and the flagging American economy—have significantly boosted its appeal. One Virginia-based organization, Numbers USA, claims that its membership grew from 5,000 to over 30,000 in the weeks after the attacks. Buchanan's *The Death of the West: How Dying Populations and Immigrant Invasions Imperil Our Country and Civilization*[1]—a deliberately confrontational jeremiad—shot to the top of Amazon.com s best-seller list within days of publication, then moved to a perch in the *New York Times* top ten. Nor does it hurt that the anti-immigrant cause boasts advocates at both ends of the political spectrum. Thus, leftists repelled by the likes of Buchanan and Brimelow could read a more congenial statement of the same case in a recent, much-discussed series in the *New York Review of Books* by the distinguished sociologist Christopher Jencks.

To be sure, immigration opponents have also had some significant setbacks. Most notably, the Republican party, which stood staunchly with them in the mid-1990's in California, is now firmly on the other side of the issue—if anything, George W. Bush has become the country's leading advocate for liberalizing immigration law. But there can be no mistaking the depth of public concern over one or another of the questions raised by the restrictionists, and in the event of more attacks or a prolonged downturn, their appeal could surely grow.

In addition to national security, immigration opponents offer arguments principally about three issues: natural resources, economics, and the likelihood that today's newcomers will be successfully absorbed into American society. On the first, restrictionists contend not only that immigrants compete with us and consume our natural resources, to the detriment of the native-born, but that their numbers will eventually overwhelm us, choking the United States to death both demographically and environmentally.

Much of Buchanan's book, for example, is devoted to a discussion of population. As he correctly notes, birth rates in Europe have dropped below replacement level, and populations there are aging. By 2050, he estimates, only 10 percent of the world's people will be of European descent, while Asia, Africa, and Latin America will grow by three to four billion people, yielding "30 to 40 new Mexicos." As the developed countries "die out," huge movements of hungry people from the underdeveloped world will swamp their territory and destroy their culture. "This is not a matter of prophecy," Buchanan asserts, "but of mathematics."

Extrapolating from similar statistics, Christopher Jencks has predicted that the U.S. population may double in size over the next half-century largely as a result of the influx of foreigners. (This is a much faster rate of growth than that foreseen by virtually any other mainstream social scientist.) Jencks imagines a hellish future in which American cities will become all but unlivable and suburban sprawl will decimate the landscape. The effect on our natural resources will be devastating, as the water supply dwindles and our output of carbon dioxide soars. (To put his arguments in perspective, Jencks finds nothing new in this pattern. Immigration has always been disastrous to our ecology, he writes: the Indians who crossed the Bering Strait 13,000 years ago depleted the continent's fauna by overhunting, and many centuries later the germs brought by Europeans laid waste to the Indians.)

Not all the arguments from scarcity are quite so apocalyptic, but all begin and end with the assumption that the size of the pie is fixed, and that continued immigration can only mean less and less for the rest of us. A similar premise underlies the restrictionists' second set of concerns—that immigrants steal jobs from native-born workers, depress Americans' wages, and make disproportionate use of welfare and other government services.

Here, groups like FAIR and CIS focus largely on the portion of the immigrant flow that is poor and ill-educated—not the Indian engineer in Silicon Valley, but the Mexican farmhand with a sixth-grade education. "Although immigrants comprise about 12 percent of America's workforce," CIS reports, "they account for 31 percent of high-school dropouts in the workforce." Not only are poverty rates among these immigrants higher than among the native-born, but, the restrictionists claim, the gap is growing. As for welfare, Krikorian points out that even in the wake of the 1996 reform that denied means-tested benefits to many immigrants, their reliance on some programs—food stamps, for example—still exceeds that of native-born Americans.

The restrictionists' favorite economist is Harvard's George Borjas, the author of a widely read 1999 book, *Heaven's Door.*[2] As it happens, Borjas did not confirm the worst fears about immigrants: they do not, for example, steal

Americans' jobs, and today's newcomers are no poorer or less capable than those who came at the turn of the 20th century and ultimately did fine in America. Still, in Borjas's estimation, compared with the native-born of their era, today's immigrants are *relatively* farther behind than, say, the southern Europeans who came a century ago, and even if they do not actually take work away from Americans, they may prompt the native-born to move to other cities and thus adversely affect the larger labor market.

As a result, Borjas contends, the presence of these newcomers works to lower wages, particularly among high-school dropouts. And because of the cost of the government services they consume—whether welfare or public schooling or hospital care—they impose a fiscal drain on a number of states where they settle. In sum, immigrants may be a boon to U.S. business and to the middle class (which benefits from lower prices for the fruit the foreigners pick and from the cheap lawn services they provide), but they are an unfair burden on ordinary working Americans, who must subsidize them with higher taxes.

Borjas's claims have hardly gone unchallenged by economists on either the Right or the Left—including Jagdish Bhagwati in a heated exchange in the *Wall Street Journal* —but he remains a much-quoted figure among restrictionists, who particularly like his appealing-sounding note of concern for the native-born black poor. Borjas's book has also greatly strengthened those who propose that existing immigration policy, which is based mainly on the principle of family unification, be changed to one like Canada's that admits people based on the skills they bring.

This brings us to the third issue that worries the anti-immigration community: the apparent failure, or refusal, of large numbers of newcomers to assimilate successfully into American society, to learn our language, adopt our mores, and embrace American values as their own. To many who harp on this theme—Buchanan, the journalist Georgie Anne Geyer, the more polemical VDARE contributors—it is, frankly, the racial makeup of today's influx that is most troublesome. "Racial groups that are different are more difficult to assimilate," Buchanan says flatly, painting a nightmarish picture of newcomers with "no desire to learn English or become citizens." Buchanan and others make much of the influence of multiculturalism and identity politics in shaping the priorities of the immigrant community; his chapter on Mexican immigrants, entitled "La Reconquista," quotes extensively from extremist Chicano activists who want, he says, to "colonize" the United States.

On this point, it should be noted, Buchanan and his followers are hardly alone, and hardly original. Any number of observers who are *favorably* disposed to continued immigration have likewise raised an alarm over the radically divisive and balkanizing effects of multiculturalism and bilingual education. Where they part company with Buchanan is over the degree of danger they perceive—and what should be done about it.[3]

About one thing the restrictionists are surely right: our immigration policy is broken. Not only is the INS one of the least efficient and most beleaguered agencies in Washington—at the moment, four million authorized immigrants are waiting, some for a decade or more, for their paperwork to be processed—but official policy, particularly with regard to Mexico, is a hypocritical sham.

Even as we claim to limit the flow of migrants, and force thousands to wait their turn for visas, we look the other way as hundreds of thousands enter the country without papers—illegal but welcomed by business as a cheap, pliable labor force. Nor do we have a clear rationale for the selection we end up making from the vast pool of foreigners eager to enter the country.

But here precisely is where the restrictionists' arguments are the least helpful. Take the issue of scarcity. The restrictionists construct their dire scenarios by extrapolating from the current flow of immigrants. But as anyone who follows these matters is aware, nothing is harder to predict than who and how many will come in the future. It is, for example, as easy today as it ever was to migrate to the U.S. from Puerto Rico, and wages on the island still lag woefully behind wages here. But the net flow from Puerto Rico stopped long ago, probably because life there improved just enough to change the calculus of hope that had been prodding people to make the trip.

Sooner or later, the same thing will happen in Mexico. No one knows when, but surely one hint of things to come is that population growth is slowing in Mexico, just as it slowed earlier here and in Europe. Over the past three decades, the Mexican fertility rate has dropped from an average 6.5 children per mother to a startling 2.5.

Nor are demographic facts themselves always as straightforward in their implications as the restrictionists assume. True, population is still growing faster in the underdeveloped world than in developed countries. But is this an argument against immigration, or for it? If they are to remain strong, countries *need* population—workers, customers, taxpayers, soldiers. And our own openness to immigrants, together with our proven ability to absorb them, is one of our greatest advantages over Japan and Europe, which face a demographic crisis as their ratio of workers to retirees adversely shifts. The demographer Ben Wattenberg has countered Buchanan with a simple calculation: "If we keep admitting immigrants at our current levels, there will be almost 400 million Americans by 2050. That"—and only that, one might add—"can keep us strong enough to defend and perhaps extend our views and values."

The argument from economics is equally unhelpful. The most commonly heard complaint about foreign workers is that they take jobs from Americans. Not only is this assertion untrue—nobody has found real evidence to support it—but cities and states with the largest immigrant populations (New York, Los Angeles, and others) boast far faster economic growth and lower unemployment than cities and states that do not attract immigrants. In many places, the presence of immigrants seems to reduce unemployment even among native-born blacks—probably because of the way immigrants stimulate economic growth.

Economists looking for a depressive effect on native-born wages have been nearly as disappointed: dozens of studies over the past two or three decades have found at most modest and probably temporary effects. Even if Borjas is right that a native-born black worker may take home $300 less a year as a result of immigration, this is a fairly small amount of money in the overall scheme of things. More to the point, globalization would have much the same effect on wages, immigrants or no immigrants. Pressed by competition from foreign imports, American manufacturers have had to change production methods and cut costs, including labor costs. If they did not, they would have to go out of business—or move to an underdeveloped country where wages are lower. In either case, the U.S. economy would end up being hurt far more than by the presence of immigrant workers—who expand the U.S. economic pie when they buy shoes and groceries and washing machines from their American neighbors and call American plumbers into their homes.

What about the costs imposed by immigrants, especially by their use of government services? It is true that many immigrants—though far from all—are poorer than native-born Americans, and thus pay less in taxes. It is also true that one small segment of the immigrant population—refugees—tends to be heavily dependent on welfare. As a result, states with large immigrant populations often face chronic fiscal problems.

But that is at the state level, and mostly in high-welfare states like California. If we shift the lens to the federal level, and include the taxes that immigrants remit to the IRS, the calculation comes out very differently: immigrants pay in more than they take out. This is particularly true if one looks at the picture over the course of an immigrant's lifetime. Most come to the U.S. as young adults looking for work—which means they were already educated at home, relieving us of a significant cost. More important, even illegal immigrants generally keep up with payroll taxes, contributing to Social Security though they may never claim benefits. According to Stephen Moore, an economist at the Cato Institute, foreign-born workers are likely to contribute as much as $2 trillion to Social Security over the next 70 years, thus effectively keeping it afloat.

The economic debate often comes down to this sort of war of numbers, but the victories on either side are rarely conclusive. After all, even 28 million immigrants form but a small part of the $12-trillion U.S. economy, and most of the fiscal costs and benefits associated with them are relatively modest. Besides, fiscal calculations are only a small part of the larger economic picture. How do we measure the energy immigrants bring—the pluck and grit and willingness to improvise and innovate?

Not only are immigrants by and large harder-working than the native-born, they generally fill economic niches that would otherwise go wanting. The term economists use for this is "complementarity." If immigrants were exactly like American workers, they would not be particularly valuable to employers. They are needed precisely because they are different: willing or able to do jobs few American workers are willing or able to do. These jobs tend to be either at the lowest rungs of the employment ladder (busboy, chambermaid, line worker in a meatpacking plant) or at the top (nurse, engineer, information-technology worker).

It is no accident that 80 percent of American farmworkers are foreign-born, or that, if there were no immigrants, hotels and restaurants in many cities would have to close their doors. Nor is it an accident that immigrants account for a third of the scientific workforce in Silicon Valley, or that Asian entrepreneurs run a quarter of the companies there. Today's supply of willing laborers from Mexico, China, India, and elsewhere matches our demand in these various sectors, and the result is good for just about everyone—business, workers, and American consumers alike.

To be sure, what is good for business, or even for American consumers, may not ultimately be good for the United States—and this is where the issue of assimilation comes in. "What is a nation?" Buchanan asks. "Is America nothing more than an economic system?" If immigrants do not come to share our values, adopt our heroes, and learn our history as their own, ultimately the nation will not hold. Immigration policy cannot be a suicide pact.

The good news is that assimilation is not going nearly as badly as the restrictionists claim. Though many immigrants start out at the bottom, most eventually join the working poor, if not the middle class. And by the time they have been here twenty years, they generally do as well as or better than the native-born, earning comparable salaries and registering *lower* poverty rates.

Nor is it true that immigrants fail or refuse to learn English. Many more than in previous eras come with a working knowledge of the language—it is hard to avoid it in the world today. Despite the charade that is bilingual education, nearly all high-school students who have been educated in this country—nine out of ten of them, according to one study—prefer English to their native tongue. And by the third generation, even among Hispanics, who are somewhat slower than other immigrants to make the linguistic shift, only 1 percent say they use "more or only Spanish" at home.

Despite the handicaps with which many arrive, the immigrant drive to succeed is as strong as ever. According to one important study of the second generation, newcomers' children work harder than their U.S. classmates, putting in an average of two hours of homework a night compared with the "normal" 30 minutes. They also aspire to higher levels of educational achievement, earn better grades, drop out less frequently—and expect only the best of their new homeland. Nearly two-thirds believe that hard work and accomplishment can triumph over prejudice, and about the same number say there is no better country than the United States. As for the lure of identity politics, one of the most thorough surveys of Hispanics, conducted in 1999 by the *Washington Post*, reported that 84 percent believe it is "important" or "very important" for immigrants "to change so that they blend into the larger society, as in the idea of the melting pot."

There is also bad news. Immigrant America is far from monolithic, and some groups do worse than others both economically and culturally. While fewer than 5 percent of Asian young people use an Asian language with their friends, nearly 45 percent of Latinos sometimes use Spanish. Close to 90 percent of Chinese parents expect their children to finish college; only 55 percent of Mexicans do. Indeed, Mexicans—who account for about a quarter of the foreign-born—lag behind on many measures, including, most worrisomely, education. The average Mexican migrant comes with less than eight years of schooling, and though the second generation is outstripping its parents, it too falls well below American norms, either for other immigrants or for the native-born.

When it comes to absorbing the American common culture, or what has been called patriotic assimilation, there is no question that today's immigrants are at a disadvantage compared with yesterday's. Many Americans themselves no longer know what it means to be American. Our schools teach, at best, a travesty of American history, distorted by political correctness and the excesses of multiculturalism. Popular culture supplies only the crudest, tinniest visions of our national heritage. Even in the wake of September 11, few leaders have tried to evoke more than a fuzzy, feel-good enthusiasm for America. No wonder many immigrants have a hard time making the leap from their culture to ours. We no longer ask it of them.

Still, even if the restrictionists are right about all this, their remedy is unworkable. Given the global economy, given the realities of politics and law enforcement in the United States, we are not going to stop—or significantly reduce—the flow of immigrant workers into the country any time soon. Businesses that rely on imported labor would not stomach it; as it is, they object vociferously whenever the INS tries to enforce the law. Nor are American citizens prepared to live with the kinds of draconian measures that would be needed to implement a significant cutback or time-out. Even in the wake of the attacks, there is little will to require that immigrants carry ID cards, let alone to erect the equivalent of a Berlin Wall along the Rio Grande. In sum, if many immigrants among us are failing to adopt our common culture, we will have to look elsewhere than to the restrictionists for a solution.

What, then, is to be done? As things stand today, American immigration policy and American law are perilously out of sync with reality—the reality of the market. Consider the Mexican case, not the only telling one but the most dramatic.

People born in Mexico now account for roughly 10 percent of the U.S. workforce, and the market for their labor is a highly efficient one. Very few recent Mexican migrants are unemployed; even modest economic upturns or downturns have a perceptible impact on the number trying to enter illegally, as word quickly spreads from workers in California or Kansas back to home villages in Mexico. This precise coordination of supply and demand has been drawing roughly 300,000 Mexicans over the border each year, although, even including minors and elderly parents, the INS officially admits only half that many.

One does not have to be a free-market enthusiast to find this discrepancy absurd, and worse. Not only does it criminalize badly needed laborers and productive economic activity. It also makes an ass of the law and insidiously corrupts American values, encouraging illegal hiring and discrimination against even lawful Mexican migrants.

Neither a moratorium nor a reduction in official quotas would eliminate this thriving labor exchange—on the contrary, it would only exacerbate the mismatch. Instead, we should move in the opposite direction from what the restrictionists demand, bringing the number we admit more into line with the reality of the market. The rationale for whom we ought to let in, what we should encourage and reward, is work.

This, as it happens, is precisely the direction in which President Bush was moving before September 11. A package of reforms he floated in July, arrived at in negotiations with Mexican president Vicente Fox, would have significantly expanded the number of visas for Mexican workers. The President's impulse may have been partisan—to woo Latino voters—but he stumbled onto the basis for an immigration policy that would at once serve America's interests and reflect its values. He put the core idea plainly, and got it exactly right: "If somebody is willing to offer a job others in America aren't willing to do, we ought to welcome that person to the country."

Compared with this, any other criterion for immigration policy—family reunification, country of origin, or skill level—sinks into irrelevancy. It makes no sense at all that three-quarters of the permanent visas available today should be based on family ties, while only one-quarter are employment-related. As for the Canadian-style notion of making skill the decisive factor, admitting engineers and college professors but closing the door to farmworkers, not only does this smack of a very un-American elitism but it disregards our all too palpable economic needs at the low end of the labor market.

The problem is that there is at present virtually no legal path into the U.S. for unskilled migrant laborers; unless they have relatives here, they have no choice but to come illicitly. If we accept the President's idea that immigration policy should be based on work, we ought to enshrine it in a program that makes it possible for those who want to work, and who can find a job, to come lawfully. The program ought to be big enough to meet market needs: the number of visas available the first year should match the number of people who now sneak in against the law, and in future years it should follow the natural rise and fall of supply and demand. At the same time, the new regime ought to be accompanied by serious enforcement measures to ensure that workers use this pipeline rather than continuing to come illegally outside it.

Such a policy makes sound economic sense—and also would provide a huge boost for immigrant absorption and assimilation. By definition, the undocumented are effectively barred from assimilating. Most cannot drive legally in the U.S., or, in many states, get regular care in a hospital. Nor, in most places, can they send their children to college. An indelible caste line separates them from other Americans—no matter how long they stay, how much they contribute, or how ardently they and their children strive to assimilate. If we want newcomers to belong, we should admit them legally, and find a fair means of regularizing the status of those who are already here illicitly.

But rerouting the illegal flow into legal channels will not by itself guarantee assimilation—particularly not if, as the President and Congress have suggested, we insist that workers go home when the job is done. In keeping with the traditional Republican approach to immigration, the President's reform package included a proposal for a guest-worker program, and before September 11, both Democrats and Republicans had endorsed the idea. If we want to encourage assimilation, however, such a system would only be counterproductive.

The cautionary model in this case is Germany, which for years admitted unskilled foreigners exclusively as temporary guest workers, holding out virtually no hope that either they or their children could become German citizens. As it happened, many of these migrants remained in Germany long after the work they were imported for had disappeared. But today, nearly 40 years later, most of them still have not assimilated, and they remain, poorly educated and widely despised, on the margins of German society. Clearly, if what we hope to encourage is the putting-down of roots, any new visa program must give participants a shot at membership in the American body politic.

But how we hand out visas is only the first step in a policy aimed at encouraging immigrant absorption. Other steps would have to include the provision of basic services like instruction in English, civics classes, naturalization programs—and also counseling in more practical matters like how to navigate the American banking system. (Many newcomers, even when they start making money, are at sea in the world of credit cards, credit histories, mortgage applications, and the like.) All these nuts-and-bolts services are as essential as the larger tasks, from overhauling the teaching of American history to eliminating counterproductive programs like bilingual education and ethnic entitlements that only breed separatism and alienation.

There can be no gainsaying the risks America runs in remaining open to new immigrants. The security perils, though real enough, are the least worrisome. Legalizing the flow of needed workers and providing them with papers will help keep track of who is here and also help prevent those who wish to do us harm from entering in the first place. The more daring, long-term gamble lies in continuing to admit millions of foreigners who may or may not make it here or find a way to fit in. This is, as Buchanan rightly states, "a decision we can never undo."

Still, it is an experiment we have tried before—repeatedly. The result has never come out exactly as predicted, and the process has always been a wrenching one. But as experiments go, it has not only succeeded on its own terms; it has made us the wonder of the world. It can do so again—but only if we stop denying reality and resolve instead to meet the challenge head-on.

Notes

1. Dunne Books, 320 pp., $25.95.
2. Reviewed by Irwin M. Stelzer in the September 1999 COMMENTARY.
3. In COMMENTARY, see, for example, Linda Chavez's "Our Hispanic Predicament" (June 1998) and "What To Do About Immigration" (March 1995), and my own "In Asian America" (July-August 2000).

NO

Patrick J. Buchanan

La Reconquista

As the [immigrant] invasion rolls on, with California as the preferred destination, sociologist William Frey has documented an out-migration of African Americans and Anglo-Americans from the Golden State in search of cities and towns like the ones they grew up in. Other Californians are moving into gated communities. A country that cannot control its borders isn't really a country anymore, Ronald Reagan warned us some twenty years ago.

Concerns about a radical change in America's ethnic composition have been called un-American. But they are as American as Benjamin Franklin, who once asked, "Why should Pennsylvania, founded by the English, become a Colony of Aliens, who will shortly be so numerous as to Germanize us instead of our Anglifying them. . . ?" Franklin would never find out if his fears were justified. German immigration was halted during the Seven Years War.

Former president Theodore Roosevelt warned, "The one absolutely certain way of bringing this nation to ruin, of preventing all possibility of its continuing to be a nation at all, would be to permit it to become a tangle of squabbling nationalities."

Immigration is a necessary subject for national debate, for it is about who we are as a people. Like the Mississippi, with its endless flow of life-giving water, immigration has enriched America throughout history. But when the Mississippi floods its banks, the devastation can be enormous. Yet, by the commands of political correctness, immigration as an issue is off the table. Only "nativists" or "xenophobes" could question a policy by which the United States takes in more people of different colors, creeds, cultures, and civilizations than all other nations of the earth combined. The river is rising to levels unseen in our history. What will become of our country if the levees do not hold?

In late 1999, this writer left Tucson and drove southeast to Douglas, the Arizona border town of eighteen thousand that had become the principal invasion corridor into the United States. In March alone, the U.S. Border Patrol had apprehended twenty-seven thousand Mexicans crossing illegally, half again as many illegal aliens crossing in one month as there are people in Douglas.

While there, I visited Theresa Murray, an eighty-two-year-old widow and a great grandmother who lives in the Arizona desert she grew up in. Her ranch house was surrounded by a seven-foot chain-link fence that was topped with coils of razor wire. Every door and window had bars on it and was wired to an alarm. Mrs. Murray sleeps with a .32-caliber pistol on her bed table, because she has been burglarized thirty times. Her guard dogs are dead; they bled to death when someone tossed meat containing chopped glass over her fence. Theresa Murray is living out her life inside a maximum-security prison, in her own home, in her own country, because her government lacks the moral courage to do its duty and defend the borders of the United States of America.

If America is about anything, it is freedom. But as Theresa Murray says, "I've lost my freedom. I can't ever leave the house unless I have somebody watch it. We used to ride our horses clear across the border. We had Mexicans working on our property. It used to be fun to live here. Now, it's hell. It's plain old hell."

While Theresa Murray lives unfree, in hellish existence, American soldiers defend the borders of Korea, Kuwait, and Kosovo. But nothing is at risk on those borders, half a world away, to compare with what is at risk on our border with Mexico, over which pass the armies of the night as they trudge endlessly northward to the great cities of America. Invading armies go home, immigrant armies do not.

Who Killed the Reagan Coalition?

For a quarter of a century, from 1968 until 1992, the Republican party had a virtual lock on the presidency. The "New Majority," created by Richard Nixon and replicated by Ronald Reagan, gave the GOP five victories in six presidential elections. The key to victory was to append to the Republican base two Democratic blocs: Northern Catholic ethnics and Southern white Protestants. Mr. Nixon lured these voters away from the New Deal coalition with appeals to patriotism, populism, and social conservatism. Success gave the GOP decisive margins in the industrial states and a "Solid South" that had been the base camp of the Democratic party since Appomattox. This Nixon-Reagan coalition proved almost unbeatable. McGovern, Mondale, and Dukakis could carry 90 percent of the black vote, but with Republicans taking 60 percent of the white vote, which was over 90 percent of the total, the GOP inevitably came out on top.

This was the Southern Strategy. While the media called it immoral, Democrats had bedded down with segregationists for a century without similar censure. FDR and Adlai Stevenson had put segregationists on their tickets. Outside of Missouri, a border state with Southern sympathies, the only ones Adlai captured in 1956 were Dixiecrat states later carried by George Wallace.

Neither Nixon nor Reagan ever supported segregation. As vice president, Nixon was a stronger backer of civil rights than Senators John F. Kennedy or Lyndon Johnson. His role in winning passage of the Civil Rights Act of 1957 was lauded in a personal letter from Dr. Martin Luther King, who hailed Vice President Nixon's "assiduous labor and dauntless courage in seeking to make Civil Rights a reality."

For a quarter century, Democrats were unable to pick the GOP lock on the presidency, because they could not shake loose the Republican grip on the white vote. With the exception of Lyndon Johnson's landslide of 1964, no Democrat since Truman in 1948 had won the white vote. What broke the GOP lock on the presidency was the Immigration Act of 1965.

During the anti-Soviet riots in East Berlin in 1953, Bertolt Brecht, the Communist playwright, quipped, "Would it not be easier . . . for the government to dissolve the people and elect another?" In the last thirty years, America has begun to import a new electorate, as Republicans cheerfully backed an immigration policy tilted to the Third World that enlarged the Democratic base and loosened the grip that Nixon and Reagan had given them on the presidency of the United States.

In 1996, the GOP was rewarded. Six of the 7 states with the largest numbers of immigrants—California, New York, Illinois, New Jersey, Massachusetts, Florida, and Texas—went for Clinton. In 2000, 5 went for Gore, and Florida was a dead heat. Of the 15 states with the most foreign-born, Bush lost 10. But of the 10 states with the smallest shares of foreign-born—Montana, Mississippi, Wyoming, West Virginia, South Dakota, South Carolina, Alabama, Tennessee, and Arkansas—Bush swept all 10.

Among the states with the most immigrants, only Texas has been reliably Republican, but now it is going the way of California. In the 1990s, Texas took in 3.2 million new residents as the Hispanic share of Texas's population shot from 25 percent to 33 percent. Hispanics are now the major ethnic group in four of Texas's five biggest cities: Houston, Dallas, San Antonio, and El Paso. "Non-Hispanic Whites May Soon Be a Minority in Texas" said a recent headline in the *New York Times*. With the Anglo population down from 60 percent in 1990 to 53 percent, the day when whites are a minority in Texas for the first time since before the Alamo is coming soon. "Projections show that by 2005," says the *Dallas Morning News*, "fewer than half of Texans will be white."

America is going the way of California and Texas. "In 1960, the U.S. population was 88.6 percent white; in 1990, it was only 75.6 percent—a drop of 13 percentage points in thirty years. . . . [By 2020] the proportion of whites could fall as low as 61 per cent." So writes Peter Brimelow of *Forbes*. By 2050, Euro-Americans, the largest and most loyal share of the electorate the GOP has, will be a minority, due to an immigration policy that is championed by Republicans. John Stuart Mill was not altogether wrong when he branded the Tories "the Stupid Party."

Hispanics are the fastest-growing segment of America's population. They were 6.4 percent of the U.S. population in 1980, 9 percent by 1990, and in 2000 over 12 percent. "The Hispanic fertility rates are quite a bit higher than the

Table 1

1996	1,045,000
1997	598,000
1998	463,000
1999	872,000
2000	898,315

white or black population. They are at the levels of the baby boom era of the 1950s," says Jeffrey Passel, a demographer at the Urban Institute. At 35.4 million, Hispanics now equal African Americans in numbers and are becoming as Democratic in voting preferences. Mr. Bush lost the African-American vote eleven to one, but he also lost Hispanics two to one.

In 1996, when Clinton carried Latino voters seventy to twenty-one, he carried first-time Latino voters ninety-one to six. Aware that immigrants could give Democrats their own lock on the White House, Clinton's men worked relentlessly to naturalize them. In the year up to September 30, 1996, the Immigration and Naturalization Service swore in 1,045,000 immigrants as new citizens so quickly that 80,000 with criminal records—6,300 for serious crimes—slipped by. [Table 1 shows] the numbers of new citizens in each of the last five years.

California took a third of these new citizens. As non-Latino white registration fell by one hundred thousand in California in the 1990s, one million Latinos registered. Now 16 percent of the California electorate, Hispanics gave Gore the state with hundreds of thousands of votes to spare. "Both parties show up at swearing-in ceremonies to try to register voters," says Democratic consultant William Carrick. "There is a Democratic table and a Republican table. Ours has a lot of business. Theirs is like the Maytag repairman." With fifty-five electoral votes, California, home state of Nixon and Reagan, has now become a killing field of the GOP.

Voting on referenda in California has also broken down along ethnic lines. In 1994, Hispanics, rallying under Mexican flags, opposed Proposition 187 to end welfare to illegals. In the 1996 California Civil Rights Initiative, Hispanics voted for ethnic preferences. In 1998, Hispanics voted to keep bilingual education. Anglo-Americans voted the other way by landslides.

Ron Unz, father of the "English for the Children" referendum that ended state-funded bilingual education, believes the LA riot of 1992 may have been the Rubicon on the road to the balkanization of California.

> The plumes of smoke from burning buildings and the gruesome television footage almost completely shattered the sense of security of middle-class Southern Californians. Suddenly, the happy "multicultural California" so

> beloved of local boosters had been unmasked as a harsh, dangerous, Third World dystopia. . . . the large numbers of Latinos arrested (and summarily deported) for looting caused whites to cast a newly wary eye on gardeners and nannies who just weeks earlier had seemed so pleasant and reliable. If multicultural Los Angeles had exploded into sudden chaos, what security could whites expect as a minority in an increasingly nonwhite California?

Except for refugees from Communist countries like Hungary and Cuba, immigrants gravitate to the party of government. The obvious reason: Immigrants get more out of government—in free schooling for their kids, housing subsidies, health care—than they pay in. Arriving poor, most do not soon amass capital gains, estates, or incomes that can be federally taxed. Why should immigrants support a Republican party that cuts taxes they don't pay over a Democratic party that will expand the programs on which they do depend?

After Ellis Island, the Democratic party has always been the first stop for immigrants. Only after they have begun to move into the middle class do the foreign-born start converting to Republicanism. This can take two generations. By naturalizing and registering half a million or a million foreign-born a year, the Democrats are locking up future presidential elections and throwing away the key. If the GOP does not do something about mass immigration, mass immigration will do something about the GOP—turn it into a permanent minority that is home to America's newest minority, Euro-Americans.

As the ethnic character of America changes, politics change. A rising tide of immigration naturally shifts politics and power to the Left, by increasing the demands on government. The rapidly expanding share of the U.S. electorate that is of African and Hispanic ancestry has already caused the GOP to go silent on affirmative action and mute its calls for cuts in social spending. In 1996, Republicans were going to abolish the U.S. Department of Education. Now, they are enlarging it. As Hispanic immigration soars, and Hispanic voters become the swing voters in the pivotal states, their agenda will become America's agenda. It is already happening. In 2000, an AFL-CIO that had opposed mass immigration reversed itself and came out for amnesty for illegal aliens, hoping to sign up millions of illegal workers as dues-paying union members. And the Bush White House—in its policy decisions and appointments—has become acutely attentive to the Hispanic vote, often as the expense of conservative principles.

America's Quebec?

Harvard economist George Borjas, who studied the issue, found no net economic benefit from mass migration from the Third World. The added costs of schooling, health care, welfare, social security, and prisons, plus the added pressure on land, water, and power resources, exceeded the taxes that immigrants contribute. The National Bureau of Economic Research puts the cost of immigration at $80.4 billion in 1995. Economist Donald Huddle of Rice University estimates that the net annual cost of immigration will reach $108 billion by 2006. What are the benefits, then, that justify the risks we are taking of the balkanization of America?

Census 2000 revealed what many sensed. For the first time since statehood, whites in California are a minority. White flight has begun. In the 1990s, California grew by three million people, but its Anglo population actually "dropped by nearly half a million . . . surprising many demographers." Los Angeles County lost 480,000 white folks. In the exodus, the Republican bastion of Orange County lost 6 percent of its white population. "We can't pretend we're a white middle class state anymore," said William Fulton, research fellow at USC's Southern California Studies Center. State librarian Kevin Starr views the Hispanization of California as natural and inevitable:

> The Anglo hegemony was only an intermittent phase in California's arc of identity, extending from the arrival of the Spanish . . . the Hispanic nature of California has been there all along, and it was temporarily swamped between the 1880s and the 1960s, but that was an aberration. This is a reassertion of the intrinsic demographic DNA of the longer pattern, which is a part of the California-Mexican continuum.

The future is predictable: With one hundred thousand Anglos leaving California each year, with the Asian population soaring 42 percent in a single decade, with 43 percent of all Californians under eighteen Hispanic, America's largest state is on its way to becoming a predominantly Third World state.

No one knows how this will play out, but California could become another Quebec, with demands for formal recognition of its separate and unique Hispanic culture and identity—or another Ulster. As Sinn Fein demanded and got special ties to Dublin, Mexican Americans may demand a special relationship with their mother country, dual citizenship, open borders, and voting representation in Mexico's legislature. President Fox endorses these ideas. With California holding 20 percent of the electoral votes needed for the U.S. presidency, and Hispanic votes decisive in California, what presidential candidate would close the door to such demands?

"I have proudly proclaimed that the Mexican nation extends beyond the territory enclosed by its borders and that Mexican migrants are an important—a very important—part of this," said President Zedillo. His successor agrees. Candidates for president of Mexico now raise money and campaign actively in the United States. Gov. Gray Davis is exploring plans to have Cinquo de Mayo, the fifth of May, the anniversary of Juarez's 1862 victory over a French army at Puebla, made a California holiday. "In the near future," says Davis, "people will look at California and Mexico as one magnificent region." Perhaps we can call it Aztlan.

America is no longer the biracial society of 1960 that struggled to erase divisions and close gaps in a nation 90 percent white. Today we juggle the rancorous and rival claims of a multiracial, multiethnic, and multicultural country. Vice President Gore captured the new America in his famous howler, when he translated our national slogan, "E Pluribus Unum," backward, as "Out of one, many."

Today there are 28.4 million foreign-born in the United States. Half are from Latin America and the Caribbean, a fourth from Asia. The rest are from Africa, the Middle East, and Europe. One in every five New Yorkers and Floridians is foreign-born, as is one of every four Californians. With 8.4 million foreign-born, and not one new power plant built in a decade, small wonder California faces power shortages and power outages. With endless immigration, America is going to need an endless expansion of its power sources—hydroelectric power, fossil fuels (oil, coal, gas), and nuclear power. The only alternative is blackouts, brownouts, and endless lines at the pump.

In the 1990s, immigrants and their children were responsible for 100 percent of the population growth of California, New York, New Jersey, Illinois, and Massachusetts, and over half the population growth of Florida, Texas, Michigan, and Maryland. As the United States allots most of its immigrant visas to relatives of new arrivals, it is difficult for Europeans to come, while entire villages from El Salvador are now here.

The results of the Third World bias in immigration can be seen in our social statistics. The median age of Euro-Americans is 36; for Hispanics, it is 26. The median age of all foreign-born, 33, is far below that of the older American ethnic groups, such as English, 40, and Scots-Irish, 43. These social statistics raise a question: Is the U.S. government, by deporting scarcely 1 percent of an estimated eleven million illegal aliens each year, failing in its constitutional duty to protect the rights of American citizens? Consider:

- A third of the legal immigrants who come to the United States have not finished high school. Some 22 percent do not even have a ninth-grade education, compared to less than 5 percent of our native born.
- Over 36 percent of all immigrants, and 57 percent of those from Central America, do not earn twenty thousand dollars a year. Of the immigrants who have come since 1980, 60 percent still do not earn twenty thousand dollars a year.
- Of immigrant households in the United States, 29 percent are below the poverty line, twice the 14 percent of native born.
- Immigrant use of food stamps, Supplemental Social Security, and school lunch programs runs from 50 percent to 100 percent higher than use by native born.
- Mr. Clinton's Department of Labor estimated that 50 percent of the real-wage losses sustained by low-income Americans is due to immigration.
- By 1991, foreign nationals accounted for 24 percent of all arrests in Los Angeles and 36 percent of all arrests in Miami.
- In 1980, federal and state prisons housed nine thousand criminal aliens. By 1995, this had soared to fifty-nine thousand criminal aliens, a figure that does not include aliens who became citizens or the criminals sent over by Castro in the Mariel boat lift.

- Between 1988 and 1994, the number of illegal aliens in California's prisons more than tripled from fifty-five hundred to eighteen thousand.

None of the above statistics, however, holds for emigrants from Europe. And some of the statistics, on low education, for example, do not apply to emigrants from Asia.

Nevertheless, mass emigration from poor Third World countries is "good for business," especially businesses that employ large numbers at low wages. In the spring of 2001, the Business Industry Political Action Committee, BIPAC, issued "marching orders for grass-roots mobilization." The *Wall Street Journal* said that the 400 blue-chip companies and 150 trade associations "will call for continued normalization of trade with China . . . and easing immigration restrictions to meet labor needs. . . ." But what is good for corporate America is not necessarily good for Middle America. When it comes to open borders, the corporate interest and the national interest do not coincide, they collide. Should America suffer a sustained recession, we will find out if the melting pot is still working.

But mass immigration raises more critical issues than jobs or wages, for immigration is ultimately about America herself.

What Is a Nation?

Most of the people who leave their homelands to come to America, whether from Mexico or Mauritania, are good people, decent people. They seek the same better life our ancestors sought when they came. They come to work; they obey our laws; they cherish our freedoms; they relish the opportunities the greatest nation on earth has to offer; most love America; many wish to become part of the American family. One may encounter these newcomers everywhere. But the record number of foreign-born coming from cultures with little in common with Americans raises a different question: What is a nation?

Some define a nation as one people of common ancestry, language, literature, history, heritage, heroes, traditions, customs, mores, and faith who have lived together over time on the same land under the same rulers. This is the blood-and-soil idea of a nation. Among those who pressed this definition were Secretary of State John Quincy Adams, who laid down these conditions on immigrants: "They must cast off the European skin, never to resume it. They must look forward to their posterity rather than backward to their ancestors." Theodore Roosevelt, who thundered against "hyphenated-Americanism," seemed to share Adams's view. Woodrow Wilson, speaking to newly naturalized Americans in 1915 in Philadelphia, echoed T.R.: "A man who thinks of himself as belonging to a particular national group in America has yet to become an American." This idea, of Americans as a separate and unique people, was first given expression by John Jay in *Federalist 2:*

> Providence has been pleased to give this one connected country to one united people—a people descended from the same ancestors, speaking the same language, professing the same religion, attached to the same principles

> of government, very similar in their manners and customs, and who, by their joint counsels, arms, and efforts, fighting side by side throughout a long and bloody war, have nobly established their general liberty and independence.

But can anyone say today that we Americans are "one united people"?

We are not descended from the same ancestors. We no longer speak the same language. We do not profess the same religion. We are no longer simply Protestant, Catholic, and Jewish, as sociologist Will Herberg described us in his *Essay in American Religious Sociology* in 1955. We are now Protestant, Catholic, Jewish, Mormon, Muslim, Hindu, Buddhist, Taoist, Shintoist, Santeria, New Age, voodoo, agnostic, atheist, humanist, Rastafarian, and Wiccan. Even the mention of Jesus' name at the Inauguration by the preachers Mr. Bush selected to give the invocations evoked fury and cries of "insensitive," "divisive," and " exclusionary." A *New Republic* editorial lashed out at these "crushing Christological thuds" from the Inaugural stand. We no longer agree on whether God exists, when life begins, and what is moral and immoral. We are not "similar in our manners and customs." We never fought "side by side throughout a long and bloody war." The Greatest Generation did, but it is passing away. If the rest of us recall a "long and bloody war," it was Vietnam, and, no, we were not side by side.

We remain "attached to the same principles of government." But common principles of government are not enough to hold us together. The South was "attached to the same principles of government" as the North. But that did not stop Southerners from fighting four years of bloody war to be free of their Northern brethren.

In his Inaugural, President Bush rejected Jay's vision: "America has never been united by blood or birth or soil. We are bound by ideals that move us beyond our background, lift us above our interests, and teach us what it means to be a citizen." In his *The Disuniting of America,* Arthur Schlesinger subscribes to the Bush idea of a nation, united by shared belief in an American Creed to be found in our history and greatest documents: the Declaration of Independence, the Constitution, and the Gettysburg Address. Writes Schlesinger:

> The American Creed envisages a nation composed of individuals making their own choices and accountable to themselves, not a nation based on inviolable ethnic communities. For our values are not matters or whim and happenstance. History has given them to us. They are anchored in our national experience, in our great national documents, in our national heroes, in our folkways, our traditions, and standards. [Our values] work for us; and, for that reason, we live and die by them.

Bush Americans no longer agree on values, history, or heroes. What one-halfof America sees as a glorious past the other views as shameful and wicked. Columbus, Washington, Jefferson, Jackson, Lincoln, and Lee—all of them heroes of the old America—are all under attack. Those most American of words, equality and freedom, today hold different meanings for different Americans. As for our "great national documents," the Supreme Court decisions that interpret our Constitution have not united us; for forty years they have divided us, bitterly, over prayer in school, integration, busing, flag burning, abortion, pornography, and the Ten Commandments.

Nor is a belief in democracy sufficient to hold us together. Half of the nation did not even bother to vote in the presidential election of 2000; three out of five do not vote in off-year elections. Millions cannot name their congressman, senators, or the Supreme Court justices. They do not care.

Whether one holds to the blood-and-soil idea of a nation, or to the creedal idea, or both, neither nation is what it was in the 1940s, 1950s, or 1960s. We live in the same country, we are governed by the same leaders, but can we truly say we are still one nation and one people?

It is hard to say yes, harder to believe that over a million immigrants every year, from every country on earth, a third of them breaking in, will reforge the bonds of our disuniting nation. John Stuart Mill warned that "free institutions are next to impossible in a country made up of different nationalities. Among a people without fellow-feeling, especially if they read and speak different languages, the united public opinion necessary to the working of representative government cannot exist."

We are about to find out if Mill was right.

POSTSCRIPT

Should America Remain a Nation of Immigrants?

Buchanan argues that the new immigration since 1968 from Mexico, other parts of Latin America, and Asia is destroying the core culture of the United States. He maintains that the new immigrants are responsible for America's rising crime rate; the increase in the number of households that are below the poverty level; and the increase in the use of food stamps, Supplemental Social Security, and school lunch programs. Furthermore, maintains Buchanan, low-income Americans sustain real wage losses of 50 percent because of competition from legal and illegal immigration.

Buchanan also asserts that America is losing the cultural war. He holds that the Republican Party's white-based majority under Presidents Richard Nixon and Ronald Reagan has been undermined by an immigrant-based Democratic Party. He notes that the two biggest states—California and Texas—are beset with ethnic enclaves who do not speak English and whose political and cultural values are outside the American mainstream.

Although Buchanan expresses feelings that are felt by many Americans today, his analysis lacks historical perspective. Ever since Columbus encountered the first Native Americans, tensions between immigrants and native-born people have existed. During the four peak periods of immigration to the United States, the host group has felt overwhelmed by the newest groups entering the country. Buchanan quotes Benjamin Franklin's concern about the German immigrants' turning Pennsylvania into a "Colony of Aliens, who will shortly be so numerous as to Germanize us instead of our Anglifying them." But Buchanan does not carry his observation to its logical conclusion. German immigration into the United States did not halt during the Seven Years War, as Buchanan contends. It continued during the nineteenth and early twentieth centuries, and Germans today constitute the largest white ethnic group in the country.

Buchanan also ignores the hostility accorded his own Irish-Catholic relatives by white, Protestant Americans in the 1850s, who considered the Irish crime-ridden, lazy, drunken ignoramuses living in ethnic enclaves who were unassimilable because of their "Papist" religious ceremonies. Irish males, it was said, often did not work but lived off the wages of their wives, who worked as maids. When menial jobs were performed mostly by Irish men, they were accused of lowering the wages of other working-class Americans. One may question whether the newest immigrants are different from Buchanan's own ancestors.

Jacoby gives a spirited defense of the newest immigrants. She dismisses the argument for increased immigration restriction after the September 11 attacks on the World Trade Center and the Pentagon by distinguishing between a terrorist and an immigrant. She contends that the estimates about a future population explosion in the country might be exaggerated, especially if economic conditions improve in Third World countries when the global economy becomes more balanced.

Jacoby stresses the positive impact of the new immigrants. Many of them—particularly those from India and other Asian countries—have contributed their skills to the computer industry in the Silicon Valley and other high-tech industrial parks across America. Jacoby also argues that even if poorer immigrants overuse America's health and welfare social services, many of them contribute portions of their pay to the Social Security trust fund, including illegal immigrants who might never receive a government retirement check. Jacoby does allow that although today's immigrants may be no poorer than those who came in the third wave at the turn of the twentieth century, today's unskilled immigrants are relatively further behind than the southern and eastern Europeans who came around 1900. This is the view of sociologist George J. Borjas in *Heaven's Door: Immigration and the American Economy* (Princeton University Press, 1999).

Most experts agree that changes need to be made in the U.S. immigration laws. Some groups, such as the Federation for American Immigration Reform (FAIR), would like to see a huge cut in the 730,000 legal immigrants, 100,000 refugees, and 200,000 illegal immigrants (Borjas's numbers) who came into America each year in the 1980s and 1990s. Borjas would add a point system to a numerical quota, which would take into account age, work experience, fluency in English, educational background, work experience, and the quality of one's job. Jacoby also favors an immigration policy that gives preference to immigrants with key job-related skills over those who use the loopholes in the law to reunite the members of their families. Unlike Buchanan, Jacoby maintains that the newest immigrants will assimilate as earlier groups did but only when their legal status as citizens is fully established.

There is an enormous bibliography on the newest immigrants. A good starting point, which clearly explains the immigration laws and their impact on the development of American society, is Kenneth K. Lee, *Huddled Masses, Muddled Laws: Why Contemporary Immigration Policy Fails to Reflect Public Opinion* (Praeger, 1998). Another book that concisely summarizes both sides of the debate and contains a useful glossary of terms is Gerald Leinwand, *American Immigration: Should the Open Door Be Closed?* (Franklin Watts, 1995).

Because historians take a long-range view of immigration, they tend to weigh in on the pro side of the debate. See L. Edward Purcell, *Immigration: Social Issues in American History Series* (Oryx Press, 1995); Reed Ueda's *Postwar America: A Social History* (Bedford Books, 1995); and David M. Reimers, *Still the Golden Door: The Third World War Comes to America,* 2d ed. (Columbia University Press, 1997) and *Unwelcome Strangers: American Identity and the Turn Against Immigration* (Columbia University Press, 1998).

ISSUE 17

Environmentalism: Is the Earth Out of Balance?

YES: Otis L. Graham, Jr., from "Epilogue: A Look Ahead," in Otis L. Graham, Jr., ed., *Environmental Politics and Policy, 1960s–1990s* (Pennsylvania State University Press, 2000)

NO: Bjorn Lomborg, from "Yes, It Looks Bad, But . . . ," "Running on Empty," and "Why Kyoto Will Not Stop This," *The Guardian* (August 15, 16, & 17, 2001)

ISSUE SUMMARY

YES: Otis L. Graham, Jr., a professor emeritus of history, maintains that the status of the biophysical basis of our economies, such as "atmospheric pollution affecting global climate, habitat destruction, [and] species extinction," is negative and in some cases irreversible in the long run.

NO: Associate professor of statistics Bjorn Lomborg argues that the doomsday scenario for earth has been exaggerated and that, according to almost every measurable indicator, humankind's lot has improved.

Historically, Americans have not been sympathetic to preserving the environment. For example, the first European settlers in the sixteenth and seventeenth centuries were awed by the abundance of land in the New World. They abandoned their Old World custom of practicing careful agricultural husbandry on their limited lands and instead solved their agricultural problems in North America by constantly moving to virgin land. The pioneers believed that the environment must be conquered, not protected or preserved.

The first real surge in the environmental movement occurred during the Progressive Era of the early twentieth century. Reformers were upset about the changes seen in America since the Civil War, such as an exploding population, massive immigration, political corruption, and the end of the frontier (as proclaimed by the 1890 census). The remedy for these problems, said the reformers, lay in strong governmental actions at the local, state, and national levels.

Environmentalists agreed that the government had to take the lead and stop the plundering of the remaining frontier before it was too late. But the movement split into two groups—conservationists and preservationists—a division that has continued in the movement to this day.

The Nixon administration pushed through the most important piece of environment regulation ever passed by the government: the National Environmental Policy Act of 1969, which established the Council for Environmental Quality (CEQ) for the purpose of coordinating all federal pollution control programs. This legislation empowered the Environmental Protection Agency (EPA) to set standards and implement CEQ policies on a case-by-case basis. The EPA thus became the centerpiece of the emerging federal environmental regulatory system.

In the late 1970s and early 1980s a new urban-oriented environmentalism emerged. The two major concerns surrounded the safety of nuclear power and the sites where toxic wastes were dumped. For years proponents of atomic power proclaimed that the technological benefits of nuclear power far outweighed the risks. Now the public began to have doubts.

More dangerous and more mysterious were the dangers from hazardous waste and pollutants stored improperly and often illegally across the country. The first widely known battle between local industry and the public occurred at Love Canal, near Niagara Falls, New York. In the 1950s a working-class neighborhood was constructed around a canal that was being used as a dump site for waste by Hooker Chemical, a local company. Although the local government denied it, cancers and birth defects in the community reached epic proportions. On August 2, 1978, the New York State health commissioner declared Love Canal a great and imminent peril to the health of the general public. President Jimmy Carter declared the Hooker Chemical dump site a national emergency, and by the following spring, 237 families had been relocated. Controversies such as Love Canal made the public aware that toxic waste dumps and the accompanying fallout were nationwide problems. Congress passed several laws in the 1980s to deal with this issue. The Superfund Act of 1980 created a $1.6 billion fund to clean up toxic wastes, and the Nuclear Waste Policy Act of 1982 directed a study of nine potential sites where the radioactive materials left over from the creation of nuclear energy could be permanently stored.

In spite of the lax enforcement of the laws under the Reagan administration, the public became alarmed again in 1988 when Representative Mike Synar (D-Oklahoma) chaired a congressional subcommittee on the environment that uncovered contamination of 4,611 sites at 761military bases, a number of which threatened the health of the nearby communities. Many of these sites still need to be cleaned up.

Is the environmental crisis real? In the following selections, Otis L. Graham, Jr., contends that the problems of global warning, habitat destruction, and species extinction are probably irreversible and unsolvable. Bjorn Lomborg argues that the doomsday scenario for the earth has been exaggerated and that, by almost every measurable indicator, mankind's lot has improved.

YES **Otis L. Graham, Jr.**

A Look Ahead

Environmental policy is about fixing a problem—a large, complex, foundational problem. From the 1960s to the end of the century, the United States engaged this problem on a wider scale and with more energy than ever before, as a part of a global, multinational effort in this direction. Seen from our experience and vantage, what are the prospects ahead of humanity and nature in the ongoing negotiation of our relationship?

Serious thought on this question usually begins not with historical inquiry but with reports from technology and the natural and social sciences, disciplines that habitually project events and trends ahead. But projecting likely futures also turns out to involve history, since formulating education guesses about what lies ahead requires us to estimate what momentum and direction we have already established strongly enough to shape that future. The two broad schools of opinion on tomorrow have been called the Cornucopian and the Malthusian, labels that exaggerate the bias of the extreme ends of debate. Let us use the terms eco-optimists, people who wind up cheerful after they concede that there are a few problems, and eco-pessimists, people who see bad outcomes but still believe that something can be done or they would not be speaking.

The conviction that the American environment offered an inexhaustible resource was of course the primal assumption shaping our national history. Pessimism about using things up came later, the chief voices including George Perkins Marsh (*Man And Nature,* 1864), Frederick Jackson Turner's thoughts on the implications of the discovery in the Census of 1890 that the era of the frontier was over, the warnings of Teddy Roosevelt, Gifford Pinchot, and others in the first and second Conservation movements (who were usually optimists at bottom). The alarm-sounding books by Vogt and Osborn in 1948 and Walter Prescott Webb's *The Great Frontier* (1952) touched on the United States only as part of a global crisis of population pressing upon depleting resources, and were influential among a limited readership. The Sixties cranked up virtually every concern to a higher volume and larger audiences, and the reception of Stanford University biologist Paul Ehrlich's *The Population Bomb* (1968)—selling over a million copies in paperback, Ehrlich being interviewed in *Playboy* magazine and receiving wide media attention—gave the message of ecocrisis a mass audience. "The battle to feed all of humanity is over," Ehrlich wrote, predicting the deaths of hundreds of millions of people in famines across the 1970s and mounting pressure upon resources and environment even in affluent societies like the United States. The Club of Rome's best-selling *The Limits to Growth* (1972), written by a team of MIT scholars led by Dennis L. Meadows, offered a melancholy projection of population pressure, resource depletion, and pollution that described a grim global slide over the next three decades into "a dismal and depleted existence," a miserable condition they called "overshoot and collapse." Eight years later the U.S. government came out in broad agreement. *Global 2000,* an interagency report commissioned by President Jimmy Carter and published in 1980, reported that "if present trends continue, the world in 2000 will be more crowded, more polluted, less stable ecologically, and more vulnerable to disruption than the world we live in now."

A counterattack against this strong current of eco-pessimism was predictable. Offer an idea that receives wide public attention in America and people will piggy-back into the limelight by providing an opposite view. Further, optimism runs deep in American history, and tends to assert itself when gloom is expressed. More important, one implication of the forecasts of ecocrisis was criticism of and demands for curbs on growth, a sentiment fundamentally and deeply alarming to the business community and other elements of American society. Another reason for stiff resistance to the very idea of eco-pessimism is its implication that there must be a larger role for government in regulating resource uses, waste disposal, and even procreation. "Mutual coercion mutually agreed upon" in the area of human fertility was the recommendation, and "freedom in a commons brings ruin to all" a memorable line, in University of California biologist Garrett Hardin's widely discussed and reprinted 1968 article, "The Tragedy of the Commons." "Free market" loyalists sensed dangerous implications—government intrusion into land and resource use, perhaps even the bedroom. A final factor attracting criticism was that the pessimists sometimes predicted with too much specificity and enthusiasm, and some of the bad things forecast did not happen, or did not happen on anything like the scale predicted or as soon as foreseen. "The Prophet Paul," as one writer dubbed Ehrlich, had indeed said in a magazine interview that "our large polluting population is responsible for air pollution that could very easily lead to massive starvation in the U.S. within the next two decades," and "I believe we're facing the brink because of population pressures." And Paul and William Paddock did predict mass starvation in China "within five or ten years" in their *Famine*—1975!

To all of this the eco-optimists responded with a spirited critique and rebuttal. One of the earliest to emerge was to become a polarizing figure who went beyond skeptical questioning of the eco-pessimists to assert an almost religious belief that more growth and more people were the formula not for disaster but for a rosy future. This was Julian Simon, a professor of marketing at the University of Illinois until, "in the midst of a depression of unusual duration," he found healing in a conversion to the cause of "having more children and taking in more immigrants." He then moved to Washington, D.C., and began a productive and influential career as the leading eco-optimist. In a cascade of essays, public appearances, and books (principally

The Ultimate Resource [1981]), Simon reversed every argument of the environmentalists. What was needed was more population, which would bring us more Mozarts and Einsteins, building the knowledge and genius sufficient to solve environmental problems. "There is no meaningful physical limit—even the commonly mentioned weight of the Earth—to our capacity to keep growing forever," was one of Simon's most reprinted remarks, as well as his paraphrase of the *Global 2000* conclusion: "If present trends continue, the world in 2000 will be less crowded, less polluted, more stable ecologically and less vulnerable to resource-supply disruption than the world we live in now."

The eco-optimist point of view had many more voices, often located in think tanks such as the Heritage Foundation or the Cato Institute whose support came from pro-capitalist foundations, corporations, and individuals. But the vulnerability of some of the language and predictions of the pessimists drew many and independent rebuttals. Journalist Gregg Easterbrook's *A Moment on the Earth* (1995) brought together an immense literature on environmental problems which he interpreted to mean that we were in fact winning the battle to preserve the environment. The air was cleaner, pollution is shrinking and will soon end, global warming is "almost certain to be avoided," and doomsday thinking "is nonsensical." Environmentalists should stop "proclaiming emergencies that do not exist." . . .

To this writer, at the end of the 1990s, the worriers have the most convincing scenarios, globally and even in the United States, as I am obliged to explain.

There would be no debate if there were not facts and arguments on both sides. Optimists point out that global population-growth projections are slightly improving, the UN Population Division now seeing the likelihood (if current trends persist, always the fundamental qualifier) of a world population reaching (this is the middle of five projections) 10.8 billion by 2050, stabilizing at 11 billion persons around 2100. Earlier estimates in the middle range for 2050 had been closer to 12 billion, with responsible demographers fearing 16 billion (or more). Population growth rates have been declining more broadly than earlier projected. This is good news, depending on how you look at it. Is ending up with the smallest bad scenario therefore good news?

In Europe, the population worry has actually veered around to a very different, "birth dearth" anxiety. Most European nations began reporting below-replacement fertility rates in the 1970s, giving rise to fears that a shrinkage of nations lay ahead. Rising immigration rates into the prosperous nations of the European Union have ensured that nations will not shrink but will give rise to a more volatile concern over national identity. Will Italy, for example, with the lowest birth rates in the world and ever recorded, still be Italy in one hundred years, when it is populated by Muslim immigrants from Albania, Algeria, and elsewhere?

Thus the world faces two demographic problems: unprecedented population growth in the poorer and underdeveloped regions where most humans live, and stabilized and even potentially shrinking nationalities (not populations, which are replenished by immigration) in Europe, Australia, and the fastest growing industrialized nation since it permitted mass immigration with a 1965 law, the United States. To simplify, the global population is going to double (not triple, as we feared two decades ago), and nations whose fertility choices lead to shrinking populations will be put back on the growth path by immigration, welcome and legal or neither. (Japan will not permit immigration, and, as probably the only nation in the world that retains control over its demographic destiny, will have to decide very shortly how much to shrink.) Out of this mixed picture, some people make doubling rather than tripling into good news, the lesser of two disasters.

The enormity of the demographic upheaval whose final century we now enter should not be trivialized by calculations that trim a couple of billion off at the end. As Bill McKibben pointed out in 1998, "The *increase* in human population in the 1990s has exceeded the *total* population in 1960. The population has grown more since 1950 than it did during the previous four million years."

While this awesome event is at the core of our difficulties, we must know much more than whether "the population bomb" will in the end be judged as earthquake at Richter 6.5 or 7.0. The first question is food supplies, then the constellation of measures of human well-being that extend from mere survival. Here I will argue that much of the apparent good news is being misinterpreted.

As the Simon–Ehrlich bets show, we move through an era in which those who measure progress in the conventional ways—looking at measures of human well-being such as food production per capita, the prices (and thus availability) of basic commodities, life expectancy, including infant mortality, automobile or home or telephone ownership, and, in most societies in the second half of the century with Africa as a major exception, per capita income—can report impressive gains, and win Simonite bets. Even measurements of "natural resources" such as timber or fossil fuels, or environmental "quality" as defined in the environmental protection statutes since the 1960s, contain some ground for optimism, a sense of winning momentum. As eco-optimist writer Gregg Easterbrook said in 1995, there has been in the United States an "astonishing, and continuing, record of success" in improving water and air quality that humans use, more recycling of wastes, expanding acreage of forests—all of this at less cost than business and anti-environmental lobbies predicted. He might have mentioned gasoline dropping briefly in 1999 to $1 per gallon in the United States decisive evidence of a "natural resource shortage" that did not, to date, follow the scenario of the Malthusians.

But shift the focus from these conventional accounting categories in measuring human welfare to measures of ecosystem health—from the economists' evidence that humans are consuming more and living better (on the whole) to the ecologists' evidence that the ecosystem foundations are eroding—and the future takes on a worrier's look. Complacency, wrote an international team of scientists in *Science* in 1998, persists because "conventional indicators of the standard of living pertain to commodity production, not to the natural resource base on which all production depends." We Americans (and Canadians, Europeans, Asians, Australians, New Zealanders, most Latin Americans) are still "making progress," enlarging our consumption and numbers—while drawing down our basic capital, the ecological foundations of the earth's limited capacity to sustain humans. Economists are accustomed to report on our well-being measured in Gross Domestic Product (GDP), but "Ecolate" (Garrett Hardin's term, meant to go along with Literate and Numerate) natural scientists are desperately trying to get the public's attention for another category of reporting: the status of the biophysical basis of our economies. Ehrlich and his colleagues offered in the second bet to measure some of these—atmospheric pollution affecting global climate, habitat destruction, species extinction—knowing the trends to be negative.

Wherever one samples the trends, they signal the depletion of ecological capital, some of it surely irreversible. Arable soil acreage shrinks by erosion, salinization, and urban development. Habitat mutilation or disturbance, and invasive species, accelerate species extinction, shrinking the range and potential benefits of biodiversity. Human pollution and harvesting sterilize the oceans. And that most temporary piece of good fortune, humanity's wonderful energy bonanza of fossil fuels, when burned, sends skyward a global blanket warming the earth and stressing every ecosystem upon it.

A powerful new conception of this capital draw-down has emerged in the phrase "ecosystem services." Described in Paul and Anne Ehrlich, *Extinction* (1981), Gretchen Daily et al., *Nature's Services* (1997), and in a lead article in *Nature* in 1997 by Robert Costanza and associates, ecosystem services are the free goods drawn upon by the human economy and taken for granted, but now rapidly contracting: pollinating crops and natural vegetation, controlling potential agricultural pests, filtering and decomposing wastes, forming soil and maintaining fertility, maintaining the gaseous composition of the atmosphere. In the *Nature* article, Costanza and his associates, in an effort to gain the attention of policymakers and public, estimated the value of ecosystem services at $33 trillion a year, or twice the world's annual GDP.

Teddy Roosevelt thought we were running out of vital resources—forests, petroleum, wildlife, places of natural beauty. He was not wrong, but we now see more deeply into the problem. Ecosystems and their services are wounded and shrink, both because of overharvesting and conversion to agricultural or urban uses, and because "what we are running out of is what the scientists call 'sinks,'" in the words of Bill McKibben, places to dump our garbage at no (apparent) cost.

As the century comes to a close, Americans cruise into more and more affluence on a remarkable economic roll, not the best climate in which to absorb the complex news of the melancholy trends in our ecological bank accounts. That side of our situation is difficult to see. Economists, journalists, and law-trained policymakers are looking in another direction, measuring conventional things with prices on them. And the vast majority of us, woefully uneducated by our schools, universities, churches, and media, have only a dim understanding of the erosion of the often distant ecological foundations of our livelihood. We have no idea of where or how our "ecological footprint" is felt. Ecological footprint—a helpful concept in the hands of ecologists who hope to measure and visualize the far-flung impacts of our urbanized communities, "the 'load' imposed by given population on nature," in the words of Mathis Wackernagel and William Rees, authors of *Our Ecological Footprint* (1996). Seen in this way, Chicago may have (let us say) cleaned up its air and wastes and restored fish to the Chicago River. All appears well locally. But to discover that city's ecological footprint requires calculation of the ecological goods and services appropriated from far away—from distant agricultural land, from oceanic and forest carbon sinks absorbing atmospheric carbon dioxide, from waterways asked to dilute and break down wastes, from fisheries and forests harvested. The calculations have not been made not only because they are immensely complicated but also because no one has fixed a price for these ecosystem disturbances or knows who or how to charge. But whatever the calculation, we can be certain that Chicagoans, and all Americans in this perspective, are, due to their affluence, "larger" (and thus their footprint larger) than people from Brazil, some of whom are clear-cutting the Amazonian rain forests and thus have a much larger footprint than the residents of the Bangladesh flood plain. Where and how the footprint disturbs nature is out of sight and off the account books of our households. But to better foresee the human future requires an accounting that reaches across jurisdictional borders and is not confined to things already assigned pricetags.

Three decades ago, alarmed writers about the future such as Paul Ehrlich, Barry Commoner, and the Club of Rome *Limits to Growth* authors occasionally used words like "bomb," "collapse," "descent into barbarism," "the death of the planet." Scientists all, they wished to gain attention, and did. But this occasional language, along with an underestimation of the role of human ingenuity, gave them the Parson Malthus problem: the disasters did not arrive on time. A generation later, lookers-ahead who come to pessimistic conclusions report with more sophistication, allow more complexity and perplexity to come through, and do not specify the date of the next famine. In *The Population Explosion* (1990), the Ehrlichs agree with T. S. Eliot that while the world might end with a "bang," it is more likely to end in a "whimper," the slow breakdown of both natural and agricultural ecosystems, with disease outbreaks, water shortages, and rising social disorder. This scenario, like most, looks to the experiences humans may expect, but there is a holocaust of sorts ahead for plant and animal life. Writer David Quammen surveyed paleontologists and found them convinced that "we are entering another mass extinction, a vale of biological impoverishment" in which "somewhere between one third and two thirds of all species" will become extinct. The resulting world will still have wildlife, of course, but only those who survived the ecological mauling by 10 billion humans. "Wildlife will consist of the pigeons and the coyotes," Quammen writes, "the black rats and the brown rats," rodents, cockroaches, house sparrows and geckos "and the barn cats and the skinny brown feral dogs . . . a Planet of Weeds."

This upcoming cascade of ecological breakdowns was increasingly seen as arriving regionally rather than uniformly around the globe. Many observers foresaw escalating problems ahead for the fast-growing giant, China, adding 13 million people a year, her thin soils eroding and cities choked with traffic, garbage, and heavily polluted air from coal combustion. In *Who Will Feed China?* (1995), Lester Brown warned that a combination of droughts and depletion of groundwater acquifers meant an imminent decline in the supply of water for Chinese farmers. Taken with conversion of farmland for urban uses, floods and erosion, agricultural production would fail to keep pace with a growing population, throwing that formerly food-sufficient nation of 1.2 billion onto world grain markets. The ripple effects would include rising grain prices and shortages in poor nations, a formula for famine and political instability.

It is the latter that increasingly draws attention. The world's poor will suffer as their numbers press ever harder upon degraded resources, but they cannot be expected always and everywhere to suffer patiently. Human conflicts between the globes' rich and poor seem likely to be a core dynamic of the difficulties ahead. Journalist Robert Kaplan caught President Clinton's attention with a 1996 article reporting on his travels along an arc of countries from Africa through the Middle East, where he found repeated examples of ecological collapse intensifying tribal and civil wars with several "failed states" losing control over national borders. In a sophisticated look out toward *The World in 2020* (1994), Hamish MacRae sees water shortages, a tightening of oil supplies, relentless habitat destruction, and unavoidable international conflict as China replaces the United States as the world's chief air polluter and thus driver of global warming. Even that Texas optimist Walt Rostow, in his recent look ahead at the twenty-first century, sees the period from the 1990s to 2025 as "a period of maximum strain on resources and the environment when global population is still expanding" and there might be, starting first in certain regions, "a global crisis of Malthusain consequences."

Rostow shares with most other forecasters a relaxed optimism about oil, not having checked lately with geologists. "With so much to worry about," Rostow writes, "why worry about energy," especially since massive new oil reserves are under development in the Caspian Sea region of central Asia?

But the time of troubles that he sees ahead in at least the first half of the twenty-first century will apparently include the next and final oil crunch. Some time in the first decade of that century, geologists are now arguing, world oil production will begin to decline and prices will rise. Whether or not political instability in the Middle East brings artificial shortages, oil production will soon begin falling behind demand, which is growing at 2 percent a year to double in 34 years. "The Petroleum Interval" for human-kind began about 140 years ago when Colonel Drake drilled oil in Pennsylvania, points out Walter Youngquist in *Geodestinies,* and will be more than 300 years from that event, "a brief bright blip on the screen of human history." No, says *Science* magazine, there is quickly gathering a consensus among geologists that "mankind will consume it all in a 2-century binge of profligate energy use." The time available to come up with alternatives is much shorter than anticipated.

Thus there seemed a shift across a broad front in the direction of eco-pessimist anticipation, laced here and there (as they had not been in the 1960s–1970s) with a qualified optimism about the possibility of technological leaps over or around some of the problems. Perhaps the decisive factor making for an overall sense of crisis was the evolving understanding of climate change. In the 1990s the scenario of global warming moved from a widely disputed hypothesis to an assumption about the planetary future, at least at the broad center of scientific and governmental opinion, augmented by some business converts, which included British Petroleum. Earth may surprise us, all admit, and not warm as predicted. But at century's end the added factor of almost certain warming and climatic instability seems like the draw of the game-killing black Queen in a game of Hearts. What will the "period of maximum strain" feel like, if greenhouse warming comes upon our overcrowded world as expected (all agree that no policy changes in any country can slow or reverse it until the second half of the . . . century)? Writer Bill McKibben imagined it "stormier" than before, both wetter and drier; spring coming earlier, summers hotter and longer; glacier meltings and retreat, rising oceans, altered ocean currents bringing abrupt climate change on shore; crop failures; millions of environmental refugees. "The next fifty years are a special time," he concluded in language suggesting difficulty in finding the right adjective but not wanting to use any of the common terms of alarm. Clearly it would not on the whole be a nice time, when wishing you to have a nice day will be enough. "The single most special thing about it may be that we are now apparently degrading the most basic functions of the planet."

From this perspective, Americans at the end of the twentieth century are enjoying an Indian Summer before the arrival of what Harvard biologist E. O. Wilson calls in understated terms "The Century of the Environment." Pleasant news and prospects surround us, by standard measures. Our own national economy as of this writing (1999) seems the only healthy, inflation-free, full-employment, steadily growing stock market booming large economy in a world of mixed performances, including the utter collapse of the system of our former rival. U.S. environmental policies and private-sector responses have produced welcome improvements in some measures of environmental and human health, and impressive institutional learning. As a people we are overweight and living longer than ever.

Yet a time of troubles looms ahead, in the view of most natural scientists and a growing number of other observers, one that will spare no country and respect no borders. Environmental problems and policy will push to the front of national and international agendas, and laterally inject themselves further into policy realms like national defense, trade, and public health. We cannot imagine how another symposium of this sort thirty years from now might assess U.S. environmental politics and policy. But since the anticipated problems a generation out into the doubling of human numbers are sure to be more formidable than the oil spills and pesticide warnings that launched in the Sixties a new era of environmental concern, our resources are also greater. It is well to briefly take stock of them.

Thirty years of serious pollution fighting has collected an impressive scientific, technological, and analytical base in American governments, universities, research centers, and corporations. Public support for environmental protection holds at high levels, even if the public is confused and misinformed about some things—relative risks of various hazards, and the basic demography of the United States and the planet. The "Brownlash" against environmentalism . . . did considerable damage but also forced some hard thinking about policy alternatives. At century's end there seems more long-term wind in the Green sails than in the Brown. Simonite denial of environmental decline is found only on the journalistic fringes, untenable any longer in the science-respecting mainstream. A steady boost in public environmental concern and education can be expected as we go to school amid future episodes of crisis—mammoth oil spills, local famine, epidemics, extreme weather disasters. The same can be said of the daily existence of Americans living amid intensifying pressures of urban congestion and suburban sprawl driven by the developed world's fastest population growth rate. These conditions will worsen and bring environmental matters to the foreground. The Green persuasion has already spread beyond its largely affluent, WASP social base and put down roots among ethnic and racial minorities in both urban and rural settings, and gathers new recruits from American religious communities, as well as from a surprisingly vigorous animal rights movement. The "business community," if that phrase has any meaning, has moved from solid hostility toward costly environmental regulations to an unevenly "Greened" or pro-active ally in lightening our ecological footprints. Environmental grassroots activism is invigorated and given intellectual and political leverage in the 1990s by the Internet, where millions of citizens exchange information and encouragement, quickly mobilize constituencies and focus political pressure.

Still, these and other assets applied to environmental repair will not be enough, for they have not yet been enough. One could read the history of environmental effort during the last four decades of the twentieth century as exposing a core defect in the campaign to realign humanity's relationship to the natural world. Environmentalism aims at what in the end? "Clean air" and "clean water" are useful phrases for media releases and legislation. But environmentalists have not communicated a compelling national goal, a vision of a future on the other side of the struggles to contain the succession of crises that growth produced. If thinking is not strategic, then it becomes tactical, and we clean up the nearby creek—but the growth path is never challenged. Americans, and apparently all others, still march to the equivalent of the Bible's injunction from Genesis 1:28: "Be fruitful, and multiply, and replenish the earth . . . and subdue it."

For a brief time in the penumbra of the Sixties, the audacious idea of realigning the purpose of American life away from perpetual national expansion seemed to make headway, as Beck and Kolankiewicz relate. "Limits to growth" was a book title and much-volleyed phrase in the early 1970s, and an intellectual high watermark in the search for a larger strategy for environmentalism came in 1972 when the Commission on Population and the American Future concluded that "no substantial benefits would result from continued growth of the nation's population" and that the nation should welcome and plan for stabilization. This was the sine qua non, a foundation on which could be built a more complete vision of what Franklin D. Roosevelt liked to call "a permanent country."

But the effort to re-aim America away from the growth path toward something else—the "stationary state" of John Stuart Mill?—foundered under intense and emotional opposition. Critics of the Rockefeller Commission's recommendation of population stabilization were quick to attach to that idea the scent of government intrusion into procreation, and to mobilize against one recommended tactic in particular, abortion rights. Then the media learned that demographers were reporting that replacement-level fertility had already been reached in the United States, a finding widely misunderstood to mean that U.S. population growth was over. Author Ben Wattenberg, among others, began to warn of a "birth dearth," and public discussion of population growth and goals slipped into a hopeless confusion through the Reaganite 1980s in which governmental policy actually aligned itself with the expansionist position of the Vatican.

By the 1990s those still concerned about population growth within the United States knew that the nation's growth rate was the fastest among industrialized nations, adding 3 million people a year (which meant a doubling time for the national population of 60–70 years), growth driven increasingly by the massive immigration released by the Immigration Act of 1965. As Beck and Kolankiewicz describe, a few environmental groups still called for U.S. (and world) population stabilization (one, Negative Population Growth, for a reduction) as one objective among many others. But most avoided the issue to sidestep the extra controversy thought to come with it. Members of the Sierra Club in 1998 forced a referendum to commit the Club to population stabilization and the reduction of immigration levels required to achieve that, and were turned back on a 60–40 percent vote by board and staff opposition, arguing not that the facts were wrong but that any position on immigration would attract criticism from ethnic spokespersons and create negative image problems.

Thus in the four decades under review, the first strategic goal on the way to "a permanent country"—population stabilization—was for a while endorsed from a presidential commission down through environmental intellectuals to the grassroots. Then it slid quietly to the margins until in 1998 the goal of capping population growth even if it required immigration limits could not carry a vote in the Sierra Club. As U.S. population surged ahead, the effort to put stabilization back on the American political agenda was blocked because it required immigration reduction, and that was not politically correct among the leadership of most environmental organizations. The entire period after the Sixties thus takes on the aspect of a vigorous and expanding environmental movement that somewhat puzzlingly lost its earlier grip on a key component of a larger strategic purpose, turning increasingly to tactical battles over this redwood grove or that city's air quality. The commitment to global as well as domestic family planning of the Kennedy-Johnson years, even Nixon's brief interest in population questions, gave way to a broad resignation about and a growing ignorance of global and especially national demographic trends. This was a part of the larger acquiescence by mainstream environmentalists in the Growth Path, after the Club of Rome had briefly stimulated a debate about establishing limits.

Of course, to redesign human values and institutions so that "growth"—in most material things, but not, as Mill pointed out, in matters of the mind and spirit—would meet limits involved a hellishly complicated set of trade-offs and calculations that only a priestly few wanted to discuss, let alone begin. American history marshals a long heritage of open frontiers and individualism against it. "Don't go to limited access!" shouted an agitated New England fisherman at a hearing on the shrinking stocks of bluefin tuna: "I don't want to be limited! That's not American!"

The easiest path of such a tectonic shift in social outlook on growth and limits, however, would be to end population growth. Indeed, in places it began to happen without a law, national policy, or much debate. Voluntarily, European, American, and some Asian women began to choose smaller families or no offspring at all, so that by the end of the 1990s some sixty countries (the United States was in the group until 1995, when immigration pushed fertility rates again above 2.1) had reached or moved below replacement-level fertility, prevented from absolute population shrinkage only by immigration from still-growing societies. At the 1994 UN Conference on Population in Cairo, 179 nations established (not unanimously; several Roman Catholic and Islamic nations objected) a plan to cap global population at 9.8 billion by 2050, an objective thought optimistic but not beyond reach. This would leave the earth swarming with 10 billion increasingly industrialized humans, and international discussion of how to reduce that burden would lead to bitter disputes over very hard choices.

One new feature of the landscape of international environmental politics, however, may force all nations to debate these choices. This is global warming. The ongoing international negotiations launched in Kyoto require all developed nations to accept binding limits on their CO2 and other greenhouse gas emissions, and eventually all nations will in one way or another come under such pressure. For the United States, our permanent ceiling, absent some scientific recalculation, has been determined to be 7 percent below 1990 emissions. A limit has finally been set, a firm number! We hope to reach it by technological innovation and conservationist discipline, and these will be indispensable. But another logic is at work. In making our reductions to get within specified levels and then in staying there, each additional person in a nation's population—by excess of births over deaths, or by immigration—reduces the allowable amount to be divided among that population. Population growth, and some forms of economic growth, now have a new and formidable opponent, the zero-sum game of Greenhouse emission containment. One could again at least imagine that time called for by the 1972 Population Commission, when the environmental restoration project could aim at goalposts that are not forever moved outward by mounting human numbers.

As to what the ultimate goal should be, the idea of calculating the earth's "carrying capacity" was years ago lifted out of population biology and used as a basis for discussing ideal human population limits and lifestyles. The concept stimulated some fresh thinking, but it had at least the disadvantage of appearing to assume that the goal was mere physical survival of the largest number of humans at any given time. Then in 1987 the World Commission on Environment and Development, or the Brundtland Commission Report, *Our Common Future,* finally brought together the global discussions of economic development and the environment that had been on separate and sometimes hostile tracks since Third World countries at Stockholm in 1972 had forced developed countries to concede that development came first and must not be impeded by environmental concerns. *Our Common Future* attempted to reconcile and join economic and environmental goals, defining "sustainable development" as "development that meets the needs of the present without compromising the ability of future generations to meet their own needs."

Those vague words devised in an attempt to bridge the perspectives of First and Third worlds boosted "sustainable development" into a position at the end of the century as "a mantra that launched a thousand conferences," in the words of one participant in such global discussions. But perhaps Sustainable Development will be more than a short-lived topic at conferences. It affirms that it is possible to reconcile environmental and economic objectives, and therefore it is necessary. It has at least the advantage over Carrying Capacity that it changes our accounting by emphasizing intergenerational equity, the passing on of not only a viable ecological base to the next generation. And the word "needs" implies a menu of human wants that goes beyond mere resources sufficient for survival to include a need for nature's spaces and vistas and textures, even for sustainable hunting and fishing. In any event, the "thousand conferences" appear to be having some results. "Indicators of Sustainability" have begun to be developed to keep track of the state of ecological and socioeconomic systems, changes in them, and cause-and-effect relationships. Canada published sustainability indicators in 1993, President Clinton's Council on Sustainable Development began a series of reports in 1994 that includes 32 indicators, the European Union has an indicators program, and the city of Seattle launched a sustainability program in 1990 that has proposed 40 indicators of the "long-term health" of the environment, population, and community. Much is unclear and ill-defined in all this activity. But the process of debating and then monitoring sustainability indicators involves, and educates, hundreds—in a city like Seattle, thousands—of participants. A "buzz word" to enhance reports and project proposals, Sustainable Development seems at this stage also a promising conception of how humans might clarify their goals, match them to the long-term viability of ecosystems, and begin to honor their obligations to posterity. Fifty or a hundred years ago, when a now forgotten word was viable, this would have been called Planning—for a different and better future than the stressful one dead ahead.

NO

Bjorn Lomborg

Commentary of Bjorn Lomborg

Yes, It Looks Bad, But . . .

We are all familiar with the litany of our ever-deteriorating environment. It is the doomsday message endlessly repeated by the media, as when *Time* magazine tells us that "everyone knows the planet is in bad shape," and when the *New Scientist* calls its environmental overview "self-destruct."

We are defiling our Earth, we are told. Our resources are running out. The population is ever-growing, leaving less and less to eat. Our air and water is more and more polluted. The planet's species are becoming extinct in vast numbers—we kill off more than 40,000 each year. Forests are disappearing, fish stocks are collapsing, the coral reefs are dying. The fertile topsoil is vanishing. We are paving over nature, destroying the wilderness, decimating the biosphere, and will end up killing ourselves in the process. The world's ecosystem is breaking down. We are fast approaching the absolute limit of viability.

We have heard the litany so often that yet another repetition is, well, almost reassuring. There is, however, one problem: it does not seem to be backed up by the available evidence. We are not running out of energy or natural resources. There is ever more food, and fewer people are starving. In 1900, we lived for an average of 30 years; today we live for 67. According to the UN, we have reduced poverty more in the last 50 years than we did in the preceding 500, and it has been reduced in practically every country.

Global warming is probably taking place, though future projections are overly pessimistic and the traditional cure of radical fossil-fuel cutbacks is far more damaging than the original affliction. Moreover, its total impact will not pose a devastating problem to our future. Nor will we lose 25–50% of all species in our lifetime—in fact, we are losing probably 0.7%. Acid rain does not kill the forests, and the air and water around us are becoming less and less polluted.

In fact, in terms of practically every measurable indicator, mankind's lot has improved. This does not, however, mean that everything is good enough. We can still do even better.

Take, for example, starvation and the population explosion. In 1968, one of the leading environmentalists, Dr Paul R Erlich, predicted in his best-selling book, *The Population Bomb,* that "the battle to feed humanity is over. In the course of the 1970s, the world will experience starvation of tragic proportions—hundreds of millions of people will starve to death."

This did not happen. Instead, according to the UN, agricultural production in the developing world has increased by 52% per person. The daily food intake in developing countries has increased from 1,932 calories in 1961—barely enough for survival—to 2,650 calories in 1998, and is expected to rise to 3,020 by 2030. Likewise, the proportion of people going hungry in these countries has dropped from 45% in 1949 to 18% today, and is expected to fall even further, to 12% in 2010 and 6% in 2030. Food, in other words, is becoming not scarcer but ever more abundant. This is reflected in its price. Since 1800, food prices have decreased by more than 90%, and in 2000, according to the World Bank, prices were lower than ever before.

Erlich's prediction echoed that made 170 years earlier by Thomas Malthus. Malthus claimed that, unchecked, human population would expand exponentially, while food production could increase only linearly by bringing new land into cultivation. He was wrong. Population growth has turned out to have an internal check: as people grow richer and healthier, they have smaller families. Indeed, the growth rate of the human population reached its peak of more than 2% a year in the early 1960s. The rate of increase has been declining ever since. It is now 1.26%, and is expected to fall to 0.46% by 2050. The UN estimates that most of the world's population growth will be over by 2100, with the population stabilising at just below 11bn.

Malthus also failed to take account of developments in agricultural technology. These have squeezed ever more food out of each hectare of land. It is this application of human ingenuity that has boosted food production. It has also, incidentally, reduced the need to take new land into cultivation, thus reducing the pressure on biodiversity.

The issues on food, population and air pollution covered here all contradict the litany. Yet opinion polls suggest that many people—in the rich world, at least—nurture the belief that environmental standards are declining. Four factors cause this disjunction between perception and reality.

The first is the lopsidedness built into scientific research. Scientific funding goes mainly to areas with many problems. That may be wise policy, but it will also create an impression that many more potential problems exist than is the case.

A second source of misperception is the self-interest of environmental groups. Though these groups are run overwhelmingly by selfless folk, they nevertheless share many of the characteristics of other lobby groups. They need to be noticed by the mass media. They also need to keep the money that sustains them rolling in. The temptation to exaggerate is surely there, and sometimes, indulged in.

In 1997, for example, the World Wide Fund for Nature issued a press release entitled Two-thirds of the World's Forests Lost Forever. The truth turned out to be nearer 20%. This would matter less if people applied the same degree of scepticism to environmental lobbying as they do to other lobby groups. But while a trade organisation arguing for, say, weaker pollution controls is instantly seen as self-interested, a green organisation opposing such a weakening is seen as altruistic—even if a dispassionate view of the controls might suggest they are doing more harm than good.

A third source of confusion is the attitude of the media. People are clearly more curious about bad news than good, and newspapers and broadcasters give the public what it wants. That can lead to significant distortions of perception: an example was America's encounter with El Niño in 1997 and 1998. This climatic phenomenon was accused of wrecking tourism, causing allergies, melting ski slopes and causing 22 deaths by dumping snow in Ohio. Disney even blamed El Niño for a fall in share prices.

A more balanced view comes from a recent article in the *Bulletin of the American Meteorological Society*. It estimated the damage caused by the 1997–98 Niño at $4bn, but the benefits amounted to some $19bn. These came from higher winter temperatures (which saved an estimated 850 lives, reduced heating costs and diminished spring floods caused by meltwaters), and from the well-documented connection between past Niños and fewer Atlantic hurricanes. In 1998, America experienced no big Atlantic hurricanes and thus avoided huge losses. These benefits were not reported as widely as the losses.

The fourth factor is poor individual perception. People worry that the endless rise in the amount of stuff everyone throws away will cause the world to run out of places to dispose of waste. Yet even if UK waste production increases at the same rate as that in the US (surely an overestimate, since the British population does not increase as fast), the total landfill area needed for 21st-century UK waste would be a meagre 100ft tall and eight miles square—an area equivalent to 28% of the Isle of Man.

Knowing the real state of the world is important because fear of largely imaginary environmental problems can divert political energy from dealing with real ones. The Harvard University centre for risk analysis has carried out the world's largest survey of the costs of life-saving public initiatives. Only initiatives whose primary stated political goal is to save human lives are included. Thus, the many environmental interventions which have little or no intention to save human lives, such as raising oxygen levels in rivers, improving wetlands and setting up natural reservations, are not considered here. We only compare those environmental interventions whose primary goal is to save human lives (as in toxin control) with life-saving interventions from other areas.

There are tremendous differences in the price to be paid for extra life-yearsby means of typical interventions: the health service is quite low-priced, at $19,000 per median price to save a life for one year, but the environment field stands out with a staggeringly high cost of $4.2m.

This method of accounting shows the overall effectiveness of the American public effort to save human life. Overall, information exists about the actual cost of 185 programmes that account for an annual expenditure of $21.4bn, which saves around 592,000 life-years. The Harvard study shows that, had the spending been used in the most cost-efficient way, 1,230,000 life-years could have been saved for the same money. Without further costs, it would have been possible to save around 600,000 more life-years or, at 10 years per life, 60,000 more human beings.

When we fear for our environment, we seem easily to fall victim to short-term,feel-good solutions that spend money on relatively trifling issues and thus hold back resources from far more important ones. When we realise that we can forget about imminent breakdown, we can see that the world is basically heading in the right direction and that we can help to steer this development process by focusing on and insisting on reasonable prioritisation. When the Harvard study shows that we forgo saving 60,000 lives every year, this shows us the cost we pay for worrying about the wrong problems—too much for the environment and too little in other areas.

This does not mean that rational environmental management and environmental investment is not often a good idea—only that we should compare the costs and benefits of such investments to similar investments in all the other important areas of human endeavour. And to ensure that sensible, political prioritisation, we need to abandon our ingrained belief in a mythical litany and start focusing on the facts—that the world is indeed getting better, though there is still much to do.

Running on Empty?

It was an axiom of the early environmentalists that we were running out of resources, and that fear underlies much of the movement's thinking on recycling, on the belief that small is beautiful, and on the need to restructure society away from its obsession with resource-consuming production. The idea has held powerful sway during 30 years of popular thinking—despite the fact that it has been clearly shown to be incorrect. Scare stories of resource depletion still turn up in the media every so often, but many environmentalists today have disavowed their earlier fears.

For many people, the 1973 oil crisis was the first evidence of finite resources. But we have long worried about running out of all kinds of materials: in antiquity, grave concerns were voiced about the future of copper and tin. The 1972 bestseller *Limits to Growth,* by the so-called Club of Rome, picked up on the old worry, claiming that gold would run out in 1981, silver and mercury in 1985, and zinc in 1990. It hasn't happened, and yet the idea held an almost magical grip on intellectuals in the 70s and 80s; and even today most discussions are predicated on the logic of Limits to Growth.

Only the economists begged to differ. One of them, Julian Simon, grew so frustrated that in 1980 he issued a challenge to the environmentalists. Since increased scarcity would mean higher prices, he bet $10,000 that any given raw material—to be picked by his opponents—would have dropped in price at least one year later. Stanford University environmentalists Paul Ehrlich, John Harte and John Holdren, stating that "the lure of easy money can be irresistible," took him on.

The environmentalists put their money on chromium, copper, nickel, tin and tungsten, and they picked a time frame of 10 years. By September 1990, each of the raw materials had dropped in price: chromium by 5%, tin by a whopping 74%. The doom-mongers had lost.

The truth is that they could not have won. Ehrlich and co would have lost, whatever they had bet on: petroleum, foodstuffs, sugar, coffee, cotton, wool, minerals, phosphates—they had all become cheaper.

Today, oil is the most important and most valuable commodity of international trade, and its value to our civilisation is underlined by the recurrent worry that we are running out of it. In 1914, the US Bureau of Mines estimated that supplies would last only 10 more years. In 1939, the US department of the interior predicted that oil would last only 13 more years. In 1951, it made the same projection: oil had only 13 more years. As Professor Frank Notestein of Princeton said in his later years: "We've been running out of oil ever since I was a boy."

Again, measuring scarcity means looking at the price. Even if we were to run out of oil, this would not mean that oil was completely unavailable, only that it would be very, very expensive. The oil-price hike from 1973 to the mid-80s was caused by an artificial scarcity, as Opec introduced production restraints. Likewise, the present high price is caused by adherence to Opec-agreed production cutbacks in the late 90s. It is expected that the price will again decline from $27 a barrel to the low $20s by 2020, bringing it well within the $17–$30 suggested by eight other recent international forecasts.

The long-term trend is unlikely to deviate much from these levels because high prices deter consumption and encourage the development of other sources of oil—and forms of energy supply. Likewise, low prices have the opposite effect.

In fact, the price of petrol at US pumps, excluding tax, stood at $1.10 in early 2001—comparable with the lowest prices before the oil crisis. This is because most of the price consists of the costs of refining and transportation, both of which have experienced huge efficiency increases.

At the same time, we have had an ever-rising prediction of the number of years' worth of oil remaining (years of consumption), despite increasing consumption. This is astounding. Common sense dictates that if we had 35 years' consumption left in 1955, we should have had 34 years' supply left the year after—if not less, because we consumed more oil in 1956 than in 1955. But the chart shows that in 1956 there were more years of reserves available.

The development for non-fuel resources has been similar. Cement, aluminium, iron, copper, gold, nitrogen and zinc account for more than 75% of global expenditure on raw materials. Despite a two- to 10-fold increase in consumption of these materials over the past 50 years, estimates of the number of years it will take to run out of them have grown. And the increasing abundance is reflected in price: the Economist's price index for raw materials has dropped by 80% since 1845.

So how can we have used ever more, and still have ever more left? The answers provide three central arguments against the limited resources approach:

1. "Known resources" is not a finite entity.

It is not that we know all the places with oil, and now just need to pump it up. We explore new areas and find new oil. But since searching costs money, new searches will not be initiated too far in advance of production. Consequently, new oil fields will be added as demand rises.

It is rather odd that anyone could have thought that known resources pretty much represented what was left, and therefore predicted dire problems when these had run out. It is like glancing into my refrigerator and saying: "Oh, you've only got food for three days. In four days you will die of starvation." But in two days I will go to the supermarket and buy more food. The point is that oil will come not only from the sources we already know, but also from many sources of which we do not yet know. The US Geological Survey has regularly made assessments of the total undiscovered resources of oil and gas, and stated in March 2000: "Since 1981, each of the last four of these assessments has shown a slight increase in the combined volume of identified reserves and undiscovered resources."

2. We become better at exploiting resources.

We use new technology to extract more oil from known oilfields, become better at finding new oilfields, and can start exploiting oilfields that were previously too expensive and/or difficult to exploit. An initial drilling typically exploits only 20% of the oil in the reservoir. Even with the most advanced techniques using water, steam or chemical flooding to squeeze out extra oil, more than half the resource commonly remains in the ground. It is estimated that the 10 largest oilfields in the US will still contain 63% of their original oil when production closes down. Consequently, there is still much to be reaped in this area. According to the latest US Geological Survey assessment, such technical improvements are expected to increase the amount of available oil by 50%.

At the same time, we have become better at exploiting each litre of oil. Since 1973, the average US car has improved its mpg by 60%. Home heating in Europe and the US has improved by 24–43%. Many appliances have become much more efficient—dishwashers and washing machines have cut energy use by about 50%.

Most nations now exploit energy with increasing efficiency: we use less and less energy to produce each dollar, euro or yen in our gross national products. Since 1880, the UK has almost tripled its production per energy use; worldwide, the amount of wealth produced per energy unit doubled between 1971 and 1992.

We also exploit other raw materials better: today, a car contains only half as much metal as a car produced in 1970. Super-thin optical fibres carry the same number of telephone calls as 625 copper wires did 20 years ago. Newspapers are printed on ever-thinner paper, because paper production has been improved. Bridges contain less steel, because steel has become stronger and because we can calculate specifications more accurately. Moreover, information technology has changed our consumption—we buy fewer things and more bits. Programs worth several hundred dollars will fit on a CD-rom made from two cents' worth of plastic.

3. We can substitute.

We do not demand oil as such, but rather the services it can provide. Mostly we want heating, energy or fuel, and this we can obtain from other sources, if they prove to be better or cheaper. This happened in England around 1600 when wood became increasingly expensive (because of local deforestation and bad infrastructure), prompting a gradual switch to coal. During the latter part of the 19th century, a similar move from coal to oil took place.

In the short run, it would be most obvious to substitute oil with other commonly known fossil fuels such as gas and coal. For both, estimates of the number of years' supply remaining have increased. Moreover, shale oil could cover a large part of our longer-term oil needs. At $40 a barrel (less than one-third above the current world price of crude), shale oil can supply oil for the next 250 years at current consumption; in total, there is enough shale oil to cover our total energy consumption for 5,000 years.

In the long run, renewable energy sources could cover a large part of our needs. Today, they make up a vanishingly small part of global energy production, but this will probably change.

The cost of solar energy and wind energy has dropped by 94–98% over the past 20 years, and have come much closer to being strictly profitable. Renewable energy resources are almost incomprehensibly large. The sun could potentially provide about 7,000 times our own energy consumption—in principle, covering just 2.6% of the Sahara desert with solar cells could supply our entire needs.

It is likely that we will eventually change our energy uses from fossil fuels towards other, cheaper energy sources—maybe renewables, maybe fusion, maybe some as yet unthought-of technology. As Sheikh Yamani, Saudi Arabia's former oil minister and a founding architect of Opec, has pointed out: "The stone age came to an end not for a lack of stones, and the oil age will end, but not for a lack of oil." We stopped using stone because bronze and iron were superiormaterials; likewise, we will stop using oil when other energy technologies provide superior benefits.

Why Kyoto Will Not Stop This

[Recently] in Bonn, most of the world's nations (minus the US) reached an agreement to cut carbon emissions. Generally, the deal was reported as almost saving the world. This is not only untrue in the scientific sense—the deal will do almost no good—but it also constitutes a very poor use of our resources to help the world.

Global warming is important: environmentally, politically and economically. There is no doubt that mankind is increasing atmospheric concentrations of carbon dioxide and that this will increase temperatures. I basically accept the models and predictions from the 2001 report of the UN's intergovernmental panel on climate change (IPCC). But in order to make the best choices for our future, we need to separate hyperbole from reality.

The IPCC bases its warning that the world might warm up by 5.8C over the coming century on an enormous variety of projections and models, a kind of computer-aided storytelling. The high-emission scenarios seem plainly unlikely. Reasonable analysis suggests that renewable energy sources—especially solar power—will be competitive with, or even outcompeting, fossil fuels by the middle of the century. This means carbon emissions are much more likely to follow the low-emission scenarios, causing a warming of about 2–2.5C.

Moreover, global warming will not decrease food production; nor is it likely to increase storminess, the frequency of hurricanes, the impact of malaria, or, indeed, cause more deaths. It is even unlikely that it will cause more flooding, because a much richer world will protect itself better.

However, global warming will have serious costs—estimated by Yale University's Professor William Nordhaus to be about $5 trillion. Such estimates are inevitably uncertain, but derive from models assessing the cost of global warming in a wide variety of areas, including agriculture, forestry, fisheries, energy, water supply, infrastructure, hurricane damage, drought damage, coastal protection, land loss caused by a rise in sea level, loss of wetlands, loss of species, loss of human life, pollution and migration. The consequences of global warming will hit developing countries hardest (primarily because they are poor and have less capacity to adapt), while the industrialised nations may benefit from a warming lower than 2–3C.

Despite our intuition that we need to do something drastic about global warming, we are in danger of implementing a cure that is more costly than the original affliction: economic analyses clearly show that it will be far more expensive to cut carbon dioxide emissions radically than to pay the costs of adaptation to the increased temperatures.

All models agree that the effect of the Kyoto protocol on the climate will be minuscule (even more so after the negotiations in Bonn). One model, by a leading author of the 1996 IPCC report, shows us how an expected temperature increase of 2.1C by 2100 will be diminished by the protocol to an increase of 1.9C. To put it more clearly, the temperature that we would have experienced in 2094 has been postponed to 2100. In essence, the Kyoto protocol does not negate global warming, but merely buys the world six years.

If Kyoto is implemented with anything but global emissions trading, it will not only be almost inconsequential for the climate, but it will also constitute a poor use of resources. The cost of such a pact, just for the US, would be higher than the cost of solving the single most pressing global problem—providing the entire world with clean drinking water and sanitation. It is estimated that the latter would avoid 2m deaths every year, and prevent half a billion people becoming seriously ill annually. If no trading mechanism is implemented for Kyoto, the costs could approach $1 trillion, almost five times the cost of worldwide water and sanitation coverage. In comparison, total global aid today is about $50bn a year.

If we were to go even further and curb global emissions to the 1990 level, the net cost would escalate to about $4 trillion extra—comparable almost to the cost of global warming itself. Likewise, a temperature increase limit would cost anything from $3 to $33 trillion extra.

Basically, global warming will be expensive ($5 trillion) and there is very little we can do about it. Even if we were to handle global warming as well as possible—cutting emissions a little, far into the future—we would save a minimal amount (about $300bn). However, if we enact Kyoto or even more ambitious programmes, the world will lose.

So is it not curious that the typical reporting on global warming tells us all the bad things it will cause, but few or none of the negative effects of overly zealous regulation? And why are discussions on global warming rarely a considered meeting of opposing views, but instead dogmatic and missionary in tone?

The problem is that the discussion is not just about finding the best economic path for humanity; it has much deeper political roots. This is clear in the 2001 IPCC report, which tells us that we should build cars and trains with lower top speeds, extols the qualities of sailing ships and bicycles, and proposes regionalised economies to alleviate transport demands.

Essentially, the IPCC is saying that we need to change individual lifestyles, move away from consumption and focus on sharing resources (eg through coownership). Because of climate change, we have to remodel our world.

The problem, as the IPCC puts it, is that "the conditions of public acceptance of such options are not often present at the requisite large scale." It goes as far as suggesting that the reason why we are unwilling to accept slower (or no) cars, and regionalised economies with bicycles but no international travel, is that we have been indoctrinated by the media, where we see TV characters as reference points for our own lives, shaping our values and identities. Consequently, the media could also help form the path towards a more sustainable world: "Raising awareness among media professionals of the need for greenhouse gas mitigation and the role of the media in shaping lifestyles and aspirations could be an effective way to encourage a wider cultural shift."

While using global warming as a springboard for wider policy goals is entirely legitimate, such goals should be made explicit: it is problematic to have an organisation which gathers important scientific data on global warming also promoting a political agenda.

Thus the lessons of the global warming debate are fivefold. First, we have to realise what we are arguing about—do we want to handle global warming in the most efficient way, or do we want to use global warming as a stepping stone to other political projects? I believe that in order to think clearly, we should try to separate the issues, not least because trying to solve all problems at one go may result in bad solutions for all areas. So I try to address just the issue of global warming.

Second, we should not spend vast amounts of money to cut a tiny slice off the global temperature increase when this constitutes a poor use of resources, and when we could probably use these funds far more effectively in the developing world. This connection between the use of resources on global warming and aiding the third world goes much deeper because the developing world will experience by far the most damage. When we spend resources to mitigate global warming, we are helping future inhabitants in the developing world; however, if we spend the same money directly in the third world, we are helping present inhabitants, and thus their descendants.

Since the inhabitants of the third world are likely to be much richer in the future, and since the return on investments in developing countries is much higher than those in global warming (about 16% to 2%), the question really boils down to: do we want to help better-off inhabitants in the third world 100 years from now a little, or do we want to help poorer inhabitants in the present third world much more?

To give an indication of the size of the problem, the Kyoto protocol is likely to cost at least $150bn a year, possibly much more. Unicef estimates that just $70–80bn a year could give all third world inhabitants access to the basics, such as health, education, water and sanitation. More important still is that if we could muster such a massive investment in the present-day developing countries, this would also put them in a much better future position, in terms of resources and infrastructure, from which to manage a future global warming.

Third, since cutting back carbon dioxide emissions quickly turns very costly and easily counterproductive, we should focus more of our efforts on finding ways of reducing the emission of greenhouse gases in the long term. Partly, this means that we need to invest much more in the research and development of solar power, fusion and other likely power sources. Given the current US investment in renewable energy research and development of just $200m, a considerable increase would seem a promising investment to achieve a possible conversion to renewable energy towards the latter part of the century.

This also means we should be more open to other techno-fixes (so-called geo-engineering). These range from fertilising the ocean (making more algae bind carbon when they die and fall to the ocean floor) and putting sulphur particles into the stratosphere (cooling the earth) to capturing carbon dioxide from fossil fuel use and returning it to storage in geological formations.

Fourth, we ought to look at the cost of global warming in relation to the total world economy. Analysis shows that even if we chose the less efficient programmes to cut carbon emissions, it would defer growth at most by a couple of years by the middle of the century. In this respect, global warming is still a limited and manageable problem.

Finally, this also underscores that global warming is not nearly the most important problem in the world. What matters is making the developing countries rich and allowing the citizens of developed countries even greater opportunities.

There are four main scenarios from the 2001 IPCC report. If we choose a world focused on economic development within a global setting, the total income over the coming century will be some $900 trillion. However, should we go down a path focusing on the environment, even if we stay within a global setting, humanity will lose some $107 trillion, 12% of the total potential income. And should we choose a more regional approach to solving the problems of the 21st century, we will stand to lose $140–274 trillion. Moreover, the loss would mainly be to the detriment of the developing countries. Again, this should be seen in the light of a total cost of global warming of about $5 trillion, and the fact that the optimal global warming policy can save us just $300bn.

If we want to leave a planet with the most possibilities for our descendants, both in the developing and developed world, it is imperative that we focus primarily on the economy and solving our problems in a global context, rather than focusing on the environment in a regionalised context. Basically, this puts the spotlight on securing economic growth, especially in the third world, while ensuring a global economy—both tasks which the world has set itself within the framework of the World Trade Organisation (WTO).

If we succeed, we could increase world income by $107–274 trillion, whereas even if we achieve the absolutely most efficient global warming policies, we can increase wealth by just $300bn. To put it squarely, what matters to our and our children's future is not primarily decided within the IPCC framework, but within the WTO framework.

POSTSCRIPT

Environmentalism: Is the Earth Out of Balance?

Graham provides a reasonably objective account of the battle between those who believe that our resources are being irrevocably depleted and those who deny that such a crisis exists and who argue that, with the exception of Africa, long-term environmental and economic trends should improve the quality of life in the future. Although he takes a more moderate stance than most writers about the environment, Graham lines up with the pessimists. According to Graham, 30 years of environmental laws have given scientists a great deal of information about the scientific problems and limits of governmental actions, and they have even provided society "with a qualified optimism about the possibility of technological leaps over or around some of the problems," such as improvements in air quality and limiting population growth. But Graham maintains that we may be "enjoying an Indian Summer" before we are overwhelmed by the more severe biophysical problems that are affecting the global climate.

Lomborg takes issue with the doomsday forecasts of the pessimists. He denies he has a conservative agenda even if his conclusions coincide with studies from right-wing think tanks such as the CATO Institute and the American Enterprise Institute (AEI). In fact, Lomborg calls himself a leftist who once belonged to Greenpeace and remains an environmentalist. A statistician by profession, Lomborg began his study of the environment in a seminar with 10 of his sharpest students at the University of Arthurs in Denmark. There he tried to refute the statistical critique of Julian Simon, whose articles and books tore apart the statistics of Paul Ehrlich and other prophets of doom. When he finished the seminar, Lomborg concluded that "a large amount of [Simon's] points stood up to scrutiny and conflicted with what we believed ourselves to know."

Miguel A. Santos, *The Environmental Crisis* (Greenwood Press, 1999) is a good starting point for examining this issue. The best historical overviews of the controversy are Hal K. Rothman's *Saving the Planet: The American Response to the Environment in the Twentieth Century* (Ivan R. Dee, 2000) and *The Greening of a Nation? Environmentalism in the United States Since 1945* (Harcourt Brace, 1998). Two excellent articles on the issue are Stewart L. Udall, "How the West Was Won," *American Heritage* (February/March 2000) and John Steele Gordon, "The American Environment," *American Heritage* (October 1993). Finally, two interesting books that reverse the traditional stances of liberals and conservatives on the environment are Gregg Easterbrook, *A Moment on the Earth: The Coming Age of Environmental Optimism* (Viking, 1995) and Peter Huber, *Hard Green: Saving the Environment From the Environmentalists: A Conservative Manifesto* (Basic Books, 1999).

Contributors to This Volume

EDITOR

LARRY MADARAS is a professor of history and political science at Howard Community College in Columbia, Maryland. He received a B.A. from the College of the Holy Cross in 1959 and an M.A. and a Ph.D. from New York University in 1961 and 1964, respectively. He has also taught at Spring Hill College, the University of South Alabama, and the University of Maryland at College Park. He has been a Fulbright Fellow and has held two fellowships from the National Endowment for the Humanities. He is the author of dozens of journal articles and book reviews.

STAFF

Larry Loeppke	Managing Editor
Jill Peter	Senior Developmental Editor
Nichole Altman	Developmental Editor
Beth Kundert	Production Manager
Jane Mohr	Project Manager
Tara McDermott	Design Coordinator
Bonnie Coakley	Editorial Assistant
Lori Church	Permissions

AUTHORS

RICHARD M. ABRAMS is a professor of history at the University of California, Berkeley, where he has been teaching since 1961. He has been a Fulbright professor in both London and Moscow and has taught and lectured in many countries throughout the world, including China, Austria, Norway, Italy, Japan, Germany, and Australia. He has published numerous articles in history, business, and law journals, and he is the editor of *The Shaping of Twentieth Century America: Interpretative Essays,* 2d ed. (Little, Brown, 1971) and the author of *The Burdens of Progress* (Scott, Foresman, 1978).

DAVID H. BENNETT is a professor of history at Syracuse University, where he specializes in modern American history and modern military history. He is the author or coauthor of numerous publications, including *The Party of Fear: The American Far Right From Nativism to the Militia Movement* (Vintage Books, 1995) and *Demagogues in the Depression: American Radicals and the Union Party, 1932–36* (Rutgers University Press, 1969). He earned his Ph.D. from the University of Chicago in 1963.

GARY DEAN BEST is a professor of history at the University of Hawaii in Hilo, Hawaii. He is a former fellow of the American Historical Association and of the National Endowment for the Humanities, and he was a Fulbright scholar in Japan from 1974 to 1975. His publications include *The Nickel and Dime Decade: American Popular Culture During the 1930s* (Praeger, 1933).

ROGER BILES is a professor in and chair of the history department at East Carolina University in Greenville, North Carolina. He is the author of *The South and the New Deal* (University Press of Kentucky, 1994) and *Richard J. Daly: Politics, Race, and the Governing of Chicago* (Northern Illinois Press, 1995).

PATRICK J. BUCHANAN is a syndicated columnist and a founding member of three public affairs shows, *The McLaughlin Group, The Capital Gang,* and *Crossfire.* He has served as senior adviser to three American presidents, ran twice for the Republican nomination for president (1992 and 1996), and was the Reform Party's presidential candidate in 2000. He is the author of *A Republic, Not an Empire: Reclaiming America's Destiny* (Regnery, 1999).

WILLIAM G. CARLETON (1903–1982) was professor emeritus at the University of Florida and author of the widely used textbook on *The Revolution in American Foreign Policy.*

CLAYBORNE CARSON is a professor of history at Stanford University in Stanford, California. He is also editor and director of the Martin Luther King, Jr., Papers Project at the university's Martin Luther King, Jr., Center for Non-Violent Social Change, which published in 2000 the fourth volume of a 14-volume edition of King's speeches, sermons, and writings. His publications include *A Knock at Midnight: Inspiration from the Great Sermons of Reverend Martin Luther King, Jr.* (Warner Books, 2000), coedited with Peter Holloran, and *Guide to American History* (Viking Penguin, 1999).

STANLEY COBEN (d. 2000) was a professor of history at the University of California, Los Angeles, for 30 years. He earned his Ph.D. in history from Columbia University in 1962, and he also taught at Princeton University.

Cohen is best known for his research on the American Red Scare of the early 1900s, and he is author of *Reform, War, and Reaction: 1912–1932* (University of South Carolina Press, 1973).

DANIEL DEUDNEY is an assistant professor in the department of political science at the Johns Hopkins University in Baltimore, Maryland. He is the author of *Pax Atomica: Planetary Geopolitics and Republicanism* (Princeton University Press, 1993).

W. E. B. DuBOIS (1868–1963) was the most important African-American intellectual of the twentieth century.

SARA M. EVANS is Distinguished McKnight University Professor of History at the University of Minnesota, where she has taught women's history since 1976. She is the author of several books including *Personal Politics: The Roots of Women's Liberation in the Civil Rights Movement and the New Left* (1979) and *Born for Liberty: A History of Women in America,* 2nd ed., (1997). Born in a Methodist parsonage in South Carolina, she was a student activist in the civil rights and antiwar movements in North Carolina and has been an active feminist since 1967.

ADAM FAIRCLOUGH is a professor at the University of Leeds, where he holds the chair of modern American history. He has written extensively on the civil rights movement and is the author of *Teaching Equality: Black Schools in the Age of Jim Crow* (University of Georgia Press, 2001) and *Race and Democracy: The Civil Rights Struggle in Louisiana, 1915–1972* (University of Georgia Press, 1999).

RICHARD M. FRIED is a professor of history at the University of Illinois at Chicago and the author of *The Russians Are Coming! The Russians Are Coming! Pageantry and Patriotism in Cold-War America* (Oxford University Press, 1998).

JOHN LEWIS GADDIS is the Robert A. Lovett Professor of History at Yale University in New Haven, Connecticut. He has also been distinguished professor of history at Ohio University, where he founded the Contemporary History Institute, and he has held visiting appointments at the United States Naval War College, The University of Helsinki, Princeton University, and Oxford University. He is the author of many books, including *The United States and the End of the Cold War: Implications, Reconsiderations, Provocations* (Oxford University Press, 1992) and *We Now Know: Rethinking Cold War History* (Oxford University Press, 1997).

F. CAROLYN GRAGLIA, a former lawyer, is a writer and lecturer living in Austin, Texas.

OTIS L. GRAHAM, JR., is a professor emeritus of history at the University of California, Santa Barbara. He is the editor of *The Public Historian* and the author or editor of many books on the environment, public policy, and modern America, including *Debating American Immigration, 1882–Present,* coauthored with Roger Daniels (Rowman & Littlefield, 2001) and *A Limited Bounty: The United States Since World War II* (McGraw-Hill, 1996).

LOUIS R. HARLAN is a Distinguished Professor of History Emeritus at the University of Maryland in College Park, Maryland. His publications include

Separate and Unequal: Public School Campaigns and Racism in the Southern Seaboard States, 1901–1915 (University of North Carolina Press, 1958) and *Booker T. Washington: The Wizard of Tuskegee* (Oxford University Press, 1983), which won the 1984 Pulitzer Prize for biography, the Bancroft Prize, and the Beveridge Prize.

JOHN EARL HAYNES is a twentieth-century political historian with the Library of Congress. He is coauthor, with Harvey Klehr and K. M. Anderson, of *The Soviet World of American Communism* (Yale University Press, 1998) and, with Harvey Klehr and Fridrikh I. Firsov, of *The Secret World of American Communism* (Yale University Press, 1996).

DAVID HEALY is a professor of history at the University of Wisconsin–Milwaukee and the author of several books and articles on U.S. relations in the Caribbean, including *Gunboat Diplomacy in the Wilson Era: The U.S. Navy in Haiti, 1915–1916* (University of Wisconsin Press, 1976). He received a B.A., an M.A., and a Ph.D. from the University of Wisconsin–Madison, and he is currently working on a book about the Latin American policies of James G. Blaine.

JOAN HOFF-WILSON is a professor of history at Indiana University in Bloomington, Indiana, and coeditor of the *Journal of Women's History.* She is a specialist in twentieth-century American foreign policy and politics and in the legal status of American women. She has received numerous awards, including the Berkshire Conference of Women Historians' Article Prize and the Stuart L. Bernath Prize for the best book on American diplomacy.

G. JOHN IKENBERRY, currently a Wilson Center Fellow, is a professor of political science at the University of Pennsylvania and a nonresident senior fellow at the Brookings Institution. He is the author of *After Victory: Institutions, Strategic Restraint and the Rebuilding of Order After Major Wars* (Princeton University Press, 2000) and *American Foreign Policy: Theoretical Essays*, 3rd ed. (Addison-Wesley Longman, 1998).

TAMAR JACOBY, a senior fellow at the Manhattan Institute, writes extensively on race, ethnicity, and other subjects. Her articles and book reviews have appeared in a variety of periodicals, including *The New York Times, The Wall Street Journal, The New Republic, Commentary,* and *Foreign Affairs*. Before joining the Institute, she was a senior writer and justice editor for *Newsweek*. Her publications include *Someone Else's House: America's Unfinished Struggle for Integration* (Basic Books, 1998).

HENRY KISSINGER, a distinguished scholar, diplomat, and writer, was the secretary of state to Presidents Richard Nixon and Gerald Ford. He has published two volumes of memoirs from those years, *The White House Years* (Little, Brown, 1979), and *Years of Upheaval* (Little, Brown, 1982).

HARVEY KLEHR is the Andrew W. Mellon Professor of Politics and History at Emory University. He is coauthor, with Kyrill M. Anderson and John Earl Haynes, of *The Soviet World of American Communism* (Yale University Press, 1998) and, with John Earl Haynes and Fridrikh I. Firsov, of *The Secret World of American Communism* (Yale University Press, 1996).

MICHAEL L. KURTZ is dean of the graduate school at Southeastern Louisiana University in Hammond, Louisiana, where he has also served as professor of history. He is editor of *Louisiana Since the Longs: Nineteen-Sixty to Century's End* (Center for Louisiana Studies, 1998).

WALTER LaFEBER is the Noll Professor of History at Cornell University in Ithaca, New York. He is the author of several major books concerning Central America, and his most recent publications include *America, Russia, and the Cold War*, 7th ed. (McGraw-Hill, 1992) and *The American Age: United States Foreign Policy at Home and Abroad Since 1750* (W.W. Norton, 1989, 1993).

ARTHUR S. LINK was a professor of history at Princeton University. He is the editor-in-chief of the Woodrow Wilson papers and the author of the definitive multivolume biography of President Wilson.

BJORN LOMBORG is an associate professor of statistics in the department of political science at the University of Aarhus in Denmark and a frequent participant in topical coverage in the European media. His areas of professional interest include the simulation of strategies in collective-action dilemmas, the use of surveys in public administration, and the use of statistics in the environmental arena. In February 2002, Lomborg was named director of Denmark's national Environmental Assessment Institute. He earned his Ph.D. from the University of Copenhagen in 1994.

RICHARD L. McCORMICK is president of Rutgers University in New Brunswick, New Jersey. Prior to that, he served as president of the University of Washington in Seattle. He received his Ph.D. in history from Yale University in 1976, and he is the author of *The Party Period and Public Policy: American Politics From the Age of Jackson to the Progressive Era* (Oxford University Press, 1986).

H. R. McMASTER graduated from the U.S. Military Academy at West Point in 1984. Since then, he has held numerous command and staff positions in the military, and during the Persian Gulf War he commanded Eagle Troop, 2d Armored Calvary Regiment in combat. He is the author of *A Distant Thunder* (HarperCollins, 1997).

THOMAS G. PATERSON is emeritus professor of history at the University of Connecticut in Storrs, Connecticut. His articles have appeared in such journals as *Journal of American History* and *Diplomatic History*, the editorial boards of which he has served on, and *American Historical Review*. A former president of the Society for Historians of American Foreign Relations, he has authored, coauthored, or edited many books, including *Contesting Castro* (Oxford University Press, 1994).

PRESIDENT'S COMMISSION ON THE ASSASSINATION OF PRESIDENT JOHN F. KENNEDY was appointed by President Lyndon Johnson on November 29, 1963, to investigate the assassination of President Kennedy and the subsequent killing of the alleged assassin and to report its findings and conclusions to him. Commonly known as the Warren Commission, after the commission's chair, Chief Justice Earl Warren, the commission's members included Representative Gerald R. Ford (R-Michigan) and Allen W. Dulles, former director of the CIA.

BRUCE J. SCHULMAN is professor of history and director of American Studies at Boston University. A frequent contributor to publications such as *The New York Times* and the *Los Angeles Times*, Schulman lives in Brookline, Massachusetts.

ROBERT A. THEOBALD (1929–1999) was a retired rear admiral before his death. He was the commanding officer of Flotilla One, Destroyers, Pacific Fleet, and was present at the Pearl Harbor attack. He testified on behalf of Admiral Husband E. Kimmel before the Roberts Commission, which had accused Kimmel of "dereliction of duty."

BRIAN VANDEMARK teaches history at the United States Naval Academy at Annapolis, Maryland. He served as research assistant on Clark Clifford's autobiography, *Counsel to the President: A Memoir* (Random House, 1991), and as collaborator on former secretary of defense Robert S. McNamara's Vietnam memoir *In Retrospect: The Tragedy and Lessons of Vietnam* (Times Books, 1995).

ROBERTA WOHLSTETTER is a historian and a member of the Steering Committee of the Balkan Institute, which was formed to educate the public on the nature of the crisis in the Balkans and its humanitarian, political, and military consequences. She has earned the Presidential Medal of Freedom, and she is coauthor of *Nuclear Politics: Fuel Without the Bomb* (Harper Business, 1978).

Index